Praise for Eva Musby and

Anorexia and Other Eating Disorders:
How to Help Your Child Eat Well and Be Well

From parents

"The most practical advice I've ever come across."

"Within three weeks our daughter has gone from eating nothing but a couple of small pieces of fruit per day to eating on six occasions each day, with three meals and three snacks. And she has even started to eat spontaneously without prompting. This is down to all the information in your book which gave us the confidence to do something which, at the time felt to be quite radical and a bit scary."

"Since reading your book my husband and I have been the perfect picture of empathy – cool, calm, collected. It works. It absolutely works."

"Amidst the chaos of those early months, the only literature that I found at all useful was your book. I was being advised to be very combative and aggressive with my daughter's eating, but your book gave me the confidence to do things in a gentler way … and she got better."

"The information in this book is lifesaving and if you had to gather all this information yourself it would take years. I have bought other books on the subject but I keep returning to this one. When I wake up in the middle of the night worrying I read this and feel reassured and empowered to carry on."

"It felt like my daughter's anorexia was winning the battle and after almost 3 years I had no strength left to fight it. I can't thank you enough for your practical advice and tips, which made total sense to me, and allowed me to begin again with renewed purpose, and my daughter has started eating again. It is so good to read advice from someone who knows exactly what we are going through."

"I know we have a long battle ahead of us, but each time I get a bit down, I read your advice and I'm filled with confidence."

"These are just the practical tips that I need and that I feel a lot of books don't address, as they are so concerned with getting the kids away from death's door, but as we have discovered that is just a first step."

"Parents are starting to understand the WHY and the WHAT they must do when a loved one has a restrictive eating disorder, but Musby does what no one else does: shares the HOW. Parents need solid tools, tips, and problem-solving. Open any page in this book and you'll find a bit of the hard-won advice that parents around the world are teaching one another.

Read this book to join the growing movement of parents who are saving their sons and daughter's futures and their lives through good information and action."

Laura Collins Lyster-Mensh, founder of parents' online community F.E.A.S.T. activist writer (circummensam.com) and author of 'Eating With Your Anorexic'

From clinicians

"Your work is a tremendous source of information and support"

Daniel Le Grange, PhD, Professor in Children's Health, Eating Disorders Director, Department of Psychiatry, UCSF. Co-author of many books and scientific articles on Family-Based Treatment with James Lock (see below)

"Eva Musby takes as her starting point Family Based Treatment (FBT) – a therapy that encourages and supports parents to engage directly with changing the maintaining behaviors of anorexia nervosa – not eating enough, over exercising and any other unhealthy strategies for keeping weight at an unhealthy low level. She provides detailed, highly accessible descriptions of what worked for her family and for other families she knows who found ways to defeat anorexia nervosa. Importantly, she provides specific and clear answers to many common questions parents struggle with: how much do we feed her? How long do we sit at the table? Will we harm our relationship with him? How long will this take?

While clinical experts are certainly a part of her story, hearing how she and her family worked out the problems makes her account compelling and heartening to parents who will identify with the dilemmas faced.

Her style is a mix of matter-of-fact statements of what worked and what didn't, and admission of the limits of her know-how. The result is a highly readable volume that offers practical solutions for parents to consider when helping their own child to recover for anorexia nervosa.

Therapists and other clinicians can learn from this book – not only about some of our own limitations and foibles that so often confuse and baffle the families we hope to help, but also about how we might better help families to understand those dilemmas and develop possible solutions to them."

James Lock, MD, PhD, Professor of Psychiatry and Pediatrics at Stanford University School of Medicine: Director of the Eating Disorder Program in the Department of Psychiatry and Behavioral Sciences. Author of many books and scientific articles including 'Help Your Teenager Beat and Eating Disorder', 'Treatment Manual for Anorexia Nervosa: A Family-Based Approach', and 'Treating Bulimia in Adolescents: A Family-Based Approach'

"I am a family therapist working in the Maudsley Child and Adolescent Eating Disorders Service. Your book is packed with helpful information for parents and has been brilliant for my patients and for our team. It conveys the right message in an accessible way; that parents are an essential resource and with the right support can find their own strengths to support their child to recover.

I often give parents the website link straight after the initial assessment, when I know the family is leaving the clinic feeling bewildered. Your book and video can help to sustain the family until we meet them again and guide them through the process of recovery. What you put across in your video about helping your child to eat really enhances what we convey to parents and families.

I also show it in multi-family groups and in teaching the Maudsley approach to other professionals around the country."

Esther Blessitt, Senior Systemic Psychotherapist, writing on behalf of the Child and Adolescent Eating Disorders Service at the Maudsley Hospital, London

"This is by far, by leagues, by legions, the most practical and outstanding advice for parents or caregivers battling an eating disorder in their child. Eva Musby helps parents see the light at the end of the tunnel, while giving them tools to chug along the entire way through the nearly airless space that same tunnel represents. It is comprehensive in its scope, but not overwhelming – every chapter has scenarios and suggestions that can only be learned and taught this well by someone who has lived this and come out the other side.

Ms. Musby clearly has a great deal of respect for caregivers and sufferers alike. There is a humility to her writing that makes it clear that every parent and child must find their own way into recovery together, but a confidence and knowledge that leaves the reader feeling more capable and calm than they imagined they could feel.

I love that this guide is evidence-informed but full of parent wisdom. This book distils all the sticky, challenging, fearsome things that both patients and their families encounter when faced with an eating disorder: from noticing the problem to finding effective treatment to refeeding and beyond….back to life and a child or adolescent who can live and eat and be free.

I will be recommending this to every parent or caregiver I encounter in my practice, as well as every health provider working with our patients. It is that good."

Dr Rebecka Peebles, MD, Co-Director, Adolescent Medicine, Eating Disorder Assessment and Treatment Program, The Children's Hospital of Philadelphia

"This is really good work. In speaking with the clear, humorous and wise voice of one parent to another, it is pretty much the best I have read […] Eva, as you know I am a pediatric eating-disorder doctor and I highly recommend [your] video for parents. Well done."

Dr Julie O'Toole, MD, MPH, founder and Chief Medical Officer, Kartini Clinic, Oregon, USA (www.kartiniclinic.com)

"This is amazing! I am truly gobsmacked. I have devoured (!) the excellent chapter on helping your child to eat, with the superb bungee-jumping analogy."

Dr E. Jane B. Morris, Consultant Psychiatrist,
The Eden Unit, Royal Cornhill Hospital, Aberdeen, UK

"As a child and adolescent psychologist specializing in eating disorders, I believe strongly that parents are the patient's most valuable resource in recovery. But when parents are in the trenches with their children, they desperately need support, guidance, and reassurance.

At last, here is a book written for parents, by a parent, which offers priceless insights from those who have gone through this horrible illness with their children and come out the other side. Parents who read this book are arming themselves with practical skills and unique perspectives that only a fellow parent can provide. I strongly recommend this book to all parents who are facing this daunting illness in their child."

Dr Sarah K. Ravin, child and adolescent psychologist
specializing in eating disorders (drsarahravin.com)

"We have been sharing the book with families in treatment and know how helpful it has been to them. A fabulous resource, written by a fellow parent who knows what it's like."

Charlotte Oakley, Clinical Lead, Connect-Eating Disorders,
NHS Greater Glasgow & Clyde, UK

"As a team dedicated to Family-Based Treatment, we have been really impressed by the information and support in your book and frequently recommend it to parents and carers of the young people we treat."

Marc Clegg, Clinical Nurse Specialist in adolescent eating disorders,
Parkview Clinic, Birmingham Children's Hospital NHS Trust, UK

"I keep 2 copies of this book in my office at all times so I can lend it out and/or highlight certain sections. It is one of the most practical, well written 'how to do this terrible job' books I have seen yet. Parents and care givers will love all the great tips and all the ways they learn to cope. Clinicians will also learn a lot about how anorexia 'acts' which is crucial to being a well informed and effective clinician."

Therese Waterhous, RDN (willamettenutritionsource.com), serving as expert to
FEAST-ED and the Academy for Eating Disorders

Anorexia and other Eating Disorders

How to help your
child eat well
and be well

Practical skills for family-based treatment,

compassionate communication

and emotional support

for parents of children and teenagers

Eva Musby

APRICA

Updated January 2020
Version 2020-01-02
Text and Illustrations Copyright © Eva Musby 2014

http://anorexiafamily.com

ISBN-13: 978-0-9930598-0-3
Published by APRICA
This book is also available in all the main ebook formats

Cover design by Andrew Brown at designforwriters.com
Cover photograph by Melody Revnak

DISCLAIMER
I'm a parent – not a doctor, therapist, psychologist or dietitian. This book is not a substitute for professional advice. Best practice is bound to evolve after this book is published. Pay attention to your instincts, ask around, read, speak to other parents, check if the version you're reading is up to date, and most importantly, keep your clinicians in the loop.

To all the loving parents

CONTENTS

Go to anorexiafamily.com/toc-detailed for a detailed table of contents with all the subheadings.

HOW THIS BOOK CAN HELP YOU

*Here's an overview of the help I'd like to offer you in this book and
some suggestions on how to find your way around the information fast.*

THE PRACTICAL AND EMOTIONAL TOOLS PARENTS ARE ASKING FOR

If your child has an eating disorder, you're likely to have many questions you want answers to, as well as a whole lot of skills you dearly want to acquire.

Yet most of us parents don't get the answers or the tools we need, even from the best professionals. We muddle through as best we can, and when we reach the light at the end of the tunnel, we say, 'I wish that two years ago, I'd known what I know now.'

Take the big question: 'How do we get our child to eat?' It was always clear to my husband and me that we should feed our child rather than leave her to her own devices, but the *how* to do this remained a mystery to us. We scoured the books and the internet; we begged the professionals for tips, but it took a whole year before we got precise answers and some coaching on how to help our child eat. Then, practically overnight, we became infinitely more effective. I see a huge need for this type of help, as illustrated by the following email a parent sent me.

> *"Your practical refeeding scenarios saved us. Until then I knew what
> we needed to do but did not know how. And it worked for us.
> Having the words and dialogue to say was what I needed when a
> mother's instinct flies out the window."*

In addition to practical questions, we need help with emotions: ours and our child's. Eating disorders can turn a happy home into a war zone. If you're like me, you'll have panicked and shouted, threatened and cried, and you're the last person your child is ready to trust. Meanwhile, you feel exhausted, incompetent and bruised.

When you get skilled at managing emotions and at communicating with compassion, it's possible to support your child no matter what.

Children can achieve wonderful things when we treat them with compassion, when we withstand their outbursts, stay persistent, and nurture trust and connection.

*"I came across your draft whilst in the middle of an emotional
meltdown, both mine and my daughter's. With your advice, I turned
the situation round. Deep breath and hand on heart. I am new to
this but learning very fast, or trying to. Some of what you say has
saved me from sinking into depths of despair."[1]*

Our daughter made rapid progress once we'd got all our external and internal ducks in a row. It's been a joy to see her thrive, and as a parent who's also a writer, it gives me huge satisfaction to pass on resources to other parents.

*"I immediately put some of your suggestions into practice with
almost instantaneous results."*

This is a big book because I cover the great many questions parents encounter along the journey. I provide plenty of signposting so that you can get the answers you need in a hurry. I guide you through a vast collection of strategies, based not only on my experience and knowledge but also on what I've learned from parents and clinicians all over the globe.

You might enjoy a companion resource to this book: Bitesize[2], a collection of very short audios, each addressing one question parents usually need help on. When you hear me giving tips or modelling parent-child dialogue, it can reinforce what you read. Also, if you have a partner who doesn't like to read, Bitesize provides a route to getting them (almost) as well informed as you.

It's my heartfelt hope that among this wealth of expertise, you will find what you need to help your child recover and for your relationship to thrive.

WHAT YOU WILL GET FROM THIS BOOK

My aim is to give you strategies for action as well as emotional support. If your child has an eating disorder, I'm assuming you're not feeling at your best right now, so I want to take good care of you. I will not give you disaster stories. This is most certainly not a misery memoir. I will do everything I can to empower you. Not because I'm a nice person, you understand, but purely because the evidence is that results are best when parents are supported in caring for their ill child.

Many parents, at some stage, have questions and doubts about the method used to treat their child. I will help you recognise the treatment approaches that are validated by research and those that are based on outdated theories.

I will offer you tools you can use right away, and then I'll build on those with more tools to help in the longer term. My intention is to support you through the entire journey to wellness.

I will address the practical questions that come up, again and again, in parent circles, such as:

- How do I get my child to eat foods she's avoided for months? To eat anything?
- Will I push him over the edge if I stop him exercising?

- The specialist is aiming at another 3 kg. Won't that make my daughter even more anxious?
- What should we do about school, about holidays?

Parents also have a whole lot of questions relating to their child's mental state and how to have a better connection. For example:

- What's going on in her head?
- What should I say when he's hysterical and wailing that he's fat?
- How can I connect when she's pushing me away?
- Rewards haven't worked, nor have threats. Is this the end of the road?

Finally, many of us sense that our power to support our children lies in the love we've had for them since the day they were born. We need emotional resources when we are sorely stretched:

- How can I stay calm when I want to scream?
- My ex hates conflict; my partner is undermining my efforts; my mother-in-law says I'm making our son worse. What can I do?
- I resent losing friends, activities, my job.
- Will my kid and I ever be close again? I miss her.

I'm offering to sit down with you over a cup of tea (tea is, of course, the answer to all of life's stressors!) and guide you. I'll give you general principles, lots of ideas for you to pick from, and lots of examples.

IS THIS BOOK FOR YOU?

If you're the parent of a child suffering from the restricting type of anorexia nervosa (i.e. they are restricting their food intake), this book is definitely for you, because that's where my experience lies. Note that a child might only meet all the diagnostic criteria for anorexia once the illness is entrenched. This book will help you to start treatment early, when it's easiest and most effective. This book is also for you if your child is anxiously following restrictive food rules. Some youngsters become malnourished from an obsessive drive to eat 'clean'. For some (usually male), the mental and physical dangers come from a diet aimed at increasing muscle bulk and weight, and from insufficient body fat.

If you're dealing with the binge-purge type of anorexia, the tools I offer will be equally relevant, as there is so much in common between the two types.

All eating disorders have big areas of overlap, so if your child has bulimia nervosa, binge-eating disorder or any other type of eating disorder, many sections of this book will also be relevant to you. I do recommend, however, that you complement the material in this book with information from other sources, as there are differences in how each type of eating disorder is best treated.

I use the word 'child' a lot. The age group I have in mind is young children and adolescents. My own daughter was 10 when anorexia hit her, then she needed some support again age 15 to 18. The type of family-based treatment at the heart of this book is backed up by good evidence from research on 12 to 18-year olds. I know of parents who have successfully used the same approach with their adult child. The communication resources I offer are not age-specific, so I believe that even if your child is an adult, you will find help in this book.

I'm referring to you as 'parents', but I'd like to include all carers in this. Sometimes the main carer is a boyfriend or a sister, not much older than the sufferer. I've also borne in mind that my readers may be single parents, or may not be a united couple.

I also would like you to feel included whatever your gender, and the same goes for your child. I hope you will be comfortable with my varied use of 'he', 'she' and 'they'.

What about the country you live in? It doesn't make any difference to the tools in this book (though of course it make a difference to the health care you have access to). I'm in Scotland, United Kingdom.

I hope this book will be helpful to clinicians, too, and that it will complement your work with families. At the very least you will get an honest insight into quite a few parents' needs, perhaps more than you do in your consulting room.

As for the emotional resources I offer, they're valid for you, me and everyone. The principles of communication, self-compassion, mindfulness and resilience are based on age-old wisdom, they have been adapted and tested in modern therapies, and they apply to all human beings of all ages.

DON'T JUST READ THIS - GET CLINICAL SUPPORT

Now for some words of caution. I care more about your child's wellbeing than about being right. I write as a mother. I was a scientist in my younger years, so I get twitchy when I come across bad science or unsupported claims. I have no qualifications in medicine, in psychology, or in the approaches I draw on, such as Family-Based Treatment (FBT), mindfulness and Nonviolent Communication (NVC). Experts in these fields have kindly checked and commented on my writings. Note that there are heated debates going on in the world of eating-disorders treatment. I'm offering you approaches that, where possible, have been scientifically tested and validated. But if I stopped there you'd be left with huge gaps. I'm filling those by suggesting strategies that worked for us and for other parents.

Keep your radar switched on. The field is evolving and there may be new, promising interventions that are missing from this book if the version you're reading is more than a couple of years old.

The tips I give might not all be suitable for your situation. Our children have many similarities, but the differences matter too. Pay attention to your instincts, ask around, read, speak to other parents.

Most importantly, make sure your child's physical wellbeing is monitored and keep your clinicians in the loop. Modern eating-disorders specialists encourage parents to exchange know-how, so you should find it possible to be open with them if I write anything that contradicts their views. I'd like this book to support how families work with experts, because collaboration and openness produces better outcomes for the children.

HOW TO USE THIS BOOK

Take the best and leave the rest

Therapists respond to their clients' needs in the present moment. I can't do this for you, so it's fine if you pick out the bits that are relevant to you and leave the rest for now.

I'm here to give you resources to change the things you have the power to change. Some things are outside our control. If you try out some of my suggestions and get nowhere, it doesn't mean you're doing anything wrong. What's much more likely is that your situation is very different and some of the tools I offer are not for you right now.

When you find strategies that are helpful, don't beat yourself up or despair when you don't manage them all the time (notice I said 'when', not 'if'). I found that my numerous 'mistakes', however much I regretted making them, were harmless in the long term. The things I did well were far more important. Be kind to yourself. We're human and we can only do our best with the resources available to us. This illness pushes us to keep learning and to develop new skills and resilience.

Jump to the chapters you need most right now

- If you'd like to understand more about what this illness is like for your child and what can be done to help her, start at the beginning of the book.
- If you're desperate for tips to get the next meal in, jump to the practical chapters (Chapters 6 to 9).
- If you've mastered meals and weight gain, see Chapters 9 and 10 for the next steps.
- Chapter 11 addresses issues around family, friends, work and money and is relevant at any stage.
- If you're researching approaches to treatment or trying to work more effectively with therapists (either your child's or your own), go to Chapter 12.
- If you're in a hurry to communicate better with your child and help her feel supported, jump to Chapters 13 and 14. They deal with emotions and are just as much part of the treatment as the earlier, practical chapters.
- If you need some emotional support before you do anything else, go straight to Chapters 13 and 15. They give you tools for first aid and help with developing long-term resilience.

Videos and other resources that complement this book

On my website anorexiafamily.com, and on my YouTube channel (Eva Musby) you will find more resources that I have created to support you. Do sign up to receive updates.

WITH A LITTLE HELP FROM MY FRIENDS

This book goes beyond my story and my views. I have gathered contributions from other parents, children in recovery, and I have had help from experts. I want to thank each and everyone one of them – and also to point out that anything less than wonderful in this book is mine, not theirs. Some of the parents and clinicians who've contributed are local, while others are all over the world, online.[3]

If you come across a quote without a name or without a link to endnotes, it's a contribution from a parent who wishes to protect their child's privacy. Apart from the researchers I quote, everybody's name is false.

Including mine.

This is not my daughter's memoir, or mine. I very much want to respect her privacy and dignity, and to credit the immense courage it took for her to withstand this illness and recover her smile.

OUR STORY IN LESS THAN TWO MINUTES

Since what I write is informed by personal experience, I'll give you a brief overview of our story.

My husband and I live in the UK and have one daughter. She was a happy, well-adjusted kid until shortly into her tenth year, when she spiralled into restricting anorexia. The trigger was a fall-out with friends. She decided to become thinner so they couldn't ever again call her fat. Besides, restricting food and rest fitted well with her school's health promotion messages. Looking back, we recognise that since the age of eight or so, she'd occasionally been checking her (perfectly fine) body in the mirror and asking if she was fat.

Our frantic attempts to help her eat and drink were to no avail, and less than six months after she first denied herself a sweet, she was admitted to the mental health ward of a children's hospital. Her food intake and her health quickly returned to normal, and for that we are very grateful. But her mind remained in the grip of the eating disorder. During her home visits we couldn't reliably feed her or make her feel secure. Much of the time, we were the enemy. So she remained a hospital patient, with progressively long spells at home and at her normal school.

The staff described her as 'stuck'. By her ninth month she'd narrowed her range of food and was again losing small amounts of weight. By month eleven we thought we could do better at home. There were hopeful days, but soon she was missing out on snacks, then on entire meals. We were now using the outpatient mental health services, who provided vague family sessions and insisted on giving our little girl individual therapy. It was fruitless. Her weight kept dropping, her mood was low, and we feared she'd spend her adolescence in and out of hospital if we couldn't find a better way to support her.

At last several things clicked into place. A specialist eating-disorders service came on board. They were receiving training from James Lock's team in Stanford in a well-validated method called Family-Based Treatment (FBT). Our new therapist followed the principles of this method, though in our case she did not go through all the standard steps. In addition to the standard weekly family sessions, she and I had regular phone discussions, where we did most of the work of reviewing and moving forward. When she gave us meal coaching at home, we became competent... at last.

That on its own might not have been enough, though. At the same time I'd been absorbing everything I could about communication – Nonviolent Communication, specifically – and mindfulness, and I was taking care of my own wellbeing, which for several months had been at an all-time low.

Now, when we took control of meals, it worked and it worked fast. I believe this is because whatever the difficulty, we were coming from an assured, well-informed and compassionate place. Within months, our girl recovered her joy in life and her closeness to us.

Two years after diagnosis, everything was back to normal – as long as she could lean on us to tell her what to eat. With time, that became less and less necessary. Every now and again she had a few minutes' crisis over her body shape, but she was mostly a happy, carefree twelve year old. Any signs of an eating disorder were few and far between. We remained discreetly vigilant – a little too discreetly, as it turned out, because she went downhill again age fifteen. It started with her secretly cutting down on school meals. With our experience it was relatively painless to keep her stable. Most of the time she was happy and enjoying a full life. But as her parents we could see that the mental symptoms were there, and they hung on – at a relatively low level – for the next three years. We sought the support of therapists, then decided we got better progress alone. By age 18 she was pretty well, and six months later we had no problem in letting her attend a local university and enjoy independent living. Improvements continued. She's now 21 and for each of us, life is sweet. Usually I think she's completely recovered. I'm also open to the possibility that she might be secretly backsliding. We've been duped before. We are ready to live with some level uncertainty, jump into action if and when necessary, and meanwhile, enjoy life.

During her main periods of illness, I let go of most of my work so as to have time for her. My husband went on working, though he had flexibility and was able to share the care at home several days a week. Since publishing this book, I have devoted my working hours to keeping myself up to date, publishing revisions, producing new resources on my website and on YouTube, creating my Bitesize audio collection and supporting parents by video-call.[4]

Everybody's story is different. My child's ups and downs will be different from your child's. At the same time, as I know through my daily contact with parents, this illness gives us much in common. I hope the resources that helped me and others will also help you.

2

HOW DOES AN EATING DISORDER AFFECT YOU AND YOUR CHILD?

What's going on in the mind of someone with an eating disorder? And what's it like for you the parent? The aim of this chapter is to lead the way to understanding and compassion for yourself and for your child.

WHAT IT'S LIKE FOR PARENTS

Eating disorders turn our lives inside out and we often despair and question whether anyone understands us. I wonder if what's going on for you is anything like this:

- You're terrified for your child, and you desperately need to know that there is hope, that your present struggles will pass, and that he will recover.

- You're missing your kid – he's hardly recognisable these days – and you dearly want him back.

- You'd do anything to make him well, yet you're never sure you're doing the right thing. You are searching high and low to know what can help him.

- It breaks your heart to see your child un-well, miserable and hungry. Every fibre in your body wants to give him solace.

- You're on duty 24 hours a day, you're ex-hausted, short of sleep, in a state of anxiety or overwhelm. Your body hurts. You wish you could be at your best for your child.

- You wish you could be more confident. You want to know that whatever happens, you will have done your very best.

- Your home has become a battleground. You'd love to find a way of keeping your cool.

- You may be in conflict with your partner, with the clinicians who are caring for your child, or with insurance companies. Doubts and disagreements drive you crazy and fill you with anger and resentment. You yearn for a supportive team and a partner who is on the same page as you.

- You're scared of the next mealtime yet you want to be a rock for your child to lean on.

- You're worn out from being a figure of hate, of being rejected or excluded. You miss being close to your child.

- When you see 'normal' families, you can't help feeling envious or resentful. You long for the closeness and harmony you used to take for granted.

- You keep reviewing the past, wondering if you are to blame (even after you learn that parents don't cause eating disorders). You agonise about every decision in case it's not helpful to his recovery. You sense that some of your relatives blame your parenting style. This is weighing you down. You need to believe in your capabilities again.

- Some of the people who are closest to you just don't get it, and this leaves you feeling isolated. You yearn for supportive, kind people who are ready to hear what it's like for you.

- Perhaps you keep your cool by switching your feelings off. Or conversely, you feel you're about to explode with anger and resentment. You want to give up or run away. Your head is full of unspeakable thoughts about your child. You are so scared, frustrated or depleted that you have no access to loving feelings.

- If you have other children, you're worried for them. They are anxious about their brother or sister, their home has become a war zone and they're not getting much of your time or attention. You might also want to protect them from developing an eating disorder, too.

- Money may be short, increasing your stress.

- You have no time or energy for fun. Perhaps you've given up your job and you miss it. Yet you want to keep anxiety or depression at bay so that you can give your child the best possible support.

- You can go from feeling low to blissfully happy in an instant, because your child has shown a sign of progress and you're suddenly full of hope.

- You've been hanging in there, coping all right, but now that the crisis has passed and your child is doing well, you find yourself weeping for no reason at all. You've been on an emotional rollercoaster for so long, you'd like to know for sure that you're all safe now.

- Things are looking up. You've found approaches that work and you're making good progress. You trust that whatever happens, you can cope with it, and you have confidence that your child will recover. You're frequently filled with gratitude, a new appreciation of life, and compassion for all of us on this eating-disorder journey.

WHAT'S GOING ON IN YOUR CHILD'S MIND?

It would be wonderful if we could read minds, but most of us have to guess what's going on in our child's head.[5] She may tell you she feels one thing but be feeling the opposite. She might not talk to you at all. Your guesses about what's going on with her might be coloured by your own irritable or judging feelings. The more you can get into your child's mind, the more you can tackle the illness effectively and compassionately.

Eating disorders generally bring on feelings of shame, worthlessness and despair. The accounts of people who have recovered offer insights into the contradictory feelings they experienced.

I'll concentrate on what your child may feel if she's malnourished and suffering from anorexia, as it's the eating disorder I know best:

- To her, food is bad in some way. It's revolting. It's dangerous. It's terrifying. It makes her feel sick. The confusing thing is that she also craves food, so there is the constant tension of conflicting thoughts and emotions. Thoughts of food occupy her every waking moment, and her dreams are full of banquets and binges. She has no peace of mind and she does what she can to calm herself momentarily, even if it comes at a price.

    *"I was obsessed with food, it was all I could think about, and even
    foods I didn't like tasted like heaven when I allowed myself to eat.
    The hunger is crippling; it makes you act really crazy."[6]*

- Her body is gross – she's sure of that. She cannot bear the look or feel of it. She wants it to be thinner, or lighter. When she looks in the mirror, she genuinely sees that she's fat[7], fatter than before breakfast. She may on the other hand see that she's too thin and think that this is unattractive, but she still feels the need to be thinner. (Note that some people with anorexia – especially young children – don't have a drive to be thinner or lighter or don't have body dysmorphia.[8])

- People tell her she's in trouble and insist that she needs help. This is a terrible threat to her peace of mind. If they take away the rules and behaviours that help her cope, it will be unbearable. People don't understand that the way she is just right for her. She's certain she's not ill; she's just doing what she needs to do to feel OK, as it's exciting or comforting.[9]

- At times she wishes she could be like everyone else, that she could eat without worry. But eating is forbidden or too stressful. Sometimes her internal tug of war is intense.

    *"You were all eating cake and I remember how it looked so delicious
    and I really wanted some. I felt so weak and so hungry and thirsty.
    I wanted it so very much, but at the same time I didn't."*

- She feels that people who comment on her eating or her exercising simply don't understand her. She cowers from people's judgement and criticism. She wishes they would accept her for who she is.

- It feels absolutely impossible to eat. She can't eat. People who insist that she eats are torturing her. When she does eat, she wants to gag, and her tummy hurts for ages. Calm, satisfaction, reassurance and relief flood over her when she manages to refuse a meal. Increasingly, hunger feels right. It is peaceful. But the hunger can also be miserable and it mirrors how empty and undeserving she feels.

- On some level she wishes someone would make her eat, would take the decisions off her.

- At times (if she has the binge-purge type of anorexia) she 'gives in' to a huge craving to eat, and then she gets in a trance and ends up eating 'too much'. (Objectively, it might indeed be lots, or it might be a tiny amount). She then has an overwhelming compulsion to get rid of the food or burn the calories. Her guilt and shame are torture.

- Exercising provides relief from the anxiety she feels from eating and is also something she *must* do. She feels horribly weak when she exercises, and on some level it's a relief if someone insists that she relaxes. Not much of a relief, though, because she still has to surreptitiously tense her muscles.

- It would be so lovely to be able to lie back on the sofa and relax. But this is not for her. She's different.

- Her body hurts. She is cold.

> *"I have haunting memories of a January school trip – walking around Alcatraz Island having eaten almost nothing all week, wrapped in four or five layers of clothing, utterly miserable, the coldest I've ever been in my life."* [10]

- She is constantly anxious, edgy, down. Self-imposed rules help to keep her mood in check. In her state of anxiety, it's good to feel in control, knowing what foods to avoid, what exercise to take, what clothes to wear. The need to rest, to sleep, to satisfy her hunger and live well are nothing next to the sense of achievement or the relief she gets from obeying rules.

- Like a drug you develop tolerance for, the rules only work for a while. To keep their anxiety-relieving effect, they need to be stepped up. She may not know where the rules came from, but now they're there, they keep multiplying and becoming ever more compelling. Yesterday she managed to exercise till midnight, so now that is the new standard.

- If someone interferes with her rules, she is distraught, and she may have to compensate by denying herself something else. Otherwise something terrible may happen, something that feels worse than death. Perhaps her tummy, which already sticks out too much, will become huge, and that feels unbearable. Perhaps terrible harm will come to her family. She may not know what will happen, but her dread is high, and she must keep herself (and her family) safe.

- The illness is like having a terrorist hold a gun to her head. She's terrified, but if she calls for help or does anything that the attacker has prohibited, she will be shot.

- She may hear a voice in her head, or visualise or feel some kind of entity that makes demands of her. It showers her with love whenever she manages to avoid eating, whenever her tummy feels empty. She then feels exuberant, euphoric. The voice is her buddy, a wonderful, loving, validating companion – which is more than can be said about all the people who have started to criticise and nag. But as the days pass, the voice makes ever-increasing demands. Appeasing it becomes a full-time job, creating unbearable anxiety. (I know of a couple of children younger than nine whose voices were absolutely real to them, and who terrified them at mealtimes, when they were alone and even when they were asleep. Whatever the sufferer's age, any small deviation from the voice's rules turn it into a terrifying bully. It tells her she's worthless, that she's a pig for eating a lettuce leaf, that her body looks revolting and that she has to atone for every morsel she's eaten.) The more stressed she is, the less she has the power to quieten or defy the eating-disorder voice.

> *"The relationship with the eating-disorder voice can feel very much like an abusive relationship, complete with Stockholm syndrome and all, as the voice screams at you, belittles you, and you have to depend on its permission for your very survival. You cling to it and are terrified of it at the same time."*[11]

- She may refer to a voice even when she knows it isn't real. It can be a welcome metaphor that helps to explain her internal conflict to herself. On the other hand she might find insulting the suggestion that she hears a voice, metaphor or not.

- After a meal the full feeling in her tummy is unbearable. It hurts. It feels wrong. She may feel like kilos of fat have suddenly sprouted on her and that she has ballooned out. She blames herself, and to add to the stress, the voice, if she has one, is screaming at her. She's filled with shame, regret and anxiety. She doesn't know what to do and she dreads the aftermath of each meal. It's better not to eat and to feel weak rather than to go through this torture.

- She's hiding food and lying about eating out with friends and no one has a clue. Lying and cheating isn't like her at all and she's ashamed of it, but this is an emergency. She has no choice. She has to protect herself. Cheating helps her restrict her calories but it also means she is alone with her thoughts and feelings.

- She feels terrible about screaming at her parents, about her violent outbursts. If any of her friends or teachers in school knew how she behaves, she would die of shame. This isn't her. Her state of stress is so high, she can't control herself. The guilt is horrible. It's awful to see her parents so hurt.

- When her parents shout at her and punish her for not eating, she loses hope. They hate her, she's sure of it. Who will help her? Who is capable? Who is willing? She is so alone.

- She's managed to keep up appearances in school. Her friends and teachers have no idea that she's in trouble. It's exhausting to keep up the pretence, and when she's back home she withdraws into herself. Yet school provides some welcome relief from the constant thoughts about food.

- Her parents lecture her about the need to eat. She kind of knows they're right, and yet somehow it doesn't apply to her. Sometimes she feels so unwell, or she's so upset about how she's missing out on life, that she wants to co-operate with treatment. But when it comes to eating, the terror returns, and she can't pick up her fork.

- She yearns for love and support.

    "I feel unloved but I don't want people to hug me. I want to be hugged and told everything's going to be okay, but if anyone touches me I'll kick off."[12]

- She thinks about food all the time. In the middle of the terrible stress she's dealing with, she can lose herself and find peace by going through cookbooks and making lists of recipes. Cooking for everyone brings relief as well. It's a bittersweet pleasure to see people eating, and she's proud of herself for remaining 'strong' and not even licking the spoon.

- The grown-ups are no use. When she shouts or chucks food in the bin, they give up and say they can't make her eat. They will not rescue her. They don't know how to rescue her. They are not capable. She is alone. She is terrified.

- She's angry that old friends aren't sticking by her any more. She's cross that people judge her. Some accuse her of being self-centred. They have no idea.

- She feels helpless, hopeless and ashamed because believes one of the many myths about eating disorders.

    "My daughter said, 'Mom, why am I doing this? Is it really because I don't want to grow up?' I said to her, 'Sweetheart, this isn't something you are choosing to do. It's not your fault. I just found some new information about this that says it's genetic. I'm so sorry that we passed this on to you. It's not your fault, it's not our fault.' Honestly, I can still see the understanding and relief that washed over her face. It was at that point that we really began to move forward with refeeding."[13]

- She feels guilty and ashamed about everything. She cannot bear the sadness and worry she's causing everybody. If she could stop it, she would. She is scared that parents and siblings will give up on her and abandon her.

- People have told her that if she continues like this, she may die. But eating feels even more dangerous, and even when she tries to eat, she can't. She is trapped.

- Life is unbearable. She hates herself. She is full of shame, believes she doesn't belong, doesn't have a rightful place in this world. She is a burden – a horrible, lazy, greedy person who harms those who used to love her. Now they hate her. Every mealtime is unbearable. If she were not alive, she would be in peace.

- Hurting herself or others sometimes provides temporary relief from anxiety, shame and guilt. Anger gives her a boost too: it sweeps away her doubts and helps her keep away from food.

- When someone does try to get through to her she pushes them away. She's not worthy of care. And if she's nasty enough, they'll give up on her and she can avoid eating.

- She knows that she might be tube-fed or admitted to hospital. The thought terrifies her, so she eats just enough to avoid this. Or she may be relieved at the prospect that, at last, she will be in the hands of some competent adults who know how to rescue her. In which case she eats even less at home.

- Therapists are a joke. You can lie to them and twist them round your little finger. It's fun but it's also desperately sad. Can nobody help her?

- People tell her she's dangerously undernourished. She wishes people would leave her alone. She is distraught because she is alone.

- Everything is a blank. Everything is so confusing. Her mind is numb. She can't feel anything, and doesn't care about anything.

WHAT IT'S LIKE ON THE WAY TO RECOVERY

I would like to think that once sufferers get the competent support of their parents and of professionals, some of the despair and isolation is replaced by a sense of hope and feelings of trust. Your child might continue to fight you but things might be quite different internally.

- Eating is still awful but it is possible. She remembers that yesterday, it was bearable. Perhaps she can manage today as well.

- Her parents and carers know when she hides food, and they don't give in when she refuses to eat. They are stronger than her eating-disorder drive, her eating-disorder voice. They help her to cut through the conflicting arguments going on in her head. In the past, she had no choice – she had to avoid food. Now, she tells her voice that she has no choice – she has to eat what her parents give her.

- However bad she gets, her parents understand her, they love her, they will never abandon her. They know what to do. They know how to help her. She will be rescued. There is hope. As one young woman said about her mother:

  "She carried me on her shoulders when it seemed anorexia would drown me."[14]

- She feels better than she did a week ago, a month ago, a year ago. Things that once scared her are now OK. It's OK to be the shape she is, and eating is good. She doesn't want to go back to the bad old days. She's willing to participate now, to learn how to keep herself safe so that this doesn't happen again. She's careful not to miss meals, not to let her weight drop.

- It's a little scary when the old feelings return, maybe when she's hungry or stressed. Will she ever be completely rid of this illness? But as time goes this happens less and less. Besides, she and her parents are now experts at nipping problems in the bud.

- She's proud of what she's achieved. Explorers and mountaineers have nothing on her when it comes to courage. She's also filled with gratitude for all the kindness and support she has received from many people along the journey.

- She's bored of talking about eating disorders. It's not her any more. It's over. She's got a life to get on with.

HOW THE BODY INTERACTS WITH THOUGHTS AND BEHAVIOURS

Fight, flight, freeze

Scientists are busy exploring the complexity of the brain, and there's still much to learn about the biology of eating disorders. For now here's a model that helps us parents be effective.

It seems that an eating disorder puts individuals in a near-constant state of anxiety, with extra spikes of terror at mealtimes. A living system's priority is safety. When it detects a threat it jumps into one of several possible safety modes, summarised as 'fight, flight or freeze'. The nervous system is going, 'We're not safe. Avoid! Attack! And if we can't, then shut down, go blank!' You have probably seen a lot of fight and flight around meals. And when your warnings and threats go unheard, when you simply can't get through to your child, when they look blank and disconnected, that might well be a sign of a 'frozen' or shut-down state.

We don't really know why with an eating disorder, food or rest or a particular body shape are perceived as threats. Many fears are not logical. I note signs of alarm in my body just thinking of a snake or of doing a bungee jump. Yet I'm sitting at my desk in complete safety. It's important for us to accept that for our children, whatever alarms them is alarming. It's their reality. They're not pretending. When we accept that, rather than expecting them to be logical or rational, we become powerful helpers.

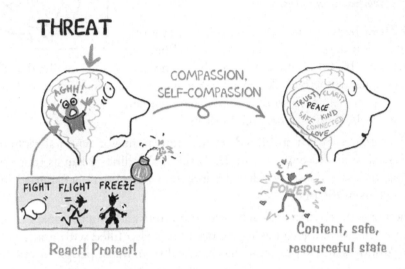

When you want to explode, 'It's only food, can't you see you need it?', imagine someone with very little vision. When they walk into your furniture and get bruised, do you berate them for being irrational? Do you tell them they ought to have seen your coffee table? No, you accept that their senses are not giving them the same information as you get. It's the same with our children. Their nervous system is receiving information that food is a threat.

The brain is wired to prioritise safety. Why waste even a second considering our values, evaluating options or seeking perspective? So to put it crudely, our safety system (much of it in the limbic brain)[15] takes over fast while the slower, rational brain functions are pretty much offline. We stay in this mode for as long as the sense of threat persists.

The route out of fight, flight or freeze is not rational talk. Instead we need to find ways of signalling to our nervous system that the threat is over. Generally that is done through physical and verbal kindness and connection. This is why in this book I will keep guiding you to use compassion – for yourself, and for your child.

Rewiring the brain

Ever since Pavlov rang bells for his dogs, scientists have studied how the mind is conditioned to react in certain ways to certain stimuli. Right now, your child's brain is wired to react to food with anxiety. When your son or daughter engages in ritual behaviours like calorie-counting or exercising, neurons fire according to a well-established pattern, calming hormones are released, and the result is sense of safety and reassurance. All this makes eating disorders hard to shift. The good news is that when a person engages in new behaviours, the brain forms new connections.

Think of tracks in the snow. If you've ever gone skiing, you'll know that if a trace has been laid, that's where your skis will go. When we support our child to eat or to refrain from purging, it's like a skier going into unmarked snow. New tracks are formed. At first they are shallow, and if there are deeper grooves nearby, that's where the skis tend to go. But if we can get the skier to go over the new tracks again and again, these will eventually become the most natural route to follow.

For the brain, the equivalent of tracks in the snow is the creation of new pathways between neurons, the strengthening of synaptic connections. You may have heard that as neurons fire together, they wire together. The same mechanism that has locked your child in their fears is the mechanism that will free her.

Malnourishment messes up the brain

Many of your child's symptoms, including their state of anxiety, depression, and irritability, are simply down to irregular, disordered eating, or to malnourishment and being underweight. You might know what it's like to be 'hangry'. And you might have noticed how dull colleagues become while they're on a weight-loss diet. In the 1940s, the effects of starvation were recorded in the now famous Minnesota Semi-Starvation Study.[16] After a few weeks on a seriously reduced diet, the men in the experiment:

- became obsessed with food; it's all they thought or talked about
- often pored over cookery books, images and descriptions of food
- became irritable, egocentric and depressed
- lost their sense of humour and isolated themselves from others

When we don't get the food we need at the times we need, the body activates a whole energy-saving system that only attends to our survival, not our wellbeing. Our fridge might be full, but if we're not feeding ourselves regularly, our body's perception is that we are in a period of scarcity. As it senses a threat to our life, it goes into fight-flight-freeze, which cuts off access to our rational and emotional intelligence. All non-essential functions are closed down to conserve energy until the famine is over.[17] This is why many of your child's physical and mental symptoms will pass with nutritional rehabilitation.

Additional effects of malnourishment for those with an eating disorder

The men in the experiment didn't have an eating disorder. They chose to starve, but they hated it and as soon as the study was over, they rushed to eat (and they didn't follow that with purging). People with a vulnerability to an eating disorder respond differently to scarcity:[18]

- An important difference is anosognosia, a neurological condition that makes an eating disorder so hard to treat. It makes people incapable of recognising that they have a problem or quite how serious it is. They fight nutrition because their current state feels right, and anything else feels awfully wrong. I imagine that, hidden away, there is always a healthy part that longs for well-being. Our children occasionally surprise us with motivation and rational thought. But undernourishment, with an eating disorder, tends to bring distorted, even delusional thinking.

- Malnourishment activates a state of threat. Normally, this focuses people on procuring food. With an eating disorder, tragically, undernourished people perceive food as terrifying. Even if they are blessed with some self-awareness and motivation, they go into fight, flight or freeze at mealtimes. Restricting food, on the other hand, temporarily brings a sense of calm or even elation to those with anorexia, something that has been linked to differences in serotonin regulation.[19]

- Many people experience weight loss through a diet or illness. Normally they regain weight because the body activates hunger and physiological mechanisms to restore weight and health. With an eating disorder, many of these mechanisms get overridden, to the extent that the more starved someone is, the more they are driven to restrict.

- Whereas starvation normally induces lethargy, eating disorders often come with a compulsion to exercise. Very young children are often afflicted by an extreme restlessness which drives them to move constantly (and at their age, it's not that they are calculating calories).

- The men in the Minnesota experiment learned to chaperone each other when they went out, to fight their urge to go get some food. The drive to eat is huge. It's probable that with any eating disorder, for most of the time, people are awfully hungry and longing to eat. With anorexia, 'I'm not hungry' protestations seem to sometimes be manipulation, and sometimes genuine. The appetite-fullness hormonal mechanisms do get disrupted. Also, people really can feel full after a tiny meal, because starvation has put the digestive system in energy-saving mode. There is still 'mental hunger', though, which those with anorexia try so much to ignore: the constant preoccupation with food, which seems to be the brain's way to get people to eat.[20]

- Normally, when you have been hungry, it feels great to finally have tucked into a big meal. With an eating disorder, when healthy hunger wins the battle against restriction, the aftermath is a cruel activation of the threat system. The person is overcome by unbearable thoughts and sensations, hence the drive to purge.

- The Minnesota men gladly ate and gained weight once the starvation phase ended. With an eating disorder there is often an intense fear of weight gain, as well as body dysmorphia: people truly see their body as grossly deformed. This glitch in the brain seems to be linked to irregular eating, as it usually gets sorted with nutritional rehabilitation. On the other hand, sufferers can continue to dislike their body for some time, even though they learn to tolerate the feeling.

- The sense of threat and anxiety seems particularly high with an eating disorder. There is a lot of self-hate, self-denial, sometimes self-harm. Some sufferers have an internal, bullying voice.

3

YOUR PART IN DIAGNOSIS

Find out how eating disorders are diagnosed, the pitfalls you can guard against, and get tips on how to get expert care without delay.

EATING DISORDER OR 'JUST' DISORDERED EATING?

If you're already getting specialist care and you're satisfied with your child's diagnosis, feel free to skip this entire chapter. My aim here is to urge parents to look for diagnosis and treatment without delay if they are worried that their child may have an eating disorder. That's because when a parent has that kind of worry, they're usually right.

When, at the more extreme end of anorexia and starvation, a child becomes scared of swallowing her own saliva, when she thinks smelling food or having a shower or putting cream on her skin might make her fat, you know this has nothing to do with a faddy diet. In the early days, though, we wonder if our child 'just' has disordered eating and body dissatisfaction – which are so common that we tend to accept them as normal.[21]

With disordered eating, people eat and exercise erratically. The might be trying to lose weight, try and fail at all kinds of diets, only eat in the evenings, fast ('for health' or weight loss), occasionally binge, vomit or use diet pills, exclude particular food groups, and become fascinated with detox, 'clean' and 'healthy' eating, 'biohacking' or extreme muscularity. Disordered eating, for some, signals the early ('prodromal') stage of an eating disorder. Intervene now, and you will find it relatively easy to bring your child back to stability before they have a diagnosable illness.[22] If your child 'just' has disordered eating, you won't be 'giving' him an eating disorder by supporting him to eat regular meals. On the contrary, you will be relieving him of his present misery, and teaching lifelong habits for happiness and wellbeing.

I know how parents hesitate to 'make a fuss' while they think their child might not have an eating disorder. Even when they suspect the illness is there, they fear it would be heavy-handed and counter-productive to start talking of eating disorders and to take charge of meals. Maybe the problem will sort itself out without intervention? Indeed, that can happen. The problem is that nobody can predict if your child will be in that category. In addition, it could take quite a few miserable years for this spontaneous recovery to take place. Then there's the problem that without treatment, some people get moderately well, but don't fully recover. The risks are just too high. Start treatment.[23]

So what signs should be ringing alarm bells? First of all, a child or adolescent losing weight, or not gaining weight. That is never OK. Notice also if your child is eating very slowly, fastidiously, using small plates, small spoons. Questioning quantities and ingredients. Cutting out major food groups. Fasting 'for health'. Becoming obsessed with cooking… for others. Commenting on body shape – theirs and others'. Exercising compulsively. Low mood and irritability.

A person with disordered eating will enjoy a feast with friends, though they think it's appropriate to make comments like, 'I really shouldn't! Oh, go on, the diet starts tomorrow!' With an eating disorder, the person is truly anxious, and they restrict or purge afterwards. When the illness is advanced, they might choose a small salad and make it last through starter, meal and dessert. Later they stop meeting friends, partly because it means eating, and partly because their state of anxiety closes them off from others.

Our children are adept at hiding signs. At first, they secretly cut out lunch in school. Then they tell us they've eaten with friends, so they don't need dinner with us. They get passionate about 'healthy' eating and exercise. We yo-yo between worry and reassurance. We're relieved that last night they happily tucked into several slices of pizza. Later we learn that the reason they allowed themselves pizza is that they skipped lunch.

There are, of course, physical signs that the body is reacting to malnourishment: thinning hair, cold hands, sore tummy, constipation, fur on the face. For those who vomit, there are specific signs as well. For lots more indicators of an eating disorder, check the endnotes.[24]

I know this stage where you are confused, where you are anxious about making a fuss over nothing. Take your child on holiday for a couple of days. If they have an eating disorder, you will see their tension rise as they try to restrict while acting normal. You will see how long it takes them to choose food off a menu. They may argue that as you both had ice-cream on the beach, you don't need dinner, and wouldn't it be nice to go for a run instead. The busiest time for referrals to eating disorder services is after holidays.

GETTING A REFERRAL FOR DIAGNOSIS AND TREATMENT

Standards set by NHS England[25] in June 2015 are providing a fantastic model for the rest of the world. Health authorities in England must now allow parents of adolescent patients to self-refer directly to the local specialist eating disorders service. Immediately, the clock starts: the treatment must begin within one week for urgent cases, four weeks for 'routine' ones.

What most parents[26] still face all over the world is the requirement to go to their family doctor, who is unlikely to have the competence to diagnose and who may not appreciate the value of early specialist intervention. In some regions, even when family doctors act swiftly, there is a long waiting list for mental health services. As Dr Rebecka Peebles says in an excellent conference video for parents and doctors, if you consulted your doctor about Stage 1 cancer, you wouldn't expect to be told to wait till it's progressed to Stage 2.[27]

There are many physical effects of malnourishment and of purging, which a doctor –ideally specialised in eating disorders – should check for. I'll mention just one important nugget from a favourite expert, Dr Jennifer Gaudiani:[28] a person can be underweight and underfed, but if they're not purging they are likely to have normal blood tests. And it's not uncommon for menstruation to continue.

The worst-case scenario is when a parent is disbelieved and branded as over-anxious or even harmful. In this section I want to help you prepare for your first visit to a doctor or specialist, so that you get what you need even if it turns out the person you're consulting doesn't have the required expertise.

When I started reading books on eating disorders, I skipped the bits that shouted, TAKE YOUR CHILD TO A DOCTOR! I wanted to read only about what *we* could do, as parents. We had a completely unscientific notion that 'medicalising' our child – having her labelled with an eating disorder – could give her an illness she might not have. Perhaps this was just a phase, we thought. When at last I consulted the family doctor on my own, five months had passed since the trigger that had made our daughter decide to cut down on sweets. Only two months before that first appointment, I'd noted in my diary that I was 'sometimes concerned' that she was hardly touching her lunch. Rapid deterioration may be a characteristic of anorexia in young children and that's what happened in our daughter's case. Each day seemed twice as bad as the previous one. Suddenly we became desperate to have specialist help, very urgently.

Our doctor recognised the signs and symptoms I described and immediately wrote a referral to Child and Adolescent Mental Health Services (CAMHS). There were delays due to administrative hiccups. We were given the surreal news that the waiting list was 12 months. I was frequently on the phone to the CAMHS receptionist to report on my daughter's worsening condition. Our struggling health service works best for those who have the education and assertiveness to push, and within two and a half weeks, we were sitting in our first session with a CAMHS nurse.

WHAT ARE THE MAIN EATING DISORDERS?

A family doctor's job is not to diagnose but to refer you to a specialist who is competent to make a diagnosis. There are hotly debated criteria to diagnose eating disorders. In most countries, diagnosis is informed by one or both of these main sources: ICD from the World Health Organisation (WHO),[29] and the more up to date DSM-5 from the American Psychiatric Association.[30]

Binge-eating disorder is characterised by recurring episodes of eating unusually large amounts of food (significantly more, in a short period of time, than most people would eat under similar circumstances), during which the person feels they have no control over their eating. Sufferers are highly distressed and are often full of guilt and shame about their binges, which happen on average at least once a week. They may go for hours or days with little or no food, battling hunger, recruiting extreme willpower, planning weight loss in great detail. If so, they could be malnourished, with medical risks just as serious as those of an underweight person.

In **bulimia nervosa**, the same criteria as for binge-eating disorder are used, and there can be just as much yo-yoing of feast and famine, but in addition there are inappropriate compensatory behaviours (purging). These could be fasting and excessive exercise but most often purging means vomiting or use of laxatives, diuretics or diet pills. The danger from these is particularly acute and regular medical checks are needed.[31]

The criteria for **anorexia nervosa** – both restricting anorexia and binge-purge anorexia – are:

- calorific restriction resulting in significantly low body weight
- intense fear of gaining weight or becoming fat, even though underweight, or persistent behaviours that prevent weight gain, even though at a significantly low weight
- disturbance in the way in which one's body weight or shape is experienced, undue influence of body weight or shape on self-evaluation, or persistent lack of recognition of the seriousness of the current low body weight

If someone meets these three criteria and also regularly binges and purges, then the diagnosis is binge-purge anorexia, not bulimia. Bulimia doesn't have the long-term weight suppression: most patients have a normal or higher than normal body weight. They may sometimes fast for a day or two but their brain is not so strongly affected by malnourishment. As a result people suffering from bulimia can usually participate in their treatment in a way that isn't possible with starving anorexia patients.

There are also classifications for rumination disorder, pica, and **avoidant/restrictive food intake disorder (ARFID)**. ARFID is a common eating disorder, often affecting people since young childhood, which covers quite a range of difficulties and causes. There may be a lack of hunger, or extreme picky eating. There may be sensory difficulties, where children cannot tolerate certain textures. Some only eat a very few bland ('beige') foods. Some have a phobia following a choking incident or a fear of vomiting (emetophobia). Some could be on the autism spectrum, though it can be tricky to untangle features of autism and those of semi-starvation. Treatment for ARFID needs to be individualised, and may be quite different from what you read in this book.

More on my website on ARFID: anorexiafamily.com/classification-eating-disorders/#arfid

OSFED (other specified feeding or eating disorder) is the most common of all eating disorders diagnoses. It is often just as serious as the other disorders and should be treated just as swiftly. When someone shows has all of the symptoms used to diagnose anorexia, bulimia or binge-eating disorder, they may get the OSFED diagnosis. The most common subcategory of OSFED is **atypical anorexia nervosa**,[32] for those who are not considered to have 'significantly low weight' (presumably as read off a BMI chart)[33], even though they might have suffered the same dangerous weight loss as someone diagnosed with anorexia. (The harmful implication is that they are not as ill.)[34] For bulimia or binge-eating disorder, OSFED includes version with 'low frequency and/or limited duration'. The recommended OSFED treatment is normally the one suitable to the most similar illness.[35] In this book, when I mention anorexia, bulimia or binge-eating disorder, please assume I am also referring to their OSFED version.

UFED (unspecified feeding or eating disorder) is often used when there is insufficient information to make a more specific diagnosis.

You may come across **eating disorders not otherwise specified (EDNOS)**. This classification was used in the previous manual, DSM-IV. Many patients who were in this category would now be diagnosed as having anorexia, bulimia or OSFED.

Some conditions seem to have all the main elements of a diagnosable eating disorders but are not presently classified as such. Some symptoms may put them in the OSFED category. Diabetes organisations report a common and dangerous disorder, **diabulimia,** suffered by people with Type 1 diabetes who restrict their insulin dose to manipulate their weight.

Many youngsters are affected by misinformed and dangerous preoccupations with health or fitness. **'Bigorexia'** or 'reverse anorexia', or an obsession with muscularity. They may also perceive themselves as puny (muscle dysmorphia).[36] A great number of boys are somewhere along a spectrum of disordered eating in order to bulk up.[37] At the worst end, they suffer from a compulsion to gain muscle weight regardless of the health and social cost, and they put their bodies through dangerous cycles of 'bulking' and 'cutting'. They only want to eat protein, they think of food only as 'fuel' and can become very ill from malnourishment and insufficient body fat. Some are at extra risk from the use of supplements[38] or anabolic steroids.

Another common phenomenon is **orthorexia**, an obsessive rigidity around eating 'healthy', 'clean', 'pure' or organic. It may involve cutting out entire food groups. As restrictions become more rigid, orthorexia can morph into anorexia. Either way, malnourishment and an obsessive mindset make it miserable or dangerous.[39]

There is also **drunkorexia**, where an alcohol drinker regularly restricts food as a way to control calories, or to become drunk faster.

'NOT THIN ENOUGH'?

If your child has lost considerable weight or is purging regularly, make sure a doctor tests for acute medical problems. Too often it's assumed that only an underweight child could be in danger, and youngsters with average or above-average weight are denied specialist care.[40] According the UK's Royal College of Psychiatrists:

> *"Young children and pre-pubescent adolescents may present without*
> *the typical features (e.g. absent periods or significantly low body mass*
> *index (BMI)) found in adults, and the behaviours associated with*

eating disorders are often covert [...] The most medically compromised patients can have a normal weight."[41]

The 'significantly low body weight' criteria ought to relate to the child's personal needs,[42] but sadly there are still clinicians who use statistical charts:

"The doctor said, 'Your son doesn't have anorexia because his BMI isn't low enough.'"

The reason some kids are not underweight is they started off overweight and have shed a lot of weight dangerously fast (and have been praised for it). Another reason might be that their parents have done an amazing job of getting them to eat in spite of everything, or that the parents took them to the doctor early.

ANOREXIA, BULIMIA, BINGE EATING: ARTIFICIAL DISTINCTIONS

It's quite common for sufferers to swing from one type of eating disorder to another. The distinctions help researchers to be consistent but they are rather artificial. Some therapists consider that the precise diagnosis is not relevant to treatment (this is called the 'transdiagnostic' model of eating disorders).[43]

Even within one recognised diagnostic category like restricting anorexia, there are individual variations. For instance among those affected many, but not all, have at some stage been afraid of swallowing their own saliva. Many, but not all, can't sit back in an armchair. Many, but not all, have a bullying or cajoling internal voice. Individuals may or may not also have a background of anxiety, trauma, depression OCD, or autism.

What is certain is that all types must be taken seriously. You don't need to be emaciated to be in unbearable mental distress and great physical danger.

AN UNLIKELY WORST-CASE SCENARIO

I want to warn you of one, very unlikely, risk of misdiagnosis, so that you can avoid it ever happening to you. If your child fits the stereotypical picture of a teenage anorexic girl, you're unlikely to have problems with diagnosis, so skip the following story.

It is not impossible that a poorly trained clinician will interpret signs of undernourishment or self-harm as child neglect or abuse and dismiss the possibility of an eating disorder. I befriended a mother who lived under the threat of child protection measures as she struggled to get help for her seven-year-old. Her requests for a second opinion were repeatedly blocked, something other clinicians find quite unbelievable and completely out of order. As I write, thanks to this woman's courage, perseverance and networking, eating disorders experts are now treating the little girl for anorexia. They're working closely with the parents and things are looking good.

I sincerely hope that the following tips will guard against you ever facing such a distressing situation.

WHAT TO TELL THE DOCTOR TO GET HELP FAST

I would recommend you do a little homework before your first visit to a doctor. Your doctor may need more than vague impressions to make a referral or diagnosis. And in some countries, like mine, they need to allocate spending responsibly. Also, you don't yet know how knowledgeable your doctor is. If your child is very young or is a boy or isn't very thin, there is a risk that an eating disorder will be dismissed out of hand.

What do I mean by homework? I mean preparing a list of symptoms, accompanied by facts and a few well-chosen anecdotes to illustrate your points. If all you tell your doctor is 'My son is hardly eating', you're dependent on your doctor's skills to draw pertinent information out of you. It's more helpful to say, 'Yesterday all he ate was such and such and all he drank was such and such. When I asked him to eat more he said, "$%#!$%!"'

Here's a list to help you prepare for your appointment. The examples relate to an eating disorder that has probably been going on for weeks or months . If your child's symptoms are milder, get him treatment before he gets to this stage:

- What your child ate and drank yesterday / this week.

- Foods your child now refuses.

- The exercise he takes. Give figures for the last week or month.

- The kind of things he thinks and talks about ('Yesterday he asked if he was fat 15 times').

- Any physical changes: weight loss, sunken eyes, dry skin, cold hands, hair loss, fine hairs on the face or body, changes in the menstrual cycle.

- Psychological changes, mood, behaviours, including any obsessions or compulsions and any self-harm. If he pinches at invisible flesh on his tummy, demonstrate it. If your child weighs himself repeatedly, say so. Also say if your child has been lying, hiding food, secretly exercising or trying to make himself sick. Describe how he resists when you try to feed him.

- If your child vomits or uses laxatives or diuretics or diet pills, flag that up, as your doctor should begin monitoring your child without delay, whether or not he's underweight.

- And finally, tell your doctor that you guess, from all the research you've done, that your child has an eating disorder and that you need some help urgently.

Consider making the first visit to the family doctor alone so that you can talk freely and with precision. If you take your child with you, be aware that he may put on a great show of being well and may lie about how little he eats or how much he exercises. If a doctor isn't aware of the extent to which an eating disorder can lead normally honest people to lie, you may be the one who's disbelieved.

Sadly there are cases of a family doctor or a psychiatrist concentrating on anxiety or obsessive-compulsive disorder (OCD) symptoms when the most urgent, life-threatening matter is an eating disorder.

If you're dealing with clinicians whose competence and expertise you're uncertain about, my tip is to concentrate on the types of symptoms I've listed above. For instance, it's not appropriate for clinicians to question you about your own – possibly traumatic – past, or to ask if you breastfed or had postnatal depression. Don't let them dig around for 'root causes' in your child's early years: this information is not relevant to diagnosis, and in the wrong hands, may land your kid with individual psychotherapy instead of specialised eating disorder treatment.

If you disagree with your family doctor, insist on an urgent referral to a specialist. If your disagreement is with a specialist, in my country the procedure is to ask your family doctor to refer you to another specialist for a second opinion. I know of families for whom this hasn't been straightforward: if this happens in your case, get an advisory body to inform you of your rights[44], and use all your networking skills to make contact with parent advocates, eating disorders specialists, paediatricians, or psychiatrists who can open doors for you when your current treatment providers are putting up barriers.

If for some reason you want to bypass your family doctor, find out who else, in your country, can do a referral.[45]

Remember, if a parent thinks their child has an eating disorder, they're most probably right. We parents know how dramatically our child has changed and how odd their behaviours have become: our task is for us to convey this to the gatekeepers.

It is accepted good practice for parents to be included in the consultation to assess a child with a suspected eating disorder. If you feel that clinicians are failing to diagnose competently, be aware that the gold standard is the Child Eating Disorders Examination Interview (Ch EDE I).[46] I never noticed it being used with my daughter.

I want to offer you one more tip in case you're having trouble being believed. Switch on the audio or video recorder on your phone while your child is acting in highly symptomatic ways. I'm not sure how ethical this seems to you, but if your purpose is to save your child's life, you can't go too wrong.

WHAT YOU DON'T WANT YOUR CHILD TO HEAR FROM A DOCTOR

I'm glad I consulted our doctor alone the first time because it allowed me to describe my child's moods and behaviours freely.

I also needed to know that the doctor wouldn't make unhelpful comments in front of my daughter. I needn't have worried, but I believe it's a valid precaution. I've heard of clinicians saying 'You're nice and slim!' or 'We all need to reduce how much fat we eat,' or 'At your age, no one wants their mum or dad telling them what to eat!' And the one I really dreaded for my innocent ten-year-old: 'So, tell me, do you make yourself vomit? Has that ever occurred to you?'

If you do consult on your own, you'll probably need to return to get your child's health checked. If your child doesn't already know his weight, I recommend that you to keep it that way. Ask for your kid to stand on the scales facing backwards. Later, when you speak to a specialist, you can discuss whether to go for open or blind weighing, but for now, your life will be much, much easier if your child doesn't make today's weight his upper limit.

"My daughter's issue was that she couldn't eat. She didn't even think about her weight before people started weighing her and commenting on weight loss. After that, every time she learned she'd put on a fraction of a pound, it was extra hard to feed her. We had to insist on blind weighing."

WHILE YOU'RE WAITING FOR A DIAGNOSIS

My own experience was good, and yours may be just as smooth. If you are less lucky, I hope that this book helps you to network, to get help, and to keep pushing. At the same time, there is much you can do for your child right now. You can get a head start and begin your part of the treatment.

More information:

For statistics on eating disorders, see anorexiafamily.com/statistics-prevalence-incidence-how-common-eating-disorders-anorexia-bulimia

4

TREATMENT: THE ESSENTIALS

The essentials for a parent who wants immediate answers: what are the main principles of the treatments covered in this book, and how long before you can expect some relief?

THE ROAD AHEAD

What does treatment look like? Here's the process that a specialised family therapy team would typically take you through. This book guides you through the many questions you will have along the way:

- Treatment starts with parents making it possible for their child to eat what they need, in spite of the anxiety stirred up by the eating disorder. Regularity matters, and daily caloric needs can be high, so the general rule is 3 meals and 3 snacks a day. This 'refeeding' or 'nutritional rehabilitation' provides a huge part of the physical and mental healing. Note that we don't lose precious time trying to build motivation: our children manage meals because we develop new skills to make it bearable for them.

  "I have been made team leader of food"

- Your child cannot achieve recovery while underweight, so if they lost weight or did not maintain a normal weight trajectory, the focus is on rapid, full weight restoration. You may wonder how your child can gain a lot of weight when they fear it so much. Weight gain is your friend as it reduces irrationality and anxiety. The general trajectory is that as weight increases, fear of weight gain eases off.

- Meanwhile parents also support their child to normalise behaviours. For instance they guard their child from vomiting, laxatives and compulsive exercise; they gradually serve foods that the eating disorder has forbidden; they facilitate the return to life in all its richness. This behavioural work brings lasting changes to the brain's perception of what is normal and perfectly fine.

- Parents learn to be firm in order to keep moving towards recovery, while also giving love, kindness, and non-judgement (I call this 'compassionate persistence'). The best current treatment is hard for our children. It requires them to walk through their version of hell. It makes all the difference that we are walking next to them. We can all bear suffering when we are feeling loved and understood. A parent's compassion also provides emotional healing, and it models emotional skills that are precious further down the line for resilience and relapse prevention.

- To achieve all this, in a first phase parents normally take charge of all things related to health – everything which the child, in their mental state, cannot do wisely for themselves. With time there is a gradual handover during which parents guide their child to re-learn and practice 'normal' behaviours, while keeping in place just the right level of safeguarding. The child recovers age-appropriate autonomy around more and more situations (resuming school, physical activity, eating with friends, going on holiday, leaving for university). By this stage, most of our sons and daughters are really well and they keep the eating disorder at bay by sticking to safe behaviours (such as regular meals and staying within a safe weight zone) – something that becomes increasingly easy. Usually this is when they are safely discharged from treatment, after some education on relapse prevention. Everybody gets on with normal living, though parents, wisely, keep a light level of vigilance. And then one day, children and parents realise that time, repetition and the pull of life have done the rest of the healing,[47] because the eating disorder thoughts and compulsions have gone, and a beautiful young soul has recovered.

I haven't mentioned hospitals, but they are essential when children are so ill that treatment at home isn't working or isn't safe. They do not provide a complete cure, but they can get the recovery process kick-started, after which parents can take over more easily. Good inpatient units make parents part of the team and skill them up to take over as soon as possible.

Food for weight restoration and stability

By now you'll have got the message about the importance of food and weight. Food is medicine for someone with an eating disorder. The brain is particularly calorie-hungry. People who binge or purge need regular meals in order to gain stability and escape a vicious cycle of obsessive restriction, terrible hunger, eating with guilt or bingeing, followed by another attempt at restriction. Children and teens need to grow and it is never OK for them to lose weight (contrary to what you might infer from media campaigns). Losing weight is especially dangerous for individuals who are vulnerable to an eating disorder because it triggers the thoughts and behaviours. Another big trigger is dipping below a certain weight: for those with a vulnerability it's crucial to be within a weight range that meets their individual, genetically programmed needs.

As a medicine for an eating disorder, food really sucks. It's the one thing sufferers fear the most in the world, and they need to swallow the pill not once, but five or six times a day, day after day. Sadly, medical science hasn't yet come up with anything that is easier for patients or their families.

If you're wondering how anyone can possibly get a child with anorexia to eat, read on. In Chapter 7 I list general principles, offer some dos and don'ts, then in Chapter 8 you can be a fly on the wall and witness an entire mealtime session. And in Chapters 13 to 15 I give you emotional tools to help you support your child meal after meal.

Train the brain: practice 'normal'

Food is fuel, but there is an additional reason why it is medicine: it seems the brain needs to relearn what is 'normal'. For instance, we serve fear foods so as to make them feel ordinary and safe again. Our children often lose the sense of what a normal portion is, what their body is supposed to look like, what it feels like when they have a sufficient level of body fat. Sometimes our children need to remember what it's like to be happy and carefree. A big treatment principle is that they shed eating-disordered habits by engaging in new behaviours. Their brains need nutrition, exposure, and time, in order to heal and form new, healthy pathways.[48] Our sons and daughters need help with this, and that's why weight-restoration should never signal the end of treatment.

Unconditional love

I mentioned how much our children need our uncritical acceptance, our unconditional love and support. This is not empty sentimentality; it's a key principle that's been validated in scientific trials.[49] We parents hold essential keys to the treatment, because families are all about love.

Your love helps your child to trust you so that together, you can tackle seemingly impossible challenges. Besides, have you noticed that anything that has any kind of importance in life comes down to love? If you yourself are presently suffering, you may already have felt how healing and empowering it is when someone hears you, understands you, accepts you.

Love is hard to put into practice in the middle of our daily storms. This is why this book offers emotional tools as well as practical ones. Feel free to jump to Chapter 13 if you feel this is what you need the most right now.

Medication

There are no drugs to cure eating disorders. But medication may assist with your child's anxiety, depression or delusional thoughts, especially at the beginning of treatment, when eating causes such high levels of distress.[50]

When does psychotherapy have a role?

You may have noticed that in my treatment outline I haven't mentioned psychotherapy. That may seem strange, because an eating disorder looks like a psychological problem. We want to talk some logic into our child. Motivate them. Find out what upset caused the eating disorder and fix it. Indeed the illness used to be treated this way but the results were poor. People don't beat the illness by talking or thinking, and that is understandable now that we know more about the physiological mechanisms which maintain an eating disorder. Family therapy for eating disorders addresses these mechanisms, which is probably why it works so much better.

The method does make space for psychotherapy, but usually at the end of treatment, when the child's mind is more free to engage. Very often there is no need for psychotherapy because once the eating disorder is beaten, your child is back. The most common psychological issues that made your child so unhappy – depression, anxiety, rigidity, delusional and obsessive thinking, compulsions – recede as the eating disorder loses its hold. When a health service won't give your child psychotherapy, it's not to save money, it's good scientific practice. Having said that, there are exceptions to every rule, and some youngsters do benefit from some psychotherapy input as an adjunct to family therapy: more on this in Chapter 12.

Disorders that ride on an eating disorder's coat tails

It's common for eating disorders to be accompanied by conditions (called 'comorbid' or 'co-occurring' conditions) that your child didn't suffer from before, such as OCD, anxiety or depression. There are also children who developed an eating disorder after they'd been suffering from other disorders, like anxiety disorders (including OCD), autistic spectrum disorder or attention deficit hyperactivity disorder (ADHD).[51] And indeed research is indicating that these conditions share a number of genes. The general rule is to treat the eating disorder as a priority because:

- it presents the greatest risk to health
- as the eating disorder recedes, some of the other problems usually do so as well
- your child probably can't engage with psychotherapy while his brain is affected by undernourishment

If a clinician suspects that your child has clinical depression, borderline personality disorder (BPD), bipolar disorder (manic depression), OCD or that he is on the autistic spectrum, don't panic quite yet. Hold the possibility lightly. I know of cases where a clinician did not have the experience to appreciate the aggression, volatility, depression, suicidality, anxiety or rigidity that an eating disorder can create to varying degrees. Often, once the child's eating disorder is successfully treated, the other diagnostic labels are dropped.[52]

FAMILY THERAPY FOR EATING DISORDERS

What I've described above is family therapy for eating disorders. There are variations, but the principles are pretty much as outlined. They worked for us, they worked for the many families whose stories I have followed, and most importantly we have scientific evidence for their effectiveness. Briefly for now (I return to this in Chapter 12), when I talk of family therapy in this book I am not talking about general or traditional family therapy, which addresses problematic relationships. For eating disorders, family therapy is simply therapy (i.e. treatment) based within the family. The method mobilises the power of parents to rescue – and then guide – their child.

The most recent review of treatments was done by England's health service: family therapy came out a clear leader for anorexia and bulimia.[53] There are similar recommendations world-wide.[54] For instance, the Canadian Paediatric Society writes:

> *"The evidence to date indicates that Family-Based Treatment (FBT)*
> *is the most effective treatment for children and teenagers with*
> *anorexia. A key component of the FBT model is that the parents*
> *are given the responsibility to return their child to physical health*
> *and ensure full weight restoration."*[55]

If you have a child or adolescent with anorexia or bulimia (or an atypical version of those), your therapist should be offering family therapy and doing their utmost to make it work for you. There are therapists who built their reputation years ago using older methods, who still don't use family therapy. I cannot understand that. I recommend you go elsewhere to maximise your child's chances of a full and swift recovery.

HOW LONG BEFORE MY CHILD IS WELL AGAIN?

Our family therapist said she expected nothing less than full recovery. Our children need hope and so do we. Treatment is a lot more effective than it used to be, and when I talk to parents whose child was ill for a long time, I usually find that the care is poles apart from what is recommended, nowadays. The depressing recovery statistics refer to old treatments. Figures vary enormously across studies and results depend on the definition given to 'recovery' and on the type of treatment (lots more in Chapter 12). In addition, our children vary in how severely the illness hits them and they vary in how quickly the treatment brings them relief.

> *"Last night, when I picked up my girl, I had forgotten to bring the*
> *snack for the ride home. She said, 'But Dad, I'm hungry.' Just*
> *matter-of-fact. So matter-of-fact that I didn't realize she had said*
> *them until a few minutes ago, nearly 12 hours later.*
> *I have waited for those two words, 'I'm hungry.' I have not heard*
> *them since I don't know when.*

ED took another hit last night. And my girl took another step. I am joyful."

Let me try and give you some indicators so you can form realistic expectations if your child is suffering from anorexia. Children who are underweight need your intense support for at least as long as it takes to get them weight-restored. You can estimate how long that will be if you plan on 0.5 to 1 kg per week of weight gain (this is the expected norm at home, and a hospital should go faster). With every meal eaten, every kilo gained, our children tend to get better physically and mentally. They manage to eat without too much cajoling... and you too gain confidence. The crisis is over. You may have more and more delightful moments when you feel that your kid is back. There can be day-to-day or week-to-week fluctuations, so if you have bad times, step back and see where you are in the overall picture.

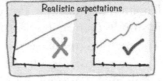

Eventually your child will reach a weight that seems to suit them (usually several kilos higher than their pre-anorexia weight), and many (but not all) of us see a big improvement in our child's mood and thinking.

The next stage of treatment is to repeatedly guide your child to practice normal behaviours (through 'exposure') and to engage in normal life. This phase is all too often rushed or even missed out, and too many youngsters go downhill again. The brain and body need time to heal before a person's recovery is secure. For instance it can take over a year for normal hunger cues to return. And it takes a lot of repetition before fears go and our children become flexible, relaxed and autonomous again.

Life will seem more normal when visits to therapists end. This typically happens 6 to 12 months after the start of family therapy, the recommended treatment for adolescents. Studies indicate that fewer than half of patients have fully recovered by then, so expect your role to continue quite a bit longer. Therapist Sarah Ravin reports that of the anorexia patients who completed treatment with her, it took between 2 and 48 months for them to achieve full recovery.[56]

In short, after weight-restoration your work will continue as you steer your child towards normality – typically 6 months of active exposure work, easing off into some more months or years where we are just vigilant.

Our children vary in how the illness hits them. Some need a lot of support for many years and their parents say that if they'd known this from the start, they could have been more patient, more resilient. But for most of us, improvements come sooner. A big push is required at the start, and as time goes on, we settle into whatever level of support our child needs. After a year or two, for most of us life feels increasingly normal, though I consider it wise to maintain some level of vigilance until our children are in their mid-twenties and their brains have fully matured.

Here are factors that usually support faster improvement and better outcomes in the case of anorexia:[57]

- Your child is treated according to the principles I outlined earlier in this chapter (food, no purging, compassionate family support, consolidating normal behaviours).

- Treatment starts as early as possible. Right away, your child gains weight at a fast rate.

- Recovery may proceed quicker if your child didn't have other mental health disorders prior to the onset of the eating disorder.

- It may seem particularly tragic when the illness hits a very young child, but this makes treatment easier and increases the chances of a swift recovery.[58]

- If time is on your side (i.e. if there's no pressure for your child to leave home), you have a better chance of future-proofing your child against relapses.

5

WHAT PARENTS NEED TO KNOW ABOUT THE CAUSES OF EATING DISORDERS

There are many outdated theories about what causes eating disorders.
Here's what you need to know so that you can focus on what matters.
If your mum thinks you gave your child an eating disorder, show her
this.

This chapter will be brief because you only really need to know three things:

- Despite a lot of research, the causes of eating disorders are still unknown (so anyone telling you your child got ill *because* – fill in the blank – doesn't know what they're talking about.

- Researchers have looked into whether parents or their parenting style might cause an eating disorder, and the answer is a very clear 'No'.

- Now concentrate on treatment

If you're interested on what is and isn't known about causation, see my page on anorexiafamily.com/cause-eating-disorder.

It's human to want to make sense of the terrible things that happen to us, and I know you will be looking for a cause, starting with 'what you did wrong'. Don't imagine for one moment that family therapy for eating disorders is interested in 'fixing' parents. 'Therapy', here, means 'treatment', and 'family' really means 'based within the family'. Modern therapists know you couldn't possibly have caused the eating disorder. They want you to stop ruminating about what you did or didn't do in the past, and instead, attend to the all-important 'now'. They give you a central role in treatment because your bond of love and your dedication make you the best person for the job.

Did everything start with bullying in school? Was it the 'healthy' eating lecture in class? Or that time a doctor, incredibly, told your child to lose weight? None of these could possibly be a single cause. Some could have provided a trigger – they might well be one element of a whole, poorly understood, complex mechanism. When your child is a lot better, you can revisit these ideas to support relapse prevention. You can't forever shield youngsters from triggers, so you will use unfortunate incidents to help your child to practise self-care skills and become more resilient.

Of course you will attend to bullying and not send your child back into a snake pit. But in terms of treating the eating disorder, theories on what might have caused the illness make no difference.

> *'I treat patients with leukemia. I don't need to know how they got it to treat them.'*[59]

There will be people around you who think your child somehow chose to have an eating disorder, or that they're vain or narcissistic or overly influenced by peers or by the media. People may also nod wisely and say, 'It's all about control, of course' or 'She didn't want to grow up' or 'It's a way for him to cope with difficult emotions'. This is all simplistic pop-psychology, and an insult to the sophisticated research going on.

> *'I wish our therapist had told us what took us so long to find out: 'This isn't anyone's fault and your child isn't doing this deliberately.'''*

If you want to shut people up fast, tell them that the illness is genetic (though that's an over-simplification because environmental factors interact with genes). If you're in a more patient mood, you might like the suggestions I make in Chapter 11.

We now know that the same genes operate to increase the risk for anorexia (we will have to wait for genome studies on other eating disorders) and several other psychiatric conditions: OCD, depression, schizophrenia and anxiety. This makes sense to all the parents whose child with anorexia also suffered from anxiety or OCD before the illness struck. Other links coming from genome studies include: attainment of academic degrees, the drive to exercise or move, some metabolic traits, and the tendency to low body-fat.[60] Please understand that genes will not, on their own, cause an eating disorder: most illnesses come from epigenetics: an interplay of genes and environment.[61]

I'll talk a little more about triggers and risk factors, as far as they are relevant to how you're going to help your child.

Weight loss and major stressors seem to be risk factors. These can trigger the illness, prolong it, or be part of what sends your child back into relapse. Conversely, the illness is presently treated and kept at bay (and there are even changes in the genes) by taking care of nutrition, weight and psychological wellbeing.

Consider also the inherited personality traits associated with anorexia: our children are often very smart, conscientious, high achieving, determined, sensitive and kind. Such traits are just lovely, but as they interact with each other and with environmental influences they can become a burden. Our children are often found to suffer from perfectionism, poor self-esteem, difficulty in set-shifting (the ability to adapt, change course, be flexible), black-and-white thinking, and a vulnerability to depression or anxiety. With this book's attention to compassion, your child will learn the art of using their personality traits to their advantage.

Be aware that most studies look at people while they're suffering from anorexia, not before, so they are not able to distinguish cause and effect. While anxiety, OCD or perfectionism often pre-date an eating disorder, plenty of parents only see these mindsets emerge while their child is malnourished. My daughter developed mental rigidity and various irrational fears while the anorexia was strong. As she recovered, she became her old emotionally intelligent self again.

Although I've mentioned possible risk factors that might help you make sense of what's happening with your child, please understand there is no simple mechanism of causation. A number of risk factors have to collectively tip someone above some threshold. You could think of it as many streams all feeding into a river. The research goes on.

Your child didn't choose to have an eating disorder

I want to emphasise that this eating disorder is in no way your child's fault. At no time does he choose any of his obnoxious, distressing or dangerous behaviours or beliefs. He is a puppet on a string. He lost his freedom the day the eating disorder took hold.

You need to get this at a very deep level, because if you're anything like what I was, blame will leak out in your words or in your body language in times of stress, right when your child most needs your support. This will hold back progress.

Even though my daughter knew that skipping meals and secrecy were likely to re-trigger the illness, and even though she was terrified of ever being ill again, at age 15 she secretly cut down on school lunches. I could blame her for that. But it is such illogical behaviour that I can only think that forces outwith her control drove her to it.

The more we let go of judgements and accept that our kids are the way they are, the more we can bring about change. Concentrate on living and breathing non-judgement and acceptance towards your child, and make that the culture in your household.

When people in recovery blame their parents

You may have come across people who had, or still have, an eating disorder, and who very much lay the blame at their parents' feet. They remember that family life was utter hell. Is it possible they had loving parents before the eating disorder hit them and the family home then turned into a war zone? Could it be, tragically, that the parents would have continued to be supportive if only they'd had better advice and access to modern treatment?

Whichever way the parents had behaved before the illness began, the eating disorder would probably have manifested itself eventually. Life, and in particular, our society, supplies triggers aplenty.

Parents with an eating disorder

Have you suffered from an eating disorder yourself? Do you presently suffer from one but manage to keep it under control? You may be scared that therapists will blame you for your child's eating disorder, or that they will consider you incapable of contributing to your child's treatment.

First, understand that because of genetics, it's very common for both child and parent to be affected by an eating disorder.

It is perfectly appropriate that you should care for your child just the same as any parent. What matters is what you do now, not what you did in the past. When James Lock and his team conducted trials to validate Family-Based Treatment, they did not exclude parents with eating disorders.

If you can get rid of any notion of shame around your own eating disorder, it will be easier for you to have unconditional acceptance of your child.

From what I've picked up through the grapevine, parents who suffer from an eating disorder are pretty good at keeping it under control while all their efforts go into supporting their child. Still, if you're struggling, do seek help. If I were king, the clinics that treat our kids would also be set up to treat parents.

The only time a therapist should be interested in your eating disorder is if it drives you to collude with your child's illness. Sure, we've all been taken in by our child's pleading and bargaining – but I'm talking about parents who actively get in the way of treatment. I have met a teenager whose mother supplied her with laxatives and helped her bin food. Clearly someone else had to take on the child's treatment – in her case, it was her older sister.

Why? Why us? How to let go

If you are losing precious energy asking 'Why?' or 'Why us?' please know that's normal. Pause, put a gentle hand on your cheek, and send yourself messages of kindness. You are suffering. It really hurts when you think you could have done something different. You so want the best for your child. May you find clarity and courage.

Self-compassion will transform the pain better than reading heaps of research. It will move you towards deep acceptance of what is, summarised by this mantra:

> *"Shit happens."*

The Serenity Prayer

The Serenity Prayer may be more to your taste:

> *'Grant me the serenity to accept the things I cannot change, courage*
> *to change the things I can, and wisdom to know the difference'*[62]

If you're finding this hard to apply, see Chapter 15 for tools that help with acceptance and letting go. These may liberate you of the torment of guilt and free up a lot of bandwidth.

Your child needs food urgently and you need all your energy for the challenging task ahead. Redirect your focus to the call for action. What's going on with your child? What are her issues and her needs right now? How can you feed her? Every day you're going to get better at it. That's what matters.

6

PRACTICAL STEPS TO HELP YOUR CHILD BEAT THE EATING DISORDER

*An eating disorder affects almost every aspect of our children's lives.
Here is an overview of what you can do to systematically weaken its
grip and get your child back.*

Helping a child with an eating disorder ought to be pretty intuitive. You just want to get your child to eat, right? Or you want her to stop bingeing or purging. But she fights you. She tells you you're making it worse, that she doesn't have a problem, that she hates you, and then she freaks you out by behaving totally out of character. You're at a loss for what to do next, and you're scared that whatever you do will make her worse.

In this chapter I cover each aspect of treatment. These are all things you can do right now to get your child well. My emphasis here is on the first phase, when you will be focusing on food – and usually weight gain. The following chapters give you more of the much-needed 'how-tos'. Then in Chapter 10 we move on to the questions that are most common after the first phase of treatment: how to bring back some normality and move towards full recovery.

Every day you have decisions to make: what to allow, what to prevent, what to try next. I'm going to tell you what worked for us and for other parents, and what experienced therapists recommend.

For every step you take, even when you encounter resistance, you are moving forward. If right now the journey I propose seems impossible to you, hang in there. Even a single tool, if it works for you, can make all the difference.

Now I don't want to overload you with things you 'should' do. I hope that one or two suggestions will stand out: things that make sense to you and that you really want to try. Things you have the energy for. Go for those and leave the rest for another time. One step at a time. Build on successes. And I want you to know, based on my very considerable experience, that it's OK to screw up sometimes. I mean, often.

Perhaps, part way through reading this chapter, you'll want to jump in and make big sweeping changes. If you're all fired up, the risk is you'll charge in like a bull and then crash at the first obstacle. Whereas your aim is to present as a competent, loving parent who can be trusted to take charge. At the end of this chapter, I offer you prompts to plan what measures and support you want to put in place.

I want to give you tools, not fear. If you read about behaviours here that your child doesn't have, be glad: there's no reason he'll ever have them. And if he does, you'll see in what follows that many don't need to be tackled right away – you can take your time, see where your priorities lie. Besides, you may get some freebies in this business: as your previously starving child regains weight, many issues can fade with no work on your part. In our case, they eventually all disappeared and we were granted every parent's wish – to get our kid back.

And also: my Bitesize audios, with models of parent-child dialogue, may help you or your partner put the following into practice[63]

FOOD AND LOVE

The two main elements of treatment

As we saw in Chapter 4, food is the main component in the treatment of an eating disorder. It provides much-needed fuel for the brain and the rest of the body. There is also healing through the regular exposure to normal eating without purging. Yet for a while, regular eating is the most scary, horrible, anxiety-inducing thing you could ask your child to do. That's where love comes in. A parent's love is a healing force. Your child will not have to walk through hell alone because you're going to be right by their side. sticking with them no matter what. It may not look like it right now, but you are building a relationship that will sustain your child's recovery and support their wellbeing for years to come.

Force-feeding? Of course not

When we use the words for nutritional rehabilitation like 'assisted eating', 'feeding' or 'refeeding', some people hear 'food police' and 'force-feeding'. Perhaps they imagine that one parent pins the child down while the other pinches the child's nostrils and shovels food in their mouth.

OK, hands up, I admit it. I've thought of it, in the darkest of my fantasies, as I sat there watching my daughter not eat, frustrated out of my mind. I bet some parents have tried to do it. We'd do anything to save our children's lives.

No, the forceful stuff is done by hospitals, not parents, and only when there is immediate danger to life. It looks like many people with anorexia accept tube-feeding, though sadly sometimes people have to be restrained. Doctors and nurses do whatever it takes to save a life.

But this isn't what we're talking about. We're talking about assisting eating at home, and that means developing all the skills that enable our children to eat what they need with absolutely no violence, physical or mental. As I show in Chapter 14, it can be done without threats, punishments, rewards or bribes. It will strengthen your relationship – that's been my experience with my daughter, and countless other parents say the same. Your child will know all through her life that she matters, that she's loved, that there is support for her no matter what, because you were her companion when she was in the darkest pit of hell. She will learn to sail her own ship because right now you are giving her a secure, peaceful harbour.

If your child needs an injection, do you tell them 'It's OK, sweetheart, never mind. I can see it's too scary for you' or do you support them through the fear and pain of it?

Our children's distress at mealtimes is horrible, but it does not harm them. Not eating harms them. Likewise, we are not fighting our children over control, choice or autonomy. We are taking charge of the elements of their life which the illness makes them unable to care for.

> *"I didn't 'get it' until another parent asked me if we were*
> *'encouraging' our son to eat or 'requiring' him to eat. None of the*
> *professionals had made the point that eating was non-negotiable."*[64]

I suffered from a version of 'food police'[65] concerns for a while. How could I bring the best out in my daughter if I took away her freedom of choice and refused to engage in the subjects that most occupied her mind?

Yet if I didn't require her to eat, she was not free. Anorexia, it seemed, had removed her ability to choose to take the most basic care of herself. It created a prison for her mind.

And so I reconciled myself with the notion that because I wanted to protect and care for her, and because food seemed to be the best treatment, I would do the equivalent of taking her for a life-saving injection, six times a day, for as many months as required. And I trusted that if I did so out of a desire to care, if I accepted and loved her, she would not feel alone in her pain.[66]

That's what parents do: we give nurturing, *and* we give structure. It's not an either/or. We take compassionate action for our kids when they simply can't take care of themselves. The day medication comes up that frees up their mind, things will be different. But for now, we feed.

Besides, there are big differences between food and a nurse's needle. Your child may be longing for you to request that she eats, as we shall see now.

GIVE YOUR CHILD CONTAINMENT AND AMMUNITION AGAINST THE EATING-DISORDER VOICE

> *"Although outwardly I must have seemed insane, inside I was*
> *secretly relieved that I was finally getting the help I needed to get my*
> *life back, and that the choice to eat was being taken away."*[67]

We get so used to our child refusing food that it's astounding when we realise that all along, a massive internal conflict was going on, and part of them was wishing they could eat, wishing it wasn't their decision.

When we remove choices from our kids, we take away internal conflicts they are incapable of handling. We give them containment, structure.

If they have an eating-disorder voice, we give them a weapon to use against it. The voice realises it's met its match and eventually quietens.

> "Deep down inside YOUR DAUGHTER WANTS YOU TO HELP HER. The disease will not let her eat; she needs to make it YOUR FAULT she is eating. You need to take the decisions away from her. Many going through this disease have a voice in their head telling them not to eat. 'Food is bad, you will get fat, you are worthless, you are a pig!' Scary to think your lovely daughter is living with this every day. Mine would say outright to me, 'Mom, you are saying I HAVE to eat this, right?' If I ever backed down, she'd come right back and say, 'You are telling me I have to eat this, right?' She needed it to be my fault she was eating it, not hers. Then she could ignore the voice in her head telling her not to eat."

If you are ever in doubt about taking away your kid's rights or freedom or dignity, think, 'Am I giving him the containment he needs?' If you were growing a fragile sapling in an area of storms and gales, would you not tie it to a pole, or enclose it in one of those transparent tube thingies? As you may have guessed, I'm not much of a gardener, but I think I would be able to gauge when a sapling needed support, and when it was strong enough to reach out on its own and claim its own space.

HEAR HOW YOUR CHILD SPEAKS IN CODE

Our children often don't express what they long for when they're plagued by internal conflicts. Or, to put it another way, because they fear retaliation from their eating-disorder voice. We can learn a lot from the stories of children who have recovered.[68] Sometimes they trick their bully by speaking in code.

> "When my ten-year-old was in the hospital I was responsible for picking her foods. The dietitians encouraged me to take it slow, but I felt differently. If my daughter asked me not to pick something, I would pick it the next day. I began to realize that for her, this was a way that she could communicate to me what she truly wanted that the eating disorder would not let her have."[69]

Have your antennae out for the hints your child may give you.

> "I became clued up to the random comments from my daughter like 'I know that if I tried an ice cream that would make you really

happy,' so I would say to myself, 'OK let's go and poke the eating disorder in the eye.'"[70]

Of course when we get a hint, we have to play along because the eating disorder bully is listening. We say, 'That's a lucky coincidence! This is exactly what I was planning to give you. No, it has nothing to do with what you just said. I'd have given you ice cream whether you wanted to or not.' Well, you might need to be a little subtler.

If you're in the habit of being transparent and truthful, forget it. You're in the presence of a hijacker, remember?

I love this dad's story of a breakthrough.

> *"D is back to school, the first time in around three months. I decided rather than overload her this morning I would add morning snack onto lunch/tea. She rang at approx 11 am — wait for it — 'I'm hungry, Dad, could you bring me a snack to school?'*
> *When I picked myself up off the floor I said yes of course, I'll be there in five minutes. Heart racing and my eyes welling up (it was emotional!), sped home, grabbed the biggest pancake. When I pulled up she was waiting, then she changed, 'No, I can't have it.' I told her she hadn't asked for it, that it was part of her meal plan, and that I was already driving that way when she rang, to bring it to her. Five minutes refusal, then she ate it.*
> *I was unashamedly crying like a baby when I went back to the garage for work, but for a change they were tears of pure joy and relief. She is my hero. Words don't do my feelings justice for how much I admire her right now."*[71]

For us, recognising a coded request was the biggest turning point in our daughter's recovery. It was like a window had sprung open, giving us a clear view of how we could help her, after a year of fumbling for the key. She'd been refusing food for several days because we had scrapped the meal plan she'd become dependent on in hospital. Her suffering was huge, but we were sticking firmly but compassionately to our decision to take charge of her meals. Her health was good enough at that point, but she was restricting and heading towards re-admission and we had nothing to lose.

Several times, she asked if I'd take her to the doctor if she continued not to eat, and if so – and this was the significant bit – would the doctor make me increase her food? Initially I had given vague answers, confused by the twisted logic of going from ordinary meals that aren't being eaten, to bigger meals that aren't eaten. But as another awful day passed, I twigged that she needed to hear a very definite yes from me. She needed a weapon against her eating-disorder voice.

So with our trusted eating-disorders clinician, we gravely and ceremoniously delivered the threat: 'You have to eat everything we serve you for the next three days, otherwise we will increase your food.'

Even though I'm sure that this is what she wanted to hear, she still found the ultimatum very distressing. But she ate. And every time she struggled, she checked:

'So if I don't eat this you'll be making me eat more?' To which we'd give an emphatic yes.

Every three days, we took our cue from her and repeated our ultimatum until two weeks had passed and the coded requests stopped, to be replaced by the occasional, half-hearted 'Do I have to eat this?' Our daughter had got used to eating everything we gave her. Presumably, the eating-disorder voice had lost its fight.

I have heard of children using written notes to communicate with their parents without their eating-disorder voice 'hearing'. Not necessarily young kids either: the voice has nothing to do with childishness. Some children message from their phone from another room. If your child can find a safe way of talking with you, your job is going to become quite a bit easier.

REMOVE CHOICES: MAGIC PLATE

For us, as for many parents, the key tool for helping our child to eat was to take control of all food and health-related decisions until they could safely do this for themselves. Some parents call this Magic Plate, and their experiences show, over and again, how effective it is.

Here's how it works. You inform your child in a clear and loving manner that from now on you and your partner will be in charge of all decisions relating to food and health. Whenever she tries to negotiate for smaller quantities, asks you to swap one food for another or refuses what you give her, you remind her that for now, you are in control, you are highly competent, and that you'd like her to trust you to take good care of her.

This is because she is physically, biologically and neurologically incapable of making competent decisions for herself in this area. She is plagued by internal conflicts that cut her off from the ability to take care of herself. For any other aspect of her life, you continue giving her age-appropriate levels of freedom and choice. But in the areas where her autonomy has already been removed by what anorexia does to her brain, you step in and make decisions until she recovers her mental health.

Six times a day (some prefer to make it five times), you ask your child to sit down and you put food in front of her. Breakfast, lunch, dinner, and snacks in between. You expect your kid to eat all of it. No negotiation.

You decide which foods to serve. You decide on quantities. The food is already plated up in the correct amounts. It's on a Magic Plate because it simply appears at the right time, and your child hasn't been involved in its preparation at all. You've kept her out of the kitchen and out of the supermarket. You don't discuss if the food quantities are greater or smaller than yesterday's or different from what the hospital used to give her. You make sure that she cannot get rid of food by hiding it or purging.

You don't ask her to choose between two types of biscuit, and you don't check whether she'd prefer cheddar or brie in her sandwich – that will come later. This spares your child the agony of decision-making when she's racked by internal conflict or being bullied by an eating-disorder voice.

Say you present your child with a choice of two biscuits. This is what might be going on in her head:

- She tries to guess which has the fewer calories. The thought of getting it wrong is highly stressful. Her eating-disorder voice won't allow her to take any risks. In the end, she's so focused on calorie avoidance that she eats neither of the biscuits, and also turns down her milk.

- She knows which biscuit has the fewer calories, and it happens to be her all-time favourite. What luck! But just as she begins to feel some pleasure, the principle of self-denial kicks in. The eating-disorder voice reminds her she's unworthy, and punishes her for enjoying food.

Of course, our children need to learn to make choices in order to recover. They will need to recover their autonomy. But that's for later, when most of the fear has gone.

Magic Plate is by no means the only method available to you. A family-based treatment therapist will not tell you to do Magic Plate; they'll ask you to devise your own way of ensuring your child eats and restores weight. Some people with eating disorders are able to participate in setting themselves challenges and in teaming up with their parents to get the motivation they need.[72] With my daughter, along with most (but not all) of the young people I've heard of, lack of motivation and strong resistance were part of the illness, and removing choices was an effective approach.

'YOU'RE MAKING ME FAT!'

As you ask your child to eat, you are highly likely to be hit with the accusation, 'You're making me fat.' Sometimes parents tell me their child isn't worried about being fat, but sadly they have to revise that the minute they serve decent portions. So how should you respond? I go into this in some detail in Chapter 14 (*'Am I fat?' How to respond*). For a quick answer right now, I suggest 'I'm so sorry you are worried. It's not helpful to talk about this. Come and look at the rainbow!'

MEAL PLANS: SHOULD YOUR CHILD DETERMINE THE MENU?

Meal plans mean different things to different people. It is sometimes just a guide to help parents who think they don't know what to feed their child. More on this later. For now, I will focus on meal plans that are created in collaboration with your child.

Meal planning with your child may seem like a good idea if he eats what he agreed to. The problem is that the plan is usually low in calories and in variety. He loses weight and his rigidity grows. Week after week you try and get him to agree to more, and you have some successes, but the trend is downwards. You are scared that if you ditch the system he will stop eating altogether, but the system is keeping him ill.

Some hospitals consider meal planning to be part of the treatment – they might call it individual nutritional counselling. There is no evidence that it's of benefit, and it presents an extra hurdle to coming home to family meals. I suspect meal planning is popular in hospitals because the catering department wants advance information. Outside hospitals, remember that people were treated with individual therapy, without the help of their family. As an eating disorder distorts the perception of portion sizes, you can see how people might need a written list of what to eat and how much… if their parents are not in charge of meals.

A dietitian who is willing to sit with a patient to do a meal plan is surely either a masochist or a saint. It can take an hour of painstaking work to change the flavour of a yoghurt. This means that another week goes by with just one new food. James Lock (who conducted randomised controlled trials on FBT, an approach which doesn't rest on meal plans) suggests this is like giving soap and water to someone suffering from OCD, in other words it reinforces rigid eating-disorder behaviours. He advises that we expose our children to varied foods as soon as possible.[73]

Anorexia typically makes people very rigid in what they consider safe. When my daughter spent weekends at home, packaged foods had to be the right brand, and everything had to be weighed accurately. I don't know if the meal plan was a necessary crutch to get her eating in hospital, but I do know it eventually became fuel for the anorexia.

In hospital, my darling girl got highly skilled at manipulating meal-planning sessions with the dietitian. With time she got the seal of approval to reduce not only her range of foods, but also her calorie intake. When I got my calculator out, I understood why her weight had started to drop.

When she was discharged from hospital, the assumption was that we would continue with the meal plan. It gave us some confidence that she would continue eating what she was accustomed to. But it was also acting as an anorexia reinforcer: we were serving the wrong kind of pizza, we hadn't used the right glass for her milk, and no way was she eating butter unless we could source the same little packets that the hospital used. In a way, the meal plan was a stick the anorexia used to beat everyone with and get its own way. My daughter could long for a slice of birthday cake, but as it wasn't on the meal plan, it was bad, dangerous and entirely forbidden. The meal plan had been allowed to gain so much power that it later proved easier to give her first chocolate brownie than to replace hospital butter portions with our own butter.

The day my daughter started recovering, rather than just stagnating or regressing, was the day we threw the meal plan away.

For her, Magic Plate proved to be anxiety-reducing. She'd ask what we were planning for dinner, and we'd say, 'It's better you find out when we serve it.' Soon, she relaxed into acceptance. We discovered that she could rise to extreme challenges if they were sprung on her without warning. The anxiety would rise in the moment and we might get an earful, but this was nothing compared to all the anorexic distress that swirled round her head if she knew what was coming.

Our children do differ in this aspect. Some recovered young people report that meal plans helped them greatly because when they knew what to expect, they felt less anxiety.[74] Presumably the adults managed to get enough on the meal plans to get progress. And the system worked because the youngsters knew that once a plan had been agreed, there was no deviating from it.

Eventually your child will have to practise walking without a crutch. He will have to become flexible about what, where, and when to eat. Whether or not meal plans work for you, at some stage you will need to get rid of them.

DO PARENTS BENEFIT FROM A MEAL PLAN?

Some clinics will give you, the parent, some kind of meal plan. These are very prescriptive, some less so. Some involve calorie-counting, and some are based on typical portion sizes for various food groups and a system of 'exchanges'. A meal plan for parents is quite different from a meal plan that's negotiated with the child. Some parents like plans because they are not confident how much to feed. They also like that the therapist holds the authority ('You have to eat it because *the experts* say so'). That's fine in the early stages, but if your child is still rigid about eating to a plan months into treatment, it's high time to bring in flexibility.

I know parents who are find meal plans a burden, especially if they prescribe foods alien to the family. Shockingly, some therapists' meal plans hinder progress: the parents sense that they could feed more, but children resist every 'extra' crumb once they've seen the plan. While there's a risk of refeeding syndrome, if you're given a meal plan, stick to it or consult clinicians. Afterwards, my view is that a meal plan should only serve as a flexible guide to *minimum* quantities, and should be scrapped as soon as it disempowers parents.

An FBT therapist will not give you a meal plan. They trust that you can work out meals for yourself. They also want your child to see *you* as the trustworthy person in charge.

WHAT IF MY CHILD DOESN'T EAT?

If you're new to this, chances are you're not asking 'What if my child doesn't eat?' but 'What about when my child doesn't eat?'

Don't expect perfection

If your child hasn't eaten for a while, or if he's been relying solely on tube-feeding, swallowing just a small amount of food is a massive victory. We need to be 100 per cent committed to feeding our children, and it's also absolutely normal to fail quite a bit. The route to recovery includes many imperfections. Anorexia may lumber people with all-or-nothing thinking, but parents don't need to join in.

> *"Sometimes, you might not succeed. MOVE ON. So it didn't work this time. You didn't stop trying to walk when you were a baby just because you toppled over a few times, did you? Keep on going."*[75]

When our daughter was in hospital, we felt like she was in a magical space where not a single meal was missed. When she was due to come home for a meal, we were terrified that if we failed to make her eat, the spell would be broken. To us, the stakes were huge. We were terrified.

The hospital assured us that missing a meal was no great deal. She wouldn't die, and neither would she get caught up in the starvation whirlpool. They were absolutely right. Even when our daughter started spending several days at a time with us, it was OK when she missed a meal. We kept an attitude of expectation that she would eat the next meal. And mostly she did.

One thing that may help you not to beat yourself up over a single failed meal is remembering that our kids' heads are full of strange rules and warped science, most of which we are ignorant of. Their secret reason for refusing a meal could be that they didn't scrunch their abdominals 23 times before getting out of bed. They may dig their heels in all afternoon, refusing lunch, arguing about how full and sick they feel, but when ten minutes later it's snack time, they may eat it with relish. You will never know why lunch was taboo, yet the snack was OK.

Plan B: when Plan A fails

Plan A is your child eating everything you want her to eat during a meal. As this is unlikely to happen 100 per cent of the time, it's a good idea to have a Plan B. This will help you make wise decisions and keep your emotions under control. You want your child to have an experience of care, not of blame or panic.

In the early days, when my daughter was unable to touch her food and I finally let her leave the table, I didn't know what to do with my face. Should I look stern and disapproving until the next meal? Should I act as though everything was just fine?

I wish I'd had this mother's clarity right from the start:[76]

> *"And if it all goes pear shaped? Well, it goes pear shaped. Move on. Just move on. Don't dwell on it, don't get your hackles up. Go to Plan B without getting angry. Whatever your Plan B may be. 'Okay, well, if you can't finish, we're going to have to Boost I suppose. That's ok. Let me get the Boost, and let's get that over with.' Calm cool confidence is key. Zero judgement, zero anger. Having a plan, and a good plan is probably the single best thing I can recommend. It will give you the confidence that you must show."*

A good Plan B should make your child safe for the next few hours. It could also consider the longer term, because what you do after this unsuccessful meal may affect how the next meal goes. For this reason, I believe Plan B should also nurture connection and unconditional acceptance.

The content of your Plan B is for you to work out with your partner and clinicians. It will depend on your child's state of health, what stage of treatment you're in, and so on. Here are some examples:

- Calling an end to the meal in a matter-of-fact way, noting (inwardly or out loud) what's been achieved, and deciding it is good enough for now. Moving on to activities that might remind your child that life can be sweet.

- Making up for uneaten food with an energy drink supplement (Boost, Ensure etc). Utterly pointless with children like mine, for whom drinking a supplement was no easier than eating, but an essential strategy for many families and part of the 'food is medicine' message.

- Cancelling an outing in order to rest. Make sure you do not present it as punishment.

- Cutting out exercise. To preserve calories, or if your child is very ill, to protect the heart. Not as a punishment.

- Lying down for a couple of hours.

- Telling your child you'll make up for the uneaten food (some, or all of it) in the next meal (after privately working out to what extent he can manage larger amounts).

> *"If she said she was too full to finish, I'd say, 'OK, I'll add it to the next snack.' Or if it was something that couldn't be reheated and re-served, 'No problem, I'll make up for it at your next meal with something else.' That usually made her gulp down the last of her food. She couldn't bear to think that the amount added to her snack might have been even just one calorie more."*

- Making the next meal bigger without making any mention of it, as all that matters right now is weight gain. Cream and butter are your friends.

- Having your child miss school, and being clear about the reasons. For instance, rest may be a medical requirement, or you may not want her to expend energy when weight gain is a priority, or you may want her at home in order to support the next meal.

- Taking her to the emergency department of the hospital.

- Taking her to clinicians who are already on board: a doctor or nurse or eating disorders unit, where you can get immediate support for the meal or for the drinking of a supplement, or for tube-feeding.

- Getting her admitted to an inpatient unit or returning her to one without delay.

> *"Our daughter managed to eat well in hospital, so when she came home for weekends, the agreement was that if she didn't finish everything on her plate, she went straight back to the ward. For a while, a nurse came to our house each mealtime, ready to take our daughter back to hospital if she didn't eat."*

- Getting her tube-fed (if she's unwilling, the mental health laws in your country would determine whether it can go ahead without her consent). Tube-feeding may sound horrible, yet many children have started their road to recovery like this.

Plan B can be just for your benefit, or it can be something you discuss with your child at a quiet time so that she doesn't hear it as a threat. For example, 'Sweetie, we've got three days to reverse this situation. We can't let your health deteriorate any more, so we'll (*insert Plan B item*) if you don't start eating everything we give you, starting from this coming lunchtime. You know that, right? Maybe it will turn out that (*Plan B item*) is what you need, but let's do everything we can for the next three days to try and avoid it.'

If your Plan B involves hospitals, you might, like some parents I know, plan for this eventuality with your medical team. The last thing you want is to queue for hours in the emergency department, only to be sent home with an instruction to 'give her a hamburger!' It has happened.

Parents tell stories of getting their kid as far as the car park of the emergency department, by which stage the child, in desperation, has drunk her energy drink. One evening I got one precious glass of water into my daughter by taking her to the out-of-hours GP service. The kind doctor was out of his depth, though he did, at least, reassure me that my daughter wasn't about to die. I used him mercilessly by insisting my daughter drank in his presence. She drank out of sheer embarrassment, poor thing.

We never had a formal Plan B – the idea never occurred to us. My husband and I played everything by ear, discussed our next move in whispers at night, and it's only with time that we realised that if our daughter failed to eat a meal, it didn't mean that we'd done anything wrong, and didn't mean that she'd never eat again.

HOW LONG SHOULD WE PERSIST WITH A MEAL?

If your child hasn't touched her food, or if she's started but now seems stuck, how long should you sit at the table with her, supporting her to eat? How long before Plan B, if you have one, should kick in?

My aim here is to show you a range of approaches, including some that I would only use as a last resort. For a break from reading, watch my YouTube video 'Stuck and not eating! Parents' meal support tips'[77], which will give you an overview of what follows.

You sit at the dinner table till everything is eaten

Many parents have saved their child's life by making it clear that mealtimes only end when all the food is eaten. After all, if you need medicine, it's not acceptable to have just half of it. School, work or fun (both for the child and the parents) are on hold until the plate is clean. Some therapists favour this approach ('Be tough on the eating disorder'), and others don't.

Details vary from family to family. Some parents have a Plan B, which they apply within an hour or so. Some persevere at the table for three, four, five hours. Some use threats of sanctions if the meal isn't finished. Many heroic parents work very hard to try to encourage, distract, entertain.

"I remember the very first day my husband and I took on refeeding our daughter D. We got through the day OK until supper time, when we gave her something with butter on it. It went on for three hours. After many attempts to engage us in circular illogical arguments, she finally asked what would happen if breakfast came and she still hadn't eaten it. I made a split second decision and calmly said to her, 'If you haven't eaten this by breakfast time, then you'll need to eat this butter as well as your breakfast.' D ate the butter about 20 minutes later. We never had a stand-off over butter again."[78]

I'll share my own experience. At various times during her anorexia I have insisted my child stay at the table until she finished her meal. In the early days, when I had insufficient skills, it ended in harsh words and tears – on both sides. Whether or not she managed the last morsel, there was a price to pay: she'd eat less for the next few meals. Much later on, when I had the skills and resources described in this book, I did occasionally make meals last a long time. But I was tracking her capabilities all along and being flexible. And I was generally more grounded and empathic.

Contrary to my experience, some parents have found that after a few painful marathon sessions, the following meals have gone smoothly. Perhaps they've given their kid a weapon to use against the anorexia: 'See, I have no choice. My parents are going to sit with me until I eat.'

If you join parent circles, you may hear the mantra 'Life stops until you eat'. It can mean a whole lot of contradictory things, so ask the speaker exactly what they mean. Sometimes it involves punishment. Sometimes it means an all-night stand-off over the last bite. Sometimes it means everything (except therapy appointments) is cancelled until the child has managed breakfast. Sometimes it means that parents reorganise their lives in order to make supporting their child an absolute priority. But most often it means accepting that some meals may become marathons.

"After 18 months of seeing this child deteriorate mentally and physically due to our inability to help her eat, 'Life stops until you eat' saved her life. For us, it meant sitting for hours over an uneaten piece of food. It shortened her suffering dramatically (six weeks) as compared to the 18 months of suffering when we didn't have that radical stance."[79]

For some parents, the mindset is really 'Life starts when you eat'.[80] You need to eat, and as soon as that's done, as soon as your body has what it needs, we can get on with our lives. This can help give the message that we're not trying to punish our child, but to keep her safe. Psychologically, it generally works better to picture what can be done rather than what can't. Compare 'You can't go on your computer till you've tidied your room!' with 'Sure, you can get back to your computer, just as soon as you've picked your clothes off the floor.'

You may like the idea of keeping your child at the table until she's eaten. It's clear, and it's consistent. But like all rigid systems, there are difficulties when it's tested to its limits. An obvious one is that your child may run away. How much do you want to forcibly bring her back to the table?

Some parents have a very strong instinct, given their child's extreme emotional instability, that marathon meals are not an option. They fear that long stand-offs will increase the risk of self-harm or suicidal impulses.

What happens when breakfast extends into snack time, which runs into lunch? Some parents add the new meal to the uneaten one, so that presumably, after a few hours, the child is expected to eat breakfast, snack and lunch. As this is probably setting the child up for failure, Plan B needs to kick in before this situation arises.

I know of a few cases where parents, in a bid to break a deadlock over dinner, have kept their child in the dining room through most of the night. Sometimes it works:

> "We sat for five hours over a bowl of ice cream, but I knew we
> would prevail, because I am able to stay up all night if I need to,
> but she can't. Indeed, she eventually ate in order to go to bed."[81]

Sometimes, though, both parent and child find the marathon session so bruising that they only try it once before opting for another approach.

If you plan to sit for many hours at the table with your child, make sure you can do so without getting so bored or desperate that you start shouting, crying or blaming. Expect your child to try everything under the sun to get you to give up. Even if you hate her behaviour, bear in mind she needs your kindness and active support all the way through (and if that sounds impossible, remember I have empathy tools for you in Chapters 13 to 15). If you encounter high levels of resistance for a long time, it's unrealistic to aim to do this by yourself. In my opinion, the marathon meal – if it's to be done in a loving manner – needs at least two carers relaying each other.

Set a time limit

None of our own clinicians were in favour of letting mealtimes go on for hours. For our daughter's home visits, the hospital suggested that we give her a 20-minute time limit. The idea was, first of all, to stop mealtimes expanding into a high-stress fight, and also that the time limit would concentrate our daughter's mind. And indeed, on some occasions, we got magic in the final three minutes. She'd pick up her fork and, in a sort of panic, gobble down her food before time ran out.

If, when the 20 minutes were over, she was still eating, of course we encouraged her to continue.

But most often, the time limit didn't particularly help. It just meant she could refuse to eat, knowing that a few minutes later she'd be free.

The use of a time limit is quite different in a hospital where a nasogastric tube might be used after the allocated number of minutes.

I believe that for some families, the work to be done isn't so much on getting the child to eat, but on getting her to eat at a good rate, free of rituals. If your child nibbles at food extremely slowly, having a time limit can be part of the work to normalise meals.

Call a halt and move on

What worked for us eventually was flexibility. Playing it by ear. While, at the same time, giving the message that we knew exactly what we were doing, that we were in charge, and that we were not in the slightest bit allowing ourselves to be manipulated. We didn't want our child to think she had any wiggle room; we wanted to protect her from the bullying of her eating-disorder voice, and at the same time, we wanted to create the conditions for success, confidence, and trust. If we allowed our daughter to get up without having finished her meal, we did so without blame, and without giving the message that there had been a failure.

I'm aware this may sound like a load of contradictions, so let me describe it (and remember there is no single way that works for every child).

A few weeks after our daughter was discharged from hospital, we asserted our takeover of all food-related decisions. She reacted to the loss of her hospital meal plan by reducing her food intake even more. During this phase, we were ready to spend 20 minutes asking her to come to the table, and when we got her there, we persisted in asking her to eat for another 20 minutes or so (the time limit was our own mental guideline – she didn't know about it). After that, if we still held no hope of success, we'd say, 'OK, one step at a time. It's entirely normal that it should be hard for you at the beginning. Next meal will be easier for you. We'll get there, don't worry. Let's forget about all this till snack time. How about doing some drawing?'

We weren't giving up, we hadn't failed, and we were still in control. This was just a process.

What we were doing is in line with what Lock and Le Grange describe in their Family-Based Treatment manual for the first few days of refeeding: parents winning small battles by getting their child to eat just one mouthful more than she was prepared to, and doing so from a mindset of uncritical acceptance.[82] To me, having your child leave food on her plate at this stage is not failure. It's the start of a virtuous cycle in which parents are empowered, the kid starts to lean on the parents, and the eating-disorder voice realises it's now facing a strong and confident opponent.

A week or so later, our daughter let go of her zero-eating stance, and thereafter some meals went on for an hour or so. We took the time to keep going, one mouthful at a time, till the plate was clean. By then we'd become reasonably skilled, our daughter knew what to expect, and the hour went by without any emotional violence.

We soon started introducing foods she'd been unable to eat for over a year. If she got stuck in spite of our best efforts, we let her off, trying to end on a successful note: 'That's fine. Enough for now. Will you help me clear up?' Or 'That's good enough. It's your first time with ice cream, so what you've achieved is absolutely fantastic. Next time it's going to be way easier.' And it was. It was always easier next time, and she knew it. Having the flexibility to judge when to call a halt helped us move her through a huge list of fear foods very fast and without our home being a battle zone.

To summarise, keep your goals in mind and call a halt when you judge your child has achieved as much as she's capable of:

- On the first day, your goal may be simply to get your kid to sit down in front of her plate.

- Then your goal will be getting her to eat one more mouthful than she was prepared to eat. Or to take one bite of a new type of food.

- Later on, your goal may be for her to eat every single thing you served her.

- And then you'll get to the day, maybe a year or two down the line, where it's OK to let your child leave some food on her plate, because you know that it's not an anorexic issue, that she's genuinely full, or that the food genuinely is disgusting. Think semolina.

Tracking your child's state of mind

As time goes on and you serve meal after meal, your child will know you are competent, focused and helpful – even though she may claim the opposite. You will become an expert at reading her body language and interpreting her words and tone of voice. You will sense when she is just about ready to take another step, and you will sense when she has done as much as is humanly possible for now. You will sense when she is open to help and when fear is making her lie or manipulate.

After a year of fumbling, I discovered that we could get great results by tracking our child's state of mind and dosing our response accordingly. It helped us bring portion sizes up to normal and to work quickly through a succession of fear foods. It seemed to help build closeness and trust.

Many parents have the opposite experience and they would urge you not to give the eating disorder any wiggle room. They announce clear rules and make sure they apply them consistently: you eat *everything* on your plate or else. My discomfort with this is that it makes the parent beholden to the rule. I want to be truly in charge, which means I want the flexibility to make decisions that I judge will best meet my child's needs at any particular moment. My message became 'Leave it to me. Trust me. Dad and I know what's right for you right now.' Although it meant that on occasion some of her meal went uneaten, more often than not I was able to support my daughter to make fast progress.

When you're learning new skills, it's easier to work to a rulebook that says this is OK and that isn't. Your piano hand must be apple-shaped. You should never put a red shirt into the white wash. You should use a ruler to draw straight lines. You should insist your child eat everything on her plate. But once you have knowledge, self-confidence and skills, you get a sense of what's needed, what's necessary, what will be most effective. Concert pianist's fingers are often flat. The colours in this red shirt don't run. And what's your straight line for, art or engineering?

If you're struggling to see how tracking and flexibility can work, in Chapter 8 you can be a fly on the wall and watch these principles being put in practice in a lunchtime scenario.

Which approach is best?

There is no right or wrong approach, only approaches that worked or didn't work for different families. Be ready to change: there's a big difference between the first week of refeeding, when you're making a leap of faith and expecting your child to overcome massive internal rules, and later on when you've established a pattern of eating, when you're feeling more skilled, and when your child is generally more on board. You may also feel very differently if right now your child is severely malnourished, or if you have room to experiment and find your feet.

Be kind to yourself

Do take into account your own capabilities. You are not an automaton. There'll be times along this journey when you have more resilience and can tackle more than at other times. If you're feeling very strong, working at a meal for hours might help you break through a deadlock. But if you tend to lose your cool after 40 minutes, it may work better for all of you to make half an hour your mental time limit.

Be kind to yourself. Although it's lovely to be consistent, it's not the end of the world if you can't stick to your chosen approach at all times.

After we ditched the hospital meal plan, it was a demanding task to get my daughter to eat, and for several days in a row all we achieved was the odd nibble. On a few occasions I gave up trying to feed my kid after just five minutes. Yes, *five* minutes (shock horror, disapproving frown). How come I didn't try harder? Well, I had not a jot of hope of success at the time, and I sensed that if I went through the motions I might explode and destroy the precious trust we were gradually building. With the resources I had at the time, it made sense.

You may wonder if there was a high price to pay for what was, in great part, self-care. In this case, it was all part of a context of relationship building. After a few days, our daughter gave me a hint about what would help her, and things started moving fast.

Our gambles are not always so successful, but that doesn't have to be the end of the world either. I have come across exhausted, frazzled parents who say they're giving up on caring for their child. They really mean it. They're cross and at the end of their tether. A few days later they're back in the saddle with renewed vigour. This is a journey of perseverance, and being kind to yourself is essential.

HOW MUCH FOOD? WHICH FOODS?

How much should you feed your child, and should you stick to the foods she finds reasonably easy? I will talk about exposure to fear foods later on. For now I'll concentrate on feeding for weight restoration.

Go fast

You are giving your child the best chances of recovery by aiming for full nutrition as quickly as possible.[83] Aim to serve full meals (3 meals and 3 snacks) as soon as possible. The exception is in the first few days of nutritional rehabilitation, where we need to guard against the possibility of 'refeeding syndrome'. It's a rare syndrome, but it can be fatal if electrolyte levels drop suddenly. The risk exists if your child has lost a large amount of weight and has been eating very little. To guard against the risk, children are monitored by a physician and given blood tests. They may also be prescribed some supplements. A physician who isn't specialised in eating disorders may not know about refeeding syndrome so it may be wise to equip yourself with scientific references ahead of your visit.[84]

Once the risk of refeeding syndrome is not an issue, the evidence is that you should go for rapid weight gain.[85]

> "[All of my adolescents] are best served getting right to their target weight, restoring steadily the whole time and nourishing their brain and bones without delay."[86]

I am labouring this point because I've been shocked to hear of parents being urged to go more slowly, with woolly arguments like 'The mental has to catch up with the physical'. This could be a legacy of times when treatment was done in individual therapy and clinicians were concerned that rapid weight gain would scare their patients away.

Aim to give your child what she needs for weight recovery, rather than what you think she'll accept. An average weight gain of 0.5 to 1 kg per week is generally recommended at home, though a hospital might aim for quite a bit more. One approach is to serve the portion sizes that your child needs, accepting that they will complain it's way too much, and that at first they may not manage it all (see earlier, 'How long should we persist with a meal?'). Another approach is to serve portions your child is likely to manage with your support, while also increasing quantities every day or so, till you reach the target quantities. This means you must withstand your child's protests at every increase and not let them slow you down. Different therapists swear by different approaches.

It is tempting to present our kids with low-stress, low-calorie foods, rather than risk 'failure' with a decent slice of lasagne. If you do that, not only will your child continue to lose weight, but chances are that very soon she'll fight to be given even less. Whatever you feed your child in the early days, she's going to object. The resistance will probably be just as strong to an 'extra' grape as to macaroni cheese. You will progress so much faster if you've gone swiftly to the foods she actually needs.

Your aim is not only to restore weight, but to restore nutrition. People with an eating disorder often have a very restricted range of low-fat or low-carb foods. This can make weight gain near-impossible, or can leave them deficient in essential nutrients. The brain, for instance, needs lipids to function correctly. Even though meals are easier for everyone with 'safe' foods, build in variety as early as you can, while remembering that fast weight restoration is the priority. Your child is less likely to recover if he sticks to a limited range of foods.[87]

'Dense' foods (high calorie for a small volume – therefore with plenty of fats) will help your child eat enough with less of a bloated stomach.[88]

How frequently should your child eat?

To help your child regain weight or remain stable, the general advice is for breakfast, lunch and dinner, plus three snacks. Which means he will be eating every two to three hours. Some people make the six meals more or less equal. Some people find six meals run into each other too much and make it five. Leaving bigger gaps between meals will probably not help. Resistance seems to grow with hunger or with a dip in blood-sugar levels. For those who binge or purge, it's essential to have regularity. With my daughter we saw resistance increase whenever mealtimes slipped, in particular during holidays. The longer we left it, the more strongly she would protest she wasn't hungry. I suspect that even well into recovery, it is helpful to time meals so that there is never a gap of more than three or four hours.

Calories or portion sizes

Feeding for weight gain is not that intuitive. Apparently we tend to underestimate how much food our kids need at this stage.[89] The main reason I see for weekly weighings is to give parents feedback. If gains are slow, either we're not feeding enough, or our child is secretly purging.

A very rough guide is that to gain 1 kg a week, a person needs an extra 1000 calories per day. At age 17 my daughter successfully took it upon herself to regain 0.5 to 1 kg per week by adding 1 litre (two very big glasses) of full fat milk to her usual meals. Another guide is to feed at least as much as the hungriest adolescent boy in the family, or 1.5 to 2 times what the adults are eating. In case you hadn't realised, adults' needs are usually lower than an adolescent's needs.

Some doctors recommend a daily multivitamin and minerals pill, or you may get more specific advice.[90]

Some youngsters need as much as two to three times their baseline amount – I've heard of some on 6000 calories a day. This is because starvation induces hyper-metabolism: extra calories are needed to just to maintain weight.[91] Some youngsters continue to need very high-calorie meals for months after weight restoration (or even for up to two years, in the experience of some parents) until their metabolism settles down again.

If you're wondering how on earth you can put so many calories into a day's meals, you might enjoy some tips I link to in the notes.[92] Nutritional supplements (Ensure, Boost, Benecalorie) may also come to your aid for a while.[93] Some children can cope with the calories in a drink better than in food, which may be why their parents can get them to have an energy drink to compensate for a tiny meal. Do some parents use cheese and oil even though this is their child's worst nightmare? Yes. Do they feel bad about it? No. If a child needs the lipids and calories to regain his health, it's the right thing to do. Do they tell their child there's oil or cream in the milkshake? No. The child is too ill to use the information wisely. If my child asked about ingredients, I replied, 'It's my job to give you what you need. Shall we watch a film tonight?'

There's a common complaint among experienced parents that their clinicians underestimate how much food their child needs. There's nothing worse than a doctor telling your child she can now eat less, when you know by experience how much she needs to maintain her weight. I recommend you request early on that these discussions are kept between adults.

Do what you can to stop your child counting calories. It's a misery-maintainer. Our children think that they will be less anxious if they know numbers, but checking makes them rigid, obsessed, and usually makes them restrict more. When my daughter was in hospital, the nurses hid the nutritional information on packaged foods, either by sticking a label on top or by painting over it with a black marker. We continued to do so for a long time at home. Some of this was symbolic: our daughter, over time, had memorised the calories on quite a few foods, and our black pen wasn't always a match for the large bold print all over the breakfast cereal. A child can also look up calories online in the blink of an eye. And so many restaurants display calorie information. But at least you are establishing the principle that calorie-counting doesn't have a place in healthy living.

Undernourishment pushes sufferers to ever greater levels of rigidity. With anorexia in particular, your child may become very attached to set portion sizes. Does this matter, if she's managing to eat and put on weight? Maybe not – you can work on variation later. But you want to avoid situations where she refuses food because she thinks there's more than usual. For instance if you always give her milk in the same glass, it might be hard for her to drink it if she believes it's a millimetre higher up the glass than usual.

So as soon as you start refeeding, do what you can do to prevent your child from mentally measuring and comparing. For example, instead of giving her a commercial pot of yoghurt, spoon it into a small bowl one day and a big bowl another day. Ideally, avoid giving reassurance that it is the very same amount. Dish out mashed potato in preference to croquettes, because if your child has five croquettes today it will be hard for her ever to have six. If you're making quiche, use different-sized tins, round or rectangular. Visit a charity shop and get crockery in a variety of sizes and shapes.

Should parents weigh food and count calories?

Although I've given you some calorie guidance, I suggest that you don't get bogged down with calorie-counting, which inevitably leads to weighing food. Many parents do a great job just guessing, and they learn from feedback when their child gets weighed.

If your child sees you calorie-counting, I suggest you present it as a temporary phase of treatment, as opposed to normal life: food is their medicine and you are making sure they get the amount they need. If you've got in a rut where your child only eats if you're measuring and counting, work on shifting this because food needs to regain its place as something a lot lovelier than medicine.

If for some reason you are weighing food, make sure your child doesn't know. Otherwise they will become very focused on accuracy, and you may have fights as they take their plate back into the kitchen to do a weight check. One gram more, and you will be accused of lying and cheating. Your stance should be that you are serving portions as is normal, by eye. And yes, there will be natural variations, which is stressful to your child, and you will help them tolerate the anxiety.

My husband and I had rough calorie guides in our heads: 500 minimum for each meal, 250-300 for each snack. I used to feel like a rabbit caught in the headlights when I planned new food, so these guides helped me feel more confident. But they could also be a hindrance because our daughter, using her massive mental database of calories, fought anything she perceived as 'more'. It became hard to shift her from the notion that lunch was 500 calories. We might have achieved quicker results by having far bigger variations in meals and snacks.

The moral is, don't let arbitrary maths take away your power! When she came home after 11 months in hospital, I attempted to build a repertoire of high-energy meals. While she was in school, I looked up calories and did the maths. But I swore that I knew how to feed her and that calorie-counting had no place in our lives. It was very freeing the day I let go of all that. Our lovely therapist, during a private phone conversation, assured me that the message we were giving our daughter was true: we *did* know how much to feed her. We could let go of calculations quite safely, and rely on our years of experience in delivering family meals. She suggested I spend my time doing something more pleasant than filling in spreadsheets. She empowered us to make food choices in the same way that, eventually, we would empower our daughter.

Finally, given that calorie-labelling is everywhere, I suggest there is no great harm in occasionally using it to guarantee a minimum. When my daughter was starting to get well and choosing a sandwich in Starbucks, I could point to the very obvious calorie label, remind her that 300 calories does not make lunch. I'd then watch with relief as she trotted off to choose some more overpriced food.

'My tummy hurts'

Some mealtimes are heartbreaking. You're asking your child to continue eating while she's wailing that she's full, that she feels sick, and that her tummy hurts. In the early days of weight regain, pain is very real, with good physical reasons. During starvation, the stomach and gut are in energy-saving mode. The stomach gets bloated and tight. There's constipation. Food isn't moving through the digestive system at the usual rate. This affects solids more than liquids (so your child may tolerate liquid supplements better than large amounts of food).[94] Regular eating fixes all these problems, and there is also specific medical advice you might want to read.[95]

Anxiety disrupts the stomach and gut, so it's normal for our children to continue feeling pain whenever meals terrify them. They also need to habituate to the sensation of a full belly. My daughter was able to eat without discomfort after a week or two of refeeding, but if for some reason she was anxious about a meal, she could instantly be sore again. When your child is in pain, provide a hot water bottle and a lot of empathy. You can also reduce the anxiety by explaining the process, normalising, and reassuring that it's not dangerous and it will pass.

Your child's food preferences

Whenever I phoned our trusted eating disorders therapist with a dilemma, she'd ask, 'What used to be normal in your family before anorexia came on the scene?' It makes sense to be guided by your pre-anorexia 'normal' because chances are that your child's new preferences and interests are driven by the eating disorder. She may be utterly conflicted as she longs for a piece of cake and fears what it would do to her, but at the very same time she may try to convince you that fruit is now her favourite dessert.

For a long time, you can assume that when she tells you that she hates milk, or suddenly wants to be vegetarian, she's driven by the eating disorder. It's a safe guess that any new 'likes' or 'dislikes' come from an attempt to reduce her anxiety. I'm vegetarian, and if your child goes veggie one day, great. But not while an eating disorder is making the decisions.

You could spend hours anxiously preparing foods you hope your child is more likely to eat. I did a lot of that in the early days, and it was like a slap in the face when my daughter turned down something she'd accepted a few days before, and which had taken me half a day of shopping and cooking (my two least favourite activities). It didn't help to make me calm and compassionate. When your child is deep in an eating disorder, her food preferences are a red herring.

Your child will probably only want low-fat versions of dairy foods and a useful rule is to only use full-fat products. This will help provide the required calories and nutritional balance and it will also reinforce the message that fat is not bad but a highly necessary part of the human diet. The same with diet versions of drinks: unless you have a clear reason for preferring sweeteners to sugar, it's not great to consider oneself beholden to 'diet' versions of anything.

Yummy foods and eating 'too much'

Our kids are scared of a great many foods, and some of the most terrifying are sometimes referred to as 'hyper-palatable' foods – or 'yummy foods' if you prefer. We're talking sweets, cakes, chips and crisps, pizza, hamburgers and hot dogs. You get the picture. If they're honest, our malnourished children will note how they crave such foods. The body knows these are life-savers: they relieve hunger fast and provide much-needed dietary fat or carbs. Psychologically, these foods have been made artificially desirable by being presented as 'treats', 'naughty' and 'junk'. When our children banned them in a bid to eat 'healthy', the alluring mystique of 'bad' food was further inflated. There is a belief that 'junk' food has such potent chemical properties that without self-control, we would never stop eating it. Yet when our beliefs don't get in the way, the body is trustworthy. In terms of desirability, cake is on a par with peaches. We are drawn to different foods, in different quantities, at different times.

In Chapter 9 I will help you introduce the foods your child craves but fears. When your child is able to eat pizza, and when pizza comes round often enough, the mystique of pizza disappears. It just becomes one of many foods they enjoy. They gain flexibility and normality. We saw our daughter make rapid progress once we helped her lose her fear of a succession of 'forbidden' foods. Her mood and thoughts seem to improve, she was able to behave like everyone else at parties and to join her friends in their café culture.

Behind the discussion around 'junk' food is a fear that it could tip our children into over-eating. What if after one bite of yummy food, a kid won't be able to stop? Is this the road to bingeing? And what about those who are currently bingeing on these foods? (More on bingeing later in this chapter.) This concern leads one expert I respect to withhold hyper-palatable foods for one year.[96] I disagree. Based on our experience and numerous parent accounts, presenting our children with all types of foods, especially those previously labelled 'bad', is beneficial.

If you see that your child is guiltily reaching out for chocolate bars, if you hear any hints that they might desire chocolate, then make chocolate more accessible, not less. Include chocolate in the meals and snacks you expect your child to eat.

What if your child has been feasting on an entire box of chocolates? The danger is not the chocolates, but compensatory restriction today or tomorrow. That may lead to even more restriction or conversely, to another feast. Stick to 3 meals, 3 snacks as normal, keep serving chocolate and any other foods your child craves, and stability will follow.

Few children are immune from society's messages about 'healthy' eating and exercise. Make it clear that all foods are good. Food is fuel, food is pleasure, and food is companionship. Different foods fit different moods and occasions, and a birthday without cake and candles doesn't sit quite right. If you are struggling with these concepts, I say more in Chapter 10 when I explain intuitive eating, and eating 'too much'.

Eating differently from the rest of the family

Our children hate that other members of the family have less on their plate. They say it's unfair and proof that we're giving them too much. That's a hump to get over. Give your child kindness for their suffering, and then the message is that each person gets what they need.

I'll state the obvious: nobody in the family should be on a weight-loss diet. That would destroy every message of health and normality that your child needs for recovery (see 'Intuitive eating' in Chapter 10 if you have no idea what I'm talking about). Putting that aside, before an eating disorder struck, members of your family were probably all eating different amounts, and that is a normality worth maintaining. In the early days I made a point of eating exactly the same as my daughter. When I returned to the quantities that were right for me, she protested, but it didn't take too long for her to get used to it. Having said, to make my task easier, I often had similar amounts for my main meals, but less of the snacks.

Given the genetic nature of eating disorders, you may yourself have had difficulties with food. If you have learned to stay well by eating what you need and no more, stick to that: your wellbeing matters. If you are still engaging in disordered eating, I know that you will do all you can to be a helpful model to your child. Parents do amazing things.

You may have a number of children who all eat different quantities and different foods. Here are some suggestions I've picked up from other parents:

- Everyone eats broadly the same thing, but as you plate up in the kitchen for the child who needs to gain weight, you add cream or other high calorie ingredients. You don't make a big announcement but you don't deny it either if they query it. And you quickly move the conversation on to other topics.

- Everyone eats the same main meals round the table, but the child who needs weight gain gets bigger snacks.

- The other children eat some meals separately with another parent or helper. This can be a relief if meals have become highly stressful.

Colds, stomach bugs and diarrhea

When you're refeeding, do your best to prevent an illness from throwing you off course. I link to some advice in the notes.[97]

TARGET BODY WEIGHT

A healthy weight range governs the wellbeing of the body, the brain, and the mind. It is necessary for recovery from an eating disorder. Without it, the eating disorder will stay. If your child has been restricting (whatever their type of eating disorder), they need to regain weight. Don't waste time over 'how much'. Their body is in famine mode. It needs nutrition and weight gain. Start refeeding and don't discuss numbers in front of your child.

Naturally, at some stage you will want to know what weight range you are aiming for. Two things are certain: your child must catch up with lost growth *and* keep growing. A child or adolescent's weight is a moving target. If you underestimate the figure, or if you hope to give your child some relief from her weight anxiety by aiming a little too low, the eating disorder will stay and you'll wonder why she is 'stuck'. This subject is so crucial that I give in-depth guidance on my website:[98]

- Weight restoration: why and how much weight gain

- Is your child's weight a gift to the eating disorder?

- What do BMI and Weight-For-Height mean?

I will outline the essentials for you in the next few pages.

First, you are wholly justified in wanting to discuss weight with clinicians. There are huge variations in opinions, beliefs, and in methods. Even the words used vary:

A weight may be described as 'ideal', 'expected', 'normal', 'healthy' or a 'target' or 'goal weight', or a 'recovery weight'. A child may be described as 'weight-restored'.

Most crucially, different clinicians might give hugely differing weight targets. They can't all be right. Far too often, a target is deliberately set low. 'Healthy' weight, for some clinicians, only means the bare minimum – the weight at which the body stops being critically impaired. Yet for the brain's health and many physiological functions, we each have our own needs body fat and weight.[99] Some therapists fear that a truly healthy weight will scare a patient away or trigger them to restrict more. As parents we can reject this shocking philosophy of resignation: we support our children to go through their fear of weight in the same way as we help them eat in spite of their terror of food.

With a youngster who is focused on muscularity, the issue will not be weight (they often have a high weight and want to gain more) but the shortage of body fat.

Individualised, or 'one-size-fits-all'?

A target weight range should be individualised to your child's needs, using their personal history (weight and height plots on a chart), genetics (based on the build of family members), skeletal frame, muscle bulk, and mental and physical state. Predictions can only be approximate: you only know a person has reached a healthy weight when they get there.

I am distressed that in spite of all the information out there, some clinicians still use a 'one-size-fits-all' method (or rather, 'middle-size-fits-all') to predict target weight. They use statistical calculators to convert a patient's age, height and gender into a target weight. Some don't even take age into account. The computer looks up the middle BMI (Body Mass Index) and churns out your child's supposedly 'ideal' weight. An app may also work out your child's 'percentile weight-for-height', where the 'ideal' is a one-size-fits-all 100 per cent weight-for-height. If a bunch of parents bought their child shoes matching the middle size sold by the shop, you would expect half the kids to end up with bleeding feet. Weight calculators present the same logical error: median BMI is lower than nature intended for half our children. Additionally, for the many malnourished kids who have some growth stunting, the 'ideal' weight corresponds to a lower height than their body needs. The use of BMI or Weight-For-Height is probably why many parents report that their child only got well after reaching a weight higher than required by the therapist. Many adults who are now symptom-free say that their mental state is only good above a certain weight threshold. If they ever dip below, symptoms return.

As I show on an example on my website,[100] a weight target individualised to your child could easily be ten kilos higher than the number churned out by an app. Statistics don't even give a decent ballpark figure.

How to use a growth chart to predict an individualised weight target

To predict a healthy weight that is likely to suit your own child, a clinician will want to plot their past height and weight data on a growth chart.[101] I take you through the steps on my website.[102] If you've not been asked for the data, then whatever weight target your child has been given will be a statistical middle-size-fits-all.

If you have no historical data for your child, no worries. Some experts see no need for a weight target anyway. Use your memory of what your child used to look like, and be like, when he was well. Show your clinicians photos of your child and of family members. And of course, keep them updated on the symptoms and behaviours you see at home.

Physical state

Blood tests, pelvic ultrasound scans[103] and measures of pubertal developments provide markers that your child is getting healthier and may have regained a healthy weight. But be careful. There doesn't seem to be any single, sure-fire physical marker of healthy weight. Different functions come back online at different times for different people. Some of the hormones that mediate appetite and metabolism take twelve months to return to normal after a large diet-induced weight loss.[104] It may take at least six months of regular periods before normal brain functioning returns.[105] In general, mental recovery lags behind physical recovery. [106]

Periods

There is a common but incorrect belief that the return of menses signals weight-restoration. Many females with anorexia have periods and become pregnant even while very underweight.[107] While on this topic, I'll flag up the converse: that even without periods, women with anorexia can and do become pregnant. Also that menses, while on the contraceptive pill, are artificial and have no benefit – quite the reverse: the starving body can't afford the monthly blood loss. Another invalid practice is to put our daughters on the combined contraceptive pill for the purpose of bone protection: this does not work.[108]

Mental state

Even when an expert has carefully worked out an individualised target weight range, it may turn out to be different by a few kilos.

> *"No more throwing things out, smashing plates, rages. She still has normal teenage rants – no getting out of those – but life is good. Keeping her above the weight where she started her period and started to eat without drama was really key. Her mental state improved after this. Interestingly, D had only lost 4–5 kg but we had to put 12 kg on her for her period to come back and her mental state to improve. I so was not expecting to have to put that much weight on her but she needed it and looks great now!"[109]*

Weight-restoration is essential for recovery, but it is not sufficient. Mental recovery usually lags behind physical restoration. You should not expect the illness to end just because your child has reached a healthy weight. Yes, there should be marked improvements in mood and mindset. It might feel like 'My kid is back'. Some honest and self-aware patients report that their constant, extreme hunger has passed, indicating that their body is now out of famine mode. But for complete healing of body and mind, more time and work are needed. See Chapter 10 for what still needs to be done to erase old fears, form new habits, re-learn 'normal', and rebuild a love of life.[110] So if your child has been declared weight-restored but their symptoms are still strong, it's possible that they need more work on 'normal', or more consolidation time, or more weight gain, or all of those.

> *"Weight recovery didn't do a magic trick for my D like I so desperately wanted it to, so I don't want to get your hopes up too much. But sustained weight and full nutrition and a lot of symptom-interruption did the trick. It got better in steps — about every six weeks we'd suddenly lurch ahead."*

Given all the uncertainties, there may be a process of nudging weight up to see if that helps. Don't let weight-stigma or fat-phobia (an unconscious bias common in both parents and therapists) get in the way.

Hindsight and lapses are, unfortunately, the best indicators of your child's healthy weight. People who considered themselves recovered (or their parents) often note that symptoms return when weight falls below a certain threshold. Nobody wants to engineer weight loss, but these incidents do provide an indication of a person's minimum weight for health.

The extinction burst – the eating disorder's final fight

You might think that your child will become more terrified and resistant with every kilo gained. If you guide them with a steady hand, that's not how it works. On the whole, mental state improves as weight goes up, presumably because the brain is getting what it needs. It's also common for our children to hit several plateaus along the journey ('I can see I was unhealthy before but I'm fine now and don't need any more'). Compassionate persistence, as always, is key.

The last of these plateaus is called the 'extinction burst'.[111] Some say it happens in the last ten pounds, some say at 90 per cent of expected body weight. It is anecdotal and in no way universal. For some youngsters, as they get close to target weight, anxiety spikes and there's an upsurge in resistance. Maybe they're terrified of overshooting? It can be disheartening for the parents, and at the same time, this is not a crisis, but a normal threshold to get over. Carry on feeding and don't even dream of stopping the weight gain. If you stop, your child will remain underweight, scared, and unrecovered.

Should your child be told a target weight?

Some clinicians tell the child the weight they're aiming at, and some don't. Your child will turn any number into their maximum, so it's incredibly unhelpful when professionals try to soften the blow with words like 'You're almost there'. A low number, given from a person in authority, will make your job extra hard further down the line.

Some skilled therapists give a generous weight target and help with the child cope with the resulting spike in anxiety. Conversely, some skilled therapists will *not* give a weight target (more on all this on my website).[112] Either way, our children need help with their fear of the unknown, as it brings up nightmare images. Try and start with an assured 'Trust us, this is what's needed'. Your child is likely to keep trying to change your mind, and I suggest you check my suggestions in Chapter 14, under the heading 'Am I fat?'

Fluctuations

While you're monitoring your child's weight, bear in mind that the scales don't show the details of the phases of repair, restoration and growth. Weight restoration is not just about regaining lost fat or muscle. Cells are repaired. Bones strengthen. Organ function, neurological, hormonal and metabolic activity are normalised. These things happen at different times and have different effects on your child's weight gain, and on how he looks and feels.

Weight gain doesn't follow a steady curve even if your child eats steadily. And of course there are considerable variations in readings at different times of day, and using different scales. You can't interpret any single reading with any certainty (a lesson your child will have to learn when they become independent). Therefore it make sense to use daily or weekly readings as part of a reward or punishment system.

A chubby-looking stage

> "She complained about dinner, and refused to eat it. I'm confused because a lot of the weight she's currently carrying is fat tissue. It is harder and harder to convince her (and myself) that this is healthy. She gained weight very quickly (up nearly 30 lbs since entering the hospital nine weeks ago. I get that she needed to gain weight (and obviously, we have done a good job of that!) but wondering whether it is good for her self-image to gain it so fast that she has an obvious belly roll?"

These concerns were raised by a mother after refeeding her daughter for 6 weeks following discharge from hospital. Three weeks later, this was the ecstatic update:

> "Things are going VERY well with my daughter. She continues to gain weight and she has grown almost an INCH since entering the hospital. Wooohoooo! It is amazing to see this growth, when I was nearly certain she was full height. Her goal now is to surpass me in height."[113]

As long as there's little muscle or padding around the belly, it's bound to bulge. Also, weight distribution after semi-starvation is not even: for a while people may look 'chubby' around their stomach and face. Eventually, the weight gets redistributed and muscles rebuild. If you (and your child) don't understand these mechanisms, you might lose your confidence to keep up the weight-gain work. This happened to me at one stage, and neither my girl's wails ('Look at my fat tummy!') nor my family's comments ('She's chubby. Do the doctors know what they're doing?') helped. Our clinicians could only give us vague explanations, and I felt judged for seeking clarity.

Was your child previously classed as overweight?

Perhaps you're concerned that your child was overweight before she started to diet, and people around you see the weight loss as positive. Remember you're aiming for health as nature intended, not what our crazy society considers desirable. If your son or daughter lost a lot of weight, it doesn't matter if they are still classed as overweight – they are malnourished, their body is in starvation mode, and they could be very ill. How much should they regain? All or most of it. Julie O'Toole is particularly good at explaining this whole weight business in her book *Give Food a Chance*, and you might enjoy some of her blogs on the subject.[114]

It is unfortunate that for a diagnosis of anorexia – as opposed to 'atypical' anorexia – a person must have 'significantly low body weight'. The distinction falsely implies that body weight matters, as opposed to physical and mental symptoms:

> *"I am one of those oh-so-lucky patients whose healthy weight rests around BMI 25-26. At BMI 24, I lost my periods, and at BMI 23, I was severely ill. No one in the eating disorders world seems to know what to do with an anorexic (and yes, I was every bit anorexic, after losing nearly 40 per cent of my body weight) who is not severely underweight according to their charts. When I explained to the doctors that I had always been heavier, stronger, more muscular than 'average', they said that it was clearly due to bingeing and that I would see that my weight would drop. Excuse me? I had not eaten in nine days; did you just say that I'm bingeing?"[115]*

Weight target discussions between clinicians and parents

Parents need open, trusting exchanges with clinicians in order to discuss weight targets. Given all the uncertainties, everyone's input is needed. This is a topic where parents can easily be judged or pathologised. A therapist may wonder if you suffer from weight bias and if you will resist the weight gain your child needs. Conversely, a well-educated parent may have to fight a low weight target, or a 'one-size-fits-all' figure given by a therapist who is not so well informed.

When my daughter was seventeen and in mild relapse, we took a stand against a CBT-E therapist's insistence that she was fine at 100 per cent weight-for-height. To me it was a no-brainer to try for more, based on her weight history, her ongoing symptoms, and on everything I know about the error of basing targets on median BMI. I could not change the clinical team's beliefs, and at the time I didn't have all the experts' quotes which are now on my website. We let go of the therapist and gradually undid the damage. In the short term, a child will go for what they want to hear, but in the longer term they know that if anyone has their back (and has done the research and put some time and care into it), it's their parents.

WEIGHING YOUR CHILD: OPEN OR BLIND?

If your child has a compulsion to weigh herself several times a day, you will no doubt have hidden the bathroom scales by now. It's a cruel paradox that while for your child, weighing is a destructive obsession, for us it's a tool to assess health status and progress with feeding.

Eating-disorder specialists tend to weigh once a week at the beginning, and later reduce the frequency. There are phases in this journey during which weighing may not be necessary: these are times you're confident that the food is going in and staying in, that other health measures are good, and that your child's mental state is improving. On the other hand, when you're gradually returning independence to your child and she's tempted to bin her sandwiches, it may help her to remember you're checking her weight. The figures will confirm that she is coping with increased levels of autonomy.

There are opposing views among therapists on whether or not your child should know her weight.[116]

Open weighing – where the patient is told their weight – is required in the manuals for Family-Based Treatment (FBT) and for cognitive behaviour therapy (CBT). When these methods were validated, researchers used open weighing, so if you don't weigh open you might be losing a crucial element for success. There are no trials to compare open and blind weighing, so we have to be guided by principles and by experience.

The argument for open weighing is that it's a form of exposure therapy. It challenges your child's eating-disordered thoughts and aims to take the emotion out of weight. It's also part of education for relapse prevention. Your child may get help to understand how weight fluctuates, how to resist interpreting any single reading, how to look at trends and stay within a healthy bracket. You can't forever protect people from knowing their weight and why should you, if you're aiming for complete recovery?

Properly done, open weighing can really pay off:

> "We did open weighing at the FBT therapist's. I worried about this
> at first but in the end I am glad we did them. Yes, we copped a lot
> of flack but our daughter got to the point where she was not afraid
> to see her weight. Now weight isn't so much an issue for her. It's like
> a shrug and move on."[117]

In the FBT and CBT manuals, therapists don't just weigh – they support the patient to deal with the emotions that come up. It's an essential therapeutic intervention. My sense is that this rarely happens. Youngsters are expected to cope, unaided, with numbers which they find terrifying. Often, they have a melt-down on the way home, they cut down on eating for the next day or the next week, and their list of fear foods grows ('Eating eggs is made me gain too fast!'). If at any stage they were given a target weight, they may use the weekly weighings to check they do not go one gram over. There is no therapeutic value in open weighing if therapists don't do the therapy. Quite the reverse.

If your therapist can't tell you how they use open weighing in a constructive way, consider blind weighing, at least until you get the lie of the land.

My daughter was weighed blind, i.e. standing with her back to the display. She was only ten, and weight was considered to be a medical issue for the grown-ups. No discussion. Ordinary kids, the argument went, don't worry about their weight. They don't weigh themselves and they don't compare their data to other children's (I wish! It seems to start around age eight or nine in my neighbourhood). Even adults, it was pointed out, don't need to check their weight: you eat what your body tells you it needs, and that's it. Any significant increase in weight, you'd know from the tightness of your clothes. My kid's job was to live her life. Our job was to feed her and monitor her health. We were promoting normal behaviour by having her not focus on weight. I was very happy with all this – it fits with my view of intuitive eating.

Her fear of weight gain resolved itself naturally as she got better. In the early days, whenever she went to a friend's house, I asked the parents to remove the scales from the bathroom. Later I wouldn't be surprised if she did weigh herself, but there were no adverse effects.

Sometimes we choose open weighing because we think our children will be re-assured that the numbers are still reasonable. I would say that doesn't tend to work:

> *"My daughter was shown where she was on a percentile chart for weight, stature and age. It reassured her to see she was still below the fiftieth-percentile weight (i.e. to her mind, skinnier than average), but an hour later, the thoughts and worries came back with a vengeance."*

Seeing numbers can be lose-lose: our children have a meltdown when they gained, and are horrified that they lost because they think they endured big meals for nothing, and they're going to be made to eat even more. They may say they want to grow tall, and that they understand that means weight gain, but in practice, the numbers are still unbearable.

Open weighing backfires if our children use the figure on the scales to regulate how much to eat or exercise or purge:

> *"My son was told he'd gained 0.1 kg. To him, that was proof that the pitiful amounts he's been eating were 'too much' and that he can't trust me. I resent these weighings. He's got quite a bit of eating to do and this is making my job harder than ever."*

With some sufferers, knowing their weight works because they have motivation on their side and a fair amount of maturity and self-awareness: they really want to recover, and they do want to monitor that they're eating enough.

There's no doubt that to be free our kids need to be relaxed about their weight readings. They need to cope if they happen to be weighed in some random health setting. They might choose weight checks as part of relapse prevention (see Chapter 10).

I am frustrated that the norm is to do open weighing at the same time as refeeding. Most of us don't insist on our child eating ice cream when they're having tremendous difficulty eating *anything*. I swear by exposure therapy, but the timing matters. Why not wait for the person to be weight-restored and for their brain to have recovered?

> *"With our ten-year-old, we did blind weights at first because with such severe pre-morbid OCD, she would totally focus on that number. She needed to eat and gain and not have more anxiety piled on when she was in an already extremely fragile state. When her weight was accidentally revealed, I think she did as well as she did because she was already weight-restored, had been for a couple of months, and had some coping skills under her belt. Yes, she still reacted badly. But not as badly as she might have had we done it when she was so malnourished that she was refusing to swallow her own spit for fear of calories."[118]*

Whenever I've had my blood pressure monitored, I've been told, 'That's fine.' The implication, which amuses me immensely, is that I couldn't possibly be interested in the figures or that I won't understand them. Yet we take growing kids with befuddled, undernourished brains, and we give them a number that means nothing without education about genetic potential, growth curves, growth spurts, daily fluctuations, and other variable which adults with university degrees struggle with.

I know of parents who wonder if a switch from open to blind weighing would help get their child unstuck. Their child has maintained a constant, low weight for months by keeping a tight control on their food intake. The parents' fear is that the child will react to the lack of data by eating even less. If you're in this situation, ask yourself whether open weighing, or the way it is being done, is contributing to the treatment or fuelling the eating disorder:

> *"For years, my daughter was told her weight. She ruminated about the number and kept herself at the lowest end. When we began FBT at age 22, the clinician did blind weights and we just fed her to see where her weight stabilized with refeeding. It was almost 20 lbs more than where the previous clinicians said she would be fine. Having blind weights freed her to just eat. She'd been weight-recovered for a year and a half when she accidentally saw her weight. She was a bit surprised by the number but she kept on eating. Once she knew her new target range, she made sure not to go below it. Even if she went over her range, it didn't have an effect on her."[119]*

Finally, one argument I've come across for open weighing is that the ensuing discussion addresses not just the young person's fears, but also the parents'. I find this slightly patronising, but fair enough: no doubt we're all affected, to some extent, by society's fat bias. So educate us! I don't see why that requires open weighing!

Blind versus open weighing is hotly debated among therapists and parents. No doubt different strategies work for different families at different times. Perhaps a number of routes are fine as long as families have the support to implement them well. If you're unhappy with your present system, work in partnership with your clinicians. The answer might be to tweak what you're doing, to give more support and education to the child, to give better explanations to the parents to bring them on board, or to completely change tack.

The practicalities of weighing

It's normal for someone with an eating disorder to try and cheat the scales. In the early stage especially, it's good practice for a clinician to test for water loading (and you can prevent your child from drinking lots before a weigh-in), and to check for any hidden, weighty objects. Your child may give up on cheating if you weigh at home at random times. At one stage I was varying the day but always weighing after breakfast, and my poor daughter was secretly forcing down large amounts of fluid every day upon waking. If accuracy is your priority, you need to use the same scales, at roughly the same time of day.[120] At home, electronic scales need to be recalibrated each time you move them.

If you decide to weigh blind, what should you say once you've noted the reading? After a few weighings, our therapist gave us the job of doing the feedback. It could be 'It's going in the right direction', but what worked best was a simple and unemotional, 'Thank you'. If our daughter asked a lot of questions, we'd stick to: 'It's all good. We're feeding you the right amounts and you're absolutely fine.'

HIDING FOOD AND LYING

The kindest thing we can do for our children is to protect them from situations in which they can lie, cheat or hide food and in which they can manipulate a situation to avoid a meal.

The pressure of eating may be so awful for your child that she will be looking for ways to reduce quantities, even by insignificant amounts. So great is her revulsion at every mouthful, that a few grains of breakfast cereal hidden in a tissue, or tucked inside her cheek, or slipped in her pocket, or dropped in a plant pot, or wiped onto her hair, make a very great difference. It may also be a way of appeasing the eating-disorder demon, a kind of bargaining that helps her to eat almost all of what you serve: 'I just *had* to eat breakfast, I had no choice, but look, I managed to avoid eating this! I am doing my best, you know.'

If you child is making a bad job of hiding her uneaten food, she may be appealing for more help: 'Just because I'm eating quite well these days, don't get complacent. I'm still struggling. (And don't let my eating-disorder voice know that I said this.)'

Our days are full of decisions we have to make in the face of uncertainty. Regarding lying and cheating, here are some options.

You might choose to be as strict as nurses in good eating disorders units. There, staff would watch her closely to stop her hiding food. They might not let her have tissues in her pockets – indeed they might not let her wear anything with pockets. They'd replace food that she had dropped. After she'd finished eating they might inspect her wide-open mouth and insist that she swallow anything hidden next to her gums. The message is that all food must be eaten. You can choose to do this at home. Hopefully, this frees your child of agonising choices (how much to eat) and compulsions (Restrict! Restrict!) and gives her greater peace of mind. Hopefully, it reassures her that you really are competent to look after her. Hopefully, if you keep closing in on the eating disorder, giving it nowhere to go, eventually it gives up.

Alternatively you could choose to pick your battles, taking the bigger picture into account. Say your child is successfully regaining weight, that she's eating without major resistance, but you find her trouser pocket is full of tissues containing pathetic little amounts of food. You could choose to not say much, and review if things get worse.

Being checked for cheating is not great for a child's dignity. Whenever you're firm, remember to make your compassion explicit: kindness and normalisation. It's normal, with an eating disorder, for previously truthful people to tell lies. If your child could avoid doing these things that shame her, she would. Our kids already have more than enough shame to bear. Let your child know that you don't judge her.

EATING RITUALS

An eating disorder can cause some people to eat extremely slowly or to pick at food, breaking it up into tiny pieces, or smearing it around on the plate. These behaviours can irritate you, so consider that for your child they are a tragic attempt to self-soothe. They might procure a sense of security, placate the eating-disorder voice, or help reduce intake. Try and judge when you can also work on practicing 'normal' behaviours to free your child of some or all of these misery-maintainers. Your priority, remember, is nutritional restoration. Be aware, also, that many rituals will vanish as your child gets better.

To work on rituals, you may use principles of exposure (more in Chapter 9). For instance you ask your child to eat their biscuit in no more than five bites, then next day, three bites. Give him empathy for his mental torment – you are asking him to give up something which relieves his anxiety. Compassionate persistence is your other tool. No, it's not OK to smear butter off the toast onto one's fingers. Try not to scream when the fingers are then wiped onto your sofa. If you care for your furniture, you might let her have some tissues … but that's just a stopgap.

EXERCISING, MOVING AND STANDING

Compulsive exercise is usually just as much part of an eating disorder food and weight. You can see it clearly in young children, who often have a desperate need to keep moving. Staying still is torture. At any age you can expect your child to obsessively tense her muscles, fidget, stand, or only sit on the edge of seats when she's been made to rest. She may secretly exercise in her bedroom or in the shower, and run to school.

In the early days, our children are often too malnourished to exercise safely, so parents have a clear mandate to make them stop, though it's usually fine to make life more enjoyable with a leisurely stroll or gentle yoga. One teen whose story I followed would go running in spite of her cardiologist's warning that it might kill her. Her dad, sadly, endorsed her sport by running with her, doggedly hanging on to his belief that exercise is always 'healthy'. Some people indiscriminately think of exercise as 'healthy', because of society's message that more is better. A truly healthy level of exercise is relative to an individual's physical state at any particular time. Anything above that is over-exercise.

Our children can appear to be fit and energetic even when their organs are under severe strain. The heart is a muscle, and like all muscles it atrophies with undernourishment. Confusingly, lab tests and vital signs often register as normal. This is because the body brings in emergency resources – at a cost – when it is starving.

The sooner we intervene with exercise compulsion, the sooner our children are freed of a source of misery. It may also help with weight recovery, of course. I used to think that was exaggerated, but I read that surprisingly more calories are needed for weight gain when our children are fidgeting or walking up and down a hospital corridor.[121]

If you don't take charge, your child's eating disorder mindset will stay unchallenged, shifting its focus from food restriction to exercise. Usually the compulsion to exercise ramps up as we get our children to eat, because they want to burn calories, prevent weight gain, or appease the eating disorder bully. Occasionally the routines are light and symbolic, but still eating-disorder-driven. They are the equivalent of leaving a few crumbs on a plate as a peace offering to the monster. If so, you might decide to pick your battles and see if time sorts it out. More often, our children put themselves through gruelling routines because that's the only way they know to soothe their anxiety. We see a kid who loves sport, and we hang on to our personal experience that movement is a mood-booster. Meanwhile our children feel famished, dizzy, weak and miserable. As one child told her mother, years later:

> "I remember wishing you would make me stop because I was so tired
> and ED would not let me stop."[122]

We might not be able to stop our kids from tensing their muscles, but we can give them containment by putting a sport on hold, by telling them they may not run or skip up and down stairs, and by requiring them to sit down when it's normal for people to sit down. We can request they refrain from exercise ('It's not for ever; we'll review later') in the same way as we request them to eat. When they comply, they need kindness and distraction because they are courageously putting aside a strategy that, in the moment, worked for them. Our role is to help them experience that not-exercising will not kill them, and that it gets easier every day. Their brain gets to learn that they are safe even when resting.

How hard it is to stop exercise varies depending on the person, the stage of the illness, and the environment. In hospital, when nurses suspect that patients are exercising in the shower, they have the bathroom door ajar to supervise from outside. They require that people lean back in sofas with their feet flat on the floor rather than on tiptoes. If you can't conjure up this level of authority at home, you might opt to gradually reduce the allowed time. This can work especially well when the exercise has a ritualistic, obsessive-compulsive flavour. Indeed physical activity is often governed by seemingly arbitrary rules. Your kid may allow herself to sit on a 20-minute journey from hospital to school, but not a ten-minute journey to meet a friend. Mine could sit for an hour of family TV every evening, but as the hands of the clock reached 8.55 p.m., the internal bully made her leap up. She also had mental rules, to the minute, about when it was OK to lie in bed.

With my daughter, it was easy to stop exercise but terribly hard to get her to sit. She complied in the ward but not at home. The hospital helped us devise elaborate reward systems which yielded a few extra minutes of sitting … as well as a great big pile of T-shirts in her wardrobe, with the price labels still on. We ditched the reward system. Some parents advise that all odd behaviours should be combated at once so as to shut down the eating disorder's outlets. We concentrated on food and hoped that our daughter's problem with sitting would sort itself out with time, weight and nutrition. Which is what happened, overnight. She had a bad cold and was feeling weak and miserable. Her sitting was, as usual, tense, avoiding the back rest. Suddenly she lay back and relaxed. I believe that on that day, she threw caution to the wind and asserted her power over her eating-disorder voice.

As usual, logic rarely works and there's little point in telling your child that tensing her muscles isn't worth it, or that a few extra minutes in bed will make no significant difference to calorie consumption or body shape. You'll most likely get roped into a discussion that fuels the eating-disorder anxiety, and at this stage, our children seek relief from anxiety by restricting and exercising.

As your child gets better you will re-introduce movement, all the time monitoring that it doesn't bolster the eating disorder. More on this in Chapter 10.

SCHOOL

When you start treatment, review whether it's beneficial for your child to go to school, and review the support and safeguards regarding eating and exercising. More on this in Chapter 10. For now, as you're in a hurry, I'll just say this: it's realistic to assume that for a while our children will cheat and lie about school meals. If they find it difficult to eat at home, chances are they are incapable of eating enough alone in school. Even with lots of calories overall, and even with a child who doesn't need weight gain, all those hours in school going hungry will give the eating disorder a daily boost.

So what to do? Some parents take time off work and keep their child home for a couple of weeks (or longer) at the beginning of refeeding. That way they can make meals last as long as required to get some successes. Once new eating habits have been established, the child can return to school, part-time if necessary, but with systems in place to ensure that every single school meal is supervised.

BEDTIME

Nights can be hard for our children. They have nightmares and come to fear sleep. While they're lying in bed, anxious and self-loathing thoughts run riot. Starvation affects sleep hormones.[123] The compulsion to exercise can make it very hard to lie still. Even when they seem to be at rest, our children may be busy following an exercise routine of tensing their muscles under the sheets.

While we should never blame or shame our kids for this behaviour, it's well worth trying to protect them from their internal bully. Many parents move their child's mattress into their own bedroom, open up the double bed to their child, or move in with the child. If that thought had even occurred to me early on, I would have done it without hesitation, and maybe it would have spared my daughter hundreds of hours of misery.

Another common reason for sharing the bedroom with your child is to prevent self-harm or suicide:

> "For many months I slept in my daughter's room and kept the
> outside doors deadlocked (sometimes even in the day) to help protect
> her from self-harm or flight (as she had several times run away either
> to exercise/purge or otherwise endanger herself). Medication also
> seemed to help, either to calm stress or assist sleep."

Children of all ages may genuinely welcome having their parents close to them, stroking them until they fall asleep, soothing, supporting. With time, they easily return to their own bedroom. I know of psychiatrists who find the idea of bed or bedroom sharing appalling. They say it's not age-appropriate. I suspect that they have Freud and sex on the mind. Well who cares what they think? Hurray for parents who follow their heart and are ready to keep their child close to them at night. I want all living beings to have comfort and safety when they need it. Every ship, large and small, needs a secure harbour.

> "My daughter did a lot of secretive standing when she was supposed
> to be in bed. The day I told her I would stay in her room until she
> fell asleep, I gave her a weapon against her anorexic voice ('See, I
> have no choice! If Mum sets up camp in my bedroom it will be
> worse for us!'). She'd already defied her internal bully over and over
> again around food and sitting, so in this case, that one 'threat' from
> a parent was all she needed to break the compulsion. Once she'd
> experienced how lovely it was to let sleep come without guilt, she sent
> her tormentor packing."

While I'm on the subject of bedtime, consider establishing regular bedtimes and preventing access to the television or internet after dark. I have come across a number of families where the person with an eating disorder cannot fall asleep till the early hours of the morning, possibly because of anxiety or depression. Their whole sleep–wake cycle goes haywire, making it very hard for them to engage with normal life or to keep to regular mealtimes. It also means the parents become exhausted and less effective.

PURGING AND BATHROOM VISITS

My daughter didn't make herself vomit. Because she was so young, we hoped that she was ignorant about purging, and we warned therapists not to even mention it. In time, we realised it had crossed her mind anyway. Although I believe that logic and lectures are generally a waste of breath, I did think it worthwhile to tell her how dangerous purging was. I hoped that if she didn't have a strong drive to purge, my warning might discourage her from trying.

Purging is common in bulimia, in restricting anorexia and in binge-purge anorexia. The word 'purge' usually refers to vomiting or misusing laxatives or diuretics, though strictly speaking it includes any inappropriate compensatory behaviour, like fasting or exercising.

What can you do about it? Since I can't speak from experience, I'll give you pointers based on what I've learned elsewhere. I urge you to look for other sources of information and advice as well, in particular if your child has an eating disorder other than anorexia.[124]

If your child purges to compensate for real or perceived bingeing, then the way forward is to support regular, satisfying meals. She will need more help if she is purging in order to avoid feeling full or feeling fat, or to flatten her stomach, or to cope with intense emotions. For her, purging may not just be about losing weight, it may also provide a temporary sense of relief or calm or it may be a form of self-punishment.

You should probably assume that your child has considered vomiting or tried it. Whether or not she has made it a habit, you can help her by giving her so much supervision that it is near impossible for her to purge. You then support her to withstand any anxiety that comes up, because you've deprived her of a behaviour that used to give her relief.

If she is not very underweight, she may also be able to take in information about the hazards of purging, and understand that it's not an effective weight control measure. Indeed, vomiting can only remove part of what she has eaten. If she is using laxatives to flatten her stomach, she may be able to understand that diarrhoea only temporarily empties her gut and has little or no effect on calorie absorption or body shape.[125]

If your child already has a purging habit, she may be completely safe, but she may also be in immediate danger from electrolyte imbalance. Make regular medical checks and blood tests an absolute priority.[126]

It seems that vomiting is quite habit-forming, and the quicker you shut down the means to do it, the better. Be aware that people who regularly throw up can become adept at doing so very quietly, very quickly, in all kinds of places, into all kinds of containers, and without even sticking fingers down their throat.

For some parents, putting a stop to purging means removing the lock on the bathroom door. They may insist that the door stays open, or ask the child to sing or count continuously. For some, the rule is you're not allowed to flush the toilet till a parent has checked it. Some mothers stay in the bathroom while their daughter showers.

A standard protective measure is to ask your kid, before each meal, if she'd like to use the toilet because you won't allow her to go for an hour after eating. This may help kill a purging habit, but be aware that some youngsters will try – and succeed – to vomit several hours after a meal. You can at least take some comfort that some of the meal has been digested.

Some parents regularly search their child's bedroom for bags of sick, laxatives or diuretics. It's against most parents' moral standards to invade their child's privacy, but these are protective measures. I suggest you recall the image of someone being held at gunpoint. It's nearly impossible for our children to resist eating disorder impulses, and I believe they need us to step in on their behalf.

As with everything related to eating disorders, expect very high levels of emotion when you prevent opportunities to purge. Plan activities that will distract and calm your child after meals. Every meal that stays inside your kid is a chance for her brain to make the connection that it's OK to eat and for the food to stay in one's stomach. It's OK to withstand the urge to rush to the bathroom. It's OK to be anxious for a while.

If you're going to take control of your child's purging behaviour, you need the same empathy resources as I describe for mealtime support, both to support your child and to support yourself. Your aim is to accept your child unconditionally. You can be sure she is giving herself a hard time for all this, and what she needs is your love and acceptance, even as you step in to stop the behaviour.

If your child is not underweight or undernourished, i.e. if her behaviour corresponds to bulimia rather than anorexia, she may have the mental capacity and motivation to collaborate in her treatment and to suggest how you can support her to stop purging. Family-Based Treatment for bulimia requires parents to take control, but it is more collaborative than for anorexia.[127] With evidence-based forms of cognitive behaviour therapy for eating disorders – an approach suitable for adults and some older teens – it is the patient who takes charge of changing her behaviour following a period of self-monitoring, record-keeping and regular eating.

BINGEING

Binge eating usually means eating unusually large amounts of food very fast, in a dazed, out-of-control state. People may plan their next binge (with a 'diet starts to-morrow' mentality) or they may find themselves bingeing in spite of their best intentions. Binges are usually associated with secrecy and shame. Our children may think they're bingeing even when quantities are objectively small. If they never eat more than three grapes for lunch, but today eat a normal meal of their own accord, in their mind that's a binge. If they wolfed down what you served them when they'd promised themselves to eat only half, in their mind that could be a binge. The issue is that they are tormented by the belief that they ate excessively, could not stop themselves, and that the only solution is more rules, more willpower.

Eating disorders that involve bingeing include binge-eating disorder, bulimia, and the binge-purge type of anorexia. It's common for people – especially longer-term sufferers – to swing from one type of eating disorder to another. Binge-eating disorder is shockingly under-diagnosed and under-treated, given that it is the most common type of eating disorder. Sufferers don't just binge, they also spend major chunks of the day or week trying to restrict, and they are usually tortured by their thoughts. Whatever the diagnosis, we should treat bingeing as seriously as restricting, not because bingeing in itself is a problem, but because it is associated with restriction and severe distress, including suicidality.

The subject of bingeing is relevant to you even if your child never, ever eats anything beyond the strict minimum you give them. Anyone who is restricting is likely to be terrified of bingeing, and this makes them rigid and rule-based. So I suggest that at a suitable time, you give your child both empathy and education on this subject. Empathy would look like, 'I'm guessing that you think about food a lot. Maybe you dream of banquets? I imagine that is quite unsettling?' If relevant you could ask, 'Are you worried that if you start eating you'll never stop? That you will flip into binge-eating?'. Give your child space to express their thoughts and fears. You can then normalise – you could tell them about the men in the Minnesota experiment,[128] or the experience of hungry people during wars. And then move on to education: see what, in the following section, might be useful for your child to hear.

It is indeed normal and healthy for malnourished people to think of food incessantly. This 'mental hunger' is a well-adapted mechanism to move us from famine to feast until our body has met its needs.[129] The drive to feast kicks in whatever the person's weight, whatever the type of restriction. It happens to those who go for much of the day without food, who cut out carbohydrates or fats, who deny themselves foods they consider 'unhealthy'. The drive to feast comes from restriction, and people get caught in a feast-restrict cycle. It's restriction, not greed or lack of moral fibre, that fuels incessant food thoughts – 'mental hunger' – whether or not there is physical hunger. That's why anorexia, bulimia and binge-eating disorder are all treated with regular meals (usually 3 meals, 3 snacks a day). Meals should be non-negotiable even – especially – after a binge.

When you talk about this with your child, reinforce that what you are doing is right both for their health and their happiness. 'Trust us, we are supporting you to eat just right so that you will get out of (or never get into) this vicious cycle, and you will reach an easy stability.'

Make sure you serve regular meals, that you do not under-feed, and that as soon as you can, you include the hyper-palatable ('yummy') foods I talked about earlier in this chapter. If your child isn't fighting hunger, if she gets to enjoy what she craves, in amounts she knows are safe and guilt-free, she may be less inclined to sneak into the bakery on the way home from school. If any of her eating is, in her mind, a binge, she may well fight you because the rest of the time she wants to restrict or exercise. As usual, your unconditional acceptance is paramount, and parents themselves need a lot of self-care.

At some stage you will be handing food choices back to your child. If they go straight into feast-famine cycling, then you've gone too fast. Take back control and consider adding in more awareness and education. You and your child may be able to identify what triggers the urge to feast. He may be hungry, in which case regular or bigger meals will solve the problem. He may have broken a self-imposed rule and gone for broke ('Today is ruined, so I might as well go on eating'). The way forward is to ditch the rules: the desired foods are available any day! Another trigger for a binge is getting drunk. Again, letting go of food rules is the way forward.

I now move onto aspects of binge-eating disorder or bulimia or binge-purge anorexia which I don't know enough about. I will tell you what I've picked up and I encourage you to do more research.[130]

Some people identify that they binge when they struggle with difficult emotions.[131] Their may need psychotherapy to make peace with a difficult past, and they might benefit from learning more effective ways to deal with feelings. At the same time, let's acknowledge that food isn't just fuel, and has a rightful place in soothing and in celebrating. Make sure all the focus doesn't go on psychological mechanisms: the feast-famine cycle matters too.

Bingeing, with or without purging, can place great strain on the whole family. Some children demand that vast quantities of food are bought and they react violently if refused. The food bills can drain the family finances. If youngsters are stopped mid-binge they may use this as confirmation that they're fat, and then restrict with renewed ardour. As with other behaviours that your child is unable to control, the best approach seems to involve parents taking charge of food intake.

Some parents are advised to prevent binges. Breaking a binge or binge-purge habit can take time and perseverance. To prevent access to food, some parents find it necessary to put locks on food cupboards and on the fridge. They check the child's bedroom for stashes of food and take measures, as best they can, to prevent after-school purchases. Some keep a check on night-time excursions to the kitchen by changing where the child or the parents sleep. When they prevent a binge or a purge, they stay with their child to help her tolerate the anxiety till it subsides. Some parents burn gallons of fuel on long drives to provide distraction and soothing.

It may be difficult to stop your child mid-binge, while she's struggling with feelings of anxiety and self-loathing. But at quieter times, away from the dinner table, she may be motivated to discuss strategies to cut out the bingeing. If she isn't severely underweight – in other words, if her brain isn't affected by undernourishment– she may be an effective partner in her own treatment. It helps that people who binge are usually very motivated to break the habit.

In many cases, parents have found success soon after taking control of purging or bingeing in the way I have described so far. But as always, there is no single solution that works for everyone.

I hear of youngsters who become absolutely single-minded in their determination to find food for a binge, or to vomit. Some parents describe their children's behaviour as impulsive, volatile, and very aggressive. I know of a few cases where therapists confused this eating-disorder-fuelled behaviour with borderline personality disorder. Furniture gets destroyed, people get punched, and the young person can run away, self-harm and threaten or attempt suicide. Sometimes it's simply not possible for parents to support their child in this way round the clock, and you may need to insist that your child is treated and kept safe in a specialised inpatient unit.

I have a friend overseas whose daughter fitted this description until recently. She suffered from poorly diagnosed and poorly treated binge-purge anorexia for most of her teenage years. When the parents prevented her from purging or bingeing or when they insisted she eat regular meals, the daughter often reacted with such violence that she'd end up in a police cell, at the cost of more trauma and of course more missed meals and weight loss. Hospitalisation stopped being an option; after a number of incidents it was hard to trust that the staff had the necessary competence. I am in awe of how these parents became masters of empathy, communication and self-compassion (more on these skills in Chapters 13 to 15). This – not hospitalisation, not psychotherapy, not threats and not locks on bathroom or cupboard doors – is what completely turned their situation around. The daughter had dreams to pursue and she became well enough to participate in her own recovery.

> *"Let your child know that you won't desert them, that you will never give up."*

In many cases the support of parents is crucial. But if your child is old enough and motivated enough to take charge of her own recovery from binge eating, then cognitive behavioural therapy (CBT) validated for eating disorders may be the treatment of choice (see Chapter 12).

POST-MEAL ANXIETY

In the early stages of refeeding, it's normal for our children to be tormented by guilt and anxiety after a meal. They think they're a failure for having eaten. The sensation in their belly is unbearable. They imagine they will become enormous overnight. No wonder they have such a compulsion to purge or exercise right away.

All this will pass as your child experiences, day after day, that horrible feelings pass. Meanwhile, plan to support your child after a meal with some form of distraction, and of course, empathy: watching a film, playing game, enjoying a friend's company, taking a drive.

> *"After I've eaten, it tends to be a lot worse; I get very guilty and worked up. After dinner, I need to do something to distract me, like TV or movies."*[132]

RUNNING AWAY

Some kids, when you start getting them to eat or when you stop them from exercising, can be so overcome with anxiety that they storm off into the street. It's fight-or-flight in action. You may have to hunt for them and bring them back home, and lock doors to stop them leaving again. Same with car doors while driving. I'd like to acknowledge how distressing this can be for everyone.

Once your child has experienced, with your compassionate help, that it's possible to endure the after-meal stress, the compulsion to go for a run is likely to fade away. What you're doing by locking doors is not only ensuring your child's safety, but also removing options, which helps to free her of internal battles.

> *"I had to lock the car doors a few times in the early days of my daughter's eating disorder, and I was terrified of making her claustrophobic. It didn't."*

SELF-HARMING AND SUICIDALITY

For some children, the level of guilt and anxiety they feel drives them to self-harm, including cutting and head-banging. This is a hard situation for parents to manage and can derail them from the task of pushing through anxiety-provoking challenges, such as feeding and preventing purging. You may have heard that young people self-harm to get momentary relief from unbearable distress, and that this is not an attempt to end their life. All the same, some children do make suicide attempts,[133] so keep consulting your clinical team and be vigilant.[134] If your child is in hospital and you believe there's a significant risk of suicide, satisfy yourself that the ward has stringent safety measures, including having a member of staff with them every minute of day and night.

You may have to physically stop the self-harm, put in place whatever supervision is needed, and remove your child's access to sharp objects. This isn't easy, because your child may so want a tool to help her deal with unbearable feelings that she may collect, hide, and secretly use any kind of item that might do the job.

> *"I created a 'safe zone' – an area as free as possible from sharp edges/hard surfaces for when things got tough, as our daughter would bash her head against anything hard and would become more distressed when we physically restrained her. We also had a backup plan with the inpatient unit that we could bring her there if her safety was at risk."[135]*

I have no experience of this, so do check out other sources of advice. I do know that parents should adopt a calm and confident stance, and avoid shaming or blaming. In other words, if you find your child's arm is injured, or if you foil a suicide attempts, promise yourself to attend to your emotions later. If your kid thinks you can't bear it, who can she lean on?

Regarding suicidality,[136] it's not that our children want to kill themselves. They want relief from a level of suffering which seems almost unbearable. Give them empathy for that, validate their feelings (more in Chapter 14). Help them notice how feelings move on, and how they move faster when they connect with someone who cares for them. Ask them to give you some kind of sign when they're feeling particularly vulnerable. At a good moment it might be worth explaining how, while they're in fight-flight-freeze it's normal that they're scrabbling for any way to stop the pain, and at the same time no decision or plan should ever be made while in that state because our wise brain is temporarily offline.

BEING COLD

When anorexia and delusional thinking are still strong, your child might believe that it is essential for her to be cold. Part of it is the crazy belief that this will make a difference to her body shape by burning calories, and part of it, I suspect, is about denial of any kind of comfort. The eating-disorder voice is not a hedonist.

> *"My daughter could accept the nurses' rules about long-sleeved shirts in the warm ward, but at home, she fought us over the thermostat and couldn't bear to stay in the living room when the fire was on. Her compulsion to only wear the lightest possible outfit passed as warmer weather came in."*

By insisting on appropriate clothing, you'll give your child some relief from their internal bully. You'll also be doing a form of exposure therapy by letting them experience that being warm and comfortable is safe. So you could insist on a woolly hat or on long sleeves in a consistent manner for a few days, and rejoice to find that your child's internal rules have gone.

It can be difficult to tackle the 'being cold' issue consistently because of weather fluctuations. You might require that your child wears a coat in cold weather, but if the weather turns warm and you allow short sleeves, you might have a renewed fight as soon as the next cold spell comes along.

You might choose to put all your fighting energy into meals and allow your child to be a little bit cold. It's heartbreaking, but it's OK for parents to take their limitations into account and to choose their battles accordingly.

COMPULSIVE BEHAVIOURS

> *"The anorexia and the OCD are definitely linked but I don't know which came first. In a way, it doesn't matter, because his weight seems to be so closely correlated with his behaviours."*

OCD is quite common with eating disorders and there's a view that eating disorders are a form of OCD. If your child is conscious of an eating-disorder voice that punishes her for eating, she may also hear it insisting on some ritual behaviours. Not obeying the voice is intensely frightening, so you may get a lot of resistance when you try to break her internal rules. She will need much compassionate support.

Some of our children get into compulsive handwashing when they fear that traces of food will enter their body and make them fat. Irrespective of how a compulsion or ritual began, it becomes the only way the person can reduce anxiety, even when rationally they know it makes no sense.

OCD, like anything you understand to be a compulsion or a rule-based, fear-avoiding behaviour, is normally treated by exposure (of which more in Chapter 9).[137] Exposure work does not require intellectual engagement on your child's part. This makes it a form of therapy that works even when your child's thinking is severely affected by malnutrition.

If your child has compulsive behaviours, in an ideal world you would treat each of them as early as possible. This would free your child of internal bullies, and also prevent habits from becoming too engrained. But in the real world, neither you nor your child have infinite resources of courage and perseverance. So I suggest that for a while, it's good enough to deal with just the most harmful behaviours and plan to treat the rest once you she can eat comfortably and has reached a healthy weight.

There's a good reason for picking this strategy. If the OCD appeared along with anorexia, many of the rituals and compulsions may vanish as your child starts to eat and gain weight. Sometimes you get something for free!

> *"Many of my daughter's odd behaviours left of their own accord within days or weeks of refeeding. The more extreme ones left first (like her terror that water – having a shower – would make her fat). Once her weight and eating habits were restored, we were left with just one, mild compulsion around how her duvet was arranged, and that too faded away after a few months of normal eating."*

If the OCD preceded the eating disorder (bearing in mind that the eating disorder might have started a lot earlier than you think), then the usual path is to treat the OCD after the child is weight-restored and the eating disorder has receded. All the same, if one OCD behaviour in particular is making your life or your child's life a misery, it might be worth trying to erase it sooner rather than later with some exposure work. Note that according to one study, systemic family therapy is more effective than Family-Based Treatment for patients with strong obsessive-compulsive symptoms.[138]

Sometimes a child's pre-existing anxiety disorder hinders progress in treating the eating disorder – for instance if it takes an hour to get a child to the table because of their handwashing. In those cases, it may be necessary to treat at least some of the OCD behaviours sooner rather than later.

BODY-CHECKING AND FAT TALK

Your kid may have a compulsion to pinch and prod himself to gauge the level of fat on his body. The mirror may reflect a cruelly distorted image. When he wails, 'I'm fat! I'm so horribly fat!' he is genuinely distressed, horrified and scared. He may freak out for an hour because of a sudden delusion that he gained several kilos over one meal. Yet at other times he might be generally okay with his changing body and the knowledge that he will gain weight.

Help your child withstand their anxiety until it passes. You might need to move them away from the mirror and stop them from measuring themselves. Forget about logic and concentrate on distraction, empathy, and modelling calm confidence. If you feel the need to reassure – and we all do – then I suggest you start with, 'I'm really sorry you are freaked out when you think of your body. It looks really painful. Now I'm asking you to trust us. This will pass. We are taking care of your body's needs, and you will be well and happy.' Then if your child is repeatedly asking for reassurance or wanting to negotiate quantities, you can move to, 'I'm sorry, honey, it's not useful to talk any longer about this.' You can start helping your child towards recovery by only talking positively about your own or your partner's body. There's more in Chapter 14 ('Am I fat?' How to respond).

CLOTHES

Some kids with an eating disorder cannot bear to wear anything except baggy clothes that cover up their bodies. This isn't about them being independent-minded teenagers, it is fear-based. I have no experience of this, but I know of parents who have intervened because their child had rigid clothing rules even after eating and weight issues had resolved. The parent made all the clothing choices for a while, so that they could gradually expose their child to the experience of wearing clothes they feared.

Clothes are also an issue when our children start regaining weight. You can't stop your child using clothes as markers of his weight gain, but you can help him not get stressed out by clothes every hour of the day.

I made it a policy not to buy my daughter clothes labelled anything smaller than '10–11 years' when she was ten. This meant that for a while, many of her clothes looked oversized and she needed belts to hold her trousers up. On one occasion, when she was starting to regain some weight, she fell in love with a skirt. I bought it for her and let her see that I was also buying the next size up. I wanted to give a clear message that I expected her to soon reach a healthy weight.

Some parents remove size labels from their child's clothes, to try to take the focus away from numbers. On the other hand, your child may be at a stage where it's good for her to challenge her thoughts about clothes sizes. Good health means children and teenagers eventually grow into adult sizes, and those range quite a bit depending on our genetic make-up.

As your child regains weight and some clothes become tight, you need to clear them out, since your child should never fit into them again. If you judge that an upfront clear-out will be too distressing for her, you can 'lose' them in the wash. Some parents buy the same item in a couple of sizes, remove labels and attempt a discreet swap when their child has gained weight. I'm not sure how often this works.

Clothes that are reasonably loose, with elastic waistbands, will help reduce your child's stress. There's nothing worse than a tight pair of jeans digging into your stomach after a meal.

As you work out how you want to tackle clothing issues, consider this: on the one hand, you may want to minimise occasions for distress and resistance, because the absolute priority is for your child to manage eating. On the other hand, you also shouldn't fear what the eating disorder fears. If she has a meltdown over an item of clothing, it's no big deal: you'll support her, and she'll learn that she can cope.

PROTECTION FROM THE INTERNET

The internet poses particular dangers. It's awash with tips for weight loss, with exercises to alter body shape, with body-obsessed pictures and motivational quotes for 'clean' eating. Ill people give advice on self-harm, suicide, appetite suppression and on how to dupe the people who care for you. Calorie-counting apps are disastrous, given that a single 'extra' calorie can be hell for our children. The web is full of recipes, food photos and cookery programs that taunt your hungry child. Even without an eating disorder, youngsters admit that Instagram selfies from people with 'perfect' bodies have a mood-lowering effect.

You may want to keep an eye on your child's online contacts: she may be supporting vulnerable friends she made in hospital, or may be getting bullied by the same gang who triggered her eating disorder.

Finally, we need to protect our children from exploitation and voyeurism. There are people who actively seek pictures of emaciated girls.

While it makes sense to block internet use early on in treatment, you'll need to weigh this up against the benefits of the internet. Social networking apps do enable our children to stay connected with real friends. With bulimia or binge-eating disorder, where sufferers want to get better, they may find helpful websites and apps. Even with a restricting eating disorder, there are sufferers who genuinely seek help, find a good website, and point their parents to it.

For complete recovery, our children will need to learn to use the internet wisely. But during treatment, they need the right level of protection. Here are some ideas for you to evaluate.

You could replace your child's phone with one that doesn't connect to the internet. You could change the password on your home's router and make sure she has no data plan on her phone. You could use parental control software for both static and mobile devices.[139] Set it to block self-harm sites and 'health'-related sites and blogs (often about calories, dieting or 'clean' eating). Family safety apps allow parents to block particular addresses, to track their child's browsing activity and get alerts about potentially dangerous conversations on social networking sites. You may be able to set up a password on your child's phone to disable internet access and prevent her from downloading apps without asking you. That way she may be able to keep some of her social networking while still being protected from the worst. You can also put passwords on all computers and ask the school and the parents of your child's friends to problem-solve with you to protect your child from harmful sites. The school will already be filtering out access to some types of site.

None of this is perfect, and if your child is determined, she may still see horrific stuff on her friends' phones during sleepovers and at school. How much you try to block depends on your assessment of your child's risk at any time. Keep tracking, rather than lock yourself into rules. With our daughter we put in controls, then relaxed them once we could trust that she would come to us whenever she came across something distressing.

Whatever measures you take, your child will probably hate them, but she'll suffer less if she senses you're acting from a place of care rather than a place of sanction and judgement.

BAKING, RECIPES AND IMAGES OF FOOD

It's common for our children to consult recipes for hours, bake elaborate creations, and get vicarious pleasure from seeing others eat the results. I believe this fuels the illness by reinforcing denial, rigidity and misguided self-control. While our daughter was ill, we didn't allow her to do any baking until she was able to enjoy eating what she'd made. On one occasion the hospital therapists argued we should let her bake at home for a charity event, as it would give her the pleasure of a 'normal' activity. To me, it was like allowing a struggling alcoholic to work in a pub.

PROTECT YOUR CHILD FROM TRIGGERS

It's good to steer our children towards normality, but some things are just too much, too soon, and they make meals extra difficult. To protect our daughter from triggers, we kept her out of the kitchen when we were cooking and didn't involve her in food shopping. We kept an eye on her reading materials. We intervened if a teacher preached 'healthy eating'. As your child gets better, they will not react so strongly to triggers, and you will be able to work on making each abnormal behaviour normal again.

YOUR SELF-CARE

Parents, we are *it!* With family therapy, our child's progress relies on us, at a time we've never been so depleted. Find ways to top-up your wellbeing with small daily pleasures, plus bigger bi-weekly mood-boosters. If you're in a couple, make sure you both become competent carers. Chapter 11 discusses partners and friends and if you don't know what to do with your grief, fear or anger, it's in Chapter 15. For now, start building a support village. You could create a WhatsApp group of friends to cheer you on, or join an online parents' group.[140] You could recruit friends and family members to help you with specific tasks. If you have a counsellor, get back into regular sessions. For your resilience and mood, treat your body like an athlete would ahead of a challenge. That means getting hugs (before problem-solving) when you're upset, and taking care of your eating and sleeping. This is a good time to ask for a thorough check-up (with my own medical history this would include B12, iron, thyroid). Explain you're on an emotional marathon and you want to be fit. You cannot function for long on will power alone.

None of this is 'selfish' (a common fear) and much of it (like hugs, or smelling a flower) is possible even in the worst crisis.

PLANNING HOW YOU WILL TAKE CHARGE

A checklist to help you prepare

If you haven't yet taken charge of your child's meals and exercising or other eating-disorder behaviours, then take a few days to get yourself ready. You'll get off to a better start and need to do fewer U-turns.

- Discuss your plans in detail with your partner so you're consistent with each other.
- Do the same with your clinicians.
- Plan how you will tell your child about the forthcoming changes and how you will talk to your other children about the illness.
- Plan a few days' menus (away from your child), to give yourself some confidence.
- Buy the first few days' food so that your child won't need to go shopping with you.
- Have both parents take a week off work (minimum). If possible, have one or both parents take longer. You may be entitled to compassionate leave.
- Discuss with the school the support you need, particularly around meals.
- Prepare hours' worth of entertainment and distraction.
- Hide the bathroom scales.
- Be prepared to cancel any arrangements that might cut short your attempts to get a meal finished.
- To avoid drama – and to intervene in case of vomiting – remove the lock from the bathroom door, and other rooms too.
- If your child is prone to self-harm, remove or lock anything she could use.
- Buy a black marker to hide nutritional information from packaged food.
- Get rid of tiny clothes.
- If you've decided your child would benefit from your presence at night, re-arrange the bedrooms.
- Plan how you will get wellbeing top-ups

A dad writes:

> "Plan how to be united when the ED does the divide and conquer thing. For the real intense ED experiences, having Dad on side can allow Mum to possibly get some level of respite."

Juggling work and other commitments

How you can possibly give your child the time and attention they need while also taking care of your family and work commitments? If you're feeling stuck, this may be a good time to take a detour to Chapters 10 and 11, where I discuss the practicalities of school, work and getting the help you need.

How to be nimble, make U-turns and still be a rock

It's natural that at first you don't yet have all the necessary skills and that you lack confidence. Fake it till you make it. With time, your child will know that you really mean business, and will trust that you're a rock they can lean on.

The FBT method prompts parents to find out what works best for them. This book gives you more help, but you will still be learning quite a lot by trial and error.

> *"My daughter has reminded me of a meal when I admitted, 'Sure, we can't actually MAKE you eat.' She says something clicked in her mind. 'Hey, in that case, why eat at all?' She remembers feeling all-powerful. And also completely abandoned."*

You will inevitably make mistakes, and that means you will have to make some U-turns. How can you look competent and reliable if you keep changing direction? How do you go from being a novice to an assured, in-control parent? How do you get some authority back, so that your child can lean on you?

With our daughter, we told her the truth: that we were now more knowledgeable. This helped when she used our past against us: 'You said that I should listen to my appetite. Well, I'm not hungry'; 'You used to tell me MacDonald's is junk food. Now you want me to eat there?!'

I'd say, 'Yes, I know that we used to talk like this when you were little. We now know a lot more. We've become experts and this is what's right for you now.'

Give yourself latitude to change your mind. Don't lock yourself into promises; don't make deals. I decided that the only thing we needed to be consistent about was that we were in charge, that we made the health-related decisions, and that these may change over time. After that, our child could protest ('You don't normally give me a dessert', 'You never said I'd have to eat in a restaurant', 'I normally only get half a pizza') but at least she couldn't accuse us of breaking promises. I'd say, 'It's true, you never had more than half a pizza on your hospital meal plan, so no wonder it's freaking you out. I'm so sorry. We're in charge now and this whole pizza is what you need.'

I noticed how our trusted eating disorders specialist empowered us in our daughter's eyes. Whenever we made a change in direction, she got us, the parents, to make the announcement. At mealtimes, my husband and I did not say, 'Eat this because so-and-so, who is a highly qualified expert, says you should.' We told our kid that *we* wanted her to eat, that *we* knew what she needed, that *we* cared deeply for her. I think she felt far better supported this way.

How to tell your child that you're taking charge

If a therapist isn't there to tell you all what to do, you may well be nervous about how to talk to your child about the illness, and how you are setting in motion the wheels of treatment. I did it all wrong. I leapt in with a fierce 'From now on, you'll eat what we say you need to eat', terrified my girl, and she dug her heels in even further. We did better a year later when she came out of hospital. We were far more assured and compassionate, and made it easier for her to trust us.

Should you tell your child he has an eating disorder? I'd say yes, though you can agree whether to call it that, or call it a 'difficulty with eating', or an illness – whatever makes it possible to act on it. I know a 9-year old who recovered from anorexia, when all along he thought of it as 'a bug'.

Expect your child to argue that they're fine as they are and don't have an eating disorder. Your empathy might go along the following lines (with pauses and time for your child to respond): 'I'm glad you feel fine. We've been worried for you. I've seen your mood go down; you've been looking quite preoccupied, alone –is that so? I'm guessing your mind is quite tense as you think about food? About weight? I'm so sorry… Sure, I totally get that you say you know what you're doing, that you don't need help. I'm wondering if it's pretty scary for you to think you might not be able to do the things that normally help you feel calmer? Like eating small amounts, losing weight – that's been helping you feel OK? I'm guessing it freaks you out to hear that's going to change? Yes, that makes perfect sense to me. I would be just the same, if someone made me give up something that I'm used to, that makes me feel better in the moment.' After a while you can express your care and offer reassurance: 'I'm so sorry, I can well imagine how it's awful for you to imagine eating more and rebuilding your weight. I'm so sorry it's so tough. We are going to support you every step of the way, with oodles of kindness and understanding. Soon you'll feel good again. You'll find it's easy to enjoy food and your mind will relearn how it all happens very safely and naturally. You're an amazing person and you have a beautiful life ahead of you.'

You will have to tell your child that you are taking charge of meals, and I know you will be nervous about that. You don't need to announce every single change in one go, and indeed you could only give details that your child asks for (they might be protecting themselves from overwhelm). For instance, if you're going to stop your son from shopping, cooking, using the internet and exercising, you might tell him about the exercising only as he reaches for his running shoes. But on the whole you do need to stop walking on eggshells, name what you see and be straight about the road ahead. 'This is an eating disorder'; 'We're going to guide you so that your life will be wonderful again'; 'Your eating has got out of sync with your needs, and we now know what to do to get you back on track'; 'Your unhappiness/stress/weak-ness/difficulties with eating have come about because you've been eating erratically and you've lost weight. We're going to take charge of meals until it's easy again for you to eat without restriction. And yes, to be well again you will have to regain the weight you lost. Yes, my darling, all the weight, back to where your body needs to be to function and for your brain to give you peace.'

Expect your child to fight most of your decisions. With any pill that's hard to swallow, give empathy and make it clear it's for a limited time. You might say that you will review in a week, a month… You are not trying to make your child happy, and you're not even looking for agreement. You're just starting the process of supporting them through something that they find distressing.

Don't do too much 'education'. When your child is upset, they don't care that you are right. Your attempts to make them see sense will only heighten their frustration because they know for sure that *they* are right. Concentrate on kindness and trustworthiness. The message is that, yes, this is hard, and you're sorry about that, and at the same time (never say 'but') that's what needs to be done. Human beings can put up with a lot if they know they are loved and understood (more on compassionate communication in Chapters 13 and 14).

Put yourself in your child's shoes. What might be going on for her when she hears that you are taking action to get her well? Voice your guesses, give her a chance to reply and tell you more, and show your sorrow and care – preferably with the aid of hugs. The following may help you get a feel for what to say, but do use your own sincere words:

- 'Oh my gosh, you think we're blaming you! That we think you're bad, or stupid? [*Pause so she can express herself*] That must be so lonely and scary. [And express your care] No way. All your behaviours are normal, given your situation. My darling, we know enough about this illness to know that you don't chose it. We're on your side.'

- 'You're looking really angry! Maybe you think we're punishing you? Like we think you're bad or stupid? Is it quite shaming for you? [*Pause so she can express herself*]. Oh my darling, I'm so sorry, it must be so lonely for you to think that. It's a horrible feeling, to feel judged. [*And express your care*] None of this is your fault. You didn't choose this any more than you'd choose to have flu. I so want you to know we're on your side.'

- 'Is it horrible for you to hear we're taking charge of your meals, because at your age, of course you want your freedom, to be able to make your own decisions? [*Pause so she can express herself*] Sure, that's really understandable – I'd be just the same. You're not a baby. You have your dignity. You know, we're not getting any pleasure from being in charge, and it's only going to be for a while, just for the things we reckon you can't yet safely do for yourself. We're looking forward to you being able to fly with your own wings again.'

- 'You're looking so sad – am I right? I wonder if you're feeling hopeless? [*Pause so she can express herself*] Yes, I get it, you can't imagine how you can bear to live like this… Gosh, I really feel for you, it's horrible to feel so low. It happens a lot at this stage of the illness [*And express your care*] Emotions pass, you know, and then the sun comes back out. We're by your side. We're doing all the right things, and one day life for you will be sweet and wonderful.

As soon as you see a sign that your child feels heard or understood, move on. Don't wait for her to be happy and grateful. She may still wail her protests, but if the force has gone out of it, if you're getting tears more than fury, this is a good time for a distracting change of scene and activity.

Try to make difficult announcements, or have tricky discussions, at times your child is relatively calm, and has something nice to do afterwards. This is easier said than done, I know. You can at least avoid mealtimes and the hour that follows them.

Oh, and just before a meal isn't ideal either. The truth is there is no perfect time, so leap in when you're ready and trust that your compassionate stance will make it OK.

Finally, take heart that your child will, at some level, be incredibly relieved that you are taking charge and that you're competent. At last, someone realises the mess she's in, someone knows how to help her, someone is going to protect her from her internal bully, from her torment, her exhaustion, her hunger. There is hope.

CONCLUSION: PARENTS TAKE CHARGE

Parents, never doubt that your child needs you to take charge of his or her recovery. They may appear capable because they can still solve quadratic equations, but this illness transforms part of their brain, robbing them of the ability to do a whole lot of things safely and wisely. For those particular things, you are their surrogate wise person. You'll carry them until their body and mind learn that normal behaviours are indeed normal and safe. Then gradually you will give your child practice at taking care of themselves until they have age-appropriate autonomy. You will have the delight of seeing your wonderful child fly with their own wings. We are so lucky that out of all the terrible mental illnesses, eating disorders are perfectly treatable. Here's one young person's account, which I think says it all:

> *"Before, I'd say, 'Mom, Dad, I'll just eat more, I really will. I don't need any more help.' And they'd say, 'Oh, good, glad to hear that.' And they'd believe me. Now, I say that same thing, and they don't believe me. They know they need to help. And knowing that they don't take my 'bullshit' is SUCH a relief. It makes me KNOW that this will end. Knowing that I can't convince my parents that I can do it on my own makes me know that I will be able to do it with them – and it all will end ... thank goodness."[141]*

7

HOW DO YOU GET YOUR CHILD TO EAT IN SPITE OF THE EATING DISORDER?

In this chapter I give you all the tips I've learned from experience, from our therapists and from other parents. I'll use a bungee-jumping analogy to illustrate principles. Later, I'll offer some examples using practical scenarios.

In the early days, most of us find it impossible to get our children to eat. We desperately hunt for treatment, and when we find it we're brought round full circle: we, the parents, are the people at the centre of our child's recovery. We need to learn how to get our kids to eat.

The tools I'm about to offer you got my child from eating practically nothing, to eating what she needed. They saw her through a whole list of foods she couldn't previously eat, and freed her up to enjoy other people's cooking and meals in cafés. These tools deal with fear and irrationality, so they're relevant to many of the challenges of anorexia and related eating disorders, including the drive to exercise or to engage in obsessive-compulsive behaviours.

Some of what I suggest may not be for you, and that's fine. We're all different. Different situations, different resources.

If you'd like to hear me explain and model some of what follows, remember that the essential FAQs are also covered in Bitesize, my library of short audio clips.[142]

And now, prepare yourself. I'm going to invite you on a bungee jump. I hope you are suitably terrified!

Actually I have no intention of raising your stress levels and I'm going to take very good care of you. The aim of this thought experiment is to help you empathise with your child, so that when you're in the middle of a meal the tools come to you instinctively and you don't have to go and consult a book.

THE GREAT BUNGEE-JUMP THOUGHT EXPERIMENT

Your child's resistance is driven by fear

One day I realised that just about every mealtime obstacle my daughter threw at us was driven by fear. This changed everything. Her behaviour might have looked like contempt, or stupidity, or rudeness, or defiance, but the eating-disorders specialist coaching us suggested that the underlying emotion was fear.

> *"Before, we knew she was having rages and tantrums, however, on the multi-family therapy week we have all learned together that it is fear and anxiety."*[143]

When we presented our daughter with a plate of pasta, she refused because she was scared. When we asked her to drink a glass of milk in a café or at home, she refused, despite having been able to drink milk in the hospital, because in this new situation she was scared. When we asked her to sit for a car journey, she was in turmoil because she was scared.

Knowing this meant that her resistance hardly pushed my buttons any more. I stopped telling myself that she wasn't trying enough, or that she was being awkward or inconsistent. Instead, much of the time, I felt deep compassion. I focused on how to ease her fear enough for her to manage the next step. And I recognised the parallels with my own challenges: I wanted to support my daughter even when I was scared.

My new understanding also meant that there was no point in lecturing her about her rudeness while she was in this state. She was a kind and considerate person normally, and I trusted that her unwelcome behaviours would disappear along with her fear. Which they did. (In Chapter 14 I suggest ways to intervene when obnoxious behaviour goes beyond what you wish to accept).

Fear is a horrible emotion. So horrible that often we fear fear, and will do anything to avoid situations we know induce fear. When we feel fear, we assume that we are in danger. Think of public speaking. Many people fear it more than anything, and yet where is the danger? Even the fear we feel as we prepare to give our speech is not dangerous. Feel the fear and do it anyway, as Susan Jeffers says in her best-selling self-help book.[144] Eat.

Ready for the bungee jump?

To help us support our children to eat even though they are frightened, let's think what it would be like to take a bungee jump. I don't know about you, but I have never even considered taking a bungee jump. Way too scary. Are you telling me I have to take a jump? Arghhh!

And to take the analogy further, let's say that I'm supposed to jump not just once but several times a day for the rest of my life.

Perhaps that's what eating feels like to our kids right now.

So, how could a friend support me to jump?

PLANNING THE CHALLENGE

I've never gone bungee jumping, but I have done some rock-climbing. I got into it by accident. As a teenager, I signed up for a holiday which I thought would involve clambering over some lumpy rock formations. When I stepped out of the minibus, I looked skywards and realised that 'rock' meant 'impossibly high cliff'. Had I seen a photograph back home, I would have signed up for the pom-pom-making class instead.

Some people will find it easier to face a challenge once they've been informed and their preferences have been taken into account. Some will get themselves all Zen with positive visualisations. Some may get reassurance from knowing what they're facing: it may not be as bad as their worst fears.

I once helped a dear friend overcome her fear of flying. She was highly motivated and spend time preparing herself for it mentally, imagining herself sitting calmly on the plane. Clearly, for her, it was helpful to have time for visualisation work. At the same time, I do believe she suffered more during that planning phase than she did during the two-hour flight.

If you were doing phobia desensitisation work, your therapist might let you choose how far you're willing to go at any moment. Knowing you're in control can help reduce your anxiety. Also, when you've done the thing you feared the most, you know you did it for yourself, and you gain the confidence that you could do it again.

But people are motivated to rid themselves of their phobias, whereas anorexia usually makes food the problem, not the solution. Also, you can live in safety while you prepare yourself mentally to go on an aeroplane or do a bungee jump, but if you have anorexia you need to eat lots, right now. And until you do, your brain acts more as your foe than your ally.

In Chapter 6 I discussed the pros and cons of devising meal plans with your child. For my daughter, the less she was involved, the better, so I guess she's like me and my accidental introduction to rock-climbing. The majority of families I know of report the same thing. But if you decide your child will benefit from preparation, do the planning with her well away from mealtimes. If I was contemplating bungee jumping, I would not want to be given choices while I'm looking down from a high platform with my blood pounding in my ears.

LOGIC DOESN'T WORK

I do hope my friend won't try logic to get me to jump. I can't think of anything more stressful than having a geek rabbiting on about Hooke's law, while I'm staring down into the abyss. Is that Young's modulus he's talking about now? He is seriously getting on my nerves. All I can think is, 'I cannot take that leap. It's too hard.' My friend says, 'But the elastic cord will hold you. Remember when we did Newton's laws in school?' I don't like the look of the rope. It looks frayed. Yes, I'm sure it's frayed. And it looks too long. I'm going to crash headfirst into the riverbed. My friend is getting impatient. I play for time by starting an in-depth argument about the elastic's tensile properties. My friend gets annoyed that I am so dense about the laws of physics, which gives me a good excuse to let off steam and scream at him. I am glad to note that while we argue, he's not making me jump. I simply cannot jump.

When we are scared (and our children are scared at each meal), our brain cannot engage with intellect or aspirations. We are thrown in a state of fight, flight or freeze, which prioritises safety (see my short YouTube video on this subject.)[145]

I still squirm when I recall that I once produced a colourful chart to show my daughter the humongous number of chocolate éclairs needed to gain just half a kilo. She looked at them and nodded wisely. Then she refused the next meal.

Parents quickly discover that rational talk at mealtimes doesn't work. In Chapter 8 I'll show you how to avoid discussing calories, quantities and metabolism. Logic may have been a good-enough tool in your toolbox for ordinary life, but with any situation where emotions run high, it's as much use as an ashtray on a motorbike.

EDUCATION: THE DINNER TABLE IS NOT A LECTURE HALL

I've noticed that my friend loves delivering lectures, so I ask him to remind me how Hooke's law applies to the bit of elastic that's supposed to support me. He's delighted that he can educate me, as this is very much a pet subject of his, and while he talks, I edge further away from the ledge. When he shuts up at last, he's really cross that I still don't trust the elastic.

As a parent I relished the chance to educate my daughter about her body needing food just like a car needs fuel, and how reducing food intake slows down metabolism and how dieting is plain stupid. It had no effect whatsoever, and at mealtimes, it distracted from the task of eating.

I learned to shut up.

> *"One thing I picked up real quick is that there is a vast difference between talking and eating. I loved to hear insightful comments coming out of my daughter's mouth that showed some sanity, but if it's not immediately backed up by eating more, then it's just a diversion tactic."*[146]

EATING PROMPTS WORK BEST

In Chapter 8 I'll show you how to avoid using logic, discussing calories, quantities and metabolism. You'll see the frequent use of eating prompts, and indeed a study[147] observing parents at work during a meal concluded that the following worked best:

- Direct eating prompts ('You've got to eat all your eggs' or 'Pick it up and eat it')

- Non-direct eating prompts ('Keep going' or 'Why don't you eat some more pasta?')

- Physical prompts (e.g. pushing the plate towards your child)

And these did not work quite as well:

- Promoting autonomy ('Do you want another one?' or 'Which one do you want?')

- Providing information ('Your body needs the calcium')

CONVERSATION TOPICS: PICK WITH CARE

My friend is very kindly trying to distract me by engaging me in conversation. He's telling me a story about his wife's shoe collection. I like that. I hardly notice that as we talk, we're moving closer to the edge. Then I ask him if his wife shares his bungee-jumping interests, and he tells me about the many jumps they've taken together. The spell is broken, I'm back to thinking about this damn jump, and what I'm thinking is that I just can't do it.

For us parents it is hard to chat about anything except the one thing we're focusing on: the food. But we can really help our kids eat by distracting them.

"When I'm having a meal I just want everyone to pretend like everything's normal. And just talk normally."[148]

Topics that you might consider off limits include calories, weight, fat, ingredients, healthy eating, and vitamins. Also don't mention junk food, fat people, skinny people, models, and diets. Keep off the subject of clothes, and don't talk about running, cycling, or the Olympics. And never, ever, mention whales or pigs.

DISTRACTION: A FIRM FAVOURITE

Given the length of the above list, no wonder many of us resort to that wondrous babysitter, the TV. We can also have meals with audio books, we can play board or card games, or the kind of games our generation used for long car journeys before DVDs and online movies were invented.

Distraction is especially great to stop anxiety building up, and that means TV and games with one family member while someone else prepares dinner. It's easier to stop anxiety rising than to lower it once it's reached a peak. With the bungee jumping, I'd be grateful for anything that might keep a lid on my stress before I reach the ledge. I would love help to be distracted while I walk to the place, while I try helmets for size, and while my harness is adjusted. If my friend and I were having a great conversation through all this, then by the time I had to take the jump, my anxiety levels would be quite a bit lower.

REASSURANCE: SUPRISINGLY NOT REASSURING

"When people say 'It's all going to be okay', I resort to thinking of all the bad things that will happen."[149]

I ask my friend when the elastic was last checked. He reminds me that I've already asked him this a hundred times. I say, OK I know it was checked this morning, but who checked it? How qualified were they? My friend explains in some detail the safety checks that were done. OMG, I hadn't even thought about metal fatigue in the hooks and clips. I want to know more about how these are tested. The more he explains, the more I believe he's humouring me. He doesn't actually know that any of this stuff is safe. I am now extremely worried about metal fatigue.

Now he lets slip another piece of information. It seems that the length of the rope is adjusted for each person depending on their weight. If it's too long, I'm going to crash onto those rocks below. Now suppose that this is my second or third jump, and that I have discovered that the method for measuring the rope isn't terribly accurate. Or that the rope is 6 mm longer today than on my previous jumps. My mind is in overdrive. Does that extra 6 mm mean I'm going to die? My friend laughs. He says the safety margins are in metres, not millimetres. I try to trust him, but as I stand on the ledge, I know I don't want to drop by even one extra millimetre.

Likewise, kids with a restrictive eating disorder keep asking for reassurance and have no sense of proportion. 'Am I fat? Will this grape make me fat? Is water really OK? How do you know you're not going to make me fat?' And if they have any information about the calories, they are going to get extremely anxious about any small variation. If  you agree to weigh their food, as we did while our daughter was on a hospital meal plan, you may be setting yourself up for arguments around a fraction of a gram: the fraction your digital scale cannot measure. If your child is anxious about his breakfast being bigger than yours or bigger than the previous day's, he might manage to eat if you reassure him that it is, beyond the shadow of a doubt, identical. But there may be a price to pay in the longer term. From now on, the only way he can feel moderately safe is to demand repeated assurances that his breakfast has not changed. As in his anxiety he is bound to see differences where there are none, the result is every breakfast becomes a fearful experience.

We have an important role in supporting our children when they are afraid or anxious, and I'll talk about this in Chapter 14. During a meal, telling our kids 'You're not fat' or 'There are no calories in water' rarely does the job.

"When I'm eating, anyone who says 'You won't get fat' makes me feel like they're lying. I don't believe a word anyone says."[150]

As a general rule, the more we offer this type of reassurance, the more reassurance our kids need. Reassurance like this doesn't reassure, sadly. Better to keep it simple: 'You're safe', 'This is what you need', 'How do I know? Because I know about these things.'

* PAUSE FOR SELF-CONNECTION *

I wonder what's going on for you right now? I wonder if you've been doing a lot of the very things I'm recommending against. And if so, you might be pretty sad, or you might be blaming yourself, or you might be relishing the thought of strangling me.

> *"I have never had any aspirations to be a nurse or a bungee-jump instructor and I am feeling resentful having to do this. Part of this is my fear that I will muck it up. I probably will choose the wrong cord and accidentally kill my daughter."*

It's painful to notice our limitations when something as important as our child's wellbeing is at stake. I imagine you might be longing for some peace and rest and acceptance, or wanting to be competent, skillful and effective, or needing some hope.

Let's take skillfulness as an example. I suggest you spend a little time acknowledging your thoughts and feelings around your skills, allowing whatever comes up, accepting this is your experience. Give yourself kindness. Bring to your awareness how this is something we all wish for, and how we humans all regularly fall short. Be compassionate: you are heroically doing the very best you can with the resources at your disposal. Now imagine what skillfulness is like, how empowering and wonderful it is, and soak in the sense of what it is like to be skillful. If this is too abstract, remember an occasion when you were skillful, competent, effective. Let your body experience what that was like. Most of all give yourself oodles of kindness and acceptance for everything you are experiencing.

The above exercise of self-compassion and savouring needs is one I'll talk more about in Chapter 13.

TRUST ME, I'M AN EXPERT

What if my friend talked me through the jump in a calm and confident voice? 'I've checked your harness. It's on correctly. You are perfectly safe. Trust me, I do bungee jumps all the time.' It turns out I couldn't have chosen a better guide. My friend is not only a qualified instructor, he is also an engineer specialised in metal fatigue and elasticky things. I am so lucky! He says, 'I can tell you this is very safe. As safe as getting out of bed in the morning. Everything's going to be just fine. On you go now, put your foot here. Good. Now this hand goes right here. Trust me, you can do it. It's safe.' I like this approach. If I had to do a bungee jump I think I'd quite like the words 'safe' and 'trust' to come up quite a few times, and I'd like to know my guide knows exactly what he's doing.

When I helped my friend overcome her fear of flying, one thing that helped immensely was to realise that pilots, engineers, mechanics and everyone involved in ensuring the safety of the flight were experts. It was humbling quite how much expertise goes into one short flight. My friend got her reassurance not so much from trying to learn *how* these people made the plane safe (this would only bring up 'But what if?' questions) but from trusting *that* they were making the plane safe.

With my daughter, at mealtimes, we learned to use the words 'safe' and 'trust' like a broken record. She never objected to them. She sometimes rebelled against words like 'anorexia' or 'medicine', but not to 'this is safe' and 'trust me' and 'I know what's right for you.'

She never explicitly said that she trusted us, and on occasion she still put up a lot of resistance to a particular food. But somehow she seemed to know we were on her side. Perhaps it's because we gave her this assurance: 'We are feeding you the right things.' We knew it was absolutely true, so I imagine that she sensed it. What also helped was our growing ability to remain in a place of unconditional love and acceptance.

Much of what I write in relation to our children applies to us parents. I did a lot better when we had the support of an eating disorders specialist whom we trusted and who treated us with respect and acceptance. Still, if you notice that right now you're unsure about how trustworthy you are, if your self-confidence is at a low ebb, there is an immediate solution: fake it.

SHOCK TACTICS: SHORT-LIVED GAINS, HIGH COSTS

Let's imagine that my friend realises that nothing will make me jump today, so he yells at me and shoves me off the edge. I fall, and yes, that's me bungee jumping. I am furious as well as terrified. That was not a good experience. Tomorrow, he won't even get me out of the house.

In the early days (my way of saying 'when I didn't know better'), there were a couple of occasions when I totally lost it. We had one stand-off over a bowl of soup. My daughter was refusing to even look at it (I'll rephrase that: 'My daughter was incapable of even looking at it'), and we knew we were losing the battle. Any day now, she'd have to go into hospital.

'Will you visit me when I'm in the ward?' she asked.

I thumped the table, stuck my face right in front of hers, and screamed, 'We won't be able to visit you if you're dead!'

I know that this was traumatic for her. I've had some mending to do, and am ready to do some more. Did she eat? Yes. She shovelled her soup down with a look of utter terror. I breathed a sigh of relief (and retreated to the kitchen to let the tears flow). She had eaten. She was going to be OK tonight. But the next day? Nothing.

Arms crossed, defiant look. She was armed to the teeth for whatever I might throw at her.

More worryingly, my outburst had signalled to her that she was on her own. It seems laughable that prior to that she was still leaning on me as a source of support. All I saw was resistance, abuse and hate. But at some level she relied on me. When I screamed at her, she gave up hope. I had to learn new skills to rebuild trust.

Death and destruction

The dinner table needs to be a place of minimum stress, and enduring lectures on death and destruction (or tube-feeding) is anxiety-raising for our kids and makes eating harder. Shoving fear in their faces pushes them into fight-flight-freeze mode, when what they really need is access to their strengths.

Health promotion experts have given up on messages of doom to promote smoking cessation. If I ever needed proof of how disempowering fear is, I got it after a PowerPoint presentation aimed at patients and their families. A psychiatrist, armed with bullet points and statistical charts, made it clear that a fate worse than death awaited us all if we didn't beat anorexia. Or if we were unlucky. Or something.

We'd known this stuff for over a year. Several times, we asked for the speaker to change tack for the sake of the young people in the room, to no avail. In hindsight I wish we'd walked out. But then I'd have missed an important bit of learning about how fear poisons both motivation and the processing of information.

My daughter, at that stage, was well into successful refeeding. She ate reliably everything we gave her, and her weight wasn't too bad. So what did the death-and-destruction talk do for her?

She refused to eat that evening. Or rather she couldn't eat. Later she was able to explain that the talk had left her extremely anxious.

If the psychiatrist's intention had been to motivate us, it failed spectacularly. We had no rush of energy to overcome obstacles and beat this terrible illness – quite the contrary. My daughter had to fight a setback, my husband was upset, and I felt helpless. It was hard to remember where I'd ever got my drive and courage from.

I have heard from professionals that some people need to be hit with hard truths to emerge from denial. I propose that a more universally effective way to guide parents or patients to acknowledge what they already know, and to give them the courage to act, is empathy.

SHOUTING, INTIMIDATING, BLAMING: COUNTERPRODUCTIVE

Let's assume my friend didn't really push me off the ledge – he resisted the urge, and now he's full of adrenalin. He's incredibly frustrated and desperate to let off steam. He screams, 'You are being so irrational! How can you be so dumb? There's a rope holding you, for goodness' sake! Every other normal person is OK with it!'

Hmm, somehow, I am no closer to jumping, but I am *this* close to shoving him off the bridge. And he's not tied on.

Screaming and fear tactics can win you a meal on a couple of occasions, but our experience was that the more we threatened, blamed, lectured or yelled, the less our daughter ate the following day. This ties in with reports that non-critical families succeed better overall in refeeding their children than those with more hostile and critical ways of interacting.[151]

Most parents I know have screamed at their kids. Sometimes we've thought, mistakenly, that a show of force or disapproval might make our child eat. Most of the time we're simply out of control.

Before you beat yourself up over the past, let me assure you that the 'non-critical families' who did so well in studies probably didn't start off non-critical. Chances are the parents exploded many times in spite of their best efforts, until they got in touch with the Zen master within. I know I did. But I also know that our journey to recovery truly began the day we got closer to being a 'non-critical family'.

Here's a dad's experience:

> *"Prior to becoming ED educated and learning how to handle ED
> havoc creation, lots of energy was spent reacting rather than
> calming. Now I think about how to calm, diffuse, and at times just
> plain ignore ED's attempts at havoc creation."*

Some parents have been taught to separate their child from the eating disorder (more on the 'externalising model' in Chapter 14). This is a tool to help you give your kid uncritical acceptance, but sometimes it's also used to let off steam: 'I hate your eating disorder! ED is a bully and a coward and I'm going to wipe the smirk off its despicable face!'

But I worry when I hear parents showing strong feelings against ED in front of their child. The danger is that your poor kid gets hit by it just the same. Her stress level at mealtimes is through the roof, and if you behave with aggression, I doubt she can stand back in a calm and mature way and believe that you're not mad at her.

What is it that blocks us parents from acting in the confident and supportive way we would like to act? Why do we blow up, and start shouting? My guess is that fear is in the driving seat. The anger, the exhaustion, the hopelessness, the head in the sand, they all come from the fear that our precious child is slipping away from us. Ultimately we are terrified that our child will die. On a day-to-day level we are scared that the next mealtime will end in failure. We're scared of flying plates and bruised shins. We're scared of our child's demonic look and we're scared of her distress. We are on high alert.

So to help our child, we are first going to have to help ourselves, acknowledge our fears, make space for our grief. Which is why equipping ourselves with emotional tools is so important.

THREATS, PUNISHMENT, AND 'CONSEQUENCES': UNNECESSARY

Back to my high ledge, and me having to leap. How about if my friend throws in a little threat: 'If you don't jump now, you are *so* not going to the party tonight!'

Good grief, I am gutted!

He says, 'If you don't jump now, I will take you to the hospital where they may force you to jump anyway, and if you don't they'll tube-feed you.'

Now I fear not only the jump but also what the doctors might do to me. My anxiety is massive. I am so stressed I can't decide. My brain is fizzing and not doing anything remotely useful. When it clears a little, I decide I really want to jump to avoid having things done to me in hospital, but as I look down, I am still utterly incapable of taking the leap.

One of the problems with the threat my friend made is that it will happen in a few hours or a few days, whereas my fear is right now in the present. I don't have any mental space to imagine the future. The further away in time, the less threats work. Smoking-cessation campaigns are more successful when they concentrate on immediate benefits (sweeter breath, money in your pocket) rather than long-term negatives (early death).

Threats can also trigger a lot of anger, rebellion or despair, and that might mean less eating.

For some anorexic kids, the threat of urgent hospitalisation and tube-feeding is the one thing that has made them complete meals at home. There are children who started eating in order to regain access to various privileges. But what if a kinder approach worked at least as well?

Consequences: a euphemism for 'punishment'?

Parents sometimes talk of establishing clear consequences (imposed on the child) for not eating. My discomfort is that 'consequence' usually means 'threat', 'penalty' or 'punishment'.

It's not uncommon for parents to say, 'If you don't eat everything on your plate, you can't play a video game. You can lie down and do homework, but not a game.'

That's a threat of punishment, right?

We wouldn't punish a child with asthma for wheezing. If we're ready to punish a child with anorexia, the implication is that they're wilfully refusing food. Whereas what the illness is doing is holding a gun to their head, screaming, 'Don't you dare eat! This will be worse than death!'

Parents who go down the 'consequences' route do so because it's the only thing that seems to work. Family therapy, which has a high rate of success, lets parents find their preferred approach. At the same time, one of its main principles is that children should receive unconditional acceptance. So how can you announce 'consequences' without your child hearing 'blame'?

One way is to choose a time when nobody is angry, certainly not in the middle of a meal crisis. That way you're more likely to stick to medical issues and to avoid blame and punishment. You'll be less driven by your own knee-jerk reactions, and you might avoid making threats you can't carry out.

Revenge

There's another problem with threats or talk of consequences: when we're under stress (as we can be when our child refuses to eat or throws food at us), it's normal for our nervous system to go into a 'fight' state. We can have an urge to punish, to hurt, to take revenge. If we can stop ourselves from making threats, it's easier to avoid tipping into aggression.

I've got better at noticing when I have an urge to punish or retaliate. I try to use it as a signal to keep my mouth shut and self-connect, even if just for a few seconds.

Bash the eating-disorder demon, not your child

If we're going to use threats or 'consequences', let's make sure they hurt the eating-disorder persona, not our child. I'm guessing that denying your child TV time deprives her of something she enjoys, and gives the eating-disorder demon a huge amount of satisfaction because he's heavily into punishment himself. Or to put it another way, switching off the TV may reinforce your child's belief that she's bad, hopeless and unworthy of good things.

What scares the demon? The possibility of being fed greater quantities, of having less choice, or being denied exercise, of ingesting calories through a nasogastric tube, and of going into hospital where nurses will not take no for an answer. If you want to make threats, those are the kinds that your child may be able to use as bargaining tools against her eating-disorder voice.

A blunt instrument

Even if threats produce some kind of breakthrough, be aware that they may lose their power after a while. For example there are hospitals where children are only allowed contact with their parents if they eat, or where they have to earn the permission to have a shower (ours did not do anything like this, thank goodness). It sounds like people, under this regime, usually eat and gain weight – enough to get the hell out of there.

I have read short accounts from patients who were treated with this type of system, who have recovered and now look back with gratitude. But my understanding is that as a general rule, people go back to restricting as soon they can get away with it.

Why routinely use such punitive methods when more humane approaches usually work better?

Threats might be one blunt tool to get us through sticky challenges, but for something that will help time and again, we need lots of other resources.

REWARDS AND BRIBES: HANDLE WITH CARE

My friend might decide against threats in favour of their positive counterparts: rewards and bribes. He says, 'If you take this jump I'll buy you some hair clips.'

I snort so much I choke.

He says, a bit dejected, 'I thought you liked hair clips.'

I roll my eyes.

He says, 'OK, how about we draw up a chart and you get a star for every jump, and for every 20 stars you get a fancy new pair of shoes?' Clearly he has no idea how scary this jump is. He expects me to do 20 of them? We spend time negotiating a reward that might motivate me. I'm starting to think I might just be able to jump, just this once, if he gives me eight hundred thousand pounds. If he does, I'll jump, but what I don't tell him is that I'm damned if I'm doing this on a regular basis.

Even for eight hundred thousand pounds, I'm not sure I can manage, so I'm relieved when my friend turns down my offer. I tell him that for ten thousand pounds, I will jump from my garden wall if he covers the ground with feather cushions. We argue. At least while we argue I'm not jumping off anything.

In general, rewards should come with a hazard warning, and I'll discuss this in more detail in Chapter 14. But how might they help you get your child to eat? Here's the deal. You eat and I'll give you smiley faces, stars, paintbrushes, money, and so on. We're talking about external motivation here, and for some families, this has worked very well.

If rewards save a single child's life, they're worth considering. But our experience of reward charts was that they might work once or twice, and then no more. We were left with nothing but ugly arguments.

If we'd used rewards for eating, how could we have kept it up? We're talking six meals a day, for months. And no, at age 10 to 11, she was not interested in stickers, and if we'd offered money, the way rewards had to keep escalating, we'd have been mortgaging our home.

External motivators were not for us, but they may be good for you, so don't let me put you off. We're talking about complex human beings here, not amoeba.

Note that gifts (with no strings attached) are quite different from rewards. I don't want to put anyone off making gifts, which at their best, are a beautiful expression of love.

INCENTIVES: A NUDGE IN THE RIGHT DIRECTION

How about incentives? 'Remember how much you wanted to take this jump?' my friend says. 'You want to raise money to go on that trip to Malawi, right?' Chances are that, quivering as I am, miles above terra firma, I don't give a damn about Malawi. I can't for the life of me remember why I ever cared about Malawi. But without Malawi, I wouldn't even have made it up to the bridge.

During mealtimes, when your kid is full of fear, your attempts to motivate her with incentives may not work. Your child isn't tuned in to the joys of life, and she may tell you where to stick your incentive. No harm in trying, though. Indeed I know of wards where placemats are decorated with incentivising images.

My daughter really wanted a family Christmas because her beloved cousins would be visiting. She knew
that to join the family for Christmas, she had to manage
meals outside the hospital. As an incentive, it wasn't bad.
It helped her some of the time.

Your child might find some courage as she remem-
bers that she wants to grow tall, or to be able to have children, or to pursue a job or
university course. Note that those are quite far into the future. Incentives may work
better if they're about a pleasurable outing this afternoon or tomorrow.

Incentives, like consequences, are best when they're about real life. Your child
might enjoy picturing her future, and if it comes from her surely that's positive. Don't
expect it to be a tool you can force on your child while she's underweight, though.
She might be able to tell you exactly how many kids she plans to have and how she's
going to travel the world, and in the same breath refuse the bagel you're handing her.

VISUALISATION: ACCESS TO INNER RESOURCES

While you're using incentives, be descriptive. As your child visualises what she longs
for, pleasurable feelings may displace stressful ones. 'Remember last year when you
were in the school play and Rebecca fell off the stage?' Bringing a smile to her lips,
or making her laugh, will help bring down anxiety levels and make it easier to eat.
Back to the bungee jump, my friend could incentivise me better by helping me access
pleasant emotions.

'It's going to be amazing going to Malawi, helping to build a school! Imagine
that! Flying out there with your friends, camping at night, getting to know the local
kids. OK, you're smiling now. Jump! Right now. Go!'

This is more than positive thinking. You're building a picture, a world, for your
child to step into and enjoy. This is about putting your kid in touch with her strengths,
the things that matter to her, that give her energy. At the opposite end are fear, con-
traction, impossibility.

This is what I mean by visualisation. I would love to think that there are therapists out there who can help our kids visualise meals in a peaceful and positive way,
in the same way as my friend, who was working on her fear of flying, worked on
visualising herself on a successful flight. But I don't believe it works like that with an
eating disorder. If it did, eating disorders could easily be cured with a few hypnother-
apy sessions, and sadly there's no evidence that they can.

PRAISE: COMPLEX AND RISKY

I talk about praise in some detail in Chapter 14, but let's stick to mealtimes for now.
What kind of praise or acknowledgement does your child need?

Thinking of bungee jumping, I would expect my friend to give me some form
of praise as I step closer and closer to the dreaded edge. Whether I would want the
praise to be wildly enthusiastic ('OMG! Isn't this amazing! Here you are about to take

your first bungee jump!') or more muted ('By Jove, this is going rather well') may depend on my personality and the culture I live in.

How does this translate to the dinner table? You say, 'Well done!' You say, 'You're doing so well.' Your child looks at you in terror, tells you what a hateful person you are, puts her fork down, and refuses to eat another bite.

What happened?

There is so much internal conflict within your child, such strong feelings of worthlessness and self-hate, that praise confuses her and ignites massive debates in her head. If she has a voice that tells her not to eat, this voice is now using your praise to beat her up.

I imagine the voice might tell her any of these things:

- 'Hey, what's going on? You tricked me! I was having a little nap, and now I hear you've been eating! Stop right now, or else!'

- 'I heard that! Do you realise you've eaten half your lunch already? You thought I wouldn't notice? How dare you defy me! I'll make you pay for this.'

- 'Emergency! Parents are the enemy. Do NOT please your parents. Remember we are at war.'

- 'If your parents are pleased, that's a sure sign you've eaten way too much. How could you be so weak and stupid?'

- 'Ah, so you had a choice! You told me you had no choice, you liar. See how relieved your parents look? Clearly, they were not expecting you to eat. You ate when you could have got away with not eating! You total loser.'

- 'You don't really believe this praise is genuine, do you? Your parents are manipulating you and treating you like a baby. Nothing about you is worthy of a compliment.'

- 'Oh dear, they really mean it. If only they knew how terrible you really are!'

Our children differ around this, but it won't take you long to notice if your child hates hearing praise during a meal. If your child has moments of respite from her bullying voice, ask her how praise affects her. But if she's at the most acute stages of anorexia, it's unlikely you can have any kind of sensible discussion. In this case it might be best to err on the side of caution, and to avoid any praise relating to her eating.

Another subtlety is to avoid sounding amazed at your child's achievements. You're trying to give the message that you've been confident all along that she could eat.

What can you do? It might seem insensitive not to acknowledge the massive effort your child is putting into every bite, but the priority is to support what works.

Some parents report that whereas 'Well done for eating your toast' is a slap in the face, 'Well done for eating in spite of your fear' is well received.

If, like us, you find that the less you talk about food, the better, then when you have an urge to praise you might say: 'OK, Keep going', 'You're doing the right thing. Another mouthful', 'Did you hear how the Mayor of London was left dangling on a zip wire today?'

When the meal is over, you might avoid saying things like, 'Good, you've eaten all your dinner.' Instead, you could spring to your feet and happily say, 'Let me show you the YouTube of the Mayor on a zip wire.'

With my own daughter, once we realised the distress praise caused her at mealtimes, we did our best to cut it out. The most we did was to acknowledge what she'd achieved: 'OK, so you've managed the yoghurt. That was exactly what you needed. Now the last bit of banana, and we can go to the park.'

Our daughter did appreciate praise at calmer times – typically in bed late at night when her voice went off duty. It was validating for her to have her efforts and achievements acknowledged. And I'm guessing that she needed hope as well. I'd say something along these lines: 'You are doing fantastically. Are you pleased with what you've achieved? Just think, this time last week you couldn't have imagined eating ice cream, but you stuck to it, and now you're even considering going to a party where there'll be ice cream!'

Actually, I probably said less than that. Mostly, I tried to give her space to share her own sense of achievement. Note that I didn't tell her that she was brave, but your own child might love to hear that. And it is, after all, the truth.

It often seems like an impossible, ungrateful task, for parents to find the right words when their child has an eating disorder. Luckily, the most powerful tool in our kit is silence. The kind of silence that speaks of empathy and unconditional love.

'IT'S YOUR MEDICINE': WORTH A GO

How about the wellbeing argument? Let's imagine that taking this jump was the only proven way of curing me of my fear of heights, just like eating is the only proven way of beating anorexia. Now, say my fear of heights is extreme and is making life a misery: I can't even go up the stairs in my own house. I know that bungee jumping will cure me, but right now, as I look down into the void, I don't care if I have to spend all my remaining years avoiding stairs. So my friend might remind me of how much I miss my pre-phobia life.

'I know you hate the look of this jump. I know you're scared. At the same time, this is your medicine. You need to take this jump to get your old life back, to get your friends back. Wouldn't you love to see Helena again? Remember how the two of you used to hang out in her attic and chat for hours? Wouldn't you love to use your upstairs bathroom? You have no choice. Come. Jump.'

I think this might help a little. The Helena bit. Forget about the upstairs bathroom – the downstairs one is fine.

'Food is your medicine' is a common mantra in our world, and it's worth giving it a go because it's the truth, and it's a brief reminder of why we are acting cruel to be kind. But also be ready to abandon it. I have, as my daughter hated the mantra – I think she experienced it as patronising and lacking in empathy. Besides, 'Food is your medicine' sounds to me rather like providing information (e.g. 'Your body needs the calcium'), which, as we saw earlier, seems to be less effective than direct eating prompts.

Note that the wellbeing argument might only work if your child is in touch, at some level, with a desire to be well.

> *"People can give me facts about weight, calories, nutrition; it will just make me worse. My voice wants me to be ill, if ill means skinny, then ill it is."*[152]

DAMAGE LIMITATION: BLAME SOMETHING OTHER THAN YOUR KID

What if, after an hour of exemplary support, my instructor completely loses his patience? He calls a colleague over. 'Here, get her unclipped. I'm off. I can't believe how stubborn she is. She's not even trying!'

This is so very human that we're all highly likely to do something similar at the dinner table at some time or another. We go into fight or flight and say things that we regret two seconds later. It's not the end of the world, but it's wise to have a few damage limitation strategies.

If your child hears an eating-disorder voice, you might say, 'I hate that bully of a voice so much. I'm sorry I shouted and scared you, but I am so incredibly cross at it. I'm not going to let it harm you. I really want you to have your smoothie.'

If your child doesn't have an eating-disorder voice, it's just as valid to say, 'I didn't mean to scare you. I'm sorry I shouted. I hate that this illness is making it so hard for you to drink your smoothie.'

This last statement, I'm guessing, is the truth. But it's not a great idea to share everything about how awful you're feeling. You don't want to panic your child – remember that you are her only hope at the moment. The message should be that even though you are mad because of a particular behaviour caused by the illness, you are confident that you will beat the eating disorder. So you might continue with: 'Anyway, darling, deep breath – I know I certainly need one – and have a sip of your smoothie.'

TEAMWORK: HAVE A BREAK, MAKE A GRACEFUL EXIT

The ultimate damage-limitation plan is to leave. It is reassuring to know that if at any time you feel out of control, you can simply go.

Imagine my bungee-jumping friend is losing patience. He's tapping his fingers, checking his watch, and he's made a couple of critical comments. I need him to continue supporting me a little longer before I am ready to jump. The more irritable he gets, the more guilty and miserable and cross I feel, and the less I think I can take this leap.

Luckily my friend has noticed what's going on inside him. He says, 'Sorry, I've just remembered I need to make a phone call. But I see my wife coming over, and I'll ask her to take good care of you.'

Looking after a child with an eating disorder can be utterly exhausting, so if you can tag-team with your spouse or find a few friends or relatives who are willing to join you at mealtimes, together you will give your kid the support she needs.

I once heard a professional say that after working on an eating-disorders ward, he understood how parents scream or give up. Staff have their limits just like we do. The difference is they can discreetly signal to each other when they need someone to take over. And unlike you, they can leave the world of eating disorders behind them after their shift. Plus, they have days off and holidays. Much of this will help them maintain an aura of cheerful competence and get our kids to eat.

If you're a single parent or if your spouse isn't as hands-on as you, make it a priority to find a solution (see Chapter 11 for some suggestions). You need someone who can relay you or who can step in and take charge of a meal while you take time out. This is especially important in the early days of refeeding, when your child is more likely to resist meals and you may be tested to your limits. Of course, this person needs to support your approach or your child will play you off against him or her. In some families, both parents take a week or two off work to begin refeeding. I know of single parents who have organised for a relative or close friend to come in at mealtimes.

Sometimes, a change of horses is just what a child needs. The break alters the atmosphere or gives him a way of saving face. So after a day of resisting food with his mother, he might accept dinner with his father, saying 'Mum's rubbish. She makes it so hard for me to eat.' (At this point, however disloyal this may seem, the father would be wise to concentrate on the next mouthful, not to contradict.)

Try and find a way to pass the relay baton with grace, so you can leave without any implication of blame. Blame has quite a debilitating effect: if your kid senses that you are judging him, it becomes extra difficult for him to eat.

Making a graceful exit does require one last effort at self-control, unfortunately. What you really want to say is, 'Right, that's it. I can't stand this. I don't care if you eat or not. This is hopeless!' Your child really doesn't need to hear this. Even if you're into honesty, notice that this is not your truth. You are only worn out in this instant.

What about this type of honesty: 'Darling, I have a terrible urge to scream or to cry, and I don't want to do it here in front of you because I really care for you. I'm going to my room for a few minutes, all right?' Ugh! If your child hears that without thinking 'This is all my fault and I'm a bad person,' she's more Buddhist than the Dalai Lama.

Personally, I would prepare an exit strategy along these lines:

- Oops, is that the time? I promised Jane I would email some stuff. Excuse me for a while.

- Oh darling, I'm so sorry, I've had a headache all day, and I need to go and lie down.

- Did my phone beep? I'll just go and check if I've received a text I'm waiting for.

- Oh dear, I really need to put a wash on for tomorrow.

- Damn, I never checked my email. I'm waiting for something important. Would you excuse me?

- Are you two OK if I get on with some work? It's all a bit hectic right now.

- I fancy a walk in this lovely evening sun. Do you mind if I nip out right now?

We had times when my husband took over one meal after another because he could remain kind and supportive, whereas I tended to fall to pieces. He was able to put a lid on his emotions and get on with the job. Sometimes I felt rotten, wishing I could do the same. But this isn't a contest. We all cope differently with the challenges of the illness. If the team is working well, it's OK for an individual to be weaker at times or to contribute in different ways.

Ask for help when you need it. It's not a sign of weakness. It is the best thing you can do for your kid.

CONTAINMENT: STAY CLOSE

Let's imagine my friend is still sticking with me, supporting me. I might like him to take the jump with me and keep hold of my hand.

A piece of advice that often comes up with anorexia is to have a parent on either side of the child, sitting very close. It didn't work for my daughter – she wanted space and could easily lash out when touched – but there were a few occasions where after a long struggle, she ate while sitting on her dad's knee. I know of teenagers who need to be gently spoon-fed.

Certainly, we shouldn't expect someone with anorexia to eat on their own – not while the illness is pushing them to cheat and hide food.

If my friend leaves me on my own on the bridge, you can bet your bottom dollar I will not jump. It's not that I don't want to. I just can't. If he asks me if I jumped, I'll tell him I did. I'm scared but I'm not stupid.

If you're struggling with the idea that you are taking away your adolescent's autonomy by making her eat, you may relate to the concept of containment. Your child may be 'falling to pieces', 'all over the place', 'thrashing about'. What you're doing for her is holding her. Imagine that you had to walk along a cliff edge blindfolded. Wouldn't you like a trusted person to hold you firmly and guide you with a confident hand?

HUMOUR: THE BEST RELAXANT

Laughter is the best relaxant of all, so I hope my bungee-jumping friend is funny. I might not laugh as I'm taking the leap, but laughing will certainly reduce my anxiety levels more than anything else, enough for me to take a step.

It's probably easier to do stand-up comedy to a bunch of metallurgists than to be genuinely funny for a child in the grip of an eating disorder. I admire the people who manage it, when the situation leans more towards drama.

Still, whenever my husband or I could lighten the moment, we tried to do so. As time went on, meals became more light-hearted. It can be fun to go through a book of jokes during dinner, or watch hilarious cat videos on YouTube, and you can't beat a seriously naughty limerick.

Humour works best when it comes from a genuine sense of fun, as this dad explains:

> *"She was freaking out over the French fries. She stuck half a dozen fries upright into her turkey burger bun. I started laughing, and, surprisingly, so did she. It broke the mood for her, and gave her such relief. I knew, soon enough, she'd eat everything."*

We had to take care with the banter – it is all too easy for a child with a brain made sensitive by an eating disorder to think you're laughing at her. On the other hand, you can't be very funny if you're being ultra-careful. Here's a supremely unorthodox take on it from one mother:[153]

> *"I'm told almost daily how much I'm hated. The other morning not only was I hated, I was wished dead, so I replied, 'I wish I would die, right now, so that in your hatred you would barbeque and eat my horrible old body and at least have SOMETHING in your stomach to keep you going through your day. THAT is how much I love you!' My D was so taken back that she laughed and the bad spell was broken for a moment."*

FEELINGS: A GOOD START

Would it help if my friend showed that he understood my feelings? He says, 'How are you feeling?' He means well, but I have heard that phrase too often and if I'm feeling anything right now, it's seriously disconnected from him.

He says, 'You're scared, right?'

I say, 'Terrified. Look how my hands are shaking.'

He says, 'Don't be scared. There's nothing to be scared about. In fact, you should be really happy: a lot of people would love a chance to do this.'

I kick him.

After he's applied arnica to his shins, he tries again. 'It looks like you're very frightened. I wonder if this is very hard for you?'

Not bad. He's certainly connected with my feelings, and this time he hasn't denied them, but where does that leave me? Possibly a little weakened, or a little stuck. A little patronised too. He's using a very, very calm voice, and it's out of tune with the level of terror I'm experiencing. He can't possibly know how I feel when he's so calm. But it's nice that he's trying to understand me. He is trying hard.

Then he blows it by saying, 'You poor thing. I don't know how you can bear it.'

I am now a limp rag.

EMPATHY: POWERFUL WHEN FOCUSED ON THE TASK

I'd prefer it if my friend's empathy went further.

'You're really scared, right? Yes, I totally get it how right now you're freaked out. A lot of people are when they're standing on the ledge for the first time. You need to know that this is safe, hmm? You want to know that you're going to be all right?'

Now I feel understood. I feel felt. What a relief!

With a bit more of this, I might be able to jump.

> *"The thing that stood out most for me in your draft was that kindness could be firm and effective. I was despairing of the sledgehammer approach to break through the resistance. Just knowing we might be able to work against anorexia in a different way, a way which had already started to feel like the only way for our daughter, changed everything. Sounds dramatic but it really was a key moment for me."*

Empathy is the most powerful tool in your entire toolbox. It is an essential tool, given that your child may not believe she's ill and that the prospect of eating is so terrible for her.

> *"You will win on the strength of your relationship rather than on the strength of your argument."* (Xavier Amador, author of *I Am Not Sick, I Don't Need Help!*)[154]

Empathy is much more than a tool, it's a beautiful way to go about our lives. I will talk about empathy in greater detail in Chapters 13 to 15, but for now, I will give you some quick pointers, because I know that you have a meal to serve within the next couple of hours.

If you'd like an empathic connection with your child, all you have to do is this: *be* with her. Soul-to-soul. One human being alongside another human being.

Is that too woolly? Here are some techniques to help get you to really connect with her.

Let go of judgements and solutions. Let go of any pressure to change your child, to yank her out of her distress, to fix her and make her happy. These things are not in your power, and they put you both under unrealistic pressure. What is in your power is to be your child's best supporter, to be by her side, and respond to her needs the best you can as they present themselves.

Ask yourself what's going on for her. What's she feeling? And what's behind these feelings that are overpowering her, and behind the words she's saying? What are her deep needs? What does she long for? This is not about what the eating disorder wants, but what's important to any human being in their quest to live a full and rich life.

At mealtimes, you don't need to look too far for the things she really wants, the absence of which scare her and make her lash out. What she wishes for, most probably, is:

- safety (she feels very scared)
- peace of mind (she feels out of control, agitated, angry)
- acceptance (she feels shame and tells herself she's not an OK person)

- kindness and support (she feels despair, hopelessness and tells herself she's all alone)
- to be understood, to feel felt (which is what empathy is all about)

She may also feel revulsion towards the food, and pain in her stomach if she's not used to eating.

So to support your child with empathy, you reflect back to her what you're guessing about her feelings and needs – and you do this from a place of kindness. You may guess wrong, but that's OK, and that's why it's usually best to phrase things as questions: she may then correct you, and then you can respond with empathy based on that information. The fight may go out of her once she knows she's been understood. Your active listening may also help put her in touch with what she didn't dare acknowledge to herself.

Here are some examples:

- 'I notice you've pushed your plate away. I wonder if you're scared?' [Feeling.] She might nod, and you'd continue: 'Ughh, it's horrible being scared. Would you like to know that this is safe?' [Tuning in to how much it matters to be safe.]
- 'I'm wondering if you're pretty stressed? [Feeling.] I bet it would be just wonderful for you to have some peace. Is that so?' [Reflecting back the peaceful quality of … peace.]
- 'Would you like to be absolutely sure I'm with you, supporting you, on your side?' [Tuning in to the deliciousness of having support.]
- 'So you say looking at this food makes you feel sick? And your stomach's hurting? [Feeling – located in the body.] Oh, that's horrible. Are you worried about it? [Feeling – emotion.] Would you like some reassurance about what might be happening in your stomach?' [Tuning in to the need for reassurance.]

You may add a validating and normalising statement, something that may help her feel less shame, less messed up, and that indicates her feelings aren't a cause for alarm. This may free her up to problem-solve.[155]

- 'I'd be stressed too if I had a voice shouting at me when I'm trying to eat.'
- 'If I thought that this piece of cake was suddenly going to make me balloon out, I'd be angry too.'

You may or may not need to continue with an action or words that may meet her needs:

- 'Darling, you're totally safe. This food is exactly what you need, and it's safe.'
- 'Let's be peaceful, even if the voice is shouting. We can eat even when it's there.'

- 'I'm by your side. See, I'll be there for you as long as you need me. You're my precious girl.' (You can do this without words; this can be silent empathy.)

- 'The revulsion and the discomfort in your stomach are quite normal, you know. It can be like that at the beginning. It does pass. And meanwhile, even though it's horrible, it's quite safe. Shall I make you a hot water bottle?'

I'll offer more guidance on empathy and conversations in Chapters 13 and 14.

Don't let empathy become a talk fest. During meals, keep this type of talk to a few minutes at the most. This is not a therapy session. Your child is at the dinner table to eat. At the same time, if your child experiences fewer negative feelings and more positive ones while at the table, it will be easier for her to eat now and next time.

If the examples I've given you here make you cringe, I must tell you the dialogues I read in other people's books make me cringe too.

> *"My daughter would scream at me if I said that stuff. She would find it patronising. She says, 'You are treating me like a baby!' Or she says, 'You are not my therapist!' Or, 'Fuck off!'"*

Something that comes from the heart, once written out of context, sounds terribly artificial. Use your own words to suit your style and your child's. As long as you're connecting, it doesn't matter what you say. Remember that empathy is just 'being with'.

It can be daunting, when our children are very reactive, to know what to say. The great news is that the best empathy can be totally silent: I will refer to it as 'silent empathy'. If your whole being is present to your child, she will get the signals. She'll get a sense that you are attuned to her. It will help her tremendously.

* PAUSE FOR SELF-CONNECTION *

How are you doing? Notice what's going on for you. Are you full of hope, interest, excitement? Are you maybe overwhelmed, confused? Or something else?

Notice what you're needing right now. Perhaps, for instance, you need a break, a bit of space. A therapist would offer you information in carefully measured-out bite-sized chunks. A therapist might also help you notice all the things you're already doing that are both loving and effective. I can't do that in a book. How about you go and do something kind to yourself, even just for a short while? Smell a flower, stroke a dog, put some music on, watch a funny hamster video.

What I'm offering you here is a little practice in mindfulness. It may help you to let go of stressful thoughts and to tune into your strengths. It is an invitation to take one step to care for yourself. Notice that it doesn't diminish the care you have for others.

SELECTIVE HEARING, BODY-SWERVING AND TRANSLATION SKILLS

We've strayed from bungee jumping, so let's return to my ledge. My friend keeps urging me on and suddenly I see red. I scream at him, 'You're the most useless bungee-jumping instructor. You're always so insensitive! And by the way there's rust on this stupid clip. Are you trying to kill me? Why are you making me do this?' Maybe I kick him.

My friend could shout back at me or storm away, and that would be his right and also quite a natural fight-or-flight reaction. He could remain calm, and correct or educate me: he's not useless, and what I see on the clip is not rust but a safety inspection mark. He could answer my 'why?' question and remind me that this bungee jump is for my benefit. He could choose to speak up for his own needs and ask me to speak with consideration.

He's perfectly entitled to respond in any of these ways. But none of these responses will help me this instant because my questions are not real questions. My words are nothing but expressions of my state of fear. What I need right now is empathy – verbal or silent.

You may experience a lot of aggression at the dinner table. It's wearing for parents, and this is why this book offers many emotional resources. Here are some pointers. Imagine your child is saying, 'You're utterly useless!'

- Revise your interpretation of what's going on, from 'I really am useless' or 'How dare she speak to me like that' to 'It's not about me.' Do a body swerve. Your child may look like he's shooting poisoned arrows at you, but each arrow is actually a plea for connection.

- Develop selective hearing: let the words whoosh right over your head and listen out for feelings (usually fear) and deep needs ('keep me safe', 'understand me', 'love me', 'help me'). If you get good at this you will remain connected far more often than you feel hurt.

- Hold onto this mantra: connect before you correct. Or if you prefer: empathy before education. The principle is that people, when they're angry or in pain, need empathy before they can take in information and before they can make space in their heart for anyone else. My bungee-jumping instructor may eventually choose to tell me about the safety mark on the clip, and may eventually ask me to speak politely, just not right now while I'm shouting.

- Treat yourself with kindness. You need empathy for yourself. I bet the Dalai Lama himself would need all his internal resources to do the job you're doing.

MIRRORING: MODEL CALM CONFIDENCE

I'm standing there, in my harness, and I like that my friend looks so calm and confident. When he first said, 'You're very scared, right?', he said it with intensity, nearly matching the intensity of my feelings. I really felt understood. Now his body language and his tone of voice are soothing.

Mirroring works on the basis that we have a tendency to unconsciously mirror what others do. So if we show calm and confidence, we draw our child towards calmer and more confident feelings and behaviour.

If you look very calm when your child is yelling how much she hates the world, she might not connect with you at all and rebel even more. So it can help to start off by almost matching the intensity of her emotions: 'You're bloody furious, right?' Then bit by bit, you speak more softly, more slowly, relaxing your body, de-escalating the tension. Your kid's mirror neurons will fire away, prompting her to feel what your body is modelling.

Both fear and confidence are contagious. We all tend to unconsciously mirror each other. If we react from a place of fear when our child refuses food, her own stress levels will rise. The eating-disorder voice will then either increase the urgency of its threats or offer a welcome refuge.

I love this analogy from another mother:[156]

> *"Imagine you've fallen and you have a deep gash on your leg. Which response do you look for in those helping you?*
> *'Aghhhhhh, OMG, there's blood, lots of blood. Oh no, I think I can see bone. I feel faint. Excuse me, I am going to be sick.'*
> *Or: 'Darling, let me sit you down over here and let's look at that scratch. Hmm, OK. Look, just rest here. It's not too bad. Let's wash the worst of it away and then we will have a better idea of what we are dealing with.'"*

We want to model internal confidence, trust, and assurance, because that will make it easier for our child to eat. At the beginning we may have to fake it, as one parent points out:[157]

> *"Know what an eating disorder is and isn't. That knowledge is your confidence. Even if you don't really feel it, you MUST fake it outwardly. Any weakness you feel must not be shown on your face, ever. You have fed your kid and dealt with your kid's stubbornness for years, in many aspects. This is not really any different. You know how to hold your ground. Do it."*

Luckily, the more we fake it, the more we feel it, so there should be fewer demands on your acting skills as you go along.

DEFUSING FEAR: REMOVE THE FEAR OF FEAR

I might appreciate my friend tackling my fear directly. 'That fear you're feeling right now, it's normal. Everyone feels like this at first. The trembling, the sick feeling you've got? Utterly normal. It's a horrible feeling, hmm? Everyone gets it the first few times.

That's the way brains work when you start bungee jumping. It means nothing. You're still safe.'

When he said 'right now', and 'at first', I relaxed a little. Before that my fear seemed to stretch out into eternity. And I was all fear and nothing but fear, whereas now, I'm me, a good stable core, with a trembling, sick feeling laid over the top. Before, I thought of myself as a pathetic freak, the only person on this ledge who can't jump. Now I know my reactions are normal, part of a process. I have hope.

My friend hasn't lost focus though. He continues, 'This jump is just right for you. It's totally safe. On you go.'

In the example above, my friend delivered a rather long speech – probably too long. With our kids, a few words may be enough, or even none. Body language, as well as what we say and don't say, do most of the talking. Whereas up to now your child may have got the message 'I am terrified we'll never get through this', she can now get 'This is all as expected and we're doing all the right things.'

Note that some people will bristle if you 'accuse' them of being scared. Work colleagues, for instance. They need to hold on to some dignity, and they may mistakenly think you're talking down to them. Hopefully this isn't the case with your child, but if it is, try and home in on the next most vibrant feeling, or water down your language. 'Freaked out' or 'concerned' might do the trick. And remember the power of silent empathy if you doubt that you can find any words that connect.

NOTICE INDICATORS OF PROGRESS

Suddenly, I'm feeling just a bit more up for this jump. I really do want to raise money for my trip to Malawi. I remember the thrill of childhood rides; maybe this will be similar. I step forward a little. Yes, I can do this. I'm shaking, but I've moved right to the edge. My friend says, 'Look, I've had enough. This is too hard for you. Let's call it a day.' He'll never know how close I was to taking that leap.

We are so tuned in to the difficulty of the task that we can overlook the huge number of signals that our child is ready to take a mouthful. So we go on pleading, arguing, or we give up – when a little silence, a little push of the plate towards her, might be all she needs.

When our eating-disorders specialists came to give us coaching, they opened our eyes to these signs.

So what should you look out for?

- Your child stops saying no.
- She doesn't get up from the table, and she doesn't run away.
- She hovers by the door, when she could simply go into the next room.
- The arguments she has made so forcefully become milder.
- Her tone of voice loses its intensity. It becomes more plaintive, more uncertain. Her repetitive stating of grievances fizzles out.
- She becomes silent.
- She stops shouting and tears come to her eyes.

- She stops telling you how much she hates you.
- She goes from hating you to hating herself (heartbreaking, but often a step towards letting go and being able to accept your support).
- She holds out some kind of olive branch, or asks for a solution that will make eating easier or will help her save face.
- She goes from an absolute no to asking for reassurance that she'll be OK, that the food won't make her fat, or that you're supporting her.
- She moves closer to you or leans on you.
- She sighs, or yawns, or her shoulders droop, or she shows some other sign of letting go.
- She straightens up and looks more assertive, more like herself.
- She looks at her plate.
- She looks at you.
- She dabs at the food on her plate as though she's testing what it would be like to actually eat it.
- She picks up a fork.

We don't get much helpful feedback in this eating-disorder business. It can be weeks or months before our child says, 'Remember when you insisted that … and I got really mad at you? It really helped that you still made me do it.' But we do get multiple bits of non-verbal feedback during mealtimes – if we're on the lookout. Then it's a question of either continuing what seems to be helping, or remaining silent for a moment to give your kid space to take the next step.

WAIT A FEW MINUTES

With experience you will get a better sense of when your child needs distraction, when he needs more prompts or soothing words, and when he needs silence. If he goes very quiet, toys with his food and hesitates, a few minutes of peace might help him gather up his courage to eat.

I imagine that if I were to take a bungee jump, I would back off if I thought my instructor might push me. Once I trusted him and sensed his support, I would like him to give me some space. This would allow me to do some reassuring self-talk and master my fear. I might want to be very still, then take a breath, count to three and jump.

HOW LONG SHOULD YOU PERSIST?

In Chapter 6 I discussed options you have if – or rather when – your child doesn't manage to eat a meal.

The bungee-jumping analogy might help you weigh up your options. Here I am, peering down into the void, with my friend constantly supporting and encouraging me. At times I scream and threaten to run away, at other times I take a few hesitant steps towards the ledge. How long should my friend keep trying to make me jump?

If he gives up too soon, I'm going to have a sense of failure, and my fear will be at least as great later when my next bungee jump is due. There's also a big risk that the next time, I will scream and shout and delay all the more in the hope that he will let me off once again.

On the other hand, he might judge that I have already achieved a major victory by coming as far as the bridge and looking down, and that I am unlikely to jump on this occasion. How can he be certain? He can't. All he can do is make a guess based on his experience, his gut feeling, his reading of my body language. Because he can't be sure, he'll not make this decision until he's tried all the tools at his disposal to help me jump.

Ideally, if my friend is experienced, competent and assured, he will have the skills to manage all this flexibly. He will be a master in tracking my state of mind and capabilities at any moment. He'll be firm when I need containment, and give me a break when I am simply unable to make the slightest step forward.

If he does let me return to the car, hopefully he won't blame me or get cross. If I'm grinning, it's out of relief, not spite. If I'm going to face this ordeal again in three hours' time, I need him to continue being on my side.

More in my YouTube: "Stuck and not eating!" [158]

FOCUS ON THE CURRENT STEP IN THE PRESENT MOMENT

I can see that my friend is trying to empathise with me, but he can't possibly know how terrible I feel.

I say, 'This is really hard. There's no way I can do this over and over again, every day.'

He says, 'Now is now. I know that you can take this jump right now.'

Really? Can I take this jump right now? My mind hovers on the possibility.

My friend says, 'I know you're perfectly capable of doing this jump here, right now. See, you're already up here, so you've done 90 per cent of the work. In fact, I'll tell you what, you've already ticked off the scariest part. All that fear you've had, working to get to this point – that's the worst bit, and you've done it. Now just bend your knees, and jump!'

It's a terrible thing for our kids to have to overcome their fears over and over again. We parents know from other people's experiences that it will get easier, and that they will eventually enjoy their food. But this is not the time to lecture or educate. To our kids, eating well on a regular basis seems impossible. Whereas the next mouthful is something they can probably manage. So keep the focus on the present moment.

Back to my bungee jump, and I try and strike a bargain. I say, 'I'll go to the edge. I'll even look down for a few seconds. But that's it. I'm not actually jumping today.'

My friend could decide to be firm in order to quieten my mind: 'You need to jump today. It's not negotiable.' But he'd be missing an opportunity. I indicated something I was ready to do, something that might be manageable. He could focus on that and say, 'Going to the edge and looking down is good. On you go, take a step forward.'

I am not stupid. I know that he hasn't said anything about my refusal to jump. But I move towards the edge, telling myself I can always turn back if it gets too hard. My friend, if he is wise, will continue to support me step by step, keeping me in the present moment, because the present is always manageable. My anxiety is about the next day, the next hour, the next second.

When your child is staring at her plate, she may try bargaining with you or she may announce her limits: 'I'll eat the pasta, but not the cheese.' Try saying, 'You're ready to eat the pasta; that's good. Have some pasta.'

Your child might start eating the pasta, and you can work on the cheese a while later: 'You've done well with the pasta. Now mix in some cheese. Yes, you can do it, it's OK.'

Your child might, on the other hand, insist on making a deal: 'But I'm not eating the cheese, remember?' You don't want to get trapped in an agreement, so you could say, 'One step at a time, darling. Let's concentrate on the pasta right now. Have a mouthful.'

Of course your child might rebel when you ask her to eat the cheese: 'I ate the pasta! You said I didn't have to eat the cheese! You're a liar.' And she might add, 'What's the point in me eating anything if you're always unhappy about it? You think I'm useless! You're always making me eat more!'

This is just run-of-the-mill anorexia talk, fuelled by the high level of fear your child is experiencing. Let the words wash over you so you can remain in touch with the whole of her. You can say, 'You need to eat everything on your plate, darling. You did well with the pasta. Now the cheese, and you're done.'

Your child is scared of the enormity of the challenge, and maybe you are too. If she's struggling with this tiny amount of cheese, how will she cope with the pizza you plan to give her tomorrow? Focusing on the present moment will help you keep your cool. You probably don't want to explain all this to your child right now, but the principle of 'one step at a time' is to break the enormity of the problem down into small manageable chunks. The first chunk should seem reasonably feasible. Once your child has achieved it, you'll help her with the next one. She may need a lot of help at each step, or you may find that things get easier as she builds up successes.

LET YOUR KID SAVE FACE AND MAINTAIN SOME DIGNITY

We all need dignity and a sense of autonomy. Sometimes we're just itching to do something to save face.

As I stand on the ledge, I feel quite humiliated: here I am, making such a fuss about this jump, and everybody's staring at me and thinking I'm a wuss. I say, 'OK, I'll jump, but first, I want another helmet. Who's the idiot who decided I had to wear yellow? If I'm going to smash onto the rocks below, I want to do it in a white helmet.'

If my friend is not a very secure guy he might react to what, to him, is an attempt to annoy him or exert power over him. The truth is this is the only pathetic way I've latched onto to preserve some dignity. Let's hope that my friend is able to choose his battles wisely.

My friend might also sense that I'm using a delaying tactic, and he should refuse to get drawn in: 'This is the helmet you need. On you go. Jump.'

That would certainly be the right thing to do, if changing helmets means a major delay and allows me to retreat from the ledge.

But if he sees that I am really close to jumping, and that I wish to salvage a little piece of autonomy with my tragic little request, he could say, 'No problem. I have a white helmet for you right here. Don't move, I'll help you put it on, and then you can jump.'

You don't want to create a rod for your own back. If you acquiesce to all kinds of demands, you could be setting yourself up for a whole lot of rituals, and each meal will become increasingly complicated and will further entrench your child in anorexic rules. Some children, for instance, insist on a particular plate or glass, and that's not about autonomy but about portion control. You may get it wrong, you may be getting manipulated – it's a risk.

If your child has a bullying eating-disorder voice, her demands might be her way of getting the voice to allow her to eat: 'I'm not really giving in to Dad. I can still decide lots of things for myself. I'll eat the ravioli but I'll show him I'm the boss. See, I'm going to wear my hair over my eyes. That'll show him.'

Maybe your child will openly tell you that she needs to save face. It's then easy for you to show her your care and respect:

> *"I was helping my daughter have some ice cream. After 20 minutes she said she thought she could eat it but it would hurt her pride, like she'd made a fuss over nothing and now she was giving in to me. I told her I totally understood that she should want some dignity and a sense of independence, and that what she was doing showed huge courage. That ice cream went from being a source of shame to one of accomplishment."*

ALL SINGING FROM THE SAME HYMN SHEET

Suppose that while my friend is trying to help me to jump, his wife turns up, along with a qualified instructor.

The wife says, 'Woah! That's a big jump for a beginner!'

The instructor says, 'No it isn't! But what I want to know is, who chose this harness?'

It's going to be impossible for me to jump under these conditions.

On the other hand, if the two newcomers reinforce what my friend is doing, I am more likely to jump.

When you are supporting your child to eat, there are a lot of variables and a lot of uncertainties. How much food should you put on that plate? Is cheese simply too difficult? Should you sit there till your child eats every last crumb, even though it's way past her bedtime? Usually there are no right or wrong answers, just decisions to be made. Sometimes in a couple, one partner tends to take a harder line than the other, and this can create a silent conflict between spouses, which kids will pick up on.

It's important to recognise that this happens, and to do everything in our power to put up a united front. We also have to make sure that there is no triangulation between clinicians, us and our child. Openness and transparency are beautiful principles, but there will be situations where parents need to speak privately with doctors or therapists. And within a couple, we need to take the time, out of our child's earshot, to discuss every detail of our approach.

What about spur-of-the-moment decisions? Sometimes, you can't even afford to exchange looks with your partner, because your child notices everything. In this case, one parent could take the lead, knowing that the other will go along with it no matter what. This may not produce the best decision, but you can always discuss and adjust later.

For example, imagine that you're in the early refeeding stage and your son asks, 'Can I have a raspberry yoghurt instead of strawberry?' Your partner thinks this is a genuine request and says yes. All you can do now is nod in agreement, even though you suspect that the real reason your son wants raspberry flavour is that it has one calorie fewer; you saw him squinting at the labels.

A few weeks down the line, when you've established parental authority over food decisions and when your child is less anxious, you might have more flexibility. Your partner could openly check with you: 'Hmm, raspberry? What do you think?' The idea is to show teamwork, not hesitation.

Sometimes you might really need to disagree with your partner because the stakes are high: 'Actually, darling, Alex went to the bathroom before lunch and there's really no need for him to go right now.' Your partner's job, now, is to agree with you, however much Alex protests.

I wouldn't be surprised if there was a strong correlation between the level of consistency between two parents and the child's rate of recovery.

GIVING UNCRITICAL ACCEPTANCE

During this whole bungee-jumping malarkey, I have done quite a lot of swearing at my friend. I've been grumpy, I've blamed him for pushing me too hard, and accused him of being a bully. In fact, if I recall, I screamed at him 'I hate you!' quite a few times. Now I feel ashamed, and I am scared that he will not want to support me any more. It's a massive relief when I realise he's totally cool about it all. He laughs: 'I expect people to scream at me. It's like women giving birth, isn't it? It just shows you're going through intense stuff.'

Our kids do a lot of shouting, kicking, walking out, and worse. The previously-mentioned study of parental mealtime strategies[159] noted that the more parents succeeded in getting their child to eat, the more negative and upset the child became. Our children's hostility is normal, and they need to know that we still accept them and will continue to support them, that they have our unconditional love. If someone was holding a gun to your head, you might swear quite a bit yourself.

Whether or not we decide to accept their behaviour is another matter. We can tell them that kicking is not acceptable. 'Please don't kick. That's not OK. Talk to me; tell me what's going on. Do you need to know that this food is safe for you?' You may decide to gloss over some of your child's words or actions, because your focus has to be on eating, and manners are a red herring. Whatever stance you choose to take about particular behaviours, make sure that you show your child your acceptance and love. And if you have cracked with the stress of a meal and told your kid things that you now regret, make time for mending.

Parents need previously uncalled-for emotional resources to do all this. The last three chapters aim to support you with these.

PUTTING IT ALL TOGETHER

Here's how one of my friends reacted to some of the suggestions in this chapter:

> "Maybe I will never be an OK bungee-jump instructor – maybe your daughter was lucky to have you."

She was actually doing heroic work, and she can recognise that now her daughter is well again.

I want you to know that until I learned differently I did all of the things I'm now warning you against. Parenthood doesn't come with an education in eating disorders. And it's not just about what you know – when my daughter had a relapse, I did some of these things all over again, because I'm a human being, not a walking textbook. But the power of love makes us dust ourselves off, give it another go, and gradually our children thrive again.

To summarise, here are the things that may help your child to eat:

- Give eating prompts.
- Distract with conversation, humour, games or television.
- Exude confidence and competence.
- Help your child visualise incentives from real life.
- Talk in terms of: 'as soon as you've eaten, then we'll do [pleasant activity]'.
- Present food as 'medicine'.
- Sit close.
- Give empathy and mirroring.
- Track any signs of progress to gauge whether to keep pushing or to pull back.
- Break down the challenge to focus on the next small step.
- Be open to letting your child save face occasionally.
- Make sure carers give a consistent message.
- Use teamwork: get someone to support you and relay you.

- Show your child unconditional love, however obnoxious her behaviour may be.

Supporting your child from a place of confidence and compassion has a cumulative effect. It may not achieve miracles right away, but after a while, when your child sees that you're consistently supportive and non-judgemental, she's more likely to let go of her armoury, shove her eating-disorder voice to the side and trust you, at least for the time it takes to eat.

8

SEE THE TOOLS IN ACTION: MEALTIME SCENARIOS

In this chapter I give you examples of things to say and not to say when you're supporting your child at mealtimes. This will help you keep calm and will help your child to pick up that fork and eat. I then offer a scenario in which parents assist their child to eat for the first time. This chapter uses many of the practical and emotional tools described throughout the book.

Let's assume you're doing everything pretty damn well. You're non-critical, accepting, determined, empathic and at times you even have a sense of humour. Even then, it would be a miracle not to encounter resistance. We found ourselves searching high and low for answers on what to actually say and do to get our child to eat, and I hope this chapter helps you in this area.

First, I'm going to offer you a very, very dull list of responses you can give to the many arguments your child may put up during a meal. It's *supposed* to be dull. It's the broken record approach. Once you've got the gist of it, you might want to skip to the following section, where I invite you to be a fly on the wall during a fictional lunchtime session. This example pulls together many of the practical and emotional tools I talk about in this book. After that I give you another example, but this time we're much further into recovery: we've built trust, we have experience, and the job of exposing and desensitising to a fear is done in one short session.

So, here goes.

WHAT TO SAY, AND WHAT NOT TO SAY WHEN YOU ARE SUPPORTING YOUR CHILD TO EAT

One very useful skill we got from being coached at home was to avoid the hooks that threatened to distract us from our task. It is not our normal style to ignore questions or to refuse to discuss things, so we had to be vigilant. We learned that we could be open to discussing some things but rarely over a meal. We saved eating-disorder-related discussions for outside mealtimes.

As we saw in our bungee-jumping analogy, the idea is to keep the focus to the task of eating and using direct eating prompts rather than providing information or choices. Often, this means you have to be a broken record. The underlying message is that yes, your child has some anxiety right now, and he also needs to eat, and he can eat while feeling awful, and you are kind and will support him throughout. 'Compassionate persistence' is your motto. You are deeply in touch with your certainty that your child is safe, that the food is what he needs and that he can trust you. Think of how you'd help your child to tolerate a medical procedure or how you dealt with his first day at school.

If your child reacts with distress or aggression, this does not mean you're doing anything wrong. Remember that for him, eating is presently a horrendous experience.

Many of the examples below show how to make a clear request ('Get started on the egg'). You can experiment whether it's useful to start with a brief statement of empathy ('Looks like the egg is difficult? I can imagine how it would be especially hard because you've not had egg for quite a while. I'm so sorry. Please get started on it'). There's more guidance on empathy on Chapter 13. Whether you say kind words or not, make your tone of voice and body language convey your compassionate, kind, non-blaming attitude. Trust that your very empathic presence offers tremendous support, often more successfully than words.

I offer the words below as guidance to get you started. You will learn what works best by trial and error. Once you're comfortable with the general principles, it is probably best you use the words that come to you naturally, as your child is then more likely to sense that you are grounded, reliable and compassionate.

Setting the scene

'Whatever you've made, I'm not having it.'
> *Please get off the computer, sweetheart. I want you sitting at the table before I serve lunch. It's ready.*

'Put it on the table, then, and I'll see if I want it.'
> *This is non-negotiable, sweetie. Please come and sit down now.*

'I don't want to.'
> *I'm turning the internet off and you need to come and sit down now. Right now please.*

[Staring silently at screen.]
> *Darling, I'm going to stand right here next to you and I'm going to keep asking you to come and sit at the table.*

'I'm not hungry. I'll eat later, I promise.'
> *This is the time to eat. Come and sit down. I'm going to sit with you and support you.*

'Leave me alone!'
> *You need to eat your snack. Let's get on with it. Come to the table now.*

'But I need to text Carla. You're always stopping me from doing what I want to do. We're making plans to meet up at the park.'
> *That sounds fun! You need your lunch first. Come and eat, and then we can talk about your plans and you can text then.*

'It's boring at the table. Why can't we watch telly?'
> *That's a good idea. Go put the telly on and I'll bring your plate over.*

'I want Dad to help me with dinner, not you.'

> *Yes, that's fine. Dad can do it tonight.*

'I want Dad to help me with dinner, not you. You're rubbish'

> *Dad's not going to be in for another hour. Right now you'll have to have your dinner with me. Is there a way I can make it easier for you?*

'Dad makes me laugh. You're boring and you're always staring at me like this.' [Crosses her eyes.]

> *OK, laughing helps you. How about we watch funny YouTube movies of cats while we eat?*

I'm not hungry

'I'm not hungry. When I was little, you said I should eat when I'm hungry. Now you want to make me fat.'

> *When you were little, you didn't have anorexia. Right now food is your medicine. Come on, start eating now. Pick up your fork. OK, keep going.*

'I feel full. That means I don't need to eat.'

> *The eating disorder has screwed up your body signals. You'll have to rely on us for now. Please continue.*

'I'm ten, for goodness' sake! What crazy kind of a mum are you, to make me eat when I don't want to!'

> *The illness makes you not want to eat, and you need what's on your plate now.* [Push the plate a little closer.]

Quantities and ingredients

'I'm not eating this; it's way too much.'

> *It's what you need. Please start eating.*

'That looks disgusting. I'm not eating it.'

> *It's what you need. Please start eating.*

'You're trying to make me fat. I'm not eating this.'

> *Please sit down again. I'd like you to eat this now.*

'I can't.'

> *I know it's really hard, sweetie. I really do. Come on, you need to eat this. Please eat some more.*

'This is way too much' [Pushes plate away.]

> *It's OK, darling. You're finding this scary just now, right? This is what you need. Please keep eating.* [Place plate back in front of her.]

'Is there butter in this?'

> *We're not discussing ingredients. This is what you need to eat to be well.*

'Ah, so that means there is butter. You're trying to make me fat. Give me one without butter and then I'll eat it.'

> *I'm sorry, my darling. Whatever's on your plate is what you have to eat. Oh, I've been dying to tell you the gross thing the dog did today!* [Funny story.]

'I told you I'm vegetarian! I'm not eating the meat.'

You need to eat everything. Would you like to start on the potatoes?

'That's more than my usual amount. [Pushes a portion to the side.] I'll eat this much, but that's extra.'

Your eating-disorder voice is having a go at you, right? I'm by your side. Just start eating. One step at a time.

'So I don't have to eat the extra, right?'

Trust me. I'm your mum and I'm caring for you. Everything on your plate is what you need.

'I normally have half a pizza. You can't give me a whole!'

This is what you need today.

'So will you be giving me less at snack time?'

Leave it to us. We're doing all the right things.

'How much more do I need to eat when I go swimming? Because today I didn't swim, remember, I just played table tennis.'

I remember. This is the right amount.

'But it's as much as last week, when I went swimming and Dad –'

It's OK, darling. This is what Dad and I planned for your snack. You get started on it.

'I want a smaller slice. One like my brother's/sister's.'

This is what you need at the moment.

'You don't put cream in your own soup. It's not fair.'

We've each got what we need for our health.

Calories

'This isn't my usual yoghurt! It's full fat, right? How many calories?' [Gets up to search for wrapping with nutritional information.]

Please come back, and sit down. [Whisk wrapping away before she gets it.] It's my job to give you what you need. Please leave it to me.

'I know yesterday's snack had 323 calories. I found the label in the bin. This is way more. How much more are you giving me? How many calories? Are you giving me more every day? If it's even one calorie more, I won't have it.'

You know we don't discuss calories. It's the eating disorder that goes on about calories. Now just continue eating.

'Are there more calories in chocolate cake or in a doughnut?'

We don't discuss calories. Please eat your cake.

'Is it more to have half a glass of milk or a full glass of orange juice?'

We know it's not helpful to discuss calories or quantities. Please drink all your milk.

Calculations

'Have you worked this out? Is it the right amount?'

Yes, it's exactly what you need.

'But you worked it out, right? The calories and all that …'

Everything on your plate is what you need. Can you continue eating please?

'But how do you know what's right. You said you weren't weighing my food so how do you know? In hospital they weighed my food.'

I know what you need. I've always known what you need. I've given you just what you need since you were born. Now there's still some pasta in your plate.

The hospital/Mum/Dad don't do it like you

'This is more than the meal plan I had in hospital. When I had pizza I never had potatoes with it, I had half a –'

This is right for you now. We're in charge now.

'But how come you give me more?'

We know what's right for you. There's no more meal plan. We're in charge. Trust us. Now get started on the pizza, OK?

'Sheila let me choose low-fat yoghurt, and she's a dietitian. You don't know anything.'

We know what you need. We make your food decisions now.'

'You filled the bottle higher than Dad does. He fills it up to here. You're trying to give me more.'

I know you're anxious right now. We don't discuss quantities.

'You don't know how much I have for breakfast. Dad always fills my breakfast bowl to here. You've got it wrong. Phone him, and he'll tell you.'

I'm doing your breakfast this morning. I'm in charge.

'When Mum prepares my smoothie for school, it reaches just this little mark on the label. Dad, you're giving me too much. I'm just tipping out the extra.' [Pours it down the sink.]

Please stop that. I'm going to fill it back to the level it was anyway. It's exactly what you need. [The tone of voice is, of course, matter-of-fact and non-blaming.]

You've changed my meals

'When I was little you gave me fruit when everyone else had crisps. You said crisps were not healthy. No way am I eating crisps now.'

I have learned a huge amount about health since you started having anorexia. This is what you need right now, to get well again.

'That's not what I normally have. You can't change things.'

I understand that worries you. That's what you're having right now. Please get started.

'Are you going to keep changing what I have for my snack?'

Yes, we're in charge now. We're going to keep giving you the foods you need. Now, please get started.

'Banana? You can't give me banana. You know I don't eat bananas. Give me grapes, I can manage grapes.'

You'll manage the banana. Trust me, you will. I wonder how Zoe got on with her blind date?

'I'm not eating that scone. You've never given me scone before. If I eat it, then you'll think it's OK to give something even harder next time.'

This scone is what's right for you right now. Each meal I give you what's right, and everything I give you is something you can manage. Have a bite now.

Hiding food

'Stop staring at me when I'm eating.'

I'll do my best to help you not feel uncomfortable, and at the same time I need to check you're not hiding or dropping any food.

'I don't know how that piece of cheese landed on the floor.'

I'll get you another/We've run out of cheese so I'm going to bring you something else to make up for it. [No blame, just matter-of-fact.]

'OK, I'm done!' [Marches to the kitchen and throws wrapper in the bin.]

I'm just going to check you've eaten it all. No, there's still a bit in there. Can you just finish this bit off, please?

'You don't even trust me!'

It's really normal for an eating disorder to make people hide food. I want to make sure you get all the food you need.

My weight

'How much did I weigh yesterday? I know I put loads of weight on, and now you're giving me lasagne and you're trying to make me even fatter. Do I weight as much as before I started dieting?'

We don't discuss weight. Please leave all this to us. Trust us, OK? Now get started on the lasagne.

'What I don't get is, how come I need to put on more weight, when I'm already on the fiftieth percentile? Lorna showed me on the graph. She showed me how –'

Sweetie, this is not the time. Would you finish your plate, please?

'But I want to understand. I'm on the fiftieth percentile line, right?'

This is the time to eat. Just a few more mouthfuls and you'll be done.

'What's my target weight? I think if I knew, it would be easier for me to eat.'

We're in charge of all that, sweetie. We're not discussing it. Another mouthful please.

'You want to make me fat!'

You're feeling anxious right now, hmm? Another spoonful, sweetie. You need this to get well again.

'You're getting this all wrong! You're going to make me fat! You're fat yourself, so how can you possibly keep me right?'

It's OK, darling. We know what we're doing and we're doing it very carefully and very well. Now keep going.

(Note that there is more help on the 'weight' questions in Chapter 14)

Got to go

'You need to take me to school. I'll eat the toast at break time in school.'

I'd like you to finish your breakfast. You need to eat all this to be well for school. Eat your toast, and then we'll go.

'But I'll be late for school!'

Yes, and I know how much you hate that. At the same time, it's important that you have breakfast.

'I need to go to the toilet.'

OK, I'll wait outside the door and then we'll finish the meal/Sorry, not for another hour. And first you need to finish your meal.

'I can't eat with everyone staring at me. I'll eat when we get home.'

You're telling yourself that people are looking at you, and you're uncomfortable, right? Won't it be great when you're comfortable eating out? I would like you to manage eating here right now. I'm supporting you. After that shall we check out the shoe shop?

Hygiene

'I'm not eating that. You touched it/it's dirty/you touched your hair and then you touched my food.'

I can see you're freaked out about it, and all the same I'd like you to eat it. It's safe. Trust me.

'That fell on the floor. I'm not eating it; it's dirty.'

I'll give you another one. Please make sure that one doesn't land on the floor.

Self-hate

'I'm fat. I'm a horrid, fat pig!' [Hysterical crying and clawing at skin.]

You're having a hard time right now, eh? I'm looking after you, sweetie. Another spoonful.

Lashing out

'You don't know how much to give me. You're fat. You're making me fat.'

I serve you what you need. Trust me.

'You're fat, you're ugly, I hate you. Mum is fat, Mum is fat! Mum's a big fat pig!' [Chanting.]

I'd like you to stop that. Now finish off those last spoonfuls and we'll find something more fun to do.

'You are so stupid, stupid, stupid!' [Gets up from the table.]

Please come back. Come on, sweetie, I can see you're scared. Trust me, OK? I'm your mum and I love you.

'I hate you!' [Kicks me.]

Ow, that really hurt! I know you're freaked out and it's making you want to lash out, and at the same time that hurt me. It's not OK. Please don't do it again. Now please continue eating.

'This stinks! No way am I eating pie.' [Throws plate at wall, or at someone.]

That's not acceptable. I know you're doing it because the eating disorder makes you so scared. All the same it's not OK to do that. There's no more pie, so we'll forget about it for today. I'll make you egg on toast right now. I'll be five minutes. Meanwhile, please stay here – you can play on your Xbox.

Emotions that distract from the task

'I hate having to eat school lunches with teachers. Mrs Mann, she's so horrible! Yesterday she said, 'What's that in your sandwich? It doesn't look very nice.' Please, I really want to eat school lunch with my friends.'

Sounds like you've had a hard time with Mrs Mann and you'd like to be with your friends more. Hmm. Tell me more about it after we've finished eating.

'We were talking about news, and Mum, there's this little girl who got kidnapped!' [Crying.]

Yes, it's horrible. You can tell me more about it later if you like. Now take a breath with me… and continue eating.

Suffering and despair

'I'm so anxious! I can't eat like this. I'll eat later.'

Yes, looks like you're anxious, and it's hard for you right now. I'm with you darling. You can manage it. Start with the egg.

'My tummy hurts. I feel sick. I can't eat this.'

It's normal for it to hurt at this stage. It's horrible, but it's not dangerous, and it will pass. It will get easier. Shall we play our story game while you're eating, so you don't notice the pain?

'You don't even care!'

It looks really tough for you at the moment. I'm with you.

'I'm not eating it!'

'Mirror what I'm doing.' (Parent picks up fork and prompts child to do the same.)

'This is too hard! I can't do it!' [Sobbing.]

I'm so sorry, my sweetie. I know it's very hard for you right now. It will get easier and easier, I promise. I know. This is so hard now, and at the same time you're safe, and you can bear it. In a few moments it will pass. I'm supporting you for as long as you need it. Have a spoonful now. [Sit very close to her, a parent on each side, unless she tells you she wants space.]

'You don't understand me!'

It's really hard for you right now? Is that what you'd like me to understand? Have a spoonful. Even if it's hard. You need to do it, and you can do it.

'This is the worst day of my life! I want to die. It would be better to be dead.'

I'm sorry it's so difficult for you right now. I love you. I'm with you. How about you snuggle right in to me while you're eating?

BE A FLY ON THE WALL: A LUNCHTIME SCENARIO

Would you like to be a fly on the wall during a mealtime? To get a feel for how it's possible for parents to make their child come to the table and eat in spite of the resistance created by the eating disorder? The following scenario and the characters are made up. This is because I'm hoping to demonstrate as many principles as I can fit in, and also because it's now a while since we were in this situation so I can't trust my memory for detail. I've also made the parents do all the things I think work best. Realistically they ought to be screwing up at regular intervals, because that's life.

I'm going to show how you can deal with some tough opposition. If your child puts up less resistance than the child in this scenario, then enjoy your (relatively) lighter challenge.

I will also show you that you don't need to succeed at every step. You can help your child just by doing 'well enough'.

I'm conscious that some of you may have been trying to help your child to eat for a very, very long time. You may be weary and what I'm describing may seem impossible or ridiculous. Perhaps you need time to mull it over, and perhaps what I'm suggesting isn't what you need. I'd hate for you to jump to the conclusion that you are failing as parents. The reality is that this is a tough illness.

Whatever stage you're at, what follows is only intended to give you ideas and support. You're bound to need to adapt things to your own situation. Again, take the best and leave the rest.

Principles

Remember the bungee jump I volunteered for in Chapter 7? We'll use those principles to make lunchtime as calm and supportive as possible. We'll also use principles of compassionate communication so that your child feels safe and understood – these are described in more detail in Chapter 13. Our intentions are:

- to be compassionate, non-blaming, non-judgemental, and to see our daughter's behaviour as driven by fear, a need to calm herself and to feel safe

- to exude competence, confidence and love – if possible this will come from deep within, and that way both words and body language will come out right

- to work as a team – we want to be consistent with each other, and to relay each other when one needs a break

- to track our child closely, so we can decide when to push for more and when to give her some slack

- to keep the focus on eating, avoiding discussions and arguments, and using tools such as humour, distraction and small steps

- to give ourselves moment-to-moment compassion in order to remain grounded in our intentions

The set-up

Let's say that these are the early days of my daughter's anorexia. My husband and I have tried to get her to eat, but each day she refuses more food and she's losing weight. Our house has become a battle zone and the anxiety levels are high all round. I do a lot of crying and shouting, and my kid retreats to her room, depressed and isolated. The clinic tells us that we can and must feed our child. At the last family session, the therapist made it clear to our daughter that we are in charge of her meals. So today, Saturday, my husband and I are determined to make a fresh start.

Preparation

We have both taken a week off work, because we've heard that refeeding is hard work at the beginning. We've warned the school we might keep our daughter home. We've done a lot of talking as a couple to make sure we're on the same page. We have two objectives: first, to make her eat, and for now we'll consider it a success if she eats more than she'd have eaten on her own. Our second objective is important for the next meals and the longer term: to build trust.

For this first meal where we're going to assert our determination to feed her, we've decided to serve vegetable quiche, pasta with grated cheese, a glass of milk and some grapes, because she managed those items a few days ago. We don't want to make things extra hard at this stage.

I've been feeling terribly vulnerable, but I've carved out 20 minutes for myself with a cup of tea, sitting with my eyes closed, getting in touch with my fears as well as my hopes. I'm now a little bit more grounded. I'd love to feel more confident and upbeat, but hopefully this is good enough. My husband went for a cycle ride – that's his way of calming himself (weird or what?).

My husband has nearly finished cooking and he'll serve up at 12.30. We're going to try to stick to a schedule as this may help reduce our daughter's anxiety.

During meal preparation

My daughter (D) walks into the kitchen. My husband (H) guides her back out, saying, 'Sweetie, I'm preparing lunch. So can you keep out of the kitchen please?' *We want to keep our daughter as calm as possible before we call her to the table. If she's involved with food preparation her anxiety will rise and it will be harder for her to eat.*

I call her back into the sitting room. 'Darling, let's continue our puzzle.'

She says, 'I need to see what Dad's cooking.'

'Ah. You'll find out very soon, when it's served. Can you see where this piece goes?'

She takes it from me, and throws it onto the half-completed puzzle.

I make a face, trying to keep the atmosphere light. 'Nope, it doesn't quite fit there!'

She shrugs and I say, 'Come on, help me do this section.'

She tries a few pieces and seems to get into it. She's standing, because sitting is against her internal rules, and I decide not to make an issue of this as my priority is for her to be as calm as possible before the meal.

After a while, I ask her to go to the toilet. 'We'll ask you to stay with us for an hour after the meal, so I'd recommend you go now.'

She storms off, muttering, 'Now I can't even have a wee without my parents watching me!' but she soon comes back and we resume the puzzle.

Getting her to the table: first attempt

At 12.30 on the dot, my husband, bless him, announces that lunch is served.

My daughter makes a few steps towards the table and hovers at the door. 'Where's the food?'

My husband says, 'Take a seat and I'll serve.' When the food is already on the table, D panics and turns away, so it's easier to bring the food once she's seated. But let's make life hard for ourselves and say that she's panicking anyway.

D clings to the doorframe. 'I don't want lunch. I'm not hungry.' I notice that she hasn't actually backed off, and she's looking at the table. That's a positive sign.

H says, 'Take a seat anyway.'

'But I'm full! I'm going to be sick if I eat.'

H says, 'Take a seat and let's do our best. You need lunch.'

'Tell me what it is and then I'll come.'

'Sorry, sweetie. Please come to the table.' He gestures encouragingly. I'm already sitting, smiling kindly at D. I'm letting my husband do the talking so that D doesn't have too much thrown at her at once, but my body language says we're on the same page.

At this stage, she might well sit down, but I can hear you saying, 'What if she doesn't?' so I'll make life hard for myself and address this now.

Getting her to the table: empathy

She marches back into the sitting room, mumbling, 'I'm not having lunch.' I notice that she hasn't run upstairs to her room, and she hasn't bolted out of the front door. That's a sign that there's hope.

I come close to her and speak very gently. 'Sweetie, I'm guessing that this is quite scary for you. Is that right?' Here I'm giving voice to what I guess she's feeling. Feeling felt is part of empathy, and my guess is she needs empathy before I ask her to go back to the table.

She shrugs. Her eyes are moist.

'I'm wondering if you'd like to know this is going to be OK for you?' I could have said 'safe' too. I'm showing her that I care about what she longs for, what she needs.

The vulnerable look she gives me makes my heart melt. When empathy hits the mark, the whole atmosphere shifts. It's now possible to move on.

I say, 'We're going to help you. We'll make it as easy as it is humanly possible for you.' I'd love to put my arm round her, but experience has shown me that she'll probably shrug me off, and I don't want to make things harder.

She sniffles, then tenses up again. 'You're just going to shout at me. You're always screaming at me.'

I try and respond to what's going on for her, not to her actual words. Whenever you hear 'always' or 'never', avoid getting hooked in an argument. When someone is exaggerating they probably need to be heard at a deeper level.

I say, 'Would you like to be sure you'll get a lot of kindness?'

She nods miserably. Much of the fight has gone out of her, and I sense that she now feels understood. I can now safely move the focus from her to me and offer the assurances I guess she needs.

I say, 'Ughh! I hate it that I shouted at you the last few meals. I am quite determined to do my very best to be kind and make things calm and easy for you. I know it makes it harder when I shout. Dad and I have learned so much in the last few days, we are now the best experts you could possibly have. Especially as we love you so much. Come on, come to the table.' *Here I'm trying to make us trustworthy in her eyes, so she can lean on us.*

Can we say she now comes to the table? I think she would. But you want to make things harder for me. OK, let's see what would happen if that didn't work?

Getting her to the table: escape

She takes a few steps towards the table (*Yay!*) and then panics and runs into the hallway, where she stands, shaking. She screams, 'I hate you! You're the worst mum in the world. All you ever do is shout at me! And you want to make me fat!'

An uninvited vision crosses my mind, in which I pin her arms behind her back and drag her, kicking and screaming into the dining room and force quiche into her mouth. At the same time, I feel like bursting into tears, because I so regret how I've handled this illness up to now, and I regret every time I lost my temper. I know I've done my best throughout, but being told I'm a bad mum pushes my buttons.

* Pause for self-connection *

I'm conscious that for some of you the above may make painful reading. If so, I invite you to pause and refuel as follows. Notice, as you're reading this, the thoughts that are going through your mind; notice what emotions come up and how your body feels. I'm describing things that no parent could possibly wish for, things that may remind you of what is happening in your home right now, or that you fear may happen. If your child is further down the recovery journey, this scenario might remind you of some bad old days and bring up old fears.

Either way, the signals from your mind and body are reminders to give yourself some emotional first aid. I propose various tools for this in Chapter 15, but for now, I'd like to offer you one technique that can help you ground yourself.

You might like to imagine your unpleasant thoughts and feelings as birds swirling up above, obscuring the sky. They are not you. They're just passing by. Can you get glimpses of the sky, from time to time? This vast, beautiful, comforting expanse of space, peace and power is always there. It contains the huge wealth of internal resources you were born with, plus those you've built up throughout your life, and the world's external resources are there too: the kindness of others, the information, the support, and also the values that words can only imperfectly describe: beauty, love, patience, gratitude, spirituality. What meaning does this expanse of sky have for you right now? When you imagine yourself being part of the sky, what are you filled with? For me, it might be a sense of acceptance, of calm, of competence. Or of strength: my fears tell me quite how much I want to see my child being well, quite how much I want to support her.

Whatever deep longings or values you find in that sky, let your whole being soak them up and be nourished by them.

If you're ready, let's continue.

Onwards

My husband and I exchange compassionate glances. It helps that he doesn't blame me. We both have our strengths and weaknesses, and we are a team.

As my daughter goes on yelling abuse at me, I remember this mantra: 'This has nothing to do with me.' This is the effect of anorexia. She is in fight-or-flight mode. I have an image of her accusations whooshing past me, leaving me intact. I put my hand on my chest and instantly feel a tiny bit more centred. I look at my daughter with softened eyes and see a terrified child in the grips of an extremely challenging illness. My fantasy of reacting with violence is appeased by the compassion I feel.

Of course I'm not going to physically drag her to the table and I'm not going to stuff food down her throat. Just like shouting, violence can work only once or twice, not in the long term.

I say, gently, 'Please come back to the table.' I deliberately don't argue with what she said. The broken record technique is my friend right now.

My husband pipes in, 'Come on, sweetie, you can do it. We're here to help you.'

She says, 'I'll come if you give me a piece of toast. I'll eat toast. I'm not eating whatever it is you cooked; it stinks.'

My husband and I look at each other. Could we get her to eat at least a piece of toast? Wouldn't that be better than nothing? Because it looks like she's going to eat zero, zilch, niente, otherwise. But no. If her eating-disorder voice learns that negotiation pays off, it will bully our poor kid to fight every single request we make of her. We're committed to giving her no choice. It's especially important that we don't budge because these are early days. Later, we may find that we can use some flexibility to support her recovery, but not yet.

I'm on the verge of telling her, 'But we're serving quiche. You're okay with quiche.' Perhaps she's fearing the worst – a tureen of melted butter sprinkled with pieces of lard laced with double cream. Perhaps if she knew it was just quiche, she'd eat. On the other hand she might instantly fear it, because eating anything is horrific for her right now. The toast is a red herring.

My husband says, 'Come and sit down. We'll eat and play a game of cards at the same time.' Notice that he hasn't responded to the toast idea, as this might lead to arguments that deflect from the task, which is to come to the table. He's adding an offer of distraction.

'I hate my life!'

I think my husband's response may well help her, but I'm going to increase the challenge in order to offer you some more tools. Here goes:

She screams, 'I'm not fucking eating!' She is grabbing at her non-existent tummy. 'I'm enormous. Look at that! Look at that flab! This is your fault. You're making me fat. I hate you!' She lunges for the front door but I'm standing in her way. She screams, 'You bitch! You fucking bitch!'

I say, with some force, 'I get it! You hate us. You hate everything that's happening to you. This is really, really hard for you!' *This is an empathic reflection. Notice that I'm not retaliating and punishing her for her language. She is in terrible turmoil and has no grip on herself. It's when she's at her most 'awful' that she needs our support more than ever.*

She stares at me, slightly shocked. We're both rather breathless. After a while I say, still with some intensity, 'You'd like to get away from all this, right? You'd like to run away and find some peace from all this and get some relief from how hard your life is?' *What I'm trying to do here is use the power of mirroring. I've started by reflecting her state of high arousal, so she can feel felt: she can see I'm really in tune with how hard this is for her. I'm giving her empathy by expressing what she probably wants so very much: some relief from this awful suffering she's in. Gradually I'm going to model a calmer state, hoping that this will rub off on her.*

I sigh and give her a fond, sad smile. 'OK, take a minute. Would it help you to have a hug?' *I've learned the hard way to check about physical contact.*

She bursts into tears. 'I hate myself. I'm such a horrible, fat, horrible person. I don't know how you can live with me! You should leave me. I'm too horrible.' *We've noticed this transition from fighting food to hating us to hating herself. Although we'd rather she didn't hate herself, we've come to welcome this shift. It's usually a signal that she's about to drop her defences and let us in.*

My husband and I make those little 'Ah' and 'Hum' noises that show we're with her. After a while, my husband moves towards her, and she leans into him. Gradually, she gets calmer. We say, 'We love you. We know the illness makes you do these things. We're sticking by you.' We really mean it. In the middle of this storm, this island of connection replenishes our strength.

And then, we get back on track. 'Come on, lunch is waiting.'

Howling in the bedroom

Frankly, I think that now she may well sit at the table and start eating. But before I take you there, I want to show you a harder situation: the one where we simply can't get her to the table or we can't get her to eat.

So let's say that after calling me a bitch, she's not lunged for the door but run off upstairs to her room. Let's assume she hasn't locked herself in. You don't want to do what we once did, which was to put our shoulder to a locked bathroom door and subject our kid to the shock of splintering wood. Better to wait it out, sit outside with a cup of tea and speak soothingly. Or even better, think ahead, and remove locks from doors.

She slams her bedroom door, and we hear her sobbing her heart out.

We give her a couple of minutes and then, gently, I speak to her through the door. 'Sweetie? Darling, I'm here for you. Would you like a few minutes on your own, or would you like me or Dad to be with you?'

She growls, 'Fuck off!'

The sobs intensify. My husband says, 'We'll come back in a few minutes.' We're not sure what's best, but we think that it might help her to have a little time on her own, knowing that we're close and were not judging her or abandoning her. Later, we might come in closer, very gently, as if taming a wild animal, or one of us might sit outside her room, letting her know we're nearby, and giving her words of support. We might try to engineer some kind of distraction to change the mood – perhaps a phone call or a visit from a friend of hers.

It may still be possible to get her to the table. Right now, she is in such a state it's difficult to imagine, and it may be beyond our capabilities. But (and I'm stepping back into our real life now) I have seen a nurse call my daughter to dinner when she was hunched up behind the door of her hospital bedroom, sobbing her heart out with despair and anger. I couldn't believe that the nurse was even attempting it. We were sent home, and later were told that there'd been no problem at all – our kid had come to the table, sobbing, and had eaten a full dinner.

Still, on this occasion we've reached the limit of what feels possible. So let's end this mini episode with us throwing in the towel.

Calling it a day ... for this meal

Our daughter is leaning against her closed door, and anything we try seems to make things worse. I wonder whether there's any chance she'll eat something if I bring it to her room. If we're watching her, does it matter if she's not sitting at the table? At least she'd be eating, but on the other hand, avoiding the dining-room table could become a new anorexic rule we'd have to fight. We might be creating a rod for our own backs. In any case, in the state she's in, I can't see her eating, even in her bedroom, even standing up.

I have started to cry silently. I am so scared for my daughter, and just now, any hope that we will ever manage to feed her has vanished. I'm thinking of all those parents who say they can do it, and I tell myself I'm pathetic and useless. Shame weighs me down. My husband looks at the end of his tether as well. Neither of us has anything left inside to conclude this successfully. In fact, if we don't throw in the towel, one of us is likely to start screaming at our child.

My husband puts his head through the door and smiles at our daughter. 'Sweetie, we're sorry this is so hard for you. We'll try again at snack time, and it will get easier. We'll keep on supporting you.' I make some kind 'hmm' noises to show her I'm on board with that.

What we're doing is marking an end to this lunchtime episode. This will enable us to get on with more cheerful and connecting activities, rather than make the whole day one long, miserable attempt at eating. He's also signalling that we will continue, meal after meal, in the same manner.

Dear reader, I don't know about you, but I need an empathy pause. First, I'll let my thoughts and feelings say what they want to say. Here goes.

This is really sad. Of course we don't want anorexia to win this battle, and we certainly don't want anorexia to 'learn' that to avoid lunch, all you have to do is retreat to your bedroom. But we've all done the very best we can, within our capabilities, in the face of an extremely destructive illness. I am devastated by the thought that my daughter, right now, is weak and hungry, and that if this goes on she may become a medical emergency. This makes me weepy and I am incredibly discouraged. I'm not sure I have the strength to deal with the next meal. I have fantasies of escaping to a quiet, luxury hotel on a tropical island for a month of lolling about in a fluffy white bathrobe.

I'm allowing my thoughts and feelings to swirl around, but I'm not hooking up to any of them: I'm not expanding on them and I'm not arguing against them. Right now it feels like I'll be stuck in tears and hopelessness for ever, but I know that feelings pass. I cradle my hands to my face and give myself kindness for everything that is going on. In a while, I trust, I will sink down into a more grounded place where I'm in tune with deep needs and longings.

My husband and I talk and talk and talk. He's shaken but he's hanging on to the knowledge that other parents, using the same approach, have succeeded. I go for a walk and one of my favourite sayings comes to mind: Grant me the serenity to accept the things I cannot change, the courage to change the things I can, and the wisdom to know the difference. I sink into a place of calm acceptance, and gradually regain a little determination to face snack time. I don't feel very strong, but I'm strong enough.

Failure?

Please remember this whole scenario is fictional and the characters are made up. But in my experience, it would be quite realistic for this strand of the story to end like this.

Snack time comes along, and to our amazement, our daughter comes to the table, cool as a cucumber, and eats without a word. Dinner and evening snack go reasonably smoothly – she cries over some grapes, but eats them all the same. In hindsight, we realise our lunchtime 'failure' was actually a major step forward. We managed one of our objectives, which was to build trust. We remained supportive and loving, while sticking to the message that we expect our child to eat. We showed her this was a new beginning, an end to our flailing about, our uncertainties, our pleading, demanding, blaming, shouting and abandonment.

We'll have more 'failures' to feed her. There will be more tears and tantrums, because we'll be exposing her to foods and situations that she fears. Generally, each of these dramas will mark a major step forward.

Sitting at the table

Shall we wind back so we can get on with a scenario in which we actually get our child to eat?

So let's say she's hesitantly come to the table. For a millisecond, she begins to sit, then she pushes her chair away and stands.

I say, 'Please sit down.'

'I don't want to. I'll eat standing up.'

What to do? Our priority is that she eats. On the other hand, at the moment mealtimes are the only time she sits. We don't want to lose that. I glance at my husband. We need to be a united front, and this is a hurdle we haven't prepared for. My hunch is to insist on her sitting for this meal. If it doesn't work, my husband and I will work out the next step, and I could also discuss it with the therapist in one of our private phone calls.

I push the chair gently towards her and say, 'I'd like you to sit down.'

She blinks.

I repeat, 'Please sit down, darling.'

She sits.

My mind dances a little jig. Yay! She could have thrown the chair at me or run away, but she sat! That's such a positive sign.

'I'm not eating this!'

My husband brings the food immediately, before she has a chance to think too much. He puts her plate and a glass of milk in front of her, and says, 'So we're watching *Friends* after this?' *It's neither a bribe nor a threat ('You're not watching a film unless you eat'); it's just something to look forward to.*

He brings my food and his. It's the same food, but unlike our daughter's, it's not pre-portioned. He sits on the other side of her, quite close. *A parent on either side can feel safe and containing, and reduces the temptation to run off.*

D snorts, 'I'm not eating this. I hate quiche.'

H says, 'That's what we'd like you to eat. Everything on your plate. And the milk and grapes. Please start eating.' *This is the start of the broken record. He doesn't argue about how she normally loves quiche.*

I say, 'What do you think about getting my mum a really simple mobile phone? She keeps forgetting how to work the one she's got.' *It's called small talk, and I'm not very good at it.*

D says, 'That's stupid. Her phone doesn't even have any apps on it.'

I notice that I feel irritated and slightly anxious by her combative tone of voice. I remind myself that right now her eating-disorder voice may be ringing alarm bells in her head, and she can't possibly be all sweetness and light.

'Sure. Her phone's dead simple. But we're talking about Gran here!' *Oh my feeble attempts at humour!*

She shrugs. 'What's wrong with the one she's got?'

I say, 'You should have seen us yesterday. We were outside the supermarket, bags all around us, her walking stick tripping people up, and she was trying to call a taxi. I couldn't work out what was taking her so long, and then I realised she was dialling over and over again and her phone wasn't even switched on. Didn't she do something like that with you last week?' *Small talk, small talk. Anything except food talk, exercise talk, fat talk, whale talk!*

D says, 'What's in this quiche. Did you put cream in it?'

Damn.

H says, 'We're in charge of your food now, sweetie. Please get started.'

I continue my story. 'She was in a right state, cursing the taxi company for not answering the phone.'

'I'm not a baby! There's nothing wrong with telling me if you put cream in!'

I can feel my heart rate going up. I'm feeling triggered. Quickly I sink into what matters to me: I so want this to work. I want to help my child.

I say, 'We're not discussing ingredients. We'd like you to eat what's on your plate. Would you make a start, please?'

'There's too much. I've never had such a big slice. And I'm definitely not having pasta as well! Are you crazy?'

H says, 'It's the right amount. It's what you need.'

Flying food

She stands up abruptly and takes a step back. Luckily, we sat her in a corner, so she can't run away without going past me. I don't think I would physically restrain her – I don't think it's justified at this stage – but I do represent a bit of a psychological barrier in the path of her escape. If I did ever really need to restrain her, I'd hope to do it in as calm and compassionate a way as humanly possible.

H says, 'Please sit down.'

She tips her plate upside down. 'Well I'm not eating that! No way!' Pasta spills onto the floor. She stamps on it, yelling again and again, 'I hate you!'

I quickly say, 'Stop that, please!'

She freezes.

I want to scream; I want to cry. This is so very, very hard. I'm scared by my daughter's aggression. She looks like she's straight out of a horror movie. Her eyes are weird.

I notice that I'm thinking these things, and that my throat is tight. Time for some emergency self-compassion. I hold my hand to my chest and imagine a dear friend enveloping me with kindness – a friend who so understands how hard this is and how utterly normal and human my reactions are. I ask myself what it is that really matters to me right now. The answer comes back right away because it's always the same. I want my child to be well. I want to help her. I look at her, and now I see not a demon, but a small, frightened child. *This is the magic of the process of self-compassion.*

I say, 'Sweetie, I'm guessing that it's very hard for you to see this food on your plate. Is that right?'

Her face twitches.

'Would you like to know that it's safe? That it's the right thing for you?' Why am I not demanding that my daughter apologises and cleans up the pasta immediately? Because of the principle 'connect before you correct'. She is suffering, and that's what matters to her right now. She will have no space for anything else until she feels understood. If I reprimand her she will remain in a state of fight or flight. She will step up the resistance or tell herself she's very alone and worthless.

Her eyes well up. I take this as a sign that we now have connection. I can now move on.

I say, 'It's what you need. We're taking good care of you.' *A popular hit on our broken record.*

She sniffs. I continue: 'Now, it's not OK to tip your food onto the table or the floor. Even when you're really upset. Please don't do it again.' *This is the 'correct' bit of 'connect before you correct'. It's optional.* 'I'm going to bring you a new plate with the same food, and we'd like you to eat it.'

I can see my husband's really upset. It doesn't help that he detests waste. I discreetly stroke his shoulder as I walk past him to prepare a new plate of food. I realise that right now, this instant, I'm feeling quite strong. However this ends up, I'm confident we're doing what can be done. I hope that if my husband needs a break, he'll make up an excuse to leave the dining room. He's held the fort for me often enough. Then I realise we're out of pasta. Never mind, I will heat up some potatoes instead, and deal with the tantrum if it comes.

'Do I have to eat this?'

My husband starts a game of cards while I warm up some more quiche and some potatoes. I join in. My daughter seems calmer, and when five minutes later I bring in her plate, she picks up a fork. But then she stops.

'You gave me potatoes. I was supposed to have pasta.'

I say, 'There's no more pasta.'

She hesitates. 'Is there more in pasta or in potatoes?' She means calories of course, but she knows the word is now taboo.

'We're in charge of your food, darling. Trust us.'

She prongs a piece of quiche with her fork. (*Yes, yes, YES!*) Then she asks, 'Do I have to eat this?'

This question is the best possible thing to come from a kid with anorexia. My guess is that she wants her eating-disorder voice to hear, loud and clear, that she has no choice whatsoever. She is bravely considering eating her food, but she needs protection. If we give her the weapon she needs, she will go into battle with it.

My husband and I both nod gravely. 'Absolutely. You have to eat this.' When you've brought your child up to make her own choices wherever possible, it feels surreal to put on such a show of determination.

Her hand is shaking. She stares at the quiche on her fork. I have an urge to encourage her, to keep trying to convince her to eat it. But we stay quiet. Our instinct tells us that she's psyching herself up to take a bite, and we don't want to break her concentration.

She eats the piece of quiche. YES! She took a bite, when she could have clamped her mouth shut, thrown it against a wall, or run away. What does that tell me? Something in her, and something in us, has made her eat. She can eat, and we're doing something right.

Eating successfully

My husband says, 'Who's got the king of spades? I know one of you has it.' We'd love to jump up and down and celebrate that first mouthful, but we're acting as though it's what we confidently expected. We could, alternatively, say 'well done', or 'I can see this has taken so much courage, you're being so brave, you can do this!' but prior experience is that her eating-disorder voice gives her hell if we're anything but neutral. (It may be the opposite with your kid, so experiment with it.)

She takes another mouthful. Then she plays a card. Then another mouthful goes in. So far so good. Every now and again she slows nearly to a halt, and my heart goes in my mouth. What if she stops? I notice that my mood has shifted. There's no logic to it, but my mind is full of catastrophic thoughts. What if she stops eating? What if we can never get her to eat enough? What if she spends the rest of her life getting tube-fed in hospital? I bring my attention back to the present. Right now, she is eating. And we're playing cards. And I'm OK. For the rest, que sera, sera. I sit more comfortably, and hold my head up, as if I was confident and well. I instantly feel a little more confident and well because of this. Not much more, but it's all I need to keep me going right now. (The tools I'm using on myself, by the way, are described in Chapter 15.)

Butter, hygiene, and 'you gave me more'

For a while, we play and she keeps eating. She's got through half her meal when she stops.

I say, 'Keep going. Do you have a Jack of diamonds?'

She says, 'This is too much. You gave me more quiche than Dad did. If I hadn't spilled my food, I wouldn't have had so much.'

H says, 'We don't discuss quantities. Please keep going till you've finished what's on your plate.' If we tried to convince her that I had served her the same amount, she would argue micrograms instead of eating.

She says, 'OK, I'll finish the quiche. But I won't eat the potatoes. I don't eat potatoes when there's butter on them.'

H says, 'Keep going, sweetie. You're doing fine. Hey, how come you had the Jack!' *He's side-stepping her attempt to negotiate.*

'Our science teacher says butter's not a healthy fat.'

'We know more about your needs than your science teacher. On you go.'

She picks up a potato between her fingers, smearing the butter onto her trousers. I say, 'Please eat your potato with your fork.'

She grumbles 'I'm not even doing anything!' But she picks up her fork.

She eats a few pieces of potato. Then she stares at her plate. 'Ughh, what's that?'
We take a look. I say, 'It's a bit of skin.'
She pushes her plate away. 'I feel sick. That's disgusting. Anyway, I'm full.'
'Please keep going.'
'It's dirty.'
I put my hand on her arm. 'It's OK, darling.'
She explodes. 'Don't touch me!'
I should have known better. I'm having to train myself out of years of motherly gestures.
'Your hands are dirty! You're rubbing butter all over my skin!'
H says, 'OK, have some more potato.'
I am so scared. This is so much more a mental illness than I first realised. How long can I keep going? Will it always be so hard? Noticing my fear, I call in my resources for self-compassion and for compassion for my child. I return my attention to the here and now. My child needs me right now, and my husband and I are doing well enough under very hard circumstances. So many other parents, so many other children, have been through this, and struggled and come out the other end. I give myself a mental hug. I look at this human being who's suffering under the grip of an illness that rules her mind and depletes her body. I remember the sweetness of holding her little hand when I used to walk her to school. I imagine the day she'll proudly introduce me to a boyfriend. These thoughts warm my heart and remind me of the preciousness of what we're doing. The ugliness of the illness fades, becomes irrelevant. I'm her mum and I'm here for her, and that's all that matters in the present.

Feeling too full

She begins to whimper. 'My tummy hurts. You don't know how hard this is. I've already eaten most of the quiche, and now I feel sick. I'm going to throw up.'
'OK, darling. This is really hard for you right now. Take a few slow breaths. Breathe with me.'
She gives it a try. She looks terrified. 'It's not working. My tummy's sore. I can't eat any more than this. I feel really sick.'
'Oh, that must be tough on you. Feeling sick is such a horrible sensation. Let's give it a minute.' I believe her. It's bad enough that she's scared; it's awful that it physically hurts too. I want her to know she's been heard; otherwise she may keep on and on trying to make us hear.
We play another round, then my husband says, 'OK now, eat some more.'
'But I'm still too full!'
'I know it's horrible. Your body isn't yet used to you having proper meals and anxiety can also mess make your tummy feel this way. But it's not dangerous. It's what you need. We're looking after you.' *I imagine it's scary as well as uncomfortable for her to eat when her stomach is hurting. This is why we're trying to normalise her sensations.*
She continues eating, but she fiddles with the pastry, so that by the time she's finished eating the quiche and potatoes and she pushes her plate away, it's full of crumbs.

The last crumbs

My husband says, 'That's good, but would you please completely finish off your plate.'

'It's finished!'

'Just eat the crumbs, and then you're done.'

'They're only crumbs.'

'Sure. Please eat them.' *He refrains from blaming her for deliberately creating those crumbs.*

'That's crazy. How can a few crumbs matter?'

This is indeed quite a paradox. The problem is that they matter to her. They scare her. It may be against her rules to completely finish a plate. It's also possible that she is using them to bargain with her eating-disorder voice: 'See? I didn't eat everything.'

She starts to cry. 'I've done so very well. I've eaten all my quiche, even though you gave me more, and all my potatoes, even with butter. And all you do is blame me and nag me, just for a few crumbs. What's the point? Next time I'll eat nothing at all.' *The intensity of this outburst makes me think that these crumbs are indeed quite important, and we'd better keep insisting that they are eaten. I'm also conscious of the anorexia's attempt to manipulate: 'If you don't back off, there'll be no eating at all next meal.' We need to show our kid that anorexia can't bully us. We're stronger than it and we can protect her.*

I say, 'You're doing well, my darling. We're totally on your side. Scoop these up onto your fork, and you should be done in a few mouthfuls. And then we can watch our film.'

She's crying now. Great big, despairing sobs. It's rotten to see her suffering like this. At the same time, I am not overwhelmed by it, which surprises me a little. I used to hate seeing my child in pain. Now I know that moods pass. Pain, sadness, fear, they all pass. They're not dangerous. My job, as I see it, is simply to be there for her so that she gets comfort from knowing she's not alone. My husband and I both make compassionate 'hmm' noises. Oh, if only I could take her in my arms, this would be so much easier!

When her crying abates a little, I say, 'On you go. Those crumbs are OK, you know. Even if you're feeling horrible. We're taking good care of you.'

She says, 'How do you know you gave me the right amount? Are you weighing my food?'

'You leave food stuff to us, darling.' She already knows, from a family therapy session, that we are not weighing food and not counting calories.

'If you're not weighing my food, how do you know it's right?'

'Keep going with the crumbs, you're nearly done.' *Body swerve!*

'But you're going to make me fat!'

'Scoop them up on your fork, go on.'

'I'm so fat! You're not giving me the right amounts and I'll get fat. You don't care.'

I'm not sure whether this is a diversion tactic so that she doesn't eat those crumbs, or whether she needs help reducing her anxiety. I say, 'Would you like to know for sure that we're keeping you safe?'

She whimpers, 'I'm so fat.' Her tone of voice has changed. It's lost its edge, its intensity. I reckon the empathy is doing its magic. I might not need to say anything more, but I offer more support: 'You're safe, my darling. Dad and I are putting a huge amount of care into looking after you. We've always known how to feed you and that's what we're continuing to do now. You can trust us.'

'And you won't make me fat?'

'Never. Now just scoop up those crumbs.'

The empathy has helped her move on. She eats. But now she's doing something weird with her mouth. My husband says, 'Are you keeping some food in your cheeks?'

'No.'

'Would you show us, please? Would you open your mouth wide?'

'Why?'

'Because I think the anorexia is making you hide food under your lip, and I'd like to check. I don't want this illness to bully you. We're the ones who care for you.' *His tone is between neutral or caring. Of course she's 'pouching', but she can't help herself. If we shame or blame her, we're adding unnecessarily to her stress, and it won't stop her trying it again next meal.*

Sighing, she works her tongue along her teeth, and eventually opens her mouth. It's clear.

'Satisfied?'

'Yes, thank you. Just your milk and grapes now, and that's you done. And then we can watch *Friends*.'

A gift

She reaches out for the glass. Her hand is shaking. Then a miracle happens. She drinks the whole lot in one go. *Sometimes, you get something for nothing. A gift. You get more and more of those freebies as time goes on.*

My husband says, 'Now the grapes, and then it's *Friends*!'

I wish we could say, 'Yay! Well done!'

Sticking by her

I'm going to make things harder to give you an example of what you can do with 'failure'.

Her face goes hard. She pushes the grapes away, saying, 'No.'

Instantly, my head begins to buzz. She's defiant, and it's pushed one of my buttons. I'm on high alert.

My husband says, gently, 'We'd like you to eat the grapes. Start with one.'

'No.' *Here's one person who won't need assertiveness training.*

'You can do it. You're nearly done.'

'There's too many. I'll have one but not the rest.'

'On you go. Get started. Start on just one grape.' It may be less overwhelming for her if the challenge is broken down, one grape at a time. At the same time she mustn't get the idea that we've made a deal. We want all the grapes to be eaten.

She eats one grape. Then stops.

I say, 'On you go. Have another grape.'

She scowls at me and pops one in her mouth. 'That's it. I'm not having any more and you can't make me.' She pushes her plate away again and crosses her arms.

Her belligerence has triggered me. I notice that right now, I see her as a rude, out of control, self-centred little shit. I notice that I feel no love for her whatsoever, that I resent the effort I'm having to put into all this, that I'm telling myself that because of her, I don't have a life any more. I notice that I am furious that she's not trying harder, I'm furious that she is the way she is. I don't like these thoughts, but the fact is they're there. I notice that I'm about to give my daughter my ultimate killer weapon: the cold shoulder. I will say nothing. I will be blameless. But my face will tell her, 'You've disappointed me. You're worthless. I wash my hands of you.' These are the things I notice, as my head buzzes and my heart races.

I apply a process of self-compassion (I'll describe it more in Chapter 13). I tell myself, with great kindness, that even though I may not like my thoughts, I completely accept my present experience. Then I ask myself, 'What do you want?' *I want her to stop her nonsense and eat all her bloody grapes.* 'And what would that give you?' *It would mean she's eaten an entire meal. And that would mean we have the ability to make her eat. And that would mean she will recover. And that would mean that she won't die.*

My hardness has melted away. She's ill. She needs my help and my love. I'm now free of knee-jerk reactions. I'm centred again.

I look at her with tenderness, and I say, 'You can eat the grapes. I know you can.'

Finishing

She looks at the plate. An excellent sign. She's going to eat it.

She picks up a grape, hesitates, then squishes it angrily.

With some coaxing, we get her to eat one more, but she squishes the following one.

Now this could go three ways. We could continue to do our best and she'd manage all the grapes. We'd say, 'Good, time to watch *Friends*,' and that would be lunch over. Or we could try our best, but get absolutely nowhere. So after 20 minutes or so of trying and trying, making sure we remained calm and supportive throughout, we'd say, 'OK, that's fine. Let's enjoy our DVD now.' In other words, we would remain neutral about the fact she didn't manage the last few grapes. No blame. No drama.

I'm going to give you one more option, so you're aware you have choices. Many parents will gasp in horror, but it's worked for us every now and again.

My husband and I are glancing at each other, trying to guess each other's position. I make a decision.

'Sweetie, no squishing please. OK, we'd like you to have two more grapes, and then we'll call it a day.'

OK, don't shoot me. I know that we should be standing firm, no wiggle room and all that. We put food on her plate and she has to eat it all.

But at this stage, my instinct is that she's unlikely to manage anyway, and that this isn't necessarily setting a precedent. Though that is indeed a risk.

What's the message we really want her to get? That we're in charge of food. That she should leave all the decision-making to us. The leftover grapes won't make any difference nutritionally, so that's out of the equation. If we keep pushing and find she's truly stuck, we're ending with anorexia getting the final word, which is a shame when we've done so well up to now. We tend to remember final words more than the middle bits. My instinct is to end this meal with a good show of being in charge. If she's going to stop anyway, we make it look like we decided she should stop, after two more grapes. It's like dumping your girlfriend before she dumps you.

She asks, 'Will you give me more later?'

'We'll give you what you need. Leave it to us.' She might suddenly eat all the grapes if she can't bear the possibility of having something 'extra' later. It doesn't prove that she's been pretending that she can't eat. It simply gives us a glimpse into her internal conflicts, the bargaining she's doing with her eating-disorder voice.

She eats the two grapes. That's two more than she was ready to eat, which in this upside-down world is a measure of success. We spring to our feet.

'DVD time!'

After the meal

As my husband fiddles about with the television (this is not a good time to clear up in the kitchen), my daughter tiptoes upstairs. I catch up with her.

'What's up?'

She says, 'I just need to get something in my room.'

'I'll get it for you. Remember we'd like you to stay with us for an hour after each meal. What would you like?' It's not impossible for her to be sick in a bag in her room. Parents of children who purge recommend supervision for one or two hours.

'I need to use the toilet.'

'Sorry. Come on, let's watch the film.'

Clearly, she is agitated. She refuses to sit down (no surprise here) and her limbs keep moving.

'I shouldn't have eaten all that. I ate so much! I'm such a pig, and I'm fat, fat, fat!' It's common for the half hour or so after a meal to be full of remorse, which is why we planned the distraction of the film. Perhaps a walk would have been better, but I'm terrified that in her agitation, she'll run in the path of a car.

The DVD is in but it's not working. She is whimpering. Suddenly she says, 'I'm going out! You can't stop me!' She finds the front door locked. 'Where's the key? I need to go out!'

She's already run away once, trying to walk or run off her anxiety. I searched for her for ages, driving up and down our streets, berating myself for not keeping her safe. I hate locking the door, but I'm hoping it's very temporary and that it won't traumatise her.

Gently, I lead her back to the sitting room. 'We're with you, darling. Are you feeling very stressed, like you want to move and run?'

She wails, 'I ate everything you gave me. Everything!' I wonder if her eating-disorder voice is beating her up for it, telling her what she did was intolerable. Telling her that she must get rid of the food any way she can.

I say, 'Would it help you to know that was just what you need? Just right? Because we're looking after you really well?'

Trembling, she whispers, 'Was it really the right amount? I won't get fat?'

'Absolutely. You can trust us. We know what we're doing.'

She sags a little, as if the fight has gone out of her. Suddenly she rolls her eyes. 'Dad, can't you even make a DVD work? You need to press the button on the side!'

The crisis is over. Her mood can change for the better so suddenly. Another gift. We all enjoy the movie, even though she watches the whole thing standing.

Debrief

Later my husband and I snatch some time to hug, talk, support each other, and plan our next move. One thing is clear: she can't be expected to eat in school while she's in this state of mind. Even if the school organised some mealtime support, we couldn't expect staff to do what we've just done.

Although we're rather in shock at the turmoil we went through with just one meal, we are amazed by what our daughter achieved, and by what we achieved. Not only did she eat what she needed (even butter on the potatoes, I remind my husband!), but we built trust as well. We established the beginnings of new habits, new expectations, which will help us with future meals. And we've proven to ourselves that we can do the one thing we most want to do: get our kid to eat.

How typical was that?

You will get many mealtimes that are way easier than this, and you may get some that are harder (though the difficulty should diminish as time goes on). I want to remind you that this scenario was fictional. I designed it to include as many setbacks and tools as I could.

How long may you be facing meals that are this demanding? If you're dealing with the legacy of several years of untreated eating disorder, your guess will be way more accurate than mine. If you're relatively new to this, I'd hazard this as a guideline: the hardest will probably be week one, and within this, the hardest will be day one, which is the one I've chosen for this example. After a week or so, your child is less likely to fight you at every step. He'll resist one or two new foods or situations, but you may find that his resistance is a little less extreme, and that you can move him on more quickly.

> *"Your words were instrumental in helping me change tack,*
> *connecting with my son and building trust between*
> *us. This led to him eating properly for a whole day and gave my wife*
> *and I a much needed day away from the front line.*
> *(Eight hours later:) While we were chatting my son helped*
> *himself to a sizeable breakfast.*
> *(Three weeks later:) Still going well with occasional lapse – about*
> *one a week when a meal or two might be missed. Otherwise 3 meals*
> *and 3 snacks daily. Anorexic thoughts appear less dominant.*

*Lapses appear to be shorter in duration too. We're getting our sense
of humour back which is also a great help."*

This chapter was a tough one. You might be full of hope and determination, or
you might be rather shaken and in need of tender love and care while you process it
all. Give yourself some kindness for whatever your experience is, and if you can, grab
a minute or an hour to do something that would nourish you right now.

9

HOW TO FREE YOUR CHILD OF FEARS AND RULES: EXPOSURE THERAPY

Our children can remain stuck in an eating disorder while they're scared of certain foods or situations. In this chapter I describe how they can be desensitised to their fears through systematic exposure. Then I give you a practical example of a desensitisation session.

DESENSITISING TO FEAR FOODS

Weight recovery and restoring nutritional balance can lessen many of the symptoms of an eating disorder, but all the same, our kids usually need our help to let go of the long list of foods they cannot eat. Think of it as 'practicing ordinary', or 'practicing normal'. The more a new behaviour is used, the more it becomes normal. The brain has plasticity. It rewires itself. Recovery means enjoying ordinary food in normal situations, such as pizza with friends in a restaurant that doesn't display calories. Eating disorders, especially anorexia, promote rigidity and rules, so your child will need your help to re-learn flexibility and freedom from rules. Bear in mind that our child are often yearning for the very foods that they deny themselves with such intensity.

WHEN TO INTRODUCE FEAR FOODS

It depends.
- Dealing with fear foods is not your priority when you're desperate for your child to eat or drink *anything* because he's terribly unwell. Just the act of eating is fearful. So before you bring in extra-scary foods you could wait until you've established a bit of a feeding habit.
- If your child is terrified of everything except apple and kale, you have no choice: weight gain is the priority, so you must serve high calorie foods. Console yourself with the thought that your child would have resisted a useless low-fat yoghurt just as fiercely as they fought your creamy pasta.

- Likewise, if your child has cut out entire food groups, such as carbohydrates or fats, you will need to re-introduce them urgently because they are essential to a functioning body and mind.

- During the weeks of refeeding, notice if your child starts to resist foods that they used to tolerate. Quiche used to work, but now they fight anything with egg in it? If the eating disorder is pulling your child down, you will have to step up your efforts in the opposite direction. Not only should you continue serving eggs, you probably should increase the range of meals.

- If your child's weight and mood are steadily improving while you serve a limited range of dishes, you have a choice. Experiment with some fear foods, or stick to what you know is working until your child is close to weight re-covery. The downside of delaying fear foods is that your child's rigidity might increase with time. But what happens more often is that weight and nutri-tional restoration has made their mind more relaxed and flexible, so fear food work is actually a lot easier.

- If weight and mood are on the up, I suggest you experiment with some fear foods while prioritising weight gain. You can always pull back if it's awful. If it works, you're on the road to faster progress. I saw this with my daughter: desensitising her to fear foods and fear situations seemed to get her un-stuck. As she managed more and more of 'ordinary', her mental state improved. I put it down to her being generally less frightened, and to enjoyment and a sense of freedom and empowerment.

- When your child has reached a weight conducive to health, your priorities switch over. Systematically work through every fear foods and situation, even if this results in some meals failing altogether, with the occasional small dip in weight. Don't leave this to chance or your child may stay trapped by mis-erable eating-disorder rules even while everyone considers them recovered.

THE MAGIC OF DESENSITISATION

A common treatment for phobias is exposure to the object of fear.[160] Repeated ex-posure desensitises us. It's like we get bored. We know nothing bad happened, so we stop being alert. The brain creates new connections, and fear reactions don't get ac-tivated any more.

This is why a fairground ride loses its edge when you go on it several times. First time, you come out of it with your body shaking even while you're laughing and telling everyone else they absolutely must have a go. Second time, it's fun. Third time, the attendant says, 'You've been here before,' smiles innocently and spins you hard. You come out shaking and raving about it all over again.

What the attendant knows is that after two exposures, there's not much fear to be had. The brain has worked it out. 'This is OK. It feels like you're falling and you scream and your heart rate shoots up, but nothing bad happens.'

I found the same when I went for some MRI scans. I feared I might be claustro-phobic, so first time round I had to work quite hard at keeping calm. I was pleased with myself when the scan finished, but the procedure wasn't over. After injecting some chemical, they put me back in for another 20 minutes. I'd been lying there for a while when I noticed I was day-dreaming. When I had a third scan a few months later I practically fell asleep.

PLAN OR SURPRISE?

One approach to desensitisation is to help your child list all their 'no' foods in order of scariness. If your child finds it helpful to be involved in meal plans, you'll want fear foods to feature on them. For example, you could agree that once a week you'll serve one new food from the scary list, starting with the easiest. Presumably you'll also start with small portions. I have heard of teens with a decent amount of motivation who are willing to plan and be challenged. For a while I assumed this approach would be hopeless with a young child, but I've learned of a seven-year-old for whom it works.

Another method is for you to decide which foods to introduce when, without discussion. I talked about the Magic Plate system in Chapter 6. This is what we did because our daughter got no benefit from negotiation and forewarning. She'd had all that in hospital, and after a year the range of foods she could tolerate was still very small.

Fear foods are, by definition, fear-inducing. You can forgive kids with anorexia for wanting to aim very low. As a parent you can aim higher and help your child cope in the moment.

I experienced this myself when my daughter became an outpatient and I had regular one-to-one phone conversations with our Family-Based Therapy specialist. I'd *consider* scrapping the stupid butter portions, I'd say I would *think* about ditching the troublesome meal plan, but at that particular moment, I did not feel *at all* brave enough to commit. In my mind, these were ideas to consider for several weeks down the line. Then often as not, a perfect opportunity would present itself that very same day, and I'd implement the change without a flutter of hesitation.

My daughter could cope much better with a fait accompli than with discussion. Occasionally she asked ahead of time what was for dinner, and we learned to deny her the information. It seems that forewarning made her eating-disorder voice go into overdrive. Her stress levels shot up and eating was harder.

For that reason, we did not introduce foods in order of scariness, but varied the difficulty. When we presented her with something easy, it gave her a pleasant, confidence-building break, and when we gave her something particularly scary, she had no reason to believe that the next challenge would be even harder.

Your own child may be totally different:

> *"If she knows what is coming for the next day, she seems to get most of the feelings out at that time and then sitting down for the meal is OK. It's like she needs to rage against it before it is OK for her to eat it."*

RIP OR TUG THE BAND-AID?

Exposure therapy for phobia is typically a gradual process, starting with the least scary situation and moving towards the most terrifying one. Each new situation is like a step up a ladder. You move up a step when you've become desensitised to the fear around the previous step. That way you never have to cope with a huge amount of fear. The method is normally used with patients who are highly motivated to rid themselves of the phobia and are willing to put some work into it. Not a luxury we enjoy with anorexia.

Another approach to phobias is 'flooding' – a full-on exposure to the object of fear. It's said to be scarier, but if it works you get faster results. In our case something close to flooding wasn't just a faster route, it was the only route. If my kid was allowed any amount of time on one step of the ladder, she fell to a lower rung. Going slowly meant going backwards.

For example, when my daughter was dependent on her old hospital meal plan, we replaced her beloved, packaged, butter portions (which were hard to get hold of) with butter cut from a normal packet. We stooped as low as telling her we were weighing the damn butter, in a futile attempt to reassure her that the quantity was identical. At this stage, the move from packaged to home-portioned butter was the only change to her meal. In terms of phobia desensitisation, that's a pretty small step up the fear ladder. But her eating-disorder voice thought differently. An entire meal could become excruciating for her because the butter on the side of the plate was not a hospital portion.

We did a kind of flooding, or 'ripping off the Band-Aid', when we told her we were not weighing foods any more. Any foods. Ever again. Of course she was distressed and fought it for a few meals, but then, she had fought just as hard over just one piece of butter. The downside with flooding is you may have chaos for anything from a day to a week. In her case, it's a risk we could live with because by then she was pretty healthy. And we had some confidence in our abilities to manage mealtimes come hell or high water. Within a few days, she'd overcome a whole lot of anxieties and stopped expecting her food to be weighed. This paved the way for the next challenges, such as eating food outside the home.

Family therapy leaves it up to parents whether they want to flood or go more gradually. The message, basically, is that either is fine. An example that James Lock *et al* give of a small-steps approach would be to give your child the correct amount of food for weight gain, but once a week ask her to eat one new food, for example, cheese. The type of cheese could be up to her.

If that's giving you a good rate of progress, and if your child is able to gradually climb up the ladder of fears without too much resistance, then enjoy it. But if you have high drama at every step, you might as well make use of all that pain to go for big gains.

> *"We ripped. Every food was a fear food. Go with your gut and what you think will work."*[161]

If you cannot achieve weight gain without fear foods, you cannot afford to spend weeks serving kale:

> *"When we were aiming for weight gain, we ripped. When we were working through the list of fear foods, we tugged."*

Because there is no proven approach that consistently works with all children, you can experiment with the ladder approach and with flooding. As long as you handle 'failure' with a positive, supportive, compassionate stance, you can try various combinations without taking huge risks.

What are the risks? That your child will throw out the entire meal, and then swear that they will not eat for the rest of the week. In practice, once refeeding has started, our children only miss one meal – sometimes two, rarely any more. If your child cannot afford to fail a meal, then don't flood. Serve a very small amount of a fear food alongside an easy meal. Even then there is a risk that your child will scrap the whole meal because of it includes a half teaspoon of full-fat hummus. Be kind and persistent.

What if your child was so freaked out over a portion of beans that she ate none of her meal? You eventually release her from the table with supportive words. Blame or antagonism would only reinforce the eating-disorder voice ('We won! Don't give an inch if your dad tries giving you beans again!'). The next day, you have choices: serve up a full portion of beans again or serve up one single bean along with some other, easy food. Or serve a quarter of a bean, and serve it at snack time instead of dinnertime, because for all you know, in your child's head there may be a rule about particular foods at particular meals. You could even ask your child to just touch the bean to her lips. Or to simply look at it. Small steps.

Personally, I would try serving a full portion of beans at least once more, because with my daughter it usually worked (this was at a time even though it broke my heart, the odd failed meal was not a catastrophe). It's as though the difficulties of the first day had prepared her for success. If that failed, I could still present her with one bean at some other meal, and build up from there.

RESPOND FLEXIBLY TO PRESENT NEEDS

You can pick your battles. Hold on to your freedom to respond to your child's needs and abilities as well as your own. There may be some very hard challenges that you can leave for later, when your child is generally better or has enjoyed the experience of success. Some foods may look easy to you but in your child's mind be associated with a strong 'no' created at a time of high stress. The 'no' may melt away as she overcomes other fears.

> *"We started with 'tugging the Band-Aid' to minimize the stress at mealtime as husband was having a very hard time with the constant battles. Our FBT therapist was not in favor of this but it was putting weight on our daughter at a reasonable rate and not tearing our family apart. After about six weeks our daughter*

> *complained about the lack of variety. I took this as my cue to go*
> *ahead and rip: she scarfed down a bacon and cheese omelette. Now*
> *we are introducing fear foods almost daily."*

CAN CHALLENGES BE TOO STRESSFUL FOR YOUR KID?

You may have got into the habit of walking on eggshells. If you demand something 'too difficult' of your child, will she have a tantrum and eat even less? Can you stress your kid too much? Will she sink further into depression or become more rebellious?

> *"My daughter's mood went from upbeat and happy (when we first*
> *started refeeding) to absolute rages and depression about 7 to 10*
> *days later. She was the lowest of the low at that point. But it was*
> *the beginning of the long climb out. At the time I remember*
> *thinking, 'This isn't helping; it's only making her worse!' But, the*
> *FBT therapist assured me it was within the bounds of normal, and*
> *that it was in fact a positive sign that the ED was on the run, and*
> *on the defensive."[162]*

Clearly, parents must aim to feed quantities sufficient for their child to achieve weight gain. But should you launch a full-scale attack on the eating disorder, or should you proceed gradually and build on successes?

> *"We'd been hesitant to push our daughter, not knowing if we would*
> *push too far and afraid of what might happen. During our multi-*
> *family therapy week, seeing the trained team push her and have*
> *confidence in her ability to meet the challenge, was empowering for us.*
> *There were a few times she was pushed to her limit and she did*
> *explode, but we felt safe being coached and knowing there was*
> *consistent support nearby. Now that we know what she can do, our*
> *comfort zone for expectations has been widened."*

For a whole year I thought the only acceptable way was one small step at a time. It's not that I was a timid mum, but I was held back by a belief that there is such a thing as going too fast and that it might make things irrevocably worse. This came from my interpretation of a reputable book on eating disorders. Eventually, several weeks after my daughter was discharged from hospital, I got bolder: she was heading downhill and we had nothing to lose. We were by then under the care of an eating disorders specialist to whom I will be eternally grateful for empowering me. When I phoned her about going the whole hog and throwing away the hospital's meal plan, she calmly assured me that was perfectly safe. I suspect she was doing a victory dance.

Once I had dealt with my own fears that challenging my kid's anorexic behaviours might somehow harm her, I did a far better job of supporting her. I also believe that on many occasions, when I presented her with a food she secretly longed for, beyond her fear there was relief.

VIRTUOUS CIRCLES AND LASTING IMPROVEMENTS

With our daughter, we built up a good head of steam by giving her new foods every day, even several times a day. On the whole, each time it was a little easier. Her stress levels when presented with a cream cake for the first time were only marginally higher than they used to be when a yoghurt was the 'wrong' flavour. My impression is that she got used to moving through fear. She learned that her fear didn't last and that it didn't kill her. She noticed that foods she was of terrified only a week before had become perfectly OK. She got confident and started to smile. Perhaps she realised at some level that she had oodles of courage.

We were in a virtuous circle, and this helped us, as parents, to continue taking on challenges. In a way, we were giving ourselves exposure therapy too, learning that we could move through our own fears. Every time we planned to give her a new fear food, we were taking the risk we'd get an earful. Or a major drama. I told myself I could handle tantrums and that all of us, my daughter included, could handle fear or distress. At the worst, we'd have a nasty half day – more likely a nasty half hour. There wasn't any real risk. Most of all, hope had been missing from our lives for a while, and suddenly we had a method that worked, and we were getting progress at an exponential rate. Having one success after another was invigorating.

Desensitisation is to me quite magical. It is remarkable how you can do something in spite of fear and discover that the fear has gone. The beauty is that the work is done once and for all. New tracks have been laid down in the brain. Your child experiences that when she breaks one of the eating-disorder demon's rules, nothing happens. The demon may kick up a fight but it doesn't kill her. She doesn't balloon overnight because there was butter on the potatoes. She learns at a deep level that she can cope, that fear is not a reason to avoid doing things, that her life is now full of successes, and that every day she is a little bit freer.

Don't beat yourself up if for you exposure therapy is not quite so easy and empowering. I know of parents who found exposure therapy tough going, but who still absolutely swear by it.

EXAMPLE: WORKING SYSTEMATICALLY THROUGH A LIST OF FEAR FOODS

How did exposure work for us? Here's how we dealt with fear foods. But first, some context: this was a time when our daughter was stuck in an anorexic mindset, was reducing her food choices and seemed headed for another hospital admission. But physically she was well. We could afford the risk of her missing a meal.

This is how we got her through a long list of fear foods. We'd give her a small chocolate brownie on a Monday evening and support her though her fear and resistance. We'd follow with another small brownie on Tuesday or Wednesday, and that was usually quite a bit easier. When we gave her a small brownie later in the week, with luck she wouldn't bat an eyelid. A larger brownie or one made by a different manufacturer might still require a little support.

The whole week wasn't exclusively about chocolate brownies: we would introduce another new food or two in between, so that our daughter had something challenging approximately once a day.

If she didn't manage a new food, we didn't fret about it. We told ourselves that if we didn't give things a try, we'd never move forward. What we'd do is serve the same food up again a few days later, though this time the portion might be a little smaller. Or we'd serve it at a time of day when we knew things were generally easier for her. We didn't want her to learn that tantrums would put us off. She usually managed the second time round.

With time, when we gave her a new food, we were able to give her a full portion right away. For instance, every time we went to the park we bought her a new type of ice cream, and she would eat the whole thing without much trouble. We systematically worked our way through the ice-cream van's menu.

EXAMPLE: FROM PACKAGED FOOD AT HOME TO THE ABILITY TO ORDER ANYTHING IN A RESTAURANT

I'll give you another example of dealing with a whole lot of big fears in small steps.

My daughter had recently managed to eat our home-cooked food instead of a very small range of packaged, processed food. This was a huge victory, but soon I shifted my ambitions to having her eat anything, anywhere (this was entirely selfish, you understand: whenever we were out shopping, it killed me not be able to stop for a cup of tea).

For her, the big difficulty was this: how could I tell her how much to eat (and stop her getting fat) if I didn't know the ingredients and therefore the calories? In addition, there was a slight anxiety about eating in new places, though I wasn't able to identify exactly what it was she feared.

Here are the steps we took:

- We visited family and brought our own home cooking. Easy.
- Back home, she ate a bit of a dish my mum had cooked to my recipe. Difficult. After one or two repeats, she could eat a whole portion.
- Then she ate a dish of my mum's (that she'd loved pre-anorexia), knowing I'd had no input in choosing the ingredients. Very difficult. After a few repeats, much easier.
- She ate one portion of my mum's cooking at my mum's house. A little stressful.
- At home, she ate a nibble of a muffin made by the local deli (i.e. unknown ingredients and quantities). Very difficult.
- Then we repeated this three or four times till she could eat an entire muffin from that deli, at home, without stress.
- After this we stopped outside the deli, I bought a muffin, and had her eat it on the street. Difficult. Repeated once or twice.

- A few days later we sat down in the deli and she ate a muffin. Somewhat stressful, but not too bad.

- After that, we returned to the same deli several times, and I chose a different food for her each time. Easier and easier.

- I took her to a different café and chose a muffin for her. (This was a step down the fear scale in terms of the food – muffins were now easy – the challenge was eating in a new place.)

- When she was comfortable with that, it was quite easy to go into all kinds of cafés and order all kinds of food.

- We realised that even when cafés were OK, restaurants or pizzerias were an obstacle. She was used to one brand of frozen pizza, so I served up a proper fresh, hot pizza from a takeaway. Very difficult.

- After a couple of repeats, we ate pizza at a restaurant she used to love.

- After that we were able to go just about anywhere and order just about anything without putting much thought into it. She started ordering herself, and for another year or so she relied on us telling her how much of the dish to eat.

My daughter didn't do any of this willingly. Your child might have a motivation to eat out, but mine didn't. Yet it worked, and just as her peer group had reached the age at which they like to hang out in cafés, my kid was ready to join the fun.

If you're wondering how, in practice, you can get your child to take even small steps when they're putting up resistance, check out the scenario at the end of this chapter, where you can be a fly on the wall in a breakfast-time desensitisation session.

WHEN CAN EXHAUSTED PARENTS TAKE A BREAK?

James Lock's team describe refeeding as being similar to climbing up a sand hill: 'You have to keep moving uphill, or the loose sand will cause you to slip back down.' If you maintain the status quo, your child's eating-disordered focus will be on reducing quantities and reducing her range of foods. If instead you present her with challenges, her anxieties will be directed only on the new food, not on meals in general. Even with the odd setback, if she blows a fuse over a new dish, she's making progress overall. That, at least, has been my experience.

At the same time, we parents need to manage our own energy. Hope and regular delights sustain us when we're making progress, but if our child seems stuck there are limits to how much we can continue without refuelling. You may have a lot of 'shoulds' in your head – I know I did: a good parent should put their child first; a good parent should support every meal 100 per cent; even, maybe, a good parent should do everything Eva Musby says. Ouch! When you create these rules for yourself, you lose a bit of your power as a willing, self-motivated agent of change. Why did you take on all these 'shoulds'? My guess is that you really wanted to support your child. So tune back into this source of wisdom and internal power, and from there, decide how best to steer the boat. This may help you to refuel before you get worn out.

You may be surprised how quickly you re-energise yourself once you have attended to your own needs. Perhaps for you this means making the next few meals really easy. Or visiting friends or catching up on some delightful sleep, while you leave someone in charge of a couple of meals, even though they're not as skilled as you are. The sand hill metaphor is not hard science. Your child may not slip back, or if she does, for all we know she may scramble back up extra fast after a break.

Perhaps exposure and desensitisation work is not what you need right now. You may sense that at present, what really matters is regular meals and steady weight gain, and you may have a strong instinct that you can achieve more with 'safe' foods. You may sense that your child's mood and confidence is so low that the last thing you want is to give her a challenge she may fail at. Perhaps life will give you a free gift (we've had quite few along this journey) and you will never need to deliberately work on exposure. Here's a surprising and happy example:

> *"I do remember worrying about the fact that my daughter became very stuck on the same diet plan and we never introduced any fear foods. I needn't have worried because actually she went from the very restricted diet plan to eating everything literally overnight."*

EXPOSURE THERAPY FOR OTHER ANXIETIES OR PHOBIAS

Once your child has no problem choosing between a chocolate and a fruit yoghurt, she may still be gripped by fear when she has to decide on food types or quantities. You could then define the issue as a fear of choice, more than a fear of food. Perhaps time will sort this out quite naturally, but if your kid is in her late teens and soon to fly the nest, then you might want to make decision-making and meal-planning one of the challenges to work on. I give an example of this in the form of a scenario at the end of this chapter.

Exposure techniques work for a lot more than food. You can tackle all sorts of eating-disorder behaviours with desensitisation if you find they're not shifting fast enough on their own. This could apply to OCD-type behaviours (my understanding is that exposure is a treatment of choice for OCD), but also to your kid being unable to sit, or her attachment to big baggy ultra-covering clothes, or to the way she chews. You could use exposure to tackle her fear of eating in company, of moderating her exercise, and even to her hateful or rejecting behaviour towards a parent. If your child is driven to purge, helping her to delay or resist acting on it is a form of exposure therapy. If once a week your child is shown how much she weighs and learns to cope with the number, I imagine that too is about desensitisation.

HOW TO MAKE EXPOSURE WORK FOR YOU

Positive experiences have more impact

The conditions that lead neurons to strengthen synaptic connections (to rewire) are 'repetition, emotional arousal, novelty, and the careful focus of attention'.[163]

Repetition is on our side when our child manages one meal after another. The careful focus of attention is what helps us parents grow resourceful as we practise mindfulness. On the other hand, I haven't found it helpful to get my daughter to focus her attention on the experience of eating – quite the contrary. Emotional arousal mostly works against us: every time your child is terrified or furious, her brain labels the situation as one to fear and avoid. When you go on a fairground ride, the emotional arousal is very much there, but it's positive.

The question is how to create positive emotions to help success stick. Positive emotions are also useful because they are reinforcing. We tend to repeat behaviours that usually make us feel good.

If you'll forgive me for likening your child to a dog, there is much to learn from the last decade or so of developments in dog or dolphin training.[164] Pavlov's bell signalled yummy food, and through repetition it conditioned dogs to lick their chops. Neural connections had been created through repeated exposure. With modern positive dog training, the signal for 'sit' is hard-wired to pleasure and butt-lowering, because it has regularly been associated with exciting treats.

With our children, before creating new tracks, we have to get them out of the deep rut they're stuck in. We pull them off what for them is a safe and reassuring track, and they become distressed. But I do wonder if there is value in trying to make exposure work as positive and successful as possible so that our kids get positive reinforcement. For that reason I used to try to challenges while my daughter was succeeding, rather than push for one more step if it was likely to end in fear and refusal. I reasoned that if she could associate efforts with the pleasure of success, this might create a positive reinforcement for the next time.

Eating a meal can leave our kids in a highly anxious state but I do wonder if, all the same, some positive reinforcement is taking place. They may not often admit to it, but it's possible that they feel some pleasure in having managed a meal, some satisfaction in having lost a fear, and even, as time goes on, some delight in savouring a piece of chocolate.

I have not read anything on this subject with respect to eating disorders, so as always, please take all this with a good dose of caution.

Plan for one variable at a time

When you plan your exposure steps, go down a few notches to a comfortable level when you introduce a new type of fear. Otherwise you might be raising stress levels higher than you intended. For example, your child might fear two things about eating out: the food itself, and being seen by others. Say she's managed to eat ice cream in a quiet corner of a café, after weeks of having just a Diet Coke. Then she's moved up to waffles, then to chips and lasagne. If you now want to get her to sit close to other diners, at the heart of the café, forget about her achievements with the food. Instead give her something easy to eat, and only return to the lasagne when she's comfortable with where she's sitting.

Repeat in a variety of situations

Generalising is a recognised step in positive dog training. Once your pooch has learned 'sit' in the house, you need to work at 'sit' in other places before you can safely show off your skills as a trainer. The brain learns:

- One thing in situation A: 'Spaghetti isn't at all scary when I eat it in hospital with a nurse.'
- It then has to learn to apply it in situation B: 'Spaghetti's fine in hospital with Dad.'
- And possibly also in situation C: 'Spaghetti's rather delicious at home with Mum and Dad.'
- And only then is it able to generalise: 'I enjoy any kind of pasta at home with any family member.'

Humans can use rational thought to generalise matters of the intellect, but here we're dealing with irrational fears. I believe that the medical system unintentionally sets us up for failure by expecting our children to eat at home when all the refeeding prior to that has been done in hospital and by nurses.

Whenever you get frustrated by rigid, rule-based behaviour, see how you might help your child to generalise by exposing her to a variety of situations in small steps. After that you may have the pleasure of noting exponential progress.

Transformed through exposure: from fear to fun

If you like dogs you might enjoy watching a video showing how a little dog called Kiko, who had 'learned' to be fearful of crossing the kitchen floor after slipping on it, gets desensitised through gradual exposure and positive reinforcement.[165] Every time the dog hears a click, she feels pleasure because she's been conditioned to equate clicking with the likely arrival of a treat. The pleasurable feeling reinforces what the dog is doing. In other words, a click sends a direct message to the brain: 'Whatever you're doing right now, do more of it!' With our kids, we can't give pleasure with food treats, but instead we can use our words and body language, our humour, love and distractions. Clicker-training for dogs won't give you a cure for an eating disorder but it may just help you appreciate how much you can help your kid shift her behaviours.

BE A FLY ON THE WALL: A DESENSITISATION SESSION

If you're struggling to imagine how it is possible to desensitise your child to a long-held fear when she won't cooperate, here's an opportunity to be a fly on the wall while someone else does the hard work.[166] As always, bear in mind that we each have our own style and our situations may be quite different. Just take what's likely to work for you.

In this example, you'll see how you can keep pushing through your child's fear while noticing cues that things are going well.

I want to desensitise my kid to the fear of dishing out her own portions. The process is similar to mealtime support at the refeeding stage, where the issue is fear of eating, but by now she hardly has any anorexic behaviours, we both have a lot of experience of overcoming scary things, and we have a secure, trusting relationship.

Here's the background for this scenario. My daughter, up to this point, has relied on us to portion out her breakfast. It's suited us to give her generous amounts so that she has enough fuel for school. Occasionally we've tried to get her to pour cereal into a bowl and she's done so with much grumbling, putting small amounts in and waiting for us to say 'when'. On the other hand she can eat freely with friends, she's fine with sleepovers, she's increasingly regaining independence around choice and quantities of foods. But a rigidity around breakfast remains, and that's what I'm tackling today.

The way I understand it, she's still bound by a rule anorexia created a couple of years ago: I must not serve my own breakfast. Anorexia has faded into the background but the rule is still there, and it may shift if she experiences that she can safely break it.

As many other things have sorted themselves out unaided, we haven't bothered with this issue up to now, trusting that time would do the work. But now there's a reason to hurry things along – soon she'll be off on a two-week school trip. It seems wise to give her more ease with serving her own breakfast.

My guiding principles are these:

- I will keep focused on the task – she will serve herself a bowl of cereal and eat it.
- I'll break down the task in tiny steps if necessary.
- I will give her my total, compassionate presence.
- I imagine she will need empathic support around anxiety, as well as a sense of safety, trust and dignity.
- I'll give myself emergency self-compassion whenever I need it.

The set-up

So, it's Saturday and my husband's out walking the dog. He's the one who usually deals with breakfast. (I barely manage to support a mug of tea on my chest first thing in the morning.) As my daughter heads to the sitting room, I say, 'Sweetie, before you switch on the TV, come and help yourself to breakfast.'

She's instantly cross. 'You do it!'

Other times, she's moaned a bit but agreed to serve herself part of the breakfast. Her aggressive refusal confirms my instinct that this is an issue I want to tackle, and I want to tackle it NOW. I like to grab opportunities when I feel ready for them. It's my way of being brave. *In hindsight, I could also have considered that it's already 9:30 a.m., that she may be hungry and she's 'more anorexic' when she's hungry. I could have left the breakfast work to another day. But that's hindsight, and we don't have to get everything perfect.*

I say, 'No, I'd like you to do it today. I'll help you.'

'I can't be arsed, Mum. You do it.' She plonks herself on the sofa and switches on the TV.

I don't argue about her language or tone of voice. She is a lovely, considerate person, and I guess that the aggression comes from fear, or, as some would say, it's the eating-disorder voice speaking. My mission is breakfast, not manners.

'Please switch off the TV. I'd like us to do your breakfast first.' I sit close to her (close to the remote control too). Standing above her feels too antagonistic. I want to signal I am by her side. And I'm ready to use the remote control if she doesn't.

'Mum, I told you, I can't be bothered.' But she does switch off the TV, which I read as an excellent sign that part of her is ready to comply. *It is helpful to mentally note all the things that are working, not just the difficulties.*

'Thanks, sweetie. Come into the kitchen. I'll help you.'

'I don't want to do it. It's boring.'

'The way you're saying it, I'm guessing you've got a bit of anxiety around this, right?' *This is me empathising with her feelings.*

'No, just can't be arsed.'

'OK. Either way I think you'll manage to do it fine.' Even though she's denied it, I am more than certain that she is not lazy but anxious, or bound by an old rule. My priority is action, but I want to do it with presence to what's going on for her.

I say, 'I'd like to see you have a little practice at it because of your school trip.' It's the truth, and it may help motivate her. She is extremely keen on the school trip.

'Oh, honestly!' Grumbling, she comes into the kitchen. Another sign that she is ready to do a lot more than it would first appear. One way to look at it is that the authentic part of her wants to do this but must appear to put up a fight to appease the last whimpers of the eating-disorder voice that has bullied her for so long. With this mental model, I as a parent get confirmation that she needs me to keep going, to leave her no get-out clause.

In the kitchen

A variety of cereal boxes sit on the counter. I put a bowl in front of her. She grabs a box of cereal and shakes cornflakes wildly into a bowl. She fills three-quarters of the bowl and then tops it with porridge oats. The dish is overflowing now. In the past she's always gone for tiny portions, and now she looks at me defiantly. I am very aware that this is a massive challenge for her, and that she may be scared or wanting to save face. Because this is my interpretation of her behaviour, her aggressive manner washes over me. I notice that I'm surprisingly not stressed, but I am vigilant to how best to steer this.

I say, 'OK, there's a bit too much in there, so put some of the oats back in the jar, and that will be you done.' I am body-swerving her provocation by remaining matter-of-fact. I have never had to tell her to reduce her portions before and am quite enjoying the chance to show that I am not on a mission to get her to eat to excess.

With some degree of violence, she pours the surplus oats back in the jar and then looks at me.

I say, 'OK, there's a bit of a mess here, but I know this is a challenge for you, so for this time, that's OK with me. You've still got a bit more than you need.' *If she'd been very upset or aggressive, I probably wouldn't have mentioned the mess, because she might grab that as something else to argue about. On the other hand, my instinct at this moment is to remind her of my preferences around polite behaviour.*

She scoops oats out of her bowl, a little more gently this time. Again, positive feedback for me that she is actually OK, and quite capable of continuing.

Next step: the milk

I say, 'OK, so now you need to pour milk over your cereal and pour some milk in this glass.' She is used to us preparing her a portion of milk in a jug. The only time I ever saw her pour milk onto her cereal was when she was with friends. So I'm giving her step-by-step instructions to make it easier for her.

She crosses her arms. 'You do it.'

'Sweetie,' I say, 'I'd like you to do it. You'll need to do it when you're on your school trip.'

'They'll serve me. I won't need to do it myself.'

'They'll serve you lunch and dinner, but not breakfast. Go on, pour some milk onto your cereal.' I'm trying to keep the discussion short and I put the focus back on action. She already knows that breakfast on her trip will be self-service.

Anxiety on the rise

She blurts out, 'I don't even want to go on the school trip.'

I'm aware of a wave of sadness washing over me. Anorexia is such a killjoy. I'm grateful it's mostly out of her life now. Her statement is so obviously driven by fear, so out of tune with her desires, that I choose to gloss over it. If I argued, she'd only argue back and get more entrenched and we'd have a pointless discussion. I trust that the instant she's succeeded with her breakfast, she'll be back on Facebook discussing the excitement of the trip with her friends.

I say, 'Go on, pour some milk.'

'Nah, I can't be bothered anyway.'

'Sweetie, I'm guessing you've got some anxiety right now, hmm?'

I use the expression 'right now' a lot, because I want to place feelings where they belong, in the present. While we are scared, it feels like the agony will never pass, and that adds to our anxiety. Also, I usually say 'You've got some anxiety' rather than 'You are anxious' to move her towards being an observer of her emotions and away from being helplessly entangled with them (some call this distancing 'defusion'). I'm keeping my manner calm and soothing, but there have been tougher occasions when I've sensed that she needed a more robust display of empathy, mirroring her intense state, to show that I get it.

I say, 'I'm sorry some anxiety's come up. I can see it's hard for you.'

She blinks a bit, and it's my cue to continue moving on. To me, the pause, the blinking, indicates that she's received the empathy. I may be wrong, but this level of feedback is as good as it gets, so I hold on to it. Connect before you correct. I assume she feels a tiny bit more understood, more supported, and that this is enough for us to continue.

'Even with anxiety, you can pour your milk. And then let's make sure there's something fun for you to watch on TV.'

This is how I see empathy working at mealtimes: acknowledge the feelings, be by your child's side, but press for action all the same. The feelings are unpleasant but shouldn't render her helpless. I'm giving her the message that she can feel the fear and do it anyway.

She bursts into tears. 'I have anxiety because of you!'

I know this is unlikely to be true and I let the comment pass. Otherwise we'll be discussing my failings for the next hour instead of getting on with breakfast. *Remember the self-talk mantra: 'It's not about you?' Remember selective hearing, so that instead of hearing accusations, you hear what really matters to your child?* I am totally confident that so far, everything has gone very well. Her anxiety was to be expected and is a lot lighter than in the early days of refeeding. The tears, to me, are a sign that she's let go of her belligerence and is a bit more attuned to her desires. Sometimes tears are part of the process, sometimes they're not. I'm sorry for her but I'm not at all worried.

I say, 'This will be easier next time, sweetie. But you can manage it right now. Pour the milk, my darling. And then you can enjoy some TV. I recorded *Would I Lie to You* yesterday.'

I'm talking about the TV to try and get her to focus on how soon her ordeal will be over and to imagine something pleasurable. I don't want to do too much of this but I reckon the odd incentive or mood-changer won't hurt.

She frowns at me. I say, in a mock serious way, 'It's a particularly hilarious one this week.'

I'm testing the waters, wondering whether I can help her shake off some of her anxiety with some laughter. But I'm not confident I can be genuinely funny right now or that she is ready to be amused.

Note that I am not telling her that TV is conditional on success. She knows she can watch TV either way. And in any case, there is no 'if', as in 'if you manage to serve your breakfast'. We are doing very well, and so it's 'when'. We have done wonders with refeeding without threats or punishments, and there's certainly no need for them today.

She gets cross: 'I don't care about TV!'

OK, I don't think she's up for lightening the mood right now. She may be hearing it as an attempt to jolly her along, a lack of empathy. Or perhaps anything I say will provoke a reaction, because she is on high alert right now. Who knows? No harm done in trying, though.

Spilling milk, then the banana challenge

She grabs the milk carton and fills her bowl to the brim. A puddle forms on the kitchen counter. Then she pours a decent amount into her glass. I'm not worried about the spillage or the aggression. Helping herself to milk at breakfast time is an important new step and that's what matters.

I say, 'The amount in the glass is good. There's too much in the bowl, so pour some out into this cup here.'

Again, she makes a mess, and I say, 'I'm not going to ask you to clean up this time, because I know this is tricky for you. Now I'll just wipe the edges of your bowl clean and you can go watch TV. But first, would you chop half this banana onto this plate?'

I don't praise her for managing to put cereal and milk in the bowl, because in her case (and children vary in this respect), even a matter-of-fact 'well done' can anger her in the heat of the moment.

Asking her to chop the banana is a bit risky. I'd rather end this session with the thrill of success than a feeling of failure, as success would surely help in a Pavlovian sort of way. But I tell myself that if she manages the banana, she'll have accomplished serving herself her entire breakfast, which may be even more affirming. As I debate this internally I check my body language so she won't guess I am hesitating. Well, I tell myself, the worst that can happen is that she'll refuse, and then I'll add it to to-morrow's task.

She protests, 'I hate banana! Why do I get banana every day, why can't I have something else? Give me something else!'

I let this pass. I know she's eaten hundreds of bananas without a problem. Discussing it would be a distraction. Note that she hasn't stormed off, she hasn't said she's not eating anything, that she even has the knife in her hand – this is all positive feedback. (OK, at other times, having an angry anorexic kid holding a knife isn't that positive, but you know what I mean.)

'On you go, darling. And then you're all done.'

Tears

She bursts into tears and sobs her little heart out. I wait a little, then I murmur, 'Can I give you a cuddle?'

She doesn't answer, so I put my arm round her. Two years ago, there was no way I could touch her when she was upset. Even now, when she's in this state, it's hard to tell. She won't actually say yes. All I can do is watch out for a small sign or touch her hand, and when she doesn't push me off, I put my arm around her shoulders.

For all I know, she is feeling not only scared but stupid and desperate. She knows a banana shouldn't be frightening. She may also be feeling guilty or ashamed of her behaviour towards me. Perhaps she is filled with hopelessness. She's probably not heard her eating-disorder voice for a long time, and this is an unwelcome blast from the past. Maybe she wonders if she'll ever be free.

I want her to know I'm by her side and that in no way am I blaming her for anything. I am very aware that what she's doing is heroic. It calls for courage and mastery, and I love how she's managing it. We applaud intrepid explorers who brave the highest peaks and the deepest oceans, but it's nothing compared to what kids do when they defy an anorexic demand or break an OCD rule. I feel totally confident that her sobs are utterly normal for a desensitising exercise, and not at all a sign of danger or failure.

She cries some more, and I give her some time, hugging her. When the crying subsides, I say, 'I'm sorry it's hard. It's a bugger, isn't it?' (empathy doesn't bring out my more refined side). 'It's going to be way easier next time; you know that, don't you? So, the banana, and then that's you all done.' *Again, some empathy, quickly followed by action.*

As she starts chopping the banana, my husband comes in from walking the dog. My daughter tries to hide her tears, but I don't want her to be ashamed of crying. I explain in a warm but matter-of-fact way that she's busy doing her own breakfast, and we're nearly there and she's doing fine.

She bursts out: 'Mum's making me anxious. She's rubbish!'

Time for another body swerve on my part. I say, 'OK, you're nearly there. Just finish chopping the banana.'

The finale

She chops and I say, 'That's you! Enjoy your TV!' *Again, I avoid even a simple 'Well done!'*

As she carries her bowl to the living room, she says to my husband, 'I hate banana. Why do you give me banana every morning?'

Wisely, he doesn't respond. She wasn't waiting for an answer anyway; she just needed to vent. We leave her in peace for a while, as our instinct is she needs to do a bit of face-saving to recover her dignity. And it might be a little harder for her to eat with us watching (and in any case breakfast is a meal she often has more or less alone in front of the TV, while we busy ourselves). But I can see enough through the open door. *Did she have this much freedom in the early stages of the illness? No way.*

For a few minutes, she watches TV without touching her food and I wonder if she's going to need my input, but then she starts eating. I join her when she's nearly done, and we watch a bit of the show together. Everything is back to normal. She is relaxed, chatty and close to me again. The rest of the day is delightful.

Debrief

I don't discuss the breakfast work with my daughter: my experience is that analysis leads nowhere. And I don't need an apology from her about the mess in the kitchen. We both know that she's not really like that.

I do discuss the events with my husband. There's an old feeling of shame or inadequacy in me that's just resurfaced. After all, he walked into the house on a perfectly ordinary day and was faced with an unexpected bit of drama and my daughter blurting out, 'Mum makes me anxious.' It turns out my husband is delighted with what's been achieved. I'm grateful that we're a team.

Reinforcement

On each of the following days, my husband or I ask her to do her own breakfast again, and she doesn't show any resistance or anxiety. Each day she asks for less feedback, needs less guidance. On the third day she even asks on her way downstairs, 'Shall I do my own breakfast?'

We make each day a little different, as we're not sure what will be on offer during the school trip. One day there's a croissant as well as cereal, another day there's brioche, and I have plans for pancakes, waffles or eggs. I also plan to get different-sized bowls from the charity shop. As it is, she soon appears so free of fear that I forget about it.

Ideally, we would get her to generalise to other situations by doing this conditioning in different places, with different people present. Some sleepovers are coming up, and I may ask the mums for some feedback.

The school trip will give her the challenge of a new environment, but also the fun of being with others, which is usually helpful. Either way, her stress will be much lower as a result of desensitisation at home.

The end

The following breakfasts are a breeze. The school trip is a total success. Were breakfasts ever an issue? It's become hard to imagine. This particular chapter seems well and truly finished. Years later, all my daughter recalls about this episode is that I was making a fuss over nothing.

I hope this scenario gives you a vision of how exposure can work, even though your situation may be different in many ways.

To recap, the skills involve remaining focused on the task, moving forward in spite of fear, tracking and judging how fast to go at any moment, and maintaining a compassionate presence.

10

THE WORK TOWARDS FULL RECOVERY

Once eating and weight gain are secure, what else do we need to do?
How do we guide our children towards normality and autonomy?
What is too much, too soon? What safeguards are needed as we
experiment? We look at school, exercise, holidays, recovering 'normal'
eating, behaviours, beliefs and body image, preparation for college,
relapse prevention, and total recovery.

STEPS TO INDEPENDENCE AND TOTAL RECOVERY

So far we've addressed the first phase of treatment, where we take charge of meals and of any behaviours that affect our child's health. The ultimate aim is for our children to have age-appropriate independence and to be free of the eating-disorder mindset. This takes practice, experimenting, monitoring, and correcting. Both body and mind need time for healing and consolidation.

Someone with a broken leg can't and shouldn't run as soon as the cast has gone. Likewise, there has to be a period of learning, practicing and consolidating after refeeding. Here are some milestones to recovery, or reasons why your child may be stuck:

- Her weight or fat/muscle ratio might need to be higher (her personal needs – not BMI charts – are what matters)
- If you were refeeding for weight recovery, she'll have learned that eating without restriction causes weight gain. Now she needs to experience that when she eats freely (and without compensating with exercise), her weight stays stable.
- She needs to experience that it's safe (and lovely) to eat a wide variety of normal foods in normal (or festive) quantities.
- She needs to experience the pleasure of exercise that is not about body shape or weight-control.
- Her metabolism may not return to normal for a while, so she may need to continue eating similar amounts as she did when weight gain was the goal. Indeed she may still be very hungry and she needs to experience that eating when hungry is safe.

- She may not have normal satiety cues for a (long) while, so she needs guidance to choose sufficient quantities. Otherwise she may involuntarily lose weight.

- She may need to maintain the snack habit, because a long gap between meals can re-activate the eating disorder.

- She needs time to experience that her body shape is fine, that it doesn't define her, and that there's a wonderful life to be lived beyond the world of shape and of food rules. She also needs time to develop wisdom and resilience in a world that is weight and diet-obsessed.

- If in spite of all this she continues to suffer from anxiety or depression, or if she has had traumas in her early life, she may now benefit from psychotherapy.

You're in charge of your child's independence

Too often, treatment stops shortly after refeeding or weight-recovery. Therapists discharge the child from care, as though there was no more work to be done. Parents dutifully back off. Youngsters leave home. When the person goes downhill, people call it 'relapse', when actually the treatment was never completed.

You should continue to be in charge, but now you are experimenting with returning small amounts of independence to your child. Compile a list of all the 'normal' things that have been derailed by the illness and work your way through it.[167] For instance you might ask your child to choose between two foods, building up to the day she can choose from a restaurant menu. You could let her select her snacks. If a main course is accompanied by peas, you could have her help herself to an adequate portion of those, while you serve the rest. You could ask her if she fancies a second helping. At first, you will be watching closely. Keep your authority to guide and correct. If the outcome is negative, no great harm will have been done. Take back control and retry days or weeks later. Don't blame your child. Keep your cool. It was just an experiment.

Some children need parents to stay in charge of some areas a long time. If they're young, there should be no pressure to rush the process, and indeed some children show little desire to make their own food choices. Be guided by their needs, capabilities and emotional age more than by their calendar age. At the other end of the spectrum there are youngsters who demand more freedom than they can safely handle.

Don't assume your child can suddenly handle any situation wisely. Don't assume they will tell you the truth if they fail. Early on your child needs to know they cannot misuse their freedom, because others are monitoring for you. For instance I describe further down how meals in school can be supervised. Later you can take more risks (such as allowing meals out with friends) while monitoring that weight, behaviours, beliefs and mood are improving. Eventually, your monitoring will be done discreetly, with a light touch, so that your child can take pride in their autonomy and in their ability to take good care of themselves.

Practice 'normal'

This whole phase of treatment and consolidation rests on principles of exposure (Chapter 9). Behaviours become normal and safe as they are repeated and the brain rewires itself. If your son or daughter is soon due to leave for college, you may speed up their autonomy by systematically working on exposure to everything they will need to do independently. If they can't keep up, better you find out now than after they've left.

Too soon or too fast

Much of what I've described is covered by Phase II of Family-Based Treatment (FBT).[168] It's shocking how often children are discharged from treatment upon weight-recovery, as though this phase didn't exist. Another common problem is when therapists rush through Phase II without consulting the parents, pushing for the child's independence too early or too fast. Yet according to the FBT manual, if the patient returns to dieting or loses weight, therapists should swiftly motivate parents to re-establish control over eating. So in principle you're on the same team. Sometimes a therapist doesn't have the complete picture. If they're not consulting you, perhaps all they see is a smart kid who presents well and who complains that their parents are overbearing. I suggest you meet the therapist alone and describe your child's behaviours.

What's too early? According to the FBT manual, Phase II can't begin until the child's weight has reached a minimum level, *and* until parents report no significant struggles with meals, *and* demonstrate a sense of relief that they can manage the

illness. If you know these criteria are not yet met, make sure your therapist knows, because your child will surely backslide if given too much freedom. Usually, 'significant struggles' with meals continue until our children are close to weight-recovered, so Phase II begins some time after that. If you suspect your child isn't yet weight-restored, bring all the data you have – pre-illness photos can help too. I know of cases where such a meeting made all the difference.

A number of parents – especially those who have seen their child repeatedly backslide – have come to the conclusion that Magic Plate should be in force until there are clear signs that the child is weight-restored, with a greatly improved mental state. This certainly worked for our daughter, and I agree. Holding on to control for longer means you speed through a lot more exposure to fearful foods and fearful situations.

We did wonder if the longer we were in charge, the harder it would take for our daughter to become independent again. Experience proved otherwise. Things happened at our child's pace, we all enjoyed how easy life had become, and we saw her become relaxed and competent around her food decisions. I believe that every human being has a drive for autonomy. If some children cling to their parents, it's a sign they need more time to build a secure base, and they need handholding while they work through their fears.

Do parents cling to their child longer than needed, driven by irrational worries – or worse, by a pathological, codependent desire to be needed? No doubt it happens, but surely it's the exception. Let's not rush to pathologise parents. Most of us have no intention to hover over our children any longer than necessary. We are tired, bored and sick of being in a carer role. We fantasize about our freedom, and about the glorious day our child can fly with their own wings. So let's validate parents' instincts. We do not and should not take our eye off the ball while risks are not properly managed. When an inexpert therapist hands our children independence and destroys the safety net, our fears are justified, not pathological. It's our job to advocate for our child and stand our ground.

Some therapists have shockingly low ambitions, incompatible with the level of recovery we now know is possible. Patients are discharged even while ridden with obsessive thoughts and behaviours around food and weight. Sometimes treatment stops at sub-optimal weight. Patients are told they are now fine and that it's time the parents backed off. This is a ticket to freedom for the eating disorder. Make a strong show of competence and expertise. Find another therapist, and if that's not possible, you can continue to treat your child by following the road map in this chapter.

WHAT TO DO ABOUT SCHOOL?

Schools have a huge role to play. I'll describe teamwork between parents, clinicians and school, from the early refeeding days all the way to recovery.

Is school a mood-booster for your child?

Your immediate priority in the early phase of treatment is nutrition and health. If school gets in the way of that, then your child shouldn't be in class. As soon as possible, though, we want our children to be engaged in normal life and friendships, as this is part of the treatment too. Usually this requires the school to join in the teamwork.

Not too fast, though. When my daughter's mood was very low, we thought of school as a welcome boost. She appeared normal there, yet she was probably obsessing about food every minute of the day. In the early days the hospital thought that keeping up appearances in school might be quite stressful for her. Their priority was to help her feel secure at home. Later, as she recovered her physical health, they helped her with a phased return to school.

Most parents are clear that the priority is health and recovery, but some still worry about missed academic opportunities. In practice, with their genetic potential, most youngsters catch up and excel. Others forge their own rewarding path. Still, there are times during treatment when we're sitting through a school ceremony, show or concert, and it hits us how our child has missed out. Notice these thoughts with compassion, and this may protect you from giving out confusing messages. We also need kind recognition for how much we put our own life on hold. Often we give up our work, and it's no fun being at home all day with a child who's in the grip of an eating disorder.

Back in the lion's den?

A very common trigger for eating disorders is an incident of bullying – usually fat-shaming. Understandably, your child may fear being thrown back in an unsafe environment, to the point of having nightmares about it. The adults often go for the 'get back on that horse' approach, on the basis that the longer you avoid a fear, the more it grows. The problem is that the fear, and the resulting unhealthy safety behaviours, may get reinforced the next time a kid makes fattist comments. I suggest you work with the school to address bullying and fat-talk (see 'risk-reduction programs' later). I also think that adults should, with great compassion, facilitate reparation from those who did the bullying. Our children could do with the healing.

I have a theory that trauma therapy has a place in these situations. In a few EMDR sessions, a youngster could be freed them of any inner programming that restricting makes them safe from bullying. I do wonder if my daughter's relapse was triggered by an incident with a friend which was rather similar to her first trigger.

School as carrot and stick?

It is incredibly tempting when your child isn't eating breakfast to snap, 'OK then, you can't go to school!' One of our therapists would hear about our daughter's week and take on the bad cop role: 'No playground for you. I'm going to tell the school nurse to keep you in during break time.'

There was no sense in making my child sit in the nurse's room, while in the playground her friends sat on their coats and chatted. We should be clear about whether we're addressing a real health need or trying to provide incentives. If the latter, our children are very likely to experience our decisions as punishments (more on rewards and sanctions in Chapter 14).

On the other hand I was very aware that if my daughter hadn't been eating or drinking, she was too weak to go to school. Perhaps, also, she should preserve the few precious calories she'd ingested – though that was debatable, as we couldn't get her to sit or lie down at home. At least at school she sat at a desk for a few hours.

So what did we do? We reserved the right to make decisions as the need arose. We minimised risks while trying to maximise the goodness our daughter got from engaging with normal life. For months, we drove her to school rather than let her walk. And if we decided not to let her go, we took care to present it as a regretful necessity, not a punishment.

Academic support

Expect the school to keep supporting your child even while he can't attend. When my daughter was in hospital, several teachers, including the Head, would turn up at case conferences. It was heart-warming to see the pride they took in supporting her recovery. With just an hour of study a day with the ward's teacher, my child kept up without any problem. This teacher liaised regularly with the school.

There is a lot your school can do, whether you are giving your child a complete break from studying, home-schooling for a while, or gently re-introducing him to classes. Increasingly, I am hearing of parents who find school staff helpful and non-judgemental.

Meals during school hours

Your child may need to progress through four levels of support for meals in school:

- Meals are so difficult and emotional (and she is perhaps so medically unwell) that she needs to stay home

- She still needs skilled support, so you meet her in the school car park, or in a room the school allocates to you. She may come home for lunch.

- She is now used to eating, so she gets one-on-one supervision from a member of staff in a separate room, possibly with some friends of her choosing. Staff give immediate feedback to parents: did she eat everything or not? They are not expected to cajole her into eating.

- The risk of her cheating is now low, so she eats in the dining room, knowing that staff are keeping a discreet eye on her, and that they will report any problems back to the parents. And that you are monitoring her weight.

My daughter reluctantly endured this type of support at times, both in primary and in secondary school. If your child hates having staff involved, give him empathy around his desire to look normal and have people treat him with respect, while also making supervision, for a limited time, non-negotiable. Our children will not recover if they are cheating and going hungry.

Some parents trust that their child will say if they didn't manage some of the food. For several years this worked well with my daughter, because she was perfectly well, and determined not to get sucked back into the eating disorder. Yet at age 15, she went downhill again. What started with smaller lunch portions quickly spiralled into major restriction. During this time she ate well at home and we weren't weighing her, so I only twigged one night when I heard her howling in fear and distress. From this experience I recommend that when recovered, our children eat in the dining room even if they bring in a packed lunch, and that staff keep a relaxed eye on them throughout their schooling. If your child is going to backslide or relapse, it's most likely to begin out of your view, with missed school meals.

'Health promotion' in schools: why, oh why?

I'll try and keep this short or I fear it will turn into a rant.

Schools commonly have 'healthy eating' and exercising on their curriculum. Food is labelled as 'healthy' or 'junk', 'good' or 'bad'. You can never eat lean enough, you can never exercise too much. Thinness is holy, while a large body is a sure sign of sloth and bad health. Schools are forced by government to weigh children, who get the idea that a low number is best. Parents receive letters informing them their

child is 'obese' and should lose weight, purely on the basis of a statistical BMI calcu-
lation.[169] Clinicians and parents often lament how health promotion messages are a
top precipitating factor for a child's eating disorder.[170]

In school my daughter has been told that sweets are bad (yet received them as a
reward for good work). She's had to keep a food diary, to read nutritional labels, to
count dietary fat units, and to watch a 'gross' liposuction video. I bet you have your
own horror stories.

What are your options?

- Education and campaigning. You could insist that only evidence-based interventions be used (this may require changes in government policy).

- Prevention. If teachers know your child is vulnerable they may warn you
when a 'health' topic is due to come up, so he can go somewhere else.

- Intervention. If you hear of nonsense being taught in one class, you can stop
it being repeated in other classes in the same year group.

- Education after the event. I spoke to teachers after discovering that my
daughter and her friends had been lined up in order of weight for a lesson
on Excel charts.

- Wait and see. When my child was told by the science teacher to keep a food
diary, we agreed I would pull her out. The pupils had to note where an 'unhealthy' food could be replaced by a 'healthy' one and they had started com-
peting with each other for who was the most virtuous. I never did need to
intervene, though. By the second lesson, my girl had turned the situation into
a game by filling her diary with made-up nonsense.

- Mending. After the liposuction video, I was glad my daughter could talk to
me about it and come to her own very sensible conclusions. If she'd thrown
a wobbly at dinner that evening, I would have gone back to the old 'no choice'
regime of the earlier refeeding days.

- Rejoice. The rubbish taught around health could be a form of exposure therapy. If you notice that your child can process 'health' talk without excessive
suffering, be happy. She's better equipped to deal with the pressures she'll
encounter in years to come.

Risk-reduction programs in schools

I am totally in favour of evidence-based programs that aim to improve body confidence. They tend to do away with 'fat talk', with shaming of larger bodies, and with
the labelling of foods as virtuous or bad. That in itself makes them well worth im-
plementing. Additionally, some have been shown to reduce new cases of bulimia or
binge-eating disorder. Careful! Programs that are not backed up by research, even if
they seem like common sense, can do harm: eating disorders may end up more stig-
matised, the session may trigger anxiety, may lead a child to diet or over-exercise, and
the information presented may serve as a how-to manual for youngsters who are
already on the eating disorders route.

On my website: Health promotion, body confidence, diets, disordered eating and obesity: what to do?

Getting school staff on board

It's increasingly the norm for schools to be proudly and actively supportive. Many are aware that eating disorders are common among their students, and they have learned what to do. If your school is anything but helpful, be persistent. Your child needs to be safe in school for years to come.

When my daughter was first ill, age ten, we hit some pretty poor attitudes in her primary school. There was one incident where a teacher wanted to exclude her from an outing for fear she would 'contaminate' the others. The problem was sorted before I got fatally apoplectic, in no small part thanks to our specialists, who educated key staff within the school. Teachers' change in attitude also coincided with the arrival of a new Head, a woman who took pride in supporting our daughter.

We each have our styles. Mine was to hug everybody. When any of these stern-looking teachers showed the slightest sign of melting, I'd burst with gratitude and give them tearful hugs. It wasn't manipulation – I really meant it, and hey, it freed them up to act human. Soon, we were doing exemplary teamwork and hugging on a regular basis.

If you're having trouble getting school staff on board, check out the schools pages on my website[171] and ask your clinicians to intervene. You might like to try the tools of compassionate communication I offer in Chapter 13. The approach applies to any situation in which human beings are interacting.

How both schools helped us

Here are some of the ways in which the school helped my daughter, age 10-11:

- They allocated a support teacher to our case. She set up meetings and ensured information flowed.

- The educational psychologist associated with the school stayed discreet (my child did not need one more therapist) but he coordinated, among other things, the transition from primary school to high school. He was also ready to provide a listening ear for my husband or me. Another educational psychologist gave my daughter some one-to-one EMDR therapy at my request. Although this was unsuccessful, I was glad to have this rare resource, and it was free.

- There were regular meetings with us parents, the school, the clinicians and the educational psychologist. We worked out how best to supervise my daughter's meals. We discussed various opportunities for her to be given roles and responsibilities that would boost her self-confidence. We tried out various ideas to help her feel secure with girls whose jeers had, more than a year earlier, caused her to start dieting, and who at times continued to trigger huge distress in her. We were quite torn about whether it would be better to change schools, and the school's willingness to try various measures made a huge difference.

- Together we planned every detail of how to make it possible and safe for my daughter to go on a week-long school trip.

- As my daughter and her friends prepared to move to the same high school, new teachers came on board to support the transition. When they allocated pupils to classes, they discreetly took account of our guesses about which girls my daughter would be happiest with and which would perpetuate her insecurities. As a result, nothing but good things came from her move to high school.

- My daughter was increasingly well and wanted to get on with her life, so most of this work went on behind the scenes.

Later, when my daughter had a setback in secondary school, the school kept an eye on her in the dining hall, never made a fuss about her coming in late, and when she got stressed about a new maths teacher, they discreetly changed her to one she found more supportive. There were some negatives, such as when teachers didn't realise that for my daughter, the drive to get top grades was unhealthy. On one occasion I had a hard time fielding off a school nurse who insisted my daughter should have one-to-one chats with her. I didn't want too many cooks, especially one who wasn't specialised.

I'm full of gratitude for the actions of many individuals who together made a whole system work so very well. I believe key ingredients are good information and a strong lead from the Head. My guess is that every single person who helped us along got pride, satisfaction and joy from their input. There was no shortage of hugs and tears on my daughter's last day of primary school. If you ever hesitate to ask for the support you need, remember that what may initially seem like a burden to someone can become an opportunity for them to make a meaningful contribution.

More on my website:

    School portal to eating, exercise & body issues[172]

    A list of issues for parents to discuss with the school[173]

    School trip or summer camp: a helpful flow chart[174]

RE-INTRODUCING EXERCISE

In Chapter 6 I discussed the issues with exercise in the early days. Most of these remain valid as your child gets better. Exercise is as an eating disorder issue, so treat it with the same care as you do food.[175]

> *"My daughter had an exercise compulsion with her eating disorder.*
> *She asked me to run cross country for 3 years . We said no. Year 4*
> *I asked her if she still wanted to. She looked at me like I was*
> *insane and said, 'No I hate running. That was my ED, Mom!'"[176]*

Once our children are weight-restored and eating without too much difficulty, we should address their behaviours and attitudes around exercise. The aim is for them to gain freedom of mind conducive to total recovery. They can have a full and healthy life, with a relaxed and happy attitude to movement. They can be in their power, free from the slave master of compulsions, of their next exercise 'fix'. For that, they need practice, and your guidance. They also need some education: the message in our society is that the more the exercise, the better, and that is just as untrue as the thin ideal.

If your son wants to get back into running soon after weight restoration, for instance, the issues might be:

- he might not manage to keep up with the extra calorie requirements

- he might not yet be fit enough

- he might not have time to eat sufficiently because the running club takes place at lunchtime or straight after school

- his motivation might be eating-disordered. If it's not, running might still trigger or reinforce eating-disordered thoughts or behaviours, especially as a while back it was very much part of the eating disorder. Would tennis not be more enjoyable?

Don't let your child return too soon – if ever – to the type of sport that got them in trouble in the first place. Help them discover new enjoyable forms of movement, and over time, help them develop a healthy, relaxed mindset that is kind to their body. Movement is life-enhancing if it is enjoyable and if it comes with social bonds, skill, art, creativity or contact with nature. Contrast this to the self-flagellation that goes on around exercise, where more (and more, and more) is better. Let's not forget that according to public health advice, all that's required is the equivalent of a few brisk walks a week. Let's steer our children away from boring, self-obsessed exercise – the type that requires intense determination and only feels good once it's over. Our children can experience the good life free of self-bullying, counting, Fitbits; free of the rules that make their lives small and sad.

We should help our children to practice a balanced, healthy mindset. That means not using exercise to appease the anxiety of a big meal, to compensate ahead of time for a feast, to control weight or to change body shape or composition. We can help them with more effective ways of dealing with emotions (Chapters 13 and 14), and let them experience that their worth is not tied to body shape. To get there, our children may need exposure to zero or moderate exercise, and this rewires the brain along the same principles as exposure to fear foods. This is a good time to help them expand their life with new (non-sporting) interests.

To help you gauge your child's mindset and whether her activities are driven by anxiety and/or the eating-disorder, notice if:

- the frequency and duration seem excessive

- she exercises to atone for a good meal

- it's the only thing that brightens her mood

- she goes to unusual lengths to fit exercise in

- she turns down fun or social activities to prioritise exercise
- she has a strong reaction when something gets in the way of exercising

Competitive sport could play right into the hands of the eating-disordered mindset as it involves a constant drive for self-improvement. There's a big difference between a weekly volleyball class and membership of a competitive running team. Some teams (and some parents) value achievement so much they lose sight of wellbeing. There are gymnastics or dancing clubs where young kids keep attending in spite of chronic joint problems. While there can be great pleasure in perfecting a skill, high expectations can reinforce self-bullying and a disconnect from the needs of both body and soul. Of particular concern are activities that favour a particular body shape. Some dance classes are about skill, music and enjoyment. Some, on the other hand, foster a culture of thinness or squeeze miserable, self-conscious teens in tight leotards. How is it acceptable to put kids on stage in fishnet tights?

Body-building attracts some of our children. You may be glad to see your son or daughter eating lots and gaining weight in their quest for more muscle, but body-building involves a highly disordered diet of cutting and bulking. Don't be tricked into thinking that body building boosts self-esteem or confidence. Your child may never reach the level of bulk or tone that they aspire to. Remember also that a 'healthy weight' is only healthy if there's enough body fat.

There is some research-based advice that people in recovery should lay off the exercise for a while to avoid relapse and to avoid medical deficiencies.[177]

I am not convinced that we know enough to give blanket recommendations, and I would encourage you to assess your child's situation carefully, after letting go of the doctrine that 'exercise is good for you'. You also need to think long and hard if your child is on the path of professional dance or athletics. There are some stories of total recovery, but also plenty of stories where the illness has dragged on.

With my daughter, age 12, once she was well I had to work out whether to let her go back to a weekly dance class. There were many positives to tip the risk-assessment scale: she got a great buzz from dancing and music; she enjoyed the skill and had a whole lot of friends there. What's more, it would have been easy to pull her out if ever things turned sour. I had to assess risks again when she wanted to accompany a friend to go running. My gut said, 'Over my dead body'. Rather than voice this, I specified a time limit for the run and guessed, correctly, that she would soon get bored of it. In fact she decided once and for all that running was seriously sad.

In her late teens, when my daughter was – to my immense frustration – given free gym membership, I reluctantly let her join on the basis that it was social. Before I let her go, we had a useful discussion in which she worked out her red flags:

- If I wanted to go more than 2 or 3 times a week
- If I wanted to go alone
- If I wanted to do more repetitions or bigger weights each time
- If I beat myself up for wanting to do less
- If it bothered me that I haven't been for ages

Gyms aren't going to go away, so if our children want to try it out while they're under our roof, maybe we should welcome the chance to guide them. I posed the question on a forum and got a whole lot of answers. Some feel that if their child wanted to join a gym it would be a sure sign of relapse. Some warn that their gym is a highly triggering environment, with incessant 'fat talk' among users, and calorie-counters and weight-loss messages everywhere. Some are confident their child can use the gym sensibly, and can just as easily not attend too. Some, like me, think that our youngsters might benefit from the practice while they're with us. And some point out that the gym is just a social place, full of teenagers 'standing around gossiping and eyeing up the boys'!

ACTIVITIES

Life is for living. There is a healing force in having our children join clubs, go out with friends, have sleepovers, and generally do what they love to do. Not only does it bring joy, but it allows our children to practice 'normal' while we provide guidance and a safety net.

We assess what might be too much, too soon. Activities must not get in the way of essential nutrition or rest., so for instance school clubs at lunchtime could be problematic. Also, is your child at a stage he can probably be trusted, or could he be manipulating you in order to go for a run or miss a meal?

If in doubt, you could ask yourself:

- What could go wrong, how badly, and how would I know?
- How quickly could I intervene?

If you withhold permission, remember to do so with compassion.

I'll give you the example of a mother whose daughter planned to spend the day in town with a friend. The agreement was joyfully made when the girl was doing well, but mealtimes had become hard again. The mother was no longer confident that her daughter would manage meals without supervision. Her first instinct was to call off the outing. Then she devised a fun way of meeting the girls for lunch. She also accepted the risk that her daughter would not manage an afternoon snack. All the same she helped her girl plan for an ice-cream, while also dropping a backup muesli bar in her bag. In her risk-benefit assessment, this was 'good enough'.

Another example: many young people have part-time work that involves preparing or serving food. My teenager accepted that until her recovery was solid, we did not want her to work with food. After all, would you put a recovering alcoholic to work in a bar?

EATING OUT

Sometimes we find, to our joy, that our child can eat better than usual in a new environment or with a new person. For my daughter, even at her most ill, having friends round could help her eat because she wanted to appear normal. But eating in cafés and restaurants was, for a while, nearly impossible.

In the early stages, if you can't avoid eating out, your priority is to get your child to eat anything, anyhow. One mum told me how her teenage son used to select his meal from the children's menu:

> *"On many occasions, after we'd ordered, I got up on a pretence of going to the toilets and chased the waiter down in order to explain that I would like a bigger portion for my son but that it was NOT to be mentioned when they served the food. My son is still unaware of this antic."*

Once you've got a handle on refeeding, you can help your child to overcome fears associated with cafés and restaurants. As with any exposure or desensitisation work, it helps to identify what makes eating out difficult (principles and examples of exposure therapy are in Chapter 9). For instance:

- Your child may fear being observed and judged by the world. She may have a rational fear (or memory) of having tears or tantrums in public.

- We parents become inconsistent because we don't want to look odd in front of strangers. We fear people judging us or judging our child. I like to think that people's opinions don't matter to me, but I do have my limits. After getting a plate of tomato pasta on my lap, I decided that 'ripping the Band-Aid', or 'flooding', wasn't going to do much for anyone's dignity. I wiped myself down and planned a series of small steps instead.

- Your child can only eat at home if strict rituals are observed, and these don't translate to other environments. Maybe your child only drinks from one particular glass. This may come from a desire to control quantities, or there may be some OCD and hygiene issues. You could work at breaking the habit at home before you venture into a café.

- Your child wants to know what's in her food, or only trusts food that you've cooked or weighed or calorie-counted. This was a big issue for us. In Chapter 9 I described how I broke it down into steps, using my mum's cooking, muffins from our local deli, and pizza takeaways.

- She may (secretly) check calories on online menus before accepting a restaurant outing. It's a crutch, and there's little you can do about it, except gradually getting her to restaurants that don't display calories. I had one or two incidents where my daughter became scared of food she's previously accepted because the calories printed on the menu were higher than she'd thought.

- There is too much choice at the buffet, too much choice on the menu. Your child's anxiety rises as multiple voices in her head argue about the benefits and dangers of each item and deny her what she fancies. I dealt with this by choosing for my daughter at the beginning and not budging from that choice for any reason. I tried to notice what her eye was lingering on in order to choose what she seemed to desire. The next step was to have her choose between two items. As often happens with exposure, the progress became exponential. When she could choose between two types of cake, it became easy for her to choose from the entire display.

- A long meal in a proper restaurant can be scarier than a snack in the local café.

- If your child finds it hard to sit, she may find it hard to take what seems like 'extra' time in a café or restaurant.

- Eating among lots of people may be harder than eating in a quiet corner.

- If she's used to strict and predictable mealtimes, it can be stressful for her to pop into a coffee shop at a random moment during a shopping trip.

- For some there's a vague sense that eating is an intimate or disgusting act. I was fascinated and appalled to learn that among my daughter's peers (aged 13–14), there were groups of girls who would not eat in front of boys.

"We go away a lot and eat out when we do, so we had to challenge eating out pretty early on. We are going abroad later on this year for over three weeks and will be eating out three times a day, so challenging this was important for us. We cancelled this trip twice because our daughter was not up for it."[178]

HOLIDAYS AND SCHOOL TRIPS: RISKY OR BENEFICIAL?

I bet we've all, at some time, imagined that a holiday might lift our child out of their eating disorder. Get them out of their routine and isolation, give them lots to enjoy! Surely they'll stop worrying about food?

In the acute stages, when getting your child to eat is a major feat, holidays are in my experience a tempting but deeply flawed idea. The illness is far too serious to be cured by a change of scene. Routine and predictability, however depressing for us parents, help our children to manage their anxieties. On several occasions, my husband and I changed our minds about going on a family holiday, quite rightly. It was good to be close to our support systems, whether it was therapists at the end of the phone, or the local supermarket that sold the one and only acceptable type of bagel, or the weekly pub music sessions that lifted my mood.

The decision to go on holiday depends on how well your child is at the time, and on how well you plan how to make meals work outside the home.[179] I would guard against using a trip as an incentive if your child's eating disorder is strong. If you overestimate his abilities and have to cancel the holiday, he may experience this as a punishment. He may also feel ashamed and guilty that the whole family is denied a trip because of him.

We resumed holidays once our daughter's anorexia was reasonably under control. In the first couple of years, trips caused her to regress a little and we had a mini crisis or two. I believe this is because she was exposed to a whole lot of stressors: new and delicious-looking foods, new choices, new places, new company. There were people of all shapes in bikinis, unpredictable activity levels, and slightly random eating times. Sometimes she was triggered by hunger because we had lost our own routine and

had forgotten to bring a snack. The challenges she encountered were quite manageable. They didn't spoil the holiday and I consider them a good learning experience
for her and for us. We were able to measure her general progress by noting that our
holidays were increasingly free of anorexia symptoms.

Planning a holiday can be relatively low risk once you've made solid progress
with feeding and trust. Your child's motivation to go may help her work through
some fears. When my daughter was starting to make progress, she managed to eat
more foods and do more sitting ahead of some trips.

What's not certain is if the improvements will stick, creating new healthy habits,
or if your child only managed to overcome obstacles by making a deal with the eating
disorder: 'I will eat and do everything needed to get on this holiday, and when I get
home I will quickly lose weight and get back to where I was – and a little bit skinnier
than that.'

When my daughter came out of hospital we pulled out all the stops, with the
help of the school, to get her onto a five-day school trip. Even before her discharge,
she'd been restricting more and more, and the trip was our last-ditch attempt to turn
her around. She'd have fun, relax, and strengthen her relationships with school
friends. Well, our daughter ate beautifully ahead of the trip, put on enough weight to
be considered safe, and had five brilliant days during which she ate well, behaved
utterly normally, and had a thoroughly good time. On her return home, she promptly
resumed her downhill journey. What turned her round was not the holiday, but our
takeover of control shortly afterwards.

Still, the trip gave her great memories and did no harm, because the school had
put in place all the protective measures we'd asked for. We'd managed the risks well.
If she'd restricted we'd have come to fetch her right away. I have a friend who took
her family on a foreign holiday against the advice of her child's doctor, and there
again, no harm was done. She'd thought it out carefully, knew exactly where they were
going and what the food was like, and was confident that her daughter would cope
well. The whole family benefited.

If your child goes on a trip without you, you're the best-placed person to assess
the risks. When my daughter was rather well, it was reasonably straightforward to let
her go on a ten-day school trip abroad. The teachers were willing to watch out for
missed meals and over-exercising, and I gave them a flowchart[180] with guidelines for
various things that might go wrong, for instance if she missed meals or refused water.
For any problem we couldn't fix by phone, we'd fly over and collect her. As the trip
involved much physical activity, I was aware that she might unintentionally lose
weight, and I considered how large the weight loss and the refeeding work might be.
In our situation, the risks seemed acceptable. The trip turned out to be a complete
success, and it contributed to our child's journey towards independence.

There is one risk that is hard to control and that made me break into a sweat:
major delays and overcrowding at airports. When our daughter was very unwell, a
volcanic ash cloud halted air traffic in most parts of Europe for as much as four
weeks. I cannot imagine how we'd have coped if we'd been on holiday in the middle
of that mess.

Between ages 15 to 18, when my daughter was affected by anorexia again, we let her go on several holidays without us. Of course we assessed the risks – poorly, in retrospect, as each time she lost weight. But something good can come from bad decisions. She had convinced herself that if only we treated her as though she didn't have anorexia, then she wouldn't have anorexia. The trips showed her that positive thinking, and having a lovely and sociable time, are not magic potions. That without support, knowing she *should* eat, and even *wanting* to eat, wasn't enough. This helped get her collaboration in preparing for university. Also, after her last trip she did the hard work of bringing her weight back up with minimal input from us. I would never advise a parent to set their child up to fail, but if you're as bad at risk assessment as I was, it's not the end of the world.

RULE-BASED OR INTUITIVE EATING?

The aim is for your son or daughter to recover completely from an eating disorder, to the point where they have no rules around food and exercise. Appetite and pleasure will naturally lead them to eat what their body needs and their weight will effortlessly stay stable. This has worked for me most pleasantly all my adult life, so I was glad to find mine was a recognised approach named 'intuitive eating'. Contrast this with governmental health agencies, who push us in the opposite direction: strongly rule-based eating. Eat your 'five a day'. Eat less of everything else, especially fats. Read nutritional labels. Don't eat 'junk' foods. Get thinner.

It's possible that the more someone has lived with food rules, the less their body and mind can achieve balance. It's also possible they were born without the intricate biological mechanisms that make it possible. For some, maybe the psychological balance is not there: their constant state of anxiety or excitement cuts them off from hunger cues, or at the opposite end, fullness signals are inaccessible because food provides the only source of comfort. Some people who consider themselves recovered from an eating disorder say that they need some level of rule-based eating because their appetite cues are unreliable guides. And that's OK as the rules are low-key and life goes on.

It's likely that your child will need rule-based eating for at least a year after you hand over control to them. During that time, neither their biology nor their mind are capable of intuitive eating. We know it can take a year for the hormones that regulate appetite to stabilise after a weight-loss diet (a physiological reason why diets don't generally work in the long term)[181]. In addition, your child's mind needs time and practice to be aware of hunger and fullness cues and to trust them. While the eating disorder raged, all their brain knew was to fight the body's signals. So rules for balanced, regular, sufficient eating are essential at first, and gradually you will see which can safely be shed or lightened. Ideally rules will morph into rough guidelines, and in some years your child may realise that their intuition is a reliable friend. Don't rush it. Treat it like a series of small, low-risk experiments. If something goes wrong, go back to what worked, and wait a while before trying again.

I hear that intuitive eating has been corrupted by some to mean, 'Trust your body as long as it's asking for low-calorie food'. That's appalling. Go to the source[182] to learn more about intuitive eating, and meanwhile, here's my take on it.

- You give yourself unconditional permission to eat what you desire, when you desire. You don't label foods as good or bad. When you exercise or when you eat foods you previously labelled as healthy, it's for the pleasure of feeling vital, not because you 'ought to'.

- You notice hunger and fullness signals. You can safely eat even when you're full because food is also about pleasure, celebration and social times. Your body will self-regulate with the appropriate appetite cues later.

- Regarding comfort eating, you notice when you are anxious or bored, and whether food provides an effective solution (if it's your only tool, broaden your range). You accept that your body will settle into the shape and size that suits it, and you don't bully your body to be different. There is no need to weigh yourself.

- Intuitive eating isn't entirely about intuition. You also factor in your knowledge of how you function. So you have breakfast even though you're too sleepy to be hungry, because you won't get a chance later that morning. If you're going to a restaurant in the evening, you might eat less than usual beforehand to make sure you have a great appetite – but not the extent of becoming 'hangry'. You eat even when fatigue or illness strips you of appetite, because you know it will help your body. You adjust for any appetite-suppressant effects of drugs, exercise or super-focused work.

- What about 'healthy eating'? If you notice you're never naturally drawn to fruit or vegetables, you add them to your meals anyway. Make it about adding foods rather than restricting foods labelled 'unhealthy'.

- A healthy nutritional balance naturally takes place over several days or weeks, not at each meal

- You never, ever, go on a weight-loss diet or count calories

- You never mess with carbs, gluten or whatever restriction is currently fashionable

Years may pass before your child can eat intuitively (if at all). Meanwhile, help them move along a continuum, from lots of rules, to light guidance. Here are some examples of rules that can be either fantastic or dreadfully limiting, depending on your child's situation:

- Eat every three or four hours (3 meals, 3 snacks) and never miss a meal

- Eat a minimum amount even when you're not hungry (it may awaken your appetite, or you may find you really don't need any more)

- Eat normal portions, based on how much they fill the plate (rather than on calorie-counts), if you can't rely on the presence or absence of hunger/desire

- If you have a genuine problem with bingeing, you might make a rule not to eat in-between your 3 meals and 3 snacks. For people who need to regain weight, on the other hand, or who never allow themselves to 'graze', that rule might be counter-productive.

- Limit the quantity or frequency of foods that usually trigger a (genuine) binge
- Weigh yourself and know which weight(s) must lead to action
- Keep to a meal plan. Plan your meals and your shopping.
- If you have ethical reasons for trying vegetarianism or veganism, wait a few years till your recovery is secure, and treat it as an experiment

There doesn't seem to be any validated method to speed up your child's progression towards having trustworthy appetite cues. You are moving in the right direction every time you do exposure work, let go of meal plans, calorie-counting and food-weighing. Our children experience that delicious foods are safe and that quantities can safely vary. Time may do its magic, as our children discover that they can shed overcautious rules *and* be stable. In addition, we parents can model something close to intuitive eating. We can become more aware of how we talk about celebration meals. We can ban 'junk' or 'naughty' from our food vocabulary. We can point out that 'detox' is our liver's daily job and that 'clean' eating is peddled by celebrities, not scientists.[183]

There are 'mindful eating' approaches[184] with lovely principles of non-judgement and awareness, and these may have a place for people who binge. For those who restrict, mindfulness is worse – usually distraction is what they need. And it would have done my daughter no good at all to be made to chew her food 30 to 50 times, or to focus on every sensation in her mouth as she masticates and swallows. I bet many of you parents are squirming along with me.

I'm aware that some parents are pretty miserable about their own relationship with food and don't feel they are a good model for their child. If that's you, I guess it's got to be a case of: 'I'm not doing great yet, but I'm working on it. And I know enough about it to help you get it right.'

So, here you are with a range of choices, from helping your child to trust her appetite, to helping her keep to safe rules. Treating everything as a series of low-risk experiments will help you safely navigate the unknowns.

What if your child eats 'too much'?

If your child is recovering from bulimia or binge-eating disorder, he is now an expert in what to do about bingeing, and so are you. With anorexia or another restricting disorder, while your child needs to gain weight, there is no such thing as eating 'too much'. They are hungry and their body is driving them towards health. The faster they gain weight, the better. The important point is to keep them to their schedule of meals and snacks even after a 'binge'.

As youngsters become weight-restored and we start giving them some autonomy around food, they need our guidance and the chance to experiment. They are terrified of over-eating. They think that without strong self-control, the floodgates will open and they will never stop. This fear is understandable, given how long self-control has been their way of life. Additionally, if their body is still pushing them to eat to repair itself after months of 'famine', our children will continue to be consumed by dreams of banquets.

Given our children's fears and lack of experience, they tend to be over-cautious. Their meal choices may consistently err on the small side. Or they may yo-yo, eating one meal with ease, then leaping back into excessive control. The eating disorder continues to distort their perceptions: a normal slice of pizza will, for a while, continue to look enormous.

For recovery to continue, our children have to experience, over and over again, that they can safely enjoy the 'feast' which their body or mind is begging for, as long as they allow the next meals to take place without restriction. They can notice how their weight and their mind stabilise.

So if you see your child ravenously digging into a mountain of food, I suggest that you validate that this is not binge-eating[185] but a healthy hunger similar to what people experience after dieting, or after starving (as the men in the Minnesota experiment).[186] Help them relax and trust the process,[187] and wait and see. The regular meals you have insisted on for the last months are treatment for both restricting and bingeing disorders. Your child is better-than-ever protected from under-eating *and* over-eating.

What if your child's eating and weight keep increasing? I have suggested 'wait and see' but is there a point at which you should intervene? Some would say 'No' (see Chapter 6 for discussion on the Minnesota experiment and on 'overshoot', and follow my links in the endnotes).[188] Continue validating your child's eating.

Conversely, you could take the view that your child needs help to find stability, and that your job is to give more guidance, or to steer them towards eating that is more rule-based because they're not (yet) capable of intuitive eating.

I myself told my daughter, rightly or wrongly, that I would not let her get fat and not let her over-eat. I promised to guide her eating until she was able to do it sensibly for herself. In practice, she never seemed to eat massive quantities so it's not a question I had to confront. When she did report having huge dinners at parties, I urged her to notice how she was still hungry the next day, and urged her to stick to regular meals even if had thoughts of restricting. I reminded her that this, far from causing over-eating, would stabilise her just as it does for those with binge-eating disorder.

If you decide that your child needs guidance because you're certain they're eating too much, then I suggest you learn from the Intuitive Eating book,[189] since much of it is aimed at over-eaters.

WHEN TO DITCH THE SCALES?

The scales can be a useful learning tool once our children are weight-recovered and still have so much to come to terms with. They assume that anything they eat will make them 'go over' and 'get fat'. When we back off at this stage, they usually drift back down. They work very hard at never going above their magic number, which means they are restricting more than during the weight-gain phase, and mentally even further from recovery. So we have a crucial role in guiding their eating so that they experience the easy balance of 'normal' life.

If you hold onto the scales, they will see how weight stays stable, with small variations, even, say, after a birthday feast. Even after Christmas, when everyone else goes on a diet. They should observe there is no need to restrict when their weight has fluctuated upwards, because it will naturally stabilise back. And if you've decided it's best for them not to know their weight, they can at least note how their clothes feel only slightly tighter at times, and how that makes no difference to their looks.

Once this phase of recovery is achieved, should your child (and from here on, all health professionals) abandon scales and numbers? That would facilitate intuitive eating, balance and freedom of mind. On the other hand, our children may not yet – or ever – have this kind of stability. No worries – neither do most adults in our weight-anxious society.

We don't know yet if for your child, the scales will be a tool for relapse prevention, or an unnecessary legacy of the illness. You will need to work it out for yourselves, and the pros and cons may change with time.

My daughter has long known what her 'action range' is. I set it at plus or minus 1.5 kg around a weight that suits her – and of course the range has moved up as she got older and taller. The deal is that while she's in the range, she can eat intuitively and not pay any attention to fluctuations. A weight at the bottom of the action range indicates she's still safe and well, but she needs to consciously eat more. A weight at the top of the range would, in principle, prompt a review of her habits, or a check for a growth spurt. In her case I'm not sure that having a top number in her 'action range' was helpful, but she wanted to know we wouldn't let her get fat. For a long time she only fluctuated between the middle and the lower number – in other words the middle number was her psychological maximum. Very frustrating! But with time, the importance given to the scales seemed to fade as she observed, over and over, that weight just takes care of itself. I have yet to see if, after a few years of stability, it will be best to bin the scales.

ADDRESSING DEPRESSION, OCD AND OTHER ANXIETY DISORDERS

In chapter 12 I explain the role of psychotherapy as a possible adjunct to family-based treatment.

TRAUMA AND RE-ENGAGING WITH LIFE TO THE FULL

An eating disorder can isolate young people from the world for a significant chunk of their young lives at a time when they would normally be growing, exploring, socialising, experimenting, and generally doing all the things adolescents need to do. Some children transition to a full life without much trouble, dealing with life's ups and downs as well as any other teenager. Others need support to catch up or readjust, because their past experiences have affected their ability to live well in the present.

If you're getting Family-Based Treatment (FBT), this is the focus of Phase III.[190] In our case it was all very seamless. Our team had always strived for my daughter to have as normal a life as possible, even while prioritising meals. They were doing this before we were even considering what I now know is Phase II, returning appropriate food control to the child.

Sometimes the eating disorder and its treatment create their own trauma. When he's ready for it, your child might appreciate the help of a trauma therapist[191].

> *'I've been suffering from an eating disorder for 12 years now and it has been very traumatic, not only for myself but for my family. The fights, the daily stressful eating regimes, hospitalisations, illnesses, psychiatrists, lack of understanding, stigma, loss of friends, education, jobs and opportunities. The experience of an eating disorder is traumatic indeed.'[192]*

I suspect that all our children will experience some grief as well as celebration. Like explorers returning from the Himalayas, they've been affected by everything they've been through. Explorers write books and go on lecture tours. Some youngsters write poems or songs. There is a need to have witnesses, to be heard, to make sense of the past.

You shouldn't expect emotional healing to be done and dusted once and for all. Every now and again, your child will remember something significant – a joy, a memory that sparks gratitude or pain. I see this in my daughter when she recalls the kindness of a nurse on the ward or her distress around a particular event. Although I've mentioned the role of therapists, I want to stress how immensely precious we parents are to our children's wellbeing. We love them, we know how fantastic they are, and we listen, listen, listen with great compassion. If you notice you're getting defensive as your child recalls difficult times with you, seek out empathy for yourself elsewhere. If you're tempted to say 'Oh well, it's all in the past. You're OK now,' remember that your child doesn't need to be told how to think or feel. He needs a kind fellow human being by his side to witness, for a few moments, the depth of the emotions he's feeling right now. He'll be able to move on in his own good time.

NORMAL TEENAGE BEHAVIOUR OR EATING DISORDER?

Whether your child is 10, 16 or 22, it's sometimes hard to know whether a conflict has the eating disorder at its root:

- His aggression or isolation could be a sign that he's missing meals and/or experiencing a setback. Be vigilant.
- When he asks for something unusual, is it a real desire or an eating-disorder ploy to burn calories or miss meals? Guess, and monitor.
- If you don't like the behaviour and you think it's not eating-disorder-driven, I suggest in Chapter 14 how you use the same nurturing and structuring skills that you have developed around food issues. They're great skills, they deliver both compassion and boundaries, so why get into authoritarianism and punishments?

THE BALANCE OF AUTONOMY AND CONTAINMENT

Our daughter wanted to regain her autonomy in some areas before others. School meals were her priority. At age 11 she hated being supervised by staff and wanted the freedom to be with her friends at break times. Of all the times we let go of some level of control, this was the only nerve-racking one. If she missed one meal a day, we were sure this would quickly cause a relapse. But we had a major safety net in place in the form of the chief dinner lady. This amazing woman had never met us and had not been included in the training delivered by our clinicians, yet she had taken it upon herself to keep a discreet eye on our daughter. If she noticed the slightest sign that my daughter was leaving food, she told the Head. I'm glad I managed to thank her properly on my daughter's final day in primary school.

What other safety measures were in place? Well, my daughter knew she was being watched by some of the teachers. She knew her friends would raise eyebrows if they saw her throw away food, and she had a strong motivation to stop being considered anorexic. She knew that if she missed meals, it would show up in her regular weigh-ins, and that we'd reinstate the supervision. Finally, we asked her to be honest with us. This was a weak measure, as we couldn't be sure how much the eating disorder would drive her to lie, but it was part of getting back into normal life.

As she got better, my daughter started enjoying her friends, and soon she was eating at their houses or in cafés. There were times when we thought there was a significant risk that she wasn't eating enough while out with friends. On those occasions we would get her home for a meal then let her out again, or we'd suggest the whole group came to eat at our house. Sometimes we accepted the risk of her under-eating with friends. For her to be happy and enjoy outings was also part of the treatment. We'd tighten up on serving good food at home, and keep vigilant.

On the whole, eating out with friends did not seem to cause her any anxiety. If she didn't know how much to eat, she copied what the others were doing. But she needed us to provide containment. When she came home she would deliver a detailed account of her food intake and expect us to adjust the evening meal accordingly. We kept our reactions relaxed. We wanted to convey that a few crisps shared with friends were hardly worth mentioning, and that we didn't need the details of what she'd had in a café if it amounted to a normal lunch. Over the months, she had less of a need to give us an intricate account of her intake. I could ask her what she'd had for lunch in the same way as any parent would.

Where my daughter had absolutely no desire for autonomy was around her meals at home. For 12 to 18 months after we took control, she wanted us to continue making all the decisions for her. Yet at the same time she would look disappointed if at snack time we gave her an apple when she was expecting a chocolate bar. She didn't want to under-eat, because that would be a wasted opportunity to enjoy good food and because she didn't want to plunge back into anorexia (something she'd been quite clear about after weight-restoration). She was also using us as insurance against over-eating.

Because we saw signs of progress, we never saw any reason to rush her. We only tried to speed things up once, when she was due to go on a ten-day school trip and needed practice in serving herself breakfast.

Once she was well, we remained vigilant around her episodic enthusiasm for baking. It seemed to develop more and more into an art. As long as she was licking spoons and eating what she'd baked, I was relaxed. But I was even happier when she engaged in non-food-related hobbies, and I would have intervened if she'd chosen work related to food preparation or serving.

Eventually my daughter regained age-appropriate autonomy. The improvements were gradual and effortless, and as you can imagine, any noticeable change thrilled us. It's a real joy to see your child casually reach out for a second helping, or chuck a few nuts in her mouth as she walks past the kitchen counter. I'm not alone in remembering the first time my daughter said, 'I'm hungry!' If you're not there yet, I can tell you, it's more wondrous than watching your baby's first steps.

With her relapse at the age of 15, we re-adjusted the safeguards. For instance we asked the school to keep an eye on her during lunch, and she knew it. This would have been overkill earlier, when she seemed to be perfectly well. I guess that until the day you are absolutely certain your child is completely recovered, you will always be assessing risks and working out how to help her live a good life.

CAUTION VERSUS YOUR CHILD'S SELF-CONFIDENCE

As they start to improve on all fronts, our children often want to think of themselves as absolutely fine. Any mention of their eating disorder is deeply irritating. To them, it can sound as though they'll forever be labelled as defective. They would like us to acknowledge how far they've come and to share their newfound confidence. When my husband pointed these things out to me, I started questioning how best to balance caution and confidence. As parents, how much should we keep urging our children to be vigilant? How much should we swoop in when there are setbacks? How much should we remind them that they remain at risk?

A year into the illness, we latched on to our specialists' attitude. She considered we were on the right track, so that's what we reflected back to our daughter. *We're doing absolutely everything that needs to be done for you to be well. We're not worried. This is an exciting and positive time. You can get on with your life.* We still kept all the necessary controls in place. The day our daughter asked to join a friend's running club, we said no. When we had a specific request to make to keep her safe, we made it. When it was still useful for her to attend specialist appointments, we

LIFE RETURNS

insisted she go. But we avoided delivering lectures about how she was still at risk. We certainly didn't present her with images of a dismal future, should she stop being careful. Our vision has always been one of total recovery. Our attitude was that we were taking care of the present, and that she could engage with life with confidence, rather than holding back with fear. We made space for time to do its healing job.

As your child's eating disorder recedes, you can increasingly make space for them to experience life's riches. A virtuous loop is created as your child spends more time enjoying friends and interests and less time agonising over food and shape.

Would our daughter have been spared a relapse, age 15, if we had lectured her more? Probably not. And if the relapse was inevitable, I'm glad she had three years of happiness and relative normality.

FIXING YOUR CHILD'S MINDSET

You are probably familiar by now with how our children improve as we help them through their fears and get them to practice 'normal'. As healthy behaviours are repeated over and over again, the brain rewires itself, making those behaviours the new normal. It's like ever-deepening tracks in the snow. And at the same time the body and brain are getting the message that the period of famine (or irregular nutrition) is over, which allows normal functions (like hunger and fullness cues) to come back online.

All this takes time. It's rare for an eating disorder to disappear as soon as there's weight recovery. According to James Lock the rule of thumb is that it takes another 6 to 12 months. Also, it may take at least six months of regular periods before full cognitive functioning can return.[193] And even after that, many of us realise that although life is now pretty easy, and an outsider might spend a week with us and not notice anything wrong, our children haven't yet reached complete recovery. The eating-disorder mindset is hanging on.

We long for a therapy that could change our child's beliefs. They could realise that their body shape is great, that butter can go generously on toast, that food is lovely, that spin classes are boring and that weight takes care of itself. It's not enough to 'educate' our children. By now, they usually have all the intellectual understanding they need, and they have strategies to favour 'safe' behaviours over eating-disorder ones. But it's still a bit of an effort, because a non-rational part of their brain continues to pull them the other way.

To my knowledge, there is no therapy that can fix a mindset. When you've done all the work and are keeping your child steady and safe, the final tool in your box is just... time.

I'll come back to the magic of time, but first I'll contradict myself by mentioning two types of therapy that might, in principle, change someone's thoughts and beliefs. First there are body-based trauma therapies[194], which work on emotions and unconscious protective mechanisms without relying on the intellect. These do succeed in dispelling long-held safety beliefs – but nobody has studied if they help with eating-disorder thinking. Then there's CBT for eating disorders, which I describe in Chapter 12. Some therapists advocate a short round of this specialised CBT after family-based treatment is over, in the hope that this will get the young person to take responsibility for themselves. But I'm not sure this has any correcting effect on the person's thinking. CBT works on behaviours, just like FBT does, only this time it's for the young person to muster the willpower for change. To my knowledge, the approach doesn't directly transform the undercurrents of emotions that tend to hijack rational thought.

TOWARDS A RELAXED BODY IMAGE

With an eating disorder, most of our children feel very distressed about their body. Even if they don't have body dysmorphia – even if what they see is reasonably accurate – they have a strong emotional drive to be different. Boys might want a lot more muscle than is achievable or safe. Meanwhile girls, mostly, want to be thin (or, as a dietitian unadvisedly promised my ten year old, 'the thin side of normal'). With regular nutrition and weight restoration, their anxiety about this tends to abate. They become able and willing to use helpful behaviours (like regular and balanced eating) even though this goes against their desire to have a different body. The journey of recovery starts with tolerating their body, on to accepting it, and then towards feeling good in it, appreciating it and perhaps even loving it (when they happen to think about it, which is not that often because they plenty of other wonderful things in their life).

In Chapter 14 I will suggest ways to respond to 'Am I fat?' questions while our children are very distressed. Here I want to cover later stages, when our children are more capable of reflection and self-awareness. We are now able to use their 'I'm fat' or 'I'm puny' complaints to steer them towards more helpful and ethical attitudes. We can provide empathy, awareness-raising, and education. As body dissatisfaction is practically the norm in the general teen population, resources now exist which we can use to help our children.[195]

We can use these to first educate ourselves and work on our own implicit biases – it would be unusual not to have them, given the society we live in. Our children are watching and learning from us all the time, so we can model an inclusive, body-neutral, fat-neutral stance as we go about daily life. 'Neutral' in the sense that we don't draw attention to anyone's appearance – so if you've noticed a new bit of sagging in your face, come to terms with it privately. You might at times enjoy modelling body-*positivity* when you smile in the mirror and dye your hair bright purple and actively show appreciation for how a body serves us so well. When our children bring biology revision home, we can marvel at the intricate mechanisms of what makes us function. When we feel moved to comment on someone's looks, we can remark on their radiance, their big smile, their open, go-ahead posture, their visible wellbeing, and how they engage with us and with life. This type of beauty speaks to all of us more than any kind of 'look'.

We can have conversations about a movie, reality show or book : reflect on how the largest (often black) kid is either the bully, or the jolly sidekick – rarely the main character. How aspirational reality shows choose thin, mostly white people, while shows designed to make us feel superior to others pick on people in larger bodies.

We can ask, 'When you see selfies like this, what reaction do you have?' This discussion can lead to a reflection on attitudes in society, in school. As our children develop values of body diversity, they may notice how rigid and judgemental they are about their own looks. They may be curious about how they attach their self-worth to a number on a scale. They may question why they give such importance to their own appearance when they have greater values. This discomfort, this 'cognitive dis-sonance', is at the basis of some evidence-based programs to foster body ac-ceptance.[196]

So experiment with opportunities for modelling and for discussion, and see what works at different stages.

Like parents, therapists can have useful conversations to move our children's thinking along. Family-Based Treatment doesn't seem to directly address distorted thinking about shape. CBT for eating disorders does have a body image component. If any of this body work is offered to your child, and if your child is willing to attend, there is probably nothing to lose.

Pause to appreciate how much you are expecting from your child. You're hoping they will accept their body, when every few minutes, they are exposed to body-sham-ing messages from our toxic society. It's a big ask. And yet our children do grow and bloom. Often they end up with a healthier, happier attitude to bodies than their peers, their relatives, their teachers, and even their clinicians.

LETTING TIME DO THE HEALING

Given that we don't have a method to directly change someone's mindset, we should appreciate the healing properties of time.

When our daughter was discharged from treatment age 12, her life was great, but healing was not complete. She'd regained a little autonomy around meals with friends but still needed us to control her food at home. She had a couple of light obsessive-compulsive behaviours which we could not shift. She was confident and happy, but if we got distracted and let her go more than three hours without food, the old symp-toms made a brief reappearance.

I'm sure many parents can relate to the uncertainty of this period. It's hard to know whether to fight every small thing with more exposure work (often with dimin-ishing returns), or to trust that time will do the rest. In our daughter's case we decided, after taking advice from James Lock's team, to not rush her. We continued to be somewhat in charge of her food… and she continued to avoid leaning back in arm-chairs if she could get away with it. Gradually, normality crept in. I reckon she was completely anorexia-free between ages 13 and 15, though of course I cannot be sure of what was going on in her mind.

Then age 15, for no clear reason she was driven to cheat on school meals all over again. We took charge again and got a good handle on her behaviours and weight. But until age 18 her mindset remained somewhat anorexic. She would boast about the huge feasts she'd have at sleepovers, but we never saw any evidence of it. Her portion sizes at home, if she was helping herself, were always just a bit on the small side. Her eyes still anxiously flitted to our plates as she compared portion sizes. Her weight tended to slip downwards whenever it reached the mid-point of her healthy range. She convinced herself that if only we backed off, we'd realise she didn't have an eating disorder – that we were creating it. Yet whenever she had a trip without us, she lost weight. When alone, she knew she needed to eat more, but kept putting it

off to the next day. She hoodwinked us about her weight, getting herself more autonomy than she was ready for. Life was good, though, especially once her hardest
exams were over. She enjoyed her friends, delighted her teachers, and learned to relax
her drive to be a super-achiever. In short, she was doing great, as long as we continued
to be somewhat in charge.

And so, once more, we were scratching our heads, wondering how to help her
recover totally. What would free her mind? And what if she was deceiving us and was
actually a lot worse than she appeared to be? We looked for more exposure work to
do, but the last obstacles didn't seem to yield. For instance we repeatedly tried to get
her used to normal amounts of butter on bread, and we tried to serve grated cheese
on top of her pasta rather than on the side, but nothing much was budging. We
struggled with uncertainty, aware that in earlier times we'd have fought those particular issues more systematically and courageously. Now we let them go because, we
told ourselves, we'd already tried. Why invite conflict day after day, with very little
result, when overall things were really good? (Or were they? Was she tricking us?)
Like many parents at this stage, we weren't sure whether we were becoming soft, or
just realistic. Whether we were neglecting important treatment work, or allowing our
girl to heal by making space for the exciting life that was calling out to her.

This is a stage which many therapists don't see because the patients look and
sound great, and are back in their normal life. Only you, the parents, know the extent
to which you are keeping your child afloat. It's not a huge effort, but you want your
child to fly with their own wings and you don't have a method for that.

All this to say that you come to a stage where your main tool is time. Time is
your friend, if you are holding your child steady and not allowing them to backslide.
You keep the safety net around your child, you continue to be present to them, you
nurture connection, you model wisdom, you are the parent they need you to be for
their emotional age. You give them a longer leash and accept moderate levels of risk
so that they can experiment, grow, enjoy normality. And while you're doing all that,
you keep breathing to manage your unease with uncertainty, and you trust in time. It
helps to return to your own full life, which you've put on hold for so long. That brings
more normality and joy to the family, which surely is good for your child. And at
regular intervals you review whether there's anything else you should be doing, just
in case you've become complacent or have allowed yourself to be hoodwinked.
Hopefully, you will realise that your child is improving and that time is indeed a healer.

For my daughter, and for countless other young people, time really has provided
the final bit of the cure. The eating-disorder mindset dissolves. Our children can't
imagine ever sinking back into their old obsessional, distorted thinking. They don't
care about their weight, they eat heartily, and they roll their eyes when their friends
obsess about diet and exercise.

No doubt you want to know how long it will take for time to complete the healing process. It depends from where you start counting. And how well you are holding
your child steady while time does the work. It might depend on their age, since the
brain goes on maturing towards adulthood. It might depend on the level of ease or
hardship (exams don't help) in their lives. In our case, the last time my daughter had
to regain weight after a holiday without us, she was 17.5 years old. At age 18.5 she

left home for a local university. She'd been weight-recovered for more than six months and her mental state was good, though the eating-disorder mindset was not entirely gone. Had she gone to a distant university, I think she'd have been at significant risk of a setback. But she was close by, we enjoyed meeting up, and she knew we were keeping an eye on her. She seemed to get more and more secure in her wellbeing. She's 20 as I write this, and she seems totally recovered.

DEALING WITH RELAPSE

If there's one thing we parents absolutely do not want, it's to see our child relapse. Coming from our child, the words 'I'm not hungry' can send shivers up our spine. Some parents are in no doubt that they are suffering from post-traumatic stress (PTSD) and a relapse highlights the need to treat it. My husband's experience was the opposite: he gained new strength, seeing that relapse was easier to cope with than he had imagined.

Personally, I have had moments when I've told myself that I couldn't get back on that horse again. But as I allow my emotions to move through me, I get the image of a spiral staircase. We cannot be stuck in a 2D loop – life keeps moving us on in another dimension. Relapse is not the same as first time round.

One way in which relapse differs from the initial illness is that you can catch it early. Admittedly, all the symptoms are not clear-cut. If your teen says her thighs are too big, is it any different from the way her friends talk about themselves? If she says she doesn't need dinner because she and her friends had pizza on the way home, should you believe her? If she eats heartily after school, is it a sign she's incredibly well, or that she's skipping lunch? You might miss the first warning signs, but you should be able to pick up the pieces before you're faced with a full-blown relapse.

Some incidents signal a setback – a blip – rather than relapse. Even when she was well, some of my daughter's symptoms reappeared during holidays. They were mild and it was easy to take back control of her food ('You need to eat this even if you're not hungry'). This immediately brought her back to baseline.

When my daughter was age 12 to 15, her recovery looked solid. I saw happiness, an increasingly relaxed attitude to food and body shape, and stability. Then alarm bells started – there was something around her mood, her conversational topics, her concerns. Increasingly, she asked for one type of food in favour of another. The picture was blurred because there were plenty of occasions when she was her old carefree self, enjoying her food. This is similar to what had happened five years earlier, when she had reduced her food intake to a small extent and hadn't yet fallen into the anorexia whirlpool.

For a while my husband and I monitored, provisionally classified the situation as a 'blip' and only intervened in a moderate way. Until one evening a tearful outburst left us in no doubt that she needed a lot more support. It turned out that she had been reducing her lunch intake in school for a couple of months. She had lost a small amount of weight but was still in what we considered her safe range. All the same, the trademark thoughts and anxieties of anorexia had returned.

Why the relapse? Just like the first time, trying to tease out causation has raised more questions than answers. Perhaps risk factors related to her age were at their highest. Her weight had been well within what normally suits her. She was happy, we had a lovely relationship, she enjoyed her friendships and exams were not a big deal. Perhaps she was re-triggered by unpleasantness with the same close friend who had fat-shamed her first time round. Or perhaps the environmental pressures were just too high: her peers were talking of getting 'beach-ready' and she decided that eating a little less would do her no harm. What is noteworthy and sad, in terms of relapse prevention, is that she knew that restriction and secrecy were a route to relapse, and she still got sucked in.

If your child is in relapse, remember that a major ingredient of treatment is unconditional acceptance. If you think that she should have known better than to mess with her eating, you will blame her for being ill again. With my daughter, I don't have all the facts, I don't understand what went on in her mind, and I don't know if it's in her power to prevent this happening again. All I know is she didn't invite this illness in.

At times she has been heart-broken to be caught in the misery of an eating disorder all over again. She had really wanted it to be over once and for all. It is distressing for her to think that if it came back once it could come back again, and she wants confidence in the future.

If your child does experience relapse, what can you expect? In our case, it was relatively easy for my husband and I to step in, take control, and get her to eat what she needed. Part of her was determined not to get sucked into the anorexia whirlpool ever again. She had more self-awareness and a greater motivation tolerate the requirement to eat. She didn't need to gain much weight. And this time round she didn't suffer from an urge to keep moving or to be cold and hadn't developed any obsessive, compulsive or destructive behaviours. Almost immediately we were able to work on maintaining a wide range of foods. She seemed happy and lived normally but the illness stayed present, as demonstrated by her weight, which always dropped after entering her healthy zone. At age 17.5, when she returned from a holiday looking decidedly underweight, she admitted that she had cheated the scales for months. For the first time she took it upon herself to regain 10 kilos fast, and we only needed to give light support.

Our daughter was hugely resistant to any form of therapy, but some months into the relapse my husband and I sought support from an FBT therapist. It was an emotional need, because this time round we had plenty of knowledge. For six months this helped settle our minds, then the sessions stopped being useful and we were glad to continue alone.

During this period of relapse I had times of being grief-stricken at being frequently rejected all over again. I made myself to use friends more and made good use of the emotional resources I had grown first time round. I also sought out a therapist for myself, which put me on the path of more growth and happiness. As a result I have refined the tools I'm sharing with you. And in the end, our daughter got well again, and just like first time round, our beautiful connection returned.

I recommend you avoid trying to guess what the future might hold, and that you bring all your strengths to dealing with the present moment to the best of your abilities.

One parent wrote this shortly after her child returned home from hospital:

> *"No matter what ups and downs we may face from here on out, we are now educated enough that we won't ever be as 'caught unaware' of the dangers. We are now wise to the realities and the signs of this illness, and we will never again be as helpless and lost as we were when this journey began. There may be tough times ahead, and we know that — but I will never have to fear that I cannot help my daughter again. I know we can. We have. And we will continue to do so, with many more tools than we had before."[197]*

EVENTS THAT ROCK THE BOAT

Until recovery is truly secure, our children's instinctive response to stress is eating-disordered. We all hate suffering, but each event is an opportunity for our children to learn resilience while they're still safe at home, under our guidance.

> *"I have honestly come to embrace these sort of incidents because they show me how my daughter reacts to them. It isn't the reaction that is important but what happens AFTER the reaction that it is crucial to determine how healthy they really are at a particular point."[198]*

A typical adolescent goes through so many challenges: friendship issues, changing bodies, sexuality, existential questions, the drive to autonomy, hormonal upheavals. And until their early twenties they're saddled with a brain that has not yet fully reached its adult structure and that favours impulsive behaviour and emotional rollercoasters. On top of that, our teens go through several years of arduous exams, and the school reinforces the belief that low marks ruin lives.

With my daughter, we held her food and weight steady through her first major exam season, but we had limited power over the manic intensity which drove her to excel. She learned from her suffering, though, and in following years adopted a far more laid-back attitude to tests, which has served her well in university.

Illnesses can also rock the boat. Things can be going well when – wham! – your child gets a virus that interrupts regular eating – enough for old symptoms re-emerge. I know of a girl, recovering from many years of binge-purge anorexia, who kept suffering from one ailment after another. Once, after three days of high fever, she could barely eat:

> *"It was a big scare for us to see the anorexic talk coming back, but between us (herself included) we got her through it. My husband being firm. Me being patient and positive, giving her attention, and dealing with the ED talk calmly. And she held on to her motivation for her studies."*

Flu vaccination might be a sensible precaution with some children, and you could also push for your child to have a bit of a weight buffer.

If your child gets tired of suffering they may be open to psychotherapy. Never underestimate, though, your power as loving parents. More on that in Chapter 14.

RELAPSE PREVENTION, PLANS AND CONTRACTS

When my daughter was discharged at age 12, we discussed relapse prevention. As she never wanted to have anorexia ever again, she easily embraced these precautions:

- she would never leave more than three or four hours between meals
- she would eat normal quantities of food and never diet or try to lose weight
- she would be truthful about what she had eaten
- she would tell us if she detected any signs of a setback, and we would help her without blaming her

Another person might consider additional precautions such as:

- she will not purge
- she will not engage in certain levels of exercise
- if she has a big meal or binges she will still eat every three or four hours
- she recognises warning signs that will trigger various levels of support
- she might track her weight (or for added safety, have a third party do it) so it stays within a healthy range
- she might ask a few trusted friends to raise the alarm if they see warning signs
- she might get regular therapy

These discussions are useful, but they don't provide enough protection for you to completely step back. In my daughter's case she often said, 'Trust me, Mum. I don't want the anorexia to come back.' Or 'I wouldn't cut down on food. I hate feeling hungry.' Yet after three good years, something made her secretly skip a meal, and it felt rewarding enough that the illness took hold again.

If the eating disorder does return it will want secrecy. By its very nature, it will tell the sufferer that all is fine as long as nobody interferes. Relapse prevention needs the input of others. For my husband and I that meant:

- promoting our daughter's happiness
- maintaining a close, trusting relationship
- giving support whenever she went through periods of stress
- we were (overly) confident that we could recognise early symptoms
- whenever we detected a setback, we temporarily took back control of her eating (at a later stage, we would discuss it and she was able to self-correct)
- occasionally, depending on her current state, we did not allow her to exercise or bake, and we denied her meals out or sleepovers with friends

- we were alert to any illness or unusual situation that might cause her weight to drop

- our intention is to be vigilant during higher-risk periods (university, new job, pregnancy, stressful life events, etc.). Hopefully after a few of these we'll know if it's safe to let go.

We caught our daughter's relapse within a couple of months and the experience leads me to flag up a few more possible measures for your consideration:

- weighing your child every two months or so and checking progress on a growth chart

- monitoring purchases in the school canteen or asking staff to do occasional spot-checks

- asking your child's friends to raise the alarm

PREPARE YOUR CHILD FOR INDEPENDENCE

To get your child ready to safely leave the nest, take stock of all the things you are currently doing, and give them supervised practice to do it for themselves. Start several months before they're due to leave home. For instance:

- Food shopping, produce good meals without this triggering eating-disorder symptoms.

- Serving himself food regularly. He needs confidence around how much to put on his plate, and how often. The same with exercise.

- Weighing himself, not weighing himself, or having someone else weigh him – these are important individual decisions to make for as long as the risk of relapse is significant.

- Eating after a night of partying and drinking.

- How to avoid studying to excess, to deal with stress and emotions.

- Recognising signs of a setback, acting on them, and learning from them.

SAFEGUARDS AS YOUR CHILD LEAVES THE NEST

Is your child ready to leave home?

Is your child's recovery stable enough for him to safely leave home? Is the treatment finished? How's the preparation for independence going? Has he had, say, a good six months symptom-free? If yes, he's probably as ready as he'll ever be and you can be really positive. If not, the risk is that by Christmas he'll need to be rescued back into your care and he will miss out on the rest of the year.

I speak to parents whose child successfully stayed home for another year, perhaps attending a short course in a local institution or enjoying a part-time job.

I also speak to parents who are sure their child will benefit from moving on and hope that a change in life will spur on recovery. My view is that it's pretty unlikely that a young person will recover overnight just because they're excited by their course and love the idea of independent living. More likely, the eating disorder will continue to affect them to some degree. There are youngsters who stumble on through their university years, unable to fully engage because they can't eat with friends, are bound to a strict exercise regime, and get horribly stressed by exams. The parents try to monitor, guide and intervene from a distance, usually with patchy information. Or they try to not think about it and hope for the best. Either way they're in a constant state of anxiety. Far better, in my view, to let a year go by to secure recovery.

Safeguards if your child is not yet recovered

If you still think your child will benefit from leaving home, what safeguards can you put in place? Some parents consult the university health or counselling service with their son or daughter. Parents insist on regular therapy and get written agreements that the service will share particular types of information. They stay in touch frequently by video call and visit often. And they get tuition insurance in case it doesn't work out.[199] It's hard work for the parents. Whether or not it works for the young person, depends on how strongly the illness affects them, and how good the local services are. A word of warning: the hear-say is that most university health centres do not treat eating disorders effectively. How could they, unless there's daily help with meals?

Safeguards if your child is well

If your child seems, as mine did, pretty secure in their recovery, it's still important to discuss safeguards (even though they will protest that talking about relapse is demoralising). While my daughter was evaluating universities, we talked about what was easy, hard or risky, what might trigger a setback, what would be the danger signs and what action she would take. She felt very confident that the anorexia was over, but conceded that the illness is sneaky and that it was wise, for a while, to have a safety net. Visiting each other for pleasure would provide a natural low-level safeguard. She agreed that supervised weight checks might be sensible but didn't want our get-togethers to be tainted with a weighing. She came up with the idea that every couple of months she'd send me a video of her weighing herself. I reckoned this low-level check was appropriate – we could always insist on a surprise weighing if we had reason to suspect she was relapsing and cheating. Another safeguard we jointly devised was to open a joint account solely for her food shopping and keep it generously topped up. That meant she would be less tempted to skimp on food.

For her, a red flag would be if one missed meal, or one exercise session, led to more missed meals, more exercise. If she couldn't stabilise on her own after two or three repetitions, she'd let us know. She thought that having me text and enquire about her next meal would stop her wobbling any further. I told her that if an eating disorder made her push us away we would take charge, inform her tutors and bring her home.

In some families this type of discussion leads to a written plan, sometimes formulated with the help of a therapist. I kept things verbal, reasoning that if my girl was assaulted by an eating disorder again, paper would hardly be an effective weapon. I must confess that I felt apprehensive about talking about these things and kept putting it off. But it worked out nicely once my daughter realised we were searching for sensible safeguards together. For some excellent guidance on preparation for college and on relapse prevention contracts, see the endnotes.[200]

My daughter had a choice of two equally good universities, one local and one three hours away. If she'd opted for the second one, I'd have probably opposed it. She was well but I consider anyone's first year of self-sufficiency presents significant risks. I wasn't ready to do long journeys to satisfy myself of her wellbeing or to intervene. Happily, she chose the local university once she knew we'd fund her independent living. As I write this edit, she's sailed through her first two years without a hitch.

IS THERE SUCH A THING AS TOTAL RECOVERY?

'Recovery' is quite an emotional word for us parents, as this is something we want so very much for our children. Our wish list is ambitious and we don't know how realistic it is. We want our kids to maintain a healthy weight with ease. We want them to live free of eating-disorder thoughts, beliefs and behaviours. We want them to be as carefree with food as they were before the eating disorder struck. We want the illness to be a thing of the past and for the risk of relapse to go down to … well … zero.

Some people, on the other hand, talk of recovery in terms of a process rather than as an endpoint. They try not to get attached to a particular outcome that is not within their control.

It is wise to embrace reality, accepting its imperfections, while also being alert to opportunities for improvement. When you've done what is in your power (taking into account your internal and external resources), ask yourself if, at the moment, your child is living well.[201] You may not like that some of his symptoms remain, but can he control risk factors with ease? Perhaps that's perfectly good enough for now or even for ever. Perhaps some other time in the future will be just right for him to address more symptoms. Perhaps time will do the healing. For now, life is to be enjoyed.

> *"Our daughter (20) is now doing well. We still worry about her, but I guess we always will. She's still having acceptance and commitment therapy (ACT) with a clinical psychologist on a regular basis, and we keep a close but discreet eye on her."*[202]

There are people who are absolutely well but know that to prevent setbacks they must observe a number of precautions. Our kids can make friends with their vulnerabilities and learn to manage their eating. Isn't that common, in this imperfect life? A violinist with a wrist injury may enjoy a lifetime of playing, as long as she always warms up and takes breaks. Living with remission is not very different from normal life, and the wisdom our children gain in the process may well help them bypass the food and weight preoccupations of the average Westerner.

"Our son is now 16 and doing great, eating freely and enjoying sports. He takes charge of making sure he gets enough, understands that he CANNOT ever lose weight, and is several inches taller and about 70 lbs heavier than at diagnosis three years ago. Take that, anorexia!"[203]

I'm conscious that by sharing my daughter's story I may be reinforcing the common belief that relapses are inevitable. Yet research indicates that relapse is the exception. Once your child is symptom-free, she has quite a solid protection against relapse.[204]

There are clinicians whom I greatly respect who do not use the word 'recovery' even though they aim to get their patients to enjoy a full, symptom-free life. They consider that the risk of an eating disorder never goes away, that the biological nature of the illness means the vulnerability is always there, and that patients are, at best, 'in remission'.[205] Personally, I know so many stories of total recovery that I think it would be unnecessary demoralising for my daughter to believe she is forever at risk. On the contrary, I have told her that every month and year that goes by anorexia-free, is money in the bank for her brain's resilience.

I like to remember that genes are not a life sentence and that biology is not set in stone. The brain constantly changes itself. It is transformed by many factors that may or may not be in our control, including good nutrition, hormonal changes, the repetition of behaviours, and the resulting strengthening of neural connections.

Our trusted eating-disorders specialist used to say, 'I don't expect anything less than total recovery.' I translated this as 'back to normal'. We were discharged long before she could verify that her expectation would come to pass. While our intention is to live well with whatever life serves us, total recovery continues to our idea of 'normal'.

While an eating disorder is taking over your child's life, it can look like it's going to stick around for ever. But for many people that's not the case at all. If you'd like to read stories of hope, there's a collection of them on the Around the Dinner Table forum.[206]

What I got loud and clear from my daughter was that she needs us to believe in her. It was very unsettling for her to see doubt in our eyes. She found it unbearable to think that this illness may hang around and pounce back on her. She really wanted us to hold up the flag of hope.

WHAT'S THE FUTURE LIKE FOR THE PARENTS?

In our video-call sessions, parents often want to know if they will forever have to be vigilant or if one day it will be safe to consider their child completely recovered.

For me and many of the 'experienced' parents who help others on forums, life has become good. As I'll explain in Chapter 15, we may even benefit from post-traumatic growth. Some of us are glad to return to a version of our previous lives, while others, like me, are moved to embark on new journeys.

It might be wise to hang on to some vigilance for a few years, and the art is to dose is right and not give it too big a space in your mind. I remind myself that we have light, non-invasive measures in place to catch a relapse reasonably soon. We won't catch trouble as fast as if we were hovering 24/7, but that's OK in our risk-benefit equation because 'normal' is good for all of us. Who knows, perhaps our daughter has experienced minor setbacks and got the satisfaction of successfully dealing with them by herself. She is as knowledgeable about relapse prevention as I am. Should she fall again, I tell myself that we have skills and a strong connection that can see us through hardships.

Life, for each of us, has become sweet. It's been an absolute delight to see her enjoy independence, and at the same time to recover our loving closeness. I expect that if things continue to go well the eating disorder will move to a box labelled 'The Past' and we will let go of the last crumbs of vigilance. Nature is on our side, as the brain is constantly evolving towards its adult structure, which it reaches around age 23-25. Sometimes our girl reflects on how her mind is increasingly secure. I rarely find a need to enquire.

Very occasionally, my mind gives me a spike of fear. What if, in spite of her happy presentation and wise talk, our girl was once again busy hoodwinking us and secretly restricting? Usually, after bringing my compassionate attention to this fear, I decide it does not have a useful function, as it's not telling me anything we haven't already planned for. Once, my husband and I consciously shelved some worried thoughts because the answers were bound to come to light later during a family holiday (and happily, we saw that our daughter was truly well). I believe it's normal for parents to have moments of fear about children who have flown the nest, and it's our job to take care of ourselves and move on.

Sometimes, though, I have wondered if my instincts are alerting me to something that needs checking out. And so, on just two or three occasions over the last two years, I have willed myself to talk rather than walk on eggshells. For instance on one occasion I couldn't work out if she looked thinner. As she hadn't sent me a weight reading for a long time, I decided to ask her for one. On another occasion, I wanted to chat about how free and secure she now felt. Such conversations can upset her at the start because she wishes the whole thing was over for all of us. I empathise. I also explain that mostly I'm delighted by how well she is, and at the same time I would feel negligent if I didn't check when I had a niggle. She understands. Sometimes she gets in touch with her sorrow for her young self who had it so tough. She gives me the answers I need, assures me that she'd come to me if she was relapsing, and we move on. Who knows – maybe one of these conversations has given her a light wake-up call, if she needed one. Or, more likely, she truly was fine, and I got the peace of mind I needed.

In short, life after our child's eating-disorder can be wonderfully normal. Like any parent, because we love our child we sometimes get visited by the fear of what could go wrong. But by now we have skills to navigate uncertainty and manage our emotions (more in Chapter 15). Chances are you will spend very little time worrying, and a lot of time being happy and grateful that life is now delicious.

PARTNERS, FRIENDS, FAMILY AND
WORK: HELP OR HINDRANCE?

*How do you get your partner, your other children, your family, to
function well as a team? What about the outside world, with its money
and work concerns, and people who don't understand this illness?*

THE LOGISTICS: HOW CAN YOU CARE FOR YOUR CHILD AND ATTEND TO YOUR OTHER COMMITMENTS?

Caring for a child with an eating disorder often requires big changes in the parents' lives. This is easier for some of us than for others. Some parents are looking after their children singlehandedly. Some have acrimonious relationships with an ex. Some have other children or elderly parents who need a lot of care. Some are going through treatment for cancer. Even in conditions that look ideal (plenty of support, financial ease etc.), caring for an ill child turns your life inside out, and every parent needs recognition for their heroic work.

For some of us the illness hits so suddenly that all we have in place is emergency measures. We take temporary leave of absence from work, and worry that our employers will run out of patience. We stop activities that used to sustain us, and we stop going to the dentist. But as the saying goes, this is a marathon, not a sprint. How can you reorganise your life so it works for you?

I would like to help you step into a place of choice and personal power. Notice that your frustrations correspond to a desire to attend to what really matters to you. Acknowledge the tensions and give yourself compassion. Remember the acceptance that comes from 'shit happens'? Look at the cards that are in your hand right now. Many of them are horrible, so it's utterly understandable that you should be suffering. What can you do with your cards? And is there any way you can buy, borrow or steal some better ones?

If you look at your own situation, you may be able to let go of perfection. You may let go of any of the 'shoulds' you've read in this book. Being with your child 24/7 to check that she eats and abstains from bingeing or purging may not be for you. You may notice that the crisis has passed, and that you can now be reasonably sure that you can leave your child at home and that she will not self-harm, or binge or purge, and that she will eat what you've agreed she would eat.

I'm going to throw some random ideas at you to see if any help you with logistics. They come from parents who are married, single, divorced, full-time workers, freelancers, and whose young or older children are at various stages of the recovery journey. Some of the ideas may be completely inappropriate for your child's needs at present, but may nevertheless give you hope for a later stage.

- Both parents take a few weeks off work to attend to the early refeeding stage.
- One parent takes compassionate sick leave for an indefinite time period. The employer is sympathetic.
- One parent gets signed off work by their doctor for stress or depression.
- One or both parents change their work from full-time to part-time, or change to shift work so that there is always someone at home.
- The child goes into hospital for inpatient treatment or into a day-care centre.
- Parents lobby for their child to be moved from a distant hospital to a closer one. (In the UK, if you know of an excellent private treatment facility, your doctor may be able to arrange access to it free of charge.)
- One parent resigns from their job.
- Grandparents or friends are roped in on a regular basis.
- A trusted agency home carer regularly turns up for lunchtimes while parents work.[207]
- The school supervises daytime meals.
- Parents resume work full-time and support meals by phone or Skype.
- Parents lay out the lunchtime meal before they go to work, and their child is likely to eat this at home without supervision.
- The child spends some time at their parent's work.
- Parents organise regular paid help or make friendly arrangements with other parents, so that their other children get support with homework and taxiing to various activities.
- This is a great time to tell your other kids that their wish to abandon competition highland dancing is granted.
- Parents put a stop to therapy sessions that are not helpful.
- Parents require more therapy consultations to take place by phone or Skype, reducing driving time.
- Parents take turns to hold the fort at home while their partner does something for their own wellbeing.
- Parents delegate more. They get a cleaner, a gardener, a dog walker, an agency carer. If they are the main carer of an elderly parent with, say, dementia, this is a time to get state or private support.

- Parents put locks on cupboards and on the fridge, or lock away knives, so that if they need to leave their child alone they minimise the risk of bingeing or self-harming.

- Parents move their bed or their child's bed so that they can keep their child safe at night and still get some sleep.

- Parents find out what financial help is on offer from authorities (medical, social work) or charities. Transport to and from medical appointments may be funded, for instance. Social work services may pay for agency carers or may give you funds for you to use as you see best (e.g. housework, taxis, or private carers of your choice).

- Parents who cannot easily leave the house get regular emotional support by phone or internet. They use helplines, parents' forums or Facebook groups, or build a relationship with a couple of trusted friends or a counsellor.

- Parents let go of the crazy notion of self-sufficiency. They ask for exactly the help they wish for and trust that others get pleasure from helping.

SINGLE PARENTS

I'd like to acknowledge that caring for an ill child on your own is a massive task. You may long for practical help, and you may long for someone to unload onto at the end of a day – someone who can empathise with you. To me, these are absolutely essential to anyone's wellbeing. I hope that some of the suggestions in the previous section help you to work out how to undertake this journey in good company.

YOUR SPOUSE OR PARTNER

It takes a huge amount of teamwork to help someone recover from an eating disorder. Every day, your child goes through a massive internal struggle to get food in his mouth or stop bingeing or purging. Any disagreement or inconsistency between carers opens up the most irresistible escape route and slows down progress. Or, as some like to put it, an eating disorder likes to triangulate – to divide and rule.

Maybe you're in a loving relationship or maybe you signed your divorce papers five years ago. Either way, it's going to take some care to be on the same page.

Teamwork is precious

> *"Since I became more than just a father on the fringes and became
> actively involved, we have been able to support the journey to recovery
> for D and the whole family."*

My husband and I are close and we trust each other. Even so, in the early days there were times when all my self-confidence drained out of me because he disagreed with the amount of food I put on our child's plate. Or he disagreed with how I had talked to her. I saw myself as I (wrongly) imagined he saw me: incompetent, over-zealous, messing everything up. The rejection I experienced from my daughter further eroded my self-confidence. Once therapists gave us a road map, things got a lot easier, but still there were dozens of small decisions to be made every day. When we could, we made them jointly. Sometimes there was no time to consult each other, but we made time for discussion later.

After a long day of caring for our daughter on my own, I was surprised to notice that I had no urge to tell my husband about my day. I wanted to distract myself or catch up with some work. Yet he felt a need to catch up, and it was useful to relate various events so that our child couldn't say, 'But Mum doesn't put butter on my toast.'

Who's the weakest link?

Being a team doesn't mean you do equal amounts of the same things, that you are clones of each other. Caring for our children involves different skills and mindsets. At times, some of us are good at the day-to-day care, while some of us are movers and shakers, fighting to get the support we need from organisations.
A dad wrote:

> *"In the early days I was not that involved, and my wife did most of the ED stuff. It was not until the big relapse that I got to take a big role. In fact I kinda took the lead and found really good treatment. Now we are down the journey to recovery, the mum–daughter thing has become the day-to-day stuff, and I am more in the background, there to help whenever the need arises and also to be first response every now and then."*

Sometimes it makes sense to take on different roles because one is the main breadwinner, or because our children offer extra resistance to one parent in particular – often (but not always) the one who has the main, day-to-day caring role.

My husband and I had interesting fluctuations in the roles we took on. In the early days I admired his patience at mealtimes. When he was home, he did the mealtime support while I eavesdropped, trying to learn from him.

About nine months into our daughter's illness, I got terribly low, and whenever he was home it was a relief to have him handle meals, while I cried in my room and tortured myself with thoughts of my inadequacies. I really needed to hear from him that I was a valid partner in my own way. I find it interesting to note that however useless I told myself I was, I could take over and do a fine job if my husband showed the slightest sign of running out of steam.

Some meals can be exhausting to see through on one's own, and it was wonderful when we could give each other a silent signal that one of us was ready to take over to give the other a break.

As you're busy reading this book and looking for answers, I wonder if you're in a similar place I was in when I was hiding away in my room, crying, reading and learning. This was a time when I seemed fragile and weak, when I hung on to shreds of dignity behind dark glasses, when I felt ashamed that I could know so much yet do so very little. I now think of this as my chrysalis stage. I was learning the principles and skills that later helped us turn our daughter around. I became strong. I became the one who took the lead and drove changes.

Try not to end up with one 'competent' (and possibly martyred) person taking on all of the caring, while the other ('useless') person becomes de-skilled and excluded from their beloved child's care. There's a lot of shame and helplessness for the parent who's pushed aside, and this may exacerbate any tendency to depression or anxiety. The child gets the harmful message that one of their parents can't be relied on. The 'competent' parent, meanwhile, carries resentment on top of the exhaustion of full-time caring, and is at risk of burnout. Watch out for this common trap, which is nobody's fault, but comes with the difficulties of the illness.

> *"In the early days, I did most of the heavy lifting in terms of cooking, plating, supervising...and it was exhausting. My husband has some anxiety issues, and remaining calm at the table was not a strength! However, he was indispensable in other ways, most importantly keeping 'the home fires burning' by working to support us all, and doing activities with our son, among other things. When we were no longer in 'crisis' mode, he was able to support our daughter at the table, but only with some strong support on my end at first... I created daily meal/snack plans that he could follow. I admit I felt it was easier to do the whole thing myself, but our therapist encouraged us to try out the written meal plan idea.....and it worked! So I had to give up my notion that only I could prep and feed what was required....and the freedom and relief it afforded to be able to actually leave the house at meal/snack times was huge. So I am now a whole-hearted supporter of giving up all control, in order to avoid caregiver fatigue!"*

At times I have turned down my husband's help because I needed to 'feel the fear and do it anyway'. The best way of dealing with my suffering was to experience some measure of success.

If you're getting help from this book, you may be very keen to get your partner to read it too. And you may be disappointed if he or she doesn't engage. To me, our differences are what make good teamwork.

> *"My husband and I agreed not to disagree with each other in front of D and that he would support me in the plan. When he disagreed with me, I asked him to read the materials that I was reading and from which I was drawing my conclusions. He thanked me but decided to agree with me on whatever. He just couldn't deal with it. But he was WONDERFUL. He shopped, cleaned, took care of our young son, entertained D when she was distressed etc, while I researched, planned and fed our daughter."[208]*

Couples under pressure

An eating disorder puts quite a few stressors on couples. If you're in this situation, you might take heart in knowing that many people report that perfection isn't required and that bad times don't last for ever.

> *"My wife and I have been together for 26 years and the closest we came to divorcing was this past March, just before we went to UCSD's intensive multi-family therapy. We came back from there a team and it was like a fresh start and it has stayed good. FBT made our marriage better and has made me a better father."*[209]

One of the mothers I know recommends that couples put their relationship very high up their priorities, making time for communication, closeness and lovemaking. I recall she's the same person who put off essential dental treatment for the whole time her daughter was ill. So clearly, we can't do it all.

You might recognise some of these common stressors.

- You may disagree on whether your child has an eating disorder or whether this is a passing phase. If your spouse seems to be 'in denial', be aware that this may be the best way he or she has, at this moment, to handle the terror and the deep grief that comes from seeing a previously brilliant child change so drastically.

- You may disagree on how best to tackle your child's behaviour. You might be convinced that refeeding and exposure is going to save your child's life, while your partner may truly believe this will, on the contrary, destroy any chances of recovery.

- You may disagree about which clinicians you can trust, and whether or not to follow a particular therapist's advice. For example:

> *"Neither the psychiatrist nor the psychologist understood anorexia. They kept telling us to back off, blaming me for interfering when my daughter kept losing weight. After a year, I fought the system, until we were at last given access to the specialist eating-disorder service, and my daughter improved. Through all this, my husband has blamed me for rocking the boat. When the psychologist put obstacles in our way, he got really cross with me. He thought surely a professional knew better than us. And he was scared we'd end up with no medical care at all. I've done all the moving and shaking on my own. I had to do it for my daughter's sake, but it's been lonely."*

- Each person is too raw, too tired, too depleted, to be able to give the other the enormous amounts of empathy needed. As a result, they may easily be triggered by what they perceive as criticism or a lack of support.

- For some it is nearly impossible to get time alone as a couple, because their child is at risk of self-harm or suicide and needs a trusted adult nearby at all times, including at night. Where I live, the health authority or social services would provide respite care if your dependent loved one was a parent with dementia. We need at least as much support when we're caring round the clock for a child.

- Each person wishes they could be more effective. They imagine or notice that their partner resents them for having screwed up.

  "In the early weeks/months when my husband was blaming me, I repeated, 'None of this is my fault or your fault. We are doing the best that we can.' When he said, 'It's because you put cheese in it,' or, 'It's because the glass is too big,' or whatever, I just repeated, 'It seems like that, doesn't it, but it isn't about any of those things. What it is about: ED finding any way to avoid letting our daughter eat. This is nobody's fault — it's just the way it is."[210]

- There may be new imbalances, as one person becomes a carer while the other becomes the sole breadwinner. One dad wrote:

  "I have taken all my leave and went part-time for three months to support refeeding. My boss has advised that he's lost some trust in me. So I have had to focus more at work. Life will be even harder if I lose my job. My wife and I discussed role clarity. She is now full-time mum and carer for my daughter. I work and earn, and provide support to my wife as well as our children. I still feel guilty that my wife carries the burden."

- Some parents who've been apart for a long time, and who have coped by keeping communication to a minimum, now find they have to work together for their child's sake. Sometimes there is a lot of anger when one parent sees the other one 'messing up' all their hard work.

- It's easy to be wonderfully compassionate with the stranger at the supermarket checkout; it's a lot more challenging with a family member in whom we've invested so much emotionally and practically, and in a situation where so much is at stake.

- Eating-disorder concerns have taken over for so long and with such intensity that the couple forgets to nurture the relationship.

Compassionate communication within a couple

It may not be possible to find solutions to every stressor in your relationship. And I don't believe it's essential to do so, as long as you are both able to talk to each other and feel understood.

Some parents have distressing stories to tell about their ex-partners, and what I read between the lines is that both parties are worried sick about their child and are using incompatible strategies to cope. What they do have in common is love for their child. This is the foundation to build on to agree on better strategies.

Check out the Nonviolent Communication tools I offer in Chapter 13.[211] They are relevant to communication with anyone, not just your child. They will help you understand each other, have compassion for each other, express what matters to you and find solutions that work.

So, for example, if your communication tends to be a bit like this: 'You don't give a damn about us! After all I do for our child, day after day, you just go and mess it up in one single day by letting her just eat carrot sticks. You've always been totally irresponsible!', you might get into the hang of expressing your intensity more like this: 'I want us to support each other. What happened with those carrot sticks? What can we do to make this work?'[212]

Help for partners in conflict

I believe that with an eating disorder, we're living in such demanding times that each partner needs outside sources of empathy and support. We need time with friends or therapists. Someone who is there just for us, whom we don't need to take care of.

> *"Our teamwork was great, but my husband really needed me to*
> *listen to him and provide emotional support, but I just couldn't do it.*
> *I was wound up so tightly that I couldn't give him any support. So*
> *we both started seeing a counsellor separately. It helped us a lot."*[213]

If you're in conflict with your partner, make sure that the outsiders you choose for support listen well and don't take sides. You are the expert in your situation.

Family therapists may provide sessions without the child, to support a warring couple and help them get on the same page. Or you could use a relationship counsellor. Personally I might also look for a trainer in Nonviolent Communication who does mediation, because they have the tools to give people the compassion they so need and to help them reach effective solutions.

SIBLINGS

I have only one child, so when it comes to the effect of an eating disorder on siblings, I can only share what I've learned from others.[214]

- Within family therapy, siblings are included in sessions because the philosophy is that the whole family is affected by an eating disorder; everyone needs support, and everyone is offered a role in the treatment. After a while, siblings may lose interest in attending sessions, but the main job is hopefully done by then. They need to hear they're not responsible for their sibling's illness, nor for their parents' distress. They should not be asked to help their sibling to eat, nor to spy on their sibling's eating in school. On the other hand they are encouraged to behave like anyone would when they see their brother or sister is distressed: with kindness, listening, hugs or doing fun things together.[215]

- Siblings need an appropriate level of education about the illness, and this will help them step out of the blame game. Work out what to tell them and how.[216] They will be picking up on all kinds of myths from peers and the media. They may become more guarded around friends if they notice any stigma around their brother or sister's illness.

- Siblings are very significantly affected, and how they're affected varies hugely from child to child, and over time. Some kids are very upset and want to help, some are scared and withdrawn, some become fed up with or distressed by the high-intensity behaviours of their siblings and some hate that family life has been turned inside out. Some feel horribly guilty because they tell themselves that they're somehow responsible for the illness, or that they could do more to help their sibling get well. They can also feel ashamed of their own outbursts, knowing that these make life harder for everyone. They need your unconditional love and acceptance, same as your ill child.

- Sometimes siblings behave in ways that make caring for the ill child harder. For instance they might comment about the amount of food served up at dinner. Perhaps they don't know better, or they're deliberately stirring up trouble. All our children need unconditional love and acceptance, and in my opinion they need more of it, not less, when they give us unwelcome behaviour (see Chapter 13). Siblings can also make things harder through no fault of theirs, when the ill child cannot bear to eat more than their brother or sister.

- Siblings have needs just like anyone. I guess that needs for security and stability and hope and fun would be particularly acute (I list typical needs of children in Chapter 13). Those needs don't need to be met exclusively by you, the parents. For instance you may not have the time to teach your child to drive, but your friend or sister might thoroughly enjoy doing so. And while mealtimes are full of drama, it can make perfect sense to allow a sibling to eat in another room or to spend more time with a trusted relative or friend.

- Siblings can be scared and upset to see their parents struggling to cope. They may minimise their own needs in order to reduce their parents' burden, telling themselves their parents are too busy or overwhelmed. The trick is to meet your child's deeper needs so that he can safely stretch in relation to everyday frustrations. So let your child see that you care, that you love him, that you do have plenty of emotional space for him, and that you are frustrated that you cannot give him your attention exactly when he needs it. Make it clear that you are resourceful, that you continue to be his loving and emotionally available parent, and you do not want him to 'protect' you by hiding his troubles. See if you can walk your talk by having at least one parent schedule regular one-on-one time with him.

- Empathic siblings may find themselves supporting you more than is appropriate to their age, capabilities and needs, so take extra care to get your emotional top-ups from other sources. Children can be very caring and they can believe that they're responsible for making us happy. They feel guilty or worried when they don't succeed. I learned to tell my daughter what was going on for me so that she didn't feel responsible for my foul mood, at a time I was overwhelmed with my elderly mother's needs. I tried to make very specific requests ('I'd like to collapse with a cup of tea and not have to check you're ready for your sleepover. Would you pack your bag and be ready to leave at 6.00 p.m.?' or 'Before you switch on the TV, I would love one huge hug!'). The idea was to spare her the misery of guessing what might next make me yell or cry.

- For a long time I imagined I was lucky to only have one child to care for when things were tough. Yet what I'm getting from other parents is that they couldn't do without the normality and companionship they get from their other children. This reminds me how wrong I can be when I'm trying to guess what's going on for others.

PREVENTION FOR YOUR OTHER CHILDREN

Because of the genetic component of eating disorders, parents fear for their other children. Siblings may be worried to that this illness will one day affect them. It seems that the risk is pretty low, and I'll suggest how you can further reduce or manage it.

If you are fearful, it may help you to remember that extra hardships don't necessarily make us weaker (more on this in Chapter 15). Resources often come as we need them. I have been humbled to discover how even with two children with an eating disorder, parents do manage, with ups and downs, same as the rest of us. I suspect that resilience has less to do with the number of affected children than with the support systems.

The few statistics we have – and they focus on anorexia – are hopeful.[217] Even with identical twins (who share the same genes), the chances of both getting anorexia is 'only' around 55 per cent. And with fraternal twins (where half the DNA is shared), this drops to 5 per cent. If your children are not twins, it is unlikely that two or more will have anorexia.

Genetics and environment are intertwined, so is there something parents or schools can do to reduce the risk of a child getting an eating disorder? Keeping weight and nutrition stable might be the best you can do. Scientists are still very unclear about causation, because when they look at the kinds of risk factors most of us think about, they find nothing or they get contradictory results. For instance, from a recent review of many studies,[218] it turns out that the only risk factor that predicts the onset or anorexia is low body mass index (the studies didn't look at genetics). The risk factors for bulimia are closer to what you'd expect: thin-ideal internalization, perceived pressure to be thin, body dissatisfaction, dieting, and negative affect (depression). For purging disorder, the only risk factor is dieting, and for binge eating disorder, not a single risk factor has been found with any level of certainty. A more recent study[219] suggests that weight in early childhood might be an indicator of genetically-driven metabolic factors linked to an eating disorder. You might want to be extra-vigilant if your toddler's weight was particularly low or high (as early as age 2 for boys and 4 for girls) or if it jumped off (downwards or upwards) its normal growth curve. These might be indicators of adolescent anorexia and bulimia respectively.

A small number of school programs that address body dissatisfaction have been shown to reduce disordered eating and eating disorders – with the exception of anorexia.[220] These programs sensitise us to how much 'weight talk' or 'fat talk' is around us – that's talk about diets or body shape, and comments on our own or other people's weight. Correlations – but not causation – have been found between 'weight talk' and disordered eating and higher weights.[221] Children take to heart messages from their parents and we can practice disengaging from weight talk.[222] Even so, this may not protect your child from an eating disorder.

Talk of prevention can trigger guilt and grief in parents, so let's acknowledge that we love our children and would never knowingly give them substandard care. It would be remarkable if parents and children were not affected by the disordered-eating, fat-phobic norms of today's world. A fish is not aware of the water it swims in. But we parents can become wiser to the messages out there, and our children can grow the ability to stay sane when all their friends are on diets.

Even with these precautions and the benefit of hindsight, prevention is a mystery. A child can grow up with a perfectly fine body weight, in an ethos of self-compassion, intuitive eating and positive body image, and still get hit by an eating disorder. Myself, and many other parents, would put their son or daughter in that category. Conversely your child probably has friends whose parents do the exact opposite, sometimes to extreme degrees, and the child doesn't have an eating disorder.

Whether or not it helps with prevention,[223] happiness levels will surely increase if you model both body confidence and intuitive eating[224]. I also believe that that we build our children's internal resources by modelling or teaching self-compassion. It's more powerful than bolstering self-esteem.[225]

As at present there is no sure-fire way to prevent a child from getting an eating disorder, we can be vigilant about early detection and intervention. We can take care to adopt habits that would make it easier to detect and treat an eating disorder. We can react to unusual weight gain or loss, and deal promptly with restrictive or irregular eating.

For instance you could favour family meals (which in any case have been shown to bring all kinds of benefits to youngsters) and not leave a child to eat on their own. You might take extra care to nurture a relationship where your child can trust you with their concerns. You might pay particular attention to fostering emotional intelligence, so that they have skills for dealing with difficult feelings. You might address any early signs of anxiety or OCD. You could try and shield your child from triggers while they're at a vulnerable age. You could watch that he eats more when he is having a growth spurt, when he's taking part in extra sports, or after an illness.

It might be wise to keep records of your children's height and weight in their early years and plot them on a growth chart. A significant deviation from their normal growth curve would be a warning sign. If your child, sadly, did develop an eating disorder, the historical data would help set realistic expectations for a healthy weight. We hardly had any pre-anorexia weights for our daughter, partly because that's the way the UK health system works, and partly because I wanted her to grow up free of weight concerns (the best-laid plans!).

Without getting obsessive about it, it must be possible to weigh and measure a child a couple of times a year, quite casually. Children are usually pleased to see how much they've grown so you could keep the focus on the height measurement.

I'll add one more thought for those of you in countries that don't have a free health service. If there are eating disorders in your family genes, choose your medical insurance with extra care to make sure you pick one that pays for more than a few hours of therapy.

FAMILY AND FRIENDS: HOW TO MAKE GOOD USE OF THEM

We need others

Support, compassion and understanding, are major human needs. Society may be in awe of hermits, and Jean-Paul Sartre may have declared that 'hell is other people', but why would anything be hell unless we cared about it? Research has shown repeatedly that human beings thrive on connection. Connection nurtures a compassionate state, which will help you be kind to yourself and to your child.

If you're used to leaning on friends and asking for help, you'll be going, 'Duh!' But please be patient with the rest of us who now need to unlearn the self-reliance habits of a lifetime. This illness has taught me to open up, allow myself to show my vulnerabilities and enjoy the fruits of human connection.

As I edit this book, I am seeing my mother's health deteriorate in heartbreaking ways. I have been amazed by how smoothly I have dealt with a succession of huge emotions and each time regained my stability. I think it's because I have literally cried on other people's shoulders.

This is a perfect time to allow yourself to be vulnerable and seek support. I don't know about you, but while my child was ill, I never felt any shame about my suffering. Most people can understand that when your kid is starving, you suffer. You're allowed to crumple. In my case, if anyone thought I was a wimp, I wasn't aware of it. There were one or two parents who knew about my daughter and failed to give me eye contact at the school gates, but I assumed they didn't know what to say and didn't want to cause me grief. If anyone saw me red-eyed, I trusted they wouldn't judge me for it. I bet they were thankful they weren't in my shoes.

There are many parents who are very isolated and who sense that friends or family have let them down. If you need help with this, I wrote a piece about it on my website:

How we lose the very friends who should be supporting us (anorexiafamily.com/lose-friends)

Self-compassion is powerful, but there's nothing to beat a really wise, compassionate friend or therapist listening to you. Their listening helps to guide your thought processes, and there is also a healing quality to being witnessed. Before you reach for antidepressants, and before you sink into despair, try getting another human soul to hear you.

Heartbreak concerning a child is nearly impossible to deal with on your own:

*"It sometimes takes only one old friend to affirm for you that you
have always been a loving mum and your child used to be a happy,
healthy, blooming child."*

If you're longing for help, use people's strengths. Pick up on what they're offering to do for you. If they're not offering, go ahead and ask, making it clear you expect
them to say no any time a task doesn't suit them. Trust that, far from being a burden,
you're contributing something to them. Humans seem wired up to connect, to contribute, to engage in meaningful work.

*"My mum has been a fantastic help – I often worried about
involving her as it was very distressing and stressful to supervise my
daughter. She has since said that being asked to help meant so much
to her as she could see we were struggling and also she and my
daughter have become very close as a result."*

You never know what a gift you're giving someone by asking for their help:

*"My mother has told me that she feels she has had a second chance
by helping with D, as I went through similar problems at that age
(genetics!) and she had always felt that they had not dealt with the
situation very well or helped me through it. So whilst I worried
about causing her too much stress, it has actually helped her to lay
some issues of her own to rest."*

Sometimes, people help simply through their presence. When friends or grandparents show up at mealtimes, some children let go of their usual violent behaviours,
for instance. Some people might love to support you with a listening ear, some might
get great satisfaction from shopping and cooking for you (personally I think that's
weird), and some will be delighted to get on the internet and the phone on your
behalf. Ask them to network for you, to research treatments, to root out sources of
practical or financial support, or to sort out legal aspects. Some friends may support
you regularly, while others may be there for you at just one critical moment.[226]

*"My starving and dehydrated D was hysterical and delusional. She
was howling, 'You're not my mum!' I had locked the door to stop her
running away and I felt completely stuck. I had a brainwave and
phoned a neighbour. I just said, 'Hi, I could really do with your
company for a short while. Please could you come right away?' My
D fled to her room out of embarrassment. Her hysterics stopped.
The neighbour sat with me, in her pyjamas, smiling and generous
and full of stories of her travels. After 20 minutes, my D joined us
and we had a really good time."*

I know a single mother who gets emotional and practical support via a
WhatsApp group she created just for the purpose, as she could not get any understanding from her own relatives. If you're not getting the depth of connection you
long for from people in your usual circles, I suggest you go hunting outside your

usual comfort zone. There are groups of people who will stay with you through your tears, who don't want to know the details of your problems, who have no urge to give advice, who are comfortable with silence, who can fill you with compassion with a loving gaze or with warm hugs. The words these groups use to describe their activities might include 'mindfulness', 'spirituality', 'holistic', 'connection', 'heart' and so on. Some will not be your cup of tea, but you have the choice to keep searching till you find something truly nourishing.

Who to tell about the eating disorder?

If we listened to our children's wishes, the eating disorder could easily become the family's shameful secret and we'd close off all possible sources of support. We'd also be doing nothing to destigmatise eating disorders. So we have to decide who we share our truth with, and to what extent. There's no right or wrong decision, and I'll share some thoughts to help you find your own way.

Our children fear being judged as stupid, bad, or weak (because they're starving or purging, or because they're not ill enough)

> *"If people in school find out I have anorexia they'll say, 'But look at her, she's not even that skinny!'" (From a girl who bravely managed to maintain a healthy weight with the help of her parents.)*

We should assume that when we use words like 'anorexia' or 'bulimia' or, 'binge-eating disorder', what this conjures up in the other person is a cocktail of judgemental and insensitive nonsense. Be honest: you used to believe it too, right? So if we tell someone our child has an eating disorder, we have to give a short explanation of what an eating disorder is and isn't.

I had a lot of sympathy for my daughter wanting me to respect her privacy, and I also knew that I needed some people to be in the know because they could help keep an eye on her or support me. The first step is to avoid energy drains:

> *"I never told my mum. She'd have phoned me every hour for news and I'd have been the one comforting her."*

> *"My mother-in-law started giving me advice, because she'd read ONE (out-of-date) book on anorexia. After that I told her as little as possible."*

My world looked like a series of concentric circles. At the centre was our daughter, me and my husband. The next circle included a very small number of family members and people like therapists, whom I'd chosen to support me. They heard my fears and my distress, they heard some of the stories that illustrated what life was like for us, and some of our dilemmas. I trusted that they accepted us unconditionally, that they didn't judge or gossip. From them I received love, encouragement, validation, some useful advice, and occasionally, practical help. When I spoke to them on the phone, I did so out of my daughter's earshot. She was aware that they knew about her illness, and although she didn't like it, she accepted it. I told her that adults need support, and that I was careful about whom I talked to and what I said.

The next couple of circles included other family members, some friends, neighbours and parents of my daughter's friends. These people knew my daughter was ill because otherwise life would have been very complicated. How else could we account for months in hospital? How else could I ask people to remove bathroom scales or to report back to me what my daughter had eaten when she went for a sleepover? With these people, I tended to keep the information rather general, leaving out the anecdotes, the juicy details. I put myself in my daughter's shoes and asked myself if they were likely to understand or if they might judge or gossip. I described her condition as an illness, a disorder of the brain, with a genetic component.

There is an intersecting circle, which includes people I talk to through eating-disorder networks, as well as you, my reader. I decided you needed some of our stories to support you on your own journey, and I use my pen name to protect my daughter's privacy. Even then, I want to respect her dignity, and so I make choices about what I share.

And finally there is most of the outside world – people who need never know about my daughter's illness. She wants to lead a normal life. She doesn't want people scrutinising what she eats, wondering how she is now, and perhaps gossiping. I'm totally on board with that.

How much should your child's friends know?

My daughter told her friends about having anorexia around the time she went into hospital. It seemed quite natural to her. They were all ten at the time, and their concern and kindness were, at times, heart-warming – to her and to me. The hospital and school linked up so that she occasionally received a group letter from her class, and one friend regularly wrote her hilarious notes. It was an important way of keeping her connected to a healthier world, when hospital was in danger of feeling like the only safe place.

A few years later, even at a time my daughter visibly lost weight again, the same friends were paying zero attention to her history (which tells me they had not pigeon-holed her as vulnerable or weird). They were talked freely of diets and thigh gaps..

My daughter absolutely did not want them to know of her relapse. She said she enjoyed being normal with them. She didn't want to be constantly reminded of the eating disorder. I understand this but I also think that if you're serious about relapse prevention, friends are part of your safety net. If one of these girls had told me that my daughter was having nothing but flavoured water for lunch, the relapse might have been no more than a blip.

There's no right or wrong answer to the question of how much to involve your child's friends. Here are a variety of views from other parents.

> *"In my opinion most tween girls are not mature enough to handle this kind of information. I frankly wish my daughter had not told any of them – at that point in time, anyway."*[227]

"Keeping it secret felt like we were opening D up to gossip. I explained the situation and condition to her closest friends, sports team, school and family while she was in hospital (with her permission, after discussing pros and cons) and have never regretted it. I explained how the disease made it difficult for D to choose to eat etc. Having all these people know has increased the circle of safety for us. In the early days, her friends were quite comfortable to text me that D had eaten, and several times they told me of problems at school. D understood that they would do that because they cared for her. For me it was worth the risk of a couple of ignorant idiots."[228]

"I think your feelings can change as time goes on and your D gets better, so my advice would be to only tell the people you absolutely need to. I agree there shouldn't be any shame with it, but let's face it, I don't want my kid to be known as 'the anorexic'."

"I thought it was great that D told her friends, until one day at school when she was pooping she looked up to find two of the girls watching her from the next stall to make sure she was not 'puking or throwing food in the toilet'. She was mortified."

LINKS WITH OTHER PARENTS IN THE SAME BOAT

I now know many parents of children with an eating disorder, but while my daughter was ill, I wasn't particularly well linked up – something I regret.

In the endnotes I recommend a number of online parents' forums, I tell you how fantastic they can be, and also suggest some precautions.[229]

"Although we were fortunate in having a good hospital, FBT therapist, supportive local family and friends, it was only on [the FEAST] site that I found experience, advice and insight from others actually 'in the trenches' and available at any time. It was truly life-saving for my daughter and sanity-saving for me."

You might also find a group that meets regularly in your area. Our own eating-disorder service set one up while our daughter was in hospital. We chose not to go, partly because meetings clashed with musical get-togethers that were nourishing, and partly because we were convinced that our stories would scare everyone else. Now, I believe that we all have plenty in common, and in any case, a competent moderator should ensure that talk doesn't degenerate into a fear fest.

Keeping your partner in the loop

Your spouse or partner may be uncomfortable with you receiving advice from others. Who is this person who writes you long emails, who knows rather a lot about your life and who might be responsible for the new approaches you insist on trying?

The two of you are the ones driving the bus. You need to be a team. If you're being influenced by others, your spouse should know about it and you should be able to discuss options together.

Supportive friends should offer a listening ear, not opinions. You and your partner are perfectly capable of sorting out your differences – you just need your cup of compassion filled. Consider difficulties not as a conflict where you take sides, but a joint dilemma.

WORK AND MONEY

In the UK, where I am, we are incredibly lucky that health care is free. It makes me feel quite good about paying taxes. My heart breaks for parents in countries where therapy costs are enormous, where treatment is often cut short, and where insurance companies need to be fought. Many of you in the United States have serious hoops to jump through.[230] I am distressed for the millions of parents in poorer countries who cannot save their children for lack of money. I am appalled that even rich countries do not put sufficient resources into the health care of young people.

Even when health care is free, an eating disorder can drain your finances. My earnings halved while our daughter was ill. Even though we didn't experience financial hardship, I still caught myself resenting how little I was earning. My tensions would bubble up whenever I discovered how much it cost to visit a psychotherapist. At one stage, when I was questioning the effectiveness of my daughter's treatment, I researched the possibility of using a private eating-disorders clinic. Suddenly I felt like a second-class citizen, facing astronomical costs for care, which at the time I blindly assumed would be superior.

My hang-ups around my loss of earnings were sometimes a cover for more personal issues, which I labelled as selfish or shallow. I didn't like neglecting my freelance business and losing the 'me time' work provided me with, yet this seemed trivial when my daughter was suffering. But there's nothing trivial about losing a source of stimulation, satisfaction and companionship. Life in carer mode can feel like a monotonous round of meals, stormy challenges and being on standby. I didn't choose for my child to be ill, but once I'd accepted that reality, I recognised that spending days in 'mum' mode was a choice I was making because it mattered to me to care for my child. If you've grown up with feminist ideals, as I have, it can also take time to get to grips with the notion that you're the main carer while your husband is the main worker. That too is a choice.

As more recently I put work on hold to deal with my daughter's relapse, I was conscious of how privileged I was to be in a position I could help her. Gratitude seems to be overriding my previous hang-ups about money and marital roles.

Money can be a tense topic even at the best of times, and it can get mixed up with all kinds of convoluted thoughts and emotions. It may help to put money back where it belongs: it's a tool, a strategy that helps us meet our needs. There may be other strategies out there. There might not, but we can't be sure while our agitation is muddying the waters and closing our minds to possible solutions. We think we're stuck, but if we make time for mindfulness, options may come up.

- You may be able to negotiate with care providers and insurance companies.

- You may be able to access finances or care from authorities such as social work services or the health service.

- Private therapists may reduce their fees once they know about your financial constraints. Psychotherapists often work that way.

- Private therapists may give you a free trial session. This may give you an idea of how effective and efficient treatment might be.

- You may not need as many sessions as you think; some may be spaced out over a longer period of time, and perhaps phone or Skype sessions are cheaper with some therapists.

- Family and even strangers may genuinely want to help you financially. You may be strapped for cash, but there are people out there who are comfortable and like to see their money put to good use. You may value your independence and autonomy, but consider that interdependence makes the world go round. It gives people genuine pleasure to help others, and money can be a good tool to do so.

Here's an example of some out-of-the-box thinking from Cathy, whose 25-year-old daughter is fully weight-restored and 'at least half-way motivated to recover'.

> *"We hired a recovery coach. This woman is a certified yoga therapist who has a background in mentoring young women with personal development and has also worked with disordered eating clients. They really hit it off. They have done yoga therapy, restaurant outings, and clothes shopping – all went very well.*
> *My daughter was convinced that she could never wear jeans again (especially skinny jeans) and has body image issues. Well, on the shopping outing, the recovery coach convinced her otherwise.*
> *The recovery coach will work with my daughter for about 12 hours per week. Her fee for those 12 hours is about the same as two hours of therapy sessions with a therapist.*
> *The way I look at it, what do we have to lose by thinking outside of the box?*

Cathy's intention wasn't to replace therapists with coaches, but she found an unusual and affordable form of additional support. And how did this creative thinking come about? It suddenly hit her that:

> *THIS IS MY LIFE. And you know what? It's not really all that bad.' And right on the heels of this state of acceptance, came this: 'My attitude is changing. Gratitude is my new attitude.'*

12

WHICH TREATMENTS WORK?

What are the principles of successful therapies? What should you look for when choosing a therapist or treatment centre? And what are the red flags for poor treatment? I tell you more about family therapy and other approaches, suggest how to work in partnership with clinicians and when it might be better to find a new team. I also highlight what to look for in psychological support for yourself.

THE PARENT'S QUEST FOR GOOD TREATMENT

In Chapter 4 I briefly outlined the essentials of treatment for an eating disorder. I want to go into more detail now, as we parents often spend a massive amount of energy searching for effective help. I will tell you about treatments that work, and what's involved. First I want to acknowledge the situation many parents are as they search for good treatment.

Evaluating therapies, therapists, questioning their methods and skills – these can be greater stressors than the day-to-day work of looking after our kids. We are entrusting our child's life to others and we need to know the care is excellent.

Leaving one team to choose another is a major decision, fraught with uncertainties. Even the most expensive private treatment providers are unlikely to collect or publish statistics on their outcomes. Sure, their beautiful websites boast the 'many' patients who achieved 'positive outcomes', but where are the numbers?[231] And what methods exactly are they using?

Countries with a national health service provide free or affordable treatment, and – in the UK at least – your child is likely to get better, up-to-date treatment on the national health than privately. But even in countries with excellent standards, some teams are overstretched and some are still poorly trained. I know of instances where a gatekeeper has failed to diagnose an eating disorder, and parents had to put up a tremendous fight to get a second opinion. If you're in this type of situation, I recommend you use advisory bodies and all the contacts you have.[232]

In countries without a national health service, such as the US, parents may be glad to have a choice of treatment provider, but often they face difficulties with medical insurance, and many accumulate large debts.

To add to parents' headaches there's the problem of distance: all over the world, families are driving huge distances on a regular basis to access treatment or to visit an ill child in hospital.

There is also the pressure of time. Every day that your child restricts food represents ground to regain later and habits to retrain. Prompt treatment gives the best chance of recovery.

In my case I also had to factor in that every therapist my daughter saw reduced her tolerance for therapy. She hated any type of approach where she was expected to sit and reveal anything about herself. I dreaded the day she'd point-blank refuse to try someone new, someone who I felt might be 'the one'.

When a restrictive eating disorder is in control, you can expect your child to resist anybody offering treatment. If a child 'hates' a particular therapist, it might be because the therapist is doing a great job of requesting that food is eaten. On the other hand if you, the adult, feel uncomfortable about any treatment provider, it matters. We need to know that clinicians are competent, we need to be comfortable with them and trust them. I became effective when we got a specialist I really gelled with. Before that I was so frustrated with our (unspecialised, non-FBT) family therapy sessions that I'd schedule support for myself right afterwards.

The bottom line is that counsellors, psychiatric nurses, psychiatrists, nutritionists and general practitioners can unwittingly lead you down harmful routes if they are not highly knowledgeable about eating disorders in children and adolescents.

On a positive note you could already be with an excellent therapist but not yet realise it. For the 11 months that my daughter was in hospital, I had no idea that some of the people sitting silently round the table at review meetings had expertise that would later help us make rapid progress. When my child returned to outpatient services I researched some private treatment options, unaware of how excellent our family therapist would turn out to be, unaware that we were getting access to the best in evidence-based treatment. I also now know that if we had been rich enough to opt for those private treatments, our ordeal would have lasted a lot longer.

EATING DISORDER TREATMENTS THAT ARE LIKELY TO CAUSE HARM

Before I tell you about treatments that have been shown to work, I will take a short detour and mention harmful approaches which, sadly, are still common. They may seem like 'common sense' if you're new to this field, as they reflect the culture we've all grown up in. Even among therapists who are committed to evidence-based approaches, it's natural for beliefs from the old models to occasionally leak through. My hope is that if you understand what's going on you can seek solutions.

The sad legacy of psychoanalysis

Roughly speaking, the treatment models that were held in high regard in the 1970s were based on the premise that patients were fighting a smothering mother, and that (as mothers and nourishment are interwoven), rejecting food was an unconscious, symbolic and desperate attempt to break free of a pathological symbiosis. Psychoanalysis was the main show in town and the brain research and epidemiological studies available to us now didn't exist. Psychoanalysts saw families in chaos over a child who wasn't eating, and they confused cause and effect. They separated patients from their parents (parentectomy) and this was thought to support the sufferer's battle for individuation. To the patients, it all made perfect sense, as their symptoms defined how they thought of themselves: 'Choosing what I eat is my way of gaining some control over my life. My parents hate me.'

There are parallels with what's happened with autism and schizophrenia. When these disorders were poorly understood, parent-blame filled the vacuum. 'Refrigerator mothers' and suspicions of sexual abuse were wheeled in to make sense of disorders that defied understanding.

Nowadays there are still many clinicians who will consider that your family is dysfunctional, that your child needs a break from the family, who will request that parents back off, and who curtail or forbid[233] hospital visits. I frequently hear of clinicians who believe that parents have issues with anxiety, depression, control, over-attachment, under-attachment, avoidance, enmeshment. In short, they see us as harmful to our children. I wonder how often that happens to the parents of children with leukaemia.

Many psychotherapists still work from the premise that the illness serves an unconscious purpose and that if the patient can gain insight into what caused them to have an eating disorder, they will be free. The model is that patients are using denial as a protective mechanism. No research has been published to validate this type of intervention.

Clinicians have a genuine desire to treat and truly believe in their methods. Why wouldn't they? The question is, what's the evidence?' Thomas Insel, the director of the National Institute for Mental Health in the US, noted with frustration:

> *"Many professionals, who have no training in neuroscience, still find*
> *a neurobiological approach to mental disorders as misguided and*
> *frankly alien to all of their experience. [...] In an earlier decade,*
> *focusing on the medical basis of cancer and AIDS helped us out of*
> *the blame and shame phases of these disorders."*[234]

The tragedy of waiting for motivation

Some forms of treatment rest on the assumption that in order to eat, a person suffering from anorexia first needs to be motivated, or somewhere on a 'readiness' scale, or on past the 'contemplation' stage within the 'motivational interviewing' cycle. This is a Catch 22 situation because not wanting to get better is part of the illness, so therapy can go on and on in an attempt to shift this conviction. When a patient has spent long enough failing to eat through lack of motivation, they are eventually forced to eat in hospital.

Some people with anorexia do have motivation – adults more so than youngsters. Even though eating is hard they have the motivation to get on with their lives, to resume an interest, to attend a university course, to hold down a job, to be able to have children. When you hear of people who voluntarily took steps to beat their eating disorder, be aware they may have been in their early twenties upwards. After adolescence, people may benefit from more maturity and brain development; perhaps they have become weary of the illness and its effects and want to recover a normal life. They still need help. Self-responsibility can get them to sign up for treatment, but when dinnertime comes round, eating is so awful that all too often, any shred of motivation slinks off, whimpering.

Making it possible to treat children and adolescents without relying on motivation is one of the great strengths of family therapy, where parents take charge of meals.

Tragically, when the only tool on offer is to build motivation, therapists and parents can resort to extremes when nothing seems to work. Watch out for the 'reaching rock bottom' principle.[235] It may sound like 'Let her experience the consequences of her choices, so she learns to take responsibility for herself.' But it equates to this: 'Let her not eat. Let her get really hungry and weak and feel awful. Let her mess up her studies and lose friends. Let her experience the consequences of her actions. When she's reached rock bottom, she'll finally see sense. Then she'll want to get better.'

I have talked to weary parents who tried this because they thought they were out of options – such as a couple who let their underweight young adult go trekking in Africa. The outcome of such gambles is always, to my knowledge, that the person hits rock bottom... and stays there, until they are once more made to eat against their will.

The fact that well-meaning therapists and loving parents are ready to use such high-risk strategies tells me two things. First, they don't appreciate that the longer a patient is malnourished, the harder anorexia is to shift, and second, they haven't received the information or support to use approaches that are far more likely to work.

THE BEST EVIDENCE-BASED TREATMENT

To choose an effective method you must examine the biggest, best quality trials. The latest expert review of these was done by NICE, the institute which reviews the treatments to be used in England's health service. England also has stringent standards for outpatient treatment. These are valuable guide wherever you are in the world, and indeed similar recommendations come from professional institutions in many countries.

For more on standards in England:

England's eating disorder treatment standard· a model for the rest of the world?

What's the best eating disorder treatment for children and young people? The very latest guideline from NICE

So what treatment is recommended by this latest review of the evidence? For anorexia and for bulimia, it's family therapy – the type of family therapy described in this

book. Only if family therapy turned out to be 'unacceptable, contraindicated or ineffective' should you consider one of the next two best approaches:

- For anorexia or bulimia: individual cognitive-behavioural therapy
  (CBT)specifically for eating disorders

- For anorexia only: adolescent-focused psychotherapy (AFP)

For binge-eating disorder, the recommendation is for a guided self-help programme, then if necessary, group or individual CBT.

The recommendations from expert institutions in many countries are less up to
date, but similar.[236]

LIP SERVICE AND WELL-MEANING IGNORANCE

What makes a treatment 'evidence-based'? The strongest evidence – the gold standard of research – comes from randomised controlled trials, in which patients are
randomly allocated to receive either the new treatment or a control treatment. The
control treatment may be a placebo, or it may be another well-established treatment.
These trials are complicated and expensive to run, and given how eating disorders
research is seriously under-funded, we only have a handful of those.

Evidence-based medicine is also made up of carefully evaluated results from
other types of studies: from the strong evidence provided by meta-analyses and systematic reviews, to the weaker evidence provided by before-and after reports and
case studies.

It takes time for a country's health service or professional associations to review
and update their recommendations. And so, official recommendations or standards
may fail to prioritise the best treatments, and may advocate approaches which recent
research has shown to be far less effective.

All self-respecting treatment providers assert their commitment to evidence-
based treatment. Parents need to spot whether that's window-dressing or the real
thing. Indeed there are many reasons why clinicians don't necessarily stick to the science.[237] One reason is human nature: most of us (therapists included) trust our opinions and suffer from an overconfidence bias. Then there is the time, expense and
logistics involved in keeping up with the literature, going to conferences, training a
whole load of staff in new approaches and providing them with quality supervision.
So you can understand how so many treatment providers – including expensive private centres – keep doing what they've been doing for the last few years. Or, as eating-
disorders researcher Glenn Waller quipped, 'There's a lot of evidence that evidence
is better than opinion, but a lot of opinion that opinion is better than evidence.'

In most places in the world it is still very hard to find therapists who are competent in family therapy or CBT for eating disorders. Some have a very poor (but un-
formed) opinion of family therapy. Even among those delivering family therapy or
CBT, there are too many who have not had specialist training in eating disorders.
They mean well but they don't know what they don't know.[238]

PRINCIPLES VALIDATED BY RESEARCH

The successes of CBT indicate that whatever the person's age and the type of eating disorder, regular meals, weight recovery and cessation of bingeing or purging behaviours are key. For adolescents, the successes of family therapy uncover the following additional principles:

- Your child hasn't consciously or unconsciously chosen to have an eating disorder, and they are not the eating disorder. Beliefs and behaviours are driven by the illness.

- There is no requirement for the child to have motivation to eat or to beat the illness, and there is no requirement for the child to have psychological insight.

- Families should be treated as a resource, not a cause or a problem.

- Parents should be empowered to feed their children and normalise their child's eating and weight, at home.

- Exposure to food and overcoming fears may be part of how the treatment works.

- Treatment should be delivered by experienced clinicians, preferably within a team specialising in the treatment of eating disorders.

FAMILY THERAPIES: THEY'RE NOT ALL THE SAME

Throughout this book, when I talk of family therapy, I mean a form that is eating disorder-focused and supported by research. There are variations in the approach but they all have this in common: where parents are a resource, not a problem. There is some harmful confusion around words like 'family therapy', 'FBT' and 'Maudsley', so I will explain more now. If you're in a hurry, just make sure that whatever you're being offered follows the main principles listed above.

Family therapy at the Maudsley Hospital

In the 1980s, after decades of treatment that separated children from their parents, Christopher Dare, Ivan Eisler, Gerald Russel and others at the Maudsley hospital in south London developed a new type of family therapy specifically for adolescents with anorexia. They made the bold decision that because there was no evidence that parents were harmful, they would use them as a resource in the treatment of their children. They produced the first empirical studies to support family treatment for adolescents with anorexia.

The Maudsley Child and Adolescent Eating Disorders Service continues to be a centre of expertise: paediatricians or child and adolescent mental health (CAMHS) units anywhere in the UK can refer a child to the service for a second opinion or for treatment.[239] For patients who need more than the outpatient service, they offer an 'intensive treatment programme' (day care), and also work closely with the inpatient unit at King's College hospital.[240]

The treatment (named family therapy for anorexia nervosa, or systemic family therapy for anorexia, or FT-AN) has evolved under the leadership of Ivan Eisler and Mima Simic and is described in an online manual.[241] The team also created Multi-family therapy (MFT)[242] where families share strategies that help their child to eat, there are joint family meals supported by therapists, and explorations of the effect of the eating disorder on family life. The team have trained professionals in family therapy and MFT worldwide, and there is currently a program of training for eating disorders therapists within CAMHS in England and Wales.[243]

The origins of Family-Based Treatment (FBT)

Daniel Le Grange, who participated in the early family therapy studies at the Maudsley Hospital, teamed up with James Lock and others in the US to conduct further randomised controlled trials on the approach. They named it Family-Based Treatment (FBT) (or FBT-AN and FBT-BN for the anorexia and bulimia versions) and many call it *the Maudsley method* or *Manualised Maudsley* or *Maudsley-FBT*). To ensure the study's therapists were consistent, they created a manual[244] (and later wrote a parent's guide: *Help Your Teenager Beat an Eating Disorder*[245]).

Nowadays there are differences between FBT and the family therapy used and taught by the Maudsley hospital. And around the world, people are developing variations on the family therapy theme while continuing to use parents as a resource in their child's treatment.[246] In the absence of studies to tell us if differences matter, we can only hope that they're small enough that whatever variant you get, you're in good hands.

The New Maudsley Method: not the same as the Maudsley Approach

Now be ready to be seriously confused.[247] A significantly different approach came out in 2007 in the book *Skills-Based Learning for Caring for a Loved One with an Eating Disorder: the New Maudsley Method*.[248] In spite of its name, it is not an update on Maudsley/FBT – indeed the book makes no reference to the approach or its authors. New Maudsley encourages a collaborative, slow 'nudging' approach that was developed for long-term adult patients. At the same time, parents are urged not to be 'accommodating' or 'enabling' of their child's eating-disorder behaviours. Progress relies on the person's motivation and 'readiness' for change within a 'motivational interviewing' model, presumably because otherwise the person might drop out of treatment. A parent who is taking charge of meals and of normalising behaviours (as described in this book) might be labelled a 'terrier', and that's not a compliment.

To reduce the confusion created by the book's title, some refer to 'New Maudsley' as 'the skills-based method' (or even 'the dolphin book'). It does have similarities to FBT: eating is not optional, parents are (depending on the patient's willingness) invited to support their loved one, and patients are treated with compassion.

The approach comes from Janet Treasure and her King's College London team in Guy's Hospital and in the adult (not the children and adolescents') service at the Maudsley Hospital. It is intended to be used in conjunction with treatment, rather than being a treatment in its own right. Its focus is on helping staff or parents to support a person, and the team's research indicates that caregivers cope better after learning the skills. It was devised for patients with severe and enduring eating disorders (SEED), mostly adults who may have been in and out of treatment for five or more years, though plenty of parents also use parts of it with their adolescents (and many of the communication principles are like those in this book).

Family therapy that is not designed for eating disorders

There's confusion around the words 'family therapy'. If family therapy doesn't follow the principles of evidence-based treatment for eating disorders, then it probably refers to general family therapy (such as systemic family therapy). There may be an assumption that the cause of the problem, and the fix, is in the way members relate to each other. There can be parent-blaming. A really old-school family therapist may even believe that having a child with eating problems serves to distract us parents from our own issues. While the family dynamics is put under the microscope, your child may lose weight, purge and over-exercise.[249] Many treatment centres say they do family therapy, and you may assume they mean FBT, but when you read carefully, it's about fixing relationships, and these places don't put parents in charge of food. If you're offered family therapy that is not specifically for eating disorders and that is not based on the Maudsley/FBT model, read on.

Systemic family therapy versus FBT

Having just warned you that systemic family therapy might be an unpleasant waste of time, I need to tell you it may actually be just as effective as FBT, according to a randomised controlled trial.[250] Let's be clear: in the trial, the systemic family therapy took a 'non-pathologising, positive view of the family system, and the current difficulties they are struggling with' and recognised that 'the family themselves will be in the best position to generate suitable solutions'. If your family therapy service doesn't truly believe this, then the results of the trial are not relevant to you. Also important: all the therapists worked in specialist eating disorder services and had an average of 6 years of experience in treating adolescent anorexia.

So how does the study's systemic family therapy differ from FBT? Well, there is 'no specific emphasis on normalisation of eating or weight, although if the family raises this issue, the therapist will help them address it.' I imagine most families would be extremely concerned about the adolescent's eating and weight, and therefore there may be quite a lot of crossover between the two approaches.

The results? Systemic family therapy is equally effective to FBT in weight restoration and reducing eating disorder symptoms at the end of treatment and at one-year follow-up. FBT leads to faster initial weight gain and significantly fewer days in hospital (policy-makers should note this cuts the cost of treatment by half), while systemic family therapy is more effective with patients with strong obsessive-compulsive symptoms.

FAMILY THERAPY: THE FIRST LINE OF TREATMENT FOR CHILDREN AND TEENS WITH ANOREXIA AND BULIMIA

To recap, there is clear evidence that that family therapy specialised for eating disorders should be your first port of call. If a treatment centre is not offering that, they are not up to date and your child will be missing out on a treatment that is twice as effective as the next best approaches.

How effective is Family-Based Treatment (FBT)?

Before family therapy came along, there was no scientific evidence that anything worked particularly well.[251] Then the Maudsley hospital conducted some trials which indicated the family approach worked. A while later Lock, Le Grange and others nailed down a protocol (a detailed manual)[252] for family therapy, called it Family-Based Treatment (FBT) and conducted more randomised controlled trials.[253]

So how successful can you expect FBT to be? First, we need to define success. Since 2010 the trials have set a high bar for 'full remission' (close to what most of us consider to be 'full recovery'). An adolescent needs to be weight restored (or very close) and their behaviours and thinking must be similar to those of youngsters without an eating disorder. With the bar set this high, average outcomes from various studies show full remission in 34 per cent of participants at the end of treatment. With the passage of time, more tend to recover, so the total figure a year after end of treatment is 40 per cent of participants.[254]

Before you lose heart over these low figures, please note that in these studies the treatment time was one year or less. That gives plenty of time for weight restoration and for improvements in thinking and behaviours, but we parents know from experience that it takes longer to get complete freedom from the eating disorder, whatever the method used. Note also that these statistics are for FBT conducted as per the manual. I think skilled and very experienced therapists can do better by modifying details to suit the individual.

I can think of another reason why the FBT statistics might be so low. I wonder if for half of the patients, weight gain was halted before they were weight-restored. Everyone's goal weight was set as 95% of the median BMI, and by definition, half of a population is above the median, and half is below. Many parents report increased success when they seek an individualised target that reflects their child's needs.[255]

We have much more hopeful figures for 'partial remission': 89 per cent of participants recovered to this level by the end of treatment.[256] When you ask how good a treatment is, it all depends on the question you ask.

It doesn't work for everyone

According to many nation's professional bodies, and in my opinion, a child or teen's best chances are with family treatment. But as the figures above show, the approach does not work for everyone. Few treatments in the medical world work for 100 per cent of patients. If FBT or other forms of family therapy aren't working for you, it's not a reflection of personal weakness. It means it's time to try something else and keep reviewing. We'll look at alternatives later in this chapter.

Research into eating disorders is, truth be told, pretty weak, for such a common and serious illness. A systematic review concluded that 'there is insufficient evidence to determine whether there is an advantage of family therapy approaches'.[257] But let's not throw the baby out with the bathwater. I believe that even if you go for individual treatment and even if you accept to step back and not take charge of meals, your child will continue to benefit from some level of support from you.

Family therapy for anorexia in young children

The studies I refer to above are for adolescents aged 12 to 18. It seems that family therapy is also the best approach for young children, who generally have little capacity for the introspection required of talking therapies, and where it is natural for parents to be in charge.[258]

FBT-TAY for anorexia in young adults

A variant of FBT, called FBT-TAY is showing promise for 17 to 25-year olds ('transition-age youth' or TAY) suffering from anorexia. It involves more teamwork, more buy-in from the young adult, and less of parents taking charge. All the same, parents are expected to make a commitment to help their child gain weight and normalise eating.[259]

FBT for bulimia

A randomised controlled trial has shown FBT to have an edge over a specialised form of cognitive behaviour therapy for adolescents with bulimia (CBT-A). Both produce similar outcomes 12 months post-treatment but FBT produces improvements sooner.[260]

FBT in those ill for over three years: no evidence

FBT trials relate to patients treated within three years of diagnosis. If your child or young adult has been ill for much longer, there is no scientific evidence to back up the used of FBT. ('No evidence', in this case, means 'it's not been studied, so we don't know'. Confusingly, sometimes 'no evidence for X' means 'trials have shown X doesn't work/isn't true'). But I know of parents who have successfully used it all the same.

> "Our D is now over 21 and was first diagnosed at 16. Three and a
> half years ago, she had a big relapse. Prior to that treatment was

not really coordinated and we had no Maudsley Family-Based
Treatment. Since we found our special educator and her Maudsley
Approach we have steadily travelled the journey to recovery and still
find the Maudsley Approach very valid for an adult child."

What happens in family therapy?

Parents can easily read both the FBT manual and the manual written by the eating disorders services at the Maudsley Hospital.[261] The differences between the two approaches are small so I will just outline how FBT works. It's an outpatient treatment lasting 6–12 months (20 to 40 sessions).[262] Therapy team members consist of one lead clinician and a co-therapist. These may be child and adolescent psychiatrists, or psychologists or social workers. They would normally have the support of a consulting team that might consist of a paediatrician, a nurse, and a nutritionist. The main treatment providers are the parents, who are the experts on their child and provide meals and loving support at home.

When you first visit an FBT therapist with your child, the focus will be on weight restoration (Phase I). You take control of your child's meals and prevent excessive exercise, bingeing or purging. The therapist ensures you and your spouse are consistent in your commitment to helping your child to eat, and clarifies the role of siblings, offering them support as well. After about ten weekly sessions, if the child is close to a healthy weight and meals are relatively stress free, Phase II begins.[263] This is a time when an age-appropriate level of control is gradually handed back to the young person. Sessions may become less frequent – the manual allocates five sessions for this phase. Finally, Phase III (three sessions or so) is about return to normal family relationships, addressing the young person's life beyond food issues, and planning for the future.[264]

This probably sounds impossibly neat and tidy, but it has to be so when you're conducting randomised controlled trials. You must control your variables. My understanding is that for many families in treatment now, phases blend in and out of each other, and there is flexibility to meet the needs of each situation.

FBT therapists: who they are and how to find them

Certified FBT therapists have been trained by Lock and Le Grange's team and are listed on the FBT training website.[265] If your therapists aren't on the list but say they're doing FBT, there may be a perfectly valid reason. They may be part way through training and supervision (as ours was), or part of a team in which key people are FBT-qualified. They may be experienced eating disorders therapists who have attended a day or two of training from James Lock or Daniel Le Grange.[266]

A therapist may have taught themselves FBT from the manual, avoiding the considerable travelling, training and certification costs.

Be ready to step in if your therapist allows outdated concepts to leak out. It can take time, self-awareness and supervision for clinicians to let go of the models they've used throughout their careers.[267]

"Our therapists were new to FBT. Early on they gave us an awful 'why did this happen in your family' session. While I think it was meant to illuminate, it actually caused us all more worry about what we possibly did wrong to cause our daughter's illness. The day our daughter heard me tell her the illness wasn't her fault, we really began to move forward."

Should your child like the family therapist?

With FBT it's important that you, the parents, feel well supported. As for your child:

"My daughter hated her ed therapist at first sight. She would swear at her, storm out of the room. You name it. That's when I knew we had found the right one. Our previous therapist was lovely but didn't push my daughter or challenge the eating disorder enough."[268]

Is it OK to tweak the method?

Earlier I listed the main principles of family therapy. But what about the details? For instance your therapist may give you a meal plan rather than putting you in charge of food choices. They observe a family meal and give you feedback on how you handle it, or they may skip that.

The most thorough research on family therapy for eating disorders was done on the FBT method as described in the FBT manual. Some argue that therapists should use that exact method. Others say that for all we know, some variations could be just as good or even better, as long as we respect the general principles. There's also a view that the less experienced therapists are, the more they should stick to manuals.

This debate is not unique to eating disorders. Evidence-based treatments are usually set out in manuals or protocols, but clinicians often want to deviate from them. Imagine a top leukaemia specialist telling a parent that in her experience, and in your particular situation, you get better results using a slightly different dosage. No research has been done to prove it, but it's not terribly different from the standard protocol, and it does offer hope of a swifter recovery.

If therapists use their clinical judgement and experience, and if their adaptions aim to suit individual patients' needs and preferences, then what they're doing is 'evidence-based *practice*'. The idea is that one size does not fit all. There is a risk that they are unintentionally discarding ingredients that are crucial to the success of the method. Unintentionally, because unless we have a great number of 'dismantling' studies (and with eating disorders, we don't) we cannot know for sure which ingredients matter and which don't.

The FBT method has been validated as a package but dismantling studies are ongoing to tease out the elements that make it successful. Some of those uncovered so far are: parents take control, parents are united, and parents are non-blaming.[269]

When a therapist changes too many elements, they are flying solo. They would need to collect a lot of data to know that what they do actually works.

As an analogy, imagine you are following a recipe to make a cake. Because your oven door doesn't close well, you lengthen the cooking time. So far so good – that's a sound judgement based on your experience. And if you don't like vanilla, you also know there's no harm in leaving that out. Now imagine you are the creative type, so you leave out quite a few ingredients and add a few new ones. If your cake ends up like a lump of rock you won't know why, unless you go back to the recipe and systematically remove or add ingredients one at a time.

Your therapist might be lacking training or rigour if he changes the recipe. Or he may have excellent reasons to adapt it to your child, and when therapists do this and write up the research, the field keeps moving forward.[270] Our own therapist told us early on that because of the stage we were at, she wasn't applying FBT by the book but using the main principles. One obvious modification she made for my eleven-year old was to use blind weighing (the manual requires open weighing). This worked for us, and as I look back I appreciate how sensitively she responded to our needs as they came up.

This book you're reading now is not pure FBT. I aim to keep to the big principles, and to inform you whenever I disagree with elements of the method.

INDIVIDUAL THERAPIES

Cognitive behavioural therapy (CBT) adapted for eating disorders

Cognitive behavioural therapy (CBT) is a common treatment for all sorts of mental health issues, and there are variants that have been adapted for eating disorders. From here on, when I talk of CBT, I will be referring to one of these specialised, evidence-based forms. (General CBT does not put enough focus on normalising behaviours and on nutritional restoration).

CBT is not as effective as a family-based approach. In England, a thorough review of all treatments led to a recommendation that CBT may be used only if a family approach is 'unacceptable, contraindicated or ineffective'.[271]

The difficulty with CBT, like any individual therapy, is that people need to eat regularly, stop purging and restore weight through their own efforts. Parents may be sidelined. This happened to us even though we had chosen the therapist with care. We were reporting on our child's difficulties with food and exercise, yet in four sessions the professional told my girl she was well, could stop weight gain, join a gym and end the therapy. It took a while to undo the damage.

However in wise and expert hands, CBT may –like other types of individual therapy – be useful in finishing off aspects of the treatment which might not have been successfully addressed in family therapy.

If you are considering CBT for your child, I recommend you read more about pros and cons on my website on anorexiafamily.com/CBT.

Adolescent focused individual therapy (AFT)

Another validated one-to-one therapy that requires patients to take charge of their own recovery is adolescent focused individual therapy (AFT). It does not seek insight into causes but focuses on the young person's ability to change their own behaviours, restore weight, and develop emotional awareness. Parents only have a supporting role.

Lock and Le Grange, who developed FBT, also wrote the manual for AFT. From their main anorexia study comparing the two treatments, they found that for most youngsters FBT works better than AFT – twice as well. But FBT doesn't work for everyone, so they concluded that 'AFT remains an important alternative treatment for families that would prefer a largely individual treatment.' [272] And indeed the recent NICE guidance for anorexia in young people[273] puts this therapy (which they name 'adolescent-focused psychotherapy for anorexia nervosa', or AFP-AN), on a par with CBT: it may be used if – and only if – a family-based approach is 'unacceptable, contraindicated or ineffective'.

Earlier I wrote some words of caution around CBT, and you should use similar precautions with AFT. You can read a lot more about it on my website anorexiafamily.com:

> Adolescent-focused therapy (AFT) for anorexia: how does it compare with family-based treatment?
>
> Adolescent-focused therapy (AFT): a guide to the joint runner-up treatment for anorexia

More individual therapies for adults

I'll mention more therapies in case your child is offered them, as they are only validated for adults. Worldwide research led NICE[274] to recommend just three approaches for anorexia in adults: CBT for eating disorders (which I described earlier), Maudsley Anorexia Nervosa Treatment for Adults (MANTRA), and Specialist Supportive Clinical Management (SSCM). If none of those three are acceptable or effective, the next best option is eating-disorder-focused focal psychodynamic therapy (FPT). I hope that in years to come, adapted forms of family-based treatment will be available to over-18s – there is not enough research to this to feature in official recommendations.

For bulimia and for binge-eating disorder in adults, NICE recommends a guided self-help programme, possibly with brief supportive sessions, and if after four weeks this proves unacceptable, contraindicate or ineffective, then CBT is to be offered.

Psychotherapy as an adjunct to family therapy

In the FBT model, psychotherapy isn't normally required, or if it is it comes much later. Psychotherapy on its own is unlikely to resolve an eating disorder – it should only be used as an adjunct. The Royal College of Psychiatrists in the UK writes:

> *"It is not psychological therapy that will turn the course at this point, but [...] skilled nutritional rehabilitation."*[275]

Most people with anorexia have some degree of anosognosia, a brain condition that makes the person unable to perceive that they are ill and need help, or unable to perceive the severity of their situation. With any eating disorder, habits, brain wiring and physiological effects are strong, and talk is not the solution.

Your child may benefit from psychotherapy if they struggle with anxiety, depression, OCD, or with life in general. As these difficulties are often manifestations of the eating disorder, it's usually recommended to go through family-based treatment and only bring in psychotherapy if issues persist. Another reason to wait is that psychotherapy has limited effectiveness on a malnourished brain.

> *"When my daughter was at her lowest weight she was OCD for sure, and bipolar was suggested, but my wife and I really put the screws down not to give her that diagnosis in her chart because it would follow her around for ever. Sure enough, once we passed a certain weight on the road to restoration it was like her brain rebooted."*[276]

Sometimes comorbids do need attention, though:

- If they persist after the eating disorder is well under control, especially if they preceded the eating disorder. One researcher says that untreated OCD increases the chances of relapse by 75 per cent.[277]

- If they are making it impossible to treat the eating disorder (too much self-harm or suicidality, too much time spent in rituals). In this case, some youngsters get medication or psychotherapy for their comorbid while family therapy for the eating disorder continues.

While most young people are highly resistant to psychotherapy, we should pay attention when someone desires psychological help early on. Some youngsters acutely feel that we have forgotten they are living, suffering human beings. Disturbingly, psychological support can be refused on the basis that it is not family-based protocol. Thankfully, many therapists are ready to assess individual needs and opportunities. I am thinking for instance of a girl who had been traumatised by fat-bullying in school. She did well from engaging in EMDR therapy at the same time as she was renourished.

If the young person is willing to engage, there can also be a place for one of the psychotherapy approaches after family-based treatment has run its course. Some young people continue to be burdened by an eating-disorder mindset after discharge, even while their weight and behaviours are well under control. There is a sense they are neither relapse-proof, nor fully recovered. At this stage, psychotherapy can impart tools for distress tolerance and emotion regulation and can help the young person get back on track with their development. I recommend that at least some of this work is done with the family, so that parents can support the use of the tools in real-life situations.[278]

All the clinicians involved should be working as a team with each other... and with you. Later in this chapter I will discuss what you can do when your child gets individual therapy and you are excluded.

Therapists don't have your parent-power

Some parents need to be reminded of their own strengths as loving, dedicated, wise mothers and fathers. They are far too quick to abdicate their power in the belief that only a therapist can fix their child's mind. Yet it is a healing balm for your child to hear *you* saying, 'Tell me more. I'm interested. I care. I feel for you.' Even when they reject you, and even when all you can do is non-verbals (and I help you with communication in Chapter 14). Sure, a trained professional may contribute something we can't provide, but therapy is only one hour a week, outside of normal life. Our children most need to be loved and supported by their own parents. There's no relationship like it. If you bring to mind your own parents, doesn't their love or withdrawal still do something to you? Whether or not you try psychotherapy for your child, remember your own precious powers.

Why would your child engage with therapy?

I have supported parents who use the family therapy approach and are also delighted with the individual therapy their child is receiving, usually for depression or anxiety. The child engages well with the therapist and learns new ways of coping with life's challenges, so that the urge to restrict or binge fades away. Sometimes old traumas are revealed and processed.

For most, though, to say that a youngster may not engage with psychotherapy can be an understatement. Commonly, they blank the therapist out, they're rude, they have to be dragged into the building, and they run away. Whatever your child is doing, it's probably normal, and for all we know, is a sign of great sanity.

My daughter's psychotherapists revealed that even without an eating disorder, most of the children and adolescents they see won't engage with them. Without a therapeutic relationship, how can individual therapy succeed?

It seems to me that youngsters are intensely private. They fear they will be judged. They feel awkward and ashamed in front of a stranger, and prefer baring their soul to their loving parents during unscheduled moments of connectedness. They hate the abnormality of being pulled out of school and in my daughter's case, they hate the ugly institutional rooms, with plastic toys piled up in the corner, and women's magazines ('Get beach-body ready!!!') in the waiting area.

If in doubt, use this reality check: are therapy sessions making your child eat as required? If the answer is no, why bother?

More on my website anorexiafamily.com:
> Don't beat up your child (or yourself) for failing in spite of therapy

HOW TO IDENTIFY EFFECTIVE TREATMENT PROVIDERS

Given that family therapy and other validated treatments may not be available to you, that no particular method is effective for everyone and that for all we know another method out there may be just as good or better, how do you choose a therapist, clinic or hospital? Or if you country has a national health service, how satisfied are you with the treatment your child is getting, and would less harm be done by walking away from it?

The no-brainers

Any service that isn't putting specialised family therapy top of their list is only paying lip service to evidence-based treatment. The website's photography may be gorgeous, but what's behind the words?

- 'We offer family therapy to improve the way family members relate to each other, resolve conflicts and communicate'. That sounds like 'fixing' the family, and has nothing to do with family therapy evidence-based for eating disorders.

- 'Your child will receive intensive psychological and emotional support in order to understand underlying factors that have contributed to her eating disorder.' Understanding (or more likely, speculating) doesn't constitute treatment.

- 'Your child will gain a deeper understanding of herself and insight into the root causes of her eating disorder.' Ditto

- 'Eating disorders are symptoms of deep, unresolved issues. You will learn how to confront these issues and the emotions they produce, and your relationship with food will stabilise.' So it might be a while before the starving youngster gets to eat. Notice the complete absence of neurobiology.

- 'All meals are eaten in a family atmosphere with our highly trained staff'. Parents, clearly, don't get a seat at the table.

- '… blank …' Nowhere does the website mention eating or weight gain.

- 'Parents may visit their child between 2 and 3pm on Sundays. Visitation privileges will be withdrawn if the child has not gained the expected daily rate.' Yes, this still exists. The last parents I talked to who went along with this eventually had to pull their child out (a tender eleven-year-old), as there was no progress.

A checklist to assess a treatment provider

If you're assessing a potential therapist (or wondering whether to stay with one that you're unsure about) I highly recommend Dr Sarah Ravin's short blog: 'Red flags: how to spot ineffective eating disorder treatment'.[279]

If the red flags are not there, you could consider the following questions, directly or indirectly, as you talk with the therapist. Have a thorough conversation, bearing these questions in mind. In case you have skipped previous chapters and are in a hurry, I indicate the desirable answer in brackets. Note that further on I also offer a checklist to assess an inpatient unit.

- What treatment will you give my child? [Family therapy/Family-based treatment, in the case of anorexia or bulimia]

- If not family therapy, why not? [At this stage, the only valid reason would be if you are unwilling or absolutely unable to take an active role]

- What will be our role (as parents) in treatment? [You will initially take charge of meals and of normalising behaviours (phase 1), then you will cautiously steer him to take back age-appropriate control (phase 2) and help him step back into a full life (phase 3)]

- Will our child have to regain the weight he lost? [Yes, and more to account for expected growth]

- What is the target weight? [We won't know until we get signs of a healthy body and a more normal mindset]

- Can we let our child be a little bit thin so he won't keep wanting to diet? [No, we're aiming for health and total recovery]

- Can we let our child exercise/purge after meals, as it relieves her anxiety? [No]

- He's used to small meals so can we reassure him they will stay small? [No, rapid refeeding is best, and I'll help you make it work]

- Should I be glad that she's banned junk food? [No food is 'junk'. We're aiming for freedom to eat without rules.]

- Will you give us a meal plan? [With FBT: no, but I'll guide you if you're unsure.][Also fine: yes, but only at the beginning, and the plan gives you plenty of flexibility]

- Can my child recover totally? [Yes]

- Did we cause the eating disorder? [No, there are many interlinked causal factors – genetic, biological, environmental – and scientists don't yet understand causation. But we can successfully treat anyway.]

- How can I stop her being so selfish and manipulative? [We will work on unconditional acceptance of your child, as it's the eating disorder that makes her this way for now.]

- Will parents be included in all sessions? [Yes – because the therapy is about guiding parents to treat their child]

- Will you provide my child with individual therapy for her anorexia/bulimia and why? [FBT: no, unless your child still has difficulties after the eating disorder is dealt with.][Also sometimes fine: yes, in conjunction with family therapy, because of the comorbid OCD/anxiety etc.]

- If you're proposing CBT, why, and can you describe the approach? [See earlier how CBT for eating disorders differs from general CBT. CBT is the go-to approach for binge-eating disorder.]

- If you propose individual therapy, how will we parents be kept in the loop? How can we inform you of behaviours we see at home? [If the therapist is vague about your involvement, beware of getting disempowered]

- My child also has autism/OCD/depression/anxiety. How will you deal with it? [Discuss how attending to this will affect eating disorder treatment. In general, eating-disorder treatment comes first]

- Will you work on giving my child insight and motivation? [That would delay the real work. Recovery doesn't require either.]

- What if my child is in medical danger, or needs psychiatric medication or hospitalisation? [We are a team, each with our specialties, and we work closely with you and each other]

- Will you help me liaise with the school, the athletics club? [Yes]

- What support will you give us as parents? [Mealtime coaching or support visits at home would be good, though uncommon. Sessions without your child can be very useful. Sessions with other families can be supportive.]

- Who trained you in family therapy? [Ideally, one of the key names in the field, and for more than the basic 2 days]

- What are your qualifications, your experience, ongoing training, experience, supervision?[280] Are you a member of eating disorders associations? Have been involved in any published research? How do you keep yourself up to date? What books or online resources do you rate highly? [Certification in FBT is quite rare, so consider it a bonus]

- What led you to work in the field of eating disorders? [Looking for a wise, compassionate attitude and commitment to total recovery.]

- Have you ever suffered from an eating disorder yourself, and if so do you still experience symptoms? [Checking the therapist will stay focused on your child's recovery]

- How many eating-disorder patients have you treated recently; how many completed the whole course of treatment; what were the outcomes after 1 or 2 years? [A tricky one, as very few clinicians collect or publish any data]

- How soon can you see my child? [If a private clinic isn't in a hurry to see a child who is losing weight, they don't appreciate the benefits of early intervention]

I suggest that at first you check out a therapist alone, to protect your child from hearing anything harmful. In my case I also didn't want my daughter to develop an intolerance to therapists.

You could also go onto online forums[281] to ask about other parents' experiences about a particular treatment centre.

Finally, trust your gut. I would be concerned about the therapist's effectiveness if I had a sense of being bossed around, patronised, hurried, judged, excluded, not listened to or not respected, if the therapist was evasive or authoritarian, and if it took tremendous perseverance to get answers. On the other hand, I wouldn't let a warm, compassionate exchange distract me from the other, more scientific requirements.

We're not looking for perfection. Some help may be better than no help. As long as the therapist doesn't disempower you in the eyes of your child, there is plenty you can do yourself.

Therapists who previously had an eating disorder

Many eating disorder therapists come to the field because of lived experience. Some disclose it, and some don't. Some only disclose it if they sense this will benefit their client (such as instilling hope).[282]

Some therapists make their eating-disorder past their unique selling point. Avoid them if they are attached to the one single approach that made them well (commonly, a spiritual epiphany), rather than evidence-based treatment.

As a general rule (I can think of some wonderful exceptions) a therapist needs to be truly recovered. Otherwise they might collude with some aspects of the illness. Our children need a strong, courageous hand to lead them through all kinds of challenges. They need someone who is comfortable with challenging eating disorder behaviours.

We also need therapists who, unlike our children, have a positive attitude to food and to body diversity. There are still clinicians who endorse a patient's desire to stay thin, irrespective of symptoms and behaviours. I'm also thinking of a therapist who told her young patient, 'Don't worry, it will be easy to maintain your weight. You'll just make sure you don't eat too much. That's what I do.'

Should you ask a therapist if they have suffered from an eating disorder and are now free of eating-disorder thoughts and behaviours? I haven't, but it's a valid question if you're non-judgemental and you make it clear your concern is for your child's treatment.

Does a therapist seem to be a bit too much into exercise (I know of one who attends the gym five times a week)? Do they consider some foods 'naughty'? Do you see them eating ridiculously small portions (a common sight, I am told, at professional conferences). When someone who is all skin and bones says they have recovered from anorexia, I have my doubts. On the other hand, there could be any number of reasons for someone having a large body.

A recovered therapist may be fantastic, and I know a few of them. Conversely I don't think their experience is an essential asset. Any good therapist should have developed both experience and empathy. There's no need for the podiatrist who treats my mum's feet to have ever had foot problems of her own.

You can be sure that your child will be scrutinising the therapists' bodies. My daughter was cared for by a number of people in very large bodies, and I wondered if that would be an issue for her, but it never seemed to be. What affected her was how they treated her. One of her favourite, most motherly nurses had a generous, cushiony body specially designed for hugging, something that gave us both great delight.

Clinicians rich in human qualities

My daughter got meaningful support from a variety of nurses and specialists, irrespective of their training. One of her hospital therapists had a psychoanalytical background, which to me might normally be a turn-off. Yet I cannot think of anyone I would want more in times of need: she could make a desiccated twig flourish, such is the power of her empathic manner and the quiet wisdom she embodies.

There was also the nurse on the ward whose hugs were pure therapy. I remember weeping with gratitude when she promised to comfort my little girl on one particularly awful night. And then there was the youngest of all those nurses, who was one of the wisest, kindest, most empathic people I've met, yet she was unqualified and no more than 25 years old.

It's no coincidence, I'm sure, that the staff who were wonderful to my husband and me were also the ones my daughter loved the most. Their humanity lit up everything in their path. I believe that their life-affirming influence lives on within my daughter now. It certainly does with me.

DISAGREEMENTS WITH CLINICIANS

Parents who read a lot can soon become more knowledgeable than a clinician who has not specialised in eating disorders. They may also be more up to date. There are big names who have treated teens for decades, and only have a vague and incorrect idea of what family-based treatment is. And there are therapists who say they 'do FBT' after just a few hours of introductory training.

You might appreciate the support of your team overall, but strongly disagree with one aspect of the treatment. That happens in a field that is moving fast. The clinician may feel threatened: they are the expert on the treatment, and who do you think you are? You are conscious that you don't know what you don't know, so at first you genuinely want a discussion. But the therapist is not hearing you. You hesitate. Perhaps you go along with their instructions for a little while. Eventually you have spent a gazillion hour on research, plus, you can see how your child, who was doing so well, is now regressing. Your team says they are 'doing FBT', yet when you speak to parents in another part of the country, with another team who is also 'doing FBT' you discover those parents got the opposite instructions.

Make an appointment without your child and discuss the issue. You are part of the team and you are officially an expert on your son or daughter. You may bring in research papers, links to conference videos, quotes from respected experts who founded or researched family therapy. I warn you though, some parents are very frustrated this has made not one jot of difference. The clinicians argue that the evidence we present them with does not apply to our child, or is not strong enough, or that their experience goes the opposite way. 'Evidence' becomes a weapon to beat each other up with. Presumably the issue is that we are trying to use logic on something that has become a highly emotional issue for all parties.

It may help to keep on the table the three foundations of 'evidence-based practice': the evidence, the clinician's expertise, *and* your family's needs and experience.

You are an expert on the latter. Describe what's happening at home and use your well-practiced skills of compassionate persistence to persist with your request. You can make change more acceptable by proposing a trial with a review date.

And sadly, nothing may work. Some parents find that treatment is so ineffective – or even harmful – that they wonder if it's time to cut their losses and run.

DROPPING UNHELPFUL TREATMENT

One seemingly trivial reason why we stay with a therapist in spite of everything is that we want to be nice. Sometimes we feel sorry for them.[283] We appreciate that they mean well and have worked very hard for us. We imagine they are so vulnerable that we will hurt their feelings if we tell them we don't want their services any more. Nobody's needs are met when you're nice.

Sometimes we put therapists on a pedestal and we fear that if we don't behave like compliant children, they will judge us. It shouldn't matter what people think of us, but humans are social animals. Sometimes we're so cross that we thrash about, blame and complain, but we're unclear about what we really want.

If your treatment team has been blaming you and excluding you, I'm guessing that your self-confidence is at an all-time low. You've been consistently told you're a worrier, that you're over-controlling, and that your child would happily eat if only you stopped trying to feed him. Your spouse may be telling you that the doctors know best, but your gut begs to differ. Perhaps you are indeed entirely wrong. On the other hand there are many examples of parents' instincts being validated after a move to a new therapist.

As you toy with the idea of walking away from a treatment provider, you may feel extremely vulnerable, alone, and somewhat reckless. Yet if you know that these people are letting your child get worse or are undermining your own work, part of you knows it's crazy to stay with them. What might be holding you back is the possibility that they're better than nothing. Do you fear that if one of them took the huff they could make it more difficult for you to get access to other health services? Are you worried about burning your bridges and being left stranded if your child gets worse? We certainly felt quite vulnerable whenever, for any reason, a relationship with a therapist came to an end, and it was good to know we could get prompt support again if we needed it. You'll need to check the situation where you live, but where I am, refusing one type of treatment would not remove the safety net; a child would still be admitted into hospital if he needed it.

If you're struggling with doubts, seek out parent-support groups to help you consider your options. You have to make these decisions for yourself, but it helps to learn from other people's experience and you may clarify your thoughts by having people hear you out.

NO GOOD TREATMENT LOCALLY?

If you can't find a good therapist locally, there are other options. Some parents travel huge distances for a few days of intensive learning and family therapy.[284] On my website I list the certified FBT therapists who can provide treatment via video call.[285] If you're in the UK your GP may acknowledge that treatment isn't meeting your needs and they may release funds for treatment elsewhere, either at an NHS centre of excellence or a private clinic.[286] If this happens, make sure you're not going from the frying pan into the fire. Do your research.

Finally, some parents bravely go it alone.

FAMILY TREATMENT THE DIY WAY

If going it alone seems daunting, be aware that you are in good company. You may benefit from reading about the experiences of people who have done this. [287]

If you're at the stage of even considering this move, I'm guessing you're already extremely well informed and very determined. At the same time, you're going to need support. At the very least, you'll need a doctor on board to monitor your child's health. In the UK we can choose our GP, so switch if you're not happy with the one you have. You need someone who's either well educated in eating disorders or who's willing to learn.

You're also bound to have all kinds of practical questions: should you let your child choose her flavour of yoghurt? Should you weigh her? Should you let her go for a sleepover? You can benefit from the experience of other therapists and other parents from all over the world through the internet.[288]

Here's from Dr Rebecca Peebles:

> *"I believe that bad therapy is worse than no therapy. So when I get a call from parents ... if they cannot access someone who can work with them and their family in a respectful manner then I guide them to Lauren Muhlheim's book, Eva Musby's book, Laura Collins and FEAST and... That's what I guide them to and I try to empower them to pull themselves up and try to do this more on their own. I know that's really scary, and I'm not saying it's ideal but it's better than working with a crummy therapist who undermines you."*[289]

PARENT-COACHING, HOME SUPPORT AND DAY TREATMENT

Some children need a trusted adult with them at all times to prevent bingeing, purging, self-harming or suicide. This task can fall on one parent, who may become starved of sleep, company and stimulation. Parents need support for the extraordinary work they are doing. They rarely get it.

When we can't manage to feed our child at home, most of us have only one option: hospitalisation. In my daughter's case, 11 months of it. Sometimes, a child needs inpatient treatment for a short while because their illness is just too strong to treat at home. Parents still need to learn how to take charge, though, because no treatment is ever completed in hospital.

In the US, eating-disorders units may offer a continuum of care: outpatient (OP), intensive outpatient (IOP), day treatment, partial hospitalisation (PHP) and inpatient (IP) or residential. In the UK we would dearly love this range of options, or at least something in between home-caring 24/7 and inpatient admission.

Everything hinges on whether we can feed our children safely at home. In Family-Based Treatment (FBT), the second session is a family meal in the therapist's office. Some family therapists (including Eisler's team at the Maudsley service) choose not to do this – and they give compelling reasons for their decision – yet I appreciate the opportunity for parents to gain confidence and pick up some tools to begin feeding their child. Shortly after my daughter was diagnosed, an office meal was scheduled on a day I had a work commitment. I have no idea if the whole of the following year would have been different had I attended. It never occurred to me to ask for another chance.

In the weekly sessions of the refeeding phase of FBT, there is normally a lot of attention given to how meals went, who said what, what helped and what didn't. The intention is to give families tools to use once at home. In our case this wasn't hands-on enough to help.

We would be able to care for our children at home so much better if outpatient services offered more home support. What we need, what we yearn for, is an experienced person to sit with us for a few meals to observe us and coach us. Sometimes we just need to break a deadlock, to get one success. If we still can't get our child to eat, we want an expert to come in and help us get our child to eat. And we need this expert to be an expert in eating disorders, someone who is part of the team, not a general health worker who doesn't understand eating disorders.

We asked for coaching at the start of our daughter's illness, then again at regular intervals. Eventually the eating disorders unit offered to come and support us over a few meals. After four lunches we'd learned everything we'd been trying to learn during 11 months of hospitalisation and countless family therapy sessions. Those four sessions gave me a big chunk of what's in this book.

Health service managers, take note: I reckon that those visits cost the service a total of six hours. Six hours, versus thousands of hours of therapy and nursing care.

If I were king, every family hit by an eating disorder would receive coaching and support at home.

Home support and day care are available in some countries or regions, and not in others. Ask, and when you get a no, don't give up. Ask other agencies too. You might get help from an organisation in your area that oversees healthcare or social-care services. You might get home support via psychiatric services. I am not advocating that you get other people to take over feeding (except to give you a break from time to time); it's best for the long term if you are empowered to do it. But if staff visit your child at home or take her out, it may be enjoyable for her while giving you some respite. A private care agency may provide a regular person you all like and you might find it surprisingly affordable. Social work will tell you what's available. They may give you access to carers or to funds. Also, check out non-profit organisations whose mission is to care for carers.

I offer coaching by video call.[290] My experience is that it doesn't take much to support disempowered parents to become supremely competent.

HOSPITALISATION AND INPATIENT TREATMENT

Given that home support or day centres are extremely scarce, thank goodness for the safety net provided by experienced inpatient units.[291] We may all hate the idea of our precious children being hospitalised, but for some of us the decision becomes a no-brainer.

An inpatient unit is a place where a child can be rescued if she needs to be medically stabilised, or when she's very undernourished and isn't having food or fluid, or when she's self-harming or suicidal, or when you cannot supervise her constantly to break a purging habit. Sometimes, if the staff cannot get a very ill child to eat any more than the parents can, they may use a nasogastric tube and provide constant supervision to ensure it stays in place.

I hope you can get your child into hospital if that's what she needs. Some parents struggle to get their child inpatient care for an eating disorder other than anorexia. Sometimes hospitals only admit or re-admit anorexic patients if their weight falls below a certain BMI threshold, independently of all the other symptoms or behaviours. I am not even close to understanding this policy.

There are many reasons why hospital staff manage to get youngsters to eat when parents can't. Your child may eat because she respects the authority of strangers or because she's embarrassed to make a scene in front of others. Her fear of being tube-fed or detained against her will may trump her fear of eating. Unlike us, nurses are not on an emotional rollercoaster 24/7. They have built up many hours of experience with a range of patients; they get coaching, support, teamwork, and sleep. In spite of all this, they notice how their emotions can occasionally flare up around a child who's not eating, and they are quite awed by what parents do.

Eating disorders inpatient units

In the old model, eating-disorders treatment takes place in a specialised eating-disorder unit (or a psychiatric ward that has some eating-disorder beds) for several weeks or months. The unit gets youngsters to gain weight (tube-feeding if necessary) and parents breathe a sigh of relief. People are discharged when their weight is restored (or close to restored), though some units also wait for patients' mental state to improve. The unit does all the work and all the major decision-making. There may be an hour's weekly family therapy and parents are invited to review meetings, but on the whole, they are onlookers. When the person returns home, she is expected to resume normal life as though she was recovered. Yet she's had no guided practice at normal living, she still fears food and weight gain. So she restricts. She may, of course, have planned this all along – she only gained weight to be allowed home. Parents may have no more power to help her eat than first time round – when they try, she may protest that the hospital didn't serve such big portions or never made her eat cheese. Youngsters then get a revolving door situation, getting re-admitted into an inpatient unit whenever the eating disorder gets too strong.

Inpatient units, increasingly, are shifting toward a more family-orientated ethos. The trailblazers make parents (and outpatient services) active members of the treatment team, along principles of family-based treatment.[292] They support increasingly long periods at home. This way, when the child is finally discharged, she is used to being skillfully accompanied by her family and the transition is more likely to be successful. Consider for instance that traditionally, dietitians in hospitals devise meal plans in collaboration with patients. The whole ethos changes when it is the parents who make the choices, and when parents are supported to help their child to eat in the unit. With this way of working, patients may be discharged much sooner, because parents have the competence to take over and take care of the transition.

Medical (paediatric) wards

Finally there is a move to using medical (paediatric) hospital wards more skillfully. For years, paediatric wards have not known what to do with a child who won't (can't) eat – their job, as they saw it, was to treat kids with asthma or heart problems, not kids with scary mental health problems. This made them eager to pass the child on to a mental health unit as soon as they'd achieved medical stabilisation. This continues to be the situation in many places, and parents tear their hair out because nobody is sitting by the child helping him to eat and checking that he doesn't bin his food. Staff may also make insensitive or unhelpful comments as they have no education, and no guidelines, relating to eating disorders.

Now some paediatric units have protocols (pathways) telling them exactly what to do, in collaboration with outpatient eating-disorders services, in order to intervene for a few days (possibly two or three weeks at the most). With this model, parents are involved and supported in the ward, so that as soon as their child's health is stabilised, they are able to resume care at home. If all goes well, the child will never need to go into a mental health or eating-disorders unit, because the family is learning and being supported all along (as a result, some inpatient mental health units are finding they now have very few eating-disorder patients, which pleases everyone except, I imagine, the business manager). This model gives a major role to outpatient family therapists, as they are a crucial resource to both parents and the paediatric ward.

Tips: when your child is in an inpatient unit

My husband and I still remember our amazement and relief when we learned that our daughter, within 20 minutes of admission, had calmly eaten a packet of crisps and drunk a glass of milk. It's a wonderful feeling, and thank goodness for safety nets provided by competent units.

There are huge variations between services, and it's a big worry for parents when hospitals don't treat them as valuable members of the team. It means that you have to be constantly on the ball, informing, requesting, checking and complaining. When your child enters a unit, don't assume anything. Be vigilant. But also recognise when your kid is in safe hands and it's OK for things to be 'good enough'.

Here are some pointers to help you work out how to manage hospital-related issues.

- Be aware that some treatment units believe in punitive or highly regimented approaches, so do your research.

- Your child will be surrounded by others with eating disorders or other mental illnesses. Ask what measures are in place to prevent patients sharing weight-loss or self-injury tips with each other. How are children shielded from other children's distressing behaviour?

  In our case, when another child with anorexia joined my daughter's ward, the two were never left on their own to share tips and tricks. When some of the children had violent outbursts, the nurses would promptly take the other kids into another room. In spite of these precautions, my daughter does seem to have learned more than I would have liked about the traumatic lives of other children. And I didn't love how she copied some of the other kids' raucous style. Yet in spite of 11 months of this, none of it stuck. And being exposed to other children's distress wasn't all bad – my daughter developed a lot of kindness and understanding for human vulnerability.

- Ask the unit what their aims are (Safety? Medical stabilisation? Weight recovery? Some level of mental recovery?) How they will decide that your child is ready for discharge.

- If the unit is not facilitating rapid weight gain, why not? (Too many units go softly-softly, hoping to build the patient's motivation.)

- Even if hospital isn't perfect, consider the whole picture. Is your child safe and gaining weight? Use the time and space to recover and to get yourself ready to take over again.

- The hospital may introduce systems you disagree with. For instance, knowing what I know now, I am sad that my eleven-year old had weekly meal-planning sessions. Within the first 20 minutes in the ward she'd managed to eat what she'd been given, so why start negotiating with her? I believe those sessions deprived her of a golden opportunity to get her to quickly expand her range of foods.

- You will fight some things, and you will accept others because the main thing is that your child is safe, gaining weight, and you can't sweat the small stuff. Once your child is back home, you can stage-manage a clear takeover, refusing to be bound by the way the hospital did things.

- The hospital should be working to give you the competence and confidence to feed your child at home as soon as possible, and to rebuild your relationship. You should have practice on the ward, and your child should come home for increasingly long spells.

- Things might have been a lot faster for us if the health service had supported us with meals at home. It might have saved my daughter from being in hospital so long – and maybe she needn't have gone in at all. When she'd been an inpatient for a few weeks, the staff helped us feed her in the ward, but it was still hard for us to get her to eat when she had home visits, and all we could get was phone support. See if you can request more, especially if you live close enough to the unit. Here's a great example of how a hospital supported a family I know: when the child came on home visits, a nurse came to support each meal until the family got the hang of it. This also reinforced the 'food is medicine' message: if the child didn't manage a meal, the nurse was ready to take her back to the ward right away.

- It grieves me when units make home visits conditional on the child managing all their food or gaining weight. In their effort to incentivise, they are not just punishing the child. They are disempowering parents and delaying an essential part of the treatment.

- We live close to the hospital and don't have other children, so it was easy for me or my husband to go in every day. For some people the journey takes several hours, and one parent ends up staying there while the other looks after the rest of the family. For some parents, sadly, phone contact is the only option for days at a time.

- I imagine that some of you will find it very distressing to think of your child being hospitalised for as long as our daughter was. Had I known it would take nearly a year, I'd have been horrified. Could it have been shorter if the unit's ethos had been different? Quite possibly. But a long stay may be necessary when a child's mental condition is particular severe, and that's nobody's fault. I have a friend whose daughter only started eating after a three-year inpatient stay with tube-feeding. The parents found ways to make this long period meaningful and rich with loving connection.

- I'm incredibly grateful that our hospital cared for our daughter while her opposition to us was extreme. If she'd been discharged before we could feed her she would have kept dipping back to critical levels and having to be re-admitted.

Parents can be overwhelmed by all kinds of emotions when their child goes into hospital. For some parents, there is little relief – there are new types of worries, decisions, frustrations. My own feelings weren't necessarily what you might expect.

- When the possibility of hospitalisation was first raised, I was horrified. My position was 'over my dead body'. Then I learned more about what hospital would be like, and realised it might be a place where my daughter would feel safe and well cared for – and this turned out to be the case.

- The speed at which anorexia gained ground was terrifying. So a few days before our daughter was due to be admitted, we were desperate for her to go in even sooner. This was a week when getting half a glass of water into her by mid-afternoon was a major victory. We believed the hospital was going to save her life, and that's what it did.

- As soon as we set foot in the ward with our daughter, we saw that she would feel well cared for. The staff acted like real human beings. Our daughter thought the place looked wonderful (to us it was old and shabby and rather depressing). This is what she wanted. As a result we were able to drive away without feeling torn, worried or guilty.

- Unlike my daughter, many children resist being in hospital. Sometimes they plead to be taken home. Sometimes they stop engaging with their parents, convinced they've been abandoned. This is extra hard for parents, who are already grappling with sadness and with multiple concerns about how their child will be treated. This is a time to get a lot of support and compassion for yourself. You will need a clear head to negotiate many details concerning your child's care.

- I felt relieved and incredibly grateful for the first few days of my daughter's hospitalisation. My mother thought I would be a wreck, and I wasn't. And I refused to feel guilty about not feeling guilty. My daughter was being rescued by competent and kind professional and this made us luckier than a whole lot of parents all over the world.

- I was also relieved that my own personal hell was over. I still had to deal with rejection and hate every day or two when I visited, but that was fine. I acknowledged that the strain on us, as loving parents, had been horrendous, and I allowed myself to enjoy some much-needed peace of mind.

- Some parents, like me, take advantage of the respite (in between numerous meetings and visits), while others fret. Some have to deal with multiple concerns about the hospital. Sometimes all is as well as can be but parents feel guilty because suddenly they hardly have anything to do. If this is you, treat yourself with as much kindness as you would treat a loved one. You're part-way through what may be a long journey. Since professionals are caring for your child, use the time to recuperate and rebuild yourself. You may need to curl up in bed and sleep, or to enjoy the company of friends. Your child needs you to be very well, so that you can advocate for her while she's in hospital and take charge when she's discharged. Rest. Have fun. And if anyone asks you how you're doing, tell them what they want to hear: that you're sick with guilt and worry.

- For me, the whole time that my daughter was in hospital was a time to educate myself about the illness and what could be done. I did a lot of reading, and I did a lot of advocating and requesting, in order to steer my daughter's care in the direction I believed was best.

- The days when my husband visited my daughter straight from work, when I would be on my own till nine at night, seemed scarily long. I got on with my work, which I do from home. Most days, though, there were meetings of some kind to go to. Both my work and my husband's suffered, though not irrevocably. I turned down any work that required me to be bright-eyed and bushy-tailed. There are professional situation where tears are not OK.

- If you cry a lot, you're in good company. I cried because I missed my daughter. I cried when I drove away from the ward and she'd not talked to me. I cried when someone treated me with kindness. I cried and fumed and pondered and planned when I disagreed with an aspect of her treatment. What I wish for you is that your child's hospital comes with such an amazing reputation that you can relax and concentrate on looking forward to your child coming home. But I suspect that for many of us parents, at some stage along the journey there are huge stresses that come from dealing with one or more clinicians with whom we disagree.

As most of you won't be contemplating having your child in hospital for nearly as long as we did, I'd like to quote a mother whose child, aged 13, was cared for at the Center for Treatment of Eating Disorders, Children's Hospital Minneapolis. It sounds like heaven.

> *"The program follows Maudsley meticulously. They do not believe in residential treatment for adolescents/teens UNLESS the patient is medically unstable, and then only for the briefest period possible. During the entire three week period in the hospital, I was encouraged to be present as much as possible. We had family meals beginning after seven days, ramping up to twice per day as we neared the date for her discharge. We got LOTS of support from the team to help us understand both the theory and the practical means for implementation. I felt very little hesitation about going home, and they made me feel as if my husband and I were competent to handle the refeeding process at home.*
> *[...]While hospitalized, there was minimal interaction with other inpatients, and always supervised. It was very well done. They had a TON of diversionary activities throughout each day, which made the stay more pleasant for my daughter (arts and crafts, music therapy, physical therapy, yoga, television shows produced in house, etc). She loved it.*
> *The nurses were, without exception, kind and generous. Also, well trained in Maudsley, and deferential to parent decisions. I really felt like an important member of the team."*

Nine weeks after her daughter returned home for Family-Based Treatment, this mum wrote:

> *"Things are going VERY well with my daughter. The ED monster hasn't shown itself in any ugly way in several weeks now. We get little glimpses (requests for one kind of food over another), but nothing that has caused me so much as to raise an eyebrow."*

Read on my website:
  Can hospital equip you for family-based treatment? A parent's inspirational account

Hospital emergency units

While I'm on the subject of hospitals, I'll say a few words about emergency departments. They generally don't get a good press in the eating-disorders world. Too often the staff don't have specialised knowledge, and so the child and parents have to endure their judgemental reactions. Families may get sent home after several hours of waiting with: 'She's fine. Just make sure she gets a sandwich when you get home.' Worse, some parents do not trust that the right tests were carried out.[293]

Some parents find emergency units very helpful, though, especially if there has been some advance joint work done through the eating disorders service.

A few days before my daughter was due to be admitted into hospital, I got really worried about her state of dehydration and I took her to an out-of-hours doctor. He told her that if she carried on, she'd end up in a medical ward, which would be a shame as she was looking forward to going into the mental health unit. So he made her promise to eat and drink as soon as she got home. I asked that she drink a glass of water right in front of him. I could see the thought bubble over his head: 'Please no! What if she doesn't drink?' It took my kid quite some effort to manage that water, but having that doctor observe her made it possible.

PARENTS AND CLINICIANS IN PARTNERSHIP

It's a no-brainer that the best results come from clinicians and parents working in partnership, and yet I've seen ultra-competent parents become powerless victims when clinicians stand on a pedestal. We really need teamwork.

> *"Our treatment team didn't get everything right but they were really open to feedback."*

A consulting room should be a place where we parents consult people who have valuable expertise to offer.[294] The minute I am a pawn in someone else's game, governed by rules I haven't agreed to, my power to be effective diminishes.

There are instances of clinicians abusing the power that comes from their position. Some intimidate, blame, and refuse to discuss options. They can do so in subtle or overt ways. Either way, we get the message that we are not OK, and we find ourselves powerless to intervene in decisions around our child's care. This can stress us out even more than the eating disorder itself. The minute we step into a consulting room we may be stripped of the qualities that makes us strong. It is remarkable that so many professionals call us Mum and Dad, as though our names were too hard to remember. I find it hilarious to see my husband being called Dad, but it drives him crazy. 'Take a seat, Dad. How are you today?' Grrr!

I wonder if we allow some clinicians to have power over us because we truly are in their hands. We come to them at a time of utter desperation. We pray they can save our child's life and bring peace back to our family. So when the sessions don't go as we wish, we keep quiet. We don't want to upset or anger the therapist, because it matters more that our child is getting treatment.

Yet partnership between clinicians and parents means jointly working out the best way forward, often on a daily or weekly basis. That requires equality and great communication. I've even heard FBT therapists described as consultants to the parents. There are times when we are exhausted and devoid of imagination and we want experts to tell us exactly what to do. And there are times when we can take the lead because we know our kid better than anyone else and we've got the hang of this illness. Clinicians have a challenging job tracking where *we're* at and what *we* need, and for that, we need to talk and assume that they can handle what we have to say.

> *"I told them they could/should give us more advice and feedback (a*
> *kind of coaching) without being afraid they were being too directive."*

Sometimes clinicians seem to lose momentum. A parent whose daughter had been ill for several years told me that the therapists seemed to just go through the motions. The parents, on the other hand, went on achieving milestones at home. When the clinicians saw progress, they seemed to become re-energised and they started offering more support.

The Nonviolent Communication framework outlined in Chapter 13 can help you sort out what's going on in your head and give you the poise to request what you really want.

A small change – even just informing the clinician of what isn't working for you – might make all the difference. The therapists may also be ready to change how they do things, and whatever they learn from you will inform how they work with their next patients. Openness and collaboration can do wonders.

Tell your clinicians about this book

If you've read this far, I am guessing you have found some tips you would like to try out. I would recommend you are open about this with your clinicians so you can work as a team. If there are disagreements, they're better out in the open. Refrain from telling therapists how they 'ought' to be working. Would you like to be told how to do your job? Instead, tell them how the book is helping you or how it supports their treatment or how you'd like to try out some of the ideas. Ask, 'What do you think? Could you have a quick look, and let us know?'[295]

Plan ahead to make sessions fruitful

When we visit therapists, we tend to let them take the lead. But sometimes the hour goes by quickly and issues that are important to us have not been addressed. We shouldn't expect our clinicians to be mind readers, and so I believe it's rational and not disrespectful to announce, before the meeting begins in earnest, the topics we really need help with. Work out your priorities with your partner and prepare a list ahead of time. Show that you two are a team, and expect your clinicians to work in partnership with you.

More family therapy without children, please

Standard FBT sessions happen with the whole family together in a room ('conjoint'). But there is validated variant ('separated' or 'parent-focused') where parents talk with the therapist separately.[296]

We had a successful variation on this theme with the therapist who cared for us after our daughter was discharged from hospital. I had a weekly phone call with her to brief her about the week's progress, tell her about our difficulties and make plans for the coming days. It kept the family meetings upbeat, and my daughter didn't get to hear things that might have brought on shame or guilt. She was also spared discussions about upcoming challenges, as we had noted this raised her anxiety and increased her resistance.

Sessions exclusively between therapist and parents can be very helpful in making sure the therapist knows everything that matters about your child. Sometimes you can feel that your therapist is barking up the wrong tree, and perhaps that's because there are things she needs to know which you haven't yet told her. If your therapist is moving your kid too fast towards independent eating, for instance (Phase II of FBT), perhaps she needs to hear how he's still hiding food or lying about eating his school lunches.

Whether a family does better with conjoint or family-focused family may depend on the parents' ability to take charge, and how much the child is able to collaborate.[297] If you see your child engaging with the therapist, then the conjoint approach may be wonderfully supportive. If your child wriggles and squirms, lies, clams up or makes rude comments, try some parent-focused sessions.

Parents want advice

I really hate it when therapists give advice I don't agree with.

Let me clarify. I don't hate advice I disagree with; what I don't like is when there's no room for discussion. As the recipient of advice, you should feel entirely free to examine it, discuss its merits and weaknesses, assess risks with the help of your expert, and then make a decision. Not only because it's your child, not only because you know her best, but also because if the advice doesn't work out and it makes your job of feeding extra hard, it's very much your problem.

What bugs me nearly as much as coercive, non-negotiable advice is the withholding of advice, the decision to be non-directive even when the parents beg for direction. Some clinicians stand by the principle that they don't have all the answers whereas we, the parents, are experts on our child and have the power to work out solutions. What doesn't work for me is when they hold back on their considerable expertise, built upon years of training and experience with families. If we were so knowledgeable about eating disorders, we wouldn't be in an expert's consulting room. We want ideas, suggestions, choices and advice, and if we're heading down a dead-end road, we want to be told.

> *'We were in this big circle of parents and young people, and this
> woman started speaking of her daughter as 'selfish'. We shifted*

uncomfortably in our seats. I glanced at the therapists, wondering
why they weren't saying something. Someone changed the subject. So
I spoke up. The woman listened and it was like she'd seen the light.
Her daughter teared up in relief. At break time, one of the
therapists thanked me for intervening. It was surreal."

If your child had a heart condition, the specialists would answer your questions, so why, with eating disorders, do parents have to do so much research and waste so much time with trial and error?

I guess I'm preaching to the choir. If you didn't want suggestions and advice, you wouldn't still be reading this book.

"I don't think every family has to start from scratch and re-invent
the wheel. Sometimes I think Maudsley professionals get so wound
up in not being directive that they end up not being supportive
enough. We felt at times that they knew what we were doing wrong
during meals but had to let us work it out rather than coach and
give feedback. This left us feeling that we were experimenting on our
child, and that we were being tested (how long would it take us to
finally find a way of supporting meals which worked?)."

Giving advice is tricky. Empathy comes first. If parents don't ask obvious questions like 'How can I get my child to eat?' then they're probably too upset to cope with the answer. That may be a reason for a therapist to hold back.

Or perhaps the reason for evasiveness is a lot simpler:

"We'd ask the therapist for tips, and she'd say we were perfectly
capable of feeding our daughter and that we'd find our own way.
That made us feel even more incompetent, because we were failing big
time. Then one day it occurred to me she probably didn't have a clue
herself. If so, I wish she'd told us straight."

But I have also seen really knowledgeable therapists keep quiet. On one occasion, I sounded out our specialist about making a major U-turn on the content of meals. She exclaimed, 'I'm so glad you asked!' Clearly, she'd been itching for us to go down this new road, but for a reason I don't understand, had waited for the impetus to come from us. Meanwhile we'd been meekly maintaining the status quo even though we hated it, because we thought it was what was expected of us.

Lock and Le Grange, the founders of FBT, teach that too much information may overwhelm rather than empower. That there is a balance to strike, as people learn by experience, from their mistakes. That being too directive can be disempowering and perhaps diminish learning.

So when we want answers, what can we parents do? I'd suggest we make our requests for advice crystal-clear. Until we do, the experts may have all sorts of reasons to hold back. So, ask, ask, and ask again.

Parents with eating disorders

Given that eating disorders have a major genetic component, it is to be expected that many parents have suffered from one themselves. Are you worried that you will be blamed or excluded from your kid's treatment if you yourself have a history of the illness?

In principle, it shouldn't be an obstacle. Family therapy has been shown to have a decent success rate, and the method doesn't exclude parents with eating disorders.

Sometimes a parent's eating disorder is still active and the child's treatment is a strong trigger.[298] In this case, a therapist will encourage you to get treatment for yourself. I imagine that there is no problem as long as the parent is on the alert for anything they do or say that contradicts what they want for their child. Even without an eating disorder, we parents are part of society, and there are unhelpful messages and misinformation around healthy eating, fatty foods and body shape that we need to untangle ourselves from.

Supporting a child who is suffering can awaken emotions from vulnerable times in our own childhood. Mindfulness helps us to take care of our children as our true self, not as a hurt, scared or angry child. For some parents, this is a springboard to healing and growth for themselves.

Empowering parents

After the terrible old days of 'parentectomies', it's a relief that enlightened therapists make parents part of the treatment team. Our need to feel competent and empowered is pretty fundamental. If this need isn't met we turn into doormats or behave like a bull in a china shop. But being empowered also helps us make decisions on the fly. We can't run to the therapist every time we hit a new variation on a problem. We may not ever feel totally competent, but we can at least aim for 'good enough'.

In addition to how we feel about ourselves, it's also absolutely essential for parents to be empowered in their child's eyes. How else can we get our child to trust us more than they trust their disordered internal talk? Our first instinct may be to lean on the expert's authority, but soon you can end up with triangulation: 'The therapist said that I didn't have to wear a hat and gloves if it's not cold outside.' Imagine having to wait a week for an appointment before you can resolve that one!

I noticed our eating disorders specialist very deliberately handing power over to us. There was one phone call where I told her of my desire to ditch the meal plan we'd inherited from the hospital. She validated that with enthusiasm. Next, I asked her how she would bring it up at our next appointment. I knew it would be a huge blow to my daughter and I expected the therapist to weigh in with her professional authority. No such luck. If I was entertaining the slightest hope that I could hide behind an expert and be shielded from my daughter's reaction, I was sorely disappointed. 'YOU will tell her,' she said. 'You and your husband are the people most competent to care for her.'

After a while my daughter started complaining as we drove to the appointments. She'd say, 'She's nice but I don't need her. YOU know how to look after me.'

Success!

Your clinical team: is everyone on the same page?

If psychotherapists, counsellors or coaches are not well integrated in an eating disorders team, we should beware of our kids getting mixed messages. It would be so unhelpful if a therapist helping a child with her anxiety, for instance, talked about diets or body shape, or pushed her to make her own food choices without the parents' agreement. The risk of this happening is quite high when big teams are involved.

At one stage, around 20 people seemed to have an interest in my daughter's care – hospital staff, outpatient staff, eating disorder experts, and even representatives from her school. That was 20 people round the table at hospital review meetings every few months.

It's an amazing feeling to see so many people rooting for your kid, scratching their heads about how best to help her, being delighted at her progress. And to have them all give us, the parents, a lot of consideration. One example of great teamwork was how my daughter's education never fell behind. The link between clinicians and school was beautifully handled. But having a lot of experts, each giving you appointments, can mean that your child gets pulled out of class or deprived of fun several times a week. Yet it might be that only one or two people are directly useful to her.

Most of all, is everyone singing from the same hymn sheet? Sometimes you can get various parties pulling in opposite directions, and your child is piggy in the middle. We had a little bit of that, though we didn't realise it at the time. For some families, the contradictions can be disastrous. Here's an extreme illustration: say you are (in my opinion) lucky and you get family therapy with a trained eating disorders specialist, who wants you, the parent, to be in charge of your child's meals. But say your underweight child also sees a dietitian who wants to negotiate meal plans with her, a doctor who says she can now stop gaining weight, a psychologist who believes that your adolescent needs independence, a something-or-another therapist who shames her for refusing dinner, and a psychiatrist who insists on one-to-one sessions to explore the reasons why, deep down, your child is using her eating disorder as a defence mechanism. See the problem?

The experts each believe in their own experience and competence. They may all believe they're up to date with the research. You can be sure they are gritting their teeth and tearing their hair out about their differences, but they do so privately. They don't discuss their colleagues with us parents. The best they can do is build bridges and hope to get others to come to their points of view, but what with hierarchies and politics and shows of respect for each other's professions, you can imagine it's not going to happen in a hurry.

It grieves me to see a child pulled in all directions and parents getting confusing messages while experts stay diplomatically silent. But what can be done? This is yet one more thing that falls on parents' shoulders. Keep asking questions. Don't be scared if you put some of the professionals' noses out of joint. Find out about people's training and what models they hold of the illness. Be your child's best advocate. Make your choices.

One mother who read a draft of this book told me, 'Cut that last bit out. You don't have any choices.' But she made important choices over and over, striving to make the best of a disjointed and ineffective treatment team.

> *"I arranged meetings with all professionals involved to get them on the same page. I threatened that otherwise I would write to the hospital board."*

Eventually she and her husband got rid of everyone except the family doctor and successfully took over their daughter's care.

WHEN YOU'RE EXCLUDED FROM YOUR CHILD'S THERAPY

Earlier I wrote about the role of individual psychotherapy as an adjunct to family therapy. 'Individual' usually means that you're firmly expected to sit in the waiting room. The therapist considers their client to be the child, not the child-parent unit. They want to give the child privacy from her parents. They will have a confidentiality agreement.

Think carefully of the pros and cons. When it works, parents are glad that their child has a private space to express themselves, heal or learn new ways of dealing with life's challenges. Everyone is on the same page, and the therapist understands your role in supporting your child most hours of the day back home.

Often, though, our children bitterly resist sessions, and because the parents don't have a good communication channel with the therapist, they have no idea if it's worth persevering. Then there are the therapists who jeopardise the work you're doing at home, because they think that family-based treatment is a shocking infringement of a young person's independence. To them you are over-controlling or codependent. They might believe that your child must be take full responsibility for their recovery, which means that parents have to back off. For some, the crucial task of adolescence is to develop autonomy, and they set about this with little regard to the loving parent-child bond. Some make unilateral decisions based on what your child says, as though your child was miraculously free of the cognitive distortions and manipulations of an eating disorder.

A therapist may take it as read that your child will want a 'private space' away from you. Even family therapists make excuses to be alone with your child – presumably checking for abuse. It can be excruciating for our children. If you are present in therapy, not only can you make it easier for your child to express themselves, but you can help integrate any learnings into daily life. It's a lot more effective than nagging your kid to fill in worksheets. The whole family can benefit from learning the tools of ACT (acceptance and commitment therapy) or DBT (dialectic behaviour therapy), for instance. Treatment for OCD requires a lot of practice in everyday situations.

If a therapist sees you as a taxi driver, I recommend you meet them alone to check out their expertise, qualifications, beliefs and methods. You are, after all, your child's advocate. The therapist's style and approach must make sense to you. Agree on two-way communication (I discuss confidentiality below). How will you update the therapist about your child's symptoms and behaviours? How will want to warn them if your child's mood plummets, or if he is facing new pressures with school, friends or a bereavement?

Conversely, what kind of thing is the therapist willing to tell you? Some will only reveal information if your child is actively suicidal. Others may agree to report if your child fails to attend a session or if their weight falls below a certain level. Some discuss with your child what they are willing to disclose in a joint session. This could be ten minutes at the end of each hour, or a longer monthly review.

Discuss the limits of the therapist's decision-making. For instance, if you're challenging your son's fear of short sleeves, it's counterproductive if the therapist tells him he should make his own clothing decisions. It's not OK for your child to be coming home – and these are real examples – saying, 'She told me I'm old enough to make my own food choices.' Or, 'She says I can join a gym.' Or 'She worked out my BMI and I don't need to gain any more weight.' Or 'She thinks you're over-protective and I should stop telling you things'.

If you haven't set up the rules of teamwork, you could quickly become disempowered and unable to support your child in the longer term. Here is a real and all-too-typical example. I know of a 15-year old who was quickly and successfully brought back to a healthy weight through family therapy, with parents taking charge. The clinical team skipped the following phases of treatment and moved her on to individual therapy. There, the therapist decreed the girl was at an age to make her own food choices. The parents sat helplessly while their girl ate her own tiny, obsessively-prepared meals alone in her bedroom. They regularly emailed the therapist a list of symptoms and requested joint sessions, but only got bland responses – about things taking time and the girl needing to learn to take responsibility. When she became medically compromised and the parents still couldn't take charge, it was a hospital that got her eating again.

I am frustrated about the wasted opportunities when parents are excluded. After my girl was discharged from hospital I moved heaven and earth for her to see an EMDR therapist. Her dieting had been triggered by a bullying incident, and she made a strong emotional connection between thinness with safety. I really hoped that now she was better, trauma therapy could help reset her beliefs.

Well, my daughter took great pride in taking the therapist for a ride. She would come home and laugh at the woman's credulity. As my girl did want help, though, she and I proposed that I should join the sessions to act as my child's intermediary, a translator of sorts. I knew what her issues where and what an EMDR therapist needed to know. Frustratingly, this psychologist thought that my presence would be weird, even though EMDR with very young kids is routinely done with the help of a parent. And so we lost our chance to give my kid resilience against similar incidents in the future. Had we succeeded, I wonder if my girl might not have dieted, some years later, when a comparable situation arose.

More on my website anorexiafamily.com:
Eating disorders: understand where psychotherapists are coming from

Confidentiality

For some parents the toughest issue around individual therapy is the professionals' stance regarding confidentiality. Mental health laws are poorly designed for illnesses like eating disorders (that have a component of anosognosia) but a skilled clinician will work at finding solutions.[299] Sadly it's also common for parents to be given a blunt: 'Your son doesn't want to speak to you. He doesn't want you to know anything about his weight or his blood test results. Sorry and goodbye.' Depending on where you live, this could start as early as age twelve.

When a twelve-year old has diabetes, are doctors as determined to withhold blood test results from parents?

A clinician may not be allowed to give you information until your child puts their consent in writing. If your son or daughter is reluctant, they may be more willing once they know they can specify an end date, and can withdraw consent any time.

A basic element of confidentiality in individual therapy is to guarantee a patient's privacy, except if what she said indicates that she (or another person) is in some kind of danger or at risk. Before sharing this information with you, the therapist would normally discuss with your child who needs to know and how to tell them.

There's an example of this in Glenn Waller's manual for CBT therapists.[300] An underweight 15-year old disclosed in therapy that she was secretly vomiting at home. Given the level of risk, the therapist decided that others needed to know, and the two discussed how and when to tell the parents.

Indeed good therapists know that a child cannot get effective support at home if information is withheld about restricting or self-harming behaviours. They know that collaboration with parents is good for everyone. They have a sensible and compassionate approach to confidentiality. They work at securing your child's agreement to involve you. Rather than making you 'the other', they nurture the power of your connection.

A very precious tool you have is that confidentiality rules only apply in one direction. You are allowed – and it would be wise – to tell your child's therapist of any worrying behaviours you are observing. The clinician has a duty to listen, even if all they say back is 'Thanks. Goodbye'. Here is some authoritative guidance on parents wishing to raise issues:

> *"The problem that many families report is lack of information*
> *[...]this often arises from overenthusiastic defence of patient*
> *confidentiality. Even if the patient has said they do not want their*
> *family to be given information, the family can still be seen and*
> *counselled in general about any issue they wish to raise, as long as*
> *information coming from the patient is not divulged."*[301]

If you decide to reveal information to a therapist, it's probably best if you have a compassionate conversation with your child about it. That way the information is flowing in all directions. If you don't feel able to do this, the therapist should be able to advise on the next steps.

We had mostly good experiences around confidentiality. For example there was an occasion when our daughter revealed in a hospital family session that something was seriously troubling her, but she refused to give any details. We were delighted to find out that her favourite young nurse was on duty that night and that our daughter was ready to speak to her. The next morning, this delightful person phoned me and assured me that the whole issue had been dealt with and that my daughter was now quite at ease. To this day I don't know what it was about, and I'm not worried about it.

It is a lot easier for us parents to let go of the need for information if we totally trust that the carers are doing an excellent job, at least as good as we would do ourselves. It's even easier if treatment fully involves parents, so that there is no issue with confidentiality in the first place.

Children above legal-age thresholds

> *"Turning 18 can put pressure on a child. Services suddenly want to refer her to the adult services. Friends and classmates start to move away from home, giving her the feeling she should do the same."*

Many parents fear that as soon as their child turns 18, she will suddenly refuse to sit down at the dinner table. In practice, many youngsters continue to accept their parents' care, even if they fight individual meals.[302] Just as my 10-year-old could have run away every morning before breakfast, 18-year-olds don't necessarily walk off just because they have the legal right to do so. And remember that the research on FBT was done on youngsters aged 12 to 18 inclusive. More recent research is looking at adaptations of the method for young adults.[303] I encourage parents to be assertive in their caring role whatever their child's age, though I appreciate that it may not be easy.

Your country's mental health laws will determine if your child can refuse treatment, if you have any decision-making power and, indeed, if you have a right to any information at all. Mental health laws do protect very ill people, making provisions to detain them and enforce treatment against their will. Some young people avoid treatment by keeping their weight very low but not so low as to get them sectioned. This is a dreadful situation, because it's part of the nature of the illness that patients don't consider themselves seriously sick, and even when they do, the fear of eating and putting on weight can be too much for them to willingly sign up for treatment.

Clinicians may be bound by law to act according to your child's wishes, even when they know and you know that this will hinder his treatment. They may not be allowed to tube-feed or to keep a child in hospital or to give you, the parents, any information or powers. In some countries these issues kick in when your child is as young as 12. Frustratingly, it seems that some professionals are so attached to the legalities that they are practically begging the young person to refuse treatment: 'OK Morgan, we would like to give you a supplement when you can't finish a meal, but it's your right to refuse. You're over-16, you've not been sectioned, and you are free to walk away any time.'

Because of mental health laws, your youngster's weight might plummet, she might discharge herself from treatment, and clinicians may not be allowed to tell you.

Parents can be on tenterhooks, hoping that their child will voluntarily accept hospitalisation or that if she's accepted treatment, she won't suddenly change her mind.

Sometimes the issue is not so much with the law as the policies of treatment providers: a clinician's focus may be on a young adult's autonomy, while our own priority is for our child to be nourished and made safe. When clinicians believe that parents are part of the problem, not part of the solution, everybody suffers.

I have friends abroad whose 18-year-old daughter had willingly entrusted herself to her parents by giving them power of attorney. In spite of this the local eating disorder services would only treat her if she checked herself in of her own accord. This was just too hard for her. She needed her parents to carry the burden of decision-making at a particularly stressful time. So what happened? She eventually got better at home, without therapists, supported by her parents.

To find out what the laws are in your country, try these internet search keywords: 'mental health law', 'detaining orders', 'section under the Mental Health Act', 'impaired decision-making ability' and 'compulsory treatment, citizen's advice'. Depending on where you live, guardianship or power of attorney[304] may offer solutions.

You have a great big lever on your child: money (assuming your child depends on you financially). I know of parents who have used the money lever to secure their child's agreement to treatment or to entice their young adult home for a spell of refeeding.

Threats always carry some risk. If you tell your child she can only live in your house if she accepts treatment, she may set up camp on the sofas of various friends. They are unlikely to help her to eat, shelter her from drink, drugs or self-harm. (As for sex, be aware that young anorexic women do become pregnant – having no period is not a reliable contraceptive.[305]) The picture doesn't have to be so bleak though: your young adult may storm out of your house but accept the care of an aunt, of your ex, of a heroic boyfriend or girlfriend. She may also return home because that's ultimately where she feels secure.

You have one huge asset: your relationship. Your child may fight you much of the time, but she is mostly fighting internal conflicts. While she is in distress you can bet she is longing to lean on you and receive your care, love and guidance.

THERAPY, COACHING AND EMOTIONAL SUPPORT FOR PARENTS

It is ironic that while children are subjected to ineffective psychotherapy, the people who badly need psychological support – the parents – only get to perform the taxi service. My hunt for emotional support began when I realised that not only was I bursting into tears on a regular basis in the most inappropriate of places (leading to a pathological attachment to my sunglasses), but for the first time in my life I'd caught myself toying with fantasies of self-harm. In those days I could withstand my child's resistance without showing my reactions, but it came at a cost. I was a pressure cooker of emotions.

At the same time I did feel powerful. I was not a depressed wreck. I was on a hero's journey,[306] with an all-important destination. I was limping and my blisters were giving me hell, but I wasn't a cripple. All I wanted was some trusted companions to bandage me up and apply healing ointments so I could continue on my mission. In short, I was like all the parents I've ever come across who are helping a child beat an eating disorder. There are parental acts of heroism going on all over the planet, day in, day out.

In an ideal world, all parents supporting a child with an eating disorder would be offered individual support (described as counselling, coaching, or psychotherapy), as well as group support. I believe this is reasonably standard if your child or your spouse is being treated for cancer. Most of us, however, have to hunt for support and pay for it.

I myself now offer individual support to parents[307] and could describe myself as a counsellor when people's needs are mainly emotional, and as a coach when people want tools to get their child to eat, to communicate better, or to manage their emotions.

If you're not familiar with therapists, counsellors or coaches, what follows may help you find what you need.

Therapists who will help you flourish

Psychotherapy (often shortened to 'therapy') refers to any kind of psychological care. Some psychotherapists (often shortened to 'therapists') are qualified clinical psychologists, some are kind people who've done a counselling or coaching course, and some are really, really loving people who have received special healing powers by a person with a direct line to God. Qualifications are no guarantee that sessions will be any different from sitting by the fire and throwing a ten-pound note in every few minutes. It's nearly impossible to know if a particular therapist will be any use until you've given them a trial run, though their websites can help you make an initial assessment.

The most common types of psychotherapies are individual (one-to-one) talking therapies, and within this category, there are gazillions of schools, models and methods. Some focus on behaviour change, some work on the past, some concentrate on the present or future. Some are based on talk, others on the body and emotions. Some are evidence-based, and some are not. What emerges from research is that the method doesn't matter as much as your connection with the person on the other side of the Kleenex box.

My own hunt for support

The day my daughter's clinicians realised how bad I felt, they got me a prompt referral to a senior psychologist. This person did psychodynamic therapy – that's therapy rooted in psychoanalysis. She couldn't relate to my request to help me build on my strengths in order to be there for my daughter, meal after meal, day after day. I guess she didn't have the tools to do it. Her approach was to have me talk about my childhood and look for insights around the harm my parents might have caused me. Warmth and kindness were not on the menu – professional detachment is seen as a virtue in many schools of psychotherapy. Nor did I have any hope she would ever see me as a fellow human being worthy of dignity and compassion. I saw myself suddenly as a bundle of potential hang-ups, contradictions and weaknesses, a helpless victim of a childhood that couldn't possibly be good enough.

Don't get stuck with a therapist like that. Indeed many therapists work on the presumption that we are deficient. Their outlook is one of illness, of alleviating misery, not flourishing or fulfilment. They see your ongoing difficulties as your failure, not theirs. Would you keep taking your car to a garage, week after week, if your car continued to gurgle and splutter?

Find someone who aims to make you well. Better than well – someone who can help you blossom, flourish and enjoy life to the full. The field of positive psychology has opened up all these possibilities.

After one session with my psychodynamic therapist, the only way for me to get prompt support was to go private. It really hurt to find out what the going rates were. But my husband and I put it in the category of 'things that come along with the illness and become a priority'.

As it turned out, an excellent psychotherapist can go a very long way. I stopped crying after one session with a new, kind therapist.[308] After four sessions I'd moved on and said a fond good-bye. I was well and felt I'd got what she had to give me, and for that I'm most grateful.

What was the magic? Good listening and reflecting skills, of course. She also taught me much of what I'm telling you in this book about anger and knee-jerk reactions. She noted my strengths and reflected back to me a picture of an OK person who could make things happen. For the first time I had someone's full, compassionate attention and that in itself was like a balm.

Meanwhile my knowledge of Nonviolent Communication was starting to come together and I was gathering lots of tools to help me be well. I discovered that whenever I was stuck, a session with a Nonviolent Communication trainer would help me move on.

With my daughter's relapse I found I wanted support again. This time I chose a therapist highly qualified in emotional freedom technique (EFT)[309] and I stuck with her for her human qualities – and because I could see immediate results. Not only did I get a boost when I needed it, I also could see my general resilience and wellbeing shooting up.

How to choose the right person for you

If you long for support, I hope you will find an excellent therapist.[310] If you're not rich, you may discover that after a couple of sessions you are strong again, and you may only need an occasional top-up every now and again. Be aware, also, that many psychotherapists adjust their rates to suit your financial situation.

One session might be enough to test a therapist out, and even before that, their website might give you some clues. Notice what's going on for you during the first session. Do you get a sense of being heard and supported? Of being held as an equal, with respect for your shared humanity? Do you feel calm and do you get a sense of assurance and relief seeping back into your body? Are you more ready to give the best of yourself at home and do you feel generally energised? If so, you've struck gold. Never mind the method – you've got yourself the therapist you need.

PhDs and top qualifications don't guarantee you will get a great therapist, though if you are suffering from trauma, depression or anxiety it would be wise to aim for someone with solid experience, training and supervision. For the rest, check out various therapists' experience and personal qualities, and see if what they offer matches your needs.

A word of caution, as your therapist may not be knowledgeable about eating disorders. They may not appreciate that your kid's behaviours are not within his control. They may be shocked by the relentless intensity of what is going on in your home. You need help with unconditional acceptance for your child, not more judgement, so be ready to educate your psychotherapist.

More on psychotherapy approaches that might be on offer to your child or yourself. Some are well worth pursuing, others possibly not. All on anorexiafamily.com/psychotherapy-eating-disorders-anorexia

Positive psychology

Nonviolent Communication (NVC) as a psychotherapy

Acceptance and commitment therapy (ACT)

Cognitive behaviour therapy (CBT)

Dialectical behaviour therapy (DBT)

Emotion-focused family therapy (EFFT)

Psychodynamic therapies

Eye-movement desensitisation and reprocessing (EMDR)

Emotional freedom technique (EFT, or 'tapping')

Cognitive remediation therapy (CRT)

Repetitive transcranial magnetic stimulation (rTMS)

Also:

Three routes out of post-traumatic stress disorder (PTSD)

13

POWERFUL TOOLS FOR WELLBEING AND COMPASSIONATE CONNECTION

How can you speak with your child so that you can guide them
through the toughest challenges, give them support, and help them
thrive? I guide you through principles of compassionate
communication. And because you need to be effective and powerful,
and because you are a role-model for your child, I also show you how
self-compassion works. If you are fearful about what to say, if your
child's emotions – and your own – are all over the place, this chapter
will help you be the confident, courageous and resilient parent your
child needs.

So far I've concentrated on practical aspects of the illness and its treatment. To be successful, we also have to regulate our emotions and speak skillfully. We know that it's unproductive to shout or blame or criticise. We don't want to be so fearful; we don't want to walk on eggshells. It's hard to be at our best, when we are anxious for our children and when they resist us with all their might. This chapter aims to make things a lot easier for you.

The tools in this chapter have allowed me to start difficult conversations with my daughter, because I had the confidence that I could steer any dialogue, however emotive, all the way to resolution and reconnection. I'm going to take you through simple principles and examples, and based on other parents' experiences, I hope they will become easy and natural.

You and your child will feel closer, which will feel good. Also, you will be modelling how to manage one's emotional life well, something few of us have been taught. Compassionate communication should make refeeding and exposure to fear foods a lot smoother. Dialogue doesn't end when you get a 'No'. Think 'compassionate persistence'.

Your child needs to experience your compassion, trustworthiness and power, and that's more likely to work when you get good at self-compassion. So I'll guide you through that later on in the chapter. It will help you be more of the person you want to be, and a secondary benefit is that you will be modelling it for your child.

"I managed to move on this afternoon from feeling incredibly upset and angry to a state of self-compassion and compassion towards my daughter. And she responded positively and moved on from her anger to a better place. She felt my compassion. It works!"

The tools in this chapter are not just for your child. They can become your everyday language with your other children, your spouse, friends, boss, your elderly parent, your dog. They make life richer.

This chapter is about principles, and the following two chapters address common situations. If you're still hungry for more, I go into more depth, with many examples, on anorexiafamily.com/NVC-communication. As always, use only what works for you, and make it your own. Also, please check out my videos and my Bitesize audio collection,[311] so you can hear examples of speech – I am aware that written examples of dialogue can seem unnatural.

The tools here use the best of what I've found in the field of Nonviolent Communication, Emotion-Focused Family Therapy, CBT and related therapies, and research on self-compassion.[312]

"I have started to work on my self-compassion. I am giving myself more understanding and I think this is indirectly making a huge difference for my daughter as well. Yes I think that is making an enormous difference."

In case compassion sounds to you like an exclusively 'soft' female skill, that's not the case. Nonviolent Communication has been used to bring together men in war-torn zones, and research on mindfulness and compassion covers all genders.

'I'M SORRY, AND I LOVE YOU'

Our aim is to move away from pointless fights:

to connection:

In the first cartoon, we first have a parent justifying themselves ('Yes I do understand you!'), and after that it all goes pear-shaped. Connection is built in the second cartoon, following this formula: *'I'm sorry, and I love you'*. You don't have to use those exact words. What matters is that you are in empathy with your child for their pain. You show it through your body language, your tone of voice, and your words. Your message is, 'I am sorry that you are suffering, and I care.' Be sincere. It will make you feel better, and it will help bring your child back to their greater self, because major needs have been met: they've received unconditional acceptance, they know they've been heard, that they matter and that they're loved.

'I'm sorry, and I love you' will help you stay away from justifying, accusing or retaliating. It will also stop you from jumping too early into reassurance, solutions or requests, which as I'll explain soon, doesn't work well at all.

Here are some more examples, and please tweak them to suit your style, as long as you show genuine kindness and concern.

> 'My tummy is sore!' *I'm so sorry my darling. I love you.*
> 'I hate my life!' *Oh sweetheart, I am so sorry how hard things are for you at the moment.*
> 'My friends think I'm weird!' *I'm sorry, honey. That sounds lonely.*
> 'Dad hates me!' *Gosh, it must be tough to feel that your own dad hates you. I am so sorry.*
> 'Piss off!' *Hey, you're really angry! That's not like you. What's up?*

What do you say afterwards? I will come to that. First, I want to give you a tip if you are already thinking that *anything* you say always makes your child worse.

SILENT EMPATHY

Silent empathy is where you think, 'I'm sorry, and I love you' without saying it out loud. Sometimes our children are in such a state that even the most wonderful words irritate them. Sometimes *we* are in such a state that we don't trust ourselves to open our mouth! This is where silent empathy can be magic.

With silent empathy, you do nothing, you say nothing. You just stay there, thinking kind thoughts towards your child. You wonder what's going on for them. What are they feeling? What matters to them so much? Don't analyse, just let your heart be open.

Your body language says, 'You're OK. I'm OK. We're safe. This is all fine. I love you.' Give a bit of eye contact to show you care, but not so much that it might be received as overpowering. If your child allows it, offer to hold their hand, offer a hug.

I'll give you an example. My child has pushed her plate away violently: 'Are you crazy? I'm not eating that!' I am scared and cross, so I give myself a few seconds of emergency self-compassion (more on that later). That's enough for me to start opening my heart to her. I think, 'I've put butter on her toast, and it's still quite new so she's probably terrified. My poor little girl... she's not chosen any of this horror. I wonder if she's very hungry, wishing she could eat in spite of her terrifying rules. I really want to help her manage it.'

This silent empathy calms me, making me more resourceful. I have more mental bandwidth to work out what to do next. Now here's the magic. I've often been amazed to see my daughter's state shift during my silence. Perhaps it's because she's got nothing to argue against. Perhaps it's because my more peaceful state is contagious. I don't know, and that's why I think it's magic. I hope it works for you. In the example above, my girl might drop her shoulders, she might whimper, 'It's not fair, I'm not eating that,' she might look at me and she might look at the toast. All brilliant signs that she's ready for me to support her to eat.

CONNECT BEFORE YOU CORRECT

What we've done so far is connection, not problem-solving. Almost everybody tends to bypass connection and jump straight to the rational, sensible stuff: seeking solutions, reassuring, giving instructions, educating. I'll refer to all that as 'Correcting'. You can be way more effective when you do 'Connecting' first. Using the same examples as above, 'Correcting' could look like this:

'My tummy is sore!' *You need the food, darling. As you keep eating, your digestive system will return to normal.*

'I hate my life!' *Things will get better once you're eating regularly and enough.*

'My friends think I'm weird!' *No they don't! Let's invite them over and you'll see how much they love you.*

'Dad hates me!' *Well you called him an idiot, so it's not surprising you're not best of pals right now. Why don't you send him a nice message and make peace?*

'Piss off!' *Use polite language please. Would you tell me what's up using polite words?*

The 'Correcting' in these examples is sensible and non-judgemental and totally appropriate. But just now it is *too* sensible! It's all about reason, and in this moment, your child has little or no access to reason because their emotions are high.

So what normally works better is to 'Connect before you Correct'. You help your child feel safe and connected, and only when their emotions have decreased do you move on to the 'Correction' bit.

When someone is shouting, or closed off, or putting up resistance, they're in a state of fight, flight, or freeze, with little access to rational thought (remember our bungee-jump?). When we use a kind voice and body language, when we show interest and non-judgement, when we make them feel cared for, their nervous system gets the message that the threat is over, and they get access to their whole intelligence again.

You may like the metaphor of the elevator. The door to reason is on the ground floor. When your child has high emotion, they might be on the 10th floor! You have to get the elevator down to the ground floor in order to have a reasonable conversation.[313]

'Correcting', having a reasonable conversation, guiding, problem-solving – these are very much part of our job as parents: we have wisdom, knowledge and reassurance to impart. We contain our kids, we provide structure – by giving guidance and setting limits. We just need to 'Connect' first. For example:

'My friends think I'm weird!' *I'm sorry, honey. That sounds lonely. Are you having a hard time? [then eventually:] I know Andy and Becky like you a lot. I propose we invite them over for a start.*

There are exceptions to the 'Connect before you Correct' rule, and that's when our children's minds are very chaotic and we sense they need clear directions, like you would if you were caught in a fire. So when our child is physically abusive, we say, 'Stop! Do not hit!' When we are helping our child to eat, direct prompts tend to work best ('Get started on the nuts') and any empathy talk needs to be brief. Here are some more examples where, depending on the context, it can work well to jump straight to 'Correct':

'There's too much cheese!' *It's what you need. Trust me. Keep going.*

'Why are you making me fat?!' *It's not useful to talk about this. Help me choose another audiobook for us.*

'I don't want to see anyone.' *I'll ask you to say hello to our friends, and if after 10 minutes you're not enjoying yourself you can go back to your room.*

In most difficult situations, though, 'Connect before you Correct' works best.

KEEP TRACKING

If your compassionate response doesn't address what's really bothering another person, then:
- they continue to fight, or
- they keep repeating themselves, going round in circles

When that happens, check that you are doing 'Connect' and haven't jumped too soon into 'Correct'. Assuming that's in order, the reason your child seems stuck is usually that your empathy has missed the mark: something else is bothering them. Possibly something deeper. So listen out for clues. Here's an example of how you might keep tracking and responding:

Child: 'My friends think I'm weird!'
You: *No they don't! Let's invite them over and you'll see.*
Child: 'Are you crazy! Then they'll definitely think I'm weird!'
(This reaction makes you realise you jumped into 'Correct', so you loop back into compassion)
You: *I'm sorry, darling. Having friends think you're weird... that sounds lonely.*
Child: 'Well I *am* weird, let's face it!'
(You take heart that your child is less hunched up, but as she's still quite stuck in anxious thinking, you keep up the compassion)
You: *Oh that's tough! Thinking that you are weird.*
Child: 'I'm not weird, I'm just not fun, you know'
(Ah, so the empathy worked. She's more relaxed, and she's worked out she's not weird after all, without any need for you to lecture her about it.)
You: *Let's invite your friends over. It will be fun.*
Child: 'I've just told you I'm not fun!'
(A sharp reminder that you jumped to 'fixing' too soon. She had an emotion around 'I'm not fun' and you didn't track it. So do so now.
You: *Oh sweetheart, it must be miserable to think you're no fun. I really feel for you.*

Keep tracking your child's state, validating her emotions, till you see a shift. Her state should keep changing, because with compassion, emotions transform or move on fast. She might get tearful, might accept a long hug, might sit more upright – all signs that she's in a more connected state. Wait a bit, because it's a real pleasure when our children come up with their own wise words, their own solutions. If that doesn't happen, now do the parently thing: reassurance, or making a suggestion, or making things happen.

Child: *Maybe I can meet Laura and Sam at the shops, that way we have stuff to do*
You: *Sure. Tell me when and I'm happy to drive you.*

Emotions can change very fast, and what matters is your child's emotion right now, not three minutes or three years ago. For instance your child is referring to a time when as a toddler he lost you in a shopping centre.
You: *That was so scary for you! You must have thought you were lost for ever.*
Your child: *You keep on and on about it like I was a baby! So patronising!*
Although you are right that your child was terrified at the time, he has moved on. So it's more connecting to ask:
You: *How do you feel now, when you think back on it?*

(If that doesn't sound natural, avoid 'What/how do you feel' and try 'What's it like for you'.)

Your child: *I'm pretty proud of myself! I can always find my way out of trouble.*

Track feelings and needs in the present moment.

KEEP CHECKING: USE QUESTION MARKS

Now comes a piece of advice I learned from Nonviolent Communication, which I think is fantastic, yet you won't often see it.

When you respond with empathy, make it brief, and finish with a question mark.

You can also imply the question with your body language, with a pause, or by saying 'Sounds like', 'I am guessing that' or 'I wonder if'. You can also say, 'Is that right?' or 'Tell me more, I'm interested.'

> Keep checking
> "Is that right?"
> "Something like that?"
> "Did I understand you correctly?"
> "Let me check I've got this"
> "I really want to understand. Is that what matters to you?"
> "Tell me more"
> "I'm really interested."
> + notice body language

Why the question mark?

- I don't actually know what my child is experiencing. I can only guess, then check. If I guessed right, my child will gladly nod and, hopefully, tell me more. If I guessed wrong, my child will correct me ('No I'm not sad, I'm furious!') and I will offer empathy – with another question mark – for what she says.

- If, on the other hand, I tell my child how she's feeling (without checking) she may well get irritated: I don't know how she feels, I never understand her, and I'm talking 'like a therapist'!

- The question mark shows I am interested in hearing more, which shows I have time and I care. This in itself reduces suffering.

- Whether or not I guessed right, my child is now connecting with her own feelings. Because I'm interested, she can express what's going on for her. This is giving her long-term skills in living well with emotions.

KEEP YOUR 'BUT' OUT OF IT

As you move from an empathetic 'Connect' to 'Correct' you might find you're using the word 'but'. Nearly everyone does, including great therapists! For example:

Child: 'Why are you serving me ice-cream! I'm not eating it!'

You: *I'm so sorry. You've not had ice-cream for a while so no wonder it's hard. But it's what you need.*

Now see the magic happen when instead of 'but', you use *'and'*, or *'and at the same time'*, or replace the 'but' with a full stop:

Connect → *'and'* → Correct

For example:

You: *I'm so sorry. You've not had ice-cream for a while so no wonder it's hard. And at the same time, it's what you need.*

keep your
'but' out of it!

Like most of us, you might be thinking of the many unskilled responses you've given your child. I know this can be painful but with practice, compassionate communication will become natural.

Did you see what I just did? I was offering empathy, and then my meaning got lost with the word 'but'! Re-read, replacing with 'and at the same time' or a full stop, and see if it helps.

OPEN QUESTION OR EMPATHY GUESS?

With someone who's very upset, anxious, or very deep in the eating disorder, open questions can't get through the chaos of their mind.

Child: 'I told you!!!! I don't want to go to school!'
You: 'What are you feeling, when you say you don't want to go to school?'
With a well self-connected person, the answer might be, 'I have some knotting in my stomach, and a sense of restlessness. Anxiety, perhaps…'
But with your child you're more likely to get, 'I just don't want to go!!!! And you're not my therapist!!! Stop being so patronising!'
What often works better is you making a guess:

You: 'Your shoulders are hunched up. Are you anxious, maybe?'

That's a guess about their feelings. They might shrug, or they might elaborate, or correct you. By asking kindly, you've made anxiety acceptable, not shameful. If you guessed wrong, you're still building connection:
'No, I'm annoyed. My friends are idiots and I can't trust them!'
Here's another example of an open question, this time about any deep needs they're trying to meet:

You: 'What would it do for you, to not go to school?'

'*What would it do for you*' can be a really good question, but again, with someone with a chaotic mind, you might not get very far. So instead, here's a guess about needs:

You: 'I'm wondering if, by not going to school, you want to keep yourself safe from the kids who bullied you?'
Or: 'I'm guessing you don't want to go to school because you want to be safe from the kids who bullied you?'

It's absolutely fine to guess wrong. Your child can reach their truth more easily when they correct your guess than when they have to answer an open question:
Child: 'No, it's more that everyone's going to ask where I've been and it will be awkward.'
At which stage you can go into a little more empathy, then on to problem-solving.

MORE TOOLS TO HELP YOU CONNECT

So far I've given you two tools to connect compassionately to your child: silent empathy, and some form of 'I'm sorry, and I love you'. That may be all you need. You're now in a compassionate mindframe and you can make the rest up as you go along. As you may want more, I'll now walk you through my diagram titled 'Connect before you Correct'. I'll offer examples of things to say and I encourage you to adapt them so they are natural to you.

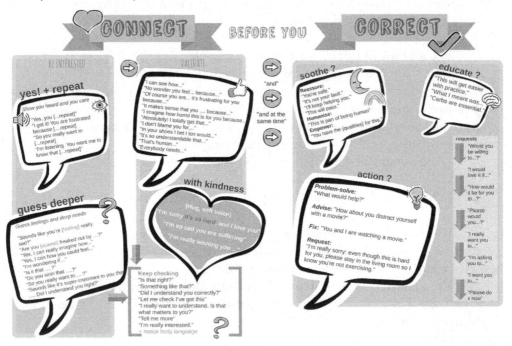

KINDNESS

First, the diagram shows a heart, indicating that whatever you say, do so with genuine kindness. This is where you say or think, 'I'm sorry, and I love you'. You are dealing with someone in a state of threat, so you'll be most effective if you can use kind touch, kind voice, and kind body language. Regarding physical touch, most of us need to check: 'May I hug you?', 'Is it OK if I hold your hand?' If you get recoil, you can say, 'That's OK, darling.' No judgement.

BE INTERESTED: 'YES!' AND REPEAT

It's natural for us to jump to a 'No', to contradict: 'No, you didn't eat too much', 'Don't be daft, nobody will stare at you', 'Of course you're not a horrible person'. We want to reassure, to make the other feel better, to fix. A short, fast response like that can be exactly what's needed, because your child is only looking for a tiny bit of reassurance. Often it works to say, 'No, it's not too much food; it's what you need'. But if your child is repeating herself or if her distress is rising, that could be because she is not feeling heard, as though her truth didn't matter.

When I coach parent I suggest they start with a 'Yes', or a nod, or some other way of agreeing and showing interest. You are never agreeing with someone's distorted beliefs. You are showing you care about what this present moment is like for them. Along with some kind of 'Yes', see if you can repeat what your child said, without it seeming odd. That way they know you've really heard them.

'My tummy is sore!' *Yes, I get it. It's really sore.*
'My friends think I'm weird!' *Ah, gosh, you think your friends see you as weird?*
'Dad hates me!' *You think he hates you?! What's up?*
'Piss off!' *I get it, you want to be left alone.*
'I hate my life!' *Yes, at the moment your life seems so very hard?*

When we deviate from our child's words, we may get their meaning wrong. So when I say, 'Yes, at the moment your life seems so very hard' my child might protest, 'No, it's boring!' No big deal. I can now give her empathy for 'boring'.

With empathy we try and repeat the other person's words, or to stay pretty close to them. Clearly we don't want to create disconnection by sounding like a cartoon parrot or a cartoon therapist. Yet if you experiment a little you might be pleasantly surprised how much people relax as they hear their words reflected back to them.

GUESS DEEPER: FEELINGS AND NEEDS

On my diagram I suggest sentence starters that show that you are interested in the other person's feelings and deep needs. In case this is new to you, I will now take you through what are feelings, what are needs, and why it's wonderful to have them heard. If you're in a hurry and the sentence starters are good enough for you, you can jump to the 'Correct' section.

BE INTERESTED: FEELINGS

People relax, feel better and become more resourceful once they sense that they've been heard and understood with acceptance – in other words when they sense our empathy. Here's how surface-level talk usually goes:

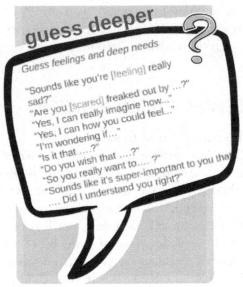

> You: 'My child will have to go into hospital!'
>
> Your friend: 'When? Which hospital?'

I bet you feel pretty lonely. A few more interactions like this and you will conclude that nobody can possibly understand you. Let's try again:

> Your friend: 'Oh I am so sorry. How are you?'
>
> You: 'He's never been away from home before.'

OK, you're not opening up too much, you're testing out the waters.

> Your friend: 'Don't worry, they'll take good care of him!'

Ouch! Let's try again:

> Your friend: 'You're worried? You need to know that people will be kind to him?'

Now you are starting to feel understood, and some of your burden is lifted. A long hug, and permission to cry, would also help.

Now for an example with your child. Here's some surface-level speech:

> Your child: 'I ate too much!'
>
> You: 'That's the eating disorder speaking. I don't speak with ED.'

Parents, I know that a therapist may have taught you to speak like this. If it works, great, but usually our children get very angry. So let's try a compassionate enquiry:

> 'You're looking very upset. What's up?'
>
> Your child: 'I had promised myself not to eat lunch.'

You: 'Is it like, you're feeling guilty?'

Your child: 'Yes. I know I have to eat, but it makes me feel guilty too.'

You: 'I'm sorry it's so hard. I love you… Shall we give the dog a bath?'

Let me tell you more about feelings, so that you can be comfortable talking about them.

The main feelings, or emotions, are 'sad, mad, bad and glad'. There's also scared, anxious, guilty, ashamed, frustrated, furious, disgusted, distressed, joyful, excited, confident, and so on.[314] Emotions live and show up in the body: a scrunched-up face, burning cheeks, tearfulness, hunched shoulders, a racing heart.

It's useful to link emotions to the body, for instance:

'You're looking fidgety. I'm wondering if you're nervous about something?'

Feelings happen. Some come from physical processes (pain, being 'hangry') and some are fed and amplified by our thoughts ('It's all hopeless!'). Either way, no feelings should ever be judged or rejected. We treat them with acceptance and kindness, because the unpleasant ones are really horrible. To be clear, we're making space for feelings, not for dreadful behaviours.

FEELING

When you're trying to spot feelings in yourself or guess the feelings in your child, don't get derailed by expressions like 'I feel that' or 'I feel like I'. These are not feelings: 'I feel that you are ignoring me', 'I feel like she's going to refuse lunch.' If you enquire further you will find feelings: 'I feel *frustration* when I tell myself you're ignoring me', 'I feel *anxiety* when I think she may go without lunch.'

One small tip: instead of saying, 'Are you feeling sad?' you can just as easily ask, 'Are you sad?' If you cut out the word 'feeling', you may sound more genuine, and be less likely to hear, 'You're not my therapist!'

Fear is an emotion to be handled with care because people tend to associate fear with weakness and a loss of dignity. Be cautious with words like 'scared' or 'frightened'. Start off with milder words, like 'concerned' or 'worried' or 'freaked out' or 'nervous'.

Me: 'Looks like seeing this omelette is freaking you out?'

On the other hand, when a person trusts you with the intensity of their emotions, meet them there. Recently my daughter used the word 'terrified' as she recalled what eating was like in the early days. So 'terrified' is the feeling I empathised with. Some parents only tell me they are 'tense', while others feel great relief sharing that they are 'petrified'.

Feelings are not dangerous and they pass

Emotions are harmless, and they pass. Yours, and your child's. They are like a wave: they rise, and just as quickly they fall again. It may be useful for your child to know that. Hopefully you can think of examples when that happened.

Apparently the average time for an emotion to move through us is only a minute and a half.[315] That's not possible when we're alone and ruminating catastrophic thoughts. A quick way of shifting emotions is to re-route one's thinking, using distraction. The best distractions engage your mind with something that generates a different emotion. What did the world do before cat videos?

The other way to help emotions move on is compassion. With your kind presence, your child might shift from anger or fear to tears. Those tears are often a gateway to more wisdom and connection. When your child is upset and you name feelings – always with a question mark – you will usually see the intensity of their distress fade.

Feelings are nobody's fault

Feelings happen, and nobody is to blame. Your child will assume that you judge their feelings, so stay clear of phrases like 'don't worry' (or 'don't be sad', 'don't be angry' or 'don't be scared'). Instead you can ask, 'Are you worried, sweetheart?'

We are used to blaming others for our feelings: 'See the distress you're causing me? It's all your fault!' It's instinctive. If I accidently bash my thumb with a hammer, my first thought will be to blame my husband for buying the wrong hammer.

Yet feelings are not directly caused by other people or by events. They come from what's going on inside ourselves, from the signals our nervous system is receiving, and from the meaning we give to what is happening.[316]

> *"My daughter often says 'You make me feel guilty!' and then acts up. Later, when she's calmer, she may say, 'This didn't happen because of what you said, Mum. It would have happened anyway.'"*

So show interest in your child's feelings, and don't be threatened by them.

> *"We were shopping together and she said, 'See, it's happening again! I want to be alone and now you're making me feel guilty because you're still here with me!' I used to defend myself or feel bad or annoyed with myself, but self-compassion is the best thing ever! I just said 'Oh' (like I was attentive to her), gave a little nod of acknowledgement and said, 'Shall we meet in half an hour?'"*

It is completely possible to care deeply for someone and not be entangled in their feelings.

BE INTERESTED: WHAT ARE THE DEEP NEEDS?

Getting empathy for feelings is lovely, and even more healing is empathy for deep needs.[317] Here's an example of connecting with feelings:

'I hate my life!' *Oh honey… You sound fed up and discouraged!*

And here's the same example, connecting with a deep need:

'I hate my life!' *Oh honey… Do you wish your life was happy and easy right now?*

I mix and match, reflecting feelings or needs or both, depending on what seems most natural and appropriate. For example:

'My friends think I'm weird!' *Ouch! That sounds awfully lonely* [feeling]. *I imagine you want friends who like you for who you are?* [need]

'That doctor was so patronising! She thinks I'm stupid!' *You're looking really cross about it* [feeling]. *Is it about wanting to be treated with dignity and respect?* [need]

Needs to look out for

I'm using the word 'needs' to describe a whole lot of positive, life-enhancing, deep universal human needs, values, longings – anything that really matters. It has nothing to do with being 'needy', quite the opposite: it's about internal power.

If there's a situation your child often struggles with, what do you think are the needs driving it? The following can be particularly important in young people:

Children and teens thrive on close connections with peers and adults, and on the unconditional love and support of their parents.

'Dad hates me!' *I can see it's really upsetting you. Do you wish you could feel close to him?*

They need to be valued, to matter.

'You'd be better off without me!' *I'm so sorry. I wonder if you really need to know how much you matter to us?*

In order to grow they also strive for autonomy, choice and independence.

'Don't tell me what to eat! I'm not a baby!' *Sure, I imagine you want independence and choice like anyone your age?*

Adolescents' brains are very different from those of adults or small children. From the ages of 10 to 23 or older, teen brains are drawn to impulsivity, big emotional highs and lows, and fight-or-flight.[318] Knowing this may help you give compassion where compassion is due.

On top of that, an eating disorder brings on a whole lot of unmet needs. I am guessing that much of the time people with an eating disorder are feeling hungry, tired, terrified, stressed, lonely or hopeless. So in addition to a whole bunch of physical needs, they long for peace, hope, closeness, support and understanding.

'Everyone will think I'm vain!' *I wonder if you want people's understanding and support, rather than ignorant judgement?*

Eating disorders also seem to fill people with a terrible loathing for themselves. They struggle with shame ('I'm not OK', 'I'm a bad person') because they can't help lying, cheating, hiding food and for some, overeating. On top of shame, there's also guilt ('I've done a bad thing') and fear ('Will my parents give up on me?') whenever they hurl abuse at their loved ones. With a distorted body image, the shame is acute, along with the belief they are a revolting and unworthy person.

"When she was really ill, she often yelled at us to leave her alone because she wasn't worth it."

The quest for identity ('Who am I?'; 'What kind of a person am I?') is particularly strong in adolescence. The need to matter is a biggie. So is the need to belong, to have a place on this earth, within the family and community. With an eating disorder in the equation, these issues are particularly painful, especially for youngsters who have been in and out of hospital and lost touch with friends and their old life.

How to enquire about someone's needs

You could ask an open question, such as:

- What do you need right now?
- Why does this matter to you?
- What is it about X that is important to you?
- If you had X (or if you didn't have Y) what would that give you?
- What comes up for you when …?
- What's going on for you?
- What would it do for you to…

For example, you are concerned that your daughter wants to stay in touch with another girl from hospital who is very ill and openly talks about self-harm. You are scared that you daughter is only interested in hearing anorexic tips.

You could say, 'I don't want you to be in touch with her', and that's fine, it's part of your parental job to protect. Or you could ask a surface-level question: 'Why do you want to message her?' and risk a surface-level reply: 'I just want to.' A 'needs' question, on the other hand, may give you some more information while also creating connection:

'I'm interested. Why is it important to you?'

Imagine the melting of your heart as your child reveals, 'Her parents don't support her like you do for me. I want to help her get well, like you helped me.' You're now in a really good position to impart your wisdom and problem-solve (tip: it's for adults, not for your struggling child, to help this girl).

Here is a guide to common needs, along with ordinary words to express them and help you connect.[319] If this is more information that you need, please jump ahead.

- *Mattering/value/unconditional love/acceptance:* Do you want to know that you matter? To be absolutely sure we love you no matter what? Is it important for you to know we want to take care of you in a way that works for you, that it matters to us?

- *Identity:* Would you like to be in touch with the real you? You want to know you can be who you really are? You want to know you're an OK person and you have a place on this earth?

- *Compassion/connection:* You want to know that we care? You wish we really understood what it's like for you?

- *Autonomy/freedom/independence:* You'd like to make your own choices/decisions about what works for you?

- *Participation:* You'd like to have a say in this?

- *Competence:* You want to be able to do what you set out to do?

- *Consistency:* Would you like to be able to count on people doing what they say they'll do?

- *Stability/predictability:* Would you like to know what's happening and when?

- *Safety/security:* You need to know that you're going to be OK? You'd like us to stick by you and keep you safe?

- *Mourning:* Are you terribly sad? Do you want me to get how sad you feel?

- *Peace:* Do you wish you could be calm and feel OK?

- *Purpose:* You want to know what this is for?

- *Fun/stimulation:* You want to have fun?

This is the basis of empathy. If you are attuned to your child's needs and your own, everything else falls into place. The connection is established.

BE INTERESTED: MAKE USE OF THE CHATTERBOX

CHATTERBOX

Our children say things that activate our knee-jerk reactions. We want to help them so we 'Correct' with logic.[320] Or, because we are hurt, we retaliate with our own harsh words. We start with a 'No', instead of curiosity. We are missing out on the chance to 'Connect'.

Child: 'You don't even care!'
Parent: 'Yes I care! I really care about you!'
Child: 'You're always criticising me!'
Parent: 'That's not true. Just now I was saying how well you did in biology.'
Child: 'You never listen to me!'
Parent: 'That's unfair! I'm listening right now!'
Child: 'Nobody likes me!'
Parent: 'Yes they do!'

When we are in a state of tension or threat, when big needs are not met, we tend to judge, exaggerate, catastrophise, re-hash the past, fear the future. It's normal. I call these types of thoughts, beliefs images or words: 'the chatterbox'.[321]

Recognise the chatterbox – in yourself, in your child, in everyone else – and use it as a signpost to deep needs. That way you can 'Connect before you Correct'.

Very often, the needs are right there in the chatterbox talk:
Child: 'You don't even care!'
Parent: 'Oh my sweetheart! You really want to know that I care?'
Child: 'You never listen to me!'
Parent: 'That's terrible! You sense I'm not listening? You need me to really listen to you?'
Child: 'Nobody likes me!'
Parent: 'I'm so sorry. It sounds painful and lonely. Everyone needs to feel liked.'
Child: 'Nobody understands me!'
Parent: 'I'm so, so sorry you don't feel understood. That sucks! It must feel so lonely! Everyone needs to be understood. You really want me to understand you better?'

Sometimes the needs are obvious when we turn around the chatterbox's words:
Child: 'You're always criticising me!'
Parent: 'Gosh, that's not good. You need to feel loved and accepted for who you are.'

The chatterbox is normal. Its beliefs and stories are usually not true, and that's fine, because they still point us towards deep needs.

VALIDATE FEELINGS AND NEEDS

In the examples above, the parent hasn't just guessed at feelings or needs, they have validated them. Having our sorrow witnessed, having our most shameful feelings heard without judgement, having someone say, 'Yes, of course this matters to you!' – this heals wounds, brings clarity, and empowers. It's what we want from good listeners, from therapists, from our nearest and dearest.

In my diagram, I suggest sentence starters that will make validation genuine and warm. Remember, you're not validating dreadful behaviours, nor distorted thinking, just universal human feelings and needs.

Notice that some of the sentence starters in the diagram use the word 'because'. Using 'because' is a great way to make yourself validate, rather than jump into fixing.[322] Take this example:

'No wonder you're freaked out by the pizza, *but* I really want to help you get back into pizza, so it's easier for you to go out with friends.'

Now let's validate with a 'because':

'No wonder you're freaked out by the pizza, *because* you've not eaten pizza in ages, and *because* you've only just started eating cheese again. So I get it that it's a big thing for you. I really want to help you get back into pizza, so it's easier for you to go out with friends.'

VALIDATE

"I can see how..."
"No wonder you feel... because..."
"Of course you are... It's frustrating for you because..."
"It makes sense that you .... because..."
"I imagine how horrid this is for you because..."
"Absolutely! I totally get that..."
"I don't blame you for...."
"In your shoes I bet I too would..."
"It's so understandable that..."
"That's human..."
"Everybody needs..."

"The key here is not to offer advice; just shut up and listen. If you must respond, respond only by affirming how hard it must be for them, and how you're here for them right here, right now."[323]

Signs that your child 'feels felt'

When can you move on to the 'Correct' bit of 'Connect before you Correct'? Or when can you stop validating your child's emotions? Sometimes we talk for too long when actually our job is done and our child is ready to move on. One of the skills I value the most is knowing when to shut up. (I'm still working on it.)

You're looking for is a sign that your child has let go of some of her reactivity and is more self-connected. You're not trying to make her happy. It's OK for her to be sad in this moment. It's OK for all her problems to not yet be solved. Watch out for signs that she has relaxed in the warmth of your empathy, that she's feeling heard and understood. She may release some tension or sigh or yawn or burp or break wind (signs of the parasympathetic nervous system in action!) or tears may come. She may open up from a closed position, stand tall and look you in the eye. With my child, if she'd been repeating a complaint or accusation over and over again, I knew my empathy has reached her when the tone of her voice changed. She could go from a passionate 'It's not fair' to a more mournful one – I used to think of it as a whimper. The conviction seemed to go out of her words, as though she was listening to herself and wondering, 'Why am I saying this? I don't even mean it. But I'm going to continue saying it a few times because, hey, it would be very odd to stop abruptly.'

Kids are particularly wonderful at switching mood in an instant once they've been heard. It's like the clouds have parted, and they're happy to move on without any further analysis.

You can't do it wrong if you are genuinely interested

It can be scary for us parents to use words. Our children are quick to jump to inter-pretations. People with eating disorders, like anyone in an anxious state, are particu-larly alert to our judgemental verbal and non-verbal language, and they give less value to our neutral or positive signals.[324]

When we're used to walking on eggshells, it takes some confidence to try a new way of talking, especially when it doesn't yet feel natural and genuine. I hope you will experience early successes and gain confidence, so that you can be truly present.

> *"I honestly thought I was going to get a 'No shit, Sherlock' or 'Ya think?' but it really worked and she opened right up."*

What if your child throws your empathic words back in your face? You always have silent empathy. You can also be honest about your intentions: 'Oh dear. I'm trying to be a better listener, because I'd love for you to feel really heard. I'd love for you to know how much I care. Is it OK if I try again?'

AND NOW AT LAST, 'CORRECT'!

We all do the 'Correct' bit of my diagram pretty naturally. We soothe, we educate, we negotiate action or problem-solve. Hopefully you will find you are more effective doing this, now that your child has moved somewhat out of their fight-flight-freeze state, because you have done the 'Connect' bit, followed by 'and' instead of 'but'. I can offer you some more tips on this part of your communication.

Soothing

When you want to soothe, you will naturally re-assure and give hope. At times, though, some things really suck, and a message that 'This will pass' could fall flat. You want to avoid empty re-assurances, stiff upper lips and vacuous cheer-leading.

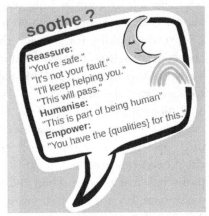

Sometimes we are soothed when we sense that our suffering is part of life. We are experi-encing the depths of what it is to be human. It may help your child to know that others are going through similar hardships.

This is also a good time to bring up your child's qualities. When we're upset we tend to forget our strengths, and it's good to be reminded of them. If our children have been ill for a long time, they have forgotten who they really are.

Educating

You might enjoy the 'education' bit now. All that logical talk you've been itching to give! This is also a time you can explain your intentions – very useful if your child has accused you of something. And everyone needs hope, so you can also impart what you know of your child, or of the illness, to do that now.

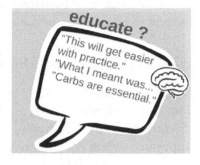

Action

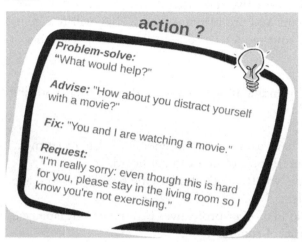

You can problem-solve, seek solutions, give advice, fix, and make requests. Because you've connected and you know what matters to your child, you should now be in a good position to 'fix' things wisely. How forceful or collaborative you are about it depends on how capable your child is of making wise decisions, and how important the outcome is to you. Let's look in more details at the art of making requests.

Make skillful requests

Some parents are used to telling their child what to do. Others find it very uncomfortable, as before the illness struck, their child didn't need much directing. With an eating disorder, we make non-negotiable requests – demands, really – like 'Please eat the yoghurt now.' We keep these for really important matters, and we make them in a non-blaming way.

There are also requests which you can make more lightly, where a 'No' is acceptable. For instance, 'I would love it if you helped me wash the dog.'

In my diagram I suggest a range of sentence-starters for requests, from negotiable to non-negotiable.

A 'No' doesn't have to be the end of the dialogue. If you really want something, keep exploring needs and problem-solving till you get a solution that suits both of you. Remember that if it's a big stretch for him, he may agree if you make agree to a time limit ('Let's try it for a week and then review').

Your child may be happy to do something for you once he understands what matters to you. Which brings me to how you express *your* feelings and needs.

HOW TO EXPRESS YOURSELF EFFECTIVELY

So far I've concentrated on empathy for another person – especially your child. Connection is a two-way thing, so expressing yourself, telling the other person what's going on for you and asking for what you want, is just as important. When you have requests to make of clinicians, it's crucial.

Because our children are in such a reactive state, they may not hear you the way you want to be heard. They will think you are blaming them. They will feel guilty about your feelings. They will hear your requests as domineering, they will rebel or get resentful. For example:

Me: 'Please would you be back by midnight, so can relax and go to sleep, knowing you are safe.'

My child: 'I'm not a baby!'

Clearly, she hasn't heard me. I have to do more 'Connect' (or bring that metaphorical elevator down to the ground floor) before I can get heard.

Me: 'No wonder it annoys you, if you think it's about being babied. At your age, of course you need some independence.'

My child: 'Well, hmmm, you're kind of over-protective.' From her body language, I class this as a 'whimper', and I reckon I can move on.

Me: 'For my own peace of mind, please. Even though I know you're sensible I will not sleep well until I know you're safely home. I'm your mum and I wouldn't be doing my job if I didn't care for you and make sure you are safe. Do you get where I'm coming from?'

That last question is to check she's heard me correctly. Distortions happen all the time. Checking and repeating is huge, for instance, in relationship counselling, and I bet you know work situations where it's also useful.

You can spell it out: 'I want to make sure I got my meaning across. Would you please tell me what you heard me say?'

My child: 'Sure. You want to know I'm safe. OK. But I warn you, when I start going to clubs, it will be more like four in the morning!'

Me: 'Thanks.'

My child: 'Anyway, I'll be back at 11:30 because that's when Ellie's parents and Daniel's parents and Rebecca's parents say they have to be home.'

NEED

'Peace of mind' and 'care' and 'safety' are expressions of my own needs, and they are non-blaming. When we express ourselves with passion and clarity from a place of 'what matters to us', we are more likely to take people along with us. It's usually more powerful than 'Do it because I say so', or 'Do it because it's high time you took responsibility for yourself'.

Expressing a need first ('I really want', 'I so love', 'It matters to me that') makes it more likely you will be heard for your real intention. For instance:

'I love seeing you and Grandma having a good time together. I'd love you to come with me today. How would that work for you?'

You could include a feeling ('I'm really sad when I realise you've not seen each other since her birthday'), but only if you're confident it will not be heard as blame.

This is true assertiveness. Position yourself in your 'Yes', state your deep (and sometimes fierce) needs, respond to objections without belittling others, and keep returning to your requests. 'Compassionate persistence', remember? Even through your tears, there's strength in saying to your child's hospital consultant: 'I need to know my child is safe. Please would you tell me what measures are in place to keep him from self-harm?' I experienced the power of upholding big needs while advocating for a family at a large, intimidating, potentially confrontational meeting of professionals, and now I swear by it.

The opposite – which we all tend to do at first – is to accuse without making clear requests ('You're not doing anything to protect my son from self-harm!'), and to whine, using 'Why?' questions ('Why are you not keeping him child safe from self-harm?').

Back to our children, most of the time we position ourselves somewhere along a continuum of truth-telling. At one end, we censure everything we say because we're in terror of their emotional outbursts. We're walking on eggshells. At the other end we aim for a high level of connection and we express ourselves with honesty, all the while choosing words that are more likely to create connection.

Don't air your chatterbox thoughts. Stick to facts.

If you're tempted to express your chatterbox thoughts about someone to their face, zip your mouth and run off to get some empathy from another source. You will not foster connection by saying, 'To be quite honest, you let me down.' You won't go far with judgements, criticisms, 'ought tos', labels ('You're a cheat'), diagnoses ('The problem with you is …') or wild accusations ('You never…').

Stick to facts. Whereas the chatterbox might say, 'You always dump your stuff on the floor for me to trip over,' the observable fact would be, 'The last few days, when you've come in, you've put your bags down on the stairs.' The chatterbox might say, 'You are doing nothing to protect my son from self-harm', the observable fact would be, 'This morning he got hold of scissors in the art therapy room'. It's easier to reach solutions when there is no hint of blame.

With our nearest and dearest, when we're suffering and not at our most mature, we *do* love to accuse, to bully, to blame, to take on the victim role. It gives temporary relief. Usually though, we regret our outbursts. It's human, and all is not lost. The mending we do afterwards can be an opportunity for some very precious connection.

Can you express your feelings?

Is it OK to share your feelings, to say 'I feel sad', or 'I feel worried?' Usually yes, as it fosters mutual compassion. But with your child… it depends.

It is pretty safe to express sorrow for your child's suffering, as in 'I'm sorry, and I love you': 'It breaks my heart that you're finding this so hard. [Pause] Have another bite.'

But how about expressing big feelings?

It's risky with anyone who is in fight-flight-freeze and has no emotional space for you. Also, the younger kids are, the harder it is for them to differentiate between themselves and others (if a sibling gets sick, or if parents fall out, they truly believe it's their fault). With an eating disorder, our children are wearing not rose-tinted glasses, but guilt-and-shame tinted ones, and this feeds their self-loathing. All this takes us away from the uncritical acceptance that has been shown to be a major factor for recovery.

When we are full of sorrow, it can be impossible to shield our child from our tears. Assume your child feels scared and guilty to see you in this state. If you're crying a lot, as I did at times, I suggest you get help so that you're not crying so often in front of your child. And when it does happen, what can you say?

Here's a tip: when expressing anything the other person could find hard to hear, it's more powerful to start with your deep, positive needs.

Compare 'I got sad when you didn't eat your meal' with, 'I have such a strong vision of you being well, and I care for you so very very much, I got sad when you didn't eat your meal.'

Here's another form of words you might like: 'The tears are because right now I am so sad to see you struggling like this because I love you so much. We're on the right path, though, and I will be fine very soon. I just need a rest so I can be myself again. May I give you a hug?'

Here's a story from when my daughter was in hospital.

The therapists thought I shouldn't try so hard to hide my tears from my daughter. They believed that if my child saw the effect her aggressive manner had on me, she would take more responsibility for her behaviour and not be so rude (confusingly, they also said it was good for our kid to take her anger out on us). When I was falling to pieces, a nurse told my daughter about it and said, 'You should start being nice to your mum.' My poor kid now had some inappropriate responsibility and guilt to deal with, as well as the deep fear that her mother would crack up and not be able to support her. Did this help her modify her behaviour? Nope. Unless you count how she withdrew from me further.

In compassionate communication terms, the nurse fed my daughter's chatterbox. More self-blame, more fear. The result was more defensiveness, more spite.

The therapists' view that my daughter would benefit from seeing how upset she 'made' me was at odds with their position that my daughter's behaviours were driven by anorexia and that she was not at fault. I see such contradictions in various writings on eating disorders, and I wouldn't be surprised if you found some in here in spite of my best efforts. It's hard to shake off old models of blame.

Your child is not your therapist

When I was suffering, I had to make a conscious decision not to burden my child with cries for moral support that were not appropriate to her age. She wasn't my pal, my partner, or my therapist. She didn't have the resources to deal with my issues. Even if the trigger for my anger wasn't connected to her but, say, to a member of the family, and even if I could trust that what I told her wouldn't fill her with guilt, she wasn't the right person to hear me out. I could need support, but just because she happened to be there didn't mean she was the right person to give it.

I want my child to know she can lean on me, but I don't want to lean on her, at least not for anything major, and that's even with the eating disorder out of the picture. I imagine that if you have several kids it must be tempting, at times, to unburden on one of the siblings who is well, especially if you and your spouse are fighting. These are all good reasons to set ourselves up with regular sources of empathy from appropriate sources.

Advice-giving: check first (in triplicate)!

When you catch yourself about to give advice, pause. Is your advice actually a request? Then make it a clear request. For instance instead of the advice, 'There are predators out there, you should be careful who you chat with online', you could make the request, 'If you ever want to chat online with someone you don't know, please check with me'. If you're fishing for reassurance, you could be direct about it: 'I'm worried about predators. Tell me what you know about keeping safe.'

Often, though, we give advice because we want to contribute to the other person. We want to help! Unfortunately, there is no greater turn-off if the person hasn't actively been seeking advice.

Here's a story that might be useful to you. It's about a mum who was scared because she knew nothing of her 23-year old's wellbeing. If she asked how treatment was going, if she asked how she could help, she got silence. The two had a trusting connection, but the daughter complained that whenever she divulged anything a bit personal, her mother fired off unwelcome advice, starting with, 'OK I understand, but why don't you try to…?' The mother is warm and knowledgeable and has great advice to give, but that's not much use if her daughter blanks her out.

I suggested to the mother how to 'Connect before you Correct' and she tells me she practiced zipping her mouth. She also reminded herself that:

> *"We have one mouth and two ears and we should use them in that ratio."*

When we spoke a few weeks later she said her daughter was now talking freely because, 'Mum, you've changed.' I was delighted because this mother, at first, had doubted she could change habits of a lifetime.

It's OK to fail. I catch myself blurting out unsolicited advice to my daughter – like how she could deal with an annoying colleague. I pull back as soon as realise what

I'm doing: 'Sorry, here I am giving you advice when you didn't ask for it. What do *you* want to do?' Sometimes she wants the advice, sometimes she doesn't.

Advice is a wonderful thing. When you started reading this book, I am guessing you were looking for advice. It is part of the pleasure of human connection that we wish to contribute to each other. The trick with advice is to offer it, not impose it: 'I'm thinking of something that might help you with this matter / I have an opinion on this. Would you like to hear it?' Observe the person carefully. It's remarkable how often they appear not to have heard, how often they don't give a clear 'Yes'. And I'm surprised how often I have an urge to dish out the advice anyway, such is my desire to contribute. If a person doesn't give you a determined 'Yes please, I could really do with some help', advice is not what they need at present. And as you already know, if their emotions are high they can't properly hear your advice before their cup of empathy is filled.

Shortly after writing this I responded to someone's email with one sentence of reassurance, and one sentence of advice ... which pretended not to be advice. I only realised I'd done this a day later. It was a good example of a mistake being a treasure because I followed up with a second, far more connecting email: my correspondent loved it and was bowled over to experience the difference.

Here's a quip from Marshall Rosenberg, NVC founder, on the subject:

> *"I'll only give advice when it is asked for in writing, notarized and in triplicate."*

SELF-COMPASSION

What for?

Self-compassion is everything I've just guided you to do for your child, but you do it for yourself. To be effective, courageous, resilient, you absolutely must practice some form of self-compassion. Do you know how many good parents, who care deeply about their child, fantasize about running off to the other side of the world? Indeed, some do. We need to toughen up for the sake of our children, and the tool to do that is not more gritting of teeth, but more kindness.

Self-compassion includes seeing the bigger picture, wisdom, courage, power, leadership, kindness, self-empathy, self-connection, being centred or grounded or mindful, presence, awareness. To be clear, self-compassion is the  opposite of – the antidote – to self-obsession, navel-gazing and being a wuss.

When I was struggling with exhaustion, despair, catastrophic thoughts, confusion or fury, self-compassion could be like pressing the Reset button. Sometimes it was more like a brilliant software upgrade. I would emerge from the process with insight and more compassion, motivation and clarity than I had imagined was possible.

The compassion your child needs from you comes directly from your own compassionate state. You are in charge of your behaviours and you make wise decisions, because you have access to your whole brain. Self-compassion is the bridge between your reactive, fight-flight-freeze state, and a state where you are yourself.

> *"Most helpful to me has been the bungee-jump metaphor and your recommendation to consider what's going on inside me while we sit at the table and she's refusing to eat. This has stopped me so many times from just screaming 'Would you JUST EAT!' when she is struggling. It has been the key thing that has permitted me to give her the space and support to work through the block. And she has so far completed every plate of food in front of her!"*

HOW TO DO SELF-COMPASSION

Self-compassion can be ridiculously simple, or quite a bit more skillful. It depends how chaotic our mind is at any moment.

Remember 'I'm sorry, and I love you'? Apply that to yourself. That's how simple it is. Another shortcut to self-compassion is this: Observe what's going on for you, and treat yourself with Kindness (OK).[325]

It's useful to experience self-compassion while being guided by someone. This is because it's not an intellectual exercise, it is a change of state, from threatened to safe. There are plenty of online resources, and if you have half an hour, I suggest you try a guided compassion audio I created. That way you can experience how self-compassion works and it will make more sense than just reading about it.[326] Self-guided audios are not everyone's cup of tea so I'll explain the steps now, with the help of my self-compassion diagram here.

The diagram has quite a lot on it, and I want to reassure you that self-compassion works with any single one of those elements. You don't have to do it all.

Pause and notice

With your child, the first step was 'Yes!' Yes, I'm paying attention. Yes, I'm interested. Do the same for yourself. Get into the habit of noticing when your body tenses, when you have an uncomfortable thought, instead of moving on fast. These days, if I see something distressing online, I deliberately press Pause and move my eyes away, long enough to breathe and let the emotion travel through me.

It might be enough to just take some deep breaths and wait. Or you might need to guide yourself through these mindfulness steps.

- "I'm telling myself that…" [what my chatterbox is saying]
- "My body feels…" [what, where?]
- "I feel" [name the emotion]
- "What really matters to me" [deep needs]

For example, we're in a café after a difficult family therapy session and I am very upset. I realise I'm scowling at the menu, so it's time to 'Pause and Notice'. I'm not in a good place to support my daughter's snack.

So I go into the toilet – thank goodness for toilets – and I close my eyes and I go: '*I'm telling myself* that the therapist is an idiot and has done incredible harm; *My* body is tense, my stomach is churning, I'm on the verge of tears, and I have an urge to punch something; *I feel* furious… no I feel scared, so very discouraged, hopeless; *What really matters to me* is…. I don't know yet, my mind is in such chaos… well obviously I didn't get the support I need to keep my girl eating… what matters to me is effective, competent support and good teamwork.'

Kindness

As soon as you've paused and noticed that you're suffering, treat yourself with kindness. Be your best, comforting friend. Use kind touch: a hand on your face, or on your heart, or in your other hand, or on your churning belly. This signals to your nervous system that you are safe, and releases the soothing hormone oxytocin.[327] Feel the warmth of your hand. Imagine it is sending

goodness into your body. These visualisations have real physical effects. If you are a very rational person (I think I am, even if I consider café toilets to be sanctuaries), then you may value self-talk and problem-solving over something as simple as physical touch. Remember that emotions don't operate at this rational level, whereas your body does.

Breathing is your friend too. There's a two-way link between body and emotions, and the breath is one of the easiest way to alter your state. People recommend different breathing patterns to self-soothe. Personally, I like to relax on every outbreath, and I find the pause before the next in-breath particularly wonderful.

You may also speak to yourself just as you would to your child: 'I'm here for you, I care about you, I'm sorry and I love you, it's OK sweetheart.' Sometimes my own self-compassion is as simple as pausing, putting a hand on my cheek and thinking 'Kind, kind, kind' for a minute or two, just like you might rub your forehead after marching into a lamppost. If you are stuck in cruel self-talk, bring to mind someone (real or imagined) who loves you, or who loves all of humanity, unconditionally.

Allow

'Allow' is about not fighting yourself – which is cruel and an energy drain. Allow your experience to be what it is. Suffering is horrible, so of course you want it to pass. Accept that you are suffering and trust that it will pass.

So as I'm leaning against the toilet wall, fuming about the terrible therapy session, I may say to myself, 'This is a moment of suffering', or 'This is really hard right now', or 'I'm really struggling' or 'I am safe right now. Trust this will pass'. This counteracts the critical, minimising self-talk which many of us do: 'I shouldn't be feeling this! I should toughen up' or 'Nice people don't feel this furious' or 'A good parent wouldn't be in this mess' No. This is your experience, right now, and it's allowed. Even more, it's horrible, so allow your emotions, with kindness.

Acceptance, non-judgement, trust: see how this is the mirror image of what you are doing for your child?

You could go a step further and also 'allow' your current external situation. Shit happens. It is what it is. If I get stuck in 'It's not fair' I lose energy. Conversely, when I give myself empathy for my suffering, I am stronger and in a far better position to change the things I can.

Our common humanity

The fight-flight-freeze state is one of isolation. Me against the world. Me alone in the world. So reflect on how your suffering is part of our shared human experience. Suffering is part of life.

Back to my café toilet, I can reflect on the thousands, the millions of parents who, for centuries, have seen experts give their child terrible advice. There are surely hundreds who, right now, are feeling exactly like I am. I can imagine ourselves giving each other our good wishes, our kindness and our understanding.

I can also normalise my reaction. My fury, my fears are normal human reactions. It's quite understandable that I should feel this way after hearing a therapist say things that will make it infinitely harder to feed my child. I feel like thumping her? I feel like crying? Many people would feel just the same.

Normalising will make you feel less isolated and will quieten the chatterbox's accusations that you are bad, sick or stupid. Hopefully by now you are in the habit of normalising your child's reactions (while still requesting different behaviours) for your child, so do it for yourself too.

Nurture

This is the bit where you get in touch with your power. What is it that matters to you, deep down? What are the positive, life-enhancing needs that are driving you?

When you're upset, at first all you can hear is your chatterbox: 'It's not fair', 'I've been badly done to', 'I'm a bad person', 'How can someone be so ignorant?', 'Why don't they read the research?' (If you're stuck in 'Why' and 'How can...' thoughts, you are haemorrhaging precious energy). When you begin to 'Pause and Notice', your mind might be too much in fight-flight-freeze to home in on what really matters. Your thoughts might be like the swirling particles in a snow globe. After a while though, the snow settles, and you get a clear view of the whole picture.

So in my toilet-sanctuary, I might think, '*I long for* good support'; '*It matters to me enormously* to have a competent person giving me trustworthy guidance'.

In Chapter 2 I considered what might be going on for you as the parent of a child with an eating disorder. My intention was to put you in touch with deep needs. I wonder if something in that list struck a chord with you and if it felt good?

Behind every painful thought or emotion are cherished values or dreams or a vision of what really matters. These life-enhancing, positive, energising needs are there for you right now, in the present moment. Nurture yourself with them. Soak them in. They're a source of strength. They take you from a scarcity mentality to a sense of abundance and possibilities.

Imagine yourself having your needs fulfilled – really visualise it, or remember what it was like when things were good.[328] Your body will feel as though it were true right now. Your situation has not changed, yet your being has flipped from victim to powerful agent. You now have a lot more energy and power and courage to go for what matters.

OK, you may not get this grand result each time, but you'll be closer.

I've been taking support from the wall in the toilet, but now I stand tall, feet anchored in the ground, head up. I give myself the gift of a wish, a blessing, a prayer: '*May I have* the support I long for.' And I bring in the wider world, all those other parents out there: '*May we all have* the support I long for.' And it feels good to include my daughter too: 'May *my precious girl be well*'. I come out of the toilet, not exactly happy, but quite a bit more myself, and I'm ready to help my child with her meal.

GET COMPASSION FROM OTHERS TOO

I've taken you through the elements of self-compassion, and again, we don't need to do it all – just one kind thought or gesture may be all that's needed to shift our state. Not always, though: we need compassion from others too. Relying entirely on yourself is not going to work for very long, and it won't work at all if you are suffering from trauma or seriously overwhelmed. We are interconnected human beings. That's why every wisdom tradition includes some kind of community – churches, monasteries, sanghas, and so on. Make sure you have regular contact with kind people. To me, a good counsellor or therapist is essential at this difficult time. People don't go up Everest single-handedly. In stories, heroes have wise elders to guide them.

WHEN TO DO SELF-COMPASSION

You could sit down with a cup of tea for a self-compassion session. Just breathe and be kind, or use the elements from my diagram, or use a recording to guide you. I did this for myself whenever I felt stuck and needed clarity, or when I was particularly upset. I would promise myself this me-time while in the middle of conflict. It helped me to hang on. Some of you may already be used to meditating once a day. If so, make sure you include the 'kindness' and 'wishes' elements I described above.

There is also emergency self-compassion, which might take just the time of one breath, before you respond to abuse. Or it might be three minutes in a café toilet. As it's short, I think it's important to promise yourself more self-care later, otherwise the psychological guard trying to protect you may keep you in fight or flight.

And there's self-compassion on the fly. I remember a situation where my daughter was arguing very hard, with some very distorted thinking, and I needed all my strength to stay present to her. I was leaning against the door frame, holding a hand to my chest, trying to give my body comfort. I was using my breath to soothe myself and thinking, 'Gosh, this is hard. Please let me be her best support. Even though I want to run away. Actually I want to collapse. It's still bearable. I'm safe. I will give myself me-time later, I promise'. On that occasion, I stayed well enough to stay present to her, and for us to reach a resolution. Again, anything so intense should come with a self-promise of tea and sympathy later.

Nowadays I think self-compassion has become my go-to reaction a few seconds after any upset. The more you do it, the more instinctive it will become. If you find you are still blowing a fuse, shouting at your child or dissolving into tears, it sounds like your head is barely above water. You need more in your life to top up your wellness levels. There's help on this in Chapter 15.

At the same time, you're not aiming for perfection. It would be lovely, but unlikely, if you could be as self-connected when your child is yelling as when you're having a spiritual experience watching a sunrise. You can aim for 'good enough'. A tiny improvement is all you need to move towards. From there, you can take the next tiny step.

WHAT IF THE FEELINGS ARE OVERWHELMING?

Most of us have gone through life ignoring our emotions for fear that they will make us worse. Self-compassion makes you tune into your emotions, and there are two reasons it makes you feel better, rather than worse. First, you are being kind to yourself, so your nervous system gets messages of safety. Second, you are connecting with your body rather than getting carried away by thoughts. But if self-compassion (or any kind of self-connection or meditation) makes you feel worse, if you are going into overwhelm, stop and do something fun or interesting. Distraction is your friend. Distraction is great for petty upsets, and it's great as an emergency tool for overwhelming feelings. In Chapter 15 I say more on 'Trauma and overwhelming fear'.

EXAMPLES OF SELF-COMPASSION

In the heat of the kitchen

This is an example from the difficult days when I was preparing meals that my daughter consistently refused (I'll rephrase that: when I was preparing meals that my daughter's illness stopped her from eating).

It starts off with internal turmoil: 'I can't bear cooking this meal. Why should I spend any time cooking? She's not going to eat it anyway. What if she never gets better? I can't bear even thinking about it. I can't go on much longer. Oh, why me? Why can't I have some peace?' *These are, of course, all chatterbox thoughts. It's natural and allowed to have them. The art is what to do next.*

I pause. For a couple of breaths, I slow down. I scan my body and find that my eyes are prickling. I hold my hand to my face, imagining a kind friend giving me some understanding.

I now know what it is I long for. 'I so want some peace. Like when things were normal and she'd come home from school, and we'd both have a hot chocolate and chat and laugh together.' *Here, I'm spending the time of a breath bathing in the lovely notion of peace and what it's like to have it. It's so relaxing that my eyes well up. My heart has softened and I'm in touch with more of the things that matter to me.* 'Oh gosh I so want her to be well and for us to laugh again. My precious little girl. May she be happy.'

I don't like cooking any more than before, but I'm now less likely to scream at my daughter if she chucks the dinner on the floor.

Recharge and continue

Another example. You've asked your child to go to bed. He refuses. You feel your temper rising. You choose to give yourself self-compassion before you say anything more.

You notice that your chatterbox is creating a string of judgements, starting with 'He's so selfish!' You take one or two slower breaths. You rephrase in your mind: '*I'm telling myself* that he's selfish'. Maybe he is, maybe he isn't.

You scan your body and find that your shoulders are tense. You are feeling tired, and you're irritated that you cannot yet get some rest. You place your hands on your shoulders and send yourself some kindness.

What do you long for? Some sleep, definitely. But you become conscious of another need: it really matters to you to nurture the connection with your child. So now you have clarity about what you want: to be receptive and to stay in dialogue for another few minutes.

Nurturing the good stuff

Now for some examples of soaking in the good stuff, of getting in touch with life-enhancing needs. For me it would be spending one second recalling the feel of my child's hand in mine when I used to walk her to school. Or two seconds smiling to myself as I imagine her wedding or graduation day. Or half a second remembering the love I feel for her every night when I watch her sleeping.

You might also recall one event involving your child for which you are grateful, something that makes your heart soar. Perhaps this morning he gave you a rare smile, and suddenly you had hope that your kid was back. Often, people minimise these joys, saying 'Mustn't get my hopes up! Mustn't tempt fate! It will all be a big disappointment!' Actually, anticipatory grief doesn't offer any protection. If your hopes are dashed, you will suffer... and you will be more ready to bounce back if in the meantime, you have nourished yourself. Athletes build up their bodies. Parents build up their wellbeing.

WRAP-UP

I've introduced you to a number of concepts that I find very helpful in communicating with others and that help me increase my resilience, courage and wisdom. I wrote a lot more about it, and it's on anorexiafamily.com/NVC-communication.

In the next chapters I offer more solutions based on communication and empathy. Chapter 14 focuses on how you connect with your child, and Chapter 15 has more tools for your own wellbeing.

More on my website:

More depth and examples on anorexiafamily.com/NVC-communication[329]

Help with compassion, self-compassion, and sleep[330]

'OK': two letters for two steps to mindfulness and compassion[331]

Compassion meditation audio guides[332]

My YouTube video: The hero's journey[333]

Examples of conversations on Bitesize, my big collection of short audios[334]

14

LOVE, NO MATTER WHAT: HOW TO SUPPORT YOUR CHILD WITH COMPASSIONATE COMMUNICATION

Has it become difficult to recognise your son or daughter? Do you struggle to help them as they flip between depression and aggression? Are you finding it hard to give unconditional love, and are you confused about rewards and punishment? In this chapter I offer you resources and examples to help you deal with common issues, communicate with compassion and build connection.

In this chapter I propose to address typical difficulties we parents experience with our children when they have an eating disorder. I'll share what served me well with my daughter, what's worked for others, and what professionals say. I'll write samples of dialogue, and do check out Bitesize, my audio collection, to hear more examples.[335]

If you skipped Chapter 13 this one should still make sense in most places, but you'll get a better grasp of matters relating to communication if you first read Chapter 13.

As always, take what's helpful, and discard the rest.

> *"My feeling, with my daughter, is that each time she goes through a mood swing or a difficult time, if we handle it calmly and compassionately and she gets through it just fine, she is learning from that. It means the next time something goes wrong, she is more likely to get through it a little more easily."[336]*

FOOD IS MEDICINE, AND LOVE IS LIFE

My connection to my child feels like my most precious weapon against the eating disorder. Food and time are crucial to healing, but humans need their souls nourished too. A parent's love is life-giving. With our love, we soothe our children's nervous systems. While our children are drawn to eating-disorder behaviours to reduce their anxiety, we are modelling for them far more effective ways to deal with all kinds of emotions. I believe that because we matter enormously to our children, and because we support them, they're able to take on major challenges in spite of their fears. We make things seem safer, calmer. Our love heals their battered self-esteem, counteracts their self-hate and guarantees that we will not abandon them.

I find this quote from a young person in recovery very moving, given the suffering brought on by the illness.

> *"What an amazing gift the eating disorder brought me and my family – the gift of communication, of love, of acceptance."*[337]

UNCONDITIONAL LOVE AND ACCEPTANCE

Unconditional love and acceptance of your child is one of the most important tools in your toolkit, both for your own benefit and your kid's. It's natural for us, in our suffering, to have all kinds of judgemental thoughts, and it's easy for these to leak out and spoil our work. I'm proposing to give you some of the principles that helped me, and also to be transparent about the mental twists and turns I underwent as I tried to be totally present to my daughter and offer her unconditional love.

'Love her even when she's down'

One afternoon, when my child was very ill, I arranged to meet a generous young woman who was recovering from anorexia. She gave me precious insights, and as we parted company I asked her, 'What is the one most important thing I should concentrate on? One thing that will make the biggest difference to my child?'

She answered without hesitation. 'Love her at all times. Even when she's down. Even when she's at her worst.'

I still get a lump in my throat when I think of this and everything it implies.

What is unconditional love and acceptance?

Unconditional love is loving our children irrespective of what they do or don't do. Love, no matter what. It's about them mattering to us. It's making them know that they are wanted, special, significant, valued, appreciated, missed, and enjoyed.

I thrive on unconditional love, and I'm a grown-up. I want my child to be nourished by that too.

I believe that it is because of our love for our kids that family therapy has been shown to work.[338] I believe the treatment is about putting love into action. Even the best residential units can't give that kind of love.

My child is more important than what she does. My relationship with her matters more than any of her achievements or behaviours. Or to put it another way, 'I'm her mum!'

Here's how I saw it when times were hard: it's easy to show her my love when all is sweetness and light, but I believe she needs it most when her behaviour is out of order. These are times when she has no resources to hand and her only tools are abuse, defensiveness, lies. If she had better ways of getting what matters to her, she wouldn't be getting in such a state. In fact, many times she's done a great job of achieving her aims peacefully. Right now she is lost. I am the person she needs to turn to. I am her anchor, her rock. I will not add to her stress, uncertainties or self-loathing by criticising her. In fact, because of the state she's in, she will be expecting me to judge her, so I will take extra care to show her my uncritical acceptance.

How about her behaviour? If she has my love, is she going to think it's OK to behave without any consideration for me?

Connect before you correct. I will address the behaviour later, if necessary. But first I will take care of our connection.

Parents can find it difficult to believe that love and acceptance work better than rewards, punishments and forceful displays of authority. They think the only alternative is to be permissive, and who wants to create a spoiled brat? Some have become masters of unconditional love and they are delighted by how well compassionate persistence works, but to them it's an abnormal, temporary way of parenting which is only appropriate to eating disorder situations. I disagree. Nonviolent Communication principles were developed with all human beings in mind. You don't need to have an eating disorder to thrive on connection and mutual respect.

Uncritical acceptance: therapeutically essential

What my young friend told me when she urged me to love my child at all times ties in perfectly with a piece of advice that emerges from research:

> *"Non-critical families seemed to succeed better overall in refeeding their children than those with more hostile and critical ways of interacting."*[339]

For family therapists, modelling uncritical acceptance towards patients is an essential therapeutic task. They're not just giving the acceptance, they're modelling it so that we, the parents learn.

Love? I'm too mad at her to feel love

No judging, no blaming, no shaming. With unconditional love and acceptance, you accept your child as she is, even when – especially when – she's behaving appallingly.

Unconditional love is not about feeling love for your child at all times.[340] We're often far too triggered to feel anything except … hmmm … rather the opposite. No worries. Feelings are not the issue here; they come and go of their own accord.

The truth is that you have love for your child. Fundamentally. All the time. You wouldn't be bothering with this book, with your research, if you didn't.

Bear with me. It's quite possible that right now you feel absolutely nothing for your child. You've gone numb. Or you despise him – you think he's selfish, weak, manipulative. Here are some blanks for you to fill in your own accusations _____ . And here are some more _____ .

Love as a value and love as a feeling

Think of love as a way of being, rather than a feeling. I have a value, something I hold most dear, a fundamental need, around my love for my child. That love is a constant. It's what made me hold her as a baby when she howled, what made me take her to the swing park even when I was longing for sleep or stimulation. It's what made me tackle the teacher who scared her and what makes me melt when she hugs me. You too have stuck by your child through sleepless nights, fevers, accidents, and tantrums. If you didn't abandon your child when he was growing up, before the eating disorder struck, then trust that you have deep, unconditional love for him. Its riches are a strength you can tap into now.

We tend to think of love as a feeling. Feelings are in the moment: 'Right now, I am bored, waiting for my child to get through her lunch, one microscopic forkful at a time', 'Right now, I am furious. She hid food in her pockets', 'Right now I hate her and resent her. I've given up my work and all my interests for her, and she's still not eating.' The feelings come about because some of your needs are crying out for attention. Perhaps you dearly wish to have some rest or peace or some time to do something more companionable or intellectually satisfying.

Feelings are waves whipped up by the wind, but love as a value, as the way of being, is a vast ocean. You can tune into it in a millisecond by imagining your daughter leaning her head on you, remembering an event when you were close, or visualising something in the future. 'I love it when my daughter laughs', 'One day I'll be sitting at her wedding service and I'll bawl my eyes out.' Do you feel yourself soften? This is one way of moving yourself out of irritation or despair.

Coping with your emotional depletion

When you bring to mind loving moments, you might find you instantly stiffen, remembering how awful your situation is. You might also realise that your actions are nowhere close to your values, because your kid is pushing all your buttons. We've surely all been there. We have too much on our plate and we are emotionally and physically depleted.

When big demands are made of your love, patience and energy, you need to refuel frequently. Top up with whatever it is that makes you feel human. As much as possible, get people to help you with some of the mealtime work, act as though you are full of love (fake it till you make it), become good at self-compassion, and urgently get yourself regular doses of tender loving care from other sources. (Plenty of tools in Chapters 13 and 15).

Teamwork helps us criticise less

Feeding your child at home is a lot easier with teamwork. There are times when we need to get someone else to do mealtime duties while we take a break and refuel. James Lock *et al* write:

> *"An overly burdened parent may show exhaustion and frustration*
> *by becoming more critical of the patient. Encourage the more*
> *energetic and perhaps less critical parent to find ways to support his*
> *or her partner in the difficult task of taking on the illness."*[341]

If you're exhausted it's practically impossible to be the person you want to be and act the way you wish to. Make it a priority to find help.

JUDGEMENTAL THOUGHTS: MY STORY

I can totally relate to research findings that uncritical acceptance is a key factor in a child's recovery. Letting go of judgements I had for my kid – in particular the thought that she ought to try harder – was a major turning point for me. After this shift in myself, I was more consistently able to open my heart to her, I was more able to support her through challenges, and I felt better too. My husband, who'd been hero-ically keeping the show on the road while I tottered on the edge of collapse, was amazed by my transformation. My ability to access unconditional love, combined with some great support from the eating disorders team, coincided with our daughter getting better. We entered a virtuous cycle: as she got better, her resistance diminished and it was easier for me to be in a compassionate state.

I'll tell you how it happened in the hope that if you too are trying to let go of judgements, your journey will be faster.

There wasn't a lot of judgement to let go of in the first place. Our attitude to our daughter had been compassionate and non-blaming for many months. The hospital talked in terms of 'your real daughter' and 'anorexia'. 'It's anorexia who stormed off into the street, not your kid. It's anorexia who howls that she's fat, not your girl.' We knew this stuff. We didn't blame our kid. Not for the illness. Not for the obnox-ious behaviours.

But I was uncomfortably aware that a tiny part of me was still judging her. I wasn't totally accepting my daughter for who she was at that moment. When I paid careful attention to my thoughts without censure, I caught a few that were not pretty. I was telling myself that she should be nice to me, that when she put up resistance, she was doing it to annoy me. I became aware of a part of me that secretly blamed her for not trying to get better. 'Why doesn't she try harder? Why is she not fighting this intruder? Why is she giving in to it? If it was me, I'd be taking on every challenge thrown at me to get better. I'd cooperate with my therapist. I'd challenge myself with fear foods. I'd talk honestly about my feelings. I'd work hard on my recovery.'

I rejected these thoughts with all my might, but they lurked on the edge of my consciousness. I could only hope that they were so quiet that my daughter would be protected from them. Yet I'm sure they leaked out through my facial expressions, though things I said and, most of all, things I didn't say. And if so, my child was probably picking up the negative signals, as people with eating disorders tend to do. In hindsight I believe that until my own attitude shifted, I could not truly be by her side. I could not be a resource she could confidently tap into, a support for her to lean on.

Would you put all your trust in someone who thinks you could be trying harder?

Wanting her to have motivation

I tried to combat my judging thoughts by remembering how nobody chooses to have an eating disorder. My kid had an illness. She had some kind of eating-disorder voice giving her hell. If she could fight this thing that was making her life a misery, she would. In other words, I tapped into how sorry I felt for her.

This left me with a bit of a problem when she was thoroughly enjoying herself. In the ward, in between the misery of family therapy sessions, she laughed and had fun with the other kids and with the nurses. They did manicures, went on shopping trips, rolled about in the soft play area and watched *X-Factor*. Much of the time, the eating-disorder voice didn't seem to be bullying her, so why, I asked myself, was she not fighting it and demanding her life back?

I knew that anorexia drives patients to resist treatment – another reason not to judge my kid, clearly. But, my thoughts argued, some anorexia sufferers do fight the illness. I'd read about them. It's only much later that I realised that any motivation to recover tends to happen in late adolescence or in adulthood, and even then people lose it at mealtimes. Motivation is such an elusive resource that family therapy does not require it.

Letting go of judgements, accepting my child as she is

I wanted to give my daughter genuine acceptance, and I didn't like my judgemental and blaming thoughts. They made my resolve fragile – I often fell flat on my face the instant my stress levels went up.

The problem is that telling yourself that you shouldn't think something doesn't stop you from thinking it. I introduced chatterbox thoughts in the previous chapter: if you try to shut it up, it rebels. I remember a turning point when I was facing a weekend on my own with my daughter. I could foresee that when she refused to eat, I would throw away weeks of self-control and scream at her. Things were very bad. She had been discharged from eleven months in hospital and she was deteriorating. It seemed like we were back at the same point we'd been at exactly a year before. I feared that my child was headed for an adolescence spent in and out of hospital.

I had an emergency phone call with a Nonviolent Communication trainer. As I told her about my fears, I found that my judgements were mixed up with hopelessness and with the fear that the illness would take my child away. I became conscious of how my thinking didn't match what was deep in me: a fierce, unconditional love of my child. There was no room for judgement in this love.

Once we have clarity, the way forward often presents itself quite naturally. I was drawn to a book on acceptance on my large to-read pile.[342] Something shifted as I read. I really did accept and let go. I accepted that this illness is the pits, that everything was horribly difficult, that I missed my daughter, and that my heart was in little pieces for what she had to go through. I accepted that there was no way of knowing what I would do if I were in her shoes, and that this was irrelevant, because the only person in her shoes was her. I accepted that what mattered was what it was like for her. I let go of thinking that things weren't fair, that things shouldn't be this way. I accepted that this was how things were right now. I tapped into a sense of trust that whatever happened, I could deal with it, even though in the present moment I had no idea what that might mean. It felt necessary to accept whatever life dished out, to let my fears speak without censure, in order to let go of shields, barriers and defence mechanisms.

I'll tell you more about acceptance and letting go in Chapter 15. These practices gave me a route to non-judgement, to genuine compassion and respect. As long as I was in a state of compassion I didn't have to make efforts to control my thoughts or what I said or how I said it.

I find compassion so effective that I now make it my go-to strategy whenever adversity strikes and judgemental thoughts reappear. With my daughter's relapse I got confirmation, again and again, of how crucial it was to open my heart. Without that openness, I suffered and I didn't do as good a job. The work is not done once and for all, but it seems that the more you do it, the better at it you get. When I blow it and have a less-than-proud moment I am generally able to regain my loving kindness faster and mend the relationship sooner. There is no 'off' switch for blame, but I hope the tools in this book help you reconnect with compassion faster and more easily. I also created some guided meditation audio resources to help you access compassion for your child.[343]

SHE LOVES YOU, EVEN WHEN SHE LOVES YOU NOT

With an eating disorder it's utterly normal for children to violently reject the people closest to them. If you're regularly on the receiving end of aggression you may be experiencing fear over and over again. Your nervous system senses danger, driving you to fight, flight or freeze. There's no space for love in this state. You can feel disconnected from any sense of caring, and that's no good for either you or your child. As one parent told me, 'All that hate wears you out.'

When my daughter smiled or gave me a hug, if was like the sunshine had broken through after six months in the Arctic. If you're getting some sun, allow yourself to savour every second of it, and later, to play it back in your mind and feel the warmth. It may bring tears and I've come to learn that's fine. I suspect it also does some much-needed care and repair.

Imagine, also, how wonderful it is for your child to suddenly feel so free, so herself, that she can express her love for you. And imagine that you give it back unconditionally. These must be the occasions when she gets a glimpse of what it's like to be well. What a huge motivator that must be.

Your son may assure you many times a day of quite how much he hates you, your daughter may try to kick you and slam the door in your face, but don't believe it. Youngsters report back, years down the line, how much they loved and missed their mum or dad, and how terrible they felt about pushing them away.

Here's what Kate, a recovered young person, wrote:

*"I remember how the illness at times made me hate my mum when
she was refeeding me and think she was trying to ruin my life and
make me miserable by forcing me to eat. It tries to destroy your
closest, most special relationship, and take away the person who loves
you and cares for you the most, who's willing to do anything to get
you better."*[344]

Why does your child 'hate' you?

Being rejected by your son or daughter is one of the top causes of suffering I see among parents – myself included. We need to sustain ourselves with compassion. It helps to realise that this state of affairs is normal, is temporary, and is not about us.

Sometimes both parents are rejected simultaneously, sometimes it's the parent who's doing most of the mealtime work, and sometimes it oscillates between the two (so that there's always one goodie and one baddie). Hey, everyone can be rejected: even the family dog and – I kid you not – the teddy bear.

The following quote comes from a child who was distraught with anxieties around food and body shape. And yet:

*"You know the worst thing about this illness, Mum? It's that you
push away the people you love the most."*

How can kids long for our love yet display such hateful behaviour? I think the answer lies, quite simply in their high level of suffering. Nobody who is well chooses to be hateful.

Imagine taking a stroll through the woods and coming across a beautiful dog, sitting by a tree. Just as you lean forward to stroke it, it roars and snaps at your hand. You are shocked and angry… until you see that its leg is mangled in a trap.[345] With our children, with the trap being invisible, it's a little harder to make sense of their rejection.

We parents can come up with many, many theories why our children 'hate' us:

- The state of fight, flight or freeze is one of disconnection and of scarcity. Everyone is a potential threat. We even hate ourselves. Contrast that with the state brought on by meditative practices, where there's a sense of abundance, safety, love, and being at one with the world.

    *"My D's treatment of me was outside her control. It was a symptom
    as sure as her starving was. She was starving herself of my love."*

- Another take on the same idea is that the brain dysfunction which causes your child to deny herself food also drives her to deny herself satisfaction of other needs, in particular her need for love.

    *"My daughter had been in hospital for four weeks. Four weeks of
    total, intense, rejection. When my birthday came up, I discovered
    she'd used her precious pocket money to buy me a present. And she'd
    made big happy birthday banners for her ward bedroom. We hugged*

and for a few delicious moments I could feel her melting in my arms, like she really wanted that hug. After that, I got the cold shoulder again for several weeks, but that hug sustained me. I knew that the indifference and rejection was only on the surface and that the love would stay alive."

- When food is reintroduced after semi-starvation, biological instabilities (e.g. serotonin uptake) make the person feel agitated and irritable. And of course, when we feed we are asking our child to give up the very behaviours that they relied on to soothe themselves.

- If our child has a phase of screaming, 'You are not my mother' (sometimes referring to some other person who's treated them kindly as their 'real' mother), that may be their way of rejecting us, but it could also be the product of a starved brain and the delusional thinking that comes with it.

- Perhaps our children, overwhelmed by their emotions and unable to self-regulate, know they'll feel calmer after a massive tantrum, and so it serves a purpose to whip themselves and everyone around them into a frenzy.

- If the disorder is all about avoiding eating, what better way than to bite the hand that feeds you? Some children are able to confide that their hostility is a deliberate ploy to make the parent to give up caring for them. Notice if your child engineers big conflicts in order to storm off to her room, declaring, 'I'm not eating now and it's all your fault!'

    "Mum, when you give me food tomorrow, if I'm really horrible to you, you've got to know I don't mean it."

- Our children have good reasons to give up on us and push us away. An eating disorder, at times, turns ordinary homes into war zones. Just when our child most needs competent support, when she needs to trust us and lean on us, we are at our worst. I certainly behaved in ways my daughter had never experienced before.

- Some suggest there is a psychological or neurological link, since infancy, between mothering and feeding, or that kids project their self-hate onto their same-sex parent. But that doesn't fit how our children can hate either parent.

- My husband thought I made an easy target for my daughter because she could see how much I cared. I observed that although I was the main baddie, she could quickly switch allegiance – and then the fact that clearly I cared was precious to her.

- Sometimes kids reject us when they are hospitalised. The message is 'You abandoned me', no matter how much we explain our reasons.

- Sometimes they feel lost and bereft because so far we've been unable to rescue them. My daughter clearly decided early on in her illness that she couldn't count on me. That must have hurt a lot. Kids rely on their parents to make it all better. It is scary for them to believe that this thing that is making their lives a misery is too big for us too.

- Finally, people with an eating disorder may be driven to push away the people who love them if they hate themselves, are full of shame, and truly believe they are unlovable. I would guess they very much want acceptance and empathy.

Your child really needs love

It might help you to know that your child may look emotionally blank or permanently angry, but like all humans she needs love. In hospital my daughter found parent figures to care for her. It was a relief for me to know she could be emotionally nourished by others while she couldn't connect with us. The kindness of some of the nurses affected her deeply, and the memories have sometimes moved her to tears of gratitude.

Showing up even when you're rejected

> *"We visited her in the closed ward up to three times a day –*
> *sometimes just long enough for her to say 'Fuck off!' We would*
> *always tell her we would be back. As we left, we'd see her look at us*
> *from the corner of her eye and we knew our visits mattered to her."*

If your kid rejects you, this is likely to pass like all the other behaviours brought on by the eating disorder. But if it doesn't, you may get some inspiration and hope from this mother:

> *"Her shut-out was complete and relentless and specific to me. If I*
> *came into a room, she left. She turned her head if she smiled in my*
> *presence so I wouldn't see it. She sat in the back seat of the car if I*
> *had to drive her somewhere. I wrote her love notes that I'd leave on*
> *her pillow, only to find them torn up in bits in her wastebasket. She*
> *would not let me touch her, even accidentally.*
>
> *Eventually she had to be given no choice – very similar to*
> *eating. We invented our own form of exposure-response therapy to*
> *basically require our D to interact with me in a civil way, over and*
> *over, every day. If I hadn't been there, every day, screwing up my*
> *courage, knocking on her door, being pleasant, ignoring the Taser*
> *eyes, smiling, she would not have recovered like this. She loves me!*
> *And this I know is my real daughter."*

Even as she rejects you, your child needs your unconditional love, which means you're going to need a lot of empathy from other sources to sustain you.

I am grateful that the hospital that took our daughter in took a firm stance about family involvement. Right from the start, their aim was to enable her to spend increasing amounts of time at home. They asked for one or both of us to visit our daughter every day whether she liked it or not. She hated it – especially when I was doing the visiting – and she expressed it with all her might. I had to trust that I was doing no harm by showing up, and that a gradual, repeated, softly-softly approach would eventually pay off. It reminded me of how one might go about taming a wild, injured animal. It was a time when I felt hugely grateful for any glimpse of connection, and I have moving memories of times she let me into her world. Small things, like once when we sat side by side and she silently leaned against me. Another time, during a stroll together, she'd been giving me a relentless tirade of accusations, when all of a sudden she quietly she put her little hand in mine. These days, we have a beautiful connection which fills me with joy.

Does your child reject your touch?

For me, the most natural way to show my love to my child is through touch. There are good reasons why holding, hugging, cuddling, stroking are instinctive soothing gestures. Touch releases oxytocin and moves people out of fight-flight-freeze. Yet like many children with an eating disorder, my daughter didn't want my touch when she was upset. She now says it's because she feared I'd be feeling for bones or fat, though I suspect the main reason was more visceral. Each time she pushed me away I had to take a deep breath in order not to blame her for how utterly bereft I felt.

> *"My daughter hated her own body and didn't want to be touched.*
> *What worked was small gestures that communicated care and love.*
> *For instance she allowed one nurse to braid her hair. And she liked*
> *it when I bought her special flowers."*

It never occurred to me to try to change my daughter's behaviour when she rejected my touch. My intention was to help her be soothed or comforted, and if physical contact triggered her, I saw it as my job to find other means, usually silent empathy. I found that once she was a little calmer, I could then ask, 'May I give you a hug?' Sometimes she was still too upset to reply, and I had to make a guess and take the risk of moving closer, hoping that this was something she actually wanted.

As the months went by, it became possible to give her physical comfort after the worst of the storm had passed. These days I feel incredibly grateful that our physical closeness has returned.

If your child pushes you away when you move in to comfort, some therapists might well advise you to back off and respect her space. But I would urge you to listen carefully to your intuition. I consider a parent–child relationship a beautiful, sacred thing. I doubt you can do any harm when you come from a place of love and acceptance. Some parents report holding their child with care, and keeping hold, until she lets go of her resistance and allows herself to be soothed.

Where's their emotional intelligence gone?

An eating disorder erodes emotional health. Our children seem to deny themselves not only nutrition, but satisfaction of all needs and desires – this is sometimes referred to as 'emotional anorexia'.[346] When they're terribly malnourished and weak, they seem spaced out and zombified, devoid of personality or soul. Starvation numbs them. This shutdown makes sense as it preserves energy and it reminds me of the frozen state of traumatised people. As we feed our children, irritation, fear and anger seem to dominate, and what we see is abusive behaviour. There can be despair as well, and moments of overwhelming grief. It can take a while before we see a smile, before we hear laughter, before we get a cuddle, or before our children are able to share anything about what's going on in their internal world. It can take even longer for them to be in tune with what they really care about and to engage with life.

In my daughter's case, I saw anorexia take an emotionally intelligent child and make her go blank. It annoyed me no end when hospital psychologists declared that she scored low in tests for emotion and mental flexibility, implying that this was her default state. If they'd seen her pre-anorexia they'd have got quite a different picture. Luckily, this confusion of cause and effect only affected my pride in my kid, not her treatment.

WHAT TO DO WITH YOUR CHILD'S ANGER

We should help our children to recognise that anger, like all emotions, comes and goes. It's part of our internal weather system. We allow the feeling, we practice self-compassion, and we give ourselves time to come out of our state of fight or flight. And during that time we control our behaviour so as not to cause harm. Your child should be clear it's not OK to act from a place of anger and cause harm. Emotional regulation isn't about having angry outbursts.

A little bit of education about anger – for yourself and perhaps for your child: it's useful to make friends with anger, so that we can allow its presence when it suddenly descends on us. We allow the anger with self-kindness, listen to any message that comes up about what matters to us, and the anger moves on.

Anger gets associated with shame and with danger, yet it's a fantastic emotion for our survival. In the face of danger, anger gets us into fight or flight fast. So it's normal that for a few seconds, our reactions are often out of proportion and unreasonable. When anger keeps stewing it's often from a sense that we are powerless and unsafe, because anger provides a temporary illusion of power and safety. When our anger hangs around, there are some unmet needs that need to be heard.

Compassion is, as usual, the way forward. Once you've given your child containment ('Do not kick!', 'Please use polite words' – more on this later), check out your child's needs. She might want to be considered, to be seen (she waves her arms about), to be heard (she shouts), to have power to meet her needs (she uses physical force) and for her needs to matter. She might long for things to be fair, or to be allowed to make her own choices. She might want safety, peace of mind, containment, to be held, understood or to have someone's loving presence. She might need some rest or a peaceful, less stimulating environment.

IS YOUR CHILD'S ANGER BETTER OUT THAN IN?

In the first few months of our daughter's illness, I was utterly confused when the hospital clinicians (and the books they recommended) advocated that we 'withstand' her angry outbursts. Apparently, blow-ups were a necessary part of the journey to recovery, and if parents intervened in any way this would compromise the healing process.

Here's how it's supposed to work. You let your child mouth off to his heart's content, swear-words and all. Your job is to stand there with a Buddha-like expression, showing that you are in no way affected and that you love him no matter what. The principle is that while he's spitting venom at you, he's not directing anger inwards. Once he's unburdened himself of his rage, he'll find some peace, and – here comes the magic – he'll then be able to eat.

Every instinct told us this was wrong. Wrong for our child's wellbeing, her dignity, her self-respect. Wrong for our relationships. Does flinging mud at their parents really enable kids to eat? If it were true, then the great majority would be cured within days.

Of course our children should know that we love them whatever their behaviour. Of course we shouldn't react to their aggression with more aggression or with blame. And I totally agree that our children should see us as solid and secure: we will not fall to pieces when they most need us. But if your child is yelling abuse, I believe he's out of control, disconnected, distressed, and driven by his state of fear (unless he's deliberately engineering a fight to avoid the next meal). He has no tools to free himself except to continue till he's exhausted. He may be calmer after his outburst, but he's paid a heavy price for it: he has to deal with shame about how he behaved, grief about hurting the people who most matter to him, and the scary knowledge that he can become seriously out of control. He may also be frightened that, although so far you haven't rebelled or broken down, you might eventually give up on him.

Emotionally, anger can feel like a pressure cooker. It keeps heating up until bang! – the safety valve explodes. But anger isn't steam. It's not a physical thing that can get 'bottled up', that drowns or suffocates people. It's a state of mind, a feeling that comes and goes. Bring the emotional level down (turn the heat off under the pressure cooker), let the person be heard, give containment, address the issues, and the anger passes.

Our brain is wired to go straight into fight, flight or freeze when it detects a threat. Anger is going to happen, whether we want it or not. The skill is to move faster from a reactive to a self-connected state. When we got tired of 'withstanding' our daughter's outbursts, my husband and I attended a course in Nonviolent Communication. I still smile as I recall that our intention was to teach our daughter to talk more nicely. Instead, the course gave us skills to respond to our daughter with empathy. Over and over again we were amazed to see how in a matter of minutes – sometimes seconds – her reactivity dipped and she reached relative calm.

We also learned to make requests in a compassionate way, so that we could, if we chose to, ask her to express her truth *and* remain polite.

The course changed our own attitudes and skills. The changes rubbed off on her. It's a good example of parenting from the inside out.[347]

IS YOUR OWN ANGER BETTER OUT THAN IN?

I used to feel really sad when I'd messed up with a cutting remark, a threat, or a rolling of the eyes. My mission was to nurture our connection, not retaliate.

Confusingly, the same therapists who told us that it was good for our daughter to externalise her anger and to see us 'withstand' it, also told me that losing my calm wasn't anything to worry about. They thought if my daughter saw the consequences of her outbursts, she would learn. The truth is she didn't learn anything except possibly that she was, surely, a despicable person who couldn't stop her own terrible behaviours.

I cannot imagine how it can be therapeutic 'teach a lesson' by giving our children as good as they've given us. If your child is out of control, it's not out of choice. If she's in such a reactive state that her behaviour is outrageous, she needs more care, support and compassion than at any other moment. She needs from you what she cannot do for herself.

If I lose my temper, it's about me. I will not make my child responsible for it.

Having said all that, from my own experience and from supporting many parents in individual sessions, I can tell you that most of us have blown a fuse at times, and we are living proof that we can be less than perfect and still, our children get well. Very occasionally, when we lose our control, it gives our children a wake-up call and they become kinder for a while. I would never plan to do it this way, but sometimes life gives us something for free.

If you want to mend your connection after losing your temper – and I recommend it because, if nothing else, it's good modelling – I suggest you stay in your power, rather than abase yourself. To do that, express deep needs. Compare 'I'm sorry I shouted' with 'I really want this house to be full of harmony and respect for each other. That's how I want to live. So now I'm sorry that I shouted.'

IT'S NOT ABOUT YOU (EVEN WHEN SHE'S MAD AT YOU)

When your child is engaging in verbal fireworks, it is natural that you should have some kind of reaction. You might want to shout back and blame her, or you might want to cry because you're blaming yourself, or you might want to shut down your love and care because hearing her is just too upsetting. Our brains are wired to do precisely this and it is pointless blaming yourself.

If you would like to stay self-connected while also taking good care of your own wellbeing, start with empathy for yourself and silent empathy for your child. I discussed both in Chapter 13, where I also suggested that nobody causes feelings in anybody else. Your child feels the way she does because of the way her mind has interpreted a situation.

Here are some mantras that may help you in the heat of the moment.

- It's not about me.
- This has nothing to do with me.
- It's all about her feelings.[348]

CHATTERBOX

You can grow your ability to translate the words that come from her chatterbox. The words themselves do not express her deep truth. But they do contain clues to her needs. So when she says, 'You don't care about me!' you could choose to hear, 'I need to know that you care. I need to matter.'

Let's say your child is yelling, 'I hate you! You never listen to me! Why are you taking me to this restaurant?'

Now imagine what it would be like for you if her words actually were, 'I want your love! I really need you to listen to me and understand me! I don't know how to help myself. Please help me. Because this restaurant thing is really awful for me.'

There is no way anyone can speak with this kind of honesty when their nervous system is sensing danger. The faster you can translate violent words into needs, the less you will be hurt.

Because these situations keep presenting themselves, you might find, increasingly, that abusive words hardly affect you. You're getting so much practice!

PUNISHMENT, SANCTIONS, CONSEQUENCES AND ULTIMATUMS

For some parents, punishments and threats have been an effective tool to get their child back into eating. If something is effective in saving a life, it has a place in your toolkit. I hope, though you will be open to trying other approaches which can work better, both for eating and for more ordinary issues. I see a lot of problems with punishments, so I'll start with that.

The word 'punishment' sounds outdated: belts, slippers, dry bread and water – who does that nowadays? Yet punishment is still alive and well. These days, we prefer to talk of 'consequences' and 'removal of privileges'. I mentioned the problem with these when we were bungee jumping.

Punishment doesn't create trust and connection, which in the longer term are most likely to bring out the behaviours you want. Punishment is more likely to break your trusting connection and lead to defiant pushback.

Some parenting gurus tell us that kids must learn the consequences of their actions. If our youngsters come in later than agreed from a party, for instance, the gurus want them grounded. I invite you to note that grounding is a set consequence – set by the parents as a punishment. It has nothing to do with the 'natural' or 'real' consequences of leaving a party late, such as the increased risk of getting mugged on the way home, or of feeling sleepy the next day.

Set consequences and punishments are more often than not a measure of how desperate we parents can feel. At first we hope to provide a deterrent ('If you don't eat/if you hit me, I'm cutting off your internet access'). When that doesn't work, we may find ourselves issuing ultimatum upon ultimatum ('If you try to hit me one more time, don't ever set foot in this house again'). We are not in our power.

When nothing seems to work, every fibre in our body wants to resort to brute force – we're in a state of fight or flight. I'm amazed how very quickly I can feel this way when I encounter resistance. If we don't de-escalate our own emotions, our knee-jerk reaction is to exert power over our kids. And they're going to do their damn best to retaliate at the earliest opportunity. Unless, that is, they are so scared that they withdraw into shame and submission.

Suppose your child is physically violent at the dinner table. Later I will offer suggestions for dealing with aggression. All the same, in the heat of the moment you might well blurt out, 'No more kicking. If you kick, I will cut your pocket money,' or, 'Right! That's it! Our outing to the shops if off. And that jacket you wanted? You're not getting it.'

Telling my child I'll cut her pocket money if she kicks me is, I believe, a threat of punishment, or an ultimatum. Refusing to buy her the jacket would be a sanction or punishment. If I told her the 'consequence' of her kicking is that a shopping outing is cancelled, this is what she might hear:

- Blame and shame: 'I'm bad and deserve punishment. I've tried and tried not to kick, but it just keeps happening. Yet my mum thinks I can stop it happening. So I must be really messed up and hopeless. I hate myself and don't deserve to a place on this earth.

- Rejection: 'She only likes me when I'm sweet. I try and try to be a normal person but it's too hard. I'm already pretending so much.'

- Alienation: 'I'm all alone. No one understands how hard this is for me.'

When parents talk of 'removing privileges', I wonder, how is it a 'privilege' for a kid to enjoy his phone or to go and see friends?

When we go against our children's wishes, it should be from a place of love and wisdom. Instead, when we punish the message is, 'I'm bigger and stronger and richer than you'. Then one day we get as good as we gave. Our children feel big and strong enough to fight back. They 'rebel', 'push back', 'test boundaries' and become 'typical teenagers'. Some professionals consider this to be the task of adolescence – the way youngsters grow into autonomous adults.

I am more drawn to expert views that we foster growth by welcoming conflict *and* working towards connection in the face of conflict. I want to model respectful dialogue so that my child learns to navigate conflicts in later life. Add to this the bigger picture – that nonviolence starts at home – and I aim to 'be the change I want to see in the world'.[349] You can have a compassionate stance without being a doormat. On the contrary, you can be incredibly persistent when you are well grounded in connection.

Don't assume that teenagers are unreasonable and antagonistic. That's a self-fulfilling prophesy. Don't drop out of their life either, because parents continue to matter enormously.[350] Nurture the connection, make clear requests, be persistent, and see your child thrive.[351]

'Take that, eating disorder!'

Some parents have been taught to separate their child from the eating disorder (ED). Over here is my lovely child, and over there is evil ED. This imagery is great if it helps you to support your child without blame. But with some parents I see that this can backfire – because ED misbehaves, ED *and* the child are made to suffer. 'ED refused breakfast, so there's no phone and no TV. ED has to learn that eating is non-negotiable.' [352] If you like seeing ED as an entity, then notice that ED likes to deny your child anything that might make her feel good. Strife and punishments play right into ED's hands. You could go so much further by picturing yourself on your child's side.

I am devastated at the idea of punishing a kid for behaviours that are driven by their eating disorder. Would you punish a kid in a plaster cast for limping? A kid with leukaemia for losing his hair? If you still believe your kid has will power over her behaviours, read about what other eating-disorder sufferers are driven to do, notice the similarities, and weep.

REWARDS AND INCENTIVES CAN BACKFIRE

While many people don't like the idea of punishment, they see rewards and incentives as a good thing. I want to show you how rewards are terribly close to punishment, and how easily they can backfire. I have found that once we mastered the art of compassionate persistence, we didn't need a reward system any more.

Let me tell you a story. In the early days our daughter's hospital devised charts of goals and rewards. During her home visits she had to sit for 30 minutes to earn a hairclip. Wearing warm clothing earned her more hairclips. When hairclips became boring, we gave her points which went towards bigger rewards such as clothing. All this became the focus of the hospital's family sessions, month after month. We tangled ourselves up in charts, ticks, stars, points, money, percentages, more money, bargaining, more ticks, more money, more maths, arguing, increasingly complex charts on Excel spreadsheets – and more arguing. The longer it went on, the less behavioural change we got. The reward system had taken on a life of its own. And so had her wardrobe. How many shirts can a girl own? My daughter, quite understandably, put all her focus in negotiating greater rewards for smaller achievements. In no time at all she was only engaging with challenges – minor ones, and only half-heartedly – when rewards were on offer. This took her further and further from her own centre, her own strengths, from the faint voice within her that wanted to heal.

One day we told the hospital we would not use rewards any more. After that our girl managed to take on all kinds of challenges. And that was through us using the skills I describe in this book.

A few words on rewards as positive reinforcement. The idea is to reward the behaviour you want to see repeated. You make your child feel good, and he'll do more of the same to keep the pleasant feeling coming. It's a benign form of manipulation, or an elementary form of behaviourism. Most things in society are set up for positive (or negative) reinforcement: gold stars in schools, awards in every field of excellence, bonuses at work.

And yet, a great number of studies have shown that rewards backfire, gradually killing off the desired behaviour.[353] Rewards tend to extinguish intrinsic motivation, replacing it with a weak external reason to do the behaviour. My daughter had no intrinsic motivation to beat anorexia, but what if she did have a desire to sit down and rest? Is it possible that by having her focus on rewards, we disconnected her from that desire?

If you still want to use rewards...

I hate to restrict your tool box, so I'll point out that in some situations, for some people, rewards have worked. Dangling a carrot may help get someone out of a rut. There are stories of kids who have eaten or overcome a compulsive behaviour because their desire for a reward trumped their fear. And when you're working on desensitising to a fear, you only need a few successes, so you won't be using rewards for months, the way we did.

If you're going to offer rewards, check that the tasks are well within your child's capabilities. Set him up for success, not failure. You promised a movie outing if he managed a fear food? Think it through. What if he can't manage all of it, and is now stuck at home with nothing to do? The lovely reward has flipped into punishment, even though he made a heroic effort to manage two thirds of the muffin.

If you want to reward the two-thirds effort, you will have to choose items that can be split into fractions. You can't have two thirds of a cinema outing but you can portion up points or money. I warn you though: a smart child will argue they managed more than two-thirds – they'll insist they got closer to three quarters, or even five eights. I challenge you to keep a clear head while all that's going on.

Incentives

Perhaps your intention is not to reward, but to incentivise and create a hopeful, positive mood. To do this, replace 'If' by 'When': '*When* you've eaten your muffin, we'll go to the movies. Use this when you're reasonably sure your child will manage most of the muffin, and have a think what you will do if he doesn't. Personally I might say, 'You've really tried and first time round it's natural it should be hard. It will get easier. Let's go and enjoy that movie!'

You may be able to make rewards truly incentivising if your child is on board – if he has some motivation to accomplish a particular task, if he welcomes a tool to help him do something he's already willing to do. This turns you two into a partnership and you're less likely to get rebellion or manipulation. In her book *Please Eat*, Beverley Mattocks describes successes when her son became enthusiastic about earning points (which led to cash).[354] To do this he had to succeed in challenges, which they agreed on in a 'contract' that they revised regularly. It seems crucial that this contract was a joint affair, not something imposed by parents.

We had a similar experience for a short while. When we started using rewards, our daughter welcomed the external motivation because she had a strong desire to manage Christmas away from the hospital. It was a success, the only success we ever had with rewards. The system failed when we continued to use it on things *we* wanted her to do, for which she had not the slightest motivation.

For more on rewards, punishments, and unconditional love:

> *Unconditional Parenting* by Alfie Kohn[355]
>
> *Hold on to Your Kids* by Gordon Neufeld and Gabor Maté[356]

HOW TO BE EFFECTIVE

You don't have to walk on eggshells

We parents know what it's like to walk on eggshells. Eating disorders often make our sons and daughters react violently and unpredictably. They accuse us of 'saying the wrong things' and then step up their restricting, bingeing or purging behaviours. So we pussyfoot around.

What if she doesn't want to tidy her room or clean her hamster's cage or stop hitting her sister? What if she storms off when Grandma's expecting a birthday visit? It's bad enough having a hard time around meals six times a day; what can we do about all the ordinary situations? Should we show her who's boss and demand what we want? Or should we say yes to everything because she has already lost her autonomy around food and health?

In Chapter 13 I introduced you to the principles of making requests, and now I propose to go into a few more details that might be particularly helpful with your child.

Teenage rudeness or eating disorder?

Parents tie themselves in knots when they try to work out if a rude behaviour is driven by the eating disorder or whether their child is being a terrible teenager. Their understanding is that if a bad behaviour is 'just teenage behaviour', then their child is being deliberately obnoxious and needs to be given 'consequences' (punishment). Otherwise the parents will look like they are condoning the behaviour, they will become a doormat, and there will be no end to the rudeness. Whereas if they believe the behaviour comes from the eating disorder, parents appreciate how well a compassionate, non-blaming, non-punitive approach works. They also understand it's unfair to punish their child for something which is not his fault.

Take the example of a teen screaming obscenities because he's run out of clean school shirts. The parents freeze, uncertain how to respond. Is it an eating-disorder issue, because their son saw his weight yesterday and because breakfast will include a fear food? If so, they have the skills to say, 'Use polite language! Now tell me, this is not like you. What's up? What is it that makes this issue so serious for you?'

But if they think their son is being a pesky teen, they go for: 'Don't you dare speak to your mother like that! Your outing with your friends is cancelled!'

I propose that you let go of these distinctions and use your wonderful compassionate communication skills for everything. You know how well they work even in the toughest of mealtime situations. If they can get your child to eat, they can also get your child to empty the dishwasher and to find a pleasing alternative to the F-word.

We can't tease apart all the factors that tipped our child's nervous system into a state of threat. Having difficult meals, having constant eating-disorder thoughts, is tough. But so is dreading an essay, or having a teacher shame you for forgetting your homework. An eating disorder puts our children in a near-constant state of stress, and so do exams.

There's an added difficulty when our children are depressed or suicidal. Punishments (like cancelling friends) are hardly going to lift their mood.

Yes, it's counter-intuitive to be compassionate when you're at the receiving end of appalling behaviour. It's strange for parents to step out of a well-worn groove to create peace, not war. There's an assumption that we can use our higher status to make our kids polite. All the same, when your child is being disrespectful, consider that they are not in choice. Human beings, when they are in choice, love harmony, connection, growth, happiness. Your child is connected to you, you are the person who gives them unconditional love, who can help them with homework and friendship issues, who gives them the stability they need to practice flying the nest. So when your teen screams at you, assume that his nervous system is in a state of threat. He's in fight-flight-freeze. He is driven by forces just as real as those of an eating disorder He does not expect love and support, though he longs for it. This makes it extra important – and extra challenging – for you to create the very connection he so needs to be his own gorgeous, wonderful self again.

Containment: you are neither doormat nor bully

With your work supporting meals, you have seen the effectiveness of compassionate persistence. Your compassionate stance is in no way permissive. You are doing an incredibly hard job, in spite of huge resistance, without needing to act like a bully. When you have lost your temper, you've quickly seen how that backfires.

Parents have two broad roles: one is nurturing, and one is structuring, or providing a container. Both attend to major needs in our children. Young children, for instance, might never get the sleep they need if we didn't insist they go to bed.

At times, children and teens lack the capacity to self-regulate effectively. When their emotions run high, they tend to get carried away by the chaos of their mind. They may wish they could stop saying things they don't really mean, and stop doing things they feel guilty about, but when they're triggered, they find it very hard to put their true self in the driving seat. It is hard for them, and at the same time we can request they keep their behaviours in check, because even while in fight or flight, humans have some level of agency. Indeed, many children who behave outrageously at home are model students in school, loved by their teachers.

And so it falls on us parents to contain our children, to give them structure – just as we place a stake next to a growing plant. We do so because our children don't have the knowledge, awareness or resources to completely look after themselves. (We adults need structure too. So many of us complain about our jobs or our routine, yet after a period of unemployment or towards the end of a long holiday, we can feel completely at sea.)

With an eating disorder, our children are living with extreme deficiency, and so days or weeks can go by without them ever being self-connected. They're probably triggered every time they think of food, every time they notice their body. Rages are commonplace.

With eating disorders, our children are horribly out of touch with some of their needs and they cling to destructive strategies. So to care for them we frequently go against their wants. An eating disorder tends to make our kids regress a few years emotionally, and so we have to adjust and allow them less autonomy than seems normal for their age, at least in the areas that are governed by the illness.

Containment is about us parents stepping in to help our children regulate their emotions and behaviours. We intervene in emotional and practical ways.

- With our empathy, we turn down the emotional heat and model a more connected state.

- We educate, we monitor, we steer, we re-direct.

- We prevent harmful behaviours with non-negotiable requests (completing meals, tube-feeding, locking doors, and so on).

To help our children recover we insist they do what they fear the most: eat, sit down, stop exercising, stop purging. Their needs for choice, independence, freedom, can't be met at such times. We can show our children that we value these needs all the same. And we can try to allow these needs to be met in as many other arenas as possible.

Requests

Demands tend to be authoritarian, while asking for nothing is the domain of the permissive doormat. The path of containment rests on making requests based on our needs and our child's needs. We're more likely to get connection, agreement, and reach a solution that works for all. And a bonus we are modelling for our child self-care and self-respect, as well as the art of dialogue.

For instance, 'Be home by eight, or there'll be trouble!' is a demand that invites rebellion, whereas you can build connection and get more of what you want by stating a need for safety: 'I want to know you'll be safe at home before the streets get dark'.

In Chapter 13 I proposed a ladder of requests, depending on your level of trust that your child can dialogue with you. There are times when we make unilateral decisions because we simply don't have the time or energy to engage in a discussion. It's not ideal, but we can still do it while acknowledging our child's needs: 'Darling, I really want you to walk the dog. I'm sorry I'm giving you no choice, and I appreciate you'd rather relax with your phone, but I'm frazzled and I want to get on with making dinner.'

In any ordinary day, we parents ask our children to do quite a number of things. Demands may, for a while, get us what we want fast, but there is a cost to our connection and wellbeing. A guide I like to use with my daughter is, 'What do I want her reason to be for doing this?'[357] To win my love? To be safe from punishment? To earn herself another pair of shoes? Will she learn that she's bad or weak, or will she exercise her strengths?

We do not create a happy world when one side bullies the other to give up on their needs, or when we act as though our needs don't matter and we turn ourselves into doormats. Compromise isn't great either – it usually means that nobody's needs are met, and you have a lose-lose situation. All too often, compromise means we 'split the resentment fifty-fifty'.[358]

I don't want to set my child up for submission, and I don't want her to think she's powerless and tip her into aggression either. And I really, truly, want her needs to matter. Young people are often heavily into fun, friends and creativity, and this surely is extremely healthy. I imagine it's a lot more important to their development than picking clothes off the floor.

At the same time, I'm unhappy when I see children who haven't been shown how to help, who don't have the experience of clearing a table or removing muddy boots and who haven't formed easy habits of saying thank you. I'm worried when I see kids who can't tolerate frustration because they are constantly protected from it. And I am sad when I see parents giving up on their own needs.

So where do you draw the line? You might find it helpful to think in terms of your boundaries.

How boundaries and limit-setting work

People commonly use the word 'boundaries' with regard to another person's behaviour. They say, 'You must give your child boundaries! He's got to learn not to swear.' But the only thing you actually have control over is what *you* will do – the boundaries are yours.[359] You decide which behaviours of your child will trigger action on *your* part. You are setting your limits.

I propose that you and your partner work out where you stand with regard to the following:

- A raised voice is OK but swearing is not?
- Swear words are OK but not when they're directed at someone who's present?
- Verbal insults wash right over you but physical acting out, such as kicking or hitting things, is off limits?
- Kicking the wall is OK but kicking people is not?
- One kick aimed at me is OK but a continued physical attack isn't?

And where do you stand with regard to more ordinary issues, like housework, screen time, and so on?

How do you decide where your boundaries lie? Your criteria might be safety, or your needs for peace, harmony, dignity or care for each other. In other words, you value your needs and attend to them. You might also set your boundaries according to your child's needs for dignity and emotional regulation. Our children don't really want to be horrible to us.

Bear in mind what your child is capable of at any time. I'm thinking of a girl who was a sweet kid, but couldn't stop herself from hitting out at staff as they tube-fed her (she's doing great now). Stay focused on your goals. Good manners didn't matter to me when eating was a priority. Mealtimes were not an effective time to try to educate; my child had a hard enough job dealing with her stress levels. But no way would I let her kick me – both for my sake and hers.

Once you've worked out your boundaries and the actions you plan to take if they're crossed, you have a choice: you can inform your child of your decisions ahead of time or you can simply implement them if and when the situation arises. If you go for the first option, talk about you and your needs: 'I want to keep us all safe, so I've made arrangements with the police that if you kick anyone, I will immediately call them so they can help us.' This will help your child not hear your decisions as threats or punishments.

If your child is able, another option is to invite him to problem-solve with you: what would help him keep a check on his behaviour? And what measures would best work for all of you if he did cross a boundary? Whether you make a unilateral decision or initiate dialogue, you're in charge of your boundaries, your self-care and your child's upbringing.

Any agreement has the potential to break down. For instance, your child may agree to eat certain foods or to stop running, but fail to comply. The trick is to steer clear of judgement when that happens. The search for solutions is back on.

One benefit of knowing your boundaries is it can help you stay cool when other people criticise your parenting. Imagine that, at a family gathering, your child sneers, 'I'm not eating this. Do you think I'm stupid?' Your mum might expect you to make a show of force to obtain polite behaviour: 'He's treating you like a doormat! You're teaching him to be a little tyrant! It's not good for him!' If the behaviour is still well within your boundaries, having a clear mind can help you stay on course.

When you don't like a behaviour – your choices

Your child is using rude language, damaging items in your house, or being violent. You are clear about your boundaries, which means that you will act if your child engages in certain behaviours. Here are some options:

- You can decide to do nothing because actually, you've revised your mental boundary. The task at hand is more important to you than pleasant behaviour. Because you're making a choice, you are more likely to stay cool. That's how I stopped noticing rude language during meals.
- You can take the time to have a 'difficult conversation' in order to restore the connection and look for solutions. I'll give an example further down.

- You could do very little in the moment, but promise yourself to make time later to talk. You will want to mend the relationship, rather than allow the hurts to fester, and you may look for ways to prevent a recurrence. For example, when a child screams profanities at you because they have run out of clean school shirts, you can use any of the options here, followed up by a conversation later: 'What's up? That language was not OK, you know that, right? We aim to treat each other respectfully in this family. I was upset for quite a while and couldn't concentrate on my work. And I bet you didn't like what happened either. I am guessing something made you very tense? What's going on?' When your connection with your child is restored, discuss how they can better handle stress, or their laundry, in the future. You can also request that in the future, they take a breath and talk politely. If they can do it in school, they can do it at home.

- You can state a need and make a clear, specific request. For example: 'I really want us to treat each other with consideration. Please don't say 'Fuck you'. You can say you're furious, and you can say you hate me right now, and you can even talk about something being 'fucking awful', but don't direct the swear words at me or Dad.' You can't stop your child from using swear words but you can make your request clear, and if that doesn't work, use some of the other suggestions.

- You can give your child your empathic presence (after giving yourself an emergency dose of compassion) and practice compassionate persistence: keep making requests for the behaviour to change, calmly and even possibly with humour. For example, 'No wonder you're upset if you have nothing to wear. It's not like you can go into class in your pink pyjamas! While you have breakfast I will iron your least dirty shirt so it looks fresh. Please have breakfast now… Seriously, trust me, this will work. I've been there. Go have breakfast.'

- You can leave the room to remove yourself from a behaviour you don't wish to tolerate. That way you don't reward poor behaviour with your attention, and as a bonus, you both get some breathing space.

- You can use the minimum level of force necessary to make everyone safe and use the de-escalation approach described in the next section. You can then request a change in behaviour, if that's realistic.

- You can (or must) call in some help if there is physical violence. Your safety is non-negotiable. In one family I know, the girl had a phase of getting into violent rages against her mother. The danger was such (and the police, in this case, so unhelpful) that the dad would restrain his daughter to give the mother a chance to escape. The girl would then stop fighting, and when her mother returned, the kid would be herself again, and full of sorrow.

  Note that the police are used to dealing with people suffering from mental health disorders, and are increasingly well trained to respond with care. Some team up with local mental health professionals.

"She was refusing to go for a blood test, punching and throwing things. Last time she was very violent and when we asked the police for help, they put my D in a cell. This time I phoned the therapist, who got the police to take my D out for a coffee to calm her down and then take her for the blood test!"

The art of the 'difficult conversation'

When your child is in fight or flight, she will create conflict with you. Conflict is fine if you can turn it into dialogue, or even a joint dilemma for the two of you to solve. You come up with effective solutions, and as a bonus, your connection gets a boost. I've heard communication coaches urging people to welcome conflict, and I won't go that far here: steering a difficult conversation takes patience and we parents are already be stretched. Still, your child does not have the emotional resources you have, so it will be up to you to take the lead and keep refuelling yourself with self-compassion. The same applies to conflicts with anyone: if you wait for the other person to be the mature one, you could be living in a war zone for a long time.

I used to dread having 'difficult conversations' with my daughter, and I would delay having them and get mildly anxious. Then one day I realised that even though I had a flutter of fear, I was actually pretty confident. I bring this up to give you the vision that this is possible, even with an illness that makes us walk on eggshells or explode with frustration. Sadly, I think the skills and confidence only come with practice, which is no fun at all. It's also much easier when you have a decent amount of trust and love in the joint bank account, and when your child isn't so ill they cannot connect.

For a while now, I have been able to start a difficult conversation reasonably soon after a worry pops up, because I know the conversation will end up fine. We might go through painful moments, but it will be bearable and do no harm. I know I can use compassionate persistence rather than give in or lose my temper. And if the resolution and connection don't happen within one conversation, we can come back to it a day or so later, and eventually both get there. Examples of times it's been especially useful to embrace difficult conversations: around planning for school trips, boyfriends, contraception, addictive substances, exercise, relapse prevention, preparing for independence, and checking that she's still well.

I am thinking of a mother who contacted me at a time she was sick with worry for her daughter, whom she suspected had lost weight in university. Because of her daughter's independence, she thought there was little she could do. You can well imagine how awful that feels. I coached her to start a 'difficult conversation'. The outcome: the daughter was relieved to be heard non-judgementally and keen to get help. They became partners in refeeding over the holidays.

Another parent who comes to mind is a mother who was very worried that her daughter was not ready to go to university, yet scared of frustrating the girl's desires and tipping her into depression. Over a couple of gentle conversations, the girl easily came round to the idea of enjoying a gap year, with lots to do at home.

Example: cutting off the Wi-Fi

Let's go through a more detailed example of a 'difficult conversation'. Let's say I've cut off my child's access to the internet, and she's screaming blue murder. My need: to protect her from harmful sites, including those that might lead her to restrict her food intake.

She says, 'You're such a bitch. You want to control everything in my life! I hate you!'

Parents have two issues: they have a duty to protect their child from the more horrifying parts of the internet. And they want to teach their child to dialogue respectfully. A classic interpretation is that my child is a teenager rebelling against her parents and that she needs to learn 'consequences': 'I will not have you call me a bitch! Because you were rude, as well as cutting off the Wi-Fi I'm banning you from TV as well. And I'm taking your phone away till Wednesday. Now say you're sorry.'

I can imagine the response: 'Right then. Sorry!!!! I don't care anyway. When I don't eat it will be your fault.' Followed by, 'I hate my life.'

Using compassionate communication I can protect my child from the internet *and* guide her to speak respectfully *and* model productive dialogue *and* help her step back into her values.

First I can say, 'Please use polite language. I'm really want to listen to your views – just use polite words.' Then I need to know more about *her* needs. Because I'm really upset at her outburst, I also have to take a second for self-compassion. I want my body language to be connecting. My own emotions are running high so I use the principle of 'fake it till you make it'.

I ask a question which often helps bring out needs: 'Why does it matter to you, to have the internet?' I'm using an 'I'm interested, I'm curious' tone of voice.

She says, 'What do you care anyway? You're just a control freak!'

I chose to ignore her chatterbox's put-down. My focus is on feelings and needs. Her anger is a clue that something really matters to her, which she needs me to hear.

I say, 'No, really, I'm interested. What does being on the internet give you?'

'Time away from annoying parents!'

Again, I let the scorn fly over my head. My attention is on needs, and having 'me time' sounds like one. 'So you'd like time to yourself? A bit of space of your own?' These are things I value too, so I'm genuinely by her side here.

But she shrugs. 'I don't want to be on my own! Some of us have friends, you know!'

I follow her lead. I say, 'I'm glad you have friends.'

She says, 'Yeah, but you don't care. You want to cut off my internet so I can't talk to them.'

Again, I ignore the taunt and concentrate on her feelings and needs. 'You like to talk with your friends? On Snapchat?'

'Duh!'

'Right, well I hadn't realised that, thanks. I thought you wanted to browse the internet.'

'I don't do that. I already know you're worried about dieting websites and Instagram. You go on and on about it; you're so boring. I just want to use Snapchat.'

I concentrate on what matters: 'Snapchat is your way of keeping in touch with all your school friends?'

'Well since I can't go to school, how else am I supposed to keep my friends?'

As she's still reactive, I keep validating her need for friendship. We'll get nowhere until she feels properly heard: 'Absolutely. I want you to keep your friends. Friends are terribly important, and you have some wonderful friends.'

NEED

'Yeah.'

Now I understand why she put up such a fight. Friends *are* important. And her need for friendship is not incompatible with my need for her to be safe. This illustrates a general principle that if there's a clash, it's around strategies, not needs.

Her body is now less tense and her tone of voice is closer to baseline. I reckon we have enough connection to move on to a search for solutions. I note – and this never ceases to amaze me – that she's more relaxed even though I haven't said she can have her way.

Now the trick is to look for strategies that meet all the needs on the table. I restate the needs because this is our common ground: 'OK, so what matters here is that you can keep in touch with friends, *and* I'd also like to keep you safe from some types of internet sites. What can we do?'

REQUEST

I'm presenting our conflict as a joint dilemma. This is why I said 'and', not 'but'.

We bounce some ideas back and forth until we have a solution that suits each of us well enough. If one of us isn't totally happy, we can agree to review by a given date.

If we can't come up with a solution I might return to my original idea to cut off the Wi-Fi. Not because I have structural power as her parent, but because I am attending to her safety. There's no call for me to be scared, guilty or apologetic about my decision. As long as she knows I've made a genuine attempt to find a solution, she may 'grieve' for what's unsatisfied, and move on.

People can be fine with needs not being met, as long as they know their needs matter and have been considered with care.

If I think it's appropriate, I can also return to how she called me a bitch: 'OK, one more thing, darling. When you called me a bitch… That really wasn't like you.'

By now she may be glad I brought the subject up. 'I know Mum, I feel awful about it. I just felt so mad. I don't like being like this and hurting you.'

We could hug and if I want, I could then bring in a little education about different brain states, fight-flight-freeze, and discuss how she proposes to stay polite even when she feels mad. A deep breath, maybe?

All this takes longer than issuing a punishment, but would you agree it accomplishes more?

DEALING WITH AGGRESSION

Immediate response to violence: protection and self-connection

There are things you can do to de-escalate aggression, and with practice (which we tend to get plenty of) you're more likely to do them instinctively. Your guiding principle throughout is to seek to be in touch with needs, both your child's and yours.

In violent situations the first step may be to protect yourself or others. In a strong voice, using clear body language, ask for a stop to any level of violence that is unacceptable to you: 'Don't kick me!', 'Put the knife down here!'[360] You're probably doing this already, as shouting 'Stop it!' is a pretty natural reaction.

If you are able to, state a need, as it may help your child to connect with you: 'I want safety! Move away from your brother right now!' or 'I really want us to treat each other with kindness. Please use polite language!'

Just as effectively, you may voice a need of your child's, so that they quickly start to feel understood. If you have no idea what to say, I suggest you pick a few words your child said and reflect them back.

For example, your kid screams 'I hate you! All the other mums let their kids go on Instagram! You're a control freak!'

You could reply, 'You wish you could use Instagram?' or 'You wish I treated you like other mums treat their kids?' or 'You'd really like more control?'

It doesn't matter exactly what you say or which part of her tirade you pick. You're signalling that you're open to hearing her, and this in itself is going to help because if she's shouting, she probably wants to be heard.

Remember also that silent empathy can be very powerful. You say very little, but your body language shows that you are stable and that you can contain your child's distress.

Composing yourself is easier said than done. In the middle of fireworks, few of us have access to a deep well of empathy. As soon as you can, see if you can connect with the place within you where there is love for her and for yourself. You are then more likely to concentrate on the behaviour and keep criticism out of the way.

Your self-connection might go like this: in the space of one breath your mind might go, '[*Feeling:*] Gosh, I hate this! I'm so sick of this! I really feel like screaming at her. [*Chatterbox:*] She's a monster! I brought her up all wrong! It's not fair I have to deal with this. [*Self-kindness:*] This is so hard. Give me courage. [*In touch with your needs:*] Yes I want to support my precious child. I can hold off shouting at her and say one supportive thing and take it from there.'

It's easier to do this when you've previously spent time reflecting on this type of situation. It gives you a shortcut for emergency situations like this. If you are too upset to get anywhere with compassion for yourself or for your child, there is magic in 'fake it till you make it'. And of course you can always walk away with an excuse, or with an dignified, 'I need time out to be myself again. I'm not abandoning you. I'll be back in 10 minutes'.

Let me give you an example. You ask your child to do something and she flares up: 'I hate you, you stupid bitch!' and she starts kicking you. In a flash, you go into self-compassion, noticing your reactions and drawing power from your desire to be safe and to be treated with consideration.

You say very firmly, 'Don't kick me. Kicking is not OK.' You don't have to be nice about this, because this really matters to you and it's non-negotiable. Your strong tone of voice may be all that's needed for your child to stop kicking, or you may need to move out of her way or to hold her still (taking care not to dig your fingers in as pain will increase her stress).

Assuming that this succeeds in getting your child to pause and maybe even give you eye contact, you might say more gently, 'I can see you're upset, so use your voice. Tell me what's going on. I am listening.'

This may not create instant peace but it's a step on the road to de-escalation. Whereas you'd be pouring oil on the fire with knee-jerk responses like 'Don't you dare call me a bitch!' or 'If you kick me one more time I'm cutting your pocket money!'

Another example: when your child is using abusive language at full volume, you can say forcefully and loudly, 'Use polite language!!!' Then more quietly, 'I want to hear what you have to say. I really do. So use polite language, in a lower tone of voice, and that will help me listen.' Note that this can work better than 'Don't shout, don't be so rude' because any sane kid will yell back that they're neither bloody shouting nor rude.

De-escalating violence

With de-escalation, you start off strong to match your child's intensity, then you model a progressively quieter, kinder tone of voice. You're juggling several things at once: giving yourself self-compassion, listening and responding to your child with compassion, making clear requests to stop aggressive behaviours, and bringing down the emotional temperature with your own body language and tone of voice. The sooner you can get yourself to a state where you're grounded, the more likely your child will also become calmer.

De-escalation can take a while, during which your child may go from one accusation to another. It can start with 'You're a control freak! Everyone else can use Instagram' then move on to, 'You gave me too much pasta at lunch!' and then, 'You never listen to me!' Usually, this is not a good time to justify yourself or to correct. Instead, look for responses that validate each of the emotions as they emerge (as explained in Chapter 13).

For instance, you could respond to the Instagram complaint with, 'Sure, I can well imagine how you'd like more freedom, because we're already in charge of your food, and because you have friends who are given that kind of freedom.' A few minutes later, when you're accused of never listening, you could say, 'I'm really sorry, that's terrible, I really want to listen and understand. Tell me more. And it will help if you speak in a lower tone of voice. Can you do that?'

This can be a feat of endurance for us parents. When you get lost, remember the simple template, 'I'm sorry, and I love you' as well as the power of silent empathy. This will save you from trying to fix problems in a hurry – usually badly. You may need to keep breathing and giving yourself compassion at every step, in order to stretch your patience a little further, just enough for the next rung on the ladder.

Finally, you'll see a sign that your child is connected to herself and to you: a sigh, a relaxation, a change in her tone of voice, or even tears. Now you can offer a hug, or a break, or move towards problem-solving, or give explanations.

Some time after this demanding exchange, you may well need to go find someone to give you some compassion for what you've been through. If you want to be in top form for your child's sake and your own, this goes in the category of essentials, not luxuries.

Your child may need more support too, as they may feel ashamed of how they treated you. So consider having a conversation later on in the day to mend the relationship and to problem-solve how to avoid such fireworks in the future. More on this 'mending' process later.

Give yourself a break

Sometimes we keep our own needs on hold for the whole length of a difficult interaction. It can be a feat of endurance. For your wellbeing, promise yourself some self-care as soon as the situation is de-escalated. When it's appropriate for you to make your exit, try to do so in a way that your child won't interpret as rejection or punishment (even if at that moment you are seething).

Suppose you've planned to go to the shops with your daughter for a fun outing. But she has a rage over lunch. Although it's not the first time, today you're vulnerable. You're feeling upset, discouraged and hugely sad.

You could say, 'I really feel for you: it looks like having lasagne for the first time freaked you out, and quite understandably. So I don't blame you for how you reacted and I'll keep supporting you. At the same time [*I don't say 'but' because that would imply what I've just said is irrelevant or untrue*] all my sense of fun has left me. I'm not at all in the mood for an outing. So I'd like to call it off and tomorrow we can see how things go. Now I'm going to my bedroom to read. This isn't to cut you out but because I reckon I'll feel better with some quiet time and after that I'll be more there for you as well. How does that sound?'

Welcome the tears after the fireworks

It might help you, as it helped us, to watch out for a progression of emotions in your child. It might start off with your child directing abuse at you. As you avoid retaliating and as you maintain a compassionate presence he might express hate towards himself. As you stay with him in empathy, with or without physical soothing, he might then move on to tears, pouring out his grief about the pains, fears and frustrations he's enduring, and he might express what he's missing and what he longs for.

We almost got to welcome the progression, because the grieving at the end seemed to serve a purpose. Each time, our daughter came out of it in a better state, with lasting improvements. These were milestones in her recovery. We certainly didn't try to provoke outpourings of grief on the grounds that they might be therapeutic.

We simply tried to be close when things got heavy for her, staying present to her through her emotions.

Sometimes it can be a lot lighter. If you manage to respond with humour when your child shouts at you, or if you can offer a distraction, you can quickly move on to something more fun.

More: listen to more examples of conversations on Bitesize, my big collection of short audios[361]

'AM I FAT?' HOW TO RESPOND

Your child is genuinely suffering

In their anxious, eating-disordered state, our children can be genuinely terrified of being fat, and indeed of any weight increase. Meltdowns are common after a weighing, or when they dress in front of a mirror (some parents choose to cover them). Our children ask obsessively, 'Am I fat? Will this make me fat?' They howl, 'I've gained too much weight! I'm so fat! I feel fat! You're making me fat!' And they demand numbers: 'What's the weight target? How many more kilos?' They perceive dreadful sensations in their body. Their vision may be distorted too. They accuse us: 'All you want is to make me fat!' Our natural reaction can be impatience, irritation, defensiveness, because this is exhausting, repetitive stuff, and sometimes it's scary how crazy it is. Let's remind ourselves that our poor child is currently being tortured by a malfunctioning brain, and that this is not for ever. However we choose to respond to the 'Am I fat?' questions, let's keep judgement out of it.

The best way for an individual to get relief from those 'I'm fat' meltdowns is, paradoxically, to regain lost weight and stick to regular meals. So keep feeding, whatever you do.

For now, when your child asks 'Will you make me fat?' you probably want some tips, and I'll give you a whole range to choose from. You are unlikely to 'convince' your child of anything, so your aim is to make the next meal work, and if at all possible, interrupt the loop of eating-disorder driven questions. This is what I'll cover here.

An opportunity to change your child's mindset

When any child, eating disorder or not, asks 'Am I fat?' thousands of parents all round the world answer, 'No, of course not' or 'No, you're beautiful.' If your child is well enough to engage in conversation – and that's a big 'if' – then it's far more helpful to model a body-neutral or body-positive stance.[362]

A reply to 'Am I fat?' could begin with, 'It doesn't matter to us what size you are' or 'No, and it would be OK if you were', or 'Yes, you are in a bigger body. And that's fine. Some might call it fat. What would you like to call it?' (The word 'fat', to me, is a non-judgemental word and I use it because it's how our kids talk, but 'living in a larger body' is currently the most accepted terminology. I suspect this will keep changing as advocacy makes its mark and I am sorry for any offence I am causing with my current use of language.)

You could explore issues of fat bias or weight stigma, and reflect on how limiting it is to define ourselves by our size rather than by our rich, wonderful life. This may help your child to let go of their imperative to be the 'right' or 'perfect' shape or weight. Gradually they will stop attaching their self-worth to their looks. And they will become sensitive to diversity, social justice and empathy. You are unlikely to manage conversations like this until your child is well on the road to recovery, and I provide more guidance on the issue of body dissatisfaction in Chapter 10.

While your child is quite ill and going through refeeding, you may appreciate the suggestions that follow.

'It's not useful to talk about it'

For weeks or months, most of our children are so anxious about their weight that any conversation increases their rigidity. Their mind is too terrified, chaotic, delusional. When a child is wailing that she can't drink water because it will make her fat, body-acceptance is hardly the issue. Someone for whom an 'extra' grape is agony is unlikely to engage in reflection about body diversity. They may agree that their best friend is both large and wonderful and even popular, but right now all they can think of is that their own body feels unbearably awful: 'It's different for me. I have to be thin. Am I fat? How much more weight do I have to gain?'

Our focus, then, has to be on creating trust and a sense of safety.

That's easier said than done. We try to find helpful words to calm our children but they distort our meaning. The same questions keep looping back, and distress levels keep rising. Meanwhile, we get more and more impatient at our impotence and they think we're judging them (which we probably are). For these reasons the best replies are short and sweet. I recommend a brief statement of empathy, then a refusal to talk about the issue, then distraction:

'I'm so sorry this is so painful to you; I so love you. It's not useful for us to talk about it. Come, let's wrap Dad's present.'

Expect your child to cling on: 'You're not saying I'm not fat, so that means I really am fat! I'm fat! I'm horribly fat!'

Keep to your script, to your broken record. Bring out the wrapping paper: 'Which one do you think Dad will like best?'

To your child, 'We're not talking about it' can be invalidating. How infuriating, how terrifying, to not have their greatest concerns addressed! So say it with kindness and non-judgement, so that your child knows you are not dismissing him or her. You could be transparent about your strategy:

'I'm sorry, darling. I'm guessing you're tense about all this and you desperately want reassurance… and we know that talking about it doesn't do that. Best to go for distraction. Would you teach me to fold a paper bird?'

Later, when the 'I am fat' questions keep recurring, you can give a shorter reply, 'Remember, sweetheart, we're not discussing that because it's not helpful.'

And of course make it clear you're not discussing food amounts or weight gain. Those are non-negotiable.

Our aim is health and happiness

Some parents find it helpful to respond (briefly) to their child's need for reassurance, but instead of engaging with 'fat' talk, they focus on health and on appreciation of the body's functionality.

'Your body will be right for you, and you will grow and thrive'.

Or 'What matters is how you will feel in your body, and how you will feel about your life, and that will be great.'

Or 'We are serving you what you need, for your body's needs. Trust us.'

Or 'We are helping you rebuild your body for health and happiness.'

Or 'We are working towards healing of your body and brain.'

Or, 'We are getting you ready for strength and energy, so we can enjoy holidays again.'

Or 'Though it's hard for you to imagine right now, you will feel good in your body / you will love how you look and feel.'

You could combine empathy, education and trust: 'It's so hard for you, because this illness distorts your perception of your body and it seems so real. As you renourish your body, your brain will get back to working beautifully.'

Your child might respond to a picture you paint of the future: 'You know, it's really normal, with an eating disorder, that at the start people have all those sensations and terrors. And then as they become healthy they feel great and they know they look great too, and they have the confidence to be themselves'.

Or how about: 'It may seem impossible for you to imagine right now, but you are going to be happy, and sparkly and your life will be rich and interesting and fun, and you won't give much thought to your eating or your looks, and when you do it will feel good – everything will fit into place really naturally. Trust me, even if right now it's hard to believe.'

This type of response works for some kids, and drives others crazy. They don't care about health, they care about being thin.

You might find that any mention of 'looks' activates more unhealthy focus on body shape. The safest is to stick to what the body does for us: energy, strong, the ability to engage in much-loved activities.

'Can't you see? You're underweight!'

You know the theory, you know it doesn't work, and you're still likely to get drawn into trying to reason with your child. Even if your kid gets a flicker of pleasure from hearing that she is dangerously underweight, a moment later, the fear springs back up: 'But I'm fatter than this morning. I can feel it here, see, here? You're making me fat!'

> *"ED will NEVER hear that the way they look is OK or 'normal'. Never. This is something I am still learning. ED*

constantly wants to engage me in the discussion of 'I'm fat' or 'My stomach is huge!' Just for grins, one day, I had her and I stand side by side and lift our shirts. I said, 'Which stomach is bigger?' Answer: Hers! Now, you must all know that I am objectively MUCH larger than her. But still the voice in her head says something very different. That was the day I stopped having those conversations. Now, I either ignore the comment, or simply say, 'We're not discussing that.'"[363]

Empathy and validation

In chapter 13 I led you through 'Connect before your Correct'. Before you try and give reassurance or education, how can you bring your child's emotional level down? Your child may move on from their 'Am I fat?' questions because with your empathic presence, it may turn out that their concerns are about something else – acceptance in their peer group, for instance. Or they may accept your 'We're not discussing it' without feeling invalidated. Or they have enough access to reason for you to engage in conversation about body-acceptance. Either way, you can't go too wrong with empathy, and if it fails, you can go straight back to 'It's not useful to talk about this.'

To connect with empathy, show interest and be genuinely curious. You can cope with whatever the response might be: 'Something about this is freaking you out. Tell me more.' Some more prompts might be:

'You seem to hate the idea of gaining weight. What is it about? ... What would it give you, to stay as you are?'

Or 'What's the worst you are imagining?'

In other words, you are inviting your child to say out loud his worst beliefs. It might seem to you like this will amplify them, but they are screaming in his head anyway. You will not be validating the beliefs, but your child's distress, given he has these beliefs. These are cruel thoughts going round his head. Hopefully, with your empathy, they will lose some of their power.

Common needs behind the 'Am I fat?' question

What might your child reveal about what drives their 'fat' questions? I'm going to suggest a few common drivers that may emerge and what a connecting response might be.

Our children's horror of weight can be pure fat phobia amplified by their anxious state: 'If I gain weight I will look gross and it will be unbearable.' An empathy response might be, 'Gosh, no wonder you're so freaked out, if you think you're going to look gross. You have a very scary image in your mind?' Or perhaps: 'Gosh, sweetheart, if I thought the person helping me get well was going to make things worse, I'd be very cross too!"

We tend to take our children's desire to be thin (and its association with beauty) very literally. The same with the desire for muscularity. But what if these desires were just how people make sense of their hyper-aroused state around food and body sensations? Centuries ago, anorexia was linked with holiness, not body shape.

With my daughter, this was quite a useful guess: 'You got called 'fat' by your friends and you worked so hard at making sure that can never happen again, by losing a lot of weight, and now you're regaining it you can't imagine how you can be safe?' To normalise and soothe, one route was: 'It makes perfect sense that you're looking for a way to feel safe. You experienced some cruel bullying. Of course you need to feel safe when you go to school.'

Even without bullying, safety could be the driver. Here are a number of empathy guesses – just one of them will do for a start: 'You have seen others getting fat-bullied and you want to protect yourself from that? You're thinking how some of your friends have smaller bodies, and skip meals, and there's this whole thin-bias culture around us, and you want to be accepted and liked? You need to be part of the in-group, where people are not bullied or left out, and you know that the dominant group judges people by their body shape? In your mind, to be a good, loveable person with friends, you need to be a particular body shape, otherwise people might not see you for who you are?' Then the validation could be: 'I can totally see how it's important to be loved and have friends and feel safe from shaming comments.' Then you could talk about friendships and being liked and being excluded, and now you've moved beyond the 'Am I fat' question to something far more real.

Another driver behind my daughter's 'fat' questions was, 'I worked so hard at losing weight, and now you're making me gain it all back, so what was the point?' At that moment, the 'Will you make me fat?' question wasn't about fat, but a call to empathy: 'I well imagine how pointless it seems to have been through so much misery, and now you have the hard work of reversing it all. You've gone through a lot. May I give you a hug?'

I think that 'Am I fat?' can also come from a really uncomfortable sensory issue: 'I see you pinching the skin on your tummy, and I wonder, is it like an uncomfortable sensation in your body?' It ties in with our children not wanting to be touched. At bedtime, just the feel of a duvet resting on the tummy area is unbearably anxiety-provoking. It's beyond logic, and the best remedy is probably empathy. 'I'm sorry it is such a horrible feeling. It will pass. Let's count five things you enjoyed today?'

Perhaps what your child needs is trust: 'You really truly have a sensation of having a large tummy, as though it was all the way out there, and that's what you're seeing in the mirror, and it's so confusing that people are telling you that's not true and you need to gain weight… and you don't know who to trust?' I told my daughter about a hypnotist who made 20 people on stage believe a pink elephant had walked in. They could see it, smell it, touch it. I put it to her that the human brain can play very convincing tricks on you. After that, it sometimes helped, in the middle of a crisis, to say, 'Remember about the hypnotism and the brain? This will pass. Now teach me to fold an origami bird.'

Problems can come up when experts give conflicting messages: 'I know you were looking up BMI charts online. Are you confused because we say one thing and the government health website says another?' You could try a little education about those charts and the misguided advice that comes with them, but your best bet is to assert your leadership: 'Trust us. We know what we're doing, we know what is right for you.'

I wonder if you and I, as we age, come to terms with changes in our body because they are gradual, and our peers are on the same journey. Our children, on the other hand, may imagine that changes are happening overnight or at an exponential rate. That's absolutely not a reason to slow down the weight gain, but we can offer empathy: 'Does it feel like from one day to the next, you could have a completely different body, and you're worried it would feel bad? You were freaked out by your last weight reading? Like it's going too fast and maybe we don't know what we're doing?'

If she's seeing the number on the scales every week, your child may need education about natural fluctuations. She may never have thought the reason her tummy is stretched after a meal is that it has no padding, and that her sluggish digestive system is keeping the food in there. She may not have made the link between getting older, growing and gaining weight. She may not be aware of water retention and monthly cycles. She might not know that with weight recovery, the tummy and face fill out first, and then it all evens out.

Sometimes it's a photo that shocks our child and leads to an 'I'm fat' meltdown. 'You saw that photo, and now you're confused what you really look like, how others see you? Is it something about feeling confident that you are accepted and welcome in the world, even when a friend aims the camera right up your nostrils?' If the time is right, consider imparting some education about distortions produced by cameras,[364] about the editing and filtering that takes place on social media, and about how the brain interprets visual cues – hence optical illusions.[365] This may help her self-soothe next time she's triggered… and hopefully she will also remind herself that we are much, much more than our looks.

If empathy is making your child seek more and more reassurance, go back to 'It's not useful to discuss this.' Either way, move on to another topic soon. Lead some kind of activity. Demonstrate that life is vast, and there is much to be enjoyed irrespective of body shape.

> *"I found that being overly empathic or reassuring made her want to fight harder as though she felt she had good reason to be distressed. For her there was only one solution (weight loss). It had us going in endless circles. ED would be trying to win my sympathy and wear me down. Over time I found it best to validate discomfort, then to be direct about her concerns and move on. I basically told her I'm sorry she feels that way about herself, we won't be cutting back and there was no point in discussing any further. I think the message she got over time was that Mom isn't going to let up and isn't overly concerned so I must be okay the way I am."[366]*

A Band-Aid: 'You're not fat'

I like to give parents lots of options, because we are busy saving a life. The next meal must be eaten. Real life is messy. So here is another strategy that is not ideal but for some, has made a child who was heading for hospital start to eat again. At one stage in my daughter's illness it worked to give her one single strong, no-nonsense, 'You're not fat', or 'We won't make you fat'. It seemed like a magic phrase she could use to soothe herself with. If she repeated the request for reassurance, we knew we'd soon be stuck in a loop, so we reverted to 'It's not useful to talk about it'.

> *"Countering a distorted cognition with actual facts is useful when we are as matter-of-fact and brief about it as we can be. 'You look perfectly fine to me. Did you notice that the azaleas are blooming?'"*[367]

'You're not fat' is a Band-Aid which might be hard work to peel off later. That's because it could reinforce your child's belief that fat is a bad thing. It also implies that you, the great arbiter of right and wrong, consider fat as wrong. When I said 'You're not fat' I didn't give any of this much thought, I was just glad that something worked. I don't think any harm was done. These days, she has no patience for fat stigma and is interested in how the Health At Every Size ethos can inform her work.

'But YOU are fat!' Model unconditional positive regard for your body

Your child may be acutely aware of everybody else's body shape, constantly comparing. They accuse you of being mean or incompetent: 'You're thin and you want to make me fat?' or 'You're fat yourself, so you're going to make me fat!'

The issue is, of course, your child's anxiety, not your own body shape. As usual, you can offer empathy and from there you can decide whether to offer reassurance or even education. Empathy might sound like, 'I imagine it's a big thing for you to trust us on something that is so stressful for you? You need to know we are competent and that we know what we are doing?'

Be aware of any buttons your child is pushing, so that you can stay in your power. I remember an eating disorder workshop in Scotland, during which the speaker stated that we all dislike our own body. I protested. So the presenter asked for a show of hands: who had a hangup about their body shape? The result, in a roomful of 60 parents, was... just about everyone.

We go on a huge learning curve when our child has an eating disorder. We can't do everything at once. If you have a larger body, chances are you have had years of being disparaged – by people close to you, by total strangers and by the medical system. I have spoken to parents who feel inadequate in family therapy because they sense (rightly or wrongly) that they are being judged for their own bigger body. As demonstrated by that show of hands at the workshop, people judge their bodies, whatever their shape or weight. So if you haven't yet reflected on how precious your body is, if you haven't yet opened up to gratitude for how it serves you, then fake it. Model owning your full self. Assert your values. Tune into your rich life. No justifying or apologising for your body, or for your eating.

When my daughter focused on my body with a look of horror, it helped when I said, 'Are you worried you're going to have a body like mine? Like... tomorrow? This body is right for me, at this stage of my life. I feel really good in it. My body wouldn't be right for you at all, at age ten. That would be really weird. And it would be odd for me to have a teen's body. Bodies change, very gradually, and our minds adapt along with them, so we're OK with it.'

Many of us mothers are experiencing menopause or perimenopause during our child's eating disorder. Our bodies are changing very fast. Our minds will eventually meet our current reality but for now, if you are not feeling appreciative, fake it till you make it. Make more of a noise about how well your body serves you. Smile in the mirror. Our children notice what we do!

Continuing with the 'You are fat so I can't trust you' taunts, another idea, if it applies to you and feels useful, is to educate. Relapse prevention has to include a very strong 'No weight-loss diets, ever' message, so consider this: 'I lost my balance because I followed loads of diets at a time I didn't know any better. Diets really screw up people's bodies and minds. You, on the other hand, are benefitting from our far greater knowledge. We are guiding you towards balance. You will get to enjoy your food, your body and your life and it will all be very natural.'

If you want more choices, consider the time-honoured principle of 'Do as I say, not as I do'. Tell your child that you are perfectly capable of feeding him the right things, even while you are working on finding a balance for yourself.

What if a child's weight used to be at the high end of the weight distribution and there's an agreement they don't need to regain quite up to that level? What if they use this to accuse you of incompetence? One suggestion is you say what I've said every time I've done a U-turn. 'Things have changed. I have learned so much since you got ill, I'm now a total expert. There are some things we have to do differently, now that we know better. We're taking extremely good care of you.'

You might prefer to keep your answers simple: 'Each to their own needs, honey. We're very good at knowing what's right for ourselves, and for you. Ever since you were a baby we've known how to feed you.' And of course there's always: 'I'm so sorry, pet, remember we found it's not helpful to talk about this.'

HYSTERICS, PANIC ATTACKS AND EXTREME ANGUISH

Sometimes the 'Am I fat?' questions aren't so much questions as hysterical episodes. They can morph into expressions of utter despair such as 'I'll never get better' or 'I can't do this any more! I don't want to live!' Or they can take a more threatening tone: 'You're useless! Tomorrow I will eat nothing! That will teach you!' Some youngsters have panic attacks. Sometimes the storms fall into a pattern – same time every night, when alone and changing into nightclothes in front of the mirror, for instance – and we can plan distractions as a preventive measure. But at times these extreme episodes come without warning.

If your child has massive, uncontrolled outbursts of emotion, you might be wondering if it's best to give him some time alone or to keep offering some kind of support, especially if your kid is shouting for you to back off because he hates you. And you might be getting tied up in knots about what to say and not say, because nothing seems to help.

What you can do is resist adding fuel to the fire. You can avoid engaging with the eating-disorder talk, and you can avoid retaliating when your child's behaviour is triggering you.

Remember that the outburst isn't about you. Your child might be banging her head against the wall, or grasping non-existent rolls of flesh round her middle, because her eating-disorder voice is screaming at her what a worthless, hateful non-person she is. Some of her anguish may come from internal conflict: she's busy fighting her eating-disorder self, furious that it has such power over her, despairing that she'll never beat it down.[368]

Her threats or fears about never recovering may strike fear in your heart, so give yourself some kindness for the state you're in, as you try to hold her emotions as well as your own. It may help you to know that her words are not prophecies. 'I give up', 'I hate myself', 'I am gross', 'I will not eat tomorrow' come from emotions that, like all emotions, will pass.

If she had access to emotional language, she might be able to say, 'I feel awful. I can hardly breathe, my stomach is churning, my throat is tight and my head is pounding. I am terrified. I wish you knew how absolutely awful this is, so awful I'm not sure I can stand another minute of it. Please hear me. Please be with me. Let me know I'm not crazy. Let me know I'm OK and you love me even though I'm screaming that I hate you.'

My guess is that most often, in these hysterical episodes, a child needs compassion more than anything. Distraction sometimes works, so it's worth trying. But if your child keeps repeating herself or upping the stakes, she might be needing to know that you really 'get' her, and until then she won't give up.

We give the greatest support simply by not panicking. While your child is hysterical she may be very scared of how out of control she is, and this adds to her panic. Her physical reactions – hyperventilating, sweating, racing heart – may convince her that she's about to die.[369] Your calm and confident presence will let her see that you're not worried about it, that this is normal, that you know these emotional waves and physical effects happen and that they pass with no harm done. These messages may come to her not so much through what you say, but through what you model. So at these difficult times, mindfulness comes to the parent's aid.

> "I used to look her in the eye and say, as if I really meant it, 'This will pass,' even though inside I was often in despair. Now she tells me this really helped her, and that she believed me."

Distress is contagious. See if the emergency self-compassion tools from Chapter 13 help you be calm. Remember that your child's emotions, though horrible, are not dangerous. Trust that all this will pass. If it's any help at all, I can tell you that in my daughter's case I'm not aware of any emotional scars.

Sometimes the best thing parents can do when their child is yelling 'Get out! Leave me alone!' is to give them some space and time: 'OK darling, I'll be downstairs, but remember I'm here for you and I love you. I'll come back in ten minutes and see how you are. Or come down as soon as you want.' The rationale for this is that your very presence is fuelling chatterbox thoughts and high emotions. Remove yourself, and your child may be able to self-soothe a tiny bit – enough to become open to your support. You don't want your child to think that you're washing your hands of her troubles, hence the importance of saying some kind words as you leave.

If your child accepts your presence in the middle of a hysterical episode, you may be able to soothe her with silent empathy, by holding her (some parents find it useful to keep holding even when the child initially resists), or by gentle talking. If she has learned breathing and relaxation techniques or has a favourite guided relaxation on her phone, help her use them. Some mums, night after night, hug their child close until she's fallen asleep. You can also buy a 'weighted blanket'; some children find these soothing at any time of day.[370]

Here are some words that, in my experience, can help bring emotions right down: 'Looks like you're very scared right now/I really get it, how awful you feel/It's such a horrible feeling/Would you like to know that you're safe?/that we're taking good care of you?/that you're going to be all right?/that the awful feelings you've got right now will pass?' I'd follow with one or two of these: 'You're safe/Remember we're in charge/We're looking after you with great care/Your feelings will pass and you'll be calm again soon, and meanwhile you're safe.'

None of this might work. If your words fuel greater reactions, silent empathy is your friend. Your child may feel your loving listening more when you're silent than when you give her empathic words.

How useful is talk later on? As your child comes down from the peak of her emotional wave, she may recall all the things that are distressing her. You might hope, as we did for a while, that by talking and by crying on your shoulder, she's healing. But I have my doubts. Talk like this can go round in circles, fuelling catastrophic thoughts and despair. There's a risk, with talk, of getting stuck in chatterbox mode, especially if your child's body is still awash with adrenalin. In an ideal world, you'd help your child connect with her deeper needs, where she might get clarity and peace. But how do you do this if her internal demons are screaming for attention?

Trapped in their nightmare

When your child is so distressed she seems out of touch with reality (when she is 'dissociating'), put talk or listening aside – even compassionate talk. Instead, direct her attention away from her nightmarish world, to the here and now. Get her away from the mirror. Instruct her to stop body-checking – give her something else to do with her hands. Bring her back to her physical senses. Direct her atten- **BODY** tion to things she can look at, hear, taste, smell or touch. One mother found she could calm her teenager by stroking her face with an ice cube. Another used a distraction technique she learned from her daughter's therapist:

> *"This really, really worked. Most important was for me to model*
> *calm. Then I'd ask my daughter to look around and tell me five*
> *things she could see. If she was hyperventilating and couldn't talk, I*
> *named objects and her eyes would follow. Next, I asked her to name*

four things she could hear, three things she could feel (sensory, not
emotion), two things she could smell and one thing she could taste."

There are endless variations on this theme. You could ask your child to look around and name anything that is red. I've had quick results running a finger on my daughter's palm and asking her to guess the letters I'm drawing.

You could give your child things to do: 'Move away from that mirror. Look this way. Good. Now put your pyjama top on. Yes, one sleeve on. Now the other sleeve. Now come and brush your teeth. Over here, in the bathroom.' In my experience this can help put someone back in touch with reality, distract from the chatterbox and give containment.

COMFORT AND REASSURANCE: WHAT WORKS AND WHAT DOESN'T

Some children can be mad at us, and still tearfully want us to stay with them, providing comfort and reassurance. Sometimes a child gets labelled 'clingy'.

This illness drives us to question our most basic instincts. Should we reassure? Should we protect? Should we give support when our child is in distress? Should we give all the closeness he asks for? Should we – and I'm including dads in this – mother?

We've already seen that reassurance is pointless when questions (such as 'Am I fat?') are driven by the eating disorder. But does that mean reassurance is generally a bad thing?

Soothing

It's a great gift when a child comes to his parents for solace. We know how to soothe, how to make those little 'hmm' noises that show we care, how to hug and enfold. This is how we nurtured our children from the day they were born, and gave them the experience of 'secure attachment'.[371] Is it ever *not* right for parents to comfort their children? I hope not.

Our children can become so isolated in their own private hell, pushing us away and thinking of us as enemies, that any opportunity for closeness is precious. If your child wants your reassuring presence at bedtime, or even at *all* times, count yourself very, very blessed.

And so I'm filled with dismay when parents occasionally report a therapist's advice to back off and let a youngster deal with his anxiety all by himself. When a child is persistent in his attempts to get help with his demons, when he keeps signalling he wants you to soothe him, I'm horrified this may label him as 'clingy'. I'm appalled that parents can be considered over-protective, codependent, or accused of babying their adolescent. I hate how a loving parent can be analysed and judged when a therapist hastily declares the child to be 'insecurely attached'. And I hate it when that parents are made to believe their love is harmful. This is not the norm, but it happens.

Here are the arguments: 'Your child must learn to be independent'; 'Your child must learn to tolerate distress'; 'If you give your child attention, you're rewarding his (anxious) behaviour'; 'You don't want to reinforce your child for being fearful'; 'Your child is 17 and 17-year-olds should sleep by themselves'.

Have you turned your child into a clingy, dependent bundle of anxiety? No. The eating disorder has done that. And your loving closeness gives him the safe space to heal and grow into adulthood.

Interdependence: it's OK to need others

I want my child to know there is no virtue in bearing her sorrows or fears alone, when there are people close by who love her and who can ease her burden.

Can you think of any times that you've been anxious? Were you perhaps longing for someone's smile, someone's presence, and were you – as I have been – grateful and empowered when you got it? Our children spend month after month after month in agony. They're grappling with issues of life, love, abandonment, hopelessness and death. Emotionally they regress, just as we all do when we've been ill or miserable for longer than we can bear. There's a saying that 'When we stress we regress'.

Imagine that you were being held at gunpoint in a hostage situation. At some point, your mother or father is allowed to visit you. Would they not hold you tight? Can you imagine them refusing to hold your hand, on the basis that you need to learn to stand on your own two feet?

I value taking responsibility for ourselves, and at the same time we are social, interdependent human beings. We thrive when we connect with others for support, kindness and empathy. It's incredibly difficult to overcome fears all by ourselves at any age. Self-soothing can only go so far. As parents under extreme stress, I'm sure you can relate to that.

I've spent a lot of my own life being an island, believing only in the value of autonomy. The day I sought support from kind people, I became infinitely more able to be the person I wanted to be. I got stronger, more compassionate, and far more capable of giving my daughter what she needed. I would love my child, likewise, to experience and value interdependence.[372]

When our nervous system feels under threat and we're in a state of fight-flight-freeze, we perceive ourselves as alone, disconnected from the world. My daughter, at times, thought that even our dog was rejecting her. It's a blessing when a human being seeks comfort from another, as it's the fastest way to bring our whole self back online. At the opposite end from fight-flight-freeze, we experience connectedness, being at one with the world and everyone. This is a highly resourceful, powerful state.

Of course, seeking comfort from others is not the only way to deal with anxiety, and it's good for our children to experience a range of strategies. There's challenging your thoughts, self-compassion, mindfulness, and there's the wonderful tool of distraction. For me, getting comfort from another human being is right there at the top.

When you welcome your child and help soothe him, you're saying, 'Your needs matter to me.' When you comfort him when he seems as clingy as a three-year-old, you're saying, 'I love and accept you the way you are, right now, at this moment.' If you turn him away or ignore him, he may learn that his needs don't matter, that they are shameful. You want to teach autonomy, but the message your child receives when you turn away is more likely to be, 'You don't matter. You are alone.'

Jumping to the rescue

You may have been told to back off on the basis that children need to learn to tolerate difficult thoughts and feelings. Some parents are reprimanded for 'jumping to their child's rescue'.

There can indeed be a problem with 'rescuing' when we are operating from our own anxious state and trying to fix our own suffering. It's a natural instinct, and at the same time it's not useful to stay there as we are not well tuned into your child's needs.

The next difficulty with rescuing is when it does not serve our intentions. Does it actually contribute to our child's wellbeing? The answer is yes, of course, if you're yanking your kid out of the path of a speeding car. But if your child is experiencing fear or discomfort, my answer is, it depends. It depends on whether the experience will leave him stronger or more terrified. Your child will benefit from dealing with fear if he's well supported and learns that fear is manageable. He will gain the confidence that he can achieve challenges and have internal resources. But if he's left to deal with fear while feeling alone and abandoned, he may form a belief that the world is a lonely and terrifying place.

I believe we're ideally placed, as parents, to judge how much protection and handholding our kids need. We sense when they are not equipped to handle a stressor and when it's not appropriate for them to even be exposed to it. That's why films come with age ratings. That's why we don't let young children watch late-night news. That's why schools have anti-bullying policies. At the other end of the spectrum, we sense when our children are likely to flourish if they manage something in spite of fear. That's what funfairs, and performing in school shows, are for. Every success you've experienced with exposure and desensitisation works on this basis.

If you're confident that you have your child's needs at heart, surely you can trust your instincts and give her a good balance of challenge and protection. Isn't that what you've been trying to do since she was born?

A good friend I made along this journey, found the perfect analogy:

> *"I was thinking back on the time my daughter started kindergarten and looked at me to check if I was feeling OK with this new place. I pretended to feel totally OK with it (even though I felt nervous leaving her in a new place) and that made her feel OK with it and enjoy it. I recognised the need to show my child confidence that she can again engage with life and enjoy it."*

More on my website anorexiafamily.com/NVC-fixing-acceptance:
'I want you to be happy': fixing, advising or contributing?

Reinforcing what?

Behaviourist principles predict that pleasant feelings reinforce behaviours. Some parents have been told that if they give their child comfort, they are providing something pleasant – a reward – in response to a fear, and that this will reinforce the fear.[373] Ouch! What you are reinforcing is that fear – like any emotion – passes, and that human connection is an excellent strategy to speed up the process.

Imagine you've just been mugged, and you're standing on the street, shocked and shaking with fear. *Scenario A:* A kind person comes over and embraces you until you become calmer. *Scenario B:* People turn away to make sure you don't get any 'rewarding' attention. You spend the night on your own, trembling. Which scenario is most likely to get you back to normal life?

Clingy, or needing comfort?

Perhaps your child never seems to have enough of you? She follows you everywhere, wants to sleep close to you, needs frequent physical touch. A typical teenager, hidden away in her room, she is not.

I'd like to tell you a short story of clinginess, if you'll forgive me for making a parallel between your child and a dog. My dog had five extremely clingy days after we got him neutered. He needed constant contact. If he wasn't on someone's lap, he just stood there, shaking, looking shell-shocked. At night he either stood frozen or paced up and down the room. He only fell briefly asleep when stroked. After a night of this, feeling slightly foolish, I abandoned my husband, and set up camp with my dog on the guest bed, where he instantly went to sleep.

I did this for a few days. Was I creating a rod for my own back? Would he forever expect to share my bed or lie on my lap while I worked? Had I fallen into the trap that if you give someone an inch, they take a mile? Nope.

After a few days, he sprang back to his old self, to his doggie cushion on the floor, his walks and his world of doggie smells and lampposts.

In short, my dog needed a comforting touch for whatever pain or shock had put him in a frozen state. Once his nervous system was back to normal, he moved on. (I was amused to talk to a great big macho man recently, who had done exactly the same thing for his great big macho dog.)

If you experience your child as clingy, I suggest you try to give her 100 per cent of what she seems to need. I trust that kids want to grow and become autonomous. Give them a safe base, a place of nurturing and comfort to which they know they can return any time, and they'll step out into the beckoning world.

As always, your own needs count as well. When we call a child 'clingy' it can be a way of saying we've run out of patience. We're running on empty. Notice if you don't have the resources to be present to your child as much as you'd like, give yourself compassion and explore what other support is available for her and for you.

Self-soothing: tools for your child

I believe that children learn to self-soothe in their own good time, when they feel secure and when they've experienced, time and again, what it's like to be soothed by their loving parents. At this stage they may welcome some tools. I've heard of older children using techniques they've learned in therapy or through relaxation audios. One of my own favourite self-soothing approaches is to get 'in flow' with an absorbing and satisfying activity, playing music being almost a guarantee of quick results.[374] So I find the following account from a mother particularly moving. Her daughter, aged seven, was battling both OCD and anorexia:

> *"A while back I gave her a little lap harp.[375] She said, 'Mom, every night my head is full of worries about what I'm going to have to eat tomorrow. But if I play the harp, I just think about the song and the notes and the worries are gone.' Later she said that when she has a bad dream that wakes her up, which happens almost every night, 'I just play the harp and it turns the witches into angels.'"*

HELPING YOUR CHILD FEEL GOOD IN HERSELF

Eating disorders bring extreme unhappiness and our children's self-esteem is often at rock bottom. Our sons and daughters are quick to beat themselves up about doing wrong (guilt) or about not being a good-enough person (shame). They have a bias towards interpreting our responses as disapproval.[376] They may be out of touch with their internal resources, even though they are using them with great courage several times a day at the dinner table. They do not think they are worthy of good things, pleasure, passion, love, or life.

Any treatment centre can provide food, but we parents provide the love that helps our children get back into the flow of life and become resilient.

In my view, the path lies in universal human needs. As I explained in Chapter 13, by this I mean values, things that matter, things that we yearn for, passions, qualities, everything that gives makes us fully alive.

- We can help our children value their needs by showing them that *we* value their needs, and by modelling how we value our own needs.

- Right away we can meet some of our children's most fundamental needs – to be loved, accepted, to belong, to be heard and understood. In other words, by giving them our compassionate presence we are contributing to their well-being. Even when they appear to be shutting us out.

- Love and acceptance don't just come from the outside: your child will benefit from internalising these so that whenever his chatterbox criticises him, he can give himself self-compassion. I'll explain more now.

Model self-compassion

Shame is 'I am a bad person.' It is toxic because it defines you as unworthy of life. When you see shame, assume there is a yearning for connection, for belonging, for acceptance. Shame can be fuelled by thoughts like, 'If people only knew what I'm really like, they'd completely reject me,' or, 'I'm such a horrible person I deserve to be forever alone.' Shame can be an existential nightmare: 'I am not worthy and have no rightful place on this earth.' Shame is terribly painful and scary, because it robs you of human connection.[377]

Self-compassion, according to research, is the best antidote to shame and is more effective than self-esteem boosters.[378] When your child's chatterbox judges her, she can come back to stability by giving herself kindness. If your efforts concentrate on building self-esteem with praise or positive affirmations, the danger is that you're trying to shoehorn in a story or a set of beliefs that clash with reality. The reality is that each of us do fail, at times.

We 'teach' our children self-compassion by giving them compassion and by modelling how we give ourselves self-compassion. If your child is receptive to learning self-compassion in a more formal way, do that too.

Praise can backfire

Let me illustrate what may happen when you give praise.[379]

Let's assume your child believes your praise is genuine, and gets a boost in her self-esteem. You say, 'You're so kind!' or, 'You're so good at drawing!' and she senses that she is a valuable person.

Sadly, she may think she's valuable *because* she is kind or good at drawing. The boost she's received is fragile. She is vulnerable to a change in the wind. A quick internet search will reveal hundreds of acts of heroic kindness, and thousands of drawings she likes more than her own. Her whole sense of self can easily crumble – what is her worth if she's, at best, average at everything?

And what if you stop loving her when you find out that there are other children who draw better than she does? The pressure is on to be the best.

Very often your praise will fail to give your child a boost. Remember when we were bungee jumping in Chapter 7? We saw how during a meal, praise can be eating-disorder hell for your child. If he is eating so well that you're happy, clearly he is disobeying his internal bully, who will now punish him.

> *"I feel worthless but when people tell me how good I am at singing or math I get angry and sad. Angry because I feel like they're lying to me; sad because I feel as if I'm failing myself and everyone else around me. A lot of the time it's a lose-lose situation. For me the praise needs to be kept to a very subtle minimum."[380]*

You don't need an eating disorder to misuse praise. Most of us have a chatterbox that interprets praise as a reason to judge and criticise. The chatterbox says, 'They think you're wonderful, but they don't know what you're really like. You're such a fraud.'

Positive affirmations: a hard sell

In your efforts to improve your child's self-esteem, you might have come across the practice of positive affirmations. I hate the damn things. You can make me say out loud 'I am a wonderful human being' a hundred times a day, I'll still manage to find arguments for and against. I will put up such intellectual resistance that the message won't have the slightest chance of reaching my subconscious or of creating new neural pathways. I accept the two-way link between thoughts and feelings, but my rational brain kicks in strongly when it knows it's being manipulated or *told* to engage in positive thinking.

So I'm wary of trying to boost a child's fragile ego with unspecific praise about how brilliant or kind she is. Especially a kid with an eating disorder, for whom shame and self-hate dominate. I really do think my kid is brilliant and kind, but if I had told her this repeatedly when anorexia was making her feel utterly worthless, what would I have achieved?

- 'Mum's only saying it to make me feel better. She doesn't actually mean it. No way am I brilliant or kind.'

- 'Mum's deluded. She may think I'm brilliant and kind, but I know I'm not. When she discovers the truth, I'll be totally alone.'

How about when the positives are clearly true? Some people believe that we build self-esteem by noticing what we're good at. Notice the achievements, notice the proud moments, give yourself praise, pat yourself on the shoulder.

To me, praising yourself raises the same problems as receiving praise from others. And there's another obstacle. Your child may see self-praise as bragging (silently or even publicly). And he'll have worked out that people who brag are a pain to be with and come across as insecure.

Gratitude and celebration

So is there nothing parents can do to help their child feel good? On the contrary. I believe we are their main conduits to wellness and wisdom, because we're there most of the time, and the parent-child connection is incredibly powerful. Not only are we helping our children when they need it, but we are surreptitiously coaching them for long-term wellbeing. Of course, if your child shows interest in learning from you, you can also openly teach them what you know. I was wary of doing that with mine but I can see how much wisdom she acquired just from us modelling and validating.

Two powerful practices we can model are gratitude and celebration. Instead of praising ourselves for what we do well, instead of trying to boost our self-esteem, we attend to what delights us, feeds our soul and gives us energy – in other words, needs.

For example, I have received both praise and thanks from parents who have read this book. My self-esteem could be boosted like this: 'I'm a great person because this reader says so.' It leaves me very vulnerable, though. What if the next email I receive is one of those pieces written entirely in capital letters? Instead, the feedback from parents is a cause for celebration. I am so very happy that I have contributed to this fellow human being. I am so very happy that I have connected, in some way, with other lives. I am so grateful that I have found a way to be part of this world.

We model celebration and gratitude by valuing our own needs and making no apologies for enjoying life. We validate our child's pleasure when their needs are met.

For instance, my daughter was into a particular video game for a while, and I bent over backwards to validate her delight in reaching higher and higher levels. First I had to let go of my judgement that the game was pointless. I struggled to get what was so great about it, so I would try and take my cues from her face.

My daughter: 'Yay! I did it! I'm on level 67! Next level I'll get an invisible cape!'

Me: 'Wow. You're getting very skilled. Looks like every level you reach, it gets more gripping?'

Which also meant she was spending more and more time sitting staring at a screen, but when your child's been down the hell hole of an eating disorder and all it entails, you don't sweat the small stuff.

You can make gratitude a bedtime habit with your child: 'Five things you're grateful for today!' Take your time. For each wonderful 'thing', express how happy you are that she enjoyed it, or draw out what it did for her that made it so wonderful. You are teaching your child to savour the good things, even in the middle of a tough day. Mine would ask me what *my* five things were, and I would make sure at least one of them was about her.

Show you care for what he cares about

Your child will have strengths and sources of wellbeing that, at present, they do not appreciate. Their sense of who they are may be tied to the eating disorder, or to school marks or a volatile friendship. You help your child grow by holding up a mirror to the full human being that she is. Highlight and reinforce her resources, strengths, passions or longings (in preference to her achievements, abilities or talents). You're bringing to her attention constants in her life, things she values or that are important to her.

Martin Seligman, who has overseen a vast body of research on positive psychology, has developed the concept of signature strengths.[381] I see a strong link between these and the 'needs' within Nonviolent Communication. Seligman advises us to recognise these strengths and use them to nurture happiness and wellbeing.

If a child plays a beautiful piece on the piano, chances are she's getting a thrill from doing it – for the sheer joy of the music and the flow of playing. If a child hands a beloved toy to a crying sibling, she is acting from qualities of care and compassion.

How do you hold up a mirror to your child? With empathy – silent or verbal. When you make comments, see if you can frame them as questions. That way you can check you guessed correctly, and you invite your child to express herself.

- 'You took good care of your friend when she was upset. You really like to care for people, don't you?'

- 'That was such a funny story you wrote. Am I right in thinking you get a buzz from doing creative work?'

- 'I'm glad to hear you laughing. Were you having the most amazing fun?'

- 'Hey, you tidied your room. Does it feel lovely and peaceful?'

By showing your own pleasure, you're giving her the all-important message that you value her needs, that you care that she gets a buzz from creative work, that you're glad she's in touch with the fun things in life, that you support that she spends time drawing if it gives her pleasure. This is unconditional love in action – 'You're OK the way you are.'

Hold a mirror up to your child's resources

When your child is suffering, when he's full of shame, self-hate or guilt, he is probably completely out of touch with his needs and strengths. He may be unaware of his internal resources.

Likewise, when you see your child so affected by the illness, it's easy to think of him as helpless. Hold in your heart the kind of person he was before he got ill. And whenever his strengths manifest themselves, make sure you acknowledge them.

But how can you do that without it sounding like praise? Let me try to demonstrate how it can work.

I want to tell you I think you're a great parent.

Believe me, you're a great parent!

Did that work for you?

When my daughter was in hospital and people told me I was a great mother, I took it to mean that they were wishing me well and doing their best to connect with me. It was heart-warming but also accentuated my isolation. I told myself they were trying to boost me because I was the one who had to do the coping. Besides, how soon before they decided I was a hopeless mum because progress wasn't fast enough?

If my praise didn't work for you, let's try something else.

- Look how in spite of all that's happening, you're still working away to support your child. Day after day, however hard it is, you have picked yourself up again. That is a real show of resilience.

- You're so full of love. I can hear it in everything you say, even when you're exhausted. You're there for your child, whatever happens.

- I love how you're searching for help, reading and gathering information, and also getting emotional support for yourself. You're doing all this with so much care and intelligence.

- You're doing a beautiful job of putting to good use all the qualities you've developed over all these years. First you used them for your work, and now your child is benefiting from them.

How did that work for you? I know it worked for me, because my sister used to say these things to me. To me it was feedback and it was hugely nourishing. My chatterbox did protest occasionally ('I'm not doing a beautiful job; I messed up just an hour ago') but on the whole I accepted the spirit of her words and they hit the spot. She was putting her finger on qualities I very much wished for.

As she was reflecting universal human needs, I trust that what she said about me pretty much applies to you as well, which is why I happily pass her words on. Feel free to add your own.

My sister helped me focus on what mattered to me and she validated my strengths. I started to notice that whenever I doubted my abilities to cope or to do a good job, her words would replay in my head and give me the boost I needed.

Because this helped me when I was in distress and needed support, I try to do the same for my daughter and for others.

If you think you'd like to reflect strengths back to your child and if you don't always have a lovely set of flowing words at hand, I trust that the message somehow comes across in compassionate silence.

Should we fight perfectionism?

Perfectionism is a personality trait associated with a higher risk for an eating disorder. Of course this doesn't mean that if you're a perfectionist you're likely to get an eating disorder, and it doesn't mean you can cure the illness simply by addressing perfectionism. Perfectionism is stressful because it's driven by fear and insecurity. Your survival depends on achieving ever-higher standards, on being better than everyone else. It's as though you have to earn the right to live on this planet. When you fail to reach your desired standard, you descend into fear and self-hate. And that makes eating-disorder behaviours particularly compelling.

During her first major set of exams, my daughter entered a kind of trance which logic couldn't penetrate. She would assure me that she had to get all As. Her intensity reminded me of the times when she insisted that water would make her fat. Once the exams were over, she recognised what a horrible state she'd got herself into, and knowing the link with anorexia, decided to practice 'good enough'. She became more aware of what she was actually interested in, rather than what provided high status. We have a running joke that she's not allowed to get more than a C in her exams.

People assume that to fight perfectionism, you need to boost self-esteem. As we saw earlier, self-compassion is far more powerful, because there's no way the best at everything – and why should we be?

We can also guide our children to increase their wellbeing *because* of their perfectionistic traits. They are so lucky to have such great staying power. Once they set their mind on something they usually achieve it with relative ease. They find it easy to concentrate and apply themselves to activities they are excited about. They lose the sense of time and get into 'flow' – a major component of happiness.[382] I'm benefiting from such qualities right now as I plough through this mass of writing.

'I've noticed': the power of having a witness

An important component of wellbeing, and a universal human need, is connection with others. We need to be heard, understood, witnessed, and when we get these things it doesn't matter half as much that many of our other needs are not being met. How does this apply to our children?

Well, they're doing heroic work to fight the eating disorder, or just to survive. Sometimes they really want that to be acknowledged and it helps them to keep going. They might want you to notice how brave they are, for instance.

Your child might hear a lot of instructions from you: 'Eat!', 'Sit!', 'You're hiding food under your lips!', 'Get back into bed!' She might think you don't notice all the efforts she makes. Maybe she's eaten something really difficult, or she's managed to sit for an entire TV programme without trying to exercise, or she's resisted the urge to hide food. Is there a way you could let her know you've noticed?

- 'I noticed how you ate a new type of yoghurt today.'
- 'You were kind to your sister when she was upset.'
- 'You did some amazing cartwheels this afternoon.'
- 'Thanks for helping clear all the chairs.'
- 'You took good care of Grandma this morning and she enjoyed seeing you.'

With my daughter, the nurses started writing her little notes on cherry-shaped pieces of paper. She stuck these onto a pretty hand-made model of a cherry tree with tissue-paper blossoms. We too made sure we wrote one or two 'cherries' each time we visited.

I think this meant a lot to her. She's kept the tree. I fall over it every time I step into the attic.

You might be able to have good 'I noticed' conversations at bedtime, or when your child's eating-disorder voice, if she has one, is quiet.

For example:

'Night, sweetie. You had a good day, didn't you?'

'Yup. My first chips in a year.' (That's 'fries' to my US friends, right?)

'That was amazing. You found it hard at the beginning, but you still did it!' *You're acknowledging her courage more than the fact she ate chips.*

You choose not to mention the fact that she showered you with abuse in a public park and tipped half the contents onto the ground. It's not her role to console you for the stress you've been through, and you don't need her to apologise: you know that for her, contemplating those chips was like someone – the eating disorder – was holding a gun to her head.

'I was really scared. But I thought, if I don't do it today, you'll make me do it another day, so I might as well have it now.'

'And then it was OK?'

'It was soooo good! I wonder if I can go to Ali's party after all. I didn't want to go because there'll be chips.'

'I'm so pleased for you. You're moving on even when you're scared, getting your-self more freedom every day. Life's getting easier, right?' *You're connecting around some deep needs here.*

'Yep. But that doesn't mean you can give me hard foods every day, eh?'

Hasn't she noticed that she's been getting several new challenging foods a day, poor thing? 'Trust me. I'm always going to give you what's right.' *You avoid discussing future meals and reinforce your role as her rock.*

'Good. Night, Mum.'

Top up the emotional bank account with love

We are well and we live well when we love ourselves. When we love ourselves we grow a huge heart with loads of space for others. Ultimately what I really want is for my child to integrate to the very core of her being the knowledge that she's an OK person. I want her to have unconditional love for and acceptance of herself, irrespec-tive of her achievements or regrets. I want her to have a sense of belonging. She has a rightful place on earth.

We can't force these attitudes onto our children, but we can model them for ourselves, and we can nurture self-love in our children by giving them our uncondi-tional love.

Unconditional love is not the norm in our society. Adults dish out stars for the best pieces of work, and set up competitions for the best piece of art. The highest achievers are put on a pedestal for all to admire, and there is no celebration of anyone else's journey. On top of that, our children have no shortage of delightful friends who are ready to point out their 'faults' ('Your hair is greasy', 'Stop following us around', 'The problem with you is you try to much'). An eating disorder adds an intense internal critic, causing self-hate and ever-increasing internal demands.

To counteract all these pressures, I want to make sure my child's emotional bank account is well topped up.[383] I want her to know that I love her, not that I love her *because* she did something.

One way I do this is to show her my love many times a day, when she's not actually doing anything in particular. I nurture the bond with a smile, a wink, a kind-ness that takes no time at all. I also aim to give her my time – to read a chapter of a book together, or to sit on her bed and chat. You'll have your own ways. If an eating disorder has driven you apart for a while, I bet you treasure those moments of close-ness.

SICK, MAD, BAD? WHAT MODEL ARE YOU USING?

Your child will have a story she tells herself about what's happening to her. Much of the time it will be 'I'm a weak and horrible person.' Lots of self-blame and self-hate, lots of hopelessness.

You too have a mental model of what's going on. It will be different if you're a neuroscientist, or a Buddhist monk, if you're new to this illness, if you've read books or if you've accumulated months of experience. It may be mostly fact-based or laden with metaphors. The story in your head will shape how you talk, and that, in turn, will transform the story your child takes in. So I suggest you notice the story you're telling and check it's as helpful as can be.

The way you talk, the way you ask your child to eat, may well change your child's story from 'It's my fault' to 'It's an illness and nobody's fault.' Your confidence will add nuances: 'We're doing exactly what's needed for you to recover once and for all,' or, 'You may always need to eat regularly, just like I am short-sighted and I remember to take glasses with me for driving.'

In some people's mind, the term 'illness' leads to 'mental illness', which may lead to 'crazy' in a permanent and alienating kind of way. The term 'brain disorder' sounds to me more like some kind of malfunction that can be fixed or managed. But your child may hear yet other things, so it's worth checking out.

With my daughter, I stressed the genetic side so that she'd know this was something that happens rather than something she had somehow brought on herself. At the same time when we talk of genetics we must be careful to correct popular, outdated and dire beliefs that genes determine our destiny (see Chapter 5).

Clinical psychologist and evolutionary biologist Shan Guisinger offers a positive take on the genetics of anorexia. Her hypothesis is that anorexia is the result of evolutionary adaptations which, in times of scarcity, enabled some individuals to restrict their eating and have boundless energy. These people's extraordinary abilities would have allowed them to lead their tribe away from famine-struck areas, keeping the focus on travel, undistracted by foraging. When the migration was over, the community gave their hero support to resume eating.[384]

As long as we can control the worst environmental factors, maybe we should celebrate the genes that predispose to an eating disorder. By nature our children are generally smart, high-achieving, conscientious, determined, sensitive, kind. The following words by genetics writer Matt Ridley may be relevant to eating disorders:

> "Perhaps schizophrenia is the result of too much of a good thing: too many genetic and environmental factors that are usually good for brain function all coming together in one individual."[385]

The externalising model: separating your child from the eating disorder

I alluded earlier to how parents are taught to separate their child from the eating disorder. It's called the externalising model and is a key principle of Family-Based Treatment (FBT). The model is that the illness has taken over our child and robbed them of their freedom. Talking this way helps everyone maintain love and engagement with the child while 'attacking' the eating disorder. Some of our children have a sense of a voice or a part within that dictates eating-disorder behaviours, so the model of ED as a separate entity inside the child may makes sense to the whole family.

I love this moving account from a young person in recovery, showing the externalising model working very well.

> *"A very close friend at school took up the role of, dare I say it? –*
> *food police, completely at her own intuition. She so quickly*
> *understood what was ED and what was me, and she 'refuses to*
> *tolerate that jerk,' as she says. One late evening, my stomach was*
> *growling and I said that I would eat 'soon'. My friend came in with*
> *oatmeal cookies, which I politely turned down. She took a cookie*
> *and put it on my lap, taking my book from my hands. 'Eat it. You*
> *are hungry and you were offered food. I don't CARE if ED*
> *doesn't like it, you EAT IT, because I don't want that jerk in my*
> *room.' I ate the cookie and, having broken ED's hold, got a glass*
> *of milk and some peanut butter."*[386]

Therapists give us the externalising tool to save us from getting too distraught or angry about our children's behaviour. We parents need frequent reminders that it's the illness (or brain functioning, or fear, or the fight-flight-freeze reaction, or biochemicals) that makes our child act up. It helps us give our kids uncritical acceptance, a major ingredient of successful treatment. It helps us feed our children in spite of the child's distress.

Any metaphor that gives you quick access to your resources is worth having in your toolbox, and remember that externalising is part of FBT, which is a well-researched treatment. Externalising is just a tool, though. After a while I found it patronising when hospital therapists kept saying, 'It's not your child who hates you, it's anorexia'; 'Your daughter didn't refuse the toast, anorexia did'; 'You have an unwelcome visitor in your family.'

After a while, how useful is it to see our child's illness as a separate, harmful entity? I'll share my thoughts on pros and cons.

The externalising model may save you giving relatives long explanations. You can tell your mother, 'I'm not telling him off because it's not his fault. He has a voice that bullies him into rejecting food.' On the other hand, it's just as quick, and possibly closer to the truth to say, 'The illness affects his brain, creating a state of extreme anxiety around food.'

Likewise, when our children are frightened or confused by an eating-disorder voice, we can label it as a demon, or we can say it's a bunch of thoughts and images generated by a malnourished or stressed brain, or one that is in a state of fight-flight-freeze.

Some parents instinctively visualise the eating disorder as a malevolent gremlin, a demon who takes over their innocent child and lies, cheats, screams and hurls food. If parents win this epic battle of good versus evil, their beloved child – who was there all along – will be set free. It helps these parents' resolve to hate the intruder, shame it, exile it or attack it till it gives up and retreats. At the very least they put on a show of protective strength or have an image of offering their kids weapons against the beast. Interestingly, the physiological signs of a state of fight-flight-freeze – the face that contorts with fury, the eyes that turn cold, the rigid body, the altered pitch of the voice –bring up images from horror movies where a child is possessed by a demon.

When parents imagine an external presence controlling their child, they can talk as though it is real: 'We don't blame you, because we know right now it's Anorexia who's shouting, not the real you', 'I don't talk to the eating disorder, but I'll talk to you', 'Don't give in to ED!' Some parents, when they're very stressed, find themselves shouting at their child, 'I hate ED!' The risk is that what our children hear is 'I hate *you!*' at a time when they are already highly strung and need help to calm down.

The externalising model is commonly offered not just to parents, but to our children, in the hope that they will judge themselves less harshly. That may be so, but be cautious with any talk of a separate entity. If your child doesn't hear an eating-disorder voice, the model may seem childish, patronising or crazy. Which doesn't do much for connection. Your child may fight you and defend her sense of who she is. How dare you say she has a horrid ED part in her. She wants to be seen as whole, as herself.

The model can be tricky if the eating disorder is currently defining everything about how your child sees herself. As far as she's concerned, she *is* the part you so hate. And you're talking of getting rid of it! So not only is she a horrible, unlovable person, she's also in danger of extermination. She'd better hold on tight to her rules. She only has herself to rely on.

If your child does visualise and hear an ED entity, be aware that it first appeared to her as a loyal friend, soulmate and protector. These days, it often turns into a bully who must be appeased. Even if your child sees herself as distinct from ED, she dare not anger it. When you threaten ED she has to side with it and fight you. If you're lucky she may sometimes rope in your help to trick ED. On just a couple of occasions, my daughter whispered food requests to me so that her bullying eating-disorder voice couldn't hear. I played along with the metaphor because it came from her and she was using it as a tool to help her eat. I doubt that she really heard a voice or totally bought into it; part of her knew it was just an image.

The externalising model has lots of pros and cons. See if you can think of about 50 more and then compare your answers with those in a fascinating paper by Kelly Bemis Vitousek.[387]

Be kind to the eating-disorder part

For me, the image of my child being hijacked by a separate entity became more of a burden than a help. Shame, attack or banishment don't make sense to me. I was drawn to nourishing my soul with compassion for my whole child, including the parts I didn't agree with, the parts that told her she was fat and that restriction is a virtue. These parts were, after all, trying to protect her from anxiety, trying to make sense of chaotic signals delivered by her brain.

As time went on, I saw my daughter more and more as a person like everyone else. I was drawn to accept the whole of my kid, just as I strive to accept the whole of myself even when it's not entirely pretty. So I began talking to her in terms that matched my own thinking: 'Right now your brain is making you do this, and we're doing the right things to make it work well again.'

Now I'm going to go out on a limb and propose we don't present our child's experience, our child's illness, as so frighteningly abnormal! We can normalise their reactions by explaining the mechanisms of fight, flight or freeze, and how these hijack our ability to think rationally, weigh up options, be wise. We can also normalise the voice, the part of our child that is driving eating-disorder thoughts and behaviours. We can show our children how we all have parts within ourselves that want to push us one way or another. Parts that, in times of stress, try to take over. For me there's the part that wants a job done and the part that procrastinates. The part that wants to be courageous and the part that finds excuses to withdraw. The part that wants me to be loving and calm, and the part that gets resentful. Right now I have a part that says I shouldn't be tired and wants to pep me up with another cup of tea. Another part is rolling its eyes because it knows a tenth cuppa will only make me jittery. Maybe one part is a tea addict and the other is annoyingly sensible, but I can be kind to both – whether or not I agree with their methods – as they both want me to feel good.

It may help our children to hear that even with their extreme eating-disorder behaviours, they are no different to any of us. We are all, to some degree, buffeted by internal conflicts and stressors. We all have parts that judge, that can't see the big picture, that take on extreme roles under extreme circumstances.

We can teach our children that we are all trying to feel good and be happy and that no part of ourselves should be demonised. Each of our parts benefits from kindness and appreciation for what they're trying to do for us, even when we disagree with their methods. Just like compassion brings the best from people, it brings the best from our parts. Our journey to wellbeing is one where our core self, our wise self, takes compassionate leadership.

So rather than tell your child how much you hate her eating-disorder voice, another option is to show a kindly interest in what needs this part of her is trying to meet. She might tell you it usually gives her a sense of control or satisfaction or comfort or peace. She may also feel safe enough to take stock and see that this doesn't work as well as she would like. If she can assume leadership, she can then give this part her appreciation for its well-meaning efforts, gradually detach from its strategies and be ready for other ways to get what she so needs. That, at least, is the hope, and you will need to see if it makes sense to you and experiment. It may work better when your child is well into recovery – I have no experience of using it with a very ill child. Note that identifying and befriending parts exists in a number of psychotherapies, including the currently popular internal family systems (IFS)[388].

TEEN BOOKS ABOUT EATING DISORDERS: TAKE CARE

Would it be useful for your son or daughter to read fiction, non-fiction or biographies about eating disorders? My opinion is that this is risky, for negligible benefits. Your child surely can't cure herself by reading. There's the risk that she will be triggered by the accounts of denial, self-hate, starvation, and over-exercising. She could be drawn to imitate the protagonist or competitively outdo him or her. If your kid is young, she may learn some 'tools of the trade' that hadn't yet occurred to her.

Not too long ago, while reading a teen novel, I found myself very much in the shoes of a first-person character. Her descent into anorexia was skillfully portrayed, and I was surprised to notice that it had an 'anorexic' effect on me. For one day, I felt repulsed by food. I'm glad to report that this passed but I shudder to think what the cost might be to someone who is vulnerable to an eating disorder.

Your child might ask for a book that will help her feel more normal and will help her understand what's happening to her. I suggest it's better she gets that through conversations with you, once you are well informed and full of empathy.

Books can be great for friends – assuming that they themselves don't have a vulnerability to an eating disorder. If your child's best friends want a better understanding of what it's like to have an eating disorder, you could give them a well chosen novel that doesn't perpetuate myths and doesn't make recovery look overly simplistic.[389]

INSPIRATION FROM SOMEONE WHO'S RECOVERED

You might know somebody who has recovered from an eating disorder, who's ready to speak with your child. The aim might be inspiration, hope, empathy, normalisation. There is a risk that this person is not quite recovered enough and will let some triggering comments through. Unless they got family-based treatment, they may show disapproval for how you have taken away some of your child's autonomy. If you're keen, I suggest you speak with this person alone first. A more 'controllable' intervention is to offer your child a well-chosen podcast.[390]

EDUCATING AND MOTIVATING YOUR CHILD

I lectured, questioned and challenged my long-suffering daughter for far too long. Whenever she had a calm moment and felt close, I would bring up something relating to the illness. I'd ask her how she was feeling, what were her hopes, what was becoming easier or harder. Then I'd drift into lecturing.

These conversations made her edgy. She wanted to relax and have fun. She wanted a break from the incessant anxiety she suffered around the eating-disorder. I knew I was out of tune with her, but I was driven to *do something* to move her forward and didn't trust that nutrition, love and normal life were enough. My husband did a far better job of playing games with her and bringing in normality. I was still working under a model I'd read about that we needed to get her to some stage of readiness for change. I was taking on the role of psychotherapist, with a child who was too young and too ill for talking therapy. It was a relief for me to let go of that.

I also recognise that education has a role when someone is close to recovered. Its purpose at that stage is not to cure but to prevent relapses.

A year down the line, when my daughter was out of hospital and looking like she'd soon have to go back in, I decided that exposure to a totally normal way of life was going to achieve more than talk. I decided I was useful when I was 'just' being present to her.

As Marshall Rosenberg, founder of the Nonviolent Communication approach said:

> "Don't just do something. Stand there."

HEART-TO-HEART TALKS

Although I stopped trying to engineer conversations with my daughter relating to her recovery, I was interested that she often brought things up when we went for a stroll, or during a car journey. So if I thought she had something on her mind, I would cajole her to accompany me on a walk. Sometimes, amazingly, emptying the dishwasher together achieved the same effect. I've often heard similar observations from parents. The key ingredient is, I believe, to have easy periods of silence.

If I were a child therapist, I would conduct my sessions during ambles in the park. I would smash up my sterile little consulting room[391] – if one of the kids hadn't already done so.

ACTIVITIES AND TIME TOGETHER

When my daughter came home from hospital I did a lot less talking and a lot more connecting. My new treatment model was that she should have a good life and should experience, as much as possible, what it's like to be well – when I wasn't asking her to eat a meal, that is. It became increasingly easy to spend relaxed time together.

Artistic and physical activities, or anything where one gets 'into flow', might not just cheer our child up, but also help the brain heal.

Our children can lose sight of who they are and what makes them tick. Their depression, anxiety and exhaustion can so easily take over. If your daughter lets you, can you cuddle up to her after a meal and play a game with her? What else could you do together that brings you close, makes her laugh and shows her that you care for her? What activities can you facilitate that will rekindle your child's zest for life?

> "While refeeding is necessary, I think it is a good thing to encourage better self-esteem and an interest in something. I totally think that it was because of her passion for music that my D started to be able to look 'at' the illness, rather than being totally immersed in it."

I'm going to give you some suggestions for activities that may help your child enjoy herself and also connect with you. I expect you'll find many of them unworkable, because so often there are terrible obstacles in the way. There's the weather, your child's state of health, her willingness to sit and stay still, how much she rejects your very presence, and countless other difficulties. Yet if you manage to find even one thing that works, your child may switch from a depressed, isolated and antagonistic stranger to something closer to her old self. She might start feeling closer to you and begin trusting you, which would be money in the bank for the stress of the next mealtime.

So, here are some ideas in no particular order: watch TV together, go through every single series of *Friends* or *The Big Bang Theory*, watch documentaries or stand-up comics, go to the cinema, read a book aloud, listen to an audio book, take an interest in your kid's online interactions, go for a stroll, walk a neighbour's dog, go window-shopping, draw or paint together, get a craft kit and build something, search the internet for a craft project, make up a story[392], plant something, do a puzzle, give your child's bedroom a facelift, sell stuff on eBay, play board games or card games, play electronic games, paint nails, braid hair, do make-up, practise doing theatrical make-up, plan a party or special event, research something (in our case, choosing a dog), go to an amusement park, go for a dip in the pool, go skating, visit a pet shop, sort photos into an album, give a gentle massage, lie next to each other and look at the clouds, snuggle up and say nothing.

I found that whatever I did, the main thing was to let go of all my own ambitions, all the work I wanted to get done, and just be there 100 per cent for my child.

To me, time spent in connection, in closeness, is money in the emotional bank. It fills up the love account, and gives us a safety margin for difficult times.

MODELLING: DO AS I DO

One reason I put so much value in emotional tools for parents is because children seem to learn so much through what we model. It's really a case of 'do as I do'. 'Do as I say' hardly has any impact.

When we behave with calm confidence in a stressful situation, our child has mirror neurons that fire away as if she was also behaving with calm confidence. In other words her brain is getting practice without any conscious effort on her part. She may even be getting the physiological benefit of this calmer state of ours. You could take this theory too far: I doubt you can learn to play the piano by idly watching pianists. All the same, modelling is a major tool in our kit.

We model calm, we model trust, we model acceptance, non-judgement, and self-awareness. We model effective communication. We model self-compassion and compassion for others and we model that needs matter. Often, we ourselves have integrated these qualities through someone modelling them for us.

Let me give you a very simple example.

Perhaps, like me, you don't want your child to get all stressed out about exams. If she's got a fine brain and plenty of motivation, failing the odd exam is hardly going to screw up her future. As you may have noticed, my motto is 'good enough' not 'perfection'. In any case, young people can go on to have a great life without succeeding in exams. So you might, like me, be on the alert if every now and again your child says, 'Maths exam tomorrow. I'm so going to fail!'

I notice that my first reaction, typically, is to reassure, reason and lecture: 'Of course you won't fail. Night after night your maths homework is fine. Just stay calm … And by the way, make sure you revise all evening, oh and also have a good night's sleep, just to be sure you're ready.'

I've noticed that if I embody qualities of calm and trust, I hardly need to say anything. I can just say 'Aha?' and look at my daughter with kindly interest. She says what she has to say, and I listen and make myself totally present to her, until finally she says, 'Anyway, I'm going to revise for 15 minutes and that will be quite enough. Mum, I really need new shoes – these ones are leaking. Can we go shopping later?'

What happens when we can't possibly model the values we want for our kids, because we're struggling with them ourselves? I have often enough regretted that I haven't been as patient and compassionate as I wanted, especially in the early days when I was learning new skills I'd never needed before. In this case self-compassion is a great value to model.

PARENT AND CHILD: OUR COMMON HUMANITY

Has it struck you that everything your child needs, you need as well?

- She gets worse with blame, so do you.
- She needs unconditional love, so do you. She is worthy of love, so are you.
- You both have some very tough action to take to save her. For her it's eating. For you it's feeding her.
- You both fear this task, and for both of you, the more you do the task the more you overcome the fear.
- When put under stress, she screams, hurls abuse or withdraws. So do you (kind of) until you get access to internal resources.
- You both need to move on with your lives.

It's not so surprising that we are so alike. We're all human beings. Eating disorders do weird stuff, but the ground rules of humanity remain.

Once I started to this I used it in several ways that empowered me:

- When I struggled to empathise with her, I looked for the parallel with myself.
- I decided that modelling wellbeing was the greatest gift I could give her.
- I reckoned that by being self-connected more often, I would be an instrument of my daughter's recovery. I now stand by this principle as I notice how people, when they are grounded and in touch with their needs, radiate an energy of wellbeing.

MENDING, APOLOGISING, AND REGRETS

After any kind of fireworks, where one or both of you lost your temper and harmed the relationship, consider the value of a mending conversation. An eating disorder will make your child react uncontrollably over and over again. You can be sure that se regrets many of her outbursts. Meanwhile your buttons have been pushed by his resistance. Let's start with the situation where you want to apologise.

There are things I regret having done to my child. There are things she was shocked by. Although I've come to terms with my regrets, I've been on the lookout for anything that is still weighing heavily on her, which may be harming her or our relationship. We parents want to mend and heal. Truth and reconciliation. As we parents deal with our own regrets and put in the mending work, we're giving our kids a model of resilience.

Sometimes there's some mending to do soon after an outburst, and sometimes there's mending to do at a later date, as our kids recover and look back on events that happened months or years ago. Sometimes we think we have cleared a painful memory, but a year later our child recalls another aspect of the event and we must be open to talking some more about it.

Apologising is only one part of mending, and sometimes we apologise only to relieve ourselves of guilt and have the other person reassure us. (An extreme example is that of a man who regularly beats his wife, following it each time with an abject apology). It's OK to check with others how they've been affected by our actions, but it's not their job to stop us from feeling guilty.

'I'm sorry': the blame game

Before I propose how to have a mending conversation, let me bring to light how most of us have learned to make apologies based on 'wrongness':

CHATTERBOX

- Guilt, self-blame: 'I did wrong.'
- Shame: 'I'm a bad person.'

Which goes hand in hand with:

- Blaming: 'You did wrong.'
- Shaming: 'You're a bad person.'

Here's how it goes: I shuffle over to my loved one, murmur 'I'm sorry' (at the back of your mind, a grown-up from your childhood is yelling, 'AND LOOK LIKE YOU MEAN IT!'), and then I list my failings, preferably with lashings of abject self-blame. The idea is that if I make myself out to be a not-OK person, my loved one will, in contrast, feel like she's a really great human being. If she has an eating disorder, wouldn't it be great if by debasing myself, I cured her of her debilitating self-hate? If only!

Here's a typical game of apology and it takes place entirely between my chatterbox and my child's chatterbox.

'I'm sorry, I did wrong. It was all my fault.'

'No, actually, it was my fault. I was the one who did wrong. I'm really sorry.'

'Well, I still feel bad about what I did.'

'I don't blame you for anything. I was totally out of order. I'm so sorry.'

In other words, if your child follows the conventional rules, your apology will stimulate guilt and shame in her.

Sometimes the other person doesn't play that game. She doesn't make herself out to be bad or wrong. Her game is to make herself right by making you out to be completely evil. So your apology fails to connect or to heal your relationship:

'I'm sorry, I did wrong. It was all my fault.'

'You bet it was! When I'm older I will write a misery memoir and you'll be really sorry.'

And sometimes our apology doesn't address the other person's pain at all:

'I'm sorry, I did wrong. It was all my fault.'

'It's always about *you*!'

The everyday 'I'm sorry, please forgive me' model doesn't give either party the empathy, listening, understanding and mending that they surely long for.[393] It deprives each of us of our authentic power, the very thing that gives us parents the strength to support our children, and which puts our children in touch with their yearning for life. Taking turns to abase ourselves doesn't seem like the basis of a great relationship. The counter-model offered by Nonviolent Communication is that both you and your child are good people trying to meet universal needs the best you can with the emotional and physical resources at your disposal.

The ingredients of mending

It's useful to spend a little time grounding yourself before a difficult conversation, so that you can steer it wisely and be a good listener. At the beginning you might get triggered by some rather bitter accusations from your child, so keep up the self-compassion and be patient with the process.

I propose these ingredients to help you with the conversation:

- *'I so regret what I did/ that I did it that way'*:

  Be explicit about what you are regretting ('I left abruptly, without a word, slamming the door, and didn't return till night-time'). Give your child a chance to tell their story, even if they exaggerate and you are itching to justify yourself.

- *'... because it had this painful effect on you'*:

  Name (and show sorrow for) the effect you guess it had on your child ('I'm so sorry you felt abandoned and scared, just when you needed support'). While your child is talking, keep validating their experience. ('So when you remember me shouting at you, you were thinking I was blaming you. Yes, no wonder you felt scared and alone. And it still feels a bit like that because you need to know you can rely on me, that I'm on your side. You want me to know you're doing your best, is that right?') Attend to the emotions or needs that come up for your child right now as they recall the event. Keep this up until you see signs of connection, of your child feeling well understood and cared for.

  This might be all you need for mending, but see if the following is also useful.

- *'Would you like to know what was going on for me?'*:

  If you explain yourself too soon, your child hear it as a load of excuses. So wait for the connection before you talk about your experience – not to justify yourself, but to attend to the relationship. Your child may imagine your intentions were evil, that you wanted to abandon them or harm them. So they may be very relieved to learn this wasn't the case. Don't stoop to self-blame, don't make yourself into a victim (don't get into a rescuer-persecutor-victim dynamic!)[394]. Keep your dignity and talk about the important needs you were trying to meet, and how you wish you'd had the wherewithal to go about meeting them in a better way.

For instance: 'When you came home and I realised you'd gone running, I was really scared for your heart. I had visions of you collapsing alone in a deserted street. You remember fight-flight-freeze? Yes well I was in flight. All I could think of was to escape from the house. Which is crazy because my state of panic was all about my love for you, and I did the opposite of showing you my love! I'm incredibly sad about that. I wish I had had the skills to calm myself enough for that not to happen. I wish I could have really been by your side.'

Keep checking how your child receives what you say: 'How does that sound?' Expect some to-and-fro here. New issues might come up.

- '... and this is what I'm going to do so that, to the best of my ability, it doesn't happen again':

'Maybe you'd like some reassurance that this couldn't happen again, that whatever happens, you'll know I'm really supporting you?' Don't make promises you can't keep!

At this stage it might also be appropriate to discuss a change in your child's behaviour, since it takes two to tango. Mending is more than just one person apologising. If your child is engaging in harmful behaviour, address it. Don't back down just because earlier you lost your cool.

After that you can check that everything is now in the clear: 'Is there anything else that's weighing on your mind?'

- [Hug]:

Finish with some connecting gesture and get on with your lives.

Be cautious about making agreements you are unhappy with. OK, you regret losing your temper during a meal, but that's no reason to agree to your child's request to cut the carbs!

And again, don't make promises that you can't be sure to keep. Early on, when my daughter's anorexia was both new and extreme, I promised her I would never shout again. I'd finally worked out that getting cross did not help her to eat, and I wanted to rebuild trust. Yet after three weeks of letting every taunt waft past my fragile Zen cocoon, I cracked. Breaking an unrealistic promise gave my poor kid one more reason not to trust me. Seriously, the best you can do is state your heartfelt intentions and promise to try your best. For example: 'I really don't want to shout at you again. I want to give you kindness and respect even when I'm triggered. That might mean I take some breaths, or a bit of alone time to calm down. I'm working on it, and I will do my very best. How does that sound?'

I wonder if these conversations seem long and complicated? If so, please remember they're smoother in real life than on the page. Besides, there isn't always a need for a drawn-out exchange. My daughter will occasionally mention a time when

I shouted, and all that's called for is for me to pause, let my heart open, and say, 'Yes, that was crap.'

Help your child to mend the relationship

When our children have an outburst and come out with rather too much abuse against us, we can help them mend the relationship. Often they themselves offer a gesture once they're calmer, and that may be plenty: a smile, a joke, a hug, a quick 'I'm sorry, I didn't mean to shout at you'.

When your child offers an apology, show you've heard it and accept it graciously. You can say, 'Thank you, sweetheart. I get that this is really not you, and that you care for me. I love you.' I think that is more powerful than a common response kind parents give, which is, 'No need to apologise. I know it's the eating disorder that made you do it, it's not your fault.'

If there is no gesture towards restoring the relationship, I worry that our kids stay stuck in a rather scary place. We can assume that however much they yell 'I hate you!' our children love us and feel terrible about causing harm. They may then avoid us, or resent us even more, and sink more into shame, depression and isolation. So how can we coach them to attend to the relationship? The norm most of us grew up with is, 'Say you're sorry!' How can we do better than that?

Here's an example of an easy alternative. Just as they kiss their child goodnight, a parent might say, 'Darling, today in the café, when you tipped your egg onto my lap, that wasn't great, right?' When they get a nod, they can move on to, 'If you feel like that again, will you please try and use words instead?'

If your child is very closed off, mending may not feel so natural. Some children stay very defensive. Some wear blinkers, forgetting the incident and resuming life as normal. They may even be extra loving or exuberant for a few hours. This is a normal defence mechanism at a time when shame would otherwise be intolerable.[395]

In these cases, take the time for a connecting conversation:

- You are bigger and wiser, so you may need to take the first step. You must be non-blaming, so do your self-compassion work first if necessary. Let your child keep their dignity. ('What happened earlier in the café… that was so not like you. I wonder if it's been pretty upsetting? What happened?')

- As your child says what happened, validate their experience. Don't take the bait if they accuse or exaggerate. ('Aha, yes, I thought so. You couldn't bear the thought of eating the egg because that was your first egg in months. And it was extra stressful because you thought people were watching and you're not yet used to cafés.')

- As you keep validating, look out for signs that your child is connecting with you. They may express their sorrow ('Mum, I feel awful that I tipped the plate onto you'). Rather than minimising the apology ('It's fine, it was nothing') acknowledge it: 'I get it, darling. You feel bad about it. It's not the kind of thing you want to be doing.' Then move on to a loving hug, and if necessary, some problem-solving for the future.

- On the other hand you child may be stuck in their shame, fearing that you judge them, that you will abandon them or punish them ('I'm a terrible person. You must hate me.') So make your unconditional love clear. This is about a behaviour, not about your child. ('I'm not blaming you. You were in fight-flight and we all know what that does to us poor humans. I want to support you to being well again so that eggs and cafés become easy. And so I can have a lovely time with you and don't spend the next hour in town with egg on my shirt.') You're expressing big needs… and a little humour can help too.

- If it seems useful and if your connection is back on line you can share more about your feelings and needs ('Yes I felt pretty shocked and upset because it's so not like you. And I really wanted you to manage this challenge so we can enjoy going out more. I know we'll get there.') This would be important if your child is very blinkered and cannot appreciate the effects of their actions.

- Our children are so sure that we blame them that it's worth checking they heard us right: 'I'm worried I didn't say that very well. Can you tell me back what you heard?'

- By now I expect your connection is good again. If you need to problem-solve, you can do so now. ('Next time we go to a café, how can we avoid this happening again?') Don't ask for promises that your child can't keep. The best any of us can do is promise to try!

Once more, be careful about any agreements you make as a result of this conversation. In the example above, your child might suggest that all would be much easier if you just didn't try any more cafés. Which is true, of course, in the short term. 'Hmm, yes that would be much easier. And at the same time that wouldn't help you move towards freedom, would it? What else might work?'

Your child might come up with a great proposal that surprises you, but what if she isn't able to engage much? You could take the lead: 'I think next time will be easier, but if – if – you're feeling quite so agitated again, how about you tell me in words? I don't mind if they're rude words, just use words, not actions, and that way other people in the restaurant won't even notice. How's that sound?… OK, I'm glad you're willing to give that a try. Let's do that for the next meal out, and then you can tell me if anything else would help you manage more easily.'

As usual, your child will find it a lot easier to agree to something if it's not for ever and is up for review.

15

HOW TO BUILD UP YOUR OWN RESILIENCE AND WELLBEING

This chapter is all about your wellbeing, your resilience, your strengths, so that you can cope right now and even flourish in the longer term. Whether you're getting ready to serve a meal or trying to cope with emotional exhaustion, you will find resources here, and nourishment for your soul.

Supporting a kid through an eating disorder is said to be a marathon, not a sprint. Many of us cower in fear of the next storm because we only barely have our heads above water. We say, 'I don't know how much more I can take.' We want stamina and endurance in order to keep going, and resilience so we can recover from knocks and move onwards and upwards with confidence.

I'm going to assume that you are now dealing with the day-to-day challenges of meals and that you have a tiny bit more time and energy to invest in your own mental wellbeing. If you've jumped straight to this chapter for emotional support and you have no idea what I mean by 'self-compassion', it might help to rewind to Chapter 13.

Developing resilience isn't just about making you feel well, though that would be a good enough reason. It's about being able to deal effectively with all the challenges you face at this difficult time – and that includes everyday things like your boiler breaking down and your aged aunt refusing to speak to you. If right now you believe your own wellbeing doesn't matter, it's still worth growing your emotional resources so that you can be in the best possible state for your child's sake.

Eating disorders often rob our children of internal resources: it's the people supporting them who open access to strength, hope, health and joy. That means mainly us, parents.

This doesn't mean you have to be happy all the time, and most of us have a lot of grieving to do. From online parents' groups it's evident that parents cry a lot, some have epiphanies after hitting rock bottom, and some have gradually grown stronger, wiser and more patient than ever before. It takes time to find our feet. It takes time to accept that our old coping mechanisms are not up to the job and to master a new set of tools.

As suffering is really not much fun, I hope that what follows will speed up your emotional journey a little.

NEW WAYS TO DEAL WITH ADVERSITY

When things were really bad, I woke every morning with a sense of dread, and my anxiety would peak before each meal. I was scared that my daughter might not eat, and I was scared of her outbursts. I desperately wanted to do a good job, to be calm and compassionate, and I did not want to react aggressively to any of her behaviours. I was frequently on the verge of tears, and on no account did I want to add to her burden by crying in front of her. I often felt I was in no fit state to support her.

My husband suffered as well. He got very weary of receiving hate day after day and he was affected by stress. But he remained functional and was able to soldier on irrespective of whether our daughter was managing meals or not. For a while he handled more than his fair share of mealtimes. This was OK: we were a team, using the abilities of each team member to the best effect. But I still had to find a way to cope on the days I was on my own, or when I wanted to give him a break. If you're a single parent and you have nobody to share some of this challenging journey with, I bet you really want to keep your emotions at a manageable level.

consistent
calm Compassionate
kind

... I WISH ....

INNER POWER
HOPE
SOLACE
SELF COMPASSION ♥
ACCEPTANCE
Letting go...

BUT HOW ?

It took me a long time to find my own way of coping, of dealing with this new thing life had thrown at us. When I found out how, I became the driver for the next stage of our journey because I knew that I could rock the boat and we would not drown.

The resources I found allowed me to be in touch with my emotions and still be effective. I believe this could help protect against exhaustion and even against post-traumatic stress disorder (PTSD).

ACCEPTANCE: WORK WITH REALITY, NOT AGAINST IT

> *"The other day I stood against my kitchen counter with my mind
> racing around the ideas that I couldn't handle this – I didn't have
> the strength – my panic level was rising. Then I said to myself,
> 'These thoughts aren't helpful'. I forced myself to stop thinking
> about my current fears and instead took the long view. I decided that
> all I could expect of myself was to do my best for my daughter at
> this moment. Even if my efforts didn't result in immediate
> perfection, I could expect change over days, weeks, month, years –
> whatever would be would be, as I gave my best in the moment. I felt
> instantly calmed and just proceeded."[396]*

Sometimes we access the power of acceptance after hitting rock bottom, but it's there for us at all times. I remember having a massive 'aha' moment when I understood how I could accept what is *and* be an agent of change.

I'd been struggling with a paradox. To get my little girl better treatment, to intervene on her behalf when things went wrong, to get her to eat in spite of her resistance, I had to be a fighter. But to retain the ability to fight – even to just function – I had to accept that things were as they were, to go with the flow, because I was on the verge of cracking up. If I accepted things and didn't fight for change, how would anything ever shift? Would we be stuck in a pitiful status quo for ever?

The tension between fight and flow lifted once I realised that acceptance is *not* apathy or resignation. It is not about abdicating, giving up, giving in, or being beaten. It is not about being passive or powerless, cowardly or weak – it actually gives you the drive to change things for the better. It is not about being indifferent or dispassionate – on the contrary it puts you in touch with what you really care about. And it is certainly not about giving our approval or endorsement to whatever is going on.

Acceptance is about accepting what is – taking stock of what is happening in the 'now' and accepting that it is our present-moment reality. Embracing our experience in the here and now. Another word for it is 'allowing'. When we allow this moment to be what it is, we stop fighting reality, we stop fighting others and we stop fighting ourselves. We step back, get a sense of perspective, and stop sweating the small stuff.

We choose life. We are *for* life, not *against* reality. This gives us drive and staying power for the things that we dearly care about.

I believe that in martial arts, power comes from going in the direction of the opponent's force, not from blocking it.

Let's be clear. Acceptance is a present-moment practice only. There is no future to accept, because it doesn't exist yet. Acceptance of the 'now' super-charges you to plan and act for a future that is meaningful to you.

What would happen if you planted a seed in a pot and partly covered it with a dish? If the seedling insisted that straight up was the only way, it would wither and die. It couldn't possibly lift the dish out of the way. For a seedling, resistance and fight is useless. Instead seedlings 'accept' that the obstacle is there and they search for life-giving light. A seedling will make its way along and around the dish, and eventually find the way out and up.

Remember the Serenity Prayer? 'Grant me the serenity to accept the things I cannot change, the courage to change the things I can, and the wisdom to know the difference.'

With acceptance we recognise our personal limits at any moment. We note aspects of our external and internal world that cannot presently be changed with willpower and that are beyond our control. For my own part, I found that accepting both my limitations and the grief this evoked made me more powerful.

It ... is ... so.

Acceptance makes sense when you're faced with unchangeable realities, such as being human, such as death or – if you're British – the weather. Acceptance also works when the obstacles in our way are presented by people. You can walk away or tell them to stop or you can try to change them, but this instant they are doing what they're doing, whether you like it or not. Having expectations of how people or the world *should* be leads to frustration and judgement, and you're less likely to take responsibility for steering your ship.

People are not billiard balls, yet they do have a tendency to follow Newton's Third Law: to every action there exists an equal and opposite reaction. Humans even take it a step further. Push me, and I will push you back even harder. This applies to our internal workings too. If we push against a part of ourselves we think shouldn't be there, it holds on to its right to exist.

On a good day, when my daughter yelled at me, I would soften into accepting that for reasons I could not fully understand, here she was, raising her voice and saying things I didn't like. When I allowed reality to be what it was, her words were more likely to wash over me, and my mind had space to work out the next step.

Now here's a paradox. With acceptance, you allow all of your present moment experience, including the parts that refuse to accept anything. Can you allow your resistance, your fury, your self-criticism, and everything about your present reaction that you don't like? Maybe you are trying hard to be an admirable person so your answer is 'No!' So now allow the 'No!' See? You can't go wrong with acceptance! What usually happens is that your resistance, when given permission to exist, transforms into something more flowing and more productive.

So when you notice thoughts that threaten to derail you – the 'What-ifs', the 'Why us?', the 'I'm not good enough' – invite yourself to allow them. Likewise with unpleasant feelings or sensations. Trust that if you don't fight them, you will better be able to withstand them and that they will pass. This frees you to focus on the task at hand.

Example: furious about your child's treatment

Let's take a situation many parents struggle with when they are appalled by the treatment their child is getting. How much energy do you want to put into fighting a therapist? Is it important for you to show that you are right and they are wrong? To prove to them how bad you think they are?

You cannot force acceptance, but you can invite it in, and the bridge from fury or victimhood to being resourceful is self-compassion. Remember Chapter 13 and the self-compassion in the café toilet after a terrible therapy session? It led to perspective and clarity about what to do next, and the energy and courage to do it.

Acceptance never implies approval or endorsement. In this example you might pull your child away from this therapist, or you might have an assertive discussion about the changes you want. If you reckon your child's treatment is harmful, it is very unlikely that acceptance will lead you to settle for the status quo.

Letting go of resistance

Another way of looking at acceptance is in terms of 'letting go'. You are letting go of your resistance to what is happening right now.

The opposite of letting go is hanging on, which you can only do for so long. Especially if you're hanging on by your fingernails. As an illustration of what letting go is like, fill up your lungs and hold your breath for as long as you can. While you're doing that, please subtract 72 from 13,287, and then subtract 72 from the result, and so on. I'm going to make myself a cup of tea, but keep going.

OK, you can breathe out now. Experience the relaxation and relief. How did the maths go? If it went well, you must be some genius when you're breathing normally.

Letting go helps you use more of your brain – the rational parts as well as the creative, intuitive ones.

Acceptance leads to creative solutions

For me the notion of acceptance and letting go was quite a revelation. Up to then I had met challenges with rigid determination – either with head-on resistance or fearful avoidance. Then one day when I was stuck and desperate I sat down with a good old cup of tea (the ultimate self-compassion tool) and experimented with accepting reality as it was. Tears flowed as I relinquished control. I expected to find peace of mind, and I did. But what surprised me was how ideas came bubbling up from nowhere.

Were all the ideas good? No way. Thank goodness for the rational mind and its ability to sort the wild and wacky from the useful. But some of them were exciting or nourishing and they opened up new avenues. One of those led to us finally getting meal coaching at home.

Here's a specific example of how acceptance leads to ideas. One dismal Thursday morning I got in touch with my fears about the upcoming weekend where I'd be alone with my daughter. She had more or less stopped eating. I was scared that I would get very depressed and lose my rag with her, which would make everything worse. Maybe she'd have to go back into hospital. As I allowed both my internal and external world to be what they were, I had a light bulb moment. I needed company! In a flash I pictured a small impromptu party, sprang out of bed and began inviting friends. I enjoyed the buzz of the preparations, I enjoyed the warmth, and the event helped me maintain a loving connection with my child.

It is far from conventional to throw a party when what most matters to you is for your starving child to eat, but in this instance I have no regrets, as it saved both of us from despair. She didn't suddenly eat well that weekend, but she did warm to life, and a day or two later things began to improve.

Letting go of a single strategy

There's another facet to letting go, and that's letting go of a particular version of the future you're attached to. When you're in a state of acceptance of the present, your mind becomes so vast that you may discover you've dropped your attachment to a particular way of doing things, a single solution to a problem, a particular path or strategy, a particular outcome. You lose any compulsion to control every detail of how things should go, you stop micro-managing.

Que sera, sera. You trust that life will unfold in a benevolent way, even though right now you may not grasp the details.

You can't force this letting go (your mind would just hang on tighter) but you can invite it in when you pause to give yourself compassion and take stock.

I want to be clear. You're not letting go of what matters to human beings – your needs, your values. Why would anyone do that? Treasure the bigger picture and keep the zest to make it happen. At the same time be open to the possibility it may not happen in quite the way you first planned.

Here's a prosaic example. Will my daughter get a well-paid secure job? That's an outcome I can easily let go of. It's only one strategy among many for something that actually matters to me – for her to enjoy a full and meaningful life. Going up the corporate ladder might be a very poor way of going about it. Life may bring her obstacles that turn out to be blessings, and her path to happiness will unfold in some other way.

We can say yes to life and let go of our attempts to control its flow. We can be open to the unknown. Instead of trying to row against the current – expending huge amounts of energy doing so, often at a cost and with little result – we can follow the flow of the river.

Can we still steer our canoe? Absolutely. Our values are our compass. Acceptance and letting go give us the mental space to keep making wise decisions. As you paddle you are bound to encounter rocks, so you'd best accept their presence and let go of your expectation that this journey will go in a straight line. As you take note of the obstacles, you can guide your canoe around them and maybe even enjoy the adventure.[397]

Sometimes I can't let go before I've considered my options. In this case I do a hypothetical letting go: for a few minutes I look at the world as if the path I am so attached to didn't exist. What would happen then? This gives me a chance to breathe into the things I fear, and to accept the things I cannot change. It makes space for a whole load of new possibilities, some of which may be a lot better than the strategy I was so set on. Or it may confirm that my initial path is the one I really want to go for, but I now do so with more clarity and peace of mind.

Now let's get real. I doubt we should be living in a constant state of letting go of strategies. Nothing much would get accomplished if we didn't stick to our better plans. To engage with life we need to get excited about particular objectives, to have goals and visions. There is a time to act with fire in your belly and a time to step back, let go and review. You can then adjust your course and follow it with renewed enthusiasm.

Example: acceptance and letting go at mealtimes

What might mealtimes look like when we use acceptance and letting go? If you try acceptance, will you get so laid back you'll stop caring and you'll let your child feed their dinner to the dog? For me, it worked the opposite way. A stance of acceptance freed up an abundance of internal resources and I grew to trust the process.

Initially, when I realised my daughter was losing weight, I fought for her to eat. I put all my will into it, and tensions rose as every small failure hurt. When I changed my stance to one of acceptance, I went on trying just as hard. I put just as much dedication into every meal. The only thing that changed was a readiness to accept whatever happened, including failure. Que sera, sera. So just before a meal, or during a meal, I often did mini letting-gos.

- I accepted that I was frightened. I allowed the uncomfortable feeling, and I found that my fear was manageable. This helped me be more present, kind and resourceful.

- I accepted that my child was in the state she was in, doing the things she was doing, saying the things she was saying, and this made me less judgemental. As a result tensions were more likely to recede and the meal was more likely to be a success.

- I accepted that she might not manage part or all of this meal. It was not in my power to control this particular outcome. I let go of my rigid expectations that nothing but success was acceptable. This made me less absorbed in catastrophic thoughts and I was more fully present to her. Of course I didn't tell her she might not manage – that would have been a self-fulfilling prophecy.

- I trusted that I would have the resources to handle whatever came up. This released me from fretting over every eventuality (such as, what if she ate the carrots but turned down the egg? What if she binned the food? What if she ran away?)

- When she reacted with hostility I accepted that this was so and I let go of thoughts that she should be different. Her reactions were not in my control, but I could choose at any moment how I would deal with them. As a result I did not suffer and panic as much, I did less retaliating and had greater access to my internal resources.

At the same time as I let go of how the meal should go, I focused on the bigger picture and on the things that were in my power. My intention was to do my best, moment by moment. To give my child my full loving presence. To trust that even if things didn't work out in this particular meal, good things would come eventually. To trust that my child had it in her to be well. A lot of work and a lot of love went into those meals. Acceptance is not laissez-faire.

When we let go of our attachment to a particular outcome, often that outcome is what we get. Other times we may get something different that is at least as good. When I let go of the idea that I *had* to get my daughter to eat everything, I was able to work harder at it and more intelligently, and on the whole she managed. And when a meal looked like a fail, often it set the scene for a leap forward soon after.

Acceptance and letting go does not guarantee success with any particular meal. As loving parents, it can be painful to consider letting go of outcomes, to accept that some things are not in our control. We want to wave a magic wand and make everything be OK. Yet our kids have an illness that makes certain behaviours incredibly difficult to change Getting them to eat or to stop exercising is not entirely within our power. In addition to that, we as parents are on a learning curve. We have limitations as well. So we do the best we can with the cards in our hand. We give our children the best of ourselves and let love be our compass.

TRUST THAT YOU HAVE RESOURCES

In order to accept and let go, you may need to make a leap of faith. I don't mean positive thinking or telling yourself that everything will turn out for the best. I'm talking about internal resources. You may need to trust:

- that you have the resources to deal with whatever life throws at you
- that if it seems the resources are not there, they will grow as and when you need them

We get access to deep resources by letting go, so annoyingly, it's a bit of a chicken and egg thing. Which I reckon is why many of us remember finding strength the day we hit rock bottom and surrendered.

Some say that what doesn't kill you makes you stronger. Some talk of how grit in the oyster produces a pearl. Yes, hardships often lead to wisdom, but unless you have a crystal ball, there are no cast-iron certainties. A big resilience tool is to trust that, whatever hard knocks life serves you in the days or years ahead, you will have access to the resources you need.

The difference between the oak tree and the reed has inspired a number of fables. Trees may stand solid and immutable, but after a storm my local park looks like a battlefield of broken trunks and limbs. Reeds, on the other hand, bend but do not break. Instead of resisting the gale, they flex with it. They might get flattened against the ground, but they straighten up again when the storm has passed.

Honestly, being a city girl, I don't know if the above is strictly true, but can we agree on it at a symbolic level? I like to think that human beings are reed-like. We all have it in us to stand tall again.

I wonder if the worst stage, the one that feels almost unbearable, is the stage when we are holding tight to the burning ship and sinking with it. I imagine that the

'40 days in the desert' theme, which crops up in a variety of spiritual stories, reflects how hardship and despair can lead to epiphany.

But it doesn't have to be so hard. We can speed up our access to resources by letting go of resistance, letting go of hyper-vigilance.

What kind of resources am I talking about? Physical strength and energy, courage, resilience, creativity, problem solving, vision, wisdom, compassion and humanity. In my case, what I most needed at the worst of times was to trust that I could bear distress and that I would remain sane.

Over the years your body and brain have built a treasure trove of skills and capabilities, and I assume you were born with a fair amount of them as well. Only a small part of the brain is used for conscious thought and deliberate action. If you enjoy creative or scientific work, you will know that insights come when your attention is elsewhere, when you've let go of deliberate effort.

I find it humbling – given the amount of formal education I've slogged through and how enamoured I am with rational thought – that much of our internal wealth is not available to the conscious mind. Rational thinking doesn't resolve emotional upheavals, nor does it lead to a sense of peace or internal power.

If it is too big a step for you to trust in the resources that are not accessible to your mind, you may relate to this analogy. Have you noticed how letting go gives you access to physical skills? If you excel at a sport or at playing a musical instrument, you probably know that to perform at your best you relinquish conscious control and trust the process. Remember what it's like to learn a new skill, like skiing or rollerblading? For me, it starts with holding myself stiffly, ready to guard against a fall. I wilfully control every movement, making it impossible for my body's natural balance to do its job. My focus on deliberate control can protect me from a serious tumble, but it will never give me speed and ease. In order to become proficient, I eventually need to let go of my protective stance and ask my controlling mind to take a back seat.

Or I need to trust that if I do fall, that's OK.

You know the move in rock 'n' roll dancing, where the girl falls backwards and just before she hits the floor, the boy supposedly catches her and throws her back up? I've done that move. Letting go of the vertical takes trust, but I had a great partner.[398] During one practice session, I dropped backwards as usual, and next thing I knew, I was flat on my back, on the floor. My partner was looking the other way, laboriously unwrapping a chocolate bar. Did that teach me never to trust him again? No, it taught me that if I fall when I am totally relaxed, there is no pain and no injury. In other words, it taught me to trust the process of letting go.

Our body also provides us with biological and neurological resources. Before you had a child, did you ever think you'd be able to change a smelly nappy, or get up six times in a night to clean up vomit and nurse your baby back to sleep? Personally I was certain I couldn't possibly function without nine hours of uninterrupted shuteye. Yet the super-human ability to do night feeds came to me.

How about when we are faced with sudden and extreme danger? I love how adrenalin kicks in in a split second, allowing us to access extraordinary speed and strength just when we need it. Nature is in no way perfect, but it does seem to provide us with tools to help us care for ourselves.

Resources are not only internal. A crisis can drive us to muster external resources. We seek out information, expertise and support from others. We find ways of paying for expert help. We get wonderful people on board. We tap into the wealth of human beings' interdependence.

We readjust and grow

It can take a massive leap of faith to believe that we can survive one storm after another.

Near my house, on a slope exposed to high winds, stands a magnificent tree. Its branches curve gracefully in one direction, reminding me of a Japanese flower arrangement. Being subjected to the rigours of the weather has not stopped this tree from thriving. You might argue that it ought to be symmetrical. Yet trees in more sheltered areas have snapped in storms, while this one still stands.

Now, I'm not saying you need to be battered by gales to become strong. There are many trees in my area that have conventional shapes, and they also withstand storms. I don't believe the universe sends us challenges to make us more enlightened, and I don't believe that we've been chosen to carry the heaviest burdens because we're special humans. I have no explanations.

The randomness and unpredictability of life can be frightening. Yet I notice that much of the time, we humans pull through. We manage to change our outlook, to live differently, to find a new kind of wellness and meaning. There must be a combination of factors (from our genes, our past, our support system and access to resources) that make different people react differently to adversity. I sense that acceptance and letting go, while nurturing a sense of what's precious, are part of it.[399]

The fear of losing one's mind

When things were tough for me I reckoned my biggest fears, in a vague, confused kind of way, were to lose myself, fall apart, crack up. I knew that it's common for parents in my situation to seek a little help from medication, and my mind blew this out of proportion. Because I was ill-informed and prejudiced against psychiatric drugs, I imagined there was no help out there beyond what I could do for myself. I told myself I had to hang on to my sanity or I'd become completely incapacitated.

If you're like me, it may be worth looking such fears in the eye. What's the worst that could happen? Depression, anxiety, aggressive or suicidal impulses? When you're ready, you might want to relax into an acceptance that all these things are possibilities. Stressors might indeed be too great for you, or the grip of the eating disorder on your child may be too strong. You may not be able to hold on to the kind of person you want to be. And just as you allow yourself to be in touch with your vulnerability, and accept that there may be some things you cannot change, you might become aware of quite how much you want to be strong and competent for the sake of yourself and of your family. See if a sense of strength bubbles up inside you: it's probably there, carrying you along even when you don't notice it.

After acceptance, resources may reveal themselves. People with depression or anxiety get psychological help or medication and they continue to function. For me, the fear of cracking up became an excellent motivator to seek out psychological support, even though the cost made my eyes water. The stress was a reality. I had to be well and take good care of myself. I also accepted that if I did become incapacitated by mental illness, that would go in the category of things I did not have the power to change.

Another major fear of mine, at one stage, was that I would not be able to bear the future if it brought more pain. What if things got a lot worse? I didn't know if I could endure a repeat of past events. I had to trust that, just as I was able to deal – well enough – with present stresses, I would deal with the future as it came. I had to trust that human beings are resilient.

I relinquished my mental model that resources are finite. I think I imagined 'coping' as a fixed quantity of coins in a medium-sized jar. I imagined there is only so much a human being can bear: too much hardship, and they go mad. Now, I believe that resources are continuously being created, and the more we're aware of how much we need them, the better they show up. Neuroscientists talk of brain plasticity. The brain learns and creates new connections throughout our lives. It doesn't matter if, like me, you're hardly a spring chicken.

Looking back, I believe I accessed resources I didn't know I had whenever I took the time to sit down, accept what was, and let go of resistance. The greater the impasse I was in, the greater the insights I got as I made peace with the world.

As we'll see later, post-traumatic growth – as opposed to post-traumatic stress disorder – is more likely among people who have experienced not just one, but several awful events. I wonder if by surviving one devastating experience, we learn, at a very deep level, to trust that resources are there when we need them. Perhaps this trust sustains us through the next challenges. It's also possible that hardships expose the limitations of our current coping strategies. We are forced to discover more effective ways of dealing with challenges in order to survive and live well. These may serve us well for years, until the next major challenge.

Some of us do crack up and disconnect from life in some way. Human beings are vulnerable, just like everything else in nature. We can only do our best to be well and to be effective. I am suggesting that mindfulness, acceptance, and letting go give us access to our best shot at doing just that.

THE BODY DRIVES THE MIND: RELAXED AND ALERT

Given that our minds and bodies are linked, you can help your mind by making your body mimic the state you'd like it to be in. You want to have acceptance, kindness, alertness? Do it with your body.

You can bring your awareness to your feet, feeling grounded and stable. You can claim your space in the world, holding your head up high and allowing your chest to expand. You are kick-starting a virtuous circle by 'tricking' your brain into believing all is well. More importantly, you're accessing the greater you – the you that has access to resources, that will care for the you that right now, is doing all the practical work and is struggling. By adopting a posture of stability, you are giving yourself a strong, compassionate presence.

If you've only got a second and you're in the middle of a stressful situation, see if you get a good enough improvement of your wellbeing by relaxing just one part of your body. You could let go of tension in your jaw, your hands, or your shoulders. You could soften your eyes. You could send all your fear and anger into your big toe. You could see what a slight smile feels like.

Do you already have a gesture your brain associates with self-connection? I often place my hand on my heart when I am at peace and grateful, and so this gesture has become an anchor, a trigger, which I can inconspicuously use any time, any place to feel more relaxed by a notch or two.[400]

And then, of course, there's breathing. Deep breathing, from the belly rather than from the chest. Let go of tensions with your out-breath. Your brain will get the message that there is no danger and its fight-or-flight response will die down.

IMAGERY TO HELP YOU GET GROUNDED AND PEACEFUL

You can combine breathing with some imagery. To help yourself reach a state of compassion, imagine that the air you breathe in soothes and softens your heart. Or visualise calm and beauty permeating your being. Then breathe out kindness into the world, or enjoy a sense of acceptance and letting go.

Here's a visualisation which I have adapted from Daniel Siegel's book *Mindsight*. Imagine your mind as a deep ocean. The surface is choppy, and sometimes it's positively wild. That's you when you're consumed by your thoughts, feelings or memories, and it's perfectly normal. And at the same time, you're a lot more than that. You're the whole, vast, stable ocean, a place that's rich in resources and that's connected to everything. Deep in the ocean, under the surface, it's calm. Your nervous system gets the message that you're safe. You can observe what's going on at the surface with serenity. Just notice. Things are clear from this place. An idea might pop up. Notice it (in my case, I have pen and paper handy to avoid the worry that I'll forget it). You can evaluate the idea later, but for now just observe that you had an idea. An emotion might wash over you. Notice where it lives in your body and allow it to be there. Tears might come. Let them flow. A wave of anger or fear may rise and crash. Your heart rate may suddenly accelerate. Observe with infinite kindness. From this place you don't need to do anything.

If water isn't your thing, you might prefer using the sky as a metaphor. You are the vastness of the sky. You have light, warmth, clarity, perspective. Clouds or flocks of birds create agitation, then they pass. Or back to the image of the airplane ride, you can experience the world from above the foggy band of cloud.

Here's another piece of imagery. You're in a cinema watching a film of what's happening to you right now. The 'you' in the film is having lots of adventures and is frequently overwhelmed with thoughts and feelings. But at any time it can step out of the screen and take a cosy seat at the back of the cinema, where the sound is turned down and everything is peaceful. It can sit back and just watch and send the 'you' in the film your compassion.

You might enjoy using imagery to get a sense of being grounded, stable, fully in your body. For me being grounded is about feeling the solid ground under my feet as well as lightness. I feel myself growing tall. You may relate to the imagery of a being a tree or a plant. You might picture yourself as a graceful reed that bends and sways but always returns, unbroken, to the vertical. Or you might want to be a solid oak that remains stable as stormy winds lash at its branches and that soaks up the warm energy of the sun as its branches reach to the sky.

Some people relate well to these images of being grounded, while others prefer the concept of being centred. You might relate to Daniel Siegel's wheel of awareness. Place yourself at the hub, right in the centre. From there you can choose to follow spokes to any part of the rim – you can choose what to place your attention on. On the rim you'll find thoughts and feelings, as well sights and sounds and smells. You'll find internal sensations and an awareness of the vastness of the external world. From the hub, you can choose to observe whatever arises on the rim. The hub is a place of deep inner peace from which you can approach all these aspects of life.

You can create your own imagery or metaphors. A friend of mine conjures up the image of a turtle when she needs to feel calm, patient and empowered.

> *"I was driving the car with my distressed child having a meltdown next to me, thinking, 'This is dangerous; I have to find a way to stay calm.' I imagined myself as a turtle. I am at least 200 years old. I have a hard, protective shell and thick skin. I am safe. I am patient. I can hold my head up high because if my child has a blow-up and I am suddenly scared, I can dive into my safe shell and come back out a moment later. It is even OK to smile a bit ... It really worked. I felt calm and immediately my child calmed down as well."*

Your favourite imagery might help soothe you a little, but not as much as you would like. Your nervous system may have good reasons to stay on the alert – during a difficult meal for example. We can act in spite of unpleasant feelings because – as long as we allow them with compassion –they're not dangerous. Feel the fear (with kindness) and do it anyway.

MINDFULNESS

Placing yourself at the centre of a wheel of awareness is an example of mindfulness, an ancient Eastern practice that is now embraced by psychotherapists. With mindfulness, you intentionally pay attention to your moment to moment experience, without judgement. More than that – and this is often forgotten – you do so with a compassionate and open heart. I think it is rash to expose yourself to difficult thoughts or emotions unless you also give yourself – or receive – kindness.

With mindfulness you bring your presence to what you're experiencing while you're experiencing it. You are stepping outside of your mind and into your body, taking a meta-perspective of what's going on internally: your thoughts, feelings and physical sensations. Mindfulness tends to quieten

CHATTERBOX

the mind and make space for your greater self, because as soon as you become aware of chatterbox thoughts, you're not so busy thinking them. The point of mindfulness is to be fully yourself in everyday life, connected to yourself and to the world around you.

Earlier I told you about the concept of acceptance, and in Chapter 13 I described self-compassion. Acceptance, self-compassion, giving your child your compassionate presence, all involve mindfulness.

The more you use opportunities to be mindful, the more your brain creates new connections and new growth, making it more and more your natural way of being.[401] If you practice being mindful during activities you enjoy, not only are you training your brain, but you're bringing stress hormones down, enhancing feel-good neurotransmitters and generally filling up your tank of wellbeing. For me this happens with music and dance. You can also train your mindfulness muscle by spending regular time in sitting meditation. There are many ways to meditate – focusing on the breath is only one of them (but remember to bring in the kindness element!). You can find courses and recordings to guide you through mindfulness, relaxation and compassion.

As this dad explains:

> *"The one thing I have done consistently over the years that has benefited me by far the most is a daily meditation practice. One of the side effects of meditation for me is seeing 'thoughts as thoughts'. Thoughts weigh nothing ... So ... I recommend meditation, even if it is just five minutes in the morning. Sitting, eyes closed, counting breaths – that's it."*[402]

More on my website:

Help with compassion, self-compassion, and sleep[403]

'OK': two letters for two steps to mindfulness and compassion[404]

Compassion meditation audio guides[405]

GOOD-ENOUGH ZEN

I used to think that through relaxation and mindfulness I could approach a meal in a totally Zen state. I used to think that this was an imperative. That I *should* get myself in a calm and benevolent frame of mind to guard against screwing up the next lunch. Well, it can be pretty stressful trying to reach a perfect level of calm six times a day when every fibre in your body is telling you that things are going to be a little bit tough. In short I would approach meals with some trepidation, aware that I wasn't quite ready for whatever would be thrown at me.

Then I got an excellent tip, which may help you too. Notice small improvements in your own state. And notice that they're good enough. Good enough for you to do what needs to be done.

I noticed that one deep breath made me let go of a small amount of tension. Or that placing my hand on my heart brought me a little closer to my resourceful self.

Or that imagining my daughter's hand in mine made me smile just a tiny bit. Or that smelling the flowers on the table made me a smidgen more trusting of the world. Small improvements are easy to create, and they may be all you need to help you through the next few minutes, or even the entire meal.

It's exactly the same with our children. They don't need to be calm and composed to manage a meal. All they need is a little something to reduce some of their tension.

Anxiety isn't a reason not to do things. You only need to reduce stress levels by a micro-unit to tackle the next micro-task. Sure, it's harmful to live with constant anxiety, but that's going to be taken care of step by step. Each time your child manages to eat, her anxiety goes down, and so does yours. With time, repetition and compassion, things will become easier.

COPING IN THE MOMENT

Feelings are in-the-moment things. In Chapter 13 I described them as waves that rise and subside. They pass. They transform into something else. Your emotions may be at rock bottom now but there is no way of predicting how they will be in ten minutes or in ten days. These days, the only certainty I have about my emotions is that they come and go, and the less I get them tangled up with my thoughts, the more likely they will move on.

When I realised that I was stressing out about the next year, the next week, or even the next hour, I decided to notice how, moment by moment, I was coping. The moment might need to be subdivided into units of milliseconds, so that I could tell myself, 'Right now, this instant, I'm actually fine.'

You could notice that the only reality is the present moment. This instant. This instant in which you are living and breathing and in which the ground is under your feet. The past is gone; the future doesn't yet exist.

I decided that if I could be fine in the present, even when things were horribly tough, I could trust I would most likely also be fine in future, present moments.

I wonder if you've ever done this with physical pain. You've bitten through a chunk of your tongue and it's hurting like hell, but just now, this second, it's bearable. And this second is OK too. And this next second. And you might even start noticing that the pain subsides, because it's not aggravated by catastrophic thoughts.

Noticing that we are coping in the moment allows us to deal with our fears one step at a time. I love this sentence from the excellent book *Parenting Your Anxious Child with Mindfulness and Acceptance* by Christopher McCurry:[406]

> *"Sometimes all we need is just a glimpse of where to go and what to do, and we can take the next step – and then the next and then the next."*

BEING IN THE MOMENT

Once I'd noticed I could cope 'in the moment', I saw the benefits of being 'in the moment' whenever I could think of it. It helped me get less entangled in judgemental or fearful thoughts. Does present-moment mindfulness mean you can't recall past events and plan the next activity? No. It means you are present to your experience, as you recall or plan. As you plan an event for tomorrow, your present-moment mindfulness brings you to notice any happy or tense reactions. You'll notice how by pausing, with kindness, tension moves on (and if it doesn't you'll plan to give it more care). Being in the 'now'[407] is part of compassion, and it fosters acceptance and trust. You may notice how perfectly fine things are in the now. You may even relish, at times, how much you're enjoying yourself.

TURN THOUGHTS AROUND: 'IS IT TRUE?'

When times were hard I got worn down with catastrophising, fearful, self-pitying or judgemental thoughts. Self-compassion (as described in Chapter 13) is the best way I know of moving on. You might also enjoy Byron Katie's method, called, 'The Work', as it's similar and supported by numerous books and videos.[408] One thing they tend not to say, which I think is crucial, is to treat yourself with infinite kindness throughout the process. You start by pinning down one of the thoughts swirling round your head and question it ('is it true?'). From here on, use your internal world more than your intellect. Bring your presence to the effect the thought has on you when you believe it. Questions like 'who would you be without the thought?' and invitations to 'turn the thought around' can get you out of a rut and bring out your internal power.

WHAT TO DO WITH FEAR

When a child has an eating disorder, we parents can be overcome by fear. We become paralysed or we thrash about blindly, neither of which is helpful to our kid. The trick is to notice the fear and allow it to be there. We can ask ourselves, 'What are you trying not to feel? What are you protecting yourself from feeling?' Allowing an unpleasant emotion, paradoxically, usually makes it go away or at least diminish. If it remains at it is, we can act effectively in spite of it.

CHATTERBOX

Fear is tied up with horrible stories from our chatterbox. They may turn out to be true, or they might not. We don't know. Who knows what life will bring? Reality is right here, in this present instant.

You may be able to attach a probability to this thing you fear. That requires logical thinking, and in order to be rational you need to move out of your state of fear into a state of compassion. We saw in Chapter 13 how to do that.

It can be liberating to acknowledge a fear. Blinkers on a horse are only useful if the horse is to follow a path determined by the rider. If you're on a ghost train, it's OK to keep your eyes shut tight – your carriage will follow the rails to the exit. But in life we want to make choices and act wisely. It helps to take in the whole picture, which includes looking danger in the eye.

Our fears are usually about a number of things that might not happen the way we want. Paradoxically, to be courageous and determined, it helps to accept that in spite of our best efforts, some things are not in our control. Uncertainty is the elephant in the room and it can be freeing to acknowledge it.

I became more effective once I had acknowledged a whole lot of thoughts that were knocking on the door of my consciousness. My daughter might not manage a meal. She might have to go into hospital. She might have to be tube-fed. She might take for ever to recover. I even allowed myself to acknowledge what I feared most: that she would die.[409]

I didn't invite all these horrible thoughts. I didn't sit there and create them. They were there anyway, nagging at me, sucking away my energy. Once I had acknowledged them, I was able to recognise them and name them whenever they popped up. I could not know if these thoughts would turn out to be true or not. My only certainty was that right now, in the present instant, things were OK. And that my experience was that resources had always turned up in times of need. My fears, which had been shape-shifting demons, transformed into tame animals. They didn't get in my way quite as much.

Recognising your fears does not mean creating a detailed movie of your worst case scenario. You could traumatise yourself over something that is unlikely to happen. If it did happen, you would be in a totally different place, with access to resources you cannot even begin to imagine. So stay in the present moment. If a horrible though comes and your belly contracts, recognise the thought, keep it at arm's length, and spend a little time being kind to yourself for the uncomfortable sensations in your belly.

Rather than stepping right in the middle of a fearful physical sensation, you can choose to bring your focus to the edge of it, staying on the outskirts. That way you have recognised that something is up that deserves your kindness. That can be just as effective a route to self-connection.

Giving yourself self-compassion for your fears is something you can do in the moment, or if that's not possible, you can promise yourself to make time for it later. For instance, when my daughter refused a dessert or threw me an insult, emergency self-compassion might do the trick (notice my fearful reaction, sense it in my body, and let it move on). But for the big things, the really scary ones, I found that I needed to put some time aside, alone. And we shouldn't and can't do all the hard stuff alone: that's what kind friends and therapists are for. Our nervous system needs connection.

When I was distressed, I waited till I had the house to myself, and then I sat in my rocking chair, closed my eyes, took the time to breathe and be present. Rather than contracting away from the fears that sprung up, I tried to relax into them, to feel them in my body. Yes, quite often that would bring tears, but that was OK. For every catastrophic thought that came up, I breathed, and I thought 'acceptance'. 'What will be will be.' Or when I was feeling extra philosophical, 'Shit happens.'

In this setting, the crying was about grieving more than about despair, about letting go instead of clinging. Sometimes I found myself shuddering a little as if the fear was finally doing what it was supposed to do and moving on. For me that was usually a sign that this particular issue would cease to cause me so much turmoil.

Usually the acceptance and letting go would make room for my mind to savour the things that most mattered to me. I'd tap into the tremendous energy of my love for my kid, the visions I had for her future, the trust that I had the power to change some things, and that whenever the opportunity arose I would be ready.

Trauma and overwhelming fear

Don't force yourself to meditate, or to go deep into self-connection, if it brings up fears that are just too scary. It's counter-productive. Some things in life require hand-holding. Meanwhile, distraction is your friend.

A number of parents suspect they suffer from post-traumatic stress disorder (PTSD). Even without it, it would be normal that some places in your mind are no-go areas – areas of trauma with a small 't'. It may seem like there are demons which, if you looked at them for too long, would turn you to stone. It's as though our mind has stationed a security guard in front of painful past situations that haven't had a peaceful resolution. The guard disables part of our brain so that we feel nothing, we freeze, we dissociate and feel numb, we go blank or foggy. Or the guard alerts the brain that a big fight reaction is called for. It feels safer to be angry than to feel fear.

All this to say that if you notice that you are getting unusually overwhelmed by an emotion, or that you have gone into some hazy dreamlike trance, it would be wise to get the support of a therapist specialising in trauma. If you get an unwelcome reaction while you are connecting with a fear, just open your eyes and connect with your senses to the outside world. Count things you see, name things you hear, describe their texture, hum a song. (There's guidance on panic attacks in Chapter 12).

More on my website: Three routes out of post-traumatic stress disorder (PTSD)

POST-TRAUMATIC STRESS OR POST-TRAUMATIC GROWTH?

It is not uncommon for parents of kids with an eating-disorder to suffer from some kind of backlash, possibly as serious as post-traumatic stress disorder, after their child's condition improves. It's by no means a general rule, but it happens. I was lucky: I did a lot of falling apart while my daughter was ill, and then felt increasingly well. But some parents end up more traumatised than their kids, something that has been observed in families where a child has recovered from cancer.

> "After my husband and I finally got our daughter to a safe stage in recovery, our bodies decided to sort of collapse on us. I kept catching bugs/viruses that went on for ages. I think our bodies know when the ED emergency is over, and then they crash! Anyway, now I'm well again."[410]

It can be scary for us parents to notice how anxious or depressed we feel and to think that this may stay with us for ever.

"It does get better, in fact it was surprising to me that I had to think hard to remember some of the things that happened, although at the time it felt like we would never get through them or forget them."

It may help you to know that PTSD is by no means inevitable and is not linked to the severity of the trauma. Martin Seligman, in his book *Flourish*, discusses survivors of traumas, in particular war veterans. In spite of what the media would have us believe, he points out that PTSD is relatively uncommon.[411] Most people return to their previous level of functioning after a brief period of depression and anxiety.

More excitingly, there is such a thing as post-traumatic growth. Seligman notes that after events producing intense depression and anxiety, a substantial number of people become not only resilient, but better than ever. Seligman gave questionnaires to 1,700 people who had suffered torture, grave illness, death of a child, rape, imprisonment and other awful events. These people had more strengths and greater wellbeing than people who had not experienced major stressors.

I can relate to that. I had months of feeling like I was cracking up while my daughter was in hospital. I carried dark glasses everywhere because I never knew when I might burst into tears. I frequently fantasised about smashing the car into a wall and feared that one day I might do so involuntarily. But I also knew that I had good reason to be distressed.

Whereas in the past I might have been ashamed of feeling low, this time I believed that my reaction was entirely normal. I sought support, learned tools and I changed. Even before my daughter began to recover, I was becoming stronger, more resourceful, more energetic than I'd ever been. When she relapsed I was also supporting my mother, who required a lot of attention because of Alzheimer's disease. The dark glasses came back out at times. But after each difficult episode I returned to wellbeing. As I edit this chapter, my daughter is well, my mother's Alzheimer has turned her into a contented Buddha, and I experience very few stressors. I live with a huge level of happiness and gratitude, way more than before our anorexia ordeals. What I'm trying to tell you is that it is possible to feel well, at times very, very well, even while your child is ill, and it's likely that once most things become easier, you will enjoy and trust life more than ever.

I hope I don't sound smug. I know I could well have continued down the tears-and-dark-glasses route, if it hadn't been for the help of some remarkable books and people. Nobody should be shamed or blamed for suffering from PTSD, depression or anxiety. Just like your child didn't choose to get an eating disorder, you didn't choose to fall apart when the stresses became too great.

If I talk of post-traumatic growth, it is not to make you out to be a failure if you're suffering right now, but to give you a vision of what may be possible.

I certainly don't feel smug when I wonder what other challenges life may bring me. How would I cope if I was faced with another relapse in my daughter's illness, combined, say, with bereavement or cancer? It happens. There are parents who are going through cancer treatment while also supporting their child through an eating disorder. I take heart from Seligman's observation that of the 1,700 people he surveyed, those who had experienced two awful events had greater strengths then people who had experienced 'only' one. And the poor bastards who had experienced three awful events fared even better. Go figure!

My intention is to give you hope for yourself and for your child. Hardships, I imagine, give us little choice but to upskill, to grow new resources that lead us to cope with bad times and live more fully in when life is sweet.

It seems that there is a strong genetic component to our wellbeing – our baseline happiness level. Yet research indicates we can flourish beyond that.[412] Our daughter's illness forced me to make use of new tools, over and over again, and I believe that's why my baseline happiness level is now way higher than it was pre-illness. I hope this will be your experience as well.

More: my YouTube video: The hero's journey[413]

MISTAKES, BLAME AND SELF-ACCEPTANCE

Judgement, from others or from ourselves, is really worth dealing with because it is quite toxic and drains you of the energy you need to be effective. It's hard for you to be present to your child if you are burdened by guilt and self-blame. Just as he needs uncritical acceptance, so do you.

Regrets: a powerful alternative to shame or guilt

A common thought that eats away at parents is, 'I should have caught the eating-disorder earlier,' or, 'If only I'd acted faster, I could have got my kid treatment before she got so stuck.'

This may be true. The earlier we take effective action to treat an eating-disorder, the faster the improvements. There are things that help recovery, and things that hinder, and most of us have done some of both. There are real, objective reasons for regret.

Differentiate these facts from the chatterbox judgements. Regret is quite different from shame or guilt. 'I should have …' is hurtful and strips you of your power. It can make you resent others who enjoyed faster successes. 'I so wish I had known …' is far more rooted in the present and can give you energy for action.

I regret and I am sad that it took us a year to find our feet and really help our daughter. I don't blame myself for it, because I know that throughout this journey I've been driven by a need for my daughter to be well. But do I wish I'd had better information sooner and more tools at my disposal? Yes. And of course this has motivated my desire to write for you.

> *"As a father, my mind is awash with the 'WHAT IF's'. I don't overly think on these or get caught up with them but they just wash in and out now and again."*

The way forward, as always, is self-compassion. Connect with needs, accept and let go. It's a form of grieving. Mourning the lost opportunities, mourning our limitations.

Regret your behaviour, love yourself

As you support your child through this illness you should expect to 'fail' and make 'mistakes', time and again. Expect to say terrible things, to shout, to cry. Even if you've got that mostly sorted out, you might still struggle with a tendency to give off passive-aggressive messages. I hate every shrug, every raised eyebrow, every frown that I directed at my daughter. And if I saw you shouting at your child over her bowl of muesli, I would hate that. What I'm hating is the behaviour. I do not hate myself, and I certainly don't hate you. I am what I am, and you are what you are. Acceptance isn't the same as complacency.

It is probably impossible to accept others, and in particular your child, if you are not living and breathing self-compassion. If you want to be present to others, it's necessary to accept yourself, what you did, and what you didn't do.

Accepting ourselves makes space in our minds and brings out the best in us. It's an essential step to gaining the self-mastery we wish for. Without self-acceptance, we can get worn out trying to do everything absolutely right.

If you're struggling to accept yourself, spend some time reconnecting with your needs and values. Perhaps you're finding your 'failures' incredibly sad and frustrating, because you're on a mission not just to feed, but to build the type of connection that will support your child's recovery. You may have a sense that the stakes are high and that you have no time to lose. Close your eyes and spend some time with the things that really matter to you. Move away from the details of what happened and tune into what you dearly want. Notice also the many ways in which you're succeeding – perhaps you take them for granted, but they are precious to your child. This self-compassion process may give you the healing you need and the drive to move on.

There are other tools that may help you. One approach using Nonviolent Communication is to get two conflicting parts of your mind to talk to each other. There's the part that hates what you did, and the part that did what you did.[414]

You could also use Byron Katie's steps in *The Work* (as mentioned above) making sure you do so with self-kindness. Or you could meditate on how what you did was good enough. You could meditate on how everything you do, you do to the best of your abilities within the resources at your disposal. And you could get real about the mistakes you've made because, as I will show you soon, mistakes are not the end of the world.

Letting go of self-judgement is not a cop-out. It's not about justifying yourself or absolving yourself of responsibility. It's not about doing nothing. It's about taking stock of where you are right now in the present so that you can take effective action in tune with your deepest values.

If you got lost on a country road, would you step out of the car and throw yourself in a thorny hedge, berating yourself for every wrong turn you took? I hope you'd work out where you are now, remind yourself of your destination, and plan a new route to get there.

Just as unconditional love for your child doesn't mean permissiveness, unconditional love for yourself doesn't mean you give up on yourself. You tune into what matters to you and go for it.

Your brain reacts to threat – live with it

The emotions around this illness are incredibly challenging. When we dwell on the what-ifs regarding our child's wellbeing, we can be overwhelmed by fear. The stakes seem high and naturally we want to do our best. Let's remember that as much as we would like God-like abilities to make our child well, some things belong to the 'shit happens' pile.

We're also dealing with challenging levels of abuse. Our children's accusations, contorted facial expressions, gestures and tone of voice are all signals of danger to our nervous system. That momentarily deprives us of our equanimity. I would be amazed if a Buddhist monk could consistently remain supportive, meal after meal, if it was their child sitting at the table fighting every mouthful.

We mean to do our best, and we're only human. During one of the updates to this book, I was supporting my daughter through a relapse. Despite my knowledge and experience, and my desire to act wisely, I was making several mistakes a day.

Yet, even as I accepted my brain's limitations, I was not giving up on what mattered to me – to help my daughter to the best of my ability. It has been my guiding light. Everything I do, including my 'mistakes', has helped me build resources towards that aim.

Mistakes can turn out fine

Remember that with an eating disorder, the feedback we receive is appallingly unreliable. We can congratulate ourselves that dinner went well, only to discover the reason our child was so relaxed is she skipped lunch. We can regret our part in causing her violent outburst and later learn her decision to fight this meal was made hours earlier – perhaps she wanted a flat tummy for a party that evening, or perhaps she was dieting ahead of a meal out with friends. And we can think we've made a mistake, and three days or three months later, learn that what we did was actually spot on.

I would sometimes beat myself up for having challenged my daughter with a food that was too difficult for her. I'd be full of regrets that a meal had ended in failure. Seeing old symptoms resurface, I believed I'd caused a setback. Yet often the story did not end there. The following day she might cope extremely well with the same food and be all smiles and self-confidence. A new milestone had been reached.

So while there are some things that clearly you don't want to do again, don't be too hasty in labelling your actions as mistakes.

What about mistakes you really regret? There's a saying in the world of eating disorders: 'Every mistake is a treasure.' [415] We cannot learn everything from books or the instructions of therapists, and our job as parents requires us to keep learning and daring. Some things we need to experience over and over again until we learn and develop the necessary skills. Each time you do something you regret, your brain has a chance to integrate better ways for next time a similar situation presents itself.

You might notice that you have some fear around the consequences of your mistakes. Yet I bet that for every child who has recovered from an eating-disorder, there is a parent who, like me, has made hundreds, thousands, of mistakes.

Mistakes can serve as an opportunity to build connection, depending on how you talk about them and mend the relationship afterwards. Your child learns and heals from what you model. While she has an eating disorder her life is full of shame and regret. If she can see how you too stumble and recover, she may learn wisdoms beyond what you could teach with words.

Do you compare yourself to others or do you use their help?

Accepting ourselves also means accepting that each of us is a valuable person, with a right to existence and wellbeing, and that it's OK to lean on others.

Whenever my husband took over because I was cracking up, I noticed some shame in me. I pictured myself as pathetic and incapable. Sure, at other times I was the driving force. But even if I'd always been the 'weak' one, that would have been the starting point for acceptance. Accept what is and concentrate on what you wish for now.

If you're struggling with self-blame and find it hard to accept yourself, relax into the discomfort and tune into the underlying needs. Perhaps it matters to you to be effective, or to contribute or to be self-reliant. Perhaps you need to know that your loved ones accept you.

I wonder if it's hard for you to hear of the successes of other parents. Do you notice any reactions of self-judgement? Any jealousy or resentment? Stick a label on it: 'Comparing Mind'. Then chuckle (because it's universal), and give yourself some compassion. When you accept your thoughts, however unwelcome they are, and when you get in touch with your feelings (behind the jealousy or hate, is there fear, possibly?), which life-enhancing, beautiful values do you unearth? Perhaps a fierce determination to be the best you can for your child?

When others judge or blame us

It can be painful to sense that the people you are looking to for connection are judging you. It hurts even more when you take their criticisms to heart and turn them into self-judgement.

Eating disorders create such extreme stresses that a whole lot of people may be trying to blame you. Therapists who work from old models may imply (subtly or bluntly) that you're a defective parent. Your partner may accuse you of making mistakes. Your friends might hear your woes and conclude there's something very wrong with you and your parenting style. I bet your child is insisting on a daily basis that if it wasn't for you, she'd be absolutely fine.

If you start with self-compassion, you may be able to create some space for compassion towards the other person. You might notice that you are judging them for judging you. You might realise that their opinions are their business and that they are doing the best they can with the resources at their disposal.

The more you can access your compassion for them and for yourself, the better you will feel.

REFUEL: ATTEND TO LIFE-GIVING NEEDS

Yes, we can stretch

If your child needs your support at mealtimes, I bet that however challenging it is, however tired or bored or frustrated you are, often enough you're willing to make him your priority.

I often postponed my desires to rest, enjoy friendships, music or the stimulation of work. I could choose to put on hold my longing for closeness with my kid, and this way many of her words washed over me. My main compass point, if I had to make a choice, was, 'What's going to help my child be well?' Because I'd worked out that most of the time that need in me trumped all the others.

Our children's needs are often our own needs. We want to nurture our kids, and so we stretch ourselves for them. If we notice we're doing this willingly, wholeheartedly, we avoid becoming martyrs. We avoid the rescuer-persecutor-victim dynamic, which is not helpful to anybody. At the same time I bet there are many times you find you've stretched further than you'd bargained for and you are of no help to anyone. So let's talk about how you can top-up your wellbeing.

Is it selfish to attend to your needs?

Anyone with a shred of common sense, when they hear what you're going through, will tell you to take care of yourself. This makes many parents bristle. 'A manicure?! What the #$%# would I do with a #$%#-ing manicure! It's a #$%#-ing break I need! Just take care of *one* meal for me! *One* meal!' The more people suggest self-care, the more alone and misunderstood we feel. Outsiders don't seem to appreciate how serious our situation is and the stress we're under.

I bet your take on self-care is that you have neither the time nor the money. What matters to you most right now is caring for your child. You might have a belief that it is virtuous to deny yourself your needs. This makes perfect sense if you believe in taking responsibility for yourself, in being strong, resilient and generous towards others. The question is, is it working?

Our children need our time and our care so urgently that inevitably, we put many of our needs on hold. I am grateful for the times I was OK even though major needs of mine could not be met. But human beings have their limits. There are some needs that, when unmet, lower our resistance. I defy anyone to be effective when sleep-deprived. It's also hard to keep going without love or empathy: we need connection with others to keep ourselves fuelled.

In general you're swimming against the tide if you have a whole lot of unmet needs, if there are not enough sources of nourishment to keep your cup full.

I suggest that the more you feed your soul, the more there is for everyone else.

Imagine a lighthouse, guiding sailors through the night back to the safety of the port. When our needs are met, we too glow, radiating life-giving energy.

Valuing what matters to you doesn't mean you ignore or compromise the needs of your loved ones. It's not an either/or situation. You can value your needs *and* those of your family.

You might not trust that your friends know that. Are you telling yourself that they would judge you for taking time off, for doing something you thoroughly enjoy when your child is so ill? Some mindfulness and compassionate communication may help you here.

Maintain the power to your child's life-support machine

Before the eating disorder came along, you might not have paid much attention to your needs. Perhaps you bumbled along like everyone else, coping reasonably well with life's ups and downs. When you felt depleted, when you were at the end of your tether, you could afford to be low until time did its usual healing job or the stressor vanished.

I'd like to argue that the strategy of ignoring or denying your needs is too pricey for you and your loved ones right now. When you're caring for a child with an eating disorder, the challenges keep coming. The fitter you are, the better you will be able to take them on. Mothers take good care of themselves during pregnancy because their health directly affects the unborn baby. Likewise an eating disorder can make our child so very low in resources that we are their life-support machine. And so we need to be plugged in to life-giving sources ourselves.

Food, exercise and sleep

BODY

We can help our mind by giving our body what it needs. Good food, obviously, and also moderate exercise, which can be a powerful antidepressant. As a dog owner I walk most days and I'm sure both the exercise and the sights and sound of nature contribute to my overall wellbeing. But you might find, as I have, that if you're feeling low, walking can encourage unhelpful ruminations. My solution is to bring along a phone loaded with audio books, podcasts and dance music.

Sleep is an issue for many of us. We don't go to bed early enough. We are kept awake by our thoughts… or our children. The result is that the next day we are less present to them. 'Sleep hygiene' tips like 'avoid emotionally upsetting conversations and activities before trying to go to sleep' are useless if your child needs lots of support at bedtime.

If you are short of sleep, do consider having a nap if at all possible. I resisted this for a while because it looked like the kind of thing you do when you're depressed. Now I think it is a sensible way of refuelling.

There are audio sleep hypnosis resources on CDs, phone apps and YouTube[416] that will lull you to sleep for an hour or even for the whole night.

Helper's high

If you find everyday caring for your child tends to lower your mood, you might be surprised at how quickly you can lift your spirits by helping others. Enjoy helper's high![417]

Now let's be practical about this. You are already doing quite enough by caring for your child (and possibly for other family members too). I'm not suggesting you should be the next Mother Teresa. I'm suggesting you notice times it feels great to contribute to other people.

Helper's high doesn't come from helping anybody in any situation. You will only get a boost if your act of kindness meets your needs and feeds your soul. Perhaps for you, the magic is in connecting with people. Or in opening to the outside world, contributing and mattering. Perhaps you thrive on intellectual stimulation or a use of your competencies, and I think this fuels a beautiful community of parents supporting each other online.

Helper's high is well worth tapping into. It may not be appropriate at times when you're completely depleted, but then again, it might be just the tonic you need.

What will feed your soul?

I really don't want to turn self-care into yet another pressure on you. You don't *have* to be strong and jolly and super-resilient. The idea is most definitely not to heap extra 'oughts' onto you. It is simply to be open to what comes up. If there's a small source of health or pleasure bubbling inside, let it flow.

Get into a habit of nurturing states where you feel good for no reason. Where you enjoy a sense of being one with the world.[418] Perhaps music or paintings do it for you, providing an instant soulful connection. Browse the internet for beautiful images and see which speak to you. There's a picture of Snoopy hugging his little bird friend, Woodstock, that thrills me every time I see it.

Do you have particular needs that are crying out for attention? I bet your time and freedom are extremely limited. Money may be an issue. Let the objections pass for now – solutions may pop up when you tune into your needs. Consider ordinary needs, like eating and sleeping well, taking exercise, laughing with friends or receiving their care, being stimulated by your work or hobbies, enjoying the support of compassionate people, and feeding your soul with the beauty of nature, music or art. Did you get a burst of goodness today inhaling a rose in a neighbour's hedge? You might not require time or money to meet a whole lot of needs. Just a readiness to let go of hyper-vigilance, and a sense of openness to opportunities.

I used to feel like nothing short of a ten-year holiday on a tropical island could possibly fill up my tank. It was humbling to find that one hour of companionship, one minute of laughter, one kind gesture from a loving person, could top me up. Wellbeing was closer to hand than I thought it was.

When you are in a terrible state, it's a great time to throw caution to the wind and try new things. But it's a shame to wait until we hit rock bottom. See if you can care for your needs now. If you're not sure you have the energy, treat it as a small experiment. The aim is to go beyond just coping. This will help nourish you and strengthen you so that you can accept the grief of unmet needs. If you resist the notion of caring for yourself, consider that it's a good thing to model for your kids. It's what you want for them, isn't it, to live life to the full?

Treasure good moments, and you will build up resilience. Shit happens, but good things happen many times a day. Be on the lookout for things to be grateful about. This will become a habit, more of your default state. Whenever you experience well-being or joy, savour it. Absorb the goodness in every cell of your body and let it take hold. Take your time.

SADNESS, MOURNING AND ... JOY

It's easy to have chatterbox thoughts around sadness and mourning. First, there's our situation: we tell ourselves that things shouldn't be as they are and life is unfair. Then we have judgemental thoughts about how we're coping. We tell ourselves that we shouldn't be so upset, that we shouldn't be suffering or that we're not going through the stages of the grieving process fast enough. Or that sadness is dangerous, that anger isn't acceptable and that people are judging us for not having pulled ourselves together. Our chatterboxes interpret what is happening in our lives, and our hearts close up with emotions like anger, anxiety or depression.

Mourning or grieving, as I understand it, is simply giving ourselves per-mission to feel what we're feeling. If we can drop into self-compassion, we are effectively mourning. We are accepting what is and allowing ourselves to feel pure sadness around this life-giving, beautiful thing that is not there any more. As we ex-perience the life and the beauty, our hearts open up.

Being fully with a need, without chatterbox baggage, means that if a source of joy or wellbeing presents itself, there's a freedom to go there. In fact, I find that sadness and joy (just like grieving and celebration), are so close together they're prac-tically one and the same thing. I guess this is why stories that blend the two can satisfy us deeply.

What's at the root of sadness, of grief? When I let go of fears, when I let go of resistance to 'what is', I believe what's left is love – something rich and joyful. I hope so. Love is where I get to when I contemplate that I am likely to outlive my mother, to outlive my little dog.

In the UK our politicians keep an eye on our happiness levels, bless them. Sci-entist often ask subjects to rate how happy they are on a scale of zero to ten. Perhaps this has contributed to a mental model I used to have of a very, very long ruler, with sad stuff at one end, and joyful stuff at the other. I imagined it would take months, years, to travel along this ruler. Having a child with an eating-disorder has taken me to both extremities, except that now this ruler has entered a multi-dimensional uni-verse where things that are poles apart are also right next to each other.

Take music, for instance. In a few minutes, it can carry your from joy to heart-wrenching sadness and back again.

I see this with dance too. I go to a Biodanza class where people are comfortable with emotions – something that came in handy when I first joined, as with my kid in hospital I was as low as could be.[419] During a dance a person can have tears streaming down their cheeks, and there'll be no expectation for them to cheer up, no fear that their suffering might be unbearable. With the next piece of music, everything can change. Even though grief may still be very present, pure joy may spring up, and you see the person dancing one great big 'yes!'. That is the flow of life, and when we engage in it we are well.

WRITING A DIARY: SELF-HELP OR RUMINATION?

Many people imagine that recording their life's ups and downs in a diary will be therapeutic. My experience is that if you're looking for self-help you should not spend any more time than necessary ruminating your thoughts.

I kept a diary in the early days of my daughter's anorexia. My aim was to spill out what came through my head. I believed that until I'd got a record of all the horrors I'd lived, I wouldn't be able to let go of them.

As I started receiving warmth and hugs and compassion and real listening, my impulse to pour everything out in notebooks disappeared. I decided that my limited time was better spent having fun and enjoying people, because those things seemed to have greater healing powers.

Looking back, I think my notebooks weren't helpful because all I was doing was engaging in chatterbox thoughts. I cried as I wrote, but it wasn't healing and didn't help me move on.

Yet for some, a diary is a tool to become more self-aware, to reflect and learn. I believe the key lies in using a self-compassion framework. Sure, let the chatterbox spill out, let the feelings be expressed. But also practice self-kindness and let your writing lead you to your needs, your strengths, your values. And of course, be ready to translate your values into action.

NEED

What works for me is to scribble lists, mind maps or to make notes based on questions from Byron Katie's *The Work*. Writing is just a prop to still the mind – the real self-help comes from the meditative work of enquiring within.

Whenever you write anything, consider how your child might react if he read it. You might love beautiful notebooks but your password-protected computer is a safer bet. It is helpful for you to pin down chatterbox thoughts to work on them but it is not helpful for your child to think that you actually believe those thoughts.

You could make brief notes of what your child is struggling with and what challenges he has overcome. That could help you get perspective, especially if you're dwelling on failed meals. Here's the executive summary from a dad's log:

> *"Ongoing total: 66 meals, of which:*
> *57 meals: eaten (86.4%)*
> *9: none of the meal eaten (all snacks) (13.6%)*
> *4: not completely finished (6.1%)"*

Finally, there is one proven self-help habit you can get into which does involve writing. Jot down, once a day, what you are grateful for.

AN ATTITUDE OF GRATITUDE

Here's how a mum, Cathy, was met by gratitude:[420]

> *'For the longest time, I felt frustrated, exhausted and even a bit
> resentful questioning, 'When will I get to have MY LIFE back
> again?'*
> *And then I changed my thinking and thought, 'Hmmm - wait a
> minute. THIS IS MY LIFE. And you know what? It's not really
> all that bad.'*
> *It could be a whole lot worse. Oh believe me, it HAS been a whole
> lot worse over these past three to five years.*
> *Today, watching my daughter pick up that fork and eat those brunch
> scrambled eggs, eat her toast, drink her orange juice ... without
> resistance and sans that vacant ED expression on her face ...
> finishing in time to spare for her to get off to work at the job she has
> been now at for over two years ... well, it put a smile on my face.*
> *My attitude is changing.*
> *Gratitude is my new attitude.*
> *As a person who recovered from anorexia myself, I look back and
> say, 'What worked?' What worked was FOOD, weight gain and
> finding happiness, loving relationships, meaningful work and
> purpose in LIFE.*
> *Happiness, love, work, purpose. Now I get to add –
> GRATITUDE.*
> *Gratitude is my NEW attitude!'*

Gratitude is good for humans. It's been shown that your level of wellbeing will increase significantly if you take a few minutes once a day to write down five things you're grateful for.[421] I'm hoping that just bringing them to my awareness is sufficient because I do quite enough writing as it is.

I've already mentioned that our brains are wired up with a negativity bias. We pay more attention and give more weight to what may be going wrong than to what's wonderful, and this may have contributed to the survival of our species. All the same, we can try to get the best of all worlds: we can be vigilant to risks *and* appreciate the good things in our lives. It may be that for every negative, you might need five positives in order to function well.[422]

A word of caution: gratitude should not be forced. It's neither a virtue nor an obligation. It's something that may bubble up from the inside when we pause to pay attention. We can prime the pump a little by staying still, opening our minds and inviting the possibility of something wonderful. Listing five items, to me, is about making space for the gratitude that is already there. It is never an 'ought'.

Gratitude goes deeper than just thinking. I like to let gratitude seep into my body and soul by remembering not just events, but how wonderful they felt and how they truly met deep needs. That's because when I first started listing things I was grateful for, it nearly backfired. If I was in a black mood, my chatterbox would barge in and remind me that the very things I'd enjoyed might be taken away from me any time. Instead of gratitude for the abundance in my life, I was getting into scarcity and fear. So I made sure that for each event I've appreciated I also dwelled on how it had filled my soul. For example when I was full of gratitude that my daughter had put her hand in mine, I let the delight of having hope and closeness sink in. Even if she didn't give me her hand for another three months, I trusted that I'd find hope and closeness in other ways.

When things were very bad I'd struggle to find five good things in my dreadful day – in fact many times I didn't even bother. I didn't want to pay lip service to the practice or turn it into a 'positive thinking' exercise – a sure-fire way of activating internal resistance. But it was good to wait and just be present. Sometimes what came up were the constants in my life, the things I wouldn't normally notice: I had food to eat, a warm house, a kind husband, and the chirping of the birds outside was peaceful.[423] I also found that when my life was full of drama and despair, a huge wave of gratitude could sweep me up when someone showed me a simple kindness.

The gratitude exercise reinforced the things that sustain me in times of trouble and that let me flourish in times of ease.

A dad wrote me this as he was struck by gratitude:

> "Every day I log on my phone brief entries on what she's eaten and maybe a little emotional check-in. AND THE REALLY COOL thing about it is that I start every entry with the same heading: "I get to save my daughter." I do that because I realized recently something profound. From the moment she was born I have always seen myself as part of what mostly all dads want: driving her to school, attending the parent meetings, celebrating report cards, watching her play games, making arrangements for college, helping her narrow down career choices, walking her down the aisle on her wedding day, holding my grandkids, etc., etc. But unlike most of those other dads, I've got one more thing to do that I never thought I'd get to do: I get to save my daughter's life. It's not that I have to. Or want. It's that I GET to. It's like I get to go to the moon or something. Ask any father what a joy it is to protect a daughter from anything. And I get to do it every day. 'Beat that!' I say to my former self. 'You never thought you'd get to do this!'"

JOY

It's time for goodbyes and I want to send you all my wishes. I so hope that you have found support in this book. For all the time I've been writing here, I have held you in my mind as a dear friend.

I'd like to finish with joy.

Is it insensitive to talk of joy when eating disorders are turning so many lives inside out? Even in normal times, it's not a popular concept. Some of us have been raised with an ethos of self-denial, where we deny ourselves not only material goods, but kindnesses and pleasures. We turn down the nourishment that makes us flourish, that sustains our wellbeing and allows us to radiate light for the benefit of others. Self-denial may have started as a spiritual aim, a quest for virtue, but to me it's more like wallowing in the mud.

I've mentioned how close to each other sorrow and joy are. An eating disorder throws us parents into the greatest suffering we've ever known. Sometimes it can seem like it will take years, and a string of miracles, for us to ever feel good again. Our children, presumably, share a similar despair.

We wait for external events to bring us happiness. And yet I believe that joy is a life force that is bubbling up in us all the time. We can put a lid on it or we can open up, enjoying and sharing its riches.

The invitation is to stoke the fires of joy.

I wonder if you've experienced something like this: you're due to go out with some friends, but you nearly cancel because you're exhausted and you're crying all the time. But you go all the same, and maybe there's good conversation or good music or good food and good cheer, and suddenly you notice how very relaxed and contented you've been feeling for the last hour.

Perhaps the switch in mood happens over small things. You notice the golden evening sun playing on the irises outside your window. Or you share your dog's delight as he chases leaves on a windy autumn walk. You're fully enjoying life for this moment in time.

I'm proposing that you not only let yourself enjoy these opportunities, but actively seek them out, because they nourish your soul and put you in touch with joy. Refuse to label yourself as someone who's sad, suffering, in distress. If you've learned anything about emotions on this journey, it's that they come and go. What remains is your drive for life.

I wonder if a moral concern might hold you back. Just as bubbles of contentment, fun, or connection percolate through you, you think, 'My kid is suffering. Right now, this very moment, she's ill. What kind of a monster am I to be feeling so wonderful?'

Even without illness in the family, it can seem wrong to enjoy life. We're reminded every time we turn on the news that somewhere in the world, people are experiencing terrible hardships. We value life's riches and we long for them to be accessible to everyone at all times. We imagine that we should show solidarity with misery by being at least a little bit miserable.

One day I was walking my dog while feeling seriously down in the dumps. I passed a few people and kept my eyes lowered; engaging with anyone, even with a silent nod, seemed like too much hard work. And then someone strode by, relaxed, open, smiling. Everything about this person said 'Life!'. I was too knotted up to give eye contact, but the light this human being shone nourished me for hours.

> *"At times our own light goes out and is rekindled by a spark from*
> *another person. Each of us has cause to think with deep gratitude*
> *of those who have lighted the flame within us." (Albert Schweitzer)*

Having had pain right inside my family has taught me the power to be gained from accepting what is, and from being open to joy. I've now experienced how it's in no way selfish – when you're embracing life, others aren't left behind, because they're nourished by your vitality. Stoking the fires of joy doesn't take away from anyone and it enriches life – mine, my family's and way beyond. My wish is for you to radiate the good things you value, because they will warm your child back to life.

I like the metaphor of the lighthouse in a beautiful article by David Spangler entitled 'Stoking the Fires of Joy'.[424] Standing strong among fierce winds and lashing waves, the lighthouse penetrates the darkness and guides ships on their journey. What use is it to anyone if we become part of the storm, when we can be part of the lighthouse?

Let's give the last joyful words to a young person on her way to recovery:

> "*I feel awake for the first time in so long ... My heart is just overflowing with appreciation for life. I cry easily now – I never had that before. I cry out of joy, out of gratitude, out of appreciation. I feel strong and comfortable in myself. I feel like I've sunken into myself. I feel okay being me. I feel like I'm becoming the person I really am. I feel like I'm living authentically ... I just feel so empowered. I feel like I can trust myself. I feel like my opinion matters. I feel like I have found my voice of self-protection, which had been missing for so long. I just feel really alive.*"[425]

THANK YOU

I am hugely grateful to a whole lot of people. I have thoroughly enjoyed telling a number of them how very much they have contributed to me and my readers, and I have a few more thank yous to make.

I want to thank the parents who have helped me make this book more relevant and rich by allowing me to quote them. Thank you also to all the parents and clinicians who offer up their knowledge on the internet, in particular those who make the FEAST site and the Around the Dinner Table forum such a top resource. Thank you to the young people whose words I reproduced here. Thank you to the parents I've become close to, whose struggles and successes I have witnessed and learned from, and to all those who commented on my manuscript. Thank you, all of you who wrote to me about your successes as you read drafts on my website. You helped me stay focused.

Thank you, Harriet Brown,[426] for your advice and your work on the Maudsley Parents website. Thank you Laura Collins[427] for your answers, and most of all for your enormous contribution, via the FEAST website and beyond, to the lives of so many families struck by an eating disorder.

Within the Nonviolent Communication community, some trainers have contributed much-needed support. Thank you, Verene Nicolas[428] for being there for me. I think with gratitude of Inbal Kashtan, who let me use some of her materials about child-friendly needs language. Thank you, Marcia Christen[429] for deepening my understanding of some Nonviolent Communication concepts. And Shona Cameron,[430] thank you for what you've given my family, as well as for your work reading, checking and commenting on sections relating to communication.

Thank you, Robert Doran,[431] for being a top-notch, dedicated and delightful editor. Also to Andrew Brown[432] for the current cover design and Melody Revnak[433] for the photograph of the giraffes.

Thank you to the eating-disorders clinicians who encouraged me right from the start and commented on the manuscript. Thank you to all the professionals who made our lives better. Thank you in particular to those who contributed to our daughter's wellbeing and supported my husband and myself.

Thank you to all the people who made tough days so much easier with their kindness – receptionists, dinner ladies, friends and total strangers.

Thank you to my husband for your steadfast tender loving care.

And finally, thank you to my daughter. For all sorts of things. Most of all, just for being you.

RESOURCES

Rather than recommending a whole lot of books, blogs and organisations here, I keep my website updated with links and articles. On my website (anorexiafamily.com) you can sign up to my mailing list for occasional messages when I've produced new resources.

You can also receive a notification whenever I produce a new video by subscribing to my YouTube channel: www.youtube.com/user/EvaMusby.

Sometimes parents are too tired and overwhelmed to read: if you or your partner are in this situation, my Bitesize audio collection[434] is for you, and it has the advantage you can hear me modelling dialogue.

Some parents know this book inside out but want more pointers for their own situation. You might enjoy some individual support from me via video call[435]. When invited, I may also speak at conferences or deliver workshops.

Do let me know how you get on, and I'm always happy to hear about mistakes or omissions in this book. I care a lot about supporting families. If this book has helped you, please help others find it by telling your clinicians and other parents about it, reviewing it online or using your social networks.

Endnotes

[1] I was delighted to hear from this mother how well they're doing now.

[2] Bitesize: anorexiafamily.com/bitesize-public/

[3] For a list of parents' online groups, see my advice on anorexiafamily.com/anorexia-nvc-mindfulness-links/anorexia-books-links-review/#Find_support_from_other_parents_internet_groups Many of the quotes in this book come from the wonderful forum Around the Dinner Table: aroundthedinnertable.org

[4] My website: anorexiafamily.com Also Bitesize, my library of short audios: anorexiafamily.com/bitesize-public. My YouTube channel: youtube.com/evamusby Subscribe to my mailing list: https://eepurl.com/bt3jf9 More on individual support from me on anorexiafamily.com/individual-support

[5] Lots more on what it feels like from Tabitha Farrar in tabithafarrar.com and her book 'Rehabilitate, rewire, recover!' amzn.to/2JpH4cf

[6] Some experts report that people with anorexia don't get any hunger signals from their brain. I've mostly come across ex-sufferers who recall extreme huger. This quote is from Tori Midoro, one of many people discussing a fascinating Ted Talk by Dr Laura Hill, titled Eating Disorders from the Inside Out. http://youtu.be/UEysOExcwrE

[7] The delusion that makes you see your body as huge when it's thin is called body dysmorphia. Most, but not all, anorexics suffer from this, and it seems to me that it's worse after meals and during times of higher stress.

[8] Ravin, S., 'Defeating the Monster: Helping Little Girls Overcome Anorexia Nervosa', http://www.blog.drsarahravin.com/eating-disorders/defeating-the-monster-helping-little-girls-overcome-anorexia-nervosa/

[9] Not recognising that one is ill – and therefore not wanting treatment – is referred to as anosognosia. Another term commonly used in the field of anorexia is 'ego-syntonic illness', meaning that it is in harmony with the patient's sense of self. In other words, people tend to like it or feel better for it.

[10] From 'Amy', commenting on Carrie Arnold's ED Bites blog: http://edbites.com/2013/08/the-trauma-of-having-an-eating-disorder/

[11] From 'hm', commenting on Carrie Arnold's ED Bites blog: http://edbites.com/2013/08/the-trauma-of-having-an-eating-disorder/

[12] From a girl with anorexia, posting on my website.

[13] From a parent on the Around the Dinner Table forum.

[14] Maya's tribute to her mother, at the All in the Mind Mental Health Awards, BBC Radio 4 (10 June 2014), http://www.bbc.co.uk/programmes/p020q4g5

[15] Some of you will have heard me talk about the limbic system (which includes the amygdala) in relation to fight or flight, of the 'triune' brain model and the 'polyvagal theory'. It turns out that these topics suffer from a blend of good science and over-simplified pop-psychology.

[16] For a fascinating first-hand account: youtu.be/hcjdPE1nDQg Also in *Give Food a Chance* by Julie O'Toole (https://amzn.to/2CivYS6). Also Todd Tucker, *The great starvation experiment* (https://amzn.to/2UCK6wE). Also a detailed article: '*They starved so that others be better fed: remembering Ancel Keys and the Minnesota Experiment*' in *The Journal of Nutrition* (June 2005) vol. 135, no. 6, pp. 1347–52, jn.nutrition.org/content/135/6/1347.full

[17] Two books for more on these mechanisms: Carrie Arnold in 'Decoding Anorexia' (https://amzn.to/2G4XQKr) and Dr Jennifer Gaudiani in 'Sick enough' (https://amzn.to/2Xa7tPR)

[18] Guisinger, S., 'Adapted to Flee Famine: Adding an Evolutionary Perspective on Anorexia Nervosa'. http://www.adaptedtofamine.com/wp-content/uploads/2015/01/guisinger-an-pr-2003.pdf

[19] Read about the serotonin/starvation cycle in Carrie Arnold's book *Decoding Anorexia* (http://amzn.to/1OY2Una).

[20] Lots more from Tabitha Farrar in tabithafarrar.com and her book 'Rehabilitate, rewire, recover!' amzn.to/2JpH4cf

[21] A study of over 80,000 US adolescents found disordered eating behaviours among 57 per cent of young women and 31 per cent of young men. Croll, J., Neumark-Sztainer, D., Story, M. and Ireland, M. J., 'Prevalence and risk and protective factors related to disordered eating behaviors among adolescents: relationship to gender and ethnicity' in *J Adolesc Health* (August 2002), vol. 31, no. 2, pp. 166-75. http://www.ncbi.nlm.nih.gov/pubmed/12127387

[22] Therapists Lauren Muhlheim and Therese Waterhous present two case studies in support of early intervention: '*Can FBT Strategies be used for early eating disorder intervention and prevention?*' in letsfeast.feast-ed.org/2014/08/can-fbt-strategies-be-used-for-early.html

See also an adaptation of FBT for the 'prodromal' or 'subsyndromal' or 'subthreshold' stage, in 'Family-based treatment for prodromal anorexia nervosa', Corine Sweeney, Katharine L Loeb, Amy Parter, Lisa Hail, Nancy Zucker. In Chapter 9 in *Family therapy for adolescent eating and weight disorders* edited by Katharine Loeb, Daniel Le Grange and James Lock, Routledge, 2015 http://amzn.to/1NN56aF

[23] Anorexia studies show that some people recover without treatment, and some don't. If you do nothing, your child may be among the relatively 'lucky' ones: it looks as though approximately 50–70 per cent of individuals with anorexia attain a complete or moderate resolution of the illness by their early- to mid-twenties. We're talking maybe five to seven years of illness or more. And what if your child is not in the lucky group? We have no way of predicting if, untreated, she would be part of the 30 to 50 per cent for whom anorexia becomes a severely disabling chronic or fatal illness. Kaye, W. H., Fudge, J. L. and Paulus, M., 'New insights into symptoms and neurocircuit function of anorexia nervosa' in *Nature Reviews. Neuroscience* (August 2009), vol. 10, pp 573–84.
http://www.nature.com/nrn/journal/v10/n8/execsumm/nrn2682.html
Regarding the mortality statistics, there is hope in a study of women followed for 10 years after diagnosis, most of whom were doing pretty well. Mustelin et al, 'Long-term outcome in anorexia nervosa in the community' in Int J Eat Disord 2015; 48:851–859, https://onlinelibrary.wiley.com/doi/abs/10.1002/eat.22415

[24] I list signs on anorexiafamily.com/school-early-detection-eating-disorder See also feedyourinstinct.com.au

[25] *Access and Waiting Time Standard for Children and Young People with an Eating Disorder. Commissioning Guide* from NHS England, June 2015. My summary: anorexiafamily.com/nhs-england-commissioning-guide-eating-disorders-access-waiting The whole doc: http://www.england.nhs.uk/wp-content/uploads/2015/07/cyp-eating-disorders-access-waiting-time-standard-comm-guid.pdf

[26] In Bev Mattock's book *When Anorexia Came to Visit: Families Talk About How an Eating Disorder Invaded Their Lives* (http://amzn.to/1bcKzbS), you can learn from the experiences of a number of UK parents as they navigated the health service. Our story is included.

[27] Video of Dr Rebecka Peebles speaking at Maudsley parents' conference on 'Eating Disorders: What Pediatricians and Parents Should Know', http://vimeo.com/50460378. I highly recommend this one-hour talk as I found it informative and empowering.

[28] Dr Jennifer Gaudiani in 'Sick enough' (https://amzn.to/2Xa7tPR)

[29] The International Classification of Diseases (ICD) from the World Health Organisation is due for revision and will probably use criteria similar to those in DSM-5. Criteria are in Chapter

V: F50. http://apps.who.int/classifications/apps/icd/icd10online2003/fr-icd.htm?gf50.htm Or for a short description: http://www.eatingdisorders.org.au/eating-disorders/what-is-an-eating-disorder/classifying-eating-disorders/icd-10

[30] The American Psychiatric Association's *Diagnostic and Statistical Manual of Mental Disorders (DSM-5)* (fifth edition) is referred to – to varying degrees – in a number of countries. More detail on my website anorexiafamily.com/classification-eating-disorders

[31] More on effects and medical checks in '*How self-induced vomiting impacts your body*' by Pamela K. Keel. edcatalogue.com/self-induced-vomiting-impacts-body

[32] Hay, P., Mitchison, D., Collado, AEL, González-Chica,DA, Stocks, N., Touyz, S. 'Burden and health-related quality of life of eating disorders, including Avoidant/Restrictive Food Intake Disorder (ARFID), in the Australian population' J Eat Disord. 2017 Jul 3;5:21 www.ncbi.nlm.nih.gov/pubmed/28680630

[33] I explain more: anorexiafamily.com/bmi-weight-for-height-wfh

[34] I explain more: anorexiafamily.com/weight-restoration-eating-disorder

[35] Examples in '*OSFED, the "other" eating disorder*' by Lauren Muhlheim verywell.com/osfed-the-other-eating-disorder-1138307

[36] More from on TakePart Live takepart.com/video/2014/11/17/eating-disorder-opposite-anorexia and on The Full Bloom Project fullbloomproject.com/podcast-episodes/boys

[37] universityofcalifornia.edu/news/22-percent-young-men-engage-disordered-eating-bulk

[38] Bryn Austin, 2019, pewtrusts.org/en/research-and-analysis/articles/2019/06/05/study-ties-some-dietary-supplements-to-medical-harms-in-children-young-adults

[39] See for instance NEDA's guide on orthorexia https://www.nationaleatingdisorders.org/orthorexia-nervosa

[40] 'Restrictive Eating Disorders Among Adolescent Inpatients', Melissa Whitelaw, Heather Gilbertson, Katherine J. Lee, Susan M. Sawyer, Pediatrics, September 2014, 134 (3) http://pediatrics.aappublications.org/content/134/3/e758

[41] Junior MARSIPAN: Management of Really Sick Patients under 18 with Anorexia Nervosa, report from the Junior MARSIPAN group, College Report CR168 (January 2012), Royal College of Psychiatrists London rcpsych.ac.uk/usefulresources/publications/collegereports/cr/cr168.aspx

[42] More from me on anorexiafamily.com/bmi-weight-for-height-wfh

[43] Christopher Fairburn, who developed and researched cognitive behaviour therapy (CBT-E), proposed a 'transdiagnostic view', arguing that bulimia, binge-eating disorder and anorexia all have the same maintaining factors that need to be targeted. Fairburn, C. G., *Cognitive Behavior Therapy and Eating Disorders* (http://amzn.to/1s6sFOj).

[44] In the UK, consult the Citizens Advice Bureau, which has an arm specialised in patients' rights.

[45] In England parents of under-18s can self-refer to their closest specialist eating disorders service. Also, anywhere in the UK, a school nurse can refer to Child and Adolescent Mental Health Services, and of course you can also change your general practitioner (GP). If you have no confidence in any of your clinicians, you can ask them to refer you to one of the country's specialist NHS units (more in Chapter 12).

[46] Christopher Fairburn developed and validated adult and child forms of therapist-led interviews (EDE-I) and self-report questionnaires (EDE-Q) to assess the presence and degree of an eating disorder. You can see the adult questionnaire at corc.uk.net/outcome-experience-measures/eating-disorder-examination. The adult questionnaire and interview are also in the CBT-E therapists' manual: Fairburn, C. G., Cognitive Behavior Therapy and Eating Disorders (https://amzn.to/2EkkMFU). The child version of the interview is named ChEDE-I.

Notice that there's a lot about shape and weight, which some people with anorexia say is not relevant to them. This questionnaire would not have done much for the 'holy anorexics' of yesteryear.

[47] O'Toole, J., 'Tincture of time', http://www.kartiniclinic.com/blog/post/tincture-of-time/

[48] For instance, Hildebrandt, T., Bacow, T., Markella, M. and Loeb, K.L., 'Anxiety in anorexia nervosa and its management using family-based treatment', *Eur Eat Disord Rev.* (January 2012) vol. 20, no. 1, pp. 1–16, http://www.ncbi.nlm.nih.gov/pubmed/22223393
For these concepts put in practice for adults, see Tabitha Farrar's book 'Rehabilitate, rewire, recover!' https://amzn.to/2Gpxnrk

[49] Family-Based Treatment (FBT), an approach validated in randomised controlled trials, relies heavily on unconditional acceptance from parents. One study indicates that the higher the 'expressed emotion' (hostility, criticisms) from fathers, the lower the chances of recovery: Daniel Le Grange, Elizabeth K. Hughes, Andrew Court, Michele Yeo, Ross D. Crosby, Susan M. Sawyer, 'Randomized Clinical Trial of Parent-Focused Treatment and Family-Based Treatment for Adolescent Anorexia Nervosa' in *J Am Academy Child & Ado Psych* (2016), vol. 55, no. 8, pp. 683–692, http://tinyurl.com/z7rwsgr

[50] Dr Julie O'Toole provides a good introduction to the role of medicines like Olanzapine, Prozac or Zoloft. 'Directly observed therapy, baby bird style, swish and swallow twice' (13 May 2011) on https://www.kartiniclinic.com/blog/post/directly-observed-therapy-baby-bird-style-swish-and-swallow-twice/ and on *Let's Feast* Blog (23 May 2014): 'Medication' letsfeast.feast-ed.org/2014/05/guest-post-by-dr-julie-otoole.html and an entire chapter in Dr Julie O'Toole's *Give Food a Chance* (https://amzn.to/2CivYS6).

[51] A good starting point to learn more about comorbid conditions is Carrie Arnold's book *Decoding Anorexia* (http://amzn.to/10Y2Una).

[52] Dr Julie O'Toole explains this beautifully in 'The many disguises of an eating disorder', http://www.kartiniclinic.com/blog/post/the-many-disguises-of-an-eating-disorder/

[53] Nice guidelines (May 2017): nice.org.uk/guidance/ng69 I explain them on anorexiafamily.com/nice-guidelines-adolescent-eating-disorder-ng69

[54] Australia/New Zealand:
Royal Australian and New Zealand College of Psychiatrists clinical practice guidelines for the treatment of eating disorders.
https://www.ranzcp.org/Files/Resources/Publications/CPG/Clinician/Eating-Disorders-CPG.aspx
US:
The National Institute of Mental Health highlights the greater effectiveness of Family-Based Treatment (also named the Maudsley approach) in 'How are eating disorders treated?', http://tinyurl.com/83frh8o. They write: 'In a therapy called the Maudsley approach, parents of adolescents with anorexia nervosa assume responsibility for feeding their child. This approach appears to be very effective in helping people gain weight and improve eating habits and moods. Shown to be effective in case studies and clinical trials … for treating eating disorders in younger, nonchronic patients.'

From the American Academy of Pediatrics:
Rosen, D. S. and the Committee on Adolescence, 'Identification and Management of Eating Disorders in Children and Adolescents', *Pediatrics, Official Journal of the American Academy of Pediatrics* (2010) vol. 126, p. 1240,
http://pediatrics.aappublications.org/content/126/6/1240.full.pdf . They write: 'Family-based interventions, nevertheless, remain an effective and evidence-based treatment strategy for adolescent AN in both open trials and randomized controlled studies … Unfortunately, family-based treatment by experienced providers is not available in all communities. Nevertheless, the essential principles of family-based treatment can still be encouraged by community providers in their work with patients and families.'

[55] Canadian Paediatric Society. Position Statement. 'Family-based treatment of children and adolescents with anorexia nervosa: Guidelines for the community physician' (Posted 1 January 2010, reaffirmed 30 January 2013). Findlay, S., Pinzon, J., Taddeo, D., and Katzman, D. K. (Canadian Paediatric Society, Adolescent Health Committee), *Paediatric Child Health* (2010) vol. 15, no. 1, pp. 31–5, http://www.cps.ca/documents/position/anorexia-nervosa-family-based-treatment

[56] Dr Sarah Ravin reports on end of treatment outcomes with her own eating-disorder patients: http://www.blog.drsarahravin.com/eating-disorders/end-of-treatment-outcomes-for-patients-with-anorexia-nervosa/

[57] For more on this, see Lock, J., 'Evaluation of family treatment models for eating disorders', *Curr Opin Psychiatry* (2011), vol. 24, no. 4, pp. 274–279. http://www.medscape.com/viewarticle/744675

[58] Ravin, S., 'Defeating the Monster: Helping Little Girls Overcome Anorexia Nervosa'. http://www.blog.drsarahravin.com/eating-disorders/defeating-the-monster-helping-little-girls-overcome-anorexia-nervosa/

Evidence that being at the younger end of the 12 to 18 range is a predictor of successful weight gain: Agras, S. W., Lock, J., Brandt, H., Bryson, S. W., Dodge, E., Halmi, K.A., Jo, B., Johnson, C., Kaye, W., Wilfley, D., Woodside, B., 'Comparison of 2 Family Therapies for Adolescent Anorexia Nervosa. A Randomized Parallel Trial.' In *JAMA Psychiatry* (September 24, 2014) http://archpsyc.jamanetwork.com/article.aspx?articleID=1910336

[59] From a doctor at an eating disorder conference http://internationaleatingdisorderadvocacy.blogspot.com/2015/05/international-conference-on-eating.html

[60] Watson, H.J., Yilmaz, Z., Thornton, L.M. et al. Genome-wide association study identifies eight risk loci and implicates metabo-psychiatric origins for anorexia nervosa. Nat Genet 51, 1207–1214 (2019) doi:10.1038/s41588-019-0439-2 Follow Cynthia M Bulik for the latest, e.g her 2019 talk on youtu.be/KduYI304iro

[61] Excellent short podcast on epigenetics of eating disorders: Howard Steigler on edcatalogue.com/episode-164-dr-howard-steiger-epigenetics-eating-disorders

[62] The serenity prayer and verses similar to it, are available on Wikipedia: http://en.wikipedia.org/wiki/Serenity_Prayer

[63] Bitesize, my library of short audios: anorexiafamily.com/bitesize-public

[64] From Jath, a mother on the Around the Dinner Table forum.

[65] You could decide to embrace the food police. As Lisa LaBorde points out in the F.E.A.S.T blog. The motto of her local police force, 'To serve and protect', perfectly describes the refeeding work of parents: http://letsfeast.feast-ed.org/2014/04/to-serve-and-protect.html

[66] In *Nonviolent Communication* there is a concept called the 'protective' or 'unilateral' use of force. When you cannot see a way to reach a collaborative solution and doing nothing would come at a major cost to you or the other, you make the best decision you can in the present moment. Your choice may be driven by a need to care for yourself or to protect or contribute to the other.

[67] This account comes from 'E.W.''s letter to the F.E.A.S.T. website, one of several letters from recovered young people, which are so worth reading in their entirety. http://www.feast-ed.org/default.asp?page=PatientLetters

[68] For a series of short and wonderful accounts from children who have recovered after being supported by their parents, check out 'Patients speak' on the F.E.A.S.T website: http://feast-ed.org.

[69] From Mamabear, posting on the Around the Dinner Table forum.

[70] From a parent, writing about their successes after reading the draft of this book.

[71] Read this dad's story here, as I've abridged it and it's a great read: http://tinyurl.com/a3yfd8p.

[72] For an example of an alternative to Magic Plate, read Bev Mattock's account of how her son Ben eventually pulled himself out of anorexia when they jointly devised 'contracts' and set up a system of rewards. This is described in her book, *Please Eat* (http://amzn.to/195YWhF). Also, if your older adolescent gets CBT he will be in charge of his food and you may just be assisting.

[73] Quoted by parents attending a talk by James Lock on 13 December 2013 at Great Ormond Street Hospital, London, and also on 2 March 2014 in Glasgow.

[74] Not from any of my experience with parents, but from youtu.be/pPSLdUUlTWE

[75] From SamHeinous, a mother, on the Around the Dinner Table forum.

[76] From SamHeinous, a mother, on the Around the Dinner Table forum.

[77] My YouTube video 'Stuck and not eating! Anorexia/restrictive eating disorders: parents' meal support tips"
https://youtu.be/BVhKXh0gLGc?list=PLVgyQbyKQSBHUbIDLlc7t3v7bN0lmLcve

[78] From Emily, posting on the Around the Dinner Table forum.

[79] From MariaEC, posting on the Around the Dinner Table forum.

[80] From Mamabear, posting on the Around the Dinner Table forum.

[81] From Gobsmacked, posting on the Around the Dinner Table forum.

[82] Lock, J. and Le Grange, D., *Help your teenager beat an eating disorder* (https://amzn.to/2IzYiVQ)

[83] *Ibid.* and 'UCSF study turns anorexia treatment on its head', *SFGate* (October 1 2013), http://www.sfgate.com/health/article/UCSF-study-turns-anorexia-treatment-on-its-head-4827675.php

[84] O'Toole, J. (2016)'Refeeding Syndrome: Hypophosphatemia', on https://www.kartiniclinic.com/blog/post/refeeding-syndrome-hypophosphatemia

Researchers have argued that the risks have been inflated: Golden, N. H., Keane-Miller, C., Sainani, K. L. and Kapphahn, C. J., 'Higher Caloric Intake in Hospitalized Adolescents With Anorexia Nervosa Is Associated With Reduced Length of Stay and No Increased Rate of Refeeding Syndrome' in *J. Adolesc. Health* (July 2013), pii: S1054–139X(13)00315–7, http://www.ncbi.nlm.nih.gov/pubmed/23830088

[85] A good predictor of success with FBT is adolescents gaining 3 or 4 lbs by week four. Doyle, P., Le Grange, D., Loeb, K., *et al*, 'Early response to family-based treatment for adolescent anorexia nervosa' in *J Eat Disord* (2010) vol. 43, pp. 659–62. http://onlinelibrary.wiley.com/doi/10.1002/eat.20764/abstract

A later study recommended a gain of at least 3.20 kg in the first 3 weeks: Le Grange, D., Accurso, E. C., Lock, J., Agras, S. and Bryson, S. W., 'Early weight gain predicts outcome in two treatments for adolescent anorexia nervosa' in *International Journal of Eating Disorders* (March 2014), vol. 47, no. 2, pp. 124–9, http://onlinelibrary.wiley.com/doi/10.1002/eat.22221/abstract

An inpatient study showed that a gain of at least .8 kg per week predicted a better year 1 outcome: Lund, B. C., Hernandez, E.R., Yates, W.R., Mitchell, J.R., McKee, P. A. and Johnson C. L., 'Rate of inpatient weight restoration predicts outcome in anorexia nervosa' in *Int. J. Eat. Disord* (May 2009), vol. 42, no. 4, pp. 301–5, http://www.ncbi.nlm.nih.gov/pubmed/19107835

Another study found that a shorter duration of illness prior to treatment beginning was a predictor of successful weight gain: Agras, S. W., Lock, J., Brandt, H., Bryson, S. W., Dodge, E., Halmi, K.A., Jo, B., Johnson, C., Kaye, W., Wilfley, D., Woodside, B., 'Comparison of 2 Family Therapies for Adolescent Anorexia Nervosa. A Randomized Parallel Trial.' In *JAMA Psychiatry* (September 24, 2014) http://archpsyc.jamanetwork.com/article.aspx?articleID=1910336

Contrary to the findings of Doyle et al 2010, this study showed there was no difference at end of treatment, and a year on, between those who had gained weight fast with FBT, or more slowly with systemic family therapy. There were fewer hospitalisations with the FBT patients, though.

[86] Dr Jennifer Gaudiani in 'Sick enough' (https://amzn.to/2Xa7tPR)

[87] Schebendach, J. E., Mayer, L. E., Devlin, M. J., Attia, E., Contento, I. R., Wolf, R. L. and Walsh, B. T., 'Dietary energy density and diet variety as predictors of outcome in anorexia nervosa.' in *Am. J. Clin. Nutr.* (April 2008), vol. 87, no. 4, pp. 810–16, http://www.ncbi.nlm.nih.gov/pubmed/18400701

[88] Dr Jennifer Gaudiani 'Sick enough' https://amzn.to/2Xa7tPR and gaudianiclinic.com/podcasts

[89] Lock, J. and Le Grange, D., *Help your teenager beat an eating disorder* (https://amzn.to/2IzYiVQ)

[90] In 'Sick enough', Dr Jennifer Gaudiani makes specific recommendations (https://amzn.to/2Xa7tPR)

[91] Marzola, E., Nasser, J. A., Hashim, S. A., Shih, P. B. and Kaye, W. H., 'Nutritional rehabilitation in anorexia nervosa: review of the literature and implications for treatment.' in *BMC Psychiatry* (2013) vol. 13, p. 290, ncbi.nlm.nih.gov/pmc/articles/PMC3829207 For a good article on hypermetabolism see Carrie Arnold: ed-bites.blogspot.co.uk/2009/01/more-on-hypermetabolism.html

[92] There are high-calorie meal suggestions from parents on the Around The Dinner Table forum: aroundthedinnertable.org/post?id=696425 for meals and aroundthedinnertable.org/post/high-calorie-snacks-5794369 for snacks. One member has a YouTube channel devoted to high-calorie recipes youtube.com/channel/UCKLW6A6sDO3ZDq8npNm8_ww. One tip from me: if your child can't cope with the sight of globules of fat, replace oil or butter with cream boiled down to a very thick consistency. Check out https://www.eatthismuch.com It generates meal plans with recipes and ingredients, for the number of calories you require.

[93] Dr Julie O'Toole, 'Practical re-feeding hints for parents: Benecalorie' https://www.kartiniclinic.com/blog/post/practical-re-feeding-hints-for-parents-benecalorie

[94] Marzola, E., Nasser, J. A., Hashim, S. A., Shih, P. B. and Kaye, W. H., 'Nutritional rehabilitation in anorexia nervosa: review of the literature and implications for treatment.' in *BMC Psychiatry* (2013) vol. 13, p. 290, http://www.ncbi.nlm.nih.gov/pmc/articles/PMC3829207/

[95] Dr Jennifer Gaudiani 'Sick enough' https://amzn.to/2Xa7tPR and gaudianiclinic.com/podcasts About serious gastro issues: Dr Philip S Mehler: edcatalogue.com/gastrointestinal-issues-impede-successful-weight-restoration-anorexia-nervosa-arfid

[96] Dr Julie O'Toole discusses hyper-palatable foods in her book *Give Food a Chance* (https://amzn.to/2CivYS6) and on her blog: https://www.kartiniclinic.com/blog/post/why-we-limit-hyper-palatable-foods-for-one-year She explains that not only do these foods create a huge amount of anxiety in patients, but that by making them no-go areas, the risk of bingeing is reduced

[97] Dr Jennifer Johnson, 'When your child with an eating disorder is sick' eatingdisordertherapyla.com/when-your-child-with-an-eating-disorder-is-sick

[98] Three articles from me: anorexiafamily.com/weight-restoration-eating-disorder ; anorexiafamily.com/target-weight-individualized-vs-bmi-eating-disorder; anorexiafamily.com/bmi-weight-for-height-wfh

[99] Anything by Dr Jennifer Gaudiani on this subject is fascinating. eatingdisorderrecoverypodcast.podbean.com/e/dr-g-metabolism and her book 'Sick enough' https://amzn.to/2Xa7tPR

[100] anorexiafamily.com/target-weight-individualized-vs-bmi-eating-disorder

[101] Charts show weight and height percentiles for particular populations
US data revised in 2000, girls: cdc.gov/growthcharts/data/set1clinical/cj41c022.pdf and boys: cdc.gov/growthcharts/data/set1clinical/cj41c021.pdf
For the UK, using data from 1990: rcpch.ac.uk/resources/uk-who-growth-charts-2-18-years. There are more US charts here: cdc.gov/growthcharts/clinical_charts.htm#Set1 If you're interested in the data sources and procedures behind the CDC charts: http://www.cdc.gov/nchs/data/ad/ad314.pdf
There is an online tool to store and plot your data on CDC and WHO charts on mygrowthcharts.com

[102] anorexiafamily.com/target-weight-individualized-vs-bmi-eating-disorder

[103] Allan, R., Sharma, R., Sangani, B., Hugo, P., Frampton, I., Mason, H. and Lask, B., 'Predicting the Weight Gain Required for Recovery from Anorexia Nervosa with Pelvic Ultrasonography', European Eating Disorders Review (2010) onlinelibrary.wiley.com/doi/pdf/10.1002/erv.982 'In some patients a higher WfH ratio or BMI, than has been conventionally recommended, is

needed to ensure reproductive maturity. A generic target WfH ratio of 90% would have been too low to support reproductive maturation in 17% of this sample.'

[104] 'Long-Term Persistence of Hormonal Adaptations to Weight Loss', Sumithran, P., Prendergast, L., Delbridge, E., Purcell, K., Shulkes, A., Kriketos, A., Proietto, J. N Engl J Med 2011; 365:1597-1604, October 27, 2011. www.nejm.org/doi/full/10.1056/NEJMoa1105816

[105] Lauren Muhlheim, 'Why full anorexia recovery is crucial for brain health. The importance of weight restoration and nutritional rehabilitation.' https://www.verywell.com/brain-starvation-and-recovery-in-anorexia-nervosa-1138303

[106] Dr Julie O'Toole on Youtube: 'Towards a definition of state not weight' youtu.be/MFL0zff5JUA and 'Setting goal weights' kartiniclinic.com/blog/post/setting-goal-weights

[107] I recommend Dr Jennifer Gaudiani's book 'Sick enough' (https://amzn.to/2Xa7tPR)

[108] FSRH (2018), fsrh.org/documents/fsrh-ceu-statement-contraception-for-women-with-eating and Dr Jennifer Gaudiani's book 'Sick enough' (https://amzn.to/2Xa7tPR)

[109] Katiejane_Aus, writing on the Around the Dinner Table forum.

[110] See Dr Julie O'Toole's comments here: https://www.kartiniclinic.com/blog/post/the-treatment-of-pediatric-anorexia-nervosa-in-2016/

[111] For instance Around the Dinner Table forum discuss the last 10 lbs http://tinyurl.com/adjyvje or Dr Anna Vinter 'The truth about anxiety during anorexia treatment' eatingrecoverycenter.com/blog/2016/05/31/truth-anxiety-anorexia-treatment-dr-anna-vinter

[112] anorexiafamily.com/weight-restoration-eating-disorder

[113] From Minnesota Mom, posting on the Around the Dinner Table forum.

[114] Julie O'Toole on healthy weight and a kid's mental state: 'Coming to terms with my daughter's genetically programmed body size' kartiniclinic.com/blog/post/coming-to-terms-with-my-daughters-genetically-programmed-body-size. Also 'Weight restoration 2.0' http://www.kartiniclinic.com/blog/post/weight-restoration-2.0 and 'Setting goal weights' https://www.kartiniclinic.com/blog/post/setting-goal-weights

[115] From LV's letter to F.E.A.S.T. website www.feast-ed.org

[116] Great podcast: Karin Kaplan Grumet: The Pros and Cons of Blind Weighing www.edcatalogue.com/episode-97-karin-kaplan-grumet-rd-cedrd-pros-cons-blind-weighing

[117] From Katiejane_Aus, posting on the Around the Dinner Table forum.

[118] From SamHeinous, posting on the Around the Dinner Table forum.

[119] From WenWinning, posting on the Around the Dinner Table forum.

[120] To learn about precautions to take in order to get a true weight, see the video Wee & Weigh by C&M ED Productions: http://youtu.be/t9Y7yv9URCU

[121] Kaye, W. H., Gwirtsman, H. E., Obarzanek, E. and George, D. T., 'Relative importance of calorie intake needed to gain weight and level of physical activty in anorexia nervosa.' In *Am. J. Clin. Nutr.* (1988) vol. 47, pp. 989–94, http://eatingdisorders.ucsd.edu/dl/docs/Relative_Importance_of_Calorie_Intake.pdf

[122] Mamabear's moving account of her child's need to be protected from a compulsion to exercise, and the lengths she had to go to: http://tinyurl.com/axgekvg

[123] Let's Feast Blog, guest post by Dr Julie O'Toole: Medication (23 May 2014), letsfeast.feast-ed.org/2014/05/guest-post-by-dr-julie-otoole.html

[124] Check out the latest on F.E.A.S.T: http://www.feast-ed.org

[125] Fairburn, C. G., *Cognitive Behavior Therapy and Eating Disorders* https://amzn.to/2EkkMFU

[126] More on effects and medical checks in '*How self-induced vomiting impacts your body*' by Pamela K. Keel. edcatalogue.com/self-induced-vomiting-impacts-body Also Dr Jennifer Gaudiani in 'Sick enough' (https://amzn.to/2Xa7tPR)

[127] The FBT manual for bulimia is: Lock and Le Grange's *Treating Bulimia in Adolescents: A Family-Based Approach* https://amzn.to/2GUwMzS

You can see the difference explained on this video with Daniel Le Grange, 'Family-Based Treatment for Bulimia Nervosa': http://maudsleyparents.org/videos.html

[128] For a fascinating first-hand account: youtu.be/hcjdPE1nDQg

[129] Plenty on this from Tabitha Farrar in tabithafarrar.com and her book 'Rehabilitate, rewire, recover!' amzn.to/2JpH4cf

[130] Check out the latest on F.E.A.S.T: http://www.feast-ed.org

[131] More on bingeing in Christopher Fairburn's books *Overcoming Binge Eating* (https://amzn.to/2Nf6mKh) and *Cognitive Behavior Therapy and Eating Disorders* (https://amzn.to/2EkkMFU) and in Glenn Waller's *Cognitive Behavioral Therapy for Eating Disorders* (https://amzn.to/2TXHQzD)

[132] From a girl suffering from anorexia, posting on my website.

[133] Having an eating disorder multiplies the risk of suicide, statistically (which doesn't mean your own child is at risk). See my graphs for suicide statistics: anorexiafamily.com/suicide-eating-disorders-statistics

[134] James Lock, speaking to parents at a seminar of the Eating Disorders Association of New Zealand (EDANZ) said, '*I think it's important to say, I hope I didn't imply that Family-Based Treatment works for everybody. Did I say that? I hope I didn't. Because it doesn't. But then antibiotics don't work for everybody either. No treatment does. Suicide trumps anorexia. It's the only thing I can think of that does. So she's truly suicidal, she apparently is? You really CAN'T keep her at home to work on these things, she HAS to be in a place where she's safe. That's not one of the things we would target, because it's too much, it's too big a problem. Most of the girls with anorexia do not have that problem. They might threaten it, they might actually get pretty serious about making their parents afraid, but very few of them actually do it – your daughter's an exception and I'm sorry about that but I don't really have an answer to that problem.*' (http://youtu.be/gqetg7LFAmo) For the parent who asked the question, this story has a happy unfolding: because they had lost trust in all the treatment providers they had tried over previous years, they committed to their daughter's care at home and concentrated on the emotional and communication aspects described in this book. The girl is now safe and making great strides towards recovery.

[135] This parent also wrote, 'It's now almost a year since diagnosis and things are looking good for my daughter and our family.'

[136] Tips for asking about suicidal thoughts: yahoo.com/lifestyle/8-gentle-ways-ask-child-220515830.html Template for a safety plan: suicidepreventionlifeline.org/wp-content/uploads/2016/08/Brown_StanleySafetyPlanTemplate.pdf

[137] For OCD and other anxiety disorders, you may enjoy *Parenting Your Anxious Child with Mindfulness and Acceptance: A Powerful New Approach to Overcoming Fear, Panic, and Worry Using Acceptance and Commitment Therapy* by Christopher McCurry (http://amzn.to/UGHdWc). Even without OCD in the picture, this book is highly relevant to the work of refeeding our children and exposing them to fear foods. Well worth reading.

[138] Agras, S. W., Lock, J., Brandt, H., Bryson, S. W., Dodge, E., Halmi, K.A., Jo, B., Johnson, C., Kaye, W., Wilfley, D., Woodside, B., 'Comparison of 2 Family Therapies for Adolescent Anorexia Nervosa. A Randomized Parallel Trial.' In *JAMA Psychiatry* (September 24, 2014) http://archpsyc.jamanetwork.com/article.aspx?articleID=1910336

[139] Try WebWatcher webwatcher.com or AVG Family Center avg.com/family-center-faq

[140] I list online parents' groups on anorexiafamily.com/anorexia-nvc-mindfulness-links/anorexia-books-links-review/#Find_support_from_other_parents_internet_groups

[141] From L's letter to the F.E.A.S.T. website http://www.feast-ed.org/default.asp?page=PatientLetters

[142] Bitesize, my library of short audios: anorexiafamily.com/bitesize-public

[143] A parent, reporting from the Intensive Multi-family Therapy Week at University of California, San Diego: http://www.aroundthedinnertable.org/post/ucsd-our-intensive-family-therapy-week-6316129

[144] Jeffers, S., *Feel the fear and do it anyway* (http://amzn.to/UBoa1g).

[145] My YouTube video 'Help your child eat with trust, not logic: the bungee jump' is at http://youtu.be/2O9nZAWCkLc?list=UU0M5B06U-R2ZUd0Cyxdggog

[146] From Jangled, writing on the Around the Dinner Table forum.

[147] 'How do parents of adolescent patients with anorexia nervosa interact with their child at mealtimes? A study of parental strategies used in the family meal session of family-based treatment'. White H., Haycraft E., Madden S., Rhodes P, Miskovic-Wheatley J., Wallis, A., Kohn M., and Meyer C. International Journal of Eating Disorders, 48 (1), p72–80, January 2015 http://onlinelibrary.wiley.com/doi/10.1002/eat.22328/abstract This study is also discussed by Dr Lauren Muhlheim in http://eatingdisordertherapyla.com/parental-direction-works-but-dont-expect-your-kid-to-be-happy-about-it-research-on-the-family-meal-in-fbt

[148] From a girl who suffers from anorexia, commenting on my website.

[149] From a girl who suffers from anorexia, commenting on my website.

[150] From a girl who suffers from anorexia, commenting on my website.

[151] From Lock, J. and Le Grange, D., *Help your teenager beat an eating disorder* (https://amzn.to/2IzYiVQ)

[152] From a girl with anorexia, posting on my website.

[153] From SCMom, writing on the Around the Dinner Table forum.

[154] Xavier Amador has developed LEAP in response to the problem of people with anosognosia (usually suffering from schizophrenia or bipolar disorder) refusing to take medicine: *I Am Not Sick and I Don't Need Help! How to Help Someone with Mental Illness Accept Treatment* (http://amzn.to/WIW1en). There are also some inspiring YouTube videos.

[155] Adding a normalising statement isn't a standard element of empathy in *Nonviolent Communication*, but it may be just what your child needs, so it's worth experimenting with. I recommend Bon Dobbs's book *When Hope Is Not Enough* (http://amzn.to/1qNGTTs) on supporting loved ones with borderline personality disorder, for more examples of validating reflections. More on http://www.anythingtostopthepain.com/

[156] Thank you to Stubbornmum, from the Around the Dinner Table forum.

[157] Also from SamHeinous, a mother on the Around the Dinner Table forum.

[158] YouTube "Sutck and not eating!" https://youtu.be/BVhKXh0gLGc

[159] 'How do parents of adolescent patients with anorexia nervosa interact with their child at mealtimes? A study of parental strategies used in the family meal session of family-based treatment'. White H., Haycraft E., Madden S., Rhodes P, Miskovic-Wheatley J., Wallis, A., Kohn M., and Meyer C. International Journal of Eating Disorders, 48 (1), p72–80, January 2015 http://onlinelibrary.wiley.com/doi/10.1002/eat.22328/abstract This study is also discussed by Dr Lauren Muhlheim in http://eatingdisordertherapyla.com/parental-direction-works-but-dont-expect-your-kid-to-be-happy-about-it-research-on-the-family-meal-in-fbt

[160] A type of exposure therapy used with anorexia is exposure and response prevention, abbreviated as ERP or EXPR. We weren't given any particular approach, but made it up as we went along.

[161] From AlwaysvigilantCAN, posting on the Around the Dinner Table forum.

[162] From Minnesota Mom, posting on the Around the Dinner Table forum.

[163] Siegel, D., *Mindsight: The New Science of Personal Transformation* (http://amzn.to/T4fW3M).

[164] Modern dog training uses 'classical' and 'operant' conditioning, and is referred to as 'positive' because new neural paths are created through pleasure, while punishment, fear or coercion hinder progress. The classic text on these principles is *Don't Shoot the Dog* by Karen Pryor

(http://amzn.to/Vtvqie), and if you'd like to see some of this in action, search for 'clicker training' videos, such as the delightful Kikopup's: http://dogmantics.com/free-videos/

[165] Video: Training Your Dog to Get Over His Fears, one of many videos by trainer extraordinaire Kikopup, which demonstrate positive dog training, based on the same brain principles used in exposure therapy: http://www.youtube.com/watch?v=3-CCJxF-9U4

[166] If you'd rather learn by laughing first, watch this four-minute video clip from The Big Bang Theory. Sheldon is getting exposure therapy to free him of his need for closure: http://youtu.be/WzWOVrhNCeQ

[167] Lauren Muhlheim puts this 'experimenting' concept really well in her excellent book '*When your teen has an eating disorder*' https://amzn.to/2EEhwUS

[168] For a wonderful description of Phase II in FBT, I refer you once again to Dr Sarah Ravin's ever-informative blog: 'Navigating Phase II', http://www.blog.drsarahravin.com/eating-disorders/navigating-phase-ii/

[169] I explain the problem with BMI in anorexiafamily.com/bmi-weight-for-height-wfh

[170] A great overview of what we know about obesity, health, and anti-obesity campaigns: Jacinta Tan, Suzana Corciova and Dasha Nicholls (2019) 'Going too far? How the public health anti-obesity drives could cause harm by promoting eating disorders' in Developments in Neuroethics and Bioethics, 2019, Volume 2, Pages 1-326. https://doi.org/10.1016/bs.dnb.2019.04.009

[171] The portal is: anorexiafamily.com/eating-disorder-policy-guidance-school Also see https://anorexiafamily.com/legal-school-plan-eating-disorder for school's statutory obligations

[172] The schools section on my website: anorexiafamily.com/eating-disorder-policy-guidance-school

[173] anorexia.com/school-eating-disorder-anorexia

[174] anorexiafamily.com/school-trips-anorexia-guide

[175] Helpful article and links from Keborah Klinger (2019): 'Similarities and differences between over-exercise and compulsive exercise' edcatalogue.com/similarities-differences-exercise-compulsive-exercise

[176] From Katie on Facebook group International Eating Disorder Family Support

[177] Dr Julie O'Toole, 'Tough calls parents have to make', kartiniclinic.com/blog/post/tough-calls-parents-have-to-make and 'Exercise and the severely anorexic patient' kartiniclinic.com/blog/post/exercise-and-the-severely-anorexic-patient She warns that exercising could prolong deficiencies in growth, metabolism and cognitive development. She uses lab tests to assess a child's readiness to resume exercise.

I am concerned that according to the CBT-E manual, even underweight patients are encouraged to engage in 'healthy exercise': Fairburn, C. G., *Cognitive Behavior Therapy and Eating Disorders* https://amzn.to/2EkkMFU

[178] From Katiejane_Aus, posting on the Around the Dinner Table forum.

[179] Good advice from Muhlheim, L. and Waterhous, T., 'Traveling with your anorexic', http://eatingdisordertherapyla.com/traveling-with-your-anorexic

[180] The flowchart I gave the teachers is at anorexiafamily.com/school-trips-anorexia-guide

[181] Sumithran, P., Prendergast L., Delbridge E., Purcell K., Shulkes A., Kriketos A., Proietto J., 'Long-Term Persistence of Hormonal Adaptations to Weight Loss' in *The New England Journal of Medicine*, 2011; 365:1597-1604. http://www.nejm.org/doi/full/10.1056/NEJMoa1105816

[182] Evelyn Tribole and Elyse Resch's book *Intuitive Eating: A Revolutionary Program That Works* (https://amzn.to/2qCZDyZ). Intuitive eating website: www.intuitiveeating.org

[183] I cheered throughout this book: A Warner, 'The angry chef' https://amzn.to/2SlV48k

[184] Mindful eating principles: for instance, The Center For Mindful Eating: http://www.thecenterformindfuleating.org/principles

[185] It looks like there's no reason to expect our children to become binge-eaters once they are weight-recovered and free of eating-disorder behaviours and thoughts. Until then it may be that

about 30 per cent of them (or according to other sources, 50 per cent) risk developing binge eating. See, for instance, Strober, M., Freeman, R. and Morrell, W., 'The long-term course of severe anorexia nervosa in adolescents: survival analysis of recovery, relapse, and outcome predictors over 10-15 years in a prospective study' in Int. J. Eat. Disord. (December 1997), vol. 22, no. 4, pp. 339–60, www.ncbi.nlm.nih.gov/pubmed/9356884

[186] For a fascinating first-hand account: youtu.be/hcjdPE1nDQg Also in *Give Food a Chance* by Julie O'Toole (https://amzn.to/2CivYS6). Also Todd Tucker, *The great starvation experiment* (https://amzn.to/2UCK6wE). Also a detailed article: *'They starved so that others be better fed: remembering Ancel Keys and the Minnesota Experiment'* in *The Journal of Nutrition* (June 2005) vol. 135, no. 6, pp. 1347–52, jn.nutrition.org/content/135/6/1347.full

[187] Plenty on this from Tabitha Farrar, e.g. 'Recovery binges' youtube.com/watch?v=JzX4hRWeJkw or from Gwyneth Olwnyn on edinstitute.org

[188] There are so many articles and discussions on parent forums. For instance: many blogs and videos by Tabitha Farrar tabithafarrar.com.

Or Emily T. Troscianko, 'Recovering from Anorexia: How and Why Not to Stop Halfway' psychologytoday.com/blog/hunger-artist/201402/recovering-anorexia-how-and-why-not-stop-halfway.
Or amazonia-love.tumblr.com/post/121882305698/why-so-much-body-fat discussing the MM (MinnieMaud) approach.

[189] Evelyn Tribole and Elyse Resch's book *Intuitive Eating: A Revolutionary Program That Works* (https://amzn.to/2qCZDyZ). Intuitive eating website: www.intuitiveeating.org

[190] Dr Sarah Ravin writes about the main issues addressed in Phase III in http://www.blog.drsarahravin.com/eating-disorders/navigating-phase-iii/

[191] I summarise trauma therapies on anorexiafamily.com/post-traumatic-stress-disorder-ptsd

[192] From Jenny, commenting on Carrie Arnold's blog, ED Bites: http://edbites.com/2013/08/the-trauma-of-having-an-eating-disorder

[193] Lauren Muhlheim, 'Why full anorexia recovery is crucial for brain health. The importance of weight restoration and nutritional rehabilitation.' https://www.verywell.com/brain-starvation-and-recovery-in-anorexia-nervosa-1138303

[194] Details on my website anorexiafamily.com/post-traumatic-stress-disorder-ptsd

[195] More educational resources on my website anorexiafamily.com/health-promotion-ED-prevention-body-obesity-school. Some therapists use *The body image workbook* by T. Cash https://amzn.to/2EYQHL4 which seems to be evidence-based. For parents to learn useful principles I like resources from Australia's Centre for Clinical Interventions although they are for body dysmorphic disorder: cci.health.wa.gov.au/resources/infopax.cfm?Info_ID=55
Lots of learning for parents in The Full Bloom Project podcast: fullbloomproject.com

[196] E.g. The Body Project. More in anorexiafamily.com/health-promotion-ED-prevention-body-obesity-school

[197] From SamHeinous, writing on the Around the Dinner Table forum.

[198] From MariaEC, posting on the Around the Dinner Table forum.

[199] See comments in kartiniclinic.com/blog/post/anorexia-nervosa-meets-thanksgiving-its-a-mess

[200] From Sarah Ravin: 'Leaving the nest: 10 tips for parents': blog.drsarahravin.com/depression/leaving-the-nest-10-tips-for-parents and 'Relapse prevention': letsfeast.feast-ed.org/2014/06/guest-post-relapse-prevention.html and podcast 'Starting college': tabithafarrar.com/podcast/dr-sarah-ravin-eating-disorders-starting-college

From Lauren Muhlheim: 'Is your young adult with an eating disorder ready for college?': eatingdisordertherapyla.com/is-your-young-adult-with-an-eating-disorder-ready-for-college and 'Eating disorder college contracts': mirror-mirror.org/college-contract.htm and 'Relapse prevention plan' mirror-mirror.org/relplan.htm

By Tabitha Farrar: 'Going to college when in recovery from an eating disorder' on mirror-mirror.org/transitioning-to-college.htm

By Carrie Arnold's account: her own thoughtful and honest relapse prevention plan edbites.com/tag/relapse-prevention

[201] Ravin, S., 'After Weight Restoration: Envisioning Recovery', http://www.blog.drsarahravin.com/eating-disorders/after-weight-restoration-envisioning-recovery/

[202] From Emily.

[203] From Jath.

[204] The relapse figures at follow-up one year after end of treatment are 10 per cent and 40 per cent for FBT and AFT respectively,: Lock, L., Le Grange, D., Agras, W.S., Moye, A., Bryson, S.W., and Jo, B., 'Randomized Clinical Trial Comparing Family-Based Treatment to Adolescent Focused Individual Therapy for Adolescents with Anorexia' in *Arch. Gen. Psychiatry* (October 2010), 67(10), pp. 1025-1032, http://tinyurl.com/a322bg7

The figures are more hopeful when you look at the longer picture. Four years after end of treatment, among 79 adolescents who had been symptom-free a year after completing either FBT or AFT, only one in each group had a relapse. Le Grange, D., Lock, J., Accurso, E. C., Agras, W. S., Darcy, A., Forsberg, S., Bryson, S. W., 'Relapse From Remission at Two- to Four-Year Follow-Up in Two Treatments for Adolescent Anorexia Nervosa' in *Journal of the American Academy of Child & Adolescent Psychiatry* (25 August 2014) http://tinyurl.com/ks3jgjt

For youngsters in an intensive inpatient treatment, nearly 30 per cent of patients had relapses following hospital discharge, prior to clinical recovery. But 'there is apparently solid protection against relapse once [recovery] is achieved': Strober, M., Freeman, R. and Morrell, W., 'The long-term course of severe anorexia nervosa in adolescents: survival analysis of recovery, relapse, and outcome predictors over 10-15 years in a prospective study' in *Int. J. Eat. Disord.* (December 1997), vol. 22, no. 4, pp. 339–60, http://www.ncbi.nlm.nih.gov/pubmed/9356884

[205] Dr Julie O'Toole, '*Is anorexia nervosa a chronic illness?*' kartiniclinic.com/blog/post/is-anorexia-nervosa-a-chronic-illness

[206] 'Road to recovery: Stories of hope'. These are brief accounts from parents whose children are now well. aroundthedinnertable.org/post/road-to-recovery----stories-of-hope-5720828

[207] A mother on the FEAST forum describes how she organised support: aroundthedinnertable.org/post/show_single_post?pid=1294886083

[208] From MariaEC, posting on the Around the Dinner Table forum.

[209] From Jangled, a father on the Around the Dinner Table forum. He's referring to a five-day intensive multi-family therapy program at the University of California, San Diego: http://eatingdisorders.ucsd.edu

[210] From a mother on the Around the Dinner Table forum.

[211] One of the best demonstrations I have seen of dialogue during conflict between a couple is in a short video by *NVC* trainer Newt Bailey, entitled 'Connected Communication Process': http://youtu.be/_eT3Cd1_n9M

I like Terry Real 'Fierce intimacy' audible.co.uk/pd/Fierce-Intimacy-Audiobook/B07FXXH91T You might also get help from 'Imago Relationships' (http://gettingtheloveyouwant.com/) and the associated book, *Getting the Love You Want: A Guide for Couples* by Harville Hendrix (http://amzn.to/14REItD). I'm also in awe of Hedy and Yumi Schleifer (http://www.hedyyumi.com) since watching their video 'Crossing the bridge' (http://amzn.to/Y6bkgi). Neither is officially based in *NVC* but the principles are the same.

[212] This is an example of what, in the *NVC* world, is called 'screaming in giraffe' (the giraffe being the symbol of *Nonviolent Communication*).

[213] From MariaEC, posting on the Around the Dinner Table forum.

[214] Read Dr Sarah Ravin: 'A Seat at the Table: Understanding and Helping the Siblings of Eating Disorder Patients', blog.drsarahravin.com/eating-disorders/a-seat-at-the-table-understanding-

and-helping-the-siblings-of-eating-disorder-patients
Also Kym Piekunka and Bridget Whitlow thought-provoking interview on facebook.com/FEASTeatingdisorders/videos/820898884952389/UzpfSTY0ODI1NjY2NTY3 MDEwMD02NTA4NDI4MTg3NDQ4MTg and 'What are siblings reporting?' edcatalogue.com/what-are-siblings-reporting
Also 'An awareness of the impact on the siblings & how they may cope' by C Varnell on CaredScotland caredscotland.co.uk/entry-recovery/recovery-6

[215] 'Insight into living with a twin sister with anorexia' youtube.com/watch?v=rXD8tdvdXQc and 'How to support a friend with an eating disorder' youtube.com/watch?v=ieSK_LYuaPA

[216] A book by Brian Lask and Lucy Watson might provide a starting point: *Can I Tell You About Eating Disorders?: A Guide for Friends, Family and Professionals* (http://amzn.to/1w0vvfS). Note that anorexia is equated with being really skinny – something which hopefully you can correct.

[217] For facts and figures around heritability of anorexia, you'll get a more rounded picture from Carrie Arnold's book *Decoding Anorexia* (http://amzn.to/10Y2Una).

[218] Stice,E., 'Interactive and Mediational Etiologic Models of Eating Disorder Onset: Evidence from Prospective Studies' in Annual Review of Clinical Psychology (2016), vol. 12, pp. 359-381, http://www.annualreviews.org/doi/abs/10.1146/annurev-clinpsy-021815-093317

[219] https://www.news-medical.net/news/20190201/Researchers-reveal-risks-of-eating-disorders-from-childhood.aspx The study is Zeynep, Y., Gottfredson, N., Zerwas, S.C., Bulik, C.M., Micali, N., 'Developmental premorbid body mass index trajectories of adolescents with eating disorders in a longitudinal population cohort' in *JAACAP* (2019), vol. 58, no. 2, pp. 191-199, jaacap.org/article/S0890-8567(18)32042-2/fulltext

[220] More on my website anorexiafamily.com/health-promotion-ED-prevention-body-obesity-school

[221] Golden N.H., Schneider M., Wood C., 'Preventing Obesity and Eating Disorders in Adolescents' in *Pediatrics* (2016) vol.130, no. 3, http://pediatrics.aappublications.org/content/pediatrics/early/2016/08/18/peds.2016-1649.full.pdf The Loth *et al (2009)* study they quote, indicating a link between parental weight talk and eating disorders is only based on the *opinions* of 27 individuals in treatment! They quote two studies showing that parental weight talk is linked to higher BMIs and more disordered eating behaviours, but these are correlations, not causation.

[222] Help for parents in The Full Bloom Project fullbloomproject.com

[223] Risk factors are just about probabilities. Think of smoking, which is a causal risk factor for lung cancer. You can avoid smoking and still get lung cancer. And not everyone who smokes gets lung cancer.

[224] I recommend two guides to feeding a child: Intuitive eating by Evelyn Tribole and Elyse Resch *Intuitive Eating: A Revolutionary Program That Works* (https://amzn.to/2qCZDyZ) and intuitiveeating.org, and evidence-based guidance from the Ellyn Satter Institute ellynsatterinstitute.org (though I am concerned about their rule to not allow food in between mealtimes)

[225] Kristin Neff's TED lecture 'The Space Between Self-Esteem and Self Compassion' on http://youtu.be/IvtZBUSplr4

[226] If you're mulling over the nature of friendships, you may enjoy the short text, 'A reason, a season, or a lifetime' (Author unknown) http://www.naute.com/love/reason.phtml

[227] From Mamabear, writing on the Around the Dinner Table forum.

[228] From Goingtobeatthis_AUS, writing on the Around the Dinner Table forum.

[229] For a list of parents' online groups, see my advice on anorexiafamily.com/anorexia-nvc-mindfulness-links/anorexia-books-links-review/#Find_support_from_other_parents_internet_groups

[230] For tips on insurance, check out DesertDweller's blog 'If you are the parent of an adult loved one with an eating disorder' desertdwellergettingon.blogspot.co.uk/2010/10/being-parent-of-adult-loved-one-with.html Ask for tips on the Around the Dinner Table forum. Check

out the 'Parent Toolkit' booklet produced by NEDA, the National Eating Disorders Association in the USA. http://www.nationaleatingdisorders.org/parent-toolkit.

[231] We have data from randomised controlled trials of FBT, but when you're choosing a therapist or centre, it's nearly impossible to have data on the percentage of patients they successfully treated. For a rare and informative exception, see Dr Sarah Ravin's series of blogs where she publishes and discusses her results: http://www.blog.drsarahravin.com/depression/a-preview-of-my-treatment-outcome-research/

[232] Search for organisations that provide information and support on patients' rights. In the UK, consult Citizens Advice Bureau. See also my 'England' and my 'Scotland' pages on my website.

[233] European countries have a marked psychoanalytical legacy. I interview parents from Switzerland on https://youtu.be/ehZ_SelFGwI Forbidding parental visits until a certain weight is reached is common in French hospitals.

[234] Thomas Insel, MD, Director of the National Institute of Mental Health, (on the 'Facts' section of the F.E.A.S.T. site) November 2010.

[235] See for instance, Beverley Mattocks' account in *Please Eat* (http://amzn.to/195YWhF). The 'rock bottom' principle has been popularised by accounts from recovered addicts, but we should not generalise to eating disorders

[236] As explained in Chapter 4. Also, The National Institute of Mental Health in the US funded a review of many forms of treatment. It concluded that 'the evidence base is strongest for the Maudsley model of family therapy for anorexia nervosa'. Keel, P. K. and Haedt, A., 'Evidence-based psychosocial treatments for eating problems and eating disorders' in *J. Clin. Child Adolesc. Psychol.* (January 2008), vol. 37, no. 1, pp. 39–61, http://www.ncbi.nlm.nih.gov/pubmed/18444053

As a result, The National Institute of Mental Health recommends FBT for the treatment of young people with anorexia: http://www.nimh.nih.gov/health/publications/eating-disorders/index.shtml

Also: Lock, J., 'Evaluation of family treatment models for eating disorders', *Curr. Opin. Psychiatry*, (2011), vol. 24, no. 4, pp. 274–9, http://www.medscape.com/viewarticle/744675

[237] Glenn Waller (2016), 'Treatment Protocols for Eating Disorders: Clinicians' Attitudes, Concerns, Adherence and Difficulties Delivering Evidence-Based Psychological Interventions' F1000 Research http://www.ncbi.nlm.nih.gov/pmc/articles/PMC4759212/

For a personal account, see 'Clinician Faces Old Ideas As She Pursues New Career' (http://www.feast-ed.org/news/news.asp?id=255447), where Dr Sarah Ravin, whose blog is consistently eye-opening and wise, explains why so many clinicians ignore evidence-based treatment.

'Show Me the Science' is another excellent article from Dr Sarah Ravin's blog: she explains how, in the world of psychology, it is quite common to find resistance to evidence-based practices. And also, how working to a manual still allows a therapist plenty of room to customise treatment to each unique patient: http://www.blog.drsarahravin.com/depression/show-me-the-science

[238] This is 'unconscious incompetence', one of four stages of competence wikipedia.org/wiki/Four_stages_of_competence

[239] South London and Maudlsey NHS Trust, Specialist Child and Adolescent Eating Disorder Service (CAEDS). https://www.national.slam.nhs.uk/services/camhs/camhs-eatingdisorders/

In North London, Great Ormond Street Hospital for Children has a Feeding and Eating Disorders Service which UK paediatricians or CAMHS can refer your child to. http://tinyurl.com/qhv63c9

In Scotland, CAMHS can refer under-12s to the inpatient psychiatric unit (which has eating disorders expertise) at the Royal Hospital for Sick Children in Glasgow.

[240] http://www.national.slam.nhs.uk/services/camhs/camhs-eatingdisorders/resources/ Ivan Eisler tells me that with these different modalities (outpatient, day care and close links with the inpatient unit), 80% of patients were discharged without any need for further eating

disorders treatment (most are simply discharged, while around 14% go on to CAMHS treatment for other problems like anxiety or depression). Could one consider these patients to have achieved full remission, as in published studies? 'We would be cautious in saying that they are all recovered as there is often a time lag between weight/eating recovery and cognitive recovery. There are certainly a proportion of people we discharge who remain troubled for some time by eating disorder thoughts, but the great majority continue to improve in this area post treatment and very few relapse (around 5-10%).' How long before patients are discharged? 'Around 25% need 6 months or less, another 25% need 18 months, and a very small proportion need 2 years or more of outpatient treatment.'

[241] Ivan Eisler, Mima Simic, Esther Blessit, Liz Dodge and team (2016), *Maudsley service manual for child and adolescent eating disorders* http://www.national.slam.nhs.uk/services/camhs/camhs-eatingdisorders/resources

[242] From Eisler, I., 'The empirical and theoretical base of family therapy and multiple family day therapy for adolescent anorexia nervosa.' In Journal of Family Therapy (2005) 27: 104-131 Includes a highly-readable description of the therapy http://tinyurl.com/nqggotg Also a study soon to be published shows better outcomes when families receive multifamily therapy as well as single family therapy: Eisler, I., Simic, M., Hodsoll, J., Asen, E., Berelowitz, M., Connan, F. et al. (in press, 2016). 'A pragmatic randomised multi-centre trial of multifamily and single family therapy for adolescent anorexia nervosa.' BMC Psychiatry.

[243] Minimum 4-day training given to experienced therapists in many UK eating-disorders teams (https://www.national.slam.nhs.uk/services/camhs/camhs-eatingdisorderstraining) (though Scotland is mostly FBT-trained). From what parents tell me or write on forums, some find multi-family incredibly helpful, while others say it wasn't for them. In the US, UCSD 's intensive multi-family therapy program (http://eatingdisorders.ucsd.edu/treatment/oneweek-intensive-treatment-programs.html) was developed with Ivan Eisler's input. It differs from the UK approach and generally gets a big thumbs up from parents.

[244] Lock, J., Le Grange, D., Agras, W. S. and Dare, C., *Treatment Manual for Anorexia Nervosa: A Family-Based Approach* https://amzn.to/2UyqXfK. This book is written for clinicians but it's totally accessible to parents and full of useful information.

[245] Lock, J. and Le Grange, D., *Help your teenager beat an eating disorder* (https://amzn.to/2IzYiVQ). This book is essential reading for parents. If you read nothing else, read this.

[246] 'Family Therapy for Adolescent Eating and Weight Disorders: New Applications', edited by Katharine L. Loeb, Daniel Le Grange, James Lock, 2015. http://amzn.to/1avbchl

[247] For more on the difference between FBT (often called 'Maudsley') and the 'New Maudsley Method, read 'Navigating the Search for True Maudsley Treatment' on the MaudsleyParents website. http://maudsleyparents.org/uofchicagoadvice.html

[248] Treasure, J., Smith, G. and Crane, A., *Skills-based Learning for Caring for a Loved One with an Eating Disorder: The New Maudsley Method*. Note that this is method is different from the so-called 'Maudsley Approach', or Family-Based Treatment (FBT) manualised by Lock, Le Grange *et al.*

Another book by the New Maudsley team is *Anorexia Nervosa. A Recovery Guide for Sufferers, Families and Friends* by Treasure, J. and Alexander, J. (Routledge Mental Health).

The website of the The New Maudsley Approach (http://thenewmaudsleyapproach.co.uk) has a practical tools for parents to help them support their (mostly adult) loved one.

[249] Fisher, C. A., Hetrick, S. E. and Rushford, N., 'Family therapy for anorexia nervosa' in *Cochrane Database Syst Rev* (April 2010), vol. 14, no. 4, CD004780, http://www.ncbi.nlm.nih.gov/pubmed/20393940 reviewed trials where interventions described as 'family therapy' were compared to other psychological or educational interventions. On the whole, there seemed to be little advantage in family therapy. In other words, don't assume that just because Family-Based Treatment works, any other form of family therapy will work too.

[250] Agras, S. W., Lock, J., Brandt, H., Bryson, S. W., Dodge, E., Halmi, K.A., Jo, B., Johnson, C., Kaye, W., Wilfley, D., Woodside, B., 'Comparison of 2 Family Therapies for Adolescent Anorexia Nervosa. A Randomized Parallel Trial.' In *JAMA Psychiatry* (2014) http://tinyurl.com/hxvltpx There were 78 adolescents receiving FBT and 80 receiving systemic family therapy. Both treatments led to similar rates of recovery at end of treatment and at 12-

month follow-up. But there were differences in other outcomes: systemic family therapy was better for adolescents who had obsessive-compulsive symptoms as well as anorexia, and FBT was better at reducing hospitalisation (median number of days 8.3 days versus 21.0 days), possibly because patients put on weight faster in the initial 8 weeks of treatment. Both types of treatment lasted 9 months.

[251] Prior to the research conducted on FBT, 'the evidence' for anorexia treatment was 'weak', the literature 'sparse and inconclusive', according to Bulik, C. M., Berkman, N., Kimberly, A. *et al*, 'Anorexia nervosa: a systematic review of randomized clinical trials' in *Int. J. Eat. Disord.* (2007), vol. 40, pp. 310–20, http://onlinelibrary.wiley.com/doi/10.1002/eat.20367/abstract

Some figures for patients not treated with FBT are available from Strober, M., Freeman, R. and Morrell, W., 'The long-term course of severe anorexia nervosa in adolescents: survival analysis of recovery, relapse, and outcome predictors over 10-15 years in a prospective study' in *Int. J. Eat. Disord.* (December 1997), vol. 22, no. 4, pp. 339–60, http://www.ncbi.nlm.nih.gov/pubmed/9356884

Here's an overview from this paper: Other review studies reported that 32 per cent to 68 per cent of people who'd had anorexia as youngsters had, some years later, a 'good outcome'. Mortality, including suicide, was 1.8 per cent to 14.1 per cent. Strober's study followed adolescents treated in one intensive inpatient unit, which provided weight-restoration, individual and family therapy. Ten to 15 years later, none of the 95 patients died. There was a 'good outcome' in 86 per cent of patients, and 76 per cent of patients made a 'full recovery'. But it took a long time to get them there: 57 to 79 months, depending on the definition of recovery.

[252] Lock, J., Le Grange, D., Agras, W. S. and Dare, C., *Treatment Manual for Anorexia Nervosa: A Family-Based Approach* https://amzn.to/2UyqXfK

[253] For a summary of the research findings on family therapy, see Rienecke, Renee D. 'Family-based treatment of eating disorders in adolescents: current insights' in *Adol health, med and therapeutics* (Jun 2017), vol. 8, pp. 69-79 https://pdfs.semanticscholar.org/d3d1/65e737dceeda802a134bd86c37b2ffda6ddf.pdf

The main studies:
Eisler, I., Dare, C., Russell, G. F. M., Szmukler, G. I., Le Grange, D. and Dodge, E., 'Family and individual therapy in anorexia nervosa: A five-year follow-up' in *Archives of General Psychiatry* (1997) vol. 54, pp. 1025–30, http://www.ncbi.nlm.nih.gov/pubmed/9366659

Lock, J., Le Grange, D., Agras, W.S., Moye, A., Bryson, S.W., and Jo, B., 'Randomized Clinical Trial Comparing Family-Based Treatment to Adolescent Focused Individual Therapy for Adolescents with Anorexia' in *Arch. Gen. Psychiatry* (2010), 67(10), pp. 1025-1032, http://tinyurl.com/a322bg7. Full remission, in this study, means a combination of a minimum of 95% of ideal body weight (given the patient's gender, age, and height) and scores within 1 standard deviation from global mean Eating Disorder Examination (EDE) norms (which means their behaviours and thoughts were within a normal range).

Were these studies done with 'easy' patients? It seems not: 26 per cent of the participants had co-morbid psychiatric disorders, and 45 per cent had previously been hospitalised.

Agras, S. W., Lock, J., Brandt, H., Bryson, S. W., Dodge, E., Halmi, K.A., Jo, B., Johnson, C., Kaye, W., Wilfley, D., Woodside, B., 'Comparison of 2 Family Therapies for Adolescent Anorexia Nervosa. A Randomized Parallel Trial.' In *JAMA Psychiatry* (September 24, 2014) http://archpsyc.jamanetwork.com/article.aspx?articleID=1910336 is another randomised controlled trial, this time comparing FBT with another form of family therapy (systemic family therapy). Success rates were lower than in the 2010 study. One possible reason I have been given in a personal communication is that the therapists had far less experience in FBT than those in the 2010 study – indeed when 210 therapy tapes were audited for 'fidelity' to the approach, the mean scores were only 4.38 on a 0 to 6 scale. Note also that the therapy, in this case, only lasted 6 months. To expect weight, mindset and behaviours to have all returned to normal within 6 months ("full remission') is very ambitious.

We also have figures for FBT used after a hospital stay: Madden S, Miskovic-Wheatley J, Wallis A, Kohn M, Lock J, Le Grange D, Jo B, Clarke S, Rhodes P, Hay P, Touyz S. 'A randomized controlled trial of in-patient treatment for anorexia nervosa in medically unstable adolescents. In Psychol Med. (2015) 45:415-427 http://tinyurl.com/j35xvzf

More statistics come from Daniel Le Grange, Elizabeth K. Hughes, Andrew Court, Michele Yeo, Ross D. Crosby, Susan M. Sawyer. 'Randomized Clinical Trial of Parent-Focused Treatment and Family-Based Treatment for Adolescent Anorexia Nervosa'. *J Am Academy Child & Ado Psych* (2016) 55 (8) pp 683–692 http://tinyurl.com/z7rwsgr

On the whole, the effect of the treatment seems to stick, and time or life also seems to bring improvements: five years after the end of FBT treatment, 80 to 85 per cent of youngsters no longer met diagnostic criteria.

Were these studies done with 'easy' patients? It seems not, in the largest study (the 2010 one), 26 per cent of the participants had co-morbid psychiatric disorders, and 45 per cent had previously been hospitalised.

Another randomised controlled trial was published in 2014, this time comparing FBT with another form of family therapy (systemic family therapy). Success rates were lower than in the 2010 study. One possible reason I have been given in a personal communication is that the therapists had far less experience in FBT than those in the 2010 study – indeed when 210 therapy tapes were audited for 'fidelity' to the approach, the mean scores were only 4.38 on a 0 to 6 scale. Note also that the therapy, in this case, only lasted 6 months. To expect weight, mindset and behaviours to have all returned to normal within 6 months ("full remission') is very ambitious. For the 78 adolescents receiving FBT, the rates were 33.1 per cent at end of treatment and 40.7 per cent at the 12-month follow up (compared to 42 per cent and 49 per cent respectively in the 2010 study). Agras, S. W., Lock, J., Brandt, H., Bryson, S. W., Dodge, E., Halmi, K.A., Jo, B., Johnson, C., Kaye, W., Wilfley, D., Woodside, B., 'Comparison of 2 Family Therapies for Adolescent Anorexia Nervosa. A Randomized Parallel Trial.' In *JAMA Psychiatry* (September 24, 2014) http://archpsyc.jamanetwork.com/article.aspx?articleID=1910336

We also have figures for FBT used after a hospital stay: Madden S, Miskovic-Wheatley J, Wallis A, Kohn M, Lock J, Le Grange D, Jo B, Clarke S, Rhodes P, Hay P, Touyz S. 'A randomized controlled trial of in-patient treatment for anorexia nervosa in medically unstable adolescents. In Psychol Med. (2015) 45:415-427 http://tinyurl.com/j35xvzf

More statistics come from Daniel Le Grange, Elizabeth K. Hughes, Andrew Court, Michele Yeo, Ross D. Crosby, Susan M. Sawyer. 'Randomized Clinical Trial of Parent-Focused Treatment and Family-Based Treatment for Adolescent Anorexia Nervosa'. *J Am Academy Child & Ado Psych* (2016) 55 (8) pp 683–692 http://tinyurl.com/z7rwsgr

On the whole, FBT seems to work with half the dose: from 20 to 24 sessions over a year are no better than 10 sessions over 6 months (but patients with significant Obsessive-Compulsive Disorder symptoms fare better with the longer dose): Lock, J., Agras, W. S., Bryson, S. and Kraemer, H., 'A comparison of short- and long-term family therapy for adolescent anorexia nervosa' in *J. Am. Acad. Child Adolesc. Psychiatry* (2005), vol. 44, pp. 632–9, http://www.ncbi.nlm.nih.gov/pubmed/15968231

[254] Statistics summarised in Daniel Le Grange et al. 'Randomized Clinical Trial of Parent-Focused Treatment and Family-Based Treatment for Adolescent Anorexia Nervosa'. *J Am Academy Child & Ado Psych* (2016) 55 (8) pp 683–692 http://tinyurl.com/z7rwsgr Daniel Le Grange told me they represent averages from up to and including 2015, all using a high bar for 'remission'. Note that the studies' weight criterion for 'remission' is over 95% of median body mass index. I explained earlier the problem with using population statistics to estimate a healthy weight target.

[255] I explain these issues in two articles: anorexiafamily.com/weight-restoration-eating-disorder and anorexiafamily.com/target-weight-individualized-vs-bmi-eating-disorder

[256] These are youngsters whose weight reached at least 85 per cent of median body mass index

[257] Fisher, CA, Skocic, S, Rutherford, KA, Hetrick, SE. Family therapy approaches for anorexia nervosa. Cochrane Database of Systematic Reviews 2019, Issue 5. cochranelibrary.com/cdsr/doi/10.1002/14651858.CD004780.pub4/information

[258] FBT and under-12s: Lock J., Le Grange, D., Forsberg, S. and Hewell, K., 'Is family therapy useful for treating children with anorexia nervosa? Results of a case series' in *J. Am. Acad. Child*

Adolesc. Psychiatry (November 2006), vol. 45, no. 11, pp. 1323-8,
http://www.ncbi.nlm.nih.gov/pubmed/17075354

Many FBT studies focus on 12 to 18-year olds, but results are similar with 9 to 13-year-olds,
according to a study of 32 children with anorexia: Lock J., Le Grange, D., Forsberg, S. and
Hewell, K., 'Is family therapy useful for treating children with anorexia nervosa? Results of a
case series' in *J. Am. Acad. Child Adolesc. Psychiatry* (November 2006), vol. 45, no. 11, pp. 1323-8,
http://www.ncbi.nlm.nih.gov/pubmed/17075354

[259] 'Young adults with anorexia: not too old for family therapy' by Eva Musby (2015)
http://www.mirror-mirror.org/treatment-for-young-adults-with-anorexia.htm See also an earlier
account: http://www.maudsleyparents.org/youngadults.html

[260] 'Randomized clinical trial of family-based treatment and cognitive-behavioral therapy for
adolescent bulimia nervosa.' Daniel Le Grange, James Lock, W. Stewart Agras, Susan W. Bryson,
Booil Jo. J Am Academy of Child & Adol Psych, 2015, 54(11) p886-894
http://www.jaacap.com/article/S0890-8567(15)00538-9/abstract
For a summary of this research, read Dr L Muhlheim (2015): 'For teens with bulimia, family
based treatment is recommended' www.eatingdisordertherapyla.com/for-teens-with-bulimia-
family-based-treatment-is-recommended

[261] Ivan Eisler, Mima Simic, Esther Blessit, Liz Dodge and team (2016), *Maudsley service manual for
child and adolescent eating disorders* http://www.national.slam.nhs.uk/services/camhs/camhs-
eatingdisorders/resources
Lock, J., Le Grange, D., Agras, W. S. and Dare, C., *Treatment Manual for Anorexia Nervosa: A
Family-Based Approach* https://amzn.to/2UyqXfK
Lots more on FBT on The Maudsley Parents website http://maudsleyparents.org

[262] On the whole, FBT seems to work with half the dose: from 20 to 24 sessions over a year are
no better than 10 sessions over 6 months (but patients with significant Obsessive-Compulsive
Disorder symptoms fare better with the longer dose): Lock, J., Agras, W. S., Bryson, S. and
Kraemer, H., 'A comparison of short- and long-term family therapy for adolescent anorexia
nervosa' in *J. Am. Acad. Child Adolesc. Psychiatry* (2005), vol. 44, pp. 632–9,
http://www.ncbi.nlm.nih.gov/pubmed/15968231

[263] For a wonderful description of Phase II in FBT, I refer you once again to Dr Sarah Ravin's
ever-informative blog: Navigating Phase II, http://www.blog.drsarahravin.com/eating-
disorders/navigating-phase-ii/

[264] Dr Sarah Ravin writes about the main issues addressed in Phase III in
http://www.blog.drsarahravin.com/eating-disorders/navigating-phase-iii/

[265] Train2treat4ed lists certified FBT therapists: train2treat4ed.com/certified-therapists-list. They
may not all be there because they have to pay to be on the site. I list those who are available to
treat via Skype on anorexiafamily.com/certified-fbt-therapists-family-based-treatment-who-
skype. The site Maudsley Parents lists FBT therapists along with some information about them:
maudsleyparents.org/providerlist.html

[266] This is now the case for all CAMHS in Scotland and many in England.

[267] Even after a year of training and weekly supervision, when 210 FBT therapy tapes were
audited, therapists did not show more than a moderate level of fidelity to the FBT approach.
Lock, L., Le Grange, D., Agras, W.S., Moye, A., Bryson, S.W., and Jo, B., 'Randomized Clinical
Trial Comparing Family-Based Treatment to Adolescent Focused Individual Therapy for
Adolescents with Anorexia' in *Arch. Gen. Psychiatry* (October 2010), 67(10), pp. 1025-1032,
http://tinyurl.com/a322bg7 The team are working on improving dissemination.

[268] From a parent on the FEAST forum:
aroundthedinnertable.org/post/show_single_post?pid=1294874899

[269] For instance, Ellison, R., Rhodes, P., Madden, S., Miskovic, J., Wallis, A., Baillie, A., Kohn, M.
and Touyz, S., 'Do the components of manualized family-based treatment for anorexia nervosa
predict weight gain?' in *Int. J. Eat. Disord.* (May 2012), vol. 45, no. 4, pp. 609–14,
http://www.ncbi.nlm.nih.gov/pubmed/22270977. This showed that parents taking control,

being united, not criticizing the patient and externalizing the illness predicted greater weight gain. Sibling support did not predict weight gain.

[270] For adaptions of FBT, read *Family therapy for adolescent eating and weight disorders* edited by Katharine Loeb, Daniel Le Grange and James Lock, Routledge, 2015 http://amzn.to/1NN56aF

[271] NICE guidance (2017): nice.org.uk/guidance/ng69 I explain it in anorexiafamily.com/nice-guidelines-adolescent-eating-disorder-ng69

[272] Lock, L., Le Grange, D., Agras, W.S., Moye, A., Bryson, S.W., and Jo, B., 'Randomized Clinical Trial Comparing Family-Based Treatment to Adolescent Focused Individual Therapy for Adolescents with Anorexia' in *Arch. Gen. Psychiatry* (October 2010), 67(10), pp. 1025-1032, http://tinyurl.com/a322bg7

Half the adolescents were given FBT, while the other half were given the most promising type of individual psychotherapy available at the time: AFT. AFT is designed to use the therapeutic relationship to foster independence, autonomy and self-management of anorexia nervosa symptoms.

The two approaches had similar results by the end of a year's treatment, but FBT proved to be superior at 6- and 12-month follow-up. For instance, a year after end of treatment, 18 per cent of the AFT group had been hospitalised, as opposed to 4 per cent in the FBT group. And of those who had achieved full remission at end of treatment, 40 per cent of the AFT participants relapsed, against 10 per cent of the FBT participants.

Four years after end of treatment, among 79 adolescents who had been symptom-free a year after completing either FBT or AFT, only one in each group had a relapse. Le Grange, D., Lock, J., Accurso, E. C., Agras, W. S., Darcy, A., Forsberg, S., Bryson, S. W., 'Relapse From Remission at Two- to Four-Year Follow-Up in Two Treatments for Adolescent Anorexia Nervosa' in *Journal of the American Academy of Child & Adolescent Psychiatry* (25 August 2014) http://tinyurl.com/ks3jgjt

Note that this talking therapy (AFT) is quite different from talking therapies where the focus is for insights into childhood traumas. With AFT, 'Patients learn to identify and define their emotions, and later, to tolerate affective states rather than numbing themselves with starvation. The therapist actively encourages the patient to stop dieting and to gain weight, and asks the patient to accept responsibility for food related issues'. Parents are only involved to 'assess parental functioning, advocate for the patient's developmental needs, and update parents on progress'.

[273] anorexiafamily.com/nice-guidelines-adolescent-eating-disorder-ng69 and https://www.nice.org.uk/guidance/ng69

[274] https://www.nice.org.uk/guidance/ng69

[275] Junior MARSIPAN: Management of Really Sick Patients under 18 with Anorexia Nervosa, report from the Junior MARSIPAN group, College Report CR168 (January 2012), Royal College of Psychiatrists London rcpsych.ac.uk/usefulresources/publications/collegereports/cr/cr168.aspx

[276] From Jangled, writing on the Around the Dinner Table forum.

[277] Blake Woodside, director of the eating disorders program at Toronto General Hospital, quoted by Carrie Arnold in her book *Decoding Anorexia* (http://amzn.to/10Y2Una). He is co-author of 'Relapse in anorexia nervosa: a survival analysis' in *Psychol. Med.* (May 2004), vol. 34, no. 4, pp. 671–9, http://www.ncbi.nlm.nih.gov/pubmed/15099421

[278] Parents report huge benefits from learning DBT skills (dialectic behaviour therapy) along with their children at UCSD's intensive family treatment aroundthedinnertable.org/post/ucsd-our-intensive-family-therapy-week-6316129

[279] Dr Sarah Ravin's blog 'Red Flags: How to Spot Ineffective Eating Disorder Treatment' is a must-read if you're on the hunt for treatment, or if you're worried about your current therapist. http://www.blog.drsarahravin.com/eating-disorders/red-flags-how-to-spot-ineffective-eating-disorder-treatment.

[280] There is no standard training path, and you cannot assume anything. Some therapists have treated eating disorders for decades using older psychological models, and it takes more than a

two-day introductory course for them to master the family-based approach. In countries without a national health service, training can be just about anything! In England, recently, the NHS overhauled eating disorder treatment for youngsters. Specialist teams were trained up fast, and all therapists must have regular supervision. Overall, the improvements have been fantastic. But there is no standard for training of therapists or supervisors. Some of these people may be treating your child or running multifamily groups after just two days' training from the team at the Maudsley's children and adolescents service. A few have had a day's introduction to FBT when James Lock visits the UK. Some have had a few hours from Janet Treasure's team on 'New Maudsley', after which they tell parents to be dolphins and incorrectly claim to be 'doing FBT'. Many don't know the difference between all these approaches and are ignorant of the manuals.

Scotland invites Lock in regularly for training in FBT. Some therapists are going through hundreds of hours of supervision from Lock's team to become certified, while others treat patients after a two-day course. Others are generalist mental health professionals with no eating-disorder specialisation.

[281] I list online forums here: anorexiafamily.com/anorexia-nvc-mindfulness-links/anorexia-books-links-review

[282] A good piece by therapists Carolyn Costin and Alli Spotts-De Lazzer: 'To tell or not to tell: therapists with a personal history of an eating disorder' https://www.edcatalogue.com/tell-not-tell/

[283] Perhaps we sense that our clinicians don't have much fun: Warren, C. S., Schafer, K. J., Crowley, M. E. and Olivardia, R., 'A qualitative analysis of job burnout in eating disorder treatment providers.' in *Eat. Disord.* (May 2012), vol. 20, no. 3, pp. 175–95, http://www.ncbi.nlm.nih.gov/pubmed/22519896

[284] UCSD: University of California, San Diego: Eating Disorders Center for Treatment and Research: http://eatingdisorders.ucsd.edu/. Among other things, they offer five-day intensive multi-family therapy.

[285] List of certified FBT therapists who do telemedicine: anorexiafamily.com/certified-fbt-therapists-family-based-treatment-who-skype

[286] The Maudsley hospital in south London provides a national eating disorders service (outpatient and daypatient) for children and adolescents https://www.national.slam.nhs.uk/services/camhs/camhs-eatingdisorders/. In north London, Great Ormond Street Hospital for Children has a Feeding and Eating Disorders Service. Both these London units accept referrals from CAMHS clinicians or consultant paediatricians anywhere in the UK and can give treatment or just a second opinion.

In Scotland, CAMHS can refer under-12s to the inpatient psychiatric unit (which has eating disorders expertise) at the Royal Hospital for Children in Glasgow.

[287] Laura Collins' book *Eating With Your Anorexic* (http://amzn.to/WoVIiI) tells the story of how her daughter was treated within the family, using principles of FBT. Harriet Brown, in *Brave Girl Eating* (http://amzn.to/YFc395), tells the story of her daughter's journey to recovery at home, also along FBT principles. The book includes useful and accessible accounts of the scientific knowledge about anorexia. Harriet Brown's article on her DIY approach to treatment: 'How to Put Together, and Work With, a Non-Maudsley Team': http://maudsleyparents.org/workingwithanonmaudsleyteam.html

[288] I list online forums here: anorexiafamily.com/anorexia-nvc-mindfulness-links/anorexia-books-links-review

[289] Rebecca Peebles (9mn57 in): youtu.be/WiC4cd4uI9U?t=597

[290] anorexiafamily.com/individual-support

[291] It's interesting to note, from Dr Sarah Ravin's experience, that 'Hospitalization during treatment with me was not related to treatment completion or treatment outcome, regardless of diagnosis.' In other words, if you're treating your child with FBT, a spell in hospital may be necessary, but after that, FBT is just as likely to succeed.

http://www.blog.drsarahravin.com/eating-disorders/a-comparison-of-treatment-outcomes-an-bn-and-ednos/

A study following youngsters after an intensive inpatient program: Strober, M., Freeman, R. and Morrell, W., 'The long-term course of severe anorexia nervosa in adolescents: survival analysis of recovery, relapse, and outcome predictors over 10-15 years in a prospective study' in *Int. J. Eat. Disord.* (December 1997), vol. 22, no. 4, pp. 339–60, http://www.ncbi.nlm.nih.gov/pubmed/9356884

[292] Stuart B. Murray, Leslie K. Anderson, Roxanne Rockwell, Scott Griffiths, Daniel Le Grange, Walter H. Kaye, 'Adapting Family-Based Treatment for Adolescent Anorexia Nervosa Across Higher Levels of Patient Care'. Eating Dis: Journal of Treatment & Prevention (2015) 23(4) http://www.tandfonline.com/doi/full/10.1080/10640266.2015.1042317

[293] Risk assessment, physical examination and more on 'Junior Marsipan: management of really sick patients under 18 with anorexia nervosa'. CR168, Royal college of psychiatrists, 2012. http://www.rcpsych.ac.uk/usefulresources/publications/collegereports/cr/cr168.aspx

[294] For an example of a clinician conveying a strong commitment to parents as partners, watch the video of Dr Rebecka Peebles speaking at Maudsley parents' conference on 'Eating Disorders: What Pediatricians and Parents Should Know' (http://vimeo.com/50460378).

[295] Advice from clinician Xavier Amador in *I am not sick and I don't need help! How to Help Someone with Mental Illness Accept Treatment* (http://amzn.to/WIW1en).

[296] Daniel Le Grange, Elizabeth K. Hughes, Andrew Court, Michele Yeo, Ross D. Crosby, Susan M. Sawyer, 'Randomized Clinical Trial of Parent-Focused Treatment and Family-Based Treatment for Adolescent Anorexia Nervosa' in *J Am Academy Child & Ado Psych* (2016), vol. 55, no. 8, pp. 683–692 http://tinyurl.com/z7rwsgr

[297] Dr Sarah Ravin (2016). *Parent-focused treatment: an attractive alternative to FBT.* http://www.blog.drsarahravin.com/eating-disorders/parent-focused-treatment-an-attractive-alternative-to-fbt/

[298] 'Weight gain & kid in recovery?' blog post by Amazonia-Love: amazonia-love.tumblr.com/post/147567439533/weight-gain-kid-in-recovery

[299] Dr Rebecka Peebles, 1:02:40 into this excellent talk: vimeo.com/50460378

[300] Waller, G., Cordery, H., Costorphine, E., Hinrichsen, H., Lawson, R., Mountford, V., Russel, K. (2007) *Cognitive Behavioral Therapy for Eating Disorders: Comprehensive Treatment Guide* (https://amzn.to/2TXHQzD)

[301] From the MARSIPAN guidelines, Royal College of Physicians, rcpsych.ac.uk/docs/default-source/improving-care/better-mh-policy/college-reports/college-report-cr189.pdf Also Amador, X., I am not sick and I don't need help! *How to Help Someone with Mental Illness Accept Treatment* (https://amzn.to/2I1p5Z0). Also DesertDweller's blog relating to caring for an adult, in particular desertdwellergettingon.blogspot.co.uk/2010/10/being-parent-of-adult-loved-one-with.html and desertdwellergettingon.blogspot.co.uk/2014/11/what-about-hipaa-and-how-to-overcome.html. For the UK, the NICE guidelines have a lot of the involvement of families: nice.org.uk/guidance/ng69

[302] Insightful account from a 40-year old: feast-ed.org/reflections-on-my-recovery-at-40-a-journey-with-my-parents

[303] Young adults with anorexia: family-based treatment for 17-25 year olds anorexiafamily.com/family-based-treatment young-adult

[304] In the UK, I think that Lasting Power of Attorney sets the bar too high to be much use: it only kicks in when the person is judged to not have the mental capacity to make decisions for themselves.

[305] Bulik, C., 'The complex dance of genes and environment in eating disorders'. An insightful one-hour lecture on YouTube. Warning: several images of skeletal people, which I could do without (http://youtu.be/zi2xXEz0Jog).

[306] My video 'The hero's journey: resilience and wellbeing for parents', youtu.be/HZgqolG3HeU

307 anorexiafamily.com/individual-support

308 She trained in the 'Human Givens' approach (http://www.hgi.org.uk/)

309 Odet Beauvoisin, certified advanced practitioner of EFT www.eftkinesiology.co.uk She can treat by video call (Skype). There is a lot of research on EFT, including some randomised controlled studies (http://www.eftuniverse.com/research-and-studies/eft-research#review). I like how the technique dovetails with mindfulness and connection to physical sensations, and how even though it looks weird, there's no bullshit.

310 Dr Sarah Ravin's tips: blog.drsarahravin.com/psychotherapy/how-to-choose-a-therapist

311 Bitesize, my library of short audios: anorexiafamily.com/bitesize-public

312 *Compassion Communication,* also called *Nonviolent Communication (NVC):* The Center for Nonviolent Communication at www.cnvc.org. I believe that NVC could do with making the 'kindness' element more explicit, while therapies that emphasize compassion could do with more emphasis on 'needs' or core values. So in this book I am blending the approaches.

Emotion-Focused Family Treatment (EFFT) provides parents with a useful framework, with excellent videos, such as youtu.be/-q3V_gkJoXE More on: mentalhealthfoundations.ca and emotionfocusedfamilytherapy.org

More resources from Kristin Neff on www.self-compassion.org or her book *Self-compassion: the proven power of being kind to yourself* amzn.to/2RXo3Qv . Also Paul Gilbert's lectures, starting from youtu.be/qnHuECDlSvE or his books, e.g. *Mindful compassion* amzn.to/2CnoZrK. Putting it all together, is Tara Brach's fantastic book *True refuge* amzn.to/2ypf81V. Also many free talks on www.tarabrach.com.

313 'Connect before you Correct' comes from Nonviolent Communication (NVC). The elevator analogy comes from Emotion Focused Family Therapy (EFFT)

314 There's a (non-exhaustive) list of feelings here: www.cnvc.org/Training/feelings-inventory

315 From Jill Bolte Taylor, neuroanatomist, in wonderful TED talk *My stroke of insight* youtu.be/UyyjU8fzEYU I can't find any details. It seems like a preposterous statement, yet I can relate to my frequent experiences of a strong emotion passing in the space of a minute or two of self-connection via 'tapping' (Emotional Freedom Technique, EFT)

316 The notion that we create our own feelings is a view shared by practitioners of mindfulness, of *Nonviolent Communication,* and of therapies like Cognitive Behaviour Therapy (CBT) and Acceptance and Commitment Therapy (ACT).

317 The main approaches I know of that include 'needs' are Nonviolent Communication (NVC) and Acceptance and Commitment Therapy (ACT). Cognitive Behavioural Therapy (CBT) stops at feelings.
You can find (non-exhaustive) lists of needs in *NVC* literature, for instance here: http://www.cnvc.org/Training/needs-inventory. But I'm going to go out on a limb and tell you not to worry about the exact words, because most of the time you're not going to use the words on these lists. If you use words like this when talking to others, they'll think you're weird and your desire to connect will be doomed.

318 For more about the brain in adolescence you might enjoy *Why Do They Act That Way?* by David Walsh (although I would throw out any parental advice about rewards and 'consequences'). Nicola Morgan's *Blame My Brain* is readable by both teens and their parents. And there's a powerful TED talk by Jill Bolte Taylor: *The neuronatomical transformation of the teenage brain* on http://tedxtalks.ted.com/video/The-Nearanatomical-Transformati

319 Quoted or adapted from *NVC* trainer Inbal Kashtan, who's a precious source of wisdom on children and all relationships. Check her out via the BayNVC's website (http://www.baynvc.org/).

320 That happens with Cognitive Behavioural Therapy (CBT), as it teaches us to dispute our thoughts

321 In *Nonviolent Communication (NVC),* what I'm calling 'chatterbox' thoughts are affectionately represented by a jackal. The giraffe represents Nonviolent Communication because it has a big heart and, being far above the ground, it can see the bigger picture.

[322] Great coaching on using 'Because' in Emotion-Focused Family Treatment (EFFT) resources such as youtu.be/-q3V_gkJoXE More on: mentalhealthfoundations.ca and emotionfocusedfamilytherapy.org

[323] From SamHeinous, a mother on the Around the Dinner Table forum.

[324] From a report by Janet Treasure, speaking at a F.E.A.S.T symposium in Nottingham (November 2012), http://www.ustream.tv/channel/feast2012-nottingham

[325] anorexiafamily.com/ok-observe-with-kindness-mindfulness-compassion

[326] Kristin Neff on self-compassion.org is the big name in self-compassion. My guided self-compassion audios are all on anorexiafamily.com/order-audio Some are on YouTube. Also, search for 'Self-compassion' or 'Kindness' on meditation apps.

[327] Kristin Neff, self-compassion.org

[328] What I write may just be a bunch of words until you've at least seen empathy in action. I recommend a recording of an in-depth telecourse by NVC trainer Robert Gonzales on the subject of self-empathy and of mourning unmet needs: 'The Living Energy of Needs: Inner Work and Empathy from the Beauty of Needs'. You can buy it from NVC Marketplace nonviolentcommunication.net or NVC Academy.

[329] https://anorexiafamily.com/NVC-communication

[330] anorexiafamily.com/compassion-and-self-compassion Also lots on YouTube, podcasts and phone apps

[331] anorexiafamily.com/ok-observe-with-kindness-mindfulness-compassion

[332] All on anorexiafamily.com/order-audio and some on youtube.com/evamusby

[333] My video 'The hero's journey: resilience and wellbeing for parents', youtu.be/HZgqolG3HeU

[334] Bitesize: anorexiafamily.com/bitesize-public

[335] Bitesize, my library of short audios: anorexiafamily.com/bitesize-public

[336] From Gobsmacked, posting on the Around the Dinner Table forum.

[337] From a letter by L, on the F.E.A.S.T. website: http://feast-ed.org/Members/PatientsSpeak/Itsnormalformetobedoubtingthis.aspx

[338] Carl Rogers made Unconditional Positive Regard a foundation of the Person-Centered approach he developed. Marshall Rosenberg, the creator of *Nonviolent Communication (NVC)* studied under Carl Rogers. To me this explains how family therapy, with its principle of 'uncritical acceptance', works so well with *NVC*.

[339] Lock, J., Le Grange, D., Agras, W. S. and Dare, C., *Treatment Manual for Anorexia Nervosa: A Family-Based Approach* https://amzn.to/2UyqXfK, quoting from research by Eisler, I., Dare, C., Russell, G. F. M., Szmukler, G. I., Le Grange, D. and Dodge, E., 'Family and individual therapy in anorexia nervosa: A five-year follow-up' in *Archives of General Psychiatry* (1997), vol. 54, pp. 1025–30, http://www.ncbi.nlm.nih.gov/pubmed/9366659

[340] Marshall Rosenberg, the creator of *Nonviolent Communication* gives an entertaining demonstration of love as a feeling, one hour into a 2000 workshop: youtu.be/UEqmZ2E1o64. Or watch the whole delicious three hours.

[341] Lock, J., Le Grange, D., Agras, W. S. and Dare, C., *Treatment Manual for Anorexia Nervosa: A Family-Based Approach* https://amzn.to/2UyqXfK

[342] The book was a French Canadian book, *La guérison intérieure par l'acceptation et le lâcher-prise* by Colette Portelance (amzn.to/14iNRHD). Later I found similar benefits in *Parenting Your Anxious Child with Mindfulness and Acceptance: A Powerful New Approach to Overcoming Fear, Panic, and Worry Using Acceptance and Commitment Therapy* by Christopher McCurry (amzn.to/UGHdWc). It could have been written for us parents working on refeeding our kids, or exposing them to fear foods. There is a lot on acceptance and letting go in buddhist resources, e.g. Sounds True (soundstrue.com)

[343] All on anorexiafamily.com/order-audio and some on youtube.com/evamusby

[344] Kate's letter on the F.E.A.S.T website is worth reading in its entirety. For another account from a child about what was going on in her when she rejected her mother, read LM's letter too

[345] Adapted from a story Tara Brach tells in her talks tarabrach.com

[346] Dr Sarah Ravin's blog: 'Emotional Anorexia': http://www.blog.drsarahravin.com/eating-disorders/emotional-anorexia/

[347] *Parenting From the Inside Out* (http://amzn.to/1pBKhAF) is the title of one of Daniel Siegel's books for parents. I'd recommend his more recent book, *The Whole-Brain Child: 12 Revolutionary Strategies to Nurture Your Child's Developing Mind* (http://amzn.to/WIHRW2) for its highly accessible account of the workings of the brain and the practical advice to help you connect with your child using the kind of tools I talk about in this book. Dan Siegel also has a whole series of short videos on YouTube: http://tinyurl.com/b9ken5p

[348] 'It's all about her feelings' is a point Bon Dobbs makes very eloquently about loved ones with Borderline Personality Disorder when describing symptoms which have a lot in common with those of anorexia: see Bon Dobbs's book *When Hope Is Not Enough* (http://amzn.to/1qNGTTs) and http://www.anythingtostopthepain.com

[349] Usually attributed to Mahatma Gandhi.

[350] Neufeld, G. and Maté, G., 'Hold on to Your Kids', amzn.to/2IMB1N8

[351] For girls' parents I highly recommend Lisa Damour, 'Untangled: guiding teenage girls through the seven transitions into adulthood' https://amzn.to/2MRT8Xe

[352] I'm a huge fan of parent forums, and I'm seriously sad when people there advocate this form of punishment as thought it was the only way to get a child to eat. It saved their child's life, but I'd like newcomers to know there are other options that have worked for other parents.

[353] Pink, D. H., *Drive: The Surprising Truth About What Motivates Us* (Riverhead Trade).

[354] Mattocks, B., *Please Eat* (http://amzn.to/195YWhF).

[355] Kohn, A., *Unconditional Parenting* (Atria Books). Alfie Kohn is *the* person to read if you want to understand the problem with rewards, praise, punishment and 'consequences'. If you work in education, do check out his other books too. amzn.to/2INd4W2

[356] Neufeld, G. and Maté, G., 'Hold on to Your Kids'. This book doesn't mention either *Nonviolent Communication* or eating disorders, but it could be a manual for either. If you or your partner recoil at anything faintly new-agey, you'll be safe with this book. amzn.to/2IMB1N8

[357] Marshall Rosenberg, creator of *NVC*, said, 'If we ask two questions, we will see that punishment never works. First: What do we want the other person to do? Second: What do we want the other person's reasons to be for doing as we request?' : http://www.nonviolentcommunication.com/freeresources/nvc_social_media_quotes.htm

[358] One of many quips attributed to Marshall Rosenberg.

[359] Bon Dobbs, in his book *When Hope Is Not Enough* (http://amzn.to/1qNGTTs) provides great clarity around the concepts of boundaries, limits, rules and threats: http://www.anythingtostopthepain.com

[360] I hope you don't need to know this, but talking about knives, I once learned that if you want someone to surrender a weapon, you're more likely to succeed by asking them to put it down in a neutral place than to hand it over to you.

[361] Bitesize: anorexiafamily.com/bitesize-public

[362] Gratitude to all those who helped directly or indirectly with this topic. You can learn more from them too:
FBT therapists Leslie Bloch and Zoë Bisbing, with whom I discuss the subject in their podcast The Full Bloom Project (fullbloomproject.com)
Rebecca Subbiah (rebeccasubbiah.com)
Health At Every Size (haescommunity.com)
Nicole McDermitt's 'An open letter to the eating disorder community' (youtu.be/S7aocdfpGFw)
Resources I collated for schools: anorexiafamily.com/health-promotion-ED-prevention-body-obesity-school

363 From Minnesota Mom, posting on the Around the Dinner Table forum.

364 Geometry of selfies youtu.be/cH2SYQ_SBwc

365 Just add water – optical illusion: youtube.com/watch?v=g7Wa3EKEkm8

366 Quote, and help on this section, from ED Mom NL edmomnl.blogspot.com on the Around The Dinner Table Facebook group facebook.com/groups/ATDTCarerSupportGroup

367 From IrishUp, posting on the Around the Dinner Table forum.

368 Beverley Mattocks, author of the book *Please Eat* (http://amzn.to/195YWhF), learned from her son Ben that when he used to beat his head against the wall and shout, it wasn't so much the anorexic demon driving the behaviour, but him trying to fight the demon.

369 For a helpful description of panic attacks, see nomorepanic.co.uk/articles/symptoms and for some tips you may use as parents, see nomorepanic.co.uk/articles/coping

370 These blankets weigh approximately 10 per cent of the child's weight. A quick internet search will reveal places to buy these or how to make your own.

371 Read Dan Siegel's books to understand the importance of 'secure attachment' and how children develop this partly through being seen and being soothed by their parents. Dan Siegel also has a whole series of short videos on YouTube: http://tinyurl.com/b9ken5p

372 I came across the concept of 'interdependence' through *NVC*.

373 Behaviourism works very well on dogs – in fact most of us have heard of its early days with Pavlov's dogs. So you may enjoy this short video from dog trainer Kikopup, explaining how you cannot reinforce fear because fear is an emotion, not a behaviour, and therefore a frightened dog *should* be comforted: http://tinyurl.com/cx9q6ao

374 The concept of flow and its relationship to happiness and well-being comes from Mihaly Csikszentmihalyi in his landmark book *Flow: The Psychology of Optimal Experience* (http://amzn.to/YPF1y7).

375 Music Maker lap harp: http://www.lap-harp.com/musicmaker.htm. This quote is from a mother on the Around the Dinner Table forum.

376 Eating disorders commonly make our children unable to recognise facial emotion, and they are more likely to interpret a neutral face as negative. Brewer, R., Cook,C., Cardi, V., Treasure J., Bird. G., 'Emotion recognition deficits in eating disorders are explained by co-occurring alexithymia' in Royal Society Open Science (Jan 2015), doi.org/10.1098/rsos.140382

377 Watch this TED talk by Brené Brown: 'The power of vulnerability' on shame and connection. http://www.ted.com/talks/brene_brown_on_vulnerability.html

378 For the difference between self-esteem and self-compassion, and to understand the importance of self-compassion, watch Kristin Neff's TED lecture 'The Space Between Self-Esteem and Self Compassion' on http://youtu.be/IvtZBUSplr4

379 For a short article on praise from an *NVC* perspective, see Inbal Kashtan: 'The Sweetest Game in Town: Contributing Without Praise', http://baynvc.org/the-sweetest-game-in-town-contributing-without-praise

380 From a girl suffering from anorexia, commenting on my website.

381 *Authentic Happiness: Using the New Positive Psychology to Realize Your Potential for Lasting Fulfilment* (http://amzn.to/15xu2gf). See also his website: http://www.authentichappiness.sas.upenn.edu

382 The concept of flow and its relationship to happiness and well-being comes from Mihaly Csikszentmihalyi in his landmark book *Flow: The Psychology of Optimal Experience* (http://amzn.to/YPF1y7).

383 I first came across the concept of an emotional bank account in Steve Covey's *The 7 Habits of Highly Effective Families*.

384 Guisinger, S., 'Adapted to Flee Famine: Adding an Evolutionary Perspective on Anorexia Nervosa'. http://www.adaptedtofamine.com/wp-content/uploads/2015/01/guisinger-an-pr-2003.pdf

[385] I recommend Matt Ridley's book *'Nature via nurture: genes, experience and what makes us human'* for how genes and environment work together (http://amzn.to/29ZPUcZ)

[386] From LV's letter to the F.E.A.S.T. website http://www.feast-ed.org/default.asp?page=PatientLetters

[387] For a very complete list of pros and cons about the externalising model (i.e. seeing your child as separate from their eating disorder, and talking to your child in those terms), I highly recommend this paper: Bemis Vitousek, K., 'Alienating patients from the 'Anorexic Self': Externalizing and related strategies', presented at Seventh International Conference on Eating Disorders, London (6 April 2005) http://tinyurl.com/bh9fjgs

[388] Internal Family Systems (IFS) http://www.selfleadership.org/about-internal-family-systems.html. The main book for it is 'Internal family systems therapy' by Richard Schwartz http://amzn.to/29xvBnC

[389] For instance Cathy Cassidy, 'Summer's Dream' amzn.to/2ODPu0d. Fiction for girls aged 8+ portraying a girl's descent into anorexia. This popular author wrote this because young girls suffering from anorexia were begging for their story to be told. She checked a couple of points with me while writing it. I particularly like how the story ends with hope (the main character finally gets help), but doesn't suffer from an overly easy, happy ending. In other words the girl doesn't suddenly pull her socks up, see sense, and get over it. I've heard a recommendation for 'The Year I Didn't Eat' by Samuel Pollen amzn.to/2WCeGXR Glancing at one chapter, it paints a most accurate picture of the illness, but it's definitely not one to give your child as it is full of calorie-counting. Also, the character seems to be getting individual therapy.

[390] For instance Tabitha Farrar's podcast 'How Family-Based Therapy saved my life — a message from a young survivor'

[391] In the UK, the National Health Service does not do interior design.

[392] You might be tempted by this simple game that creates prompts for story ideas: Rory's Story Cubes: http://www.storycubes.com/products/rorys-story-cubes/

[393] I've come across the concept of 'apologising' to your child in an eating disorders treatment called Emotion-Focused Family Treatment (EFFT).

[394] Look up the 'Karpman triangle' e.g. en.wikipedia.org/wiki/Karpman_drama_triangle

[395] Bon Dobbs's description of this sudden mood change among people suffering from Borderline Personality Disorder matches some of eating disorder experiences anythingtostopthepain.com

[396] From PapyrusUSA, writing on the Around the Dinner Table forum.

[397] For some lovely river metaphors, see Coelho, P., 'Nine steps to transform yourself into a river': http://paulocoelhoblog.com/2012/07/11/be-like-a-river/

[398] This video takes only 14 seconds and memorably illustrates the notions of trust: http://youtu.be/wPOgvzVOQig

[399] The ultimate account of this is from concentration camp survivor Viktor E. Frankl in his book *Man's Search for Meaning* (http://amzn.to/18PaXYm).

[400] Pavlov showed that in dogs, a trigger (a bell) can instantly create an emotional state because earlier, the brain learned to associate the two. Neuro-Linguistic Programming (NLP) uses this principle to create 'anchors': gestures associated with a desired state.

[401] Siegel, D., *Mindsight: The New Science of Personal Transformation* https://amzn.to/2XAGP2W

[402] From Jangled, writing on the Around the Dinner Table forum.

[403] anorexiafamily.com/compassion-and-self-compassion Also lots on YouTube, podcasts and phone apps

[404] anorexiafamily.com/ok-observe-with-kindness-mindfulness-compassion

[405] All on anorexiafamily.com/order-audio and some on youtube.com/evamusby

[406] McCurry, C., *Parenting Your Anxious Child with Mindfulness and Acceptance: A Powerful New Approach to Overcoming Fear, Panic, and Worry Using Acceptance and Commitment Therapy*

(http://amzn.to/UGHdWc). This book could have been written for us parents working on refeeding our kids, or exposing them to fear foods. Well worth reading.

[407] Lots of people enjoy Eckhart Tolle's books and YouTubes on being in the moment. *The Power of Now* (http://amzn.to/1oHm5Q0).

[408] 'The Work' of Byron Katie. Free resources and links to books on http://www.thework.com. There are many YouTube videos: http://www.youtube.com/user/TheWorkofBK

[409] If – and only if – this seems right for you right now, here is some help for letting go of fears around death, which is often the elephant in the room of our minds. You will probably cry but may also gain much freedom from suffering: Byron Katie does 'The Work' with a mother whose daughter died in a car accident. http://youtu.be/xS76V7GhfAc I also recommend the many free videos of Tara Brach https://www.youtube.com/user/tarabrach as well as for you to get support (e.g. EMDR or EFT).

[410] From Emily, a parent on the Around the Dinner Table forum.

[411] In his book, *Flourish* (http://amzn.to/1pBKhAF), Martin Seligman discusses PTSD. Martin Seligman is the founder of Positive Psychology, an approach based on research, and described in *Authentic Happiness: Using the New Positive Psychology to Realize Your Potential for Lasting Fulfilment* (http://amzn.to/15xu2gf).

[412] Seligman, M., *Authentic Happiness: Using the New Positive Psychology to Realize Your Potential for Lasting Fulfilment* (http://amzn.to/15xu2gf). Also Greater Good Science Center ggsc.berkeley.edu

[413] My video 'The hero's journey: resilience and wellbeing for parents', youtu.be/HZgqolG3HeU

[414] Marshall Rosenberg, creator of *Nonviolent Communication*, talks about regret and the inner educator in a 2000 workshop. https://youtu.be/UEqmZ2E1o64?t=8607. This takes you to 2:23 and this topic lasts 6 minutes. He uses the world 'jackal', which I've called 'chatterbox' in this book. I also give an example of an internal mediation process on my website: anorexiafamily.com/internal-conflict-parent-eating-disorder

[415] 'Every mistake is a treasure' is a motto that I believe comes from Janet Treasure's eating disorder team in London.

[416] I guide you to my favourites on anorexiafamily.com/compassion-and-self-compassion

[417] Joan Z. Borysenko lists helper's high as one of several proven tools for resilience in *It's Not the End of the World: Developing Resilience in Times of Change* (http://amzn.to/1BxLlyN).

[418] Neuroanatomist Jill Bolte Taylor vividly describes the effects she observed when a stroke incapacitated her left brain. Watch her TED talk, 'My stroke of insight', http://www.ted.com/talks/jill_bolte_taylor_s_powerful_stroke_of_insight

[419] I wholeheartedly recommend Biodanza to all of you, wherever you are in the world, and irrespective of whether you have two left feet. The thing to do is to search the internet for your nearest class and then just go. Give it a try. Do not look at the naff photos, do not look at videos that may make you cringe, just go.

[420] Extract from a message posted by Cathy on the Around the Dinner Table forum. In the same message she reported a whole lot of out-of-the-box ideas to support her daughter, some of which I quoted in the section on money. Gratitude freed up her mind.

[421] Martin Seligman reports about research on the benefits of gratitude in *Authentic Happiness: Using the New Positive Psychology to Realize Your Potential for Lasting Fulfilment* (http://amzn.to/15xu2gf). See also his website: http://www.authentichappiness.sas.upenn.edu

[422] Marano, H. E., 'Our brain's negative bias', http://www.psychologytoday.com/articles/200306/our-brains-negative-bias

[423] I love this Gratitude meditation by Jayadevi: youtu.be/8pGFjzdGUGo Search for 'Gratitude' on meditation apps as well

[424] Spangler, D., 'Stoking the fires of joy' in *Yes! Magazine*, http://www.yesmagazine.org/issues/finding-courage/624. It's only a page long. Read it and enjoy!

[425] From L's letter to the F.E.A.S.T. website http://www.feast-ed.org/default.asp?page=DecApril2010L

[426] Harriet Brown, http://www.harrietbrown.com

[427] Laura Collins, http://www.circummensam.com

[428] Verene Nicolas, Nonviolent Communication trainer, http://www.verenenicolas.org

[429] Marcia Christen, certified trainer with the Center for Nonviolent Communication, www.compassionate-language.com

[430] Shona Cameron, certified trainer with the Center for Nonviolent Communication, http://www.withunity.co.uk

[431] Robert Doran, editor: http://robert-edits.com

[432] Andrew Brown, Kazoo Publishing (www.kazoopublishing.com) and Design for Writers (www.designforwriters.com)

[433] Melody Revnack (melodyrevnakphotography.com) and Dreamstime (www.dreamstime.com)

[434] https://anorexiafamily.com/bitesize-public

[435] More on individual support from me and prices on anorexiafamily.com/individual-support

Made in the USA
Middletown, DE
06 March 2020